Christoph Wille
Gerry High
James F. Causey
Rob Scrimger
David Gulbransen
Glen Martin

Sams Teach Yourself MCSE Internet Information Server 4

IN 14 DAYS

SAMS PUBLISHING

Sams Publishing is an independent entity from Microsoft Corporation, and not affiliated with Microsoft Corporation in any manner. This publication may be used in assisting students to prepare for a Microsoft Certified Professional Exam. Neither Microsoft Corporation, its designated review company, nor Sams Publishing warrants that use of this publication will ensure passing the relevant Exam. Microsoft is either a registered trademark or trademark of Microsoft Corporation in the United States and/or other countries.

Sams Teach Yourself MCSE Internet Information Server 4 in 14 Days

Copyright © 1998 by Sams Publishing

All rights reserved. No part of this book shall be reproduced, stored in a retrieval system, or transmitted by any means, electronic, mechanical, photocopying, recording, or otherwise, without written permission from the publisher. No patent liability is assumed with respect to the use of the information contained herein. Although every precaution has been taken in the preparation of this book, the publisher and authors assume no responsibility for errors or omissions. Neither is any liability assumed for damages resulting from the use of the information contained herein.

International Standard Book Number: 0-672-31294-8

Library of Congress Catalog Card Number: 98-84487

Printed in the United States of America

First Printing: May, 1998

00 99 98   4 3 2 1

Interpretation of the printing code: the rightmost double-digit number is the year of the book's printing; the rightmost single digit, the number of the book's printing. For example, a printing code of 98-1 shows that the first printing of the book occurred in 1998.

Printed in the United States of America

Trademarks

All terms mentioned in this book that are known to be trademarks or service marks have been appropriately capitalized. Sams Publishing cannot attest to the accuracy of this information. Use of a term in this book should not be regarded as affecting the validity of any trademark or service mark.

Executive Editor
John Kane

Acquisitions Editor
Danielle Bird

Development Editor
Stacia Mellinger

Managing Editor
Sarah Kearns

Project Editor
Christopher Morris

Copy Editors
Gayle Johnson,
Audra McFarland

Indexer
Tim Wright

Technical Editor
Christoph Wille

Production
Betsy Deeter
Lisa England

Overview

	Introduction	xv
1	Internet Information Server—The Basics	2
2	IIS Architecture and Components	42
3	Configuring IIS 4.0	84
4	The WWW Server	118
5	The FTP Service	154
6	Internet Information Server Security	180
7	Microsoft Certificate Server	220
8	The SMTP Server	260
9	The NNTP Server	288
10	Microsoft Index Server	318
11	Programmability	354
12	Performance Tuning	386
13	Site Analysis	432
14	Troubleshooting	470
A	Practice Exam	502
	Index	522

Contents

1 Internet Information Server—The Basics — 2
    Objectives 3
    Internet Information Server: A Brief History 4
    IIS 4.0: Installation Prerequisites..7
        System Requirements and Recommendations 7
        System Configuration Considerations 9
        Other Pre-Installation Considerations 11
    Installing Internet Information Server..11
        Beginning the Installation 12
        Running Setup..21
        Unattended Setup 23
    Basic Configuration 24
        Introduction to Microsoft Management Console..................................25
        Basic FTP Configuration 31
        Basic WWW Configuration...32
    Testing the IIS Installation 33
    Changes Made to Windows NT by Internet Information Server 35
    Lab 38
        Questions..38
        Answers to Questions...40
        Exercise 41

2 IIS Architecture and Components — 42
    Objectives 44
    Internet Information Server Architecture 44
        Static Content Delivery Architecture 45
        Dynamic Content Delivery/Application Architecture 51
        IIS Content Delivery Architecture: Putting It Together 57
    Additional IIS Features 59
        —FTP Features 59
        HTTP Features 61
        Application Delivery Features 63
        Database Access Features 66
    IIS System Administration 67
        IIS Administration Architecture 67
        Administration Features 69
    Additional Components 64
        Microsoft SMTP Service 75
        Microsoft NNTP Service 75
    Choosing an Implementation Strategy 76
    Lab 77
        Questions..77
        Answers to Questions...81

3 Configuring IIS 4.0   84

Objectives 85
Working with the Microsoft Management Console 86
   Snap-Ins 88
   Creating and Using Custom Consoles 88
   Managing Downlevel Web Servers 94
Overview of the Metabase..98
   Purpose of the Metabase 98
   Editing Tools 99
   Backing Up and Restoring the Metabase 100
   Relocating the Metabase and the Backup Folder 102
IIS Configuration 105
Configuring MIME Mappings 106
The Windows NT Registry..108
   Global Registry Entries 109
   Service-Specific Registry Entries..110
   WWW Service Registry Entries 110
   FTP Service Registry Entries 112
Lab 113
   Questions..113
   Answers to Questions...115
   Exercise 116

4 The WWW Server   118

Objectives 119
Configuration Options for the WWW Service 120
   Configuration in the ISM 120
   Looking at the Configuration Tabs 120
Web Sites 122
   Adding IP Addresses to Windows NT 122
   Creating a New Web Site 123
   Web Sites Using IP Addresses Versus Host Headers 126
Directories 127
   Home Directory...128
   Virtual Directories 129
   Directory Properties 131
   Redirections 134
Key Items to Configure..135
   Configuring Web Site Identification 136
   Assigning Site Operators 137
   Defining Default Documents..138
   Setting Directory Security 139
   Modifying HTTP Headers..141
   Configuring ISAPI Filters 142
   Customizing Error Messages 142
   Modifying Performance Parameters 144

Lab	148
Questions	148
Answers to Questions	150
Exercise	151

5 The FTP Service · 154

Objectives	155
Creating and Managing FTP Sites	156
Creating an FTP Site	156
Configuring FTP Site Identification	157
Setting FTP Messages	159
Managing Security Accounts	160
Setting Access Permissions	163
Disconnecting Users	164
Setting Connection Limits	165
Setting Listing Styles	166
FTP Directories	167
Virtual Directories	167
Annotating Directories	171
Setting TCP/IP Restrictions	173
Lab	175
Questions	175
Answers to Questions	177
Exercise	178

6 Internet Information Server Security · 180

Objectives	182
Understanding IIS Security	182
Basic Security	183
Allowing (and Controlling) Anonymous Access	183
Using Clear Text Authentication	185
NT Challenge/Response	187
Restricting Access by IP Address/Domain Name	188
Configuring Basic Security Using Home Directory Settings	191
Advanced Security	196
Encryption Overview	196
Considerations	205
Adding Security from NT	205
Setting Directory and File Level Permissions	205
Disabling Other Services Running on the IIS Computer	208
TCP/IP Advanced Security	210
User Account Issues	211
Lab	213
Questions	213
Answers to Questions	216
Exercises	217

7 Microsoft Certificate Server · 220

Objectives	221

Certificate Basics	222
Encryption	222
Digital Signatures	223
Certificates	223
Usage Scenarios for Certificate Server	224
Enterprise-Level Internetworking	225
Partner Internetworking	225
Customer Registration	226
Certificate Server Features	226
Policy Independence	226
Transport Independence	227
Standards	227
Key Management	227
Reliability	228
Scalability	228
Installing and Configuring Certificate Server	228
Installing (and Configuring) a Root CA	229
Installing a Non-Root CA	232
Installing the Certificate Authority Certificate	233
Enrolling Certificates	236
Web Server Enrollment Page	236
Web Server Enrollment Via Key Manager	241
Client Enrollment	243
Administering Certificate Server	247
The Certificate Log Administration Utility	248
The Certificate Server Queue Administration Utility	249
Revoking Certificates	250
Backing Up and Restoring Configuration	251
Replacing Damaged or Missing CA Certificates	252
Command-Line Utilities	253
Lab	256
Questions	256
Answers to Questions	258
Exercise	259

8 The SMTP Server — 260

Objectives	261
SMTP Overview	262
Processing Messages	264
Delivering Local Messages	264
Delivering Remote Messages	264
Installing SMTP Service	265
Configuring SMTP Service	266
Using the SMTP Service Manager (HTML)	267
Components	268
Directories	269
Configuring the SMTP Site	269

	Configuring Domains	271
	Managing Messages	272
	Configuring Delivery	273
	Configuring Security	275
	Monitoring and Performance Tuning	276
	Monitoring System Processes	276
	Monitoring Message Transactions	277
	Monitoring SMTP Performance	278
	Troubleshooting SMTP	281
	System Troubleshooting	281
	Troubleshooting SMTP Services	282
	Troubleshooting Delivery	282
	Lab	283
	Questions	283
	Answers to Questions	285
	Exercises	286

9 The NNTP Server   288

	Objectives	289
	Introducing Microsoft NNTP Service	290
	Standards Support	290
	Ease of Administration	291
	Security Features	291
	Understanding the Basics of Microsoft NNTP Service	292
	Subscribing to Groups	292
	Posting Articles	293
	Reading Articles	293
	Data Structures	294
	When to Use NNTP Service	294
	A Private News Server	295
	A Public News Server	295
	Installing NNTP Service	296
	Configuring NNTP Service	297
	Using Internet Service Manager for NNTP Service	298
	Restricting Operator Access	300
	Restricting Access to Newsgroups	301
	Managing NNTP Service	303
	Creating Newsgroups	303
	Editing and Deleting Newsgroups	305
	Defining Newsgroup Limits	305
	Using Virtual Directories	306
	Generating Control Messages	308
	Restricting Control Messages	308
	Optimizing Performance	308
	System Monitoring Tools	309
	Rebuilding NNTP Service	310
	Verifying Connectivity	311

Lab	312
Questions	312
Answers to Questions	314
Exercises	314

10 Microsoft Index Server   318

Objectives	319
Roles for the Index Server	320
Indexing Web Sites	320
Document Warehousing	320
Installing the Index Server	321
Configuration Options for the Index Server	322
The HTML Administration Tool	322
Configuration in the Microsoft Management Console	324
Looking at the Properties	330
The Indexing Process	333
Working with the File System	333
Filters	334
Word Breakers	335
Normalizer	335
Merges	336
Querying the Index Server	338
Types of Queries	338
Performance Issues	344
Monitoring Performance	344
Lab	346
Questions	346
Answers to Questions	348
Exercises	349

11 Programmability   354

Objectives	355
Server-Side Programming	356
Active Server Pages	356
ISAPI	357
CGI	359
Internet Database Connector	360
Server-Side Scripting with Active Server Pages	361
Supported Scripting Languages	363
Available Objects	364
Connecting to a Database	367
Windows Scripting Host	374
Running Scripts	374
Available Objects	374
Available Sample Scripts	375
Active Directory Services Interface	375
Metabase	376
IIS Admin Objects	377

Lab 379
    Questions..379
    Answers to Questions..382
    Exercise 383

12 Performance Tuning   386

Objectives 387
IIS Performance Issues 388
    Balancing Performance and Function......................................388
    Factors That Limit Performance..389
Tools for Analyzing Network Performance 389
    NETSTAT 390
    Network Monitor..391
Performance Monitor 395
    How to Use Performance Monitor...396
    Key Areas of Concern 401
    IIS Counters 403
Using Content Analyzer to Analyze a Web Site...............................424
Lab 426
    Questions..426
    Answers to Questions..428
    Exercises 429

13 Site Analysis   432

Objectives 433
Introduction to Microsoft Site Server Express.................................434
    Components Included in Site Server
      Express 2.0 434
    Installing Site Server Components 435
Logging Site Activity..436
    Log Formats..438
    Log Storage and Generation Scheduling 444
    Converting Log Files to NCSA Format 446
Usage Import and Report Writer 446
    Importing Log Files..447
    Analyzing Log Files 450
    Automating Usage Import and Report Writer 452
Content Analyzer 458
    WebMaps...458
    Reports..462
Lab 464
    Questions..464
    Answers to Questions..466
    Exercise 468

14 Troubleshooting   470

Objectives 471
Principles of Troubleshooting 472

Information Is Your (Only) Ally	473
Visualize the Points of Failure	474
Changes Are Your Enemy	474
Commercial Software Bugs Don't Cause *That* Many Problems	475
Don't Rule Out Software Bugs	475
Don't Be Afraid to Ask for Help	476
Troubleshooting TCP/IP	477
PING	477
TRACERT	479
NSLOOKUP	480
IPCONFIG	480
NETSTAT	481
ARP	482
TCP/IP Troubleshooting Methodology	482
Troubleshooting the IIS Installation Process	483
IIS Security Problems	484
Problems with Anonymous Access	484
Users Can't Access Resources	485
Anonymous Users Have the Same Rights as Local or Domain Users	488
Applications Do Not Execute Properly	489
Access to Remote Content Directories Is Denied	489
Troubleshooting Database Access Problems	490
The Browser Client Receives a 502 (Bad Gateway) Error	490
An Attempt to Access SQL Server Results in a `Not defined as a valid user of a trusted SQL Server` Connection Response	490
Insufficient Connections on SQL Server	491
IIS Is Unable to Log to the Remote SQL Server Database	491
Troubleshooting Index Server Query Problems	491
Queries Don't Return Documents That Exist and Match Criteria	492
Queries Return Documents from Unwanted Directories	492
Queries Aren't Returning Documents from Remote Virtual Directory Roots	493
Troubleshooting Host Headers	494
Older Web Browsers Don't Support Host Header Names	494
Host Header Names Can't Be Resolved	494
Lab	495
Questions	495
Answers to Questions	498
Exercises	499

A Practice Exam   **502**

Questions	502
Answers	516

About the Authors

Christoph Wille

Christoph Wille, MCSE, MCSD and MCP-IT, works as a network consultant and assists companies in planning and deploying Internet-connected networks. He also works as a programmer, specializing in the area of server-side programming, including SQL Server, IIS4, and Exchange. However, this work doesn't prevent him from writing client-side code. Christoph has authored or contributed to several books, including *Sams Teach Yourself MCSE TCP/IP in 14 Days*, *Unlocking Active Server Pages*, and *MCSE TestPrep: Windows NT Server 4*. He can be reached via e-mail at `Christoph.Wille@softwing.com`. Visit his company's Web site at `http://www.softwing.com` for free information and downloads in various areas of his expertise.

Gerry High

Gerry High, MCSE, MCSD, is the technical director for Empower Trainers and Consultants in Kansas City, Missouri, a Microsoft-only consulting and training company. Gerry consults on Internet and intranet development using IIS, Active Server Pages, SQL Server, and Visual C++/Visual Basic.

James F. Causey

James F. Causey, originally trained as a military historian, is an MCSE and MCP-IT living in Bloomington, Indiana. He works for Indiana University, where he performs upper-level technical support, Windows development, systems and network administration, and training tasks for computing professionals. He is the lead author of *Windows NT Installation, Configuration, and Customization* for Sams Publishing, and has contributed to *High-Performance Networking Unleashed*, *Networking Essentials Unleashed*, and *Sams Teach Yourself Windows NT Server: MCSE Edition*, also from Sams. When not working or writing about computers, James contributes to an Internet-based magazine dealing with high-end audio equipment. He has some non-technological hobbies as well.

Rob Scrimger

Rob Scrimger, MCT, MCSE, with nearly twenty years of experience with computers, has amassed a strong and varied background in the Information Technology field. His background includes support for many different network and computer operating systems and applications, as well as hardware service and support, and programming in database systems and other systems.

David Gulbransen

David Gulbransen has been employed as an information systems professional for over eight years. He began his career with the Indiana University Departmental Support Lab as an analyst/manager, overseeing a consulting group responsible for advising University departments on technology deployment. After an appointment as the Computing Support Specialist for the School of Fine Arts, David left the Midwest for a position as the Manager of Information Systems at Dimension X, a Java tools development company. While there, he grew the information systems environment from a small UNIX-based shop to a shared UNIX-NT environment serving customers as diverse as Fox Television, MCA Records, Intel, and Sun Microsystems. Upon the purchase of Dimension X in 1997 by Microsoft, David returned to the Midwest to found Vervet Logic, a software development company developing XML and Web tools for new media development. Some of his other titles include *Creating Web Applets with Java*, *The Netscape Server Survival Guide*, *Special Edition Using Dynamic HTML*, and the upcoming *MCSE Training Guide: Internet Explorer Administration Kit*. David holds B.A. degrees in computer science and theater from Indiana University.

Glen Martin

Glen Martin, MCT, MCSE, has a varied background including technical support, training, and network administration for one of the computer industry's leading service providers. He currently devotes most of his time to delivering Microsoft Official Curriculum classes, with a focus on Internet Systems.

Acknowledgments

One of the things developers usually don't like to do is write, be it status reports or anything else. Some developers even get paralyzed when they have to write. Though writing was never a big problem for me, it was a problem to explain things thoroughly and from the ground up, not leaving out details that are important to novices (details that you might not even think about anymore when you are used to a technology).

I want to thank the people at Macmillan who helped me get started with writing and pointed me to where I left out the critical information (besides, well, the usual errors). A special thanks goes to Danielle Bird, who hired me as an author in the first place, and later for this book, of course. She has been involved in all writing projects that I have worked on so far and has helped me a great deal.

For this project, special thanks goes to Stacia Mellinger, who did a great job as a development editor—working with time-constrained networking people is sometimes a problem. Furthermore, I want to thank all the other authors on this book for putting up with me. As a technical editor, my comments are sometimes very short and blunt. Thanks, guys!

Finally, and most importantly, I want to thank my family for their continual support throughout all my book projects.

Christoph Wille

Introduction

by James F. Causey

As Windows NT and Microsoft Networking grow in popularity in corporate environments all over the world, more and more people are investing the time and effort necessary to learn about NT and its supporting technologies. One of the best ways to demonstrate expertise in these areas is by becoming certified by Microsoft to support them; hence, more and more people are working toward Microsoft Certified Systems Engineer (MCSE) certification. Since you're reading this book, I assume that you're one of those people.

Of the many electives that potential MCSEs can take, one of the more popular exams is *Implementing and Supporting Internet Information Server 4.0*. At the time this book was written, this was a very new exam, just out of beta testing. In fact, its predecessor, *Implementing and Supporting Internet Information Server 3.0 and Microsoft Index Server 1.0*, is still available and still valid as part of the MCSE course work.

In this Introduction we'll look at the MCSE certification process and examine where this course fits in. We'll examine how this book is designed to help you pass the course, see some suggestions for using this book to prepare, and discuss some tips and strategies for taking the test itself.

The MCSE Course Track

Microsoft offers a surprisingly broad range of certifications, and the *Implementing and Supporting Internet Information Server 4.0* exam fits into several of them. Let's look at the MCSE, MCSE+Internet, and MCP-IT (Microsoft Certified Professional: Internet Technologies) ratings.

Microsoft Certified Systems Engineer

In order to be certified by Microsoft as a Systems Engineer, you must pass six different courses. First, you must pass four *core technologies* exams. Figure I.1 describes the various exams available in the core technologies series.

Figure I.1.
The MCSE core technologies requirements.

MCSE Core Technologies Requirements: NT 4.0 Track
Exam 70-067: Implementing and Supporting Microsoft Windows NT Server 4.0
Exam 70-068: Implementing and Supporting Microsoft Windows NT Server 4.0 in the Enterprise
Exam 70-064: Implementing and Supporting Microsoft Windows 95   or   Exam 70-073: Implementing and Supporting Microsoft Windows NT Workstation 4.0
Exam 70-058: Networking Essentials

Throughout this book, when we reference MCSE certification procedures, requirements, or other information, we'll be focusing on the NT 4.0 track. There's little reason for anyone who doesn't already have NT 3.51 certification to focus on that track anymore.

As you can see, the Core Technologies exams focus on an essential knowledge of networking (*Networking Essentials*), Windows NT Server (*Implementing and Supporting Windows NT Server 4.0* and *Windows NT Server 4.0 in the Enterprise*), and Microsoft's core desktop platforms (*Windows 95* and *Windows NT Workstation*). Passing any of these courses entitles you to Microsoft Certified Professional certification.

Whenever Microsoft says that you may take one exam *or* another, this doesn't mean that you can't be certified in both products. It simply means that only one of the listed certifications will apply to a higher-level certification such as MCSE.

Introduction xvii

In addition to the four core technologies exams, you must take an additional two exams from a list of electives, as shown in Figure I.2.

Figure I.2.
The available MCSE elective exams.

MCSE Electives: NT 4.0 Track
Pass two of the following:
Exam 70-013: Implementing and Supporting Microsoft SNA Server 3.0 or Exam 70-085: Implementing and Supporting Microsoft SNA Server 4.0
Exam 70-018: Implementing and Supporting Microsoft Systems Management Server 1.2
Exam 70-021: Microsoft SQL Server 4.2 Database Implementation or Exam 70-027: Implementing a Database Design on Microsoft SQL Server 6.5
Exam 70-022: Microsoft SQL Server 4.2 Database Administration for Microsoft Windows NT or Exam 70-026: System Administration for Microsoft SQL Server 6.5
Exam 70-037: Microsoft Mail for PC Networks 3.2 – Enterprise
Exam 70-059: Internetworking with Microsoft TCP/IP on Microsoft Windows NT 4.0
Exam 70-075: Implementing and Supporting Microsoft Exchange Server 5
Exam 70-077: Implementing and Supporting Microsoft Internet Information Server 3.0 and Microsoft Index Server 1.1 or Implementing and Supporting Microsoft Internet Information Server 4.0
Exam 70-078: Implementing and Supporting Microsoft Proxy Server 1.0 or Exam 70-088: Implementing and Supporting Microsoft Proxy Server 2.0
Exam 70-079: Implementing and Supporting Microsoft IE 4.0 by Using the IEAK

Once you've passed six courses from the MCSE track, you're certified as an MCSE.

Microsoft Certified Systems Engineer + Internet

The MCSE+Internet rating is a relatively new certification that is based on the original MCSE. In order to receive the MCSE+Internet certification, you must pass a total of nine exams. Of these nine exams, seven are required core examinations, as shown in Figure I.3.

Figure I.3.
The MCSE+Internet core requirements.

MCSE+ Internet Core Technologies Requirements
Exam 70-067: Implementing and Supporting Microsoft Windows NT Server 4.0
Exam 70-068: Implementing and Supporting Microsoft Windows NT Server 4.0 in the Enterprise
Exam 70-064: Implementing and Supporting Microsoft Windows 95   or   Exam 70-073: Implementing and Supporting Microsoft Windows NT Workstation 4.0
Exam 70-058: Networking Essentials
Exam 70-059: Internetworking with Microsoft TCP/IP Microsoft Windows NT 4.0
Exam 70-077: Implementing and Supporting Microsoft Internet Information Server 3.0 and Microsoft Index Server 1.1   or   Exam 70-087: Implementing and Supporting Microsoft Internet Information Server 4.0
Exam 70-079: Implementing and Supporting Microsoft Internet Explorer 4.0 by Using the Internet Explorer Administration Kit

In addition, MCSE+Internet candidates must take two exams from a pool of available electives. The list of potential MCSE+Internet electives is shown in Figure I.4.

Figure I.4.
The available MCSE+Internet elective exams.

MCSE+ Internet Elective Exams
Exam 70-026: System Administration for Microsoft SQL Server 6.5
Exam 70-027: Implementing a Database Design on Microsoft SQL Server 6.5
Exam 70-076: Implementing and Supporting Microsoft SQL Exchange Server 5   or   Exam 70-081: Implementing and Supporting Microsoft Exchange Server 5.5
Exam 70-078: Implementing and Supporting Microsoft Proxy Server 1.0   or   Exam 70-088: Implementing and Supporting Microsoft Proxy Server 2.0
Exam 70-085: Implementing and Supporting Microsoft SNA Server 4.0

The MCSE+Internet certification is both very recent and more rigorous than the traditional MCSE. Thus, it can be a more lucrative certification to strive for, since it covers a wider range of products.

Microsoft Certified Professional: Internet Technologies

Microsoft provides another, smaller certification that you should be aware of: the Microsoft Certified Professional in Internet Technologies, or MCP-IT. You can become an MCP-IT by passing three courses:

- Internetworking with TCP/IP
- Implementing and Supporting Windows NT Server
- Implementing and Supporting Microsoft Internet Information Server 3.0 with Microsoft Index Server 1.0 *or* Implementing and Supporting Internet Information Server 4.0

With the advent of the new MCSE+Internet certification, it's unclear what the status of the MCP-IT rating will be, particularly since all the courses in the MCP-IT requirements are also part of the MCSE+Internet requirements.

By now, you've probably noticed that the *Implementing and Supporting Internet Information Server 4.0* exam is a common denominator between all these certifications. Let's talk about the reasons why it's an excellent exam to take.

Why Internet Information Server 4.0?

There are a number of excellent reasons to make Internet Information Server 4.0 part of your MCSE track:

- It is part of three certifications: MCSE, MCSE+Internet, and MCP-IT.
- Deploying and delivering technology via the Internet or via corporate intranets is exploding in popularity all over the world.
- The technologies included with IIS 4.0 integrate many of the new application and management tools that will be crucial to NT's future (with the release of NT 5.0).
- The ability to develop and support Internet/intranet solutions using Web servers will be a crucial requirement of NT systems administrators in the near future.

Network administrators in today's work environment *must* be confident in administering Internet Information Server in order to succeed. Even if your network doesn't currently use IIS, it will eventually, whether to provide internal information in a corporate intranet or to create a presence on the Internet itself. There's no quicker way to prove your IIS 4.0 knowledge on a résumé than by having this certification, and there's no more intense way to shore up your IIS knowledge than by preparing for this exam!

How This Book Is Organized

As you might have guessed from its title, this book was designed to help you pass the *Implementing and Supporting Internet Information Server 4.0* exam. We've combined our experience with the test itself and with competing preparation materials to design the best possible tool for giving you the skills and confidence necessary to pass the exam with flying colors.

The book is split into 14 chapters, each designed to be tackled in a single day. Like a good classroom course, each chapter (day) provides a mix of useful elements, beginning with a list of fast facts. These facts are pulled from the chapter and offer a unique opportunity for last-minute study. The next section in the chapter lists objectives for that chapter, as formulated by Microsoft (see the next section). The meat of the chapter follows, with conceptual explanations; instructional, hands-on tutorials; and illustrations. Each chapter ends with a lab section that offers both questions and answers as well as walk-through exercises. These elements are aimed at giving you valuable and real practice as you prepare for what you will be asked on the exam.

The appendix contains an extensive practice exam, offering you more opportunity to (actively) prepare for taking the Microsoft IIS 4.0 exam.

Test Objectives

The official curriculum for the *Implementing and Supporting Internet Information Server 4.0* exam includes a number of specific objectives. The tearcard at the front of this book lists every objective and subobjective defined by Microsoft, cross-referenced with the location in this book where you can find that material.

How to Use This Book

Whether you're brand new to Internet Information Server or a wizened guru, this book can help you prepare.

- *Beginners.* Read this book from cover to cover. Go through each day slowly and carefully, and be sure to follow along on your own system or with pencil and paper through the exercises. Take the practice tests carefully, and if you miss any questions, study the relevant sections again. After you've completed each day's exercises, it would be extremely valuable for you to take several days to implement what you've learned in a real-world networking environment, either at home or at work, to hone your skills and solidify your understanding.

- *Competent technicians.* A large number of IT professionals have varying degrees of expertise with IIS but don't feel comfortable calling themselves experts (particularly if their expertise lies mainly in previous versions of IIS). If you fall into this category, start by reading the first few theory chapters closely, and work through the exercises and practice questions. Many people who are perfectly comfortable serving some Web pages via IIS lack an essential understanding of how IIS works, so shoring up these areas of understanding is crucial. Work through the practice tests for each day, and study the chapters you're not completely comfortable with.
- *Advanced Internet administrators.* Even Internet service gurus will find this book useful, whether to refresh their knowledge of IIS specifics or to help them apply their knowledge to the NT environment. Work through the various practice tests, as well as the outline from the preceding section, and carefully review the material on which your knowledge is the least sharp. Microsoft is concerned about a number of specific skills, some more commonly used than others, and reviewing potential test questions can help you pass the test with ease.

What You Need in Order to Use This Book Effectively

In order to be assured of getting the best possible use from the material in this book, it's best if you have the following prerequisites:

- *Familiarity with Windows NT Server and Windows NT Workstation.* In fact, if you have passed (or can pass) the Microsoft Certification tests *Implementing and Supporting Windows NT Workstation* and *Implementing and Supporting Windows NT Server,* you should have all the operating system knowledge necessary to use this material.
- *Familiarity with the basics of networks.* It's best if you've already passed (or can pass) the *Networking Essentials* exam.
- *Familiarity with TCP/IP configuration and administration.* If you've passed (or can pass) the *Internetworking with Microsoft TCP/IP in Windows NT 4.0* exam, you'll have this prerequisite covered.

We'll cover some of the material needed from these prerequisites in this book in order to make certain that you're adequately prepared for the *Implementing and Supporting Internet Information Server 4.0* exam. However, in order to fully understand everything covered in this book, you'll need to be familiar with the topics listed in the tearcard at the front of this book.

Taking the Test

After long, arduous hours of study and practice, you feel ready to accept the challenge of taking the *Implementing and Supporting Internet Information Server 4.0* exam. There are some things you should know when you schedule your test, and on test day, that can make the process much smoother.

Scheduling the Test

The certification tests are entirely administered by Sylvan Prometric. Call (800) 755-EXAM to schedule your tests. You'll need the following information the first time you schedule a test:

- Your full name
- Your Social Security number
- Your address
- Your telephone number
- An appropriate method of payment (Sylvan accepts credit cards and checks)

If you call again to schedule future tests, you'll simply be asked for your Social Security number and your payment information. The operator will help you choose the Sylvan testing center most convenient to you and help you schedule a test during a free time slot at that location.

Each test costs $100. You can schedule tests as soon as there are slots available at your chosen testing center (although you must give at least one business day's notice to register). You can also call back and change your testing dates as late as one day in advance. You might find it convenient to pay for all your tests ahead of time and to schedule the specific tests later when you have a better idea of when you'll be available to take them.

Preparing for Test Day

Hopefully, when the time for your test rolls around, you'll be quite prepared to pass the exam. The day before your test, do a final review of the course material, glancing over everything but focusing primarily on any areas in which you feel a little shaky. Make sure you eat a healthy meal and get a good night's sleep before the exam.

The morning of the test, again, focus on eating healthily, and relax. Your preparations should leave you with a feeling of optimism and confidence for the test. It's not a bad idea to go over last-minute review items again before the test, but don't panic and race through everything or try to cram.

If there are any specifics about which you're not 100-percent confident, it's easy to think, "I don't need to go over that. I'm sure I'll remember it or they won't cover it much on the test." People often think this about specific configuration options or syntax issues that are easy to look up in a real-world situation. Thus, people tend to believe that they won't be heavily questioned on these topics. I've found myself in this position several times. Each time, I received a nasty surprise when I sat down to take the test. If you have felt this way, take a few minutes to glance over the specifics again. The few minutes taken will add some needed points to your score and help prevent having your confidence shaken when you sit down to take the exam.

What to Expect from the Test

Sylvan Prometric tests are administered entirely on computer, using a testing format very similar to the practice tests on the CD-ROM included with this book. They are generally given in a monitored environment (to prevent cheating), and the Prometric software doesn't let you switch to or run any other applications.

The test will consist of a number of different question types, including the following:

- Multiple choice with one correct answer
- Multiple choice with more than one correct answer
- Scenarios in which you evaluate a given solution
- Scenarios in which you provide the most appropriate solution
- Fill-in-the-blank questions
- Simulation questions, in which you perform a designated task using a simulation of the Microsoft Management Console

Some questions are very ambiguous, and you're expected to pick the best possible answer. Some questions are actually poorly written and very difficult to answer.

Each question has a Mark option, allowing you to mark the question for later review. Each question can also be left incomplete.

Once you've run through each of the questions (there are usually 49 questions on the *IIS* exam), you're given a chance to review your answers. The questions you marked for review are highlighted, as well as the ones you didn't complete (although you can review and change any answer).

Once you're confident that you've done the best you can, you submit your questions, and your answers are recorded. Next, you're given the opportunity to comment on individual questions. After your comments are submitted, your test is graded, and you're told whether you passed or failed, as well as your percentage score for each section of the test. You can't find out which questions you missed.

After reviewing your score, you're given an opportunity to comment on the test itself, and you're asked to fill out a survey about yourself and your test-preparation process.

Test Strategies

The strategies for taking the MCSE tests are very similar to those for any standardized test. Perhaps the most important is attitude. Coming into the test confident in your knowledge and excited about getting your certification is critical to passing the test. You can gain this confidence and excitement by taking care of yourself and allowing yourself plenty of time before exam day to study, review, and prepare.

Once the test has begun, be sure to read each question carefully and thoroughly before selecting an answer. If you're not sure about a question, make your best guess, and mark the question for later review, since later questions often give you knowledge to help you make a more informed decision. If you have no idea about a question, leave it incomplete.

If you run into a question about which you have absolutely no clue, don't let it blow your mind. Just mark it and move on. You'll probably be able to make an intelligent guess later based on information from other questions.

Once you've made your first pass through the test, it's time to review. Take a look at the questions you marked or didn't answer, and separate them into three levels of certainty:

- *High certainty.* You're pretty sure about the answer, but you wanted to take another look.
- *Medium certainty.* You think you can make a good guess.
- *Low certainty.* You have no idea at all, or you think it could be a couple of different answers.

Address the questions in that order. Work slowly, and try not to second-guess yourself. Feel free to put questions off even more. You can go through this evaluation-and-review process again and again.

Once you've done all you can with the tough questions, go ahead and submit your answers. The key throughout this entire process is to stay relaxed and focused. Many times, questions that blew my mind when I sat down to take the test turned out to be not that hard at all after I'd had some time to mull them over. Just make sure you don't exceed your time limit (usually about 1½ to 2 hours per test).

Summary

We've looked at the MCSE testing process, the *Implementing and Supporting Internet Information Server 4.0* exam, and strategies and methodologies for using this book to help you prepare for and pass your test. Next, we'll begin the 14 days, starting with the basics of Internet Information Server 4.0.

TEST DAY FAST FACTS

Here are a few fast facts about this chapter that you may want to know ahead of time. Also, don't forget that these facts provide great last-minute study material.

- IIS 4.0 can serve WWW (World Wide Web) and FTP (File Transfer Protocol) data, create and present powerful Web-based applications, serve outbound SMTP mail, and use NNTP for discussion groups.

- IIS 4.0 includes a number of additional products to enhance its functionality, including Microsoft Index Server, Microsoft Transaction Server, Microsoft Message Queue Server, Microsoft SMTP Server, Microsoft NNTP Server, Microsoft Certificate Server, and other products.

- IIS 4.0 is available only in the NT Option Pack.

- You must already have Internet Explorer 4.01 or higher installed in order to use the services in the NT Option Pack.

- The NT Option Pack can be installed from CD-ROM, from a local or network drive, or via the Internet.

- The NT Option Pack also supports unattended installation.

Day 1

Internet Information Server–The Basics

by James F. Causey

When Microsoft began focusing heavily on Internet technologies, one of their keys to exploiting this market was their World Wide Web server product called Internet Information Server, or IIS. IIS has grown in the past few years from being a fast but simple free HTTP server product to being a powerful enterprise data and application service platform. The Internet Information Server 4.0 exam reflects this change, covering products and technologies that didn't exist when the previous version of IIS debuted.

Throughout the next 14 days, you'll learn every aspect of the IIS 4.0 platform. As with any such discussion, however, it's good to begin at the beginning. Today, that's exactly what we'll do.

In this chapter, we'll discuss the basics of IIS 4.0. We'll look at what the product is and does, and at the history of the Internet Information Server. We'll also discuss how the product has grown and what it includes.

Then we'll discuss the basics of installing and configuring the product and verifying that your installation and setup work. Finally, we'll briefly discuss some of the changes that an IIS 4.0 installation brings to a Windows NT Server.

Objectives

This chapter helps you prepare for the Microsoft Exam by covering the following objectives:

- Install IIS
- Configure a Microsoft Windows NT Server 4.0 computer for the installation of IIS
- Identify differences to a Windows NT Server 4.0 computer made by the installation of IIS

TEST DAY
FAST FACTS

- Microsoft's new system and service management tool, the Microsoft Management Console, is included in the NT Option Pack as the primary administration interface.

- You can test the functionality and configuration of your IIS server with standard Web browsers and FTP clients.

- IIS makes a number of modifications to your NT installation, including creating user contexts for anonymous IIS authentication and Web application management, monitoring of the default TCP ports for FTP and HTTP access, and the addition of default serving directories and management tools.

1.1. Internet Information Server: A Brief History

Until a couple of years ago, the Internet was a relatively obscure technology. Its use was growing steadily but relatively slowly, and it was known only to students and faculty at academic institutions and to individuals in the technology field. However, roughly three years ago, its popularity and use exploded, due to the advent of the World Wide Web.

Originally developed at CERN, the World Wide Web (WWW) is a virtual construct made up of documents that can be easily viewed and navigated using a graphical browsing tool (called a *Web browser*). World Wide Web documents are defined using a language called HTML (Hypertext Markup Language). HTML defines a standard method for Web browser software to render and display WWW documents and to allow users to navigate using *hyperlinks*, areas of the document that link to other documents.

The World Wide Web relies on TCP/IP, using a protocol called HTTP (Hypertext Transfer Protocol) that runs on top of TCP/IP. HTML documents are served to Web browsers using HTTP by *Web servers*. Thus, Web servers can be thought of as the backbone of the World Wide Web. Figure 1.1 illustrates this principle.

Figure 1.1.
The World Wide Web relies on Web servers to handle and serve browser requests for HTML documents.

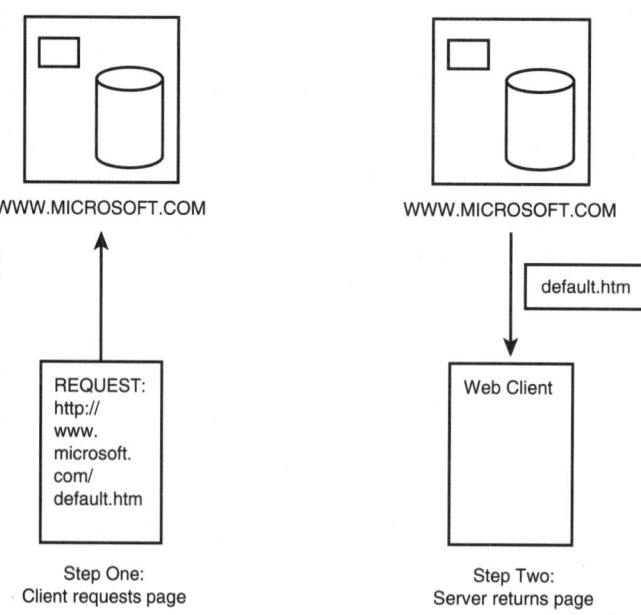

The very first Web servers were produced by the same people who provided the early, primitive Web browser software. One major source for both server and browser software was the National Center for Supercomputing Applications (NCSA) at the University of Illinois; NCSA's Mosaic browser (written by Marc Andreesen, who later went on to found Netscape) and HTTPD server quickly propagated across the Internet as de facto standards. Later, the W3C (World Wide Web Consortium) was formed as an international standards body to develop and promote standards for use on the Web.

Most early Web server software ran only on UNIX, the most common—and at first the only—network operating system on the Internet (in fact, the most popular Web server on the Internet, Apache, runs only on UNIX). As the World Wide Web exploded in popularity, however, many companies began development of Web server software for other platforms. One important potential for this development was Microsoft's Windows NT, due to its nature as a secure, reliable network operating system with integrated support for TCP/IP (the standard protocol for Internet communications). However, Microsoft itself moved slowly at first. Therefore, the first Web servers for Windows NT were produced by third parties and freeware/shareware developers.

In the mid-1990s, however, Microsoft suddenly realized the importance of the Internet as an enterprise business tool, and they moved rapidly to integrate their desktop and server products with Internet-ready solutions. Their two major products in this market are:

- *Internet Explorer.* A Web browser.
- *Internet Information Server.* A Web server.

Internet Information Server was originally designed to provide three different types of Internet services:

- *HTTP/WWW services*, for supplying and displaying HTML files on the Internet.
- *FTP (File Transfer Protocol) services*, which allow remote clients to upload files to and download files from the Internet Information Server. This integrated FTP server replaced the original standalone FTP server included with Windows NT.
- *Gopher services*, for providing simple documentation and information over the Internet in a text-based system.

Day 1: Internet Information Server—The Basics

 Note Beginning with version 4.0, Gopher services are no longer supported by IIS.

As Internet Information Server has matured, however, its scope has expanded. Internet Information Server is now designed to provide a wide range of application services on the Internet, including

- Support for Web services using HTTP, including support for HTTP version 1.1.
- Full support for file transfer services using FTP.
- Powerful security features, integrated with the security architecture of Windows NT.
- Programmability through Web-standard CGI, as well as ISAPI applications and ASP scripting.
- Site analysis and content management through Microsoft Site Server Express.
- Full text and object indexing with rich searching capabilities. This ability is implemented by Microsoft Index Server.
- Authentication and verification services for Internet clients, as well as certificate generation using Microsoft Certificate Server.
- E-mail transfer and relay, using Microsoft SMTP (Simple Mail Transport Protocol) Server.
- Internet newsgroup access, using Microsoft NNTP (Network News Transport Protocol) Server.
- Dynamic authentication, page generation, and application services, using ISAPI (Internet Service Application Programming Interface) extensions and filters and CGI (Common Gateway Interface) applications, as well as Active Server Pages (ASP).
- Complete database application access and manipulation via the Internet Database Connector (IDC) and ActiveX Data Objects (ADO), as well three-tier application services with Microsoft Transaction Server (MTS) and Microsoft Message Queue Server (MSMQ).
- Integration into Microsoft's future directory service architecture, the Active Directory.

Clearly, Internet Information Server is a powerful, flexible platform for creating full-featured Internet and intranet solutions.

1.2. IIS 4.0: Installation Prerequisites

We're just about ready to run through a sample installation of IIS 4.0. Before we begin, however, let's go over some prerequisites.

1.2.1. System Requirements and Recommendations

Internet Information Server 4.0 is a powerful and flexible product; however, in order to take advantage of these features, you must meet some basic system requirements.

As of this writing, Internet Information Server 4.0 was distributed only in the NT Option Pack, a set of tools and add-ons for Windows NT. The NT Option Pack is available both from Microsoft's BackOffice Web site (http://backoffice.microsoft.com/) and on CD-ROM.

First, you must be using Windows NT Server 4.0, with Service Pack 3 or later installed. IIS 4.0 will not run on Windows NT Workstation or any version of Windows NT prior to 4.0 SP3.

The NT Option Pack includes NT Service Pack 3 and will install it if necessary before installing the rest of the Option Pack components.

Users of Windows NT Workstation 4.0 can install the latest version of Peer Web Services for NT Workstation—which includes many of the features of IIS 4.0—using the NT Option Pack. However, Peer Web Services (or PWS, for short) does not include all of the functionality of Internet Information Server. For that reason (and because the exam focuses on IIS), this book will focus on the features and functionality of IIS 4.0; however, much of the information also applies to PWS.

Day 1: Internet Information Server—The Basics

Next, you must already have Internet Explorer 4.01 or later installed. The various applications included in the Windows NT Option Pack (particularly, the Windows Scripting Host engine) rely on code distributed with IE 4.0 only. Keep in mind that you are not prevented from using any other manufacturer's browser software on your server; however, you must have IE 4.01 or later on your system in order to successfully install the Option Pack.

When you install Internet Explorer 4.01 on your server, you may find it expedient to choose the Browser Only installation option. It's smaller (roughly 14–15MB), takes less time to download, and lacks many of the gimcracks and thingamabobs rarely needed on a back-end server (including the often-dreaded Shell Integration tools), but it still includes the required components for the Windows NT Option Pack.

In addition to these operating system prerequisites, Microsoft specifies some basic hardware requirements for the Windows NT Option Pack. Table 1.1 lists Microsoft's minimum system hardware requirements for the Windows NT Option Pack, which includes IIS 4.0. (We'll discuss why we're installing the entire Option Pack and not just IIS in the section "Installing IIS," later in this chapter.)

Table 1.1. Minimum hardware requirements for the Windows NT Option Pack.

Hardware Component	Requirement
CPU	Intel 486DX-66 MHz
RAM	32 MB
Free disk space	50 MB
Monitor/video resolution	VGA (640×480, 16 color)
Other	Network Adapter Card or RAS connection (optional; needed in order to publish documents over the network)
	3X CD-ROM drive (optional; needed in order to install from CD-ROM)

A cursory examination of the above requirements reveals that they are *extremely* conservative and are an absolute bare minimum set of requirements. In reality, you'd need to be something of a masochist to run a product as complex as IIS 4.0 on a 486; basic HTML requests might not be too terribly slow, but simple administration tasks would be quite painful.

In an attempt to be more realistic, Microsoft specifies the recommendations for minimum hardware that are listed in Table 1.2.

Table 1.2. Minimum recommended hardware for NT Option Pack.

Hardware Component	Recommended Minimum
CPU	Intel Pentium 90-MHz
RAM	64 MB
Free disk space	200 MB
Monitor/video resolution	Super VGA (800×600, 256 colors)
Other	Network Adapter Card or RAS Connection (optional; needed in order to publish documents over the network; high-speed connection strongly recommended for production sites)
	6X CD-ROM drive (optional; needed in order to install from CD-ROM)

These recommendations are far more realistic. Keep in mind that this is a recommended *minimum* configuration; depending on how your IIS installation will be used and configured and the load that will be placed on it, you may need to use much more powerful hardware.

We'll discuss performance considerations, with more specific guidelines for selecting hardware for particular needs, throughout the rest of the fourteen days. However, Day 12, "Performance Tuning," focuses specifically on performance tuning.

1.2.2. System Configuration Considerations

When planning for the installation of your Internet Information Server, you should address a few system configuration considerations that will improve both the general performance of your Windows NT Server and its performance under IIS.

IIS performance will be limited by the same potential bottlenecks as any other service provided by Windows NT Server. These bottlenecks include:

- System memory
- Network connection
- Persistent storage/disk configuration
- Number and speed of CPU(s)

A. System Memory

When serving raw, plain HTML files, probably the single greatest bottleneck to the server's ability to respond to document requests (besides available network bandwidth) is the amount of RAM on the server. The more memory available to the server, the more easily it will be able to cache frequently requested documents in memory, which reduces costly fetches from disk. In addition, having available physical memory will make other IIS tasks go more quickly; Index Server, for instance, will be able to hold more index data in RAM, reducing the need to fetch data from the persistent master index on disk. (See Day 10, "Microsoft Index Server," for more information on this technology.)

It will also allow more concurrent applications, both those used by IIS and those used by other demands on the server, to work without excessive paging activity. To put it bluntly, RAM is a very good thing; you should always strive to have lots of it.

B. Network Connection

Another major bottleneck on the potential performance of your Internet server is available network bandwidth. Depending on the popularity of your site, the number of HTTP requests made against it, and the size of the data being downloaded, a popular site can saturate all but the fastest of Internet links—and you might be amazed at how quickly. This can be a major concern if, as with most Internet servers, your system is sharing a network connection with other systems (such as your corporate WAN). Make a careful estimate of the load and potential popularity of your site when allocating network resources for the server.

C. Persistent Storage/Disk Configuration

The speed with which your NT Server can fetch data from disk is an important factor in the overall performance of your IIS installation. It affects both the ability to rapidly fetch data that is requested by clients and the system's ability to handle internal disk usage requests for system files, applications, and virtual memory access. On a heavily used Web server, optimizing your disk configuration (by using technologies such as disk arrays and techniques like spanning swap files across multiple disk spindles) can provide dramatic performance benefits.

D. Number and Speed of CPU(s)

On a basic Internet server that provides standard static HTML documents, the CPU is rarely a bottleneck. However, complex sites using the full range of dynamic page generation, security features, and application functionality available with IIS 4.0 can tax the CPU's ability to handle multiple tasks. With these configurations, using a faster processor can provide a significant improvement. Even more dramatic benefits are often seen when using multiple CPUs.

1.2.3. Other Pre-Installation Considerations

Because of the relative ease of installing and configuring Windows NT Server, it's often tempting for systems administrators to view the process of performing modifications to the system as trivial. This attitude normally backfires in unforeseen, painful, potentially job-threatening ways. When you're performing a major system configuration task such as installing the Windows NT Option Pack, it's wise to take a few precautions beforehand:

1. *Make sure you have a good backup.* This means not only making certain your backup jobs have been running, but assuring yourself that the media required to restore your most recent data is reliable. You should also make certain that you have a recent Emergency Repair Disk (it might not be a bad idea to make another one right before the installation) and a recent backup of your system's partition and volume information (from the Disk Administrator tool).

2. *Run a test installation on a non-production system.* It's always nice, if feasible, to run your first major installation of a product on a dedicated test server or a non-mission-critical server in order to find any hidden pitfalls or problems and to familiarize yourself with the product before installing on your production system.

3. *Run your production installation outside working hours.* When feasible (assuming you don't have a 24-by-7 operation), performing your production installation and configuration outside of standard working hours (or, if impossible, outside of peak usage hours) reduces the chance that any problems that come up will severely inconvenience your users. If possible, it's best to perform the work over a weekend so you have plenty of time to recover from disaster if necessary.

4. *Run the installation from CD, a local drive, or a local network share instead of from the Internet.* This makes the installation run significantly quicker and allows you to recover more rapidly from a failure.

1.3. Installing Internet Information Server

Now that you've carefully prepared your server and yourself for the installation process, it's time to actually install Internet Information Server 4.0. Because Microsoft has chosen to provide IIS 4.0 only as a part of the Windows NT Option Pack, we're going to run through the process of installing the Windows NT Option Pack. However, we'll forgo installing the components not directly related to IIS 4.0, which will cut down on the complexity of the installation.

1.3.1. Beginning the Installation

When you're ready to install IIS 4.0, take a couple of quick steps beforehand:

1. Uninstall any beta versions of Internet Information Server.
2. Stop any currently running IIS services.

The method for starting the installation of the Windows NT Option Pack depends on how you're performing the installation: from CD-ROM (such as a Microsoft Select CD) or from Microsoft's IIS Web site. Follow the appropriate instructions.

A. Starting the Installation from CD

To start the installation from CD, place the Option Pack CD in your CD-ROM drive. If Autorun is not disabled, Setup will begin automatically. If Setup does not begin automatically, open the following HTML file

```
<CD drive letter>:\setupcd\winnt.srv\default.htm
```

using Internet Explorer 4.01 or later, replacing *<CD drive letter>* with the drive letter of your system's CD-ROM drive.

B. Starting the Installation via the Internet

Starting the installation through the Internet is slightly more complicated and significantly more time-consuming.

> If you're installing over the Internet, get comfortable and be patient. There are a lot of steps involved in downloading the necessary setup files, and some of them seem repetitive and frustrating. If at all possible, run your installation from a CD-ROM. If this isn't an option, it's a good idea to download the files and keep them around for future installations so you don't have to go through this irritating process more often than necessary.

To begin, launch your copy of Internet Explorer 4.01 (or later) and open up the IIS Web site, located at the following URL:

```
http://www.microsoft.com/iis/
```

Figure 1.2 shows the Microsoft Internet Information Server 4.0 Web home page.

1.3. Installing Internet Information Server   13

Figure 1.2.
Begin your IIS installation from Microsoft's IIS home page.

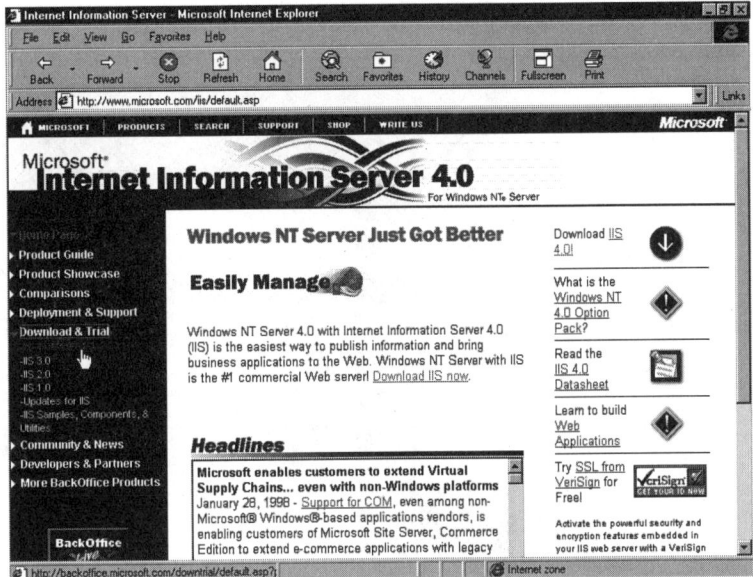

> **Note**
> Keep in mind that Microsoft revises the design of their Web pages at a near-frantic pace. Because the screen shots in this chapter were taken from the Web at the time this book was written, you may find that these pages have a completely different appearance by the time you visit.
>
> In addition, be careful about using the URLs from the screen shots because there's no guarantee that Microsoft will continue to use those URLs for the same function in the future. Though it's tedious to navigate through all the seemingly repetitive links, to be safe, always begin your downloads from the IIS home page URL (`http://www.microsoft.com/iis/`).

On the first page, click on Download and Trial in the toolbar on the left in order to display the option to install IIS 4.0/PWS 4.0. Alternatively, you can click the Download IIS 4.0! link on the right side of the screen to continue. The next screen you'll see is the BackOffice Download and Trial Center shown in Figure 1.3.

On this screen, it's rather obvious which link you need. Click on Microsoft Internet Information Server 4.0 to continue the download process and move on to the Windows NT Option Pack Download and Trial Center page shown in Figure 1.4.

Figure 1.3.
IIS 4.0 can be downloaded from the BackOffice Download and Trial Center.

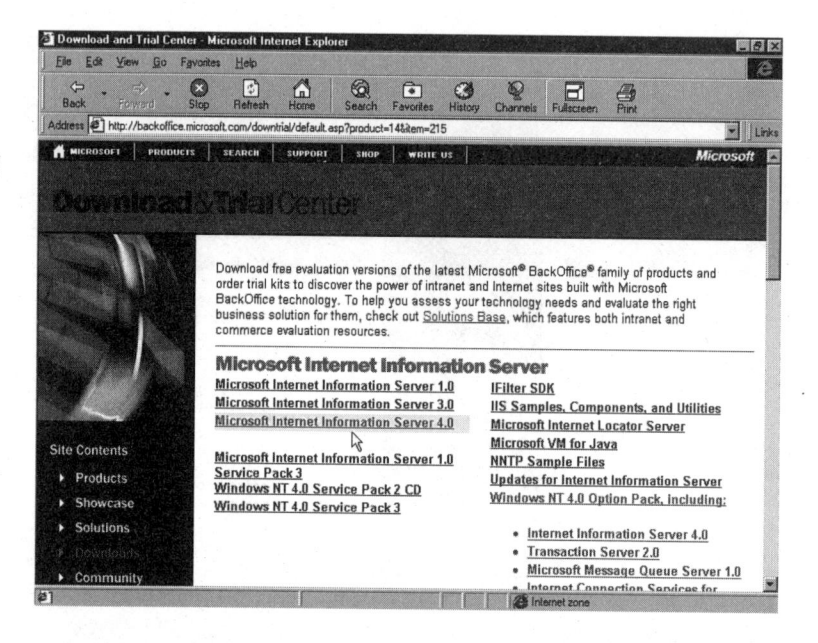

Figure 1.4.
The Windows NT 4.0 Option Pack Download and Trial Center is where you actually begin the arduous process of downloading IIS 4.0.

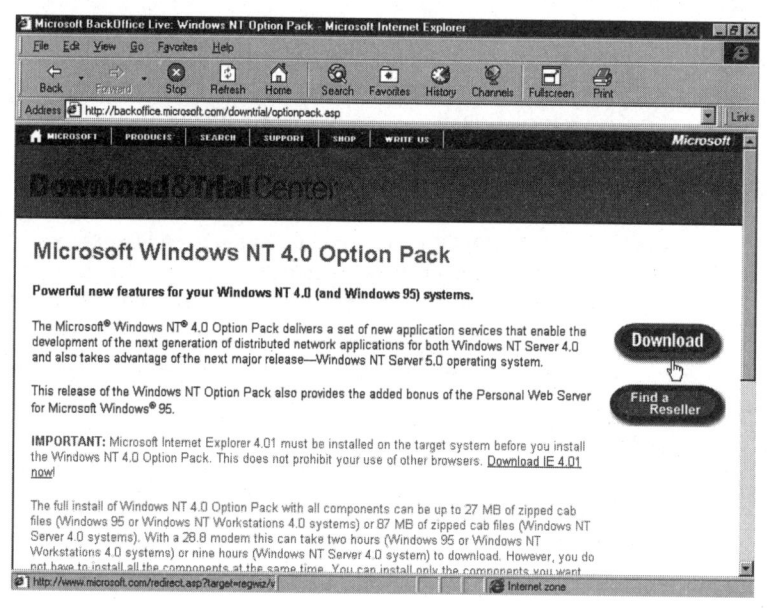

On this page, you're warned of the time and free disk space required to install the Option Pack, as well as the Internet Explorer 4.01 requirement. To move on, click the big Download button on the right side of the screen.

1.3. Installing Internet Information Server | 15

On the next page, you'll be required to verify some personal information in order to continue the download. The required fields are marked with a big, pretty red asterisk (see Figure 1.5). Enter the required information, and then click the Next button at the bottom of the form.

Figure 1.5.
Give Microsoft the required marketing information so you can download your free Web server.

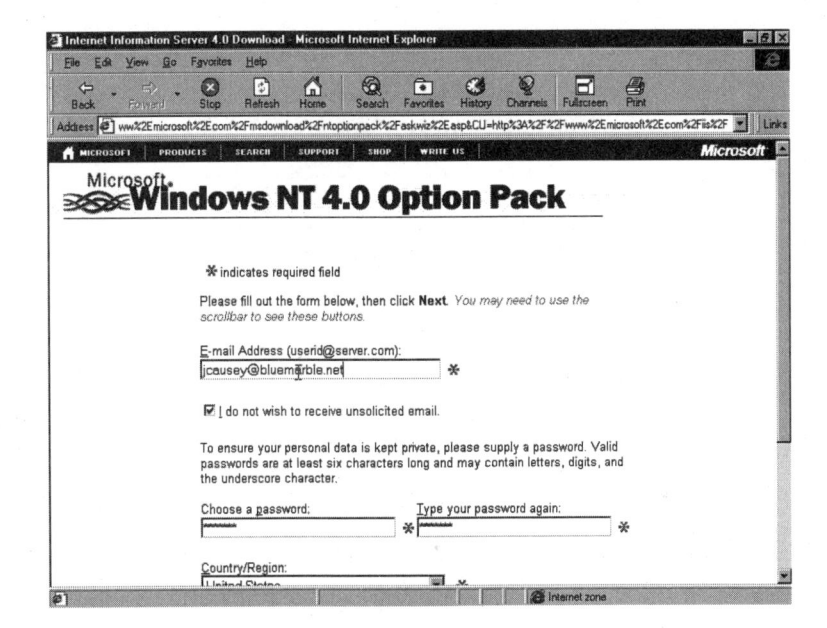

> **Note:** This irritating registration page appeared during my test installations whether or not I'd already registered. Apparently, the presence of the registration cookie on my server was not enough to avoid the process; however, it did let the Microsoft Web page pre-enter most of my required information.

After all that work, you've finally reached Download Step 1! See Figure 1.6 for a glimpse of this anticlimactic Web page.

This page offers two download options. If you're downloading the Option Pack from a system running Windows, click Option 1; if not, or if you just want to download the whole shebang for later installation, click Option 2.

We're going to assume you clicked Option 1. That brings you to Download Step 2, which is displayed in Figure 1.7.

Figure 1.6.

Download Step 1 lets you pick what type of download you want to perform.

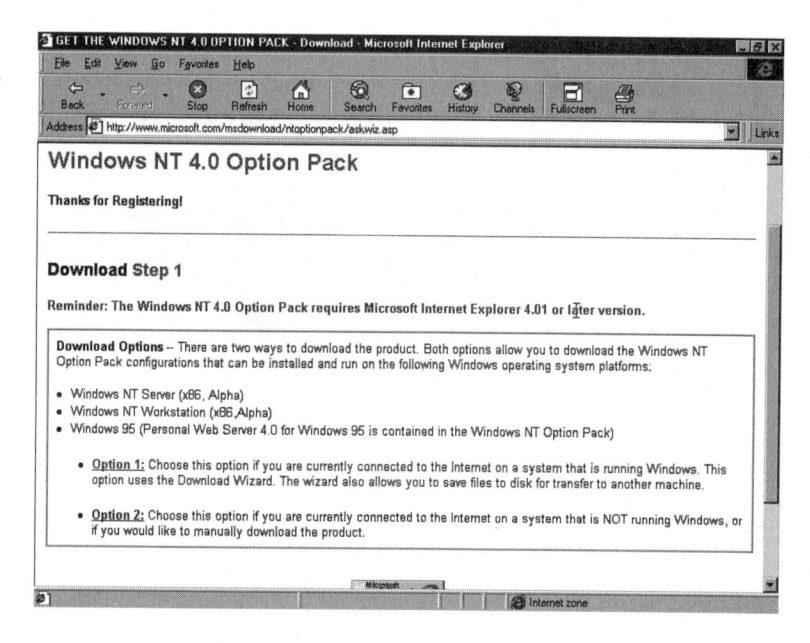

Figure 1.7.

Download Step 2 lets you select the operating system on which you'll be running the Download Wizard.

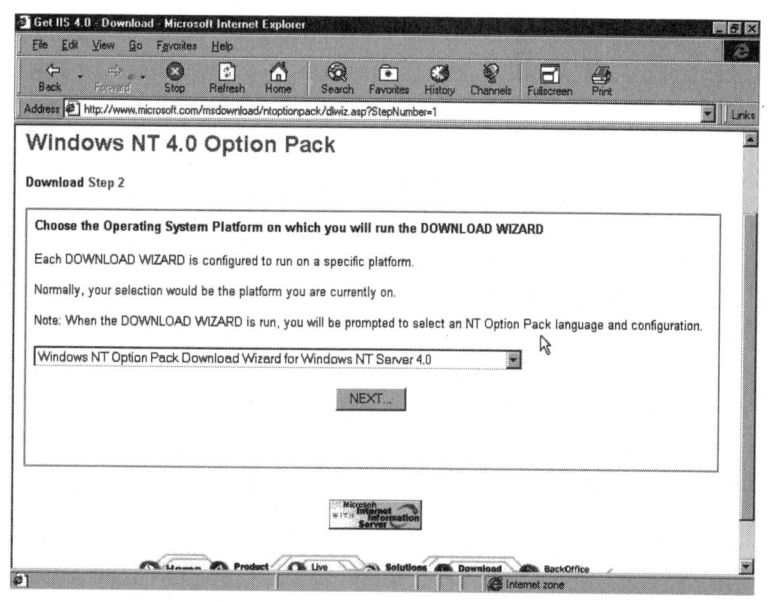

Use the drop-down box to pick which operating system you're currently running, and then click the Next button. The Download Step 3 screen appears, in which you

1.3. Installing Internet Information Server

select your desired language. Select the language you'll be using, and then click the Next button. For this example, we'll assume you selected U.S. English.

The next screen allows you to pick a download location (see Figure 1.8). For fastest downloads, you should pick the site nearest you. Select a site and click its Download from this site… button to continue. For this example, I chose ConXion USA in Washington DC.

Figure 1.8.
Select the download site nearest you in Download Step 4.

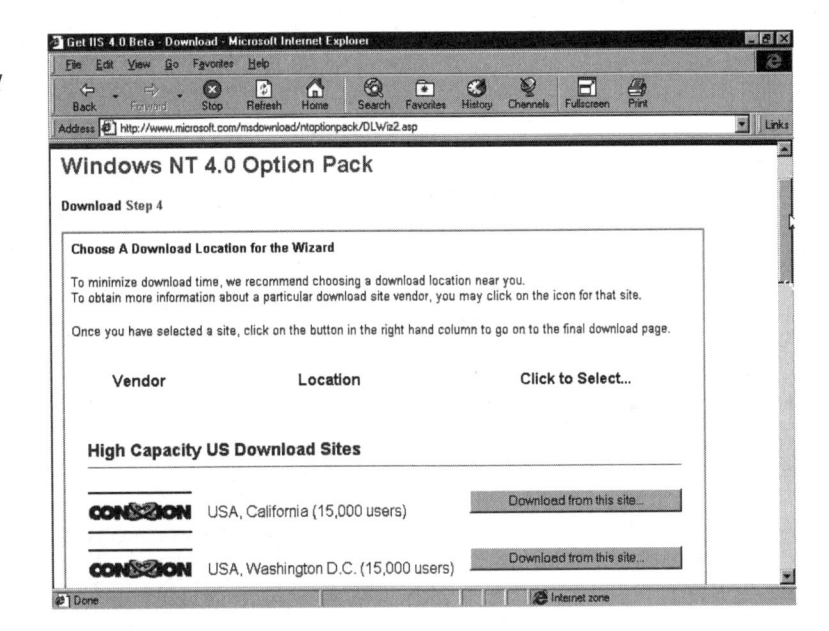

With Step 5, you're just about ready to actually begin the download. If you're not completely exasperated yet, click the link under Item to be Downloaded: to begin downloading the Option Pack Download Wizard (see Figure 1.9).

If you're using IE 4.01 to perform this process (as we recommended earlier), you'll be presented with the dialog box shown in Figure 1.10.

In this dialog box, you can save the Download Wizard in a directory so you can open it up later, or you can open it immediately. Because the Wizard itself is not particularly large and does not contain the required installation files, you don't gain very much by saving it for later. Select open this file from its current location, and then click OK to continue. You'll be presented with the End-User License Agreement (EULA) for the Windows NT Option Pack; when you're done reading it, click Yes to move on.

Day 1: Internet Information Server—The Basics

Figure 1.9.
Begin the actual download process in Download Step 5.

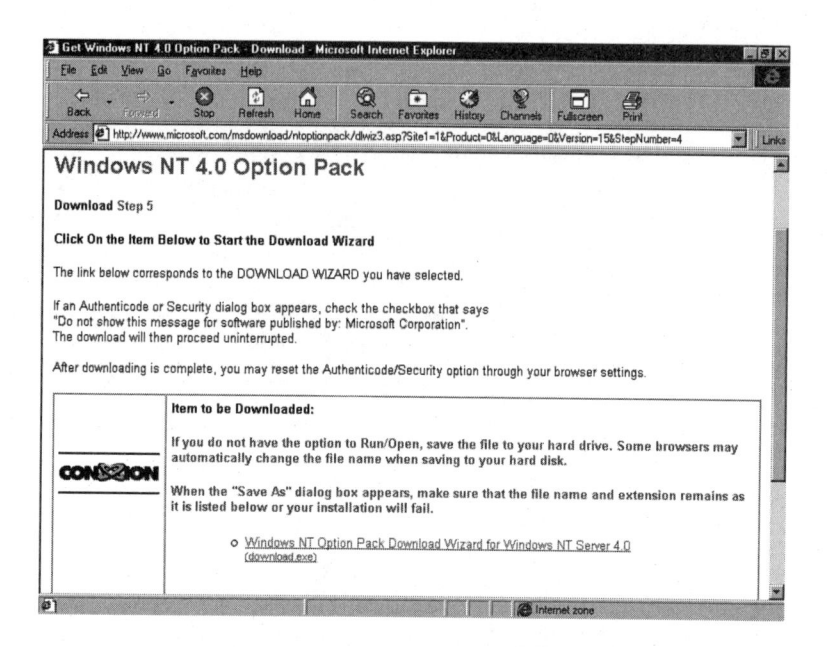

Figure 1.10.
Internet Explorer 4.01 asks if you want to open the Download Wizard immediately or save it for later.

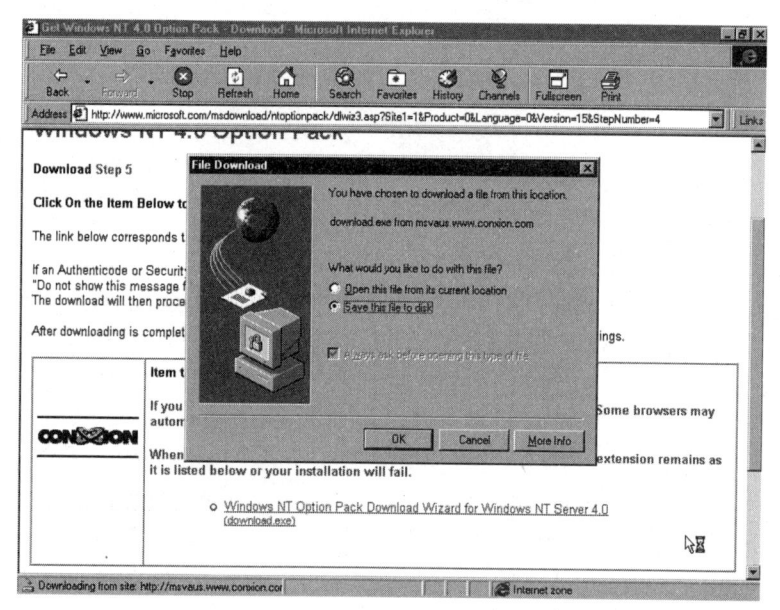

The Download Wizard unpacks some needed files and displays the Download Options dialog box shown in Figure 1.11. This dialog box allows you to either begin

1.3. Installing Internet Information Server   19

the installation or download all the required installation files for later use. For this example, go ahead and select Install and click Yes.

Figure 1.11.
The Download Options dialog box allows you to either begin the installation or download the installation files without running it.

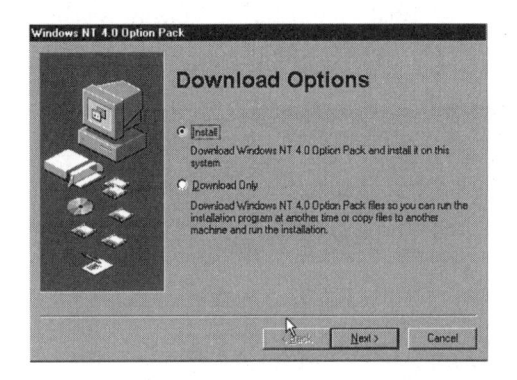

Next you'll be presented with a list of installation options. You can choose either a Typical, Minimal, or Full Installation of IIS 4.0. For this example, select Full Installation to have all possible installation options. If you don't need every potential IIS component, you might want to choose one of the other options. Click Next to continue.

Next you'll be asked where you want to place the installation files, as shown in Figure 1.12.

Figure 1.12.
The Destination Folder dialog box lets you select where to place the installation files.

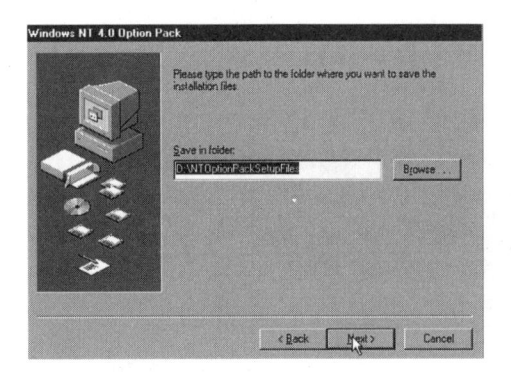

> **Note** Keep in mind that this folder is not the final destination for the installed product; it's merely the directory that will hold the setup files after they're downloaded.

Enter a directory or use the default one provided, and then click Next to continue.

The Download Wizard displays a message while it briefly generates a list of available download sites for the installation files. Once the list is generated, it is displayed in the Download Location dialog box, which is shown in Figure 1.13.

Figure 1.13.

In the Download Location dialog box, select a site to download the installation files from.

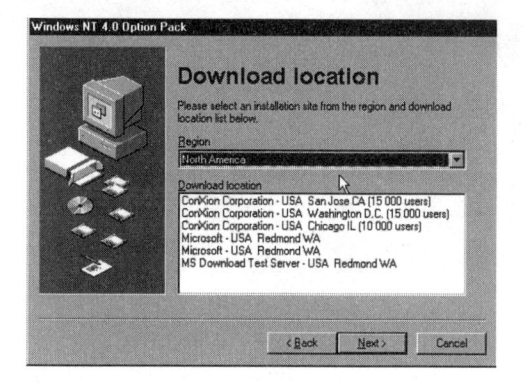

Select a region and location from which to download the installation files and click Next to continue (I selected ConXion's Washington DC site again).

The Download Wizard then generates a list of files to download and displays a message while doing so. When that list is complete, the download process (finally!) begins (see Figure 1.14).

Figure 1.14.

The Download Wizard finally begins downloading the necessary installation files.

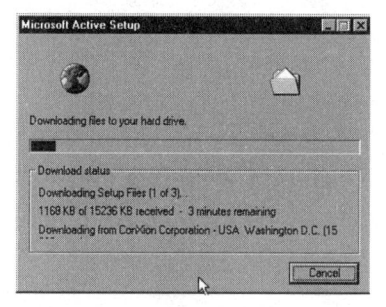

Depending on how much traffic is on the Internet at the time of your download and how busy your selected download server is, this process may take a while. Over a T3-equivalent connection on my test server, the process took nearly 15 minutes during non-peak hours.

When the download of installation files is complete, the Download Wizard informs you that you can now disconnect from the Internet.

In case you're not paying attention, the Download Wizard will go ahead and run Setup 10 seconds after the dialog box is first displayed. Either wait for the countdown, or if you're feeling impatient, click OK to run Setup. Congratulations! After all that work, you're finally ready to install Internet Information Server 4.0.

1.3.2. Running Setup

Whether you're running from CD or over the Internet, you've finally fired up SETUP.EXE. Setup begins by initializing important data and scanning for system requirements. At this point, you'll be informed if you're lacking any important requirements (if you don't have IE 4.01, for example, or if you're not running Windows NT Server 4.0). In addition, if you're already running a previous version of IIS, you'll be informed that the Gopher service, no longer included with IIS, will be disabled.

When Setup is done initializing, you'll see the opening dialog box shown in Figure 1.15. Click Next to continue.

Figure 1.15.
The actual installation begins with the Windows NT Option Pack Setup opening dialog box.

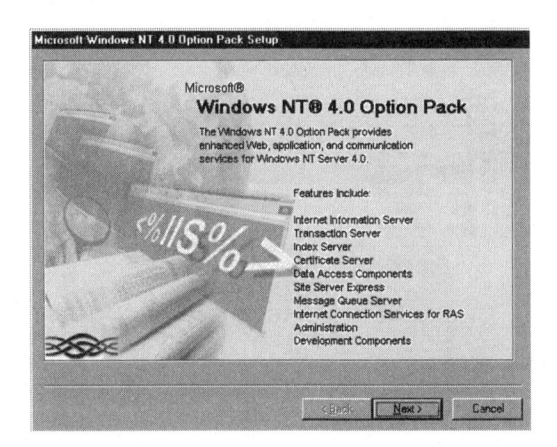

The next dialog displays the EULA for the Option Pack. If you're running this installation over the Internet, you'll probably recognize this. Read Microsoft's license requirements, and then click Accept to continue.

If you're installing the Windows NT Option Pack on top of a system that's already running a previous version of Internet Information Server, you'll see the dialog box shown in Figure 1.16. If you only want to upgrade your current copy of IIS, select Upgrade Only. However, if you want to upgrade and have the option to add some of the new features of IIS 4.0, select Upgrade Plus.

Day 1: Internet Information Server—The Basics

Figure 1.16.
The Windows NT Option Pack will upgrade older versions of IIS.

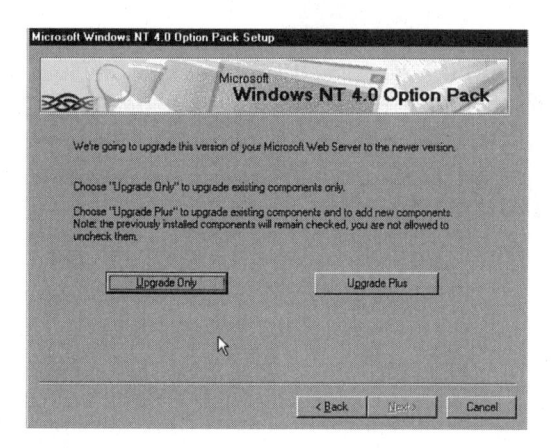

Next Setup displays the Select Components dialog box, in which you can select which components of the Windows NT Option Pack you want to install (see Figure 1.17).

Figure 1.17.
The Select Components dialog box lets you determine which parts of the Windows NT Option Pack to install.

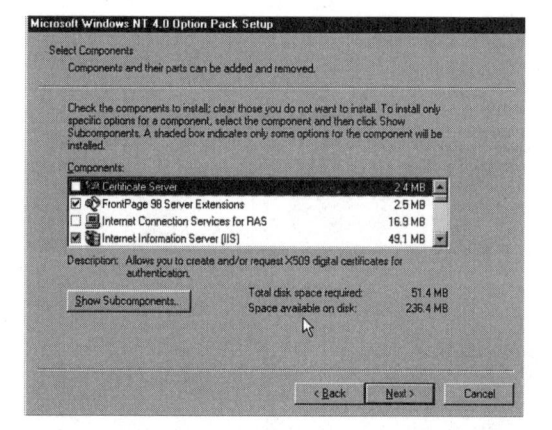

Because this book is about Internet Information Server 4.0, at the very least you'll probably want to leave the Internet Information Server (IIS) option selected. Many of the components also have subcomponents that you can install. Click the Show Subcomponents... button and select or deselect the desired subcomponents. When you're satisfied that you've selected the components you need, click Next to continue.

> **Note:** For more information on the components included with IIS, see Day 2, "IIS Architecture and Components." Each component that's relevant to Internet Information Server is also discussed in detail in its own chapter in the book.

Depending on the components you selected, Setup displays configuration information for specific system components. (Some of these component-specific dialog boxes will be discussed later in this chapter in the section "Component-Specific Installation Issues"; other information is available in the chapters for each of the optional components.) When Setup finishes the configuration, it begins to unpack, install, and configure your selected options.

> **Note**
> This process can take quite a while, depending on the speed of your system and the number of components you selected. During one of my test installations, I selected all IIS-relevant components on a Pentium-75 MHz with 32 MB of RAM running Windows NT Server; Setup took more than an hour to complete the installation process!

When Setup finishes the installation, you'll see the final Setup dialog box displayed in Figure 1.18.

Figure 1.18.
At long last, the installation is complete.

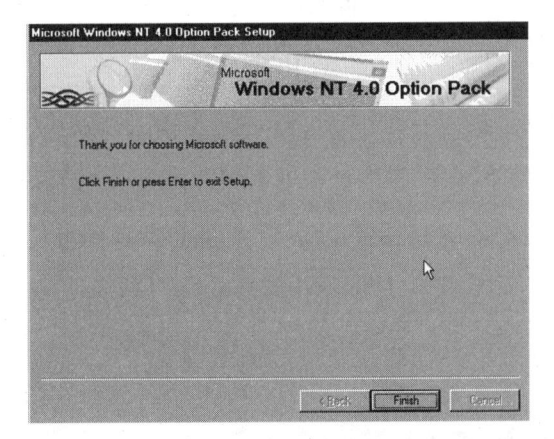

Click Finish to exit Setup. The installer finalizes some program settings and then prompts you to restart the server. Select Yes to restart. After a lot of work and no small number of steps, your installation of Internet Information Server 4.0 is complete!

1.3.3. Unattended Setup

Sometimes you might want to run the Windows NT Option Pack Setup without having to walk through the installation options. This is handy when you already know which options you need or when you want to perform the installation on multiple servers. To run Setup that way, use the following steps:

1. Place the Option Pack CD in the CD-ROM drive, or put a complete copy of the installation files on the local drive or a network share.
2. Open up the NT Command Prompt and navigate to the directory where the Option Pack's SETUP.EXE is located.
3. At the command prompt, type the following command:

```
setup.exe /u:<path to unattend.txt>
```

Replace the `<path to unattend.txt>` parameter with a qualified path to the file UNATTEND.TXT (the unattended setup script that you've generated). Sample UNATTEND.TXT files can be found in the \inetsrv\ subdirectory of the Option Pack setup files.

You can also modify or add to a previous Option Pack installation in unattended mode. To do so, use the following steps:

1. Open up the NT Command Prompt and navigate to your system's %windir%\system32 directory.
2. Type the following command:

```
sysocmgr.exe /I:<path to iisv4.inf> /c /u:<full path to unattend.txt>
```

Replace the `<path to iisv4.inf>` parameter with a qualified path to the file iisv4.inf, which contains information on your current Option Pack installation; this file is normally found in your system's %windir%\system32\setup directory.

Many components of the Windows NT Option Pack have interdependencies; make certain that you consult the documentation for the Option Pack before generating your unattend.txt file and test the file before using it in a production setup.

1.4. Basic Configuration

Now that you can install the Internet Information Server, let's look at some of the fundamental issues behind its configuration. If you're new to Internet Information Server, this will be a welcome introduction to the array of tools and options. If you're familiar with previous versions of IIS, this will allow you to familiarize yourself with the new configuration toolset.

We'll begin by looking at the Microsoft Management Console (MMC), Microsoft's new standard tool for administering system services. We'll then move on to a brief overview of the configuration of the FTP and WWW services. With a basic understanding of these two services and the MMC, you'll be able to perform basic Web and FTP serving tasks using IIS 4.0.

1.4.1. Introduction to Microsoft Management Console

Over the past several years, as Windows NT has gained popularity, Microsoft has attempted to expand its feature set and appeal to new audiences. Recently, as the product has comfortably gained command of the corporate desktop and workgroup server markets, Microsoft has begun to eye the larger enterprise market as the next objective for Windows NT.

NT's advanced architecture, rich feature set, and graphical user interface give it a number of advantages for approaching this new market. However, concerns about the product's scalability, reliability, and enterprise management abilities remain. Until these concerns are addressed, the traditional "big iron" of the enterprise market will continue to rule their segment of the market.

Microsoft is investing a huge amount of time, money, and energy in addressing these concerns both in current versions and with the next major release—Windows NT 5.0. One of the concerns they're beginning to address as we speak is manageability.

Traditionally, Windows NT has provided a series of easy-to-use, graphical tools—such as User Manager for Domains and Server Manager—for managing the system. However, these tools are scattered throughout the system. It's often extremely difficult for new administrators to determine exactly which tool performs which task, and finding those tools can often be daunting. In addition, many management tasks cannot be carried out easily across a network for multiple systems, requiring administrators to find creative, complex solutions for large-scale networks.

Microsoft is attempting to address this problem with a new tool: the Microsoft Management Console (MMC).

A. What Is the MMC?

Microsoft Management Console is Microsoft's new tool for providing administrators with a centralized system- and application-management workspace. MMC was designed with a few specific goals in mind:

- *Centralization*

    Right now, administrative applications are scattered between the Control Panel and the Administrative Tools program folder. New tools that are installed can place their configuration applications in either of these places—or anywhere else for that matter. This requires the system administrator to learn where each tool resides, which can make performing tasks that require interrelated actions between configuration tools a virtual nightmare. With MMC, the administrator will be able to perform all system administration and management tasks through a centralized interface.

- *Extensibility*

    Microsoft Management Console is designed with an extensible architecture, allowing both Microsoft and third-party tool vendors to easily provide administrators with the ability to manage all system tools through the MMC interface. In fact, MMC is designed to make the development of MMC extensions easier than developing standalone configuration programs.

- *Customization*

    Every system is different, with different needs, goals, and services. In addition, every administrator works in different ways. Microsoft Management Console is designed to encourage and support these facts flexibly; system administrators can design their own consoles using the tools and shortcuts they need, and they can save those consoles for later use.

By the time Windows NT 5.0 is released, Microsoft Management Console will act as the standard interface for system and enterprise administration functions. Microsoft is already beginning to move tools and technologies into the MMC world, as is evidenced by the Windows NT Option Pack's reliance on MMC as its management interface.

B. MMC Architecture

The Microsoft Management Console is, at its core, nothing more than a simple framework. It has no inherent management behavior; instead, it is merely an interface for other management tools, called *snap-ins*. Snap-ins are tools written to use the MMC interface that perform administrative tasks. In addition, the MMC provides support for *extension snap-ins*, which can be thought of as child snap-in tools used by parent snap-ins to extend their abilities and functionality. The systems administrator can select from a range of available snap-ins and extension snap-ins to create a customized MMC console, or *tool*, which he can then use to perform his common administration tasks. Figure 1.19 illustrates this relationship.

The administrator saves his tool configurations to an .msc file, which remembers his custom snap-in settings for later use.

Figure 1.19.
Administrators use MMC to gather and arrange snap-ins into a tool.

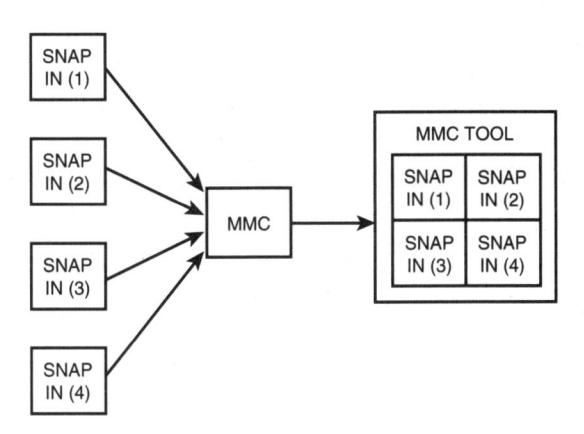

C. MMC Interface

The Microsoft Management Console runs as a 32-bit Windows MDI (Multiple Document Interface) application. This allows individual snap-ins to be run in their own windows within the larger context of the tool.

When invoked without an .msc file, the Microsoft Management Console starts up with a blank console and no other subwindows. Figure 1.20 shows MMC's initial state.

Figure 1.20.
The Microsoft Management Console appears as a clean slate when no snap-ins are installed.

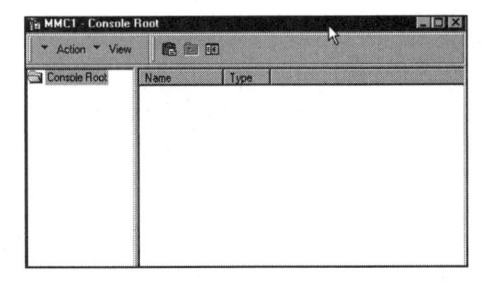

In this first screen, you can see the standard array of menus and controls provided by the MMC, as well as the Console Root subwindow. The Console Root closely resembles the Windows NT Explorer application; to see this resemblance more clearly, maximize the Console Root window, as in Figure 1.21.

The Console Root contains, by default, a splitter bar and two panes: a scope pane on the left and a detail pane on the right. The scope pane shows a list of the snap-ins currently installed in the tool, along with their various options and extension snap-ins. The detail pane displays more detailed information provided by the snap-ins themselves and provides much of the actual administrative interface. Figure 1.22 shows an MMC tool with the snap-ins for Internet Information Server and Microsoft Transaction Server installed.

Figure 1.21.
The Console Root in the MMC resembles the Windows NT Explorer.

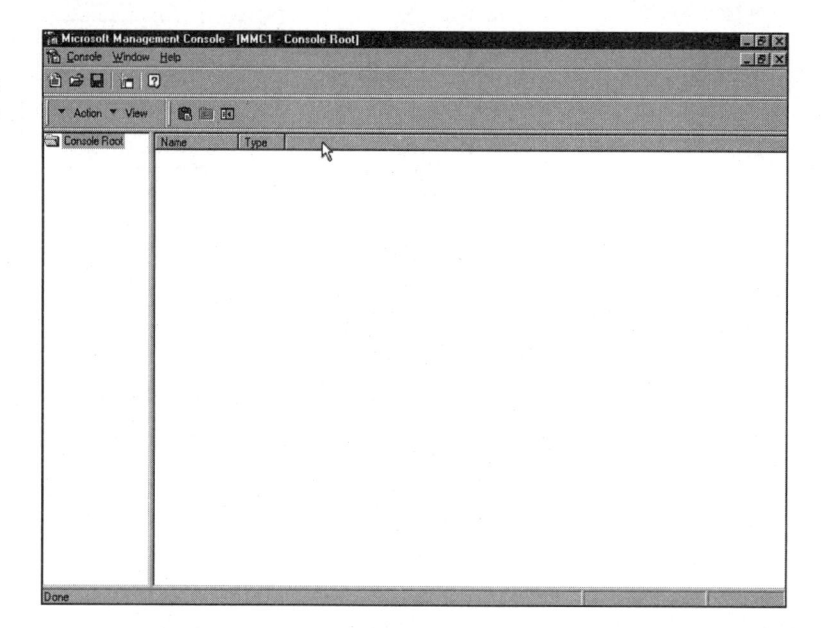

Figure 1.22.
Here's an example of a saved console: the IIS.MSC tool with IIS and MTS snap-ins installed.

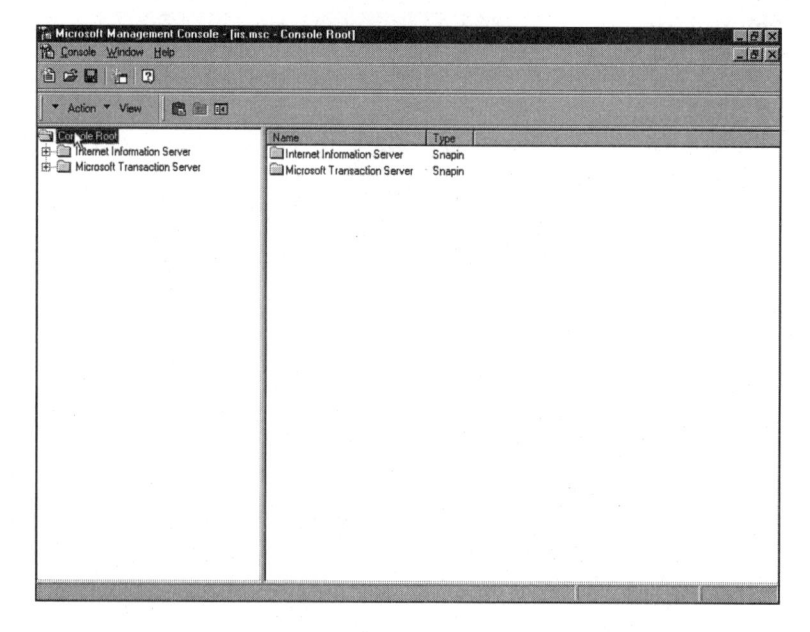

A snap-in listed in the scope pane can be expanded by clicking on the plus sign in the tree. This displays a drop-down list of available configuration options for that snap-in (see Figure 1.23).

Figure 1.23.
In the scope pane, the administrator can customize the configuration options he or she wants to view.

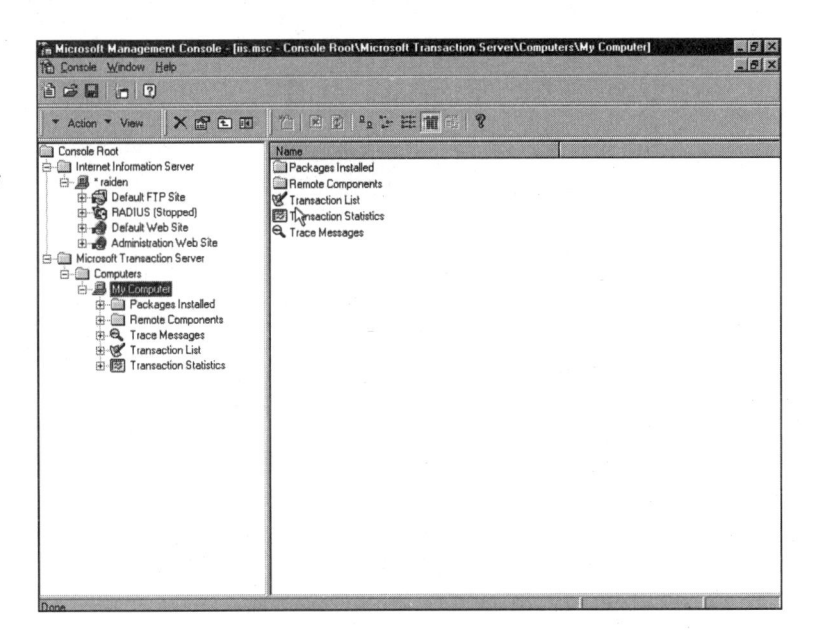

The administrator can then select an option in the scope pane and manipulate it either through the interface provided in the detail pane on the right or via options available from a right-click context menu like the one shown in Figure 1.24.

The MMC also enables you to add and remove snap-ins from the current tool. To invoke the Add/Remove Snap-In dialog box, click on the Console menu and select Add/Remove Snap-Ins. In the dialog box that appears, you can manipulate the tool's list of snap-ins (as in Figure 1.25) and snap-in extensions (see Figure 1.26) that are registered with the Microsoft Management Console.

Now that we've briefly examined the Microsoft Management Console, let's look at the snap-ins for configuring Internet Information Server's FTP and WWW services.

Figure 1.24.
Right-click on an object in the scope pane to access a context-driven list of options.

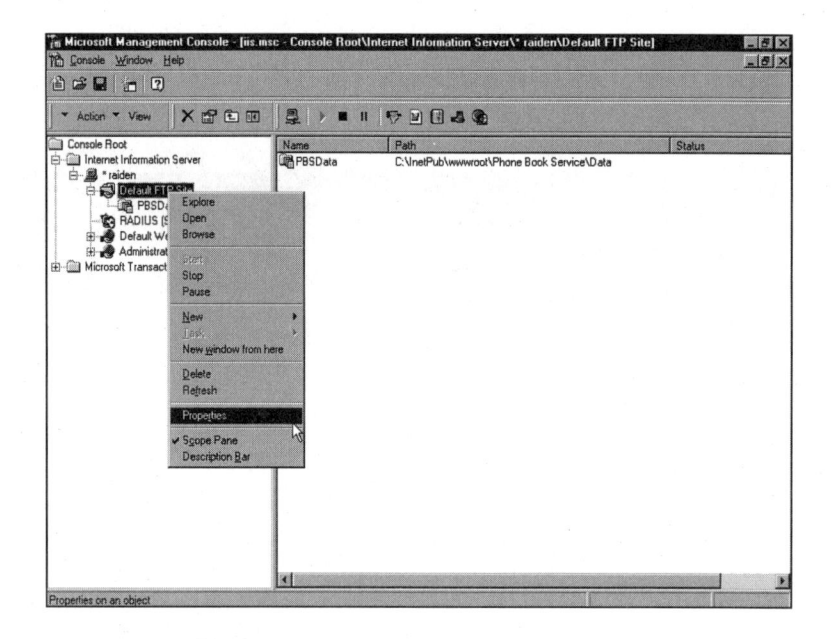

Figure 1.25.
MMC allows you to add snap-ins to the current tool or remove them from it.

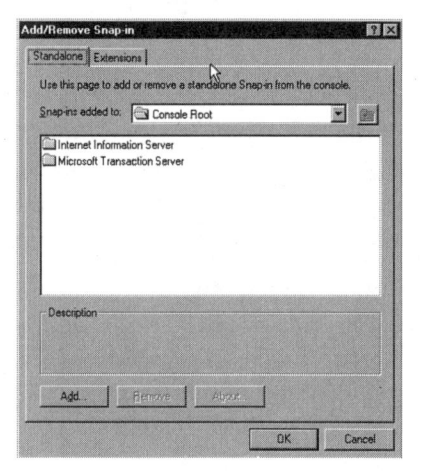

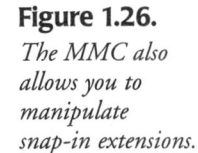

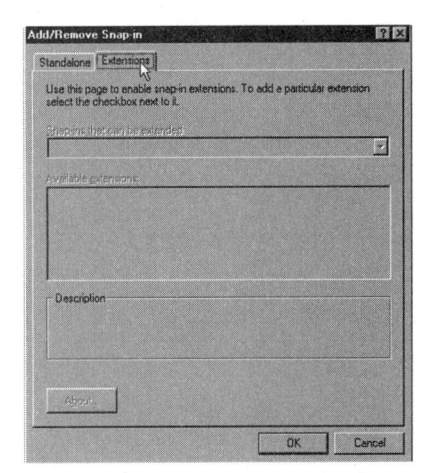

Figure 1.26.
The MMC also allows you to manipulate snap-in extensions.

> **Note:** For more detailed information on the Microsoft Management Console, see Day 3, "Configuring IIS 4.0." Tools with their own MMC snap-ins will be covered throughout this book.

1.4.2. Basic FTP Configuration

Most FTP configuration tasks can be performed through the Internet Information Server snap-in. To view the properties for the FTP service, expand the scope of the IIS snap-in until Default FTP Site is visible. Then right-click on Default FTP Site and select Properties from the context menu (see Figure 1.27).

The FTP Service Properties dialog box appears, in which you can configure nearly every pertinent option for the system's FTP server. Figure 1.28 shows this dialog box.

By default, the service is configured to allow anonymous read-only access. You'll learn how to test this access in the upcoming section, "Testing the IIS Installation."

> **Note:** For more information on configuring the FTP service, see Day 5, "The FTP Service."

Figure 1.27.
The FTP service's context menu in MMC lets you manipulate the FTP service.

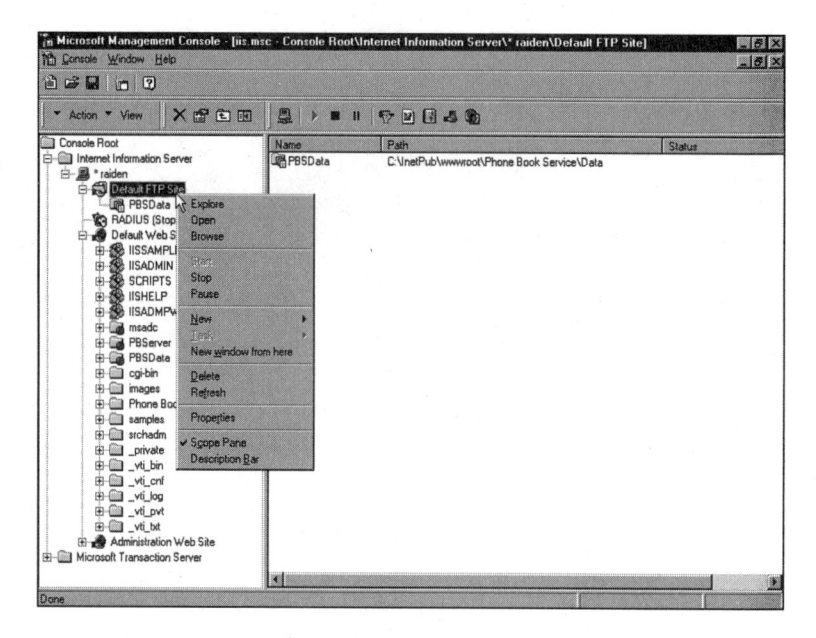

Figure 1.28.
Selecting the Properties option brings up configuration options for the default FTP server site.

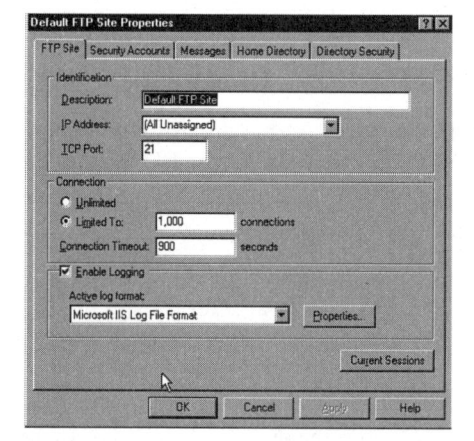

1.4.3. Basic WWW Configuration

Accessing the configuration of IIS' WWW service is also quite simple. Expand the scope for the Internet Information Server snap-in until you can see the Default Web Site entry. Right-click on Default Web Site and select Properties to open the Default Web Site Properties dialog box shown in Figure 1.29.

Figure 1.29.
This Properties dialog box shows the current configuration properties for the Default Web Site.

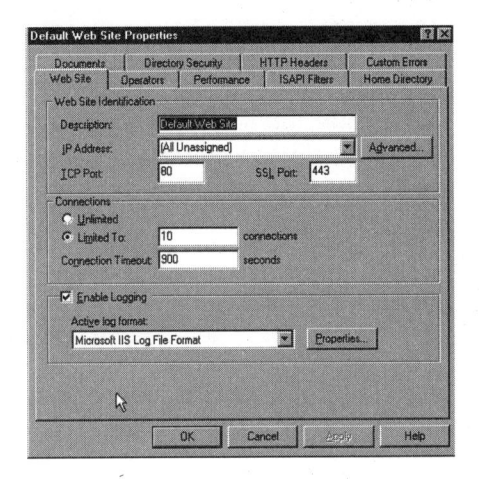

> **Note:** For more information on configuring the WWW service, see Day 4, "The WWW Server."

1.5. Testing the IIS Installation

Whether you're testing the default installation provided by Microsoft or testing your own pages and configuration later, the only truly reliable test method is to connect to your IIS server using the appropriate client tools.

To test the FTP server, go to the Windows NT Command Prompt and type:

```
ftp localhost
```

This launches the FTP client and connects you to your own IP address.

> **Note:** If you're not familiar with the LOCALHOST alias or other IP addressing issues, you can get a quick review in Day 14, "Troubleshooting."

At the username prompt, type anonymous. When prompted for your password, type your email address in the form *<username>@<domain>*. If the FTP site is configured properly, you'll be allowed to log in. See Figure 1.30 for an example of a successful login.

Day 1: Internet Information Server—The Basics

Figure 1.30.
The default IIS installation should allow for simple read-only anonymous logins.

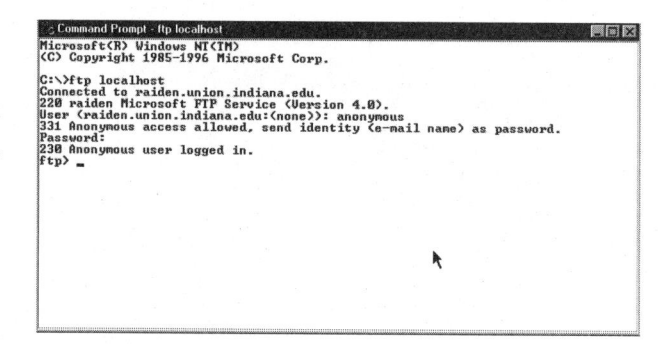

```
Microsoft(R) Windows NT(TM)
(C) Copyright 1985-1996 Microsoft Corp.

C:\>ftp localhost
Connected to raiden.union.indiana.edu.
220 raiden Microsoft FTP Service (Version 4.0).
User (raiden.union.indiana.edu:(none)): anonymous
331 Anonymous access allowed, send identity (e-mail name) as password.
Password:
230 Anonymous user logged in.
ftp>
```

Testing WWW access is even simpler. To do so, simply launch your browser and type the following in the URL field:

`http://localhost/`

If the WWW site is configured properly, you'll see the default installation home page, shown in Figure 1.31.

Figure 1.31.
The default IIS installation should also allow you to view the default HTML files.

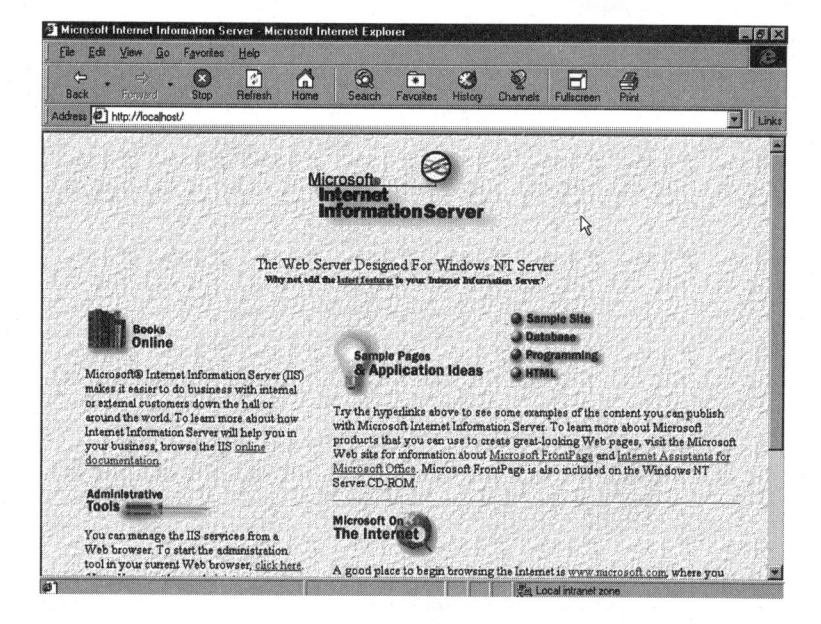

Whenever you develop new services using IIS, you should always test them for proper functionality using an actual Web browser and FTP clients both from the server itself and over the network.

> **Test Tip**
> When you're testing production Web services, it's a good idea to also test your FTP and WWW services from another workstation on the network to make certain that network connectivity is working properly on your IIS server.

1.6. Changes Made to Windows NT by Internet Information Server

The installation program of the Internet Information Server performs a number of changes to Windows NT. First, IIS creates, by default, an \INETPUB directory in the root of the installation hard drive. This directory contains a number of subdirectories, including the following:

- *\FTPROOT.* The home directory for the default FTP site.
- *\WWWROOT.* The home directory of the default WWW site.
- *\SCRIPTS.* The default directory for IIS scripts.
- *\IISSAMPLES.* A directory for holding sample pages and objects for the sample Web sites.

The number of directories the installation creates depends on which services you chose during Option Pack installation. The default directories created by a sample IIS installation are shown in Figure 1.32.

Figure 1.32.
A default IIS installation creates a number of service directories on the installation drive.

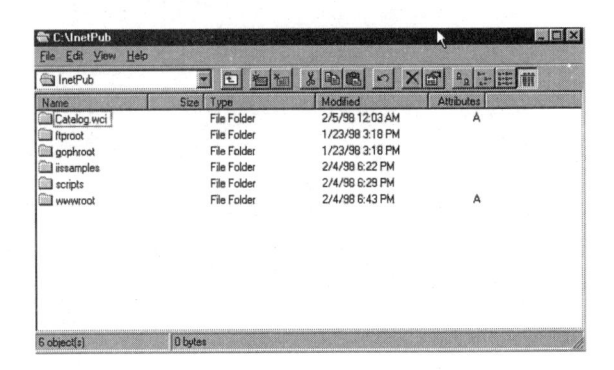

Day 1: Internet Information Server—The Basics

> **Note:** You are not required to use these default directories for serving files; the various directories can be configured to use nearly any directory on your local hard drive, as well as directories available over network shares.

Second, IIS creates program folders containing shortcuts for the various applications you've chosen, as illustrated in Figure 1.33. As you can see in the figure, Internet Information Server's program group includes shortcuts to the FrontPage Server Administrator tool, the preconfigured Internet Service Manager MMC console, and the HTML version of the Internet Service Manager.

Figure 1.33.
The Windows NT Option Pack installation creates shortcuts for configuring and administering services.

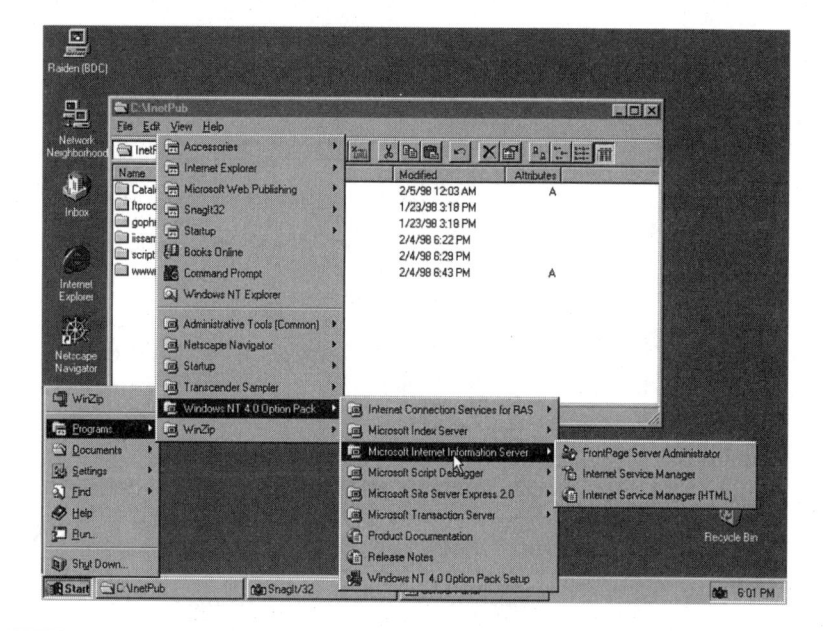

Third, IIS installs new control panels for those services that require them, such as the Microsoft Transaction Server's DTC (Distributed Transaction Coordinator) control panel (see Figure 1.34).

Fourth, IIS installs a number of system services, depending on which services were selected at the time of installation. These services include the FTP Publishing Service, the WWW Publishing Service, and the MS DTC service.

Figure 1.34.

The Windows NT Option Pack services often install new control panels.

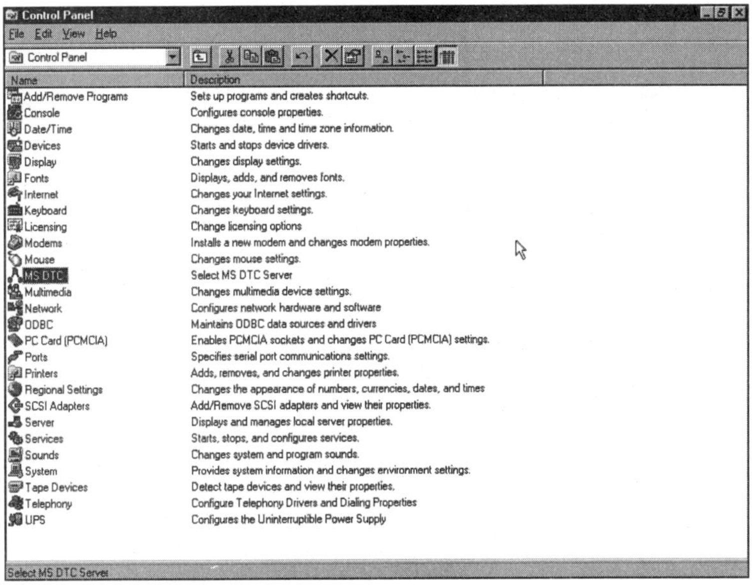
Control Panel
File Edit View Help
Control Panel
Name
Description
Add/Remove Programs
Sets up programs and creates shortcuts.
Console
Configures console properties.
Date/Time
Changes date, time and time zone information.
Devices
Starts and stops device drivers.
Display
Changes display settings.
Fonts
Displays, adds, and removes fonts.
Internet
Changes your Internet settings.
Keyboard
Changes keyboard settings.
Licensing
Change licensing options
Modems
Installs a new modem and changes modem properties.
Mouse
Changes mouse settings.
MS DTC
Select MS DTC Server
Multimedia
Changes multimedia device settings.
Network
Configures network hardware and software
ODBC
Maintains ODBC data sources and drivers
PC Card (PCMCIA)
Enables PCMCIA sockets and changes PC Card (PCMCIA) settings.
Ports
Specifies serial port communications settings.
Printers
Adds, removes, and changes printer properties.
Regional Settings
Changes the appearance of numbers, currencies, dates, and times
SCSI Adapters
Add/Remove SCSI adapters and view their properties.
Server
Displays and manages local server properties.
Services
Starts, stops, and configures services.
Sounds
Changes system and program sounds.
System
Provides system information and changes environment settings.
Tape Devices
Detect tape devices and view their properties.
Telephony
Configure Telephony Drivers and Dialing Properties
UPS
Configures the Uninterruptible Power Supply
Select MS DTC Server

Test Tip

In previous versions of IIS, you could stop and start the entire product by using the W3SVC service. Now you must instead use the IISADMIN service to control the entire product. For more information on these services, see Days 3, 4, and 5.

Fifth, after an IIS installation,Windows NT's TCP stack will begin listening to the ports used for IIS services. By default, HTTP listens to port 80, and FTP listens to port 21.

Last, an IIS installation creates the new user IUSR_<*computername*> on the server (or in the domain, if the installation server is a domain controller). This user represents the user context for anonymous connections to the IIS server. For example, if IIS were installed on a server named RAIDEN, the anonymous user would be named IUSR_RAIDEN.

If Microsoft Transaction Server is installed, it will also create a user, named IWAM_<*computername*>. This account represents the user context for the Web Application Manager.

Note

For more information on anonymous authentication and the Web Application Manager, see Day 2, "IIS Architecture and Components."

Lab

This lab consists of review questions pertaining to this chapter and provides an opportunity for you to use walk-through exercises to apply the knowledge you've learned.

Questions

1. John has just installed Internet Information Server using the default serving directories. Which of the following is the default directory for serving HTML files via IIS? (Choose the best answer.)

    A. \inetsrv\wwwroot

    B. \iis4\wwwroot

    C. \inetsrv\htmlroot

    D. \iis4\httproot

    E. \inetsrv\httproot

2. Following the installation listed in question 1, which of the following is the default directory for the FTP server? (Choose the best answer.)

    A. \iis4\downloads

    B. \inetsrv\downloads

    C. \inetsrv\ftproot

    D. \inetsrv\downloadroot

3. Which of the following is NOT a service provided by Internet Information Server? (Choose the best answer.)

    A. World Wide Web services via HTTP

    B. Internet firewall services via Microsoft Proxy Server

    C. File transfer services via FTP

    D. Internet certificate issuance via Microsoft Certificate Server

4. You need to reinstall IIS on your server, but you'd like to be able to script it to run unattended. Assuming you've generated your answer file correctly, which of the following is a valid command to start an unattended upgrade setup of the Windows NT Option Pack? (Choose the best answer.)

A. sysocmgr.exe /unattended:c:\unattend.txt

B. setup.exe /l:c:\winnt\system32\setup\iisv4.inf /c /u:c:\unattend.txt

C. unsetup.exe /u:c:\unattend.txt

D. sysocmgr.exe /l:c:\winnt\system32\setup\iisv4.inf /c /u:c:\unattend.txt

5. Which of the following is the default extension for a Microsoft Management Console custom console? (Choose the best answer.)

    A. .mct

    B. .mcs

    C. .mmc

    D. .msc

6. Which of the following services are provided by Internet Information Server 4.0? (Select all correct answers.)

    A. HTTP

    B. FTP

    C. Gopher

    D. SMTP

7. What types of tools can be developed for Microsoft Management Console? (Select all correct answers.)

    A. Device drivers

    B. Snap-ins

    C. Snap-in extensions

    D. Virtual DOS machines

8. Which of the following are valid requirements for installing the Windows NT Option Pack? (Select all correct answers.)

    A. Internet Explorer 4.01

    B. Internet Explorer 3.01

    C. Netscape Communicator 4.01

    D. Microsoft Systems Management Server

9. Microsoft Management Console will not be available until Windows NT 5.0 is released.

    A. True

    B. False

10. Internet Information Server 4.0 can be downloaded as a standalone product.

    A. True

    B. False

Answers to Questions

1. **A.** The default HTML directory for IIS is \inetsrv\wwwroot. The other directories are not created by default.

2. **C.** The default FTP directory for IIS is \inetsrv\ftproot. The other directories are not created by default.

3. **B.** IIS provides World Wide Web and FTP sevices, and includes Microsoft Certificate Server. Microsoft Proxy Server, however, is a seperate product.

4. **D.** To start an unattended upgrade setup of the NT Option Pack, use sysocmgr.exe /1:<qualified path ot iisv4.inf> /c/u:<qualified path to unattend.txt>. The other answers are not valid.

5. **D.** Microsoft Management Console saves tool configurations in files with the extension .msc.

6. **A, B, D.** IIS 4.0 includes a WWW service, an FTP service, and an SMTP service; however, it no longer supports Gopher.

7. **B, C.** Microsoft Management Console supports snap-ins and snap-in extensions.

8. **A.** The NT Option Pack requires that Internet Explorer 4.01 or later be installed.

9. **B.** False. Microsoft Management Console is included in the NT Option Pack.

10. **B.** False. Internet Information Server 4.0 is included only in the NT Option Pack.

> **Note:** This exercise addresses the following objective:
> - Installing IIS

Exercise

This exercise re-examines the process of installing Internet Information Server. Perform the following steps:

1. Connect to Microsoft's IIS Web page (http://www.microsoft.com/iis/) and download the Windows NT Option Pack files for later installation. Download the files in whatever language you prefer and from the site nearest to you.

2. When you have the files in a convenient location, begin a complete (or full) installation of IIS 4.0.

3. After the IIS installation is complete, test your installation's functionality via a Web client and an FTP client.

TEST DAY FAST FACTS

Here are a few fast facts about this chapter that you may want to know ahead of time. Don't forget that these facts also provide great last-minute study material.

- IIS integrates with Windows NT Server to provide security for HTTP and FTP connections.

- FTP sites can allow anonymous authentication, or they can require the use of clear-text usernames and passwords (or any combination thereof).

- Web sites can allow anonymous access, they can require the use of clear-text usernames and passwords, or they can require the use of Windows NT Challenge/Response encrypted authentication (or any combination thereof).

- CGI applications require the creation and deletion of a process for each application request.

- ISAPI applications can be run within the process context of IIS itself or in their own processes. Microsoft Transaction Server can be used to keep ISAPI processes alive as long as there are pending requests, thus improving performance.

- ISAPI programs can be extensions or HTTP filters.

- The WAM (Web Application Manager) handles the execution of ISAPI programs, ASP scripts, and component extensions.

Day 2

IIS Architecture and Components

by James F. Causey

In Day 1, "Internet Information Server—The Basics," one of the basic topics was the essential question: *What is Internet Information Server?* Our answer, while adequate, was not complete, as you probably realized when you saw all the additional tools and options during the NT Option Pack setup. This probably became even more obvious if you spent any time paging through the massive amount of documentation included with the product.

This chapter attempts to address the question a lot more thoroughly. We're going to discuss the architecture of the Internet Information Server product and its included available components. In the process, we're going to try to help you get a grip on the complete, rich set of features and functionality provided by the Internet Information Server platform. Armed with that knowledge, you'll be able to approach the remaining twelve chapters prepared to learn the more specific task-oriented knowledge. You'll also be able to envision the different ways you can implement IIS 4.0 to perform the Internet and intranet serving and application tasks you may encounter in the future.

IIS 4.0 includes a vast number of components. However, for the IIS 4.0 exam, Microsoft focuses primarily on the major components used for developing advanced Internet/intranet servers. These components include the following:

- FTP Service
- HTTP Service
- Microsoft Transaction Server
- Microsoft SMTP Service
- Microsoft NNTP Service
- Microsoft Index Server
- Microsoft Certificate Server

Because the exam focuses so heavily on these components, this book also focuses on them. In this chapter, we'll help you gain an understanding of these components by describing how they're incorporated into the Internet Information Server platform. Then, throughout the remaining twelve chapters, you'll learn the information you need to implement these services and construct solutions using these components. With this combination of architectural theory and practical implementation, you'll be ready to tackle the Microsoft objective, "Choose the appropriate technology to resolve specified problems," on the exam.

We'll begin by discussing the basic architecture of the Internet Information Server and how it performs the delivery of both static and programmatic content in unison with Windows NT Server. We'll then talk about the additional features of the Internet Information Server that make it a powerful data and application servicing platform. Next, we'll discuss the administration features of IIS 4.0. We'll then look at those components not

Test Day Fast Facts

- IIS 4.0 supports a number of HTTP 1.1 extensions that improve performance and add functionality.

- Microsoft Transaction Server provides developers with a simple method of supporting transaction-based processing.

- Microsoft Message Queue Server provides developers with a simple method of supporting process-to-process and application-to-application communications, even over heterogeneous networks.

- IIS includes a wide range of options for accessing back-end databases, including Access, Microsoft SQL Server, Oracle, Sybase, and many others.

- IIS can be administered via the Microsoft Management Console, via the World Wide Web, via scripts (with the help of the Windows Scripting Host), or via third-party applications.

- Microsoft Index Server provides flexible indexing and search functions for a wide range of objects on a Web server.

- Microsoft SMTP Service provides applications with a way to send outbound mail to administrators.

- Microsoft NNTP Service allows for the creation of discussion groups (or newsgroups).

- Microsoft Certificate Server allows organizations to generate their own digital certificates, which can be used for identification and authentication purposes.

previously touched on in our discussion up to that point (SMTP and NNTP). Finally, the last section in the chapter lets you in on how to draw upon all the preceding information in order to choose an implementation for your system (another objective to be addressed on the exam).

We strongly encourage you to spend some time thoroughly reading this chapter, whether you're new to IIS or whether you're a veteran from previous versions. In either case, you're probably not fully aware of all the flexibility and power provided by IIS 4.0, and this chapter can help you understand the breadth of those individual features and how they can be integrated into a single, powerful solution.

Objectives

This chapter helps you prepare for the Microsoft Exam by covering the following objectives:

- Choose the appropriate technology to resolve specified problems. (Technology includes WWW service, FTP service, Microsoft Transaction Server, Microsoft SMTP Service, Microsoft NNTP Service, Microsoft Index Server, and Microsoft Certificate Server.)
- Choose an implementation strategy for an Internet site or an intranet site for standalone servers, single-domain environments, and multiple-domain environments.
    - Choose the appropriate operating system on which to install IIS.
    - Resolve host header name issues by using a HOSTS file, DNS, or both.

2.1. Internet Information Server Architecture

Internet Information Server was designed from the ground up to provide basic, fundamental Internet/intranet services while including the latest capabilities to provide a cross-platform application deployment platform. It provides all these features while maintaining tight integration with the Windows NT Server.

We'll begin our discussion of the IIS product architecture by looking at the most basic functionality: delivery of static content. Serving static content is the simplest IIS architectural concept to understand, but it also provides the fundamentals for all other types of IIS data and application services. We'll describe the generic architectural mechanisms, as well as any specifics or catches that apply specifically to the delivery of files using FTP and static HTML files. When that's done, we'll move on to discuss how IIS performs Web-hosted application services and delivery of dynamic content.

2.1.1. Static Content Delivery Architecture

The delivery of static content can be seen as the most baseline service provided by Internet server products today. The delivery of this content includes the ability to serve files via the FTP protocol and deliver HTML pages that do not require dynamic modification or generation services.

The IIS product has always included the ability to serve static content to intranet and Internet clients while maintaining tight coupling with the features of the underlying operating system. This integration allows IIS to provide a high level of functionality and security.

Let's break up the process of serving static data into a few steps; then we'll look at the big picture.

> **Note:** Throughout the rest of this chapter, we'll be discussing many of the features and options of the Internet Information Server platform. For the most part, we'll avoid the technical details of implementing and configuring each option right now; those details are covered in the remainder of this book. For now, just try to get a solid handle on the range of functionality available with an IIS system.

A. Step One: The Client Establishes a Connection

The first step in any data transfer using IIS involves the establishment of a communications session by the remote client. This process is initiated when the client application—whether a Web browser or an FTP application—contacts the appropriate TCP port on the server and requests a connection. (If you're not familiar with the concept of TCP ports and sockets, or if you need a little refresher, check out the TCP/IP review in Day 14, "Troubleshooting.")

The IIS processes on the server "listen" to the appropriate ports for the services they're supporting in order to respond to client connection requests. This is done by requesting that the NT network stack signal the processes when a connection attempt is made. When this signal is received, if the appropriate IIS signal process decides to allow the connection (which it does as long as the maximum number of connections has not been exceeded and the client's address is not restricted from connecting to the server), it opens a socket to the remote client and establishes a session—again via the network stack. This process is illustrated in Figure 2.1.

Figure 2.1.
The Internet Information Server uses the NT TCP/IP protocol stack to monitor potential connections.

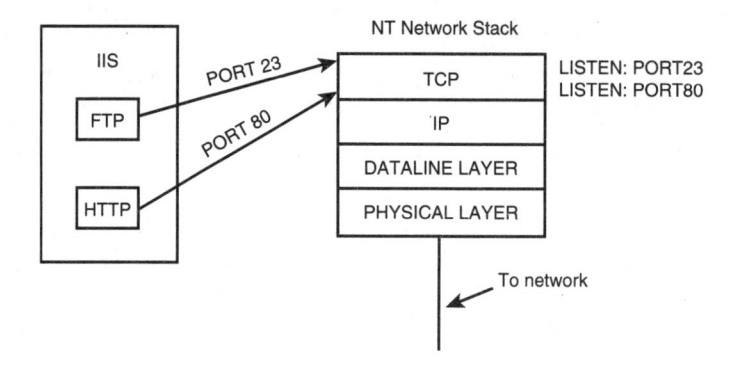

This connection process has one important variation between the FTP and HTTP services. With FTP, after the session is established, it is maintained for the entire period within which a client wishes to perform tasks and is closed only at the specific request of either the server or the client (in the event that the client user disconnected, authentication failed, or a timeout was signaled).

HTTP, on the other hand, normally establishes one session *for each object being requested.* This means that for each Web page, graphics file, or other object displayed on a page, the client must negotiate a new session, download the data, and disconnect. This repetitive, time-consuming behavior wastes network bandwidth and reduces performance.

> **Note:** The W3C (World Wide Web Consortium, a neutral body that develops standards for World Wide Web protocols and usage) has addressed this problem in a number of different fashions (including HTTP Keep-Alives) that are supported in IIS 4.0; we'll discuss these potential solutions in the section "HTTP Features," later in the chapter.

B. Step Two: Client Authentication

Now that a session has been established, the IIS needs to authenticate the client session to determine what rights and privileges, if any, the client should have on the server. This authentication is performed using Windows NT's Security Account Manager (SAM). IIS establishes an identity for the client system and then passes that identity and password, if necessary, on to the SAM for the server (or for the domain, if the server is participating in a Windows NT domain). The SAM consults the security accounts database to determine if that identity is valid, and based on that result, IIS either allows the session to continue or breaks off the connection. This process is illustrated in Figure 2.2.

Figure 2.2.
Internet Information Server works with the Windows NT Security Account Manager to authenticate client sessions.

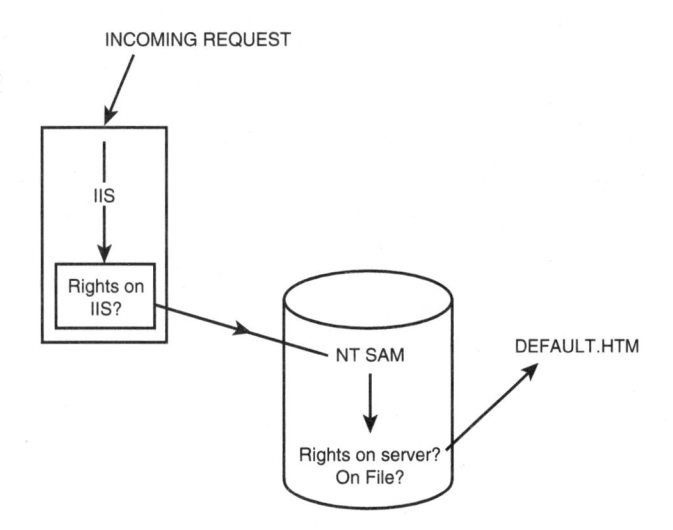

INCOMING REQUEST

IIS

Rights on IIS?

NT SAM

Rights on server? On File?

DEFAULT.HTM

The identity established by the remote client can take one of two forms:

- Anonymous
- User-specific

These forms of identification are covered in detail in the next two sections.

Anonymous

Anonymous access dates back to the initial days of the FTP protocol. FTP has traditionally been used not only to allow normal system users to log in and transfer files, but also to provide a convenient repository for users across the Internet to freely download files (and, occasionally, to upload files to public archives). This anonymous access scheme is also normally used by Web servers to allow anyone to access and view HTML files.

The method in which the identity "anonymous" is established differs between FTP and HTTP. With FTP, the client passes the server the username "anonymous" when prompted; if anonymous access is enabled on the server, the client is then asked to provide the server with the email address of the client user as the password. This convention allows FTP server administrators to better monitor the use of their systems.

With HTTP, however, the client simply requests the specified document, and if no identity is included in the request and anonymous access is allowed for the requested object, it's transferred to the Web client.

Although the methods of establishing anonymous identity differ between the two protocols, they are both handled similarly by IIS. IIS uses a specific user in the system (or domain) SAM database to represent anonymous Internet access to the system by either WWW or FTP clients. That user is, by default, named IUSR_<computername> (for example, on a system named RAIDEN, the account is named IUSR_RAIDEN). When a client authenticates using the anonymous identity, all her requests are run within the context of the NT anonymous user, as illustrated in Figure 2.3.

Figure 2.3.
Internet Information Server uses a specific NT user account to represent anonymous access.

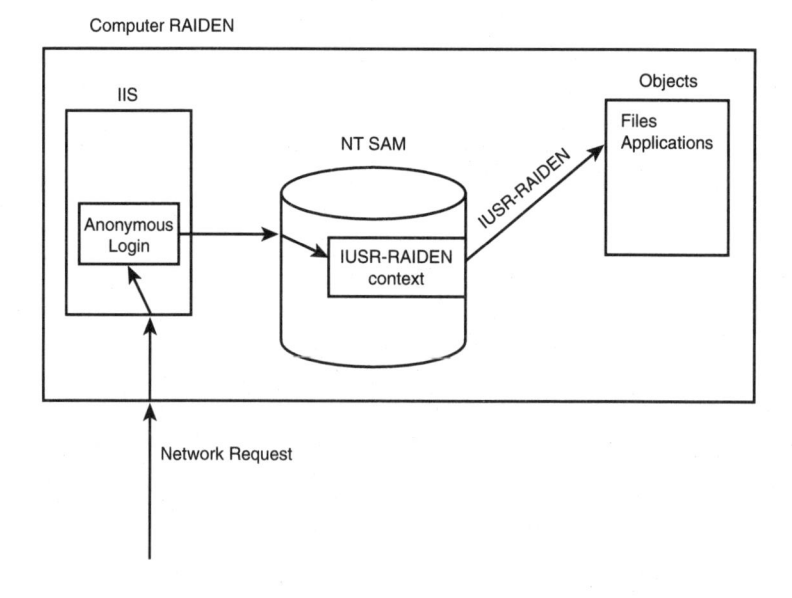

Anonymous FTP user access is often used by corporations or organizations who wish to make libraries of software (such as product updates or hardware drivers) available to anyone on the Internet. Anonymous HTTP user access is the traditional method of providing content on the World Wide Web that anyone can view.

User-Specific

With user-specific access, a client must identify himself to the Internet Information Server using a specific username and password that are valid on the NT server. This method is used when the Web site administrators wish to make content available only to certain individuals or groups (such as when a corporation provides confidential information on its corporate intranet). As with anonymous access, this is implemented in different ways for the FTP and HTTP services.

With FTP, the client is prompted for a username and password when the session is first established. That username and password are passed by IIS on to the NT SAM as described earlier. Then the SAM either accepts or rejects the authentication, and IIS either allows the session to continue or disconnects the remote client.

With HTTP, user-specific access works a little bit differently. When a Web client requests a particular file, the server responds by instructing the client to prompt for a username and password. The client returns that username and password to IIS, which then authenticates the request in the same way as with FTP. If the authentication succeeds, the server returns the requested data; if not, it returns an error message.

IIS supports two distinct methods for establishing user-specific identities. The first is Basic Authentication, in which the username and password gathered by the client are passed in clear-text to the server. This is the simplest method and is supported by all modern web clients and FTP clients, but it is rather insecure because anyone who can access the packets containing the username and password with protocol analyzer software can steal that information.

The second, more secure, mechanism is called Windows NT Challenge/Response Authentication, or NTLM (NT/LAN Manager). With this mechanism, the username and password used by the client to log into the Windows workstation are automatically passed to the IIS server. This method is both simpler for the client user and more secure because the NTLM authentication protocol encrypts the username and password. However, NTLM is currently supported only by Internet Explorer version 2.0 or later.

> **Note:** NT/IIS security interaction is discussed in more detail in Day 6, "Internet Information Server Security."

> **Test Tip:** Keep in mind that the FTP server supports only Basic Authentication; thus, if you require user-specific authentication, your users' NT usernames and passwords will be transferred insecurely across the network. Because NTLM is not supported for FTP access, it is recommended that you allow anonymous access to your FTP site only in order to prevent your system's usernames and passwords from being transmitted in the clear.

> **Note:** Internet Information Server also supports the development of custom authentication mechanisms using ISAPI filters. For more information on this, see the section "Internet Server Application Programming Interface (ISAPI)," later in the chapter.

C. Step Three: Processing of Client Requests

After a client has been authenticated via either anonymous or user-specific security, IIS can run that client session within the context of the selected user (either the system anonymous user or the specifically logged-in user). Each request to download or upload a file or switch into a directory is checked separately in two ways:

- First it's checked against the rights allowed by the configuration of IIS (which can allow read or write access to a particular Web or FTP site and can also process the request using a custom ISAPI filter).
- Then it's checked against the NT Access Control List (ACL for short) for the particular requested object.

> **Test Tip:** NT cannot perform authentication at the file system level unless NTFS is used for the IIS file space because the FAT file system does not support ACL attributes.

See Figure 2.4 for an illustration of the IIS security authentication process.

Figure 2.4.
Internet Information Server checks for security violations on each separate client object request.

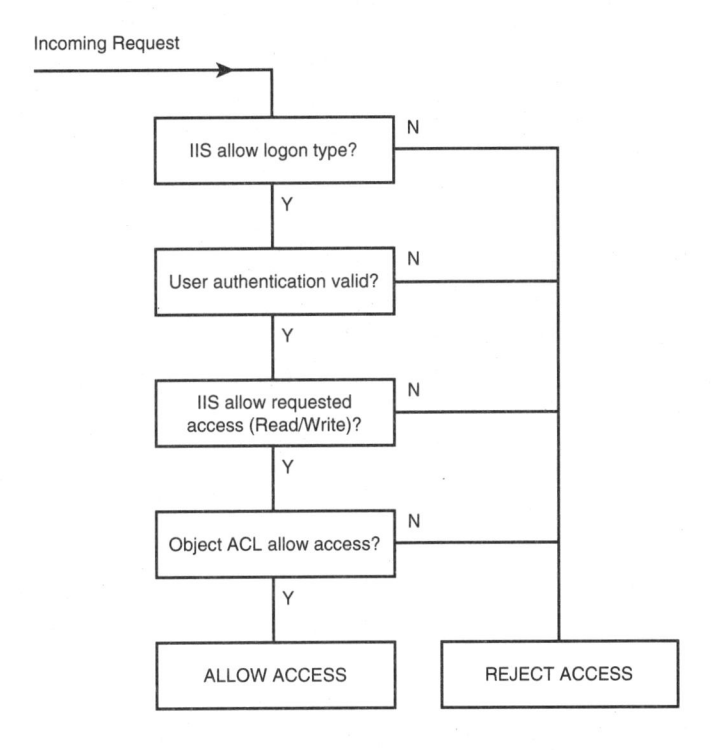

```
Incoming Request
       │
       ▼
┌─────────────────────┐   N
│ IIS allow logon type? ├──────┐
└──────────┬──────────┘      │
           │ Y                │
           ▼                  │
┌─────────────────────┐   N   │
│ User authentication valid? ├─┤
└──────────┬──────────┘      │
           │ Y                │
           ▼                  │
┌─────────────────────┐   N   │
│ IIS allow requested │       │
│ access (Read/Write)? ├──────┤
└──────────┬──────────┘      │
           │ Y                │
           ▼                  │
┌─────────────────────┐   N   │
│ Object ACL allow access? ├──┤
└──────────┬──────────┘      │
           │ Y                │
           ▼                  ▼
   ┌──────────────┐    ┌──────────────┐
   │ ALLOW ACCESS │    │ REJECT ACCESS│
   └──────────────┘    └──────────────┘
```

If both IIS and the NT SAM allow the specified client access, IIS performs the requested task. For a file read request, it uses standard NT mechanisms to read the file from disk and then transfer that file to the client over TCP/IP. For a file write request, the process works in reverse: IIS receives the file from the requesting client and then asks NT to write it to disk.

Those are the basic steps for delivering static content. Now picture them working together as an integrated whole. Figure 2.5 shows the architecture used by IIS for delivering static content.

2.1.2. Dynamic Content Delivery/Application Architecture

As the World Wide Web matured, so did expectations for its abilities. Originally designed as a method to provide static content, the Web quickly evolved to incorporate more sophisticated capabilities, which enabled it to provide dynamic content delivery. Of particular interest to Web site developers were the following capabilities:

- To receive information from the client using forms and other data-gathering mechanisms

- To dynamically generate and modify Web pages
- To deliver Web-enabled versions of enterprise application services that traditionally ran on local workstations or on mainframes

Figure 2.5.
Internet Information Server integrates tightly with Windows NT to provide static content.

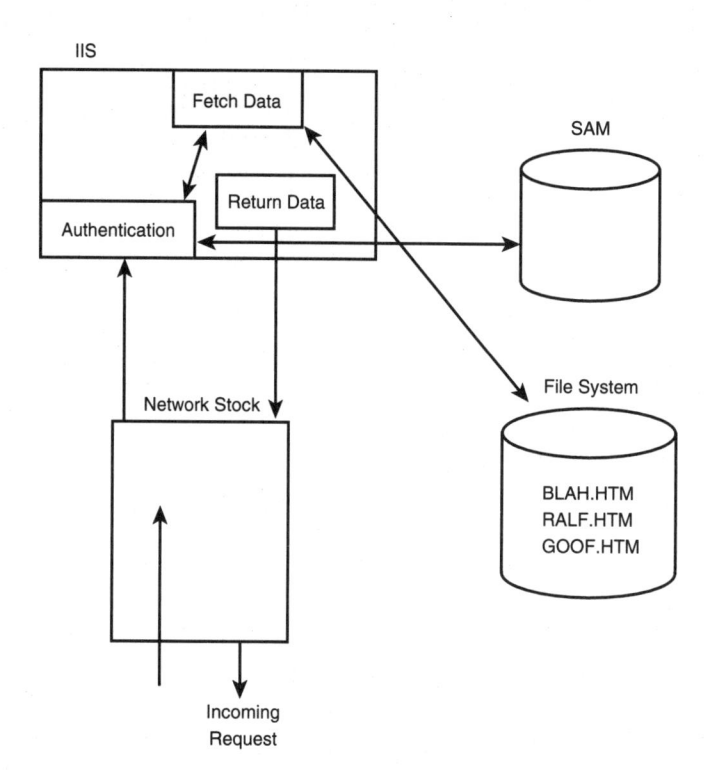

Internet Information Server 4.0 supports a number of different mechanisms for delivering this functionality. In this section, we'll review those mechanisms (CGI, ISAPI, ASP, and server-side Java) and how they're integrated with Windows NT.

A. Common Gateway Interface (CGI)

Perhaps the earliest and most widely supported method of providing application functionality via the World Wide Web is CGI, the Common Gateway Interface. CGI specifies an application programming interface for passing parameters to executable files or scripts via the URL sent from the client, for allowing those programs to dynamically generate page content in reply, and for performing other application tasks on the back-end, as illustrated in Figure 2.6.

2.1. Internet Information Server Architecture   53

Figure 2.6.
CGI allows Web clients to pass parameters to applications on the server, which can then perform tasks such as dynamic page generation.

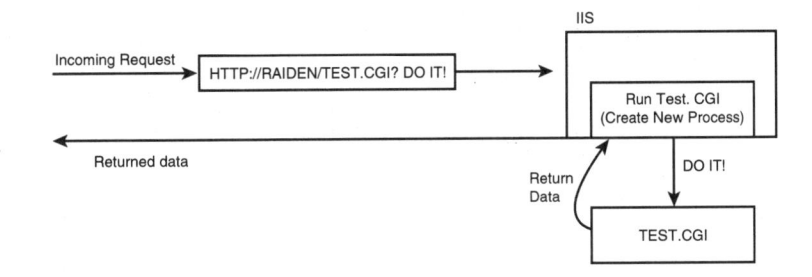

CGI is highly flexible and can be used to support both compiled executable programs and interpreted scripts. This capability allows a wide range of individuals to develop dynamic Web-based applications using their preferred development tools (whether those tools are scripting languages or traditional compiled languages).

CGI can be thought of as the lowest common denominator for web-hosted applications, as it is supported by nearly every Web server on every platform. Because it is so generic, however, CGI does not integrate tightly with the features of NT Server or the special abilities of the Internet Information Server.

In addition, CGI is rather inefficient. Every invocation of a CGI request causes the server to start a new process on the server to run the executable and then to destroy that process when the request has been served. While this works well enough on most UNIX platforms where the lowest degree of OS scheduling resolution lies at the process level, Windows NT's purely-threaded environment makes the creation and destruction of entire processes an expensive process. On a heavily loaded server, this expense can begin to take its toll on the server's performance, and it severely limits the scalability of CGI-based solutions.

B. Internet Server Application Programming Interface (ISAPI)

ISAPI can be thought of as Microsoft's answer to the limitations of CGI. ISAPI provides a way for developers to generate compiled, Windows NT-native applications that take full advantage of the features of both Windows NT and the Internet Information Server. ISAPI applications—which are implemented as dynamic link libraries (dll's) so they can be run in-process with IIS—can be developed with any Win32-capable compiling development environment, including Microsoft's Visual C++. As Win32 applications, ISAPI programs have all the capabilities of a traditional Windows program or service, including the capability to use COM (Component Object Model) and DCOM (Distributed COM) components to extend their functionality.

In previous versions of IIS, ISAPI applications always ran within the process context of the Internet Information Server itself. This eliminated the primary performance cost of CGI applications, allowing ISAPI programs to reduce the amount of load placed on the server for application execution tasks. This in-process execution is still the default context for ISAPI program execution in IIS 4.0.

However, running extension applications within the context of the server has a drawback. If the ISAPI program becomes unreliable or crashes, it can potentially affect the stability of Internet Information Server itself. In an environment where multiple ISAPI-based applications are run, this risk increases significantly because ISAPI applications can interfere with each other as well as with IIS (see Figure 2.7).

Figure 2.7.
IIS normally executes ISAPI applications in-process, enhancing performance but reducing reliability.

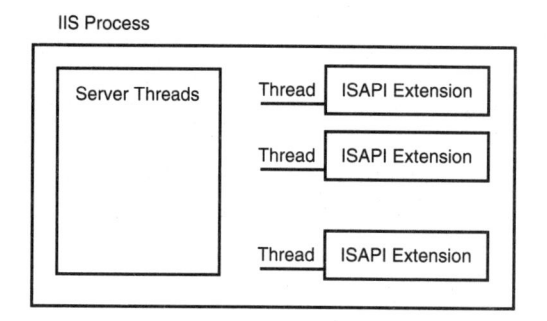

IIS 4.0 addresses this concern with the inclusion of a new component: the Web Application Manager, or WAM for short. WAM is a COM object that provides application management services for IIS, including communication between the IIS and applications themselves. When an ISAPI application is executed—depending on how it was developed—either the application can be scheduled in-process, or it can use the facilities of Microsoft Transaction Server to launch a new, separate process for the application. Microsoft refers to this capability as *crash protection* because an out-of-process ISAPI program cannot crash other ISAPI programs or the Internet Information Server itself. In addition, if an out-of-process ISAPI program does terminate abnormally, MTS can detect the status of the program's WAM and can attempt to re-start it, limiting the downtime of application services that rely on that program. This ability is often referred to as *crash recovery*. Figure 2.8 illustrates these points.

In addition, WAM attempts to continuously keep an ISAPI program's process alive for as long as requests for it are available in order to minimize the cost of process generation and destruction (in contrast with CGI, which creates and destroys a new process for each individual CGI request). The Web Application Manager integrates tightly with Microsoft Transaction Server for much of its functionality; we discuss Microsoft Transaction Server in the section "Microsoft Transaction Server," later in this chapter.

Figure 2.8.
The WAM in IIS 4.0 can execute applications out-of-process for increased reliability.

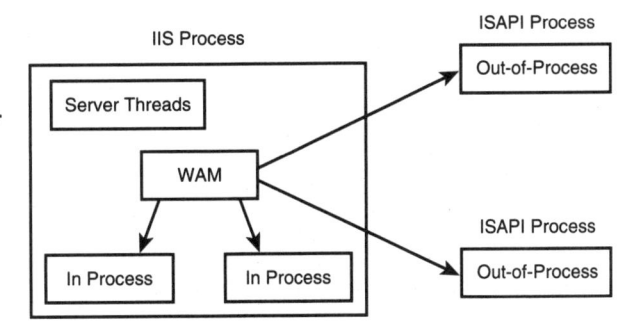

IIS supports two kinds of ISAPI applications:

- ISAPI extensions
- ISAPI filters

An *ISAPI extension* is an application designed to extend the functionality of IIS, as we've discussed throughout this section. ISAPI extensions can be used to perform most common Web application tasks, such as dynamic page generation and database integration. For example, an ISAPI extension could be used to dynamically generate a web page based on information gleaned from a Web browser.

ISAPI filters can be used to receive various events during the processing of HTTP requests. Therefore, ISAPI filters can perform a number of different functions, including authentication and security filtering, Web page redirection, data translation, and other tasks.

ISAPI is a powerful method for extending the functionality of Internet Information Server without having to sacrifice reliability or performance. For more information on ISAPI extensions and filters, see Day 11, "Programmability."

C. Active Server Pages (ASP)

ISAPI provides a powerful and flexible method for supporting Web-hosted applications. However, it retains one major drawback for many people: ISAPI applications must be developed and compiled for the Win32 API using traditional tools such as

C++. Many Web developers lack the skills or experience necessary to perform the sometimes-difficult task of developing compiled applications. With Active Server Pages, Microsoft addressed this problem yet maintained most of the advantages of ISAPI.

Active Server Pages is one of the IIS-specific technologies designed to enhance the functionality and reliability of Web-based application services. ASP is the part of Internet Information Server that allows Web developers to embed script-based application processing directly into HTML pages. This allows developers to provide dynamic content generation, database integration, and other Web application tasks with a minimum investment in new languages or Windows-specific development knowledge.

Active Server Pages is language-neutral, and can support any script for which interpreters are available. ASP already supports common scripting languages such as VBScript, JavaScript, and Perl. The scripts are interpreted at run-time by ASP and require no compilation. In addition, ASP scripts can call upon COM components running on the server to enhance their functionality.

ASP scripts and integrated components are normally run within the same process as IIS to improve their performance. However, under IIS 4.0, ASP scripts are managed by the WAM, which means that scripts and components can utilize crash protection to run out-of-process for maximum reliability. See Figure 2.9 for an illustration of the ASP architecture.

Figure 2.9.
Active Server Pages allows scripts embedded in HTML documents much of the power and flexibility of ISAPI or CGI applications.

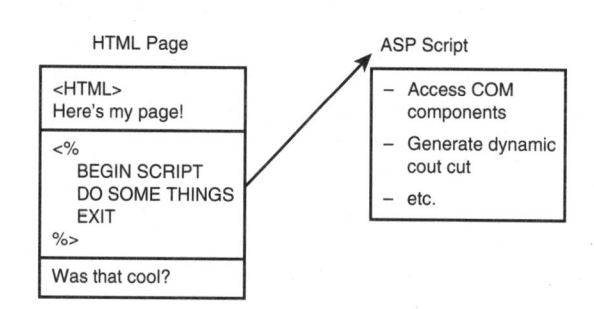

HTML Page
```
<HTML>
Here's my page!
<%
  BEGIN SCRIPT
  DO SOME THINGS
  EXIT
%>
Was that cool?
```

ASP Script
- Access COM components
- Generate dynamic cout cut
- etc.

Active Server Pages provides a method for non-programmers to develop robust, reliable applications for Internet Information Server without the expense or learning curve of a traditional programming environment. However, because ASP scripts are interpreted, they cannot match the potential performance of compiled ISAPI extensions. In addition, ISAPI extensions can natively access all services provided by the Win32 API, whereas ASP must often be extended with additional components to access that functionality (when it's practical to do so at all).

D. Server-Side Java

IIS 4.0 includes the ability to execute server-side components developed using the Java language. This allows Web application developers to use Java for components that execute on the server instead of in client windows. Server-side Java components can be invoked by Active Server Pages in the same way that a COM component is invoked. The IIS JVM includes a number of powerful features, outlined here:

- *Java 1.1 support.* The IIS JVM supports the version 1.1 specification for Java, which includes a number of enhancements.
- *Multiple access contexts.* Traditionally, Java components execute within a "sandbox," which prevents Java programs from having potentially damaging access to the system. The IIS JVM also supports the capability for certain Java components to execute outside this sandbox, providing more power and flexibility to the Java developer.
- *Integration with COM components.* The IIS JVM allows Java applets to access standard COM objects as though they were Java JavaBean objects. In addition, it provides a method for traditional COM objects outside the JVM to access JavaBeans as though they were COM objects.

2.1.3. IIS Content Delivery Architecture: Putting It Together

Now that you know the ways in which IIS can make both static and programmatic content available, you should be ready to merge your knowledge of the two.

Although we've discussed the delivery of static files and dynamically generated content as two distinct organisms, the two are normally intertwined in a standard Internet site. In fact, most Web users don't (and shouldn't) have to understand the distinction between the two; they simply enter the name of a starting URL and follow hyperlinks until they achieve their desired goals.

For this reason, IIS needs to be able to seamlessly merge the two types of content at runtime. Figure 2.10 shows how IIS routes requests for different types of documents.

Figure 2.10.
Internet Information Server routes each document request to the appropriate services whether the document is static or requires programmatic intervention.

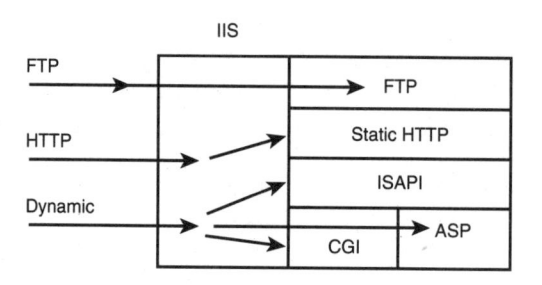

```
                            IIS
              ┌──────────────────────────┐
    FTP       │                          │
  ─────────►  │                      ────┼──► FTP
              │                          │
    HTTP      │                      Static HTTP
  ─────────►  │                          │
              │                      ISAPI
    Dynamic   │                          │
  ─────────►  │                          ├──► ASP
              │                      CGI │
              └──────────────────────────┘
```

> **Note:** For the sake of simplicity, the security procedures used by IIS are ignored in the following discussion. Refer to the section "Static Content Delivery Architecture" for more information on IIS' security procedures and integration with NT security. More information on security for Web applications is available in Day 11.

As you can see in Figure 2.10, the document-request process begins when a remote web client issues an HTTP request to the Internet Information Server. When IIS processes the request, it determines whether the page being requested is merely raw static HTML, or whether it requires programmatic intervention (such as an ASP script, CGI application, or ISAPI extension).

> **Note:** Often when you're using elements such as ISAPI filters, even requests for static HTML can require programmatic intervention. However, we've tried to stratify the distinction to make the architecture a little easier to understand.

If the requested document is static HTML, IIS' job is easy: It simply fetches the document (normally from disk, though frequently used documents may be cached in RAM for faster access) and sends it to the requesting client.

However, if the requested document requires programmatic intervention, the process is somewhat more complex. IIS begins the process of providing programmatic content by consulting the Web Application Manager, which maintains a mapping of program objects to processes and threads. If the application is already running, the WAM routes the request to that element (either running on a thread within IIS' process or in a process of its own). If the application is not running, WAM launches that application (again, either in-process or out-of-process) and then passes on the request. The applications themselves are responsible for returning their display data to IIS, which then forwards the data to the Web client.

2.2. Additional IIS Features

Up to this point, we've covered the essential basics needed to understand how IIS serves up content. Now that you understand these basics, let's look at some of the features of the Internet Information Server that make it a powerful content delivery platform.

2.2.1. –FTP Features

The File Transfer Protocol server is a rather basic feature of IIS 4.0 and is not particularly complex. However, it does include a number of features (some of which are similar to the features of the HTTP server) that make it a useful addition to the IIS suite. These features include:

- Integrated security
- Flexible access logging
- Messages and annotations
- FTP sites

A. Integrated Security

The FTP server takes full advantage of the security features of IIS, including:

- The capability to select between anonymous and user-specific authentication (though it lacks the ability to use NTLM authentication)
- The capability to restrict types of file access both through IIS itself and at the file system level using NTFS security attributes
- The capability to restrict access to the site by IP address

B. Flexible Access Logging

The FTP server can take full advantage of IIS' logging features. For more information on logging in IIS, see the section "Administration Features," later in this chapter.

C. Messages and Annotations

IIS' FTP server can display a custom message at logon and logoff time and another message when the server already has its maximum number of client connections. In addition, the administrator can create annotations that remote users will see as they move into each directory of the FTP site.

D. FTP Sites

IIS 4.0 allows administrators to create FTP *sites*. Sites combine a number of powerful features. The first is the capability to place multiple server names—each with its own IP address (and, if desired, TCP port)—on a single IIS system, as illustrated in Figure 2.11.

Figure 2.11.
IIS allows administrators to run multiple FTP sites on one IIS system.

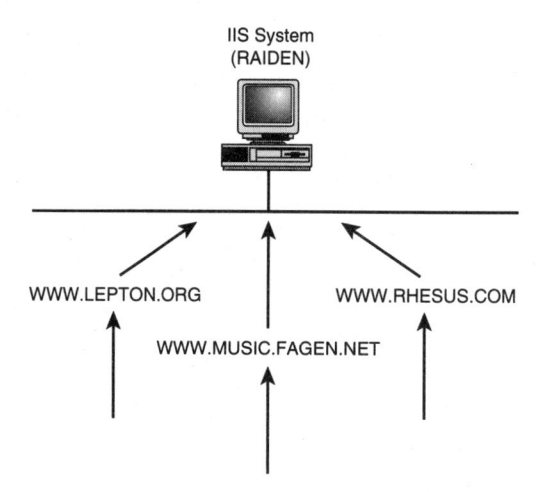

The second is the capability to use *virtual directories*. With virtual directories, an IIS administrator can use disparate directories scattered across one or multiple computers as though they were in a custom directory tree within a single site (see Figure 2.12).

Sites combine the flexibility of these features with the added capability to administer each site as an organic whole, and they enable the administrator to delegate administration features of each site to others. This means administrators can allow other individuals to maintain and configure many of the important parameters of their own sites on the IIS system without being able to affect or damage other sites or the system as a whole. Figure 2.13 illustrates this concept.

Figure 2.12.
IIS also allows administrators to generate virtual directory trees using directories scattered across multiple systems.

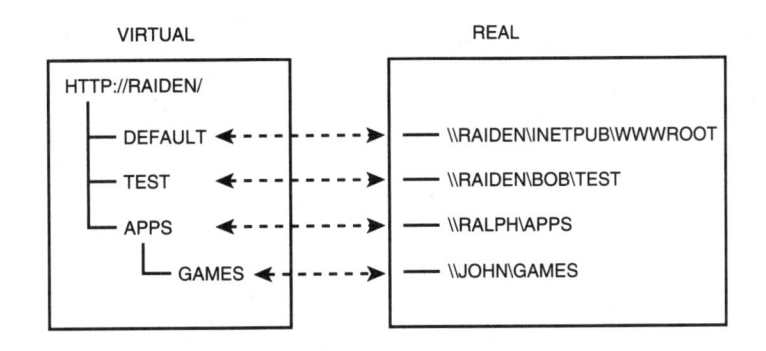

```
        VIRTUAL                              REAL
   ┌────────────────────┐              ┌──────────────────────────────┐
   │ HTTP://RAIDEN/     │              │                              │
   │   ├─ DEFAULT  ◄----┼--------------┼── \\RAIDEN\INETPUB\WWWROOT   │
   │   ├─ TEST     ◄----┼--------------┼── \\RAIDEN\BOB\TEST          │
   │   └─ APPS     ◄----┼--------------┼── \\RALPH\APPS               │
   │        └─ GAMES ◄--┼--------------┼── \\JOHN\GAMES               │
   └────────────────────┘              └──────────────────────────────┘
```

Figure 2.13.
Through the use of sites, IIS administrators can delegate the administration of different Web or FTP sites located on the same IIS system.

IIS (RAIDEN)
- WWW.BLAH.COM (Administrator: RAIDEN\JANEP)
- FTP://NEWWORLD.UN.ORG (Administrator: RAIDEN\PARANOID)
- WWW.SOCKS.COM (Administrator: RAIDEN\SOCKS)

Sites are discussed further in the section "Administration Features," later in this chapter.

2.2.2. HTTP Features

The most common, and most complex, use of IIS installations is for serving data over the World Wide Web with HTTP. IIS 4.0 includes the following powerful features in the HTTP server:

- Integrated security
- Flexible access logging
- Support for HTTP 1.1
- Web sites

A. Integrated Security

IIS uses its integration with Windows NT Server to provide powerful security both at the IIS level and when using NTFS file and directory permissions. IIS can also use anonymous and user-specific authentication, and it supports the use of NTLM security with browser clients that support this feature. IIS can also restrict access to Web sites by IP address and/or domain name.

B. Flexible Access Logging

Like the FTP server, IIS' HTTP server takes full advantage of its logging capabilities (as discussed in the section "Administration Features," later in this chapter).

C. Support for HTTP 1.1

IIS' HTTP server is compliant with version 1.1 of the HTTP standard. IIS automatically detects whether a browser client supports the features of HTTP 1.1 or only the features of the older 1.0 standard, and then it provides the appropriate responses for each.

IIS implements the following HTTP 1.1 features:

- *Persistent connections.* As you learned earlier, HTTP normally requires that a client establish a new connection for each object within an HTML page. For complex documents, this is an extremely inefficient process. With the use of *persistent connections* (also known as *HTTP Keep-Alives*), the client can remain connected to the server and continue to request objects for a specified period of time without having to break the connection and then reconnect, greatly reducing the load on the server and client, as well as reducing wasted network bandwidth.

- *Pipelining.* Browser clients also normally wait for each request sent to a Web server to be fulfilled before sending another request. With *pipelining*, a browser client can send multiple requests to the server at once and then wait for all of them to be fulfilled. This reduces wasted bandwidth and speeds the delivery of content to the browser.

- *Transfer Chunk Encoding.* Transfer chunk encoding allows dynamically generated pages (such as those generated by Active Server Pages) to be broken up into chunks of varying sizes, each with its own headers. These chunks can then be more efficiently transmitted over TCP/IP.

- *HTTP PUT and DELETE instructions.* HTTP 1.1 extends the types of instructions that can be sent by a Web browser to include PUT and DELETE. This allows a browser client with sufficient privileges to upload files to a Web site and delete files on that site using standard HTTP instead of having to log in with FTP or connect a network drive.

- *Host Headers.* With Host Headers, an IIS server can direct requests from Web clients to the appropriate site on the system and reply with the correct document to the remote client. This allows IIS to provide multiple sites without requiring a different IP address for each server, which is required for traditional virtual servers.

> **Test Tip**
> In order to use Host Headers for your sites, all your potential browser clients must be HTTP 1.1-compliant. If you cannot guarantee this, you'll have to use a different IP address for each site to make certain that all potential clients have the ability to properly access your sites.

D. Web Sites

IIS' Web server supports the capability to provide *sites*, just as with the FTP server, which we discussed earlier. The sites allow the administrator to use multiple server names and addresses, virtual directory trees, and delegated administration. In addition, ISAPI filters can be associated with various Web sites, allowing each site to use a different set of filters.

2.2.3. Application Delivery Features

We've already discussed many of the application delivery features of the Internet Information Server, such as the capability to use CGI, ISAPI, and ASP for delivering custom web solutions. We've also mentioned the WAM, which provides both crash protection and crash recovery for web applications. IIS 4.0 includes two components that extend application features and provide the background architecture for some of the features we've already discussed:

- Microsoft Transaction Server (MTS)
- Microsoft Message Queue Server (MSMQ)

A. Microsoft Transaction Server

Microsoft Transaction Server (MTS) is a powerful tool that provides application developers with the ability to easily take advantage of *transactions*. A transaction provides a way of dividing up application tasks into units that succeed or fail as a whole even if the unit consists of multiple steps or involves many different components and other applications (see Figure 2.14).

Figure 2.14.

A transaction succeeds or fails as a whole even if it requires multiple complex steps.

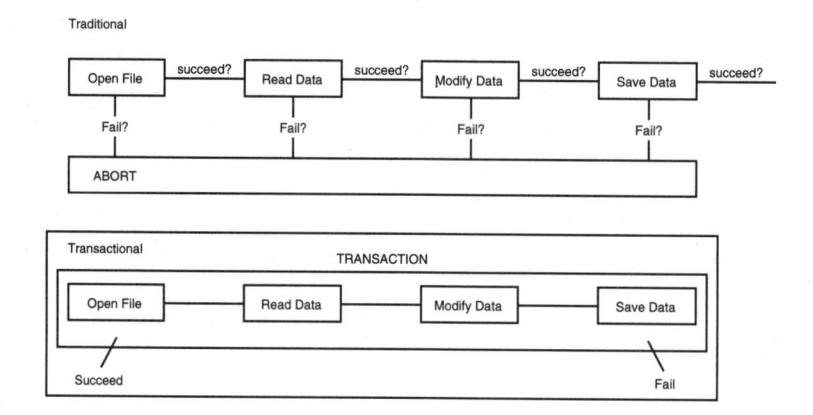

When using transactions, server applications can automatically deal with faults such as application or system crashes without corrupting or damaging data. This greatly enhances fault-tolerance.

By definition, a transaction must support the following properties (often referred to as *ACID*):

- *Atomicity.* A transaction *always* completes. It either completes successfully and commits all of its effects and changes, or it aborts and completely rolls back all effects and changes. No in-between state can be allowed to exist.
- *Consistency.* The effects and changes of a transaction are always correct and complete modifications of an object's state.
- *Isolation.* If multiple transactions are executing concurrently, they will be isolated from one another's effects and changes until transactions are completed. No transaction will be able to access objects in an inconsistent state.
- *Durability.* After a transaction commits, its effects and changes are persistent, even across applications or system failure. If a failure occurs before a transaction can complete, the transaction must be able to successfully abort or commit during recovery in order to prevent data from remaining in an inconsistent state.

Microsoft Transaction Server provides applications and components the capability to implement the ACID properties without having to manage the complex minutiae of such processes. This frees up application developers from managing low-level system resources in a multi-user environment, while still giving them a high level of fault tolerance and scalability.

MTS supports transactions not only in ISAPI applications, but also in ASP scripts and components used by ASP scripts. MTS also provides the facilities used by the WAM to keep program component processes alive as long as new requests are available, increasing the performance of those applications and of the server itself.

B. Microsoft Message Queue Server

Microsoft Message Queue Server (MSMQ) provides developers with a mechanism to easily support inter-process and inter-application communication services. The process of managing communications between different applications, particularly across heterogeneous networks, is a difficult one, which requires a huge amount of development time for powerful server-based applications. This process is made even more difficult when messages need to be managed between applications or systems that may currently be down.

MSMQ handles the complexities of communicating between processes and applications. It deals flexibly with networks and protocol independence. It also handles synchronous and asynchronous messaging services. The application developer only has to code for the generic MSMQ interface, and the product handles the rest. Much as with MTS, this frees up the developer to focus on the application instead of dealing with the complex system- and network-specific difficulties of communicating between applications.

MSMQ's automatic handling of communication also allows front-end applications to be disconnected from back-end services. In some cases, this separation causes the server's performance to improve because it no longer has to wait for a reply from the back-end services before replying to the browser client.

MSMQ also integrates with MTS, allowing developers to include the transmission and retrieval of MSMQ messages into transaction units.

Together, MTS and MSMQ provide developers the ability to quickly and easily build powerful, scalable, fault-tolerant server applications on the IIS platform.

C. Microsoft Script Debugger

Microsoft Script Debugger allows developers to perform standard application debugging services (such as watching variables, setting breakpoints, and stepping through code) with Active Server Pages scripts. Script Debugger can also scan ASP scripts for problems in syntax or logic and can help diagnose runtime errors.

2.2.4. Database Access Features

Of all the tasks commonly performed by web-hosted applications, at one point or another the vast majority involve the ability to access a database of information. The ability to query a database for information and/or modify a database with information is crucial to giving developers maximum functionality for their Web-hosted programs. IIS 4.0 includes methods by which developers can access databases, whether those databases are located on the same system or on remote database servers. Those methods are:

- Internet Database Connector
- ActiveX Data Objects (ADO)
- Remote Data Services (RDS)

A. Internet Database Connector

The Internet Database Connector is an older technology, originally implemented in the first version of Internet Information Server. It allows Web developers to easily generate HTML documents that query or update remote databases using ODBC and to return results based on those actions. Its use has gradually been supplemented by the use of embedded ASP scripts accessing data via other interfaces.

B. ActiveX Data Objects (ADO)

ADO is a set of COM interfaces that provide developers with quick, simple interfaces for accessing underlying data sources. ADO interfaces rely on Microsoft's OLE-DB database access architecture, which provides both standard database functionality and extended features. ADO objects also allow applications to treat many non-database sources, such as file systems, spreadsheet-style applications, and other sources via similar COM interfaces. ADO is primarily intended for users of Active Server Pages, for whom the added flexibility and functionality of the ADO objects is extremely useful because it's difficult to extend the functionality of ODBC through script languages.

C. Remote Data Services (RDS)

RDS is a technology that enables Web clients to easily view and manipulate data returned by application programs in a graphical format, using easily extendible COM objects. Figure 2.15 illustrates how these technologies interact to provide developers with a high degree of power and flexibility in generating Web-hosted data access applications.

Figure 2.15.
IIS 4.0 includes a number of powerful components that allow developers to easily generate applications that interact with back-end data stores.

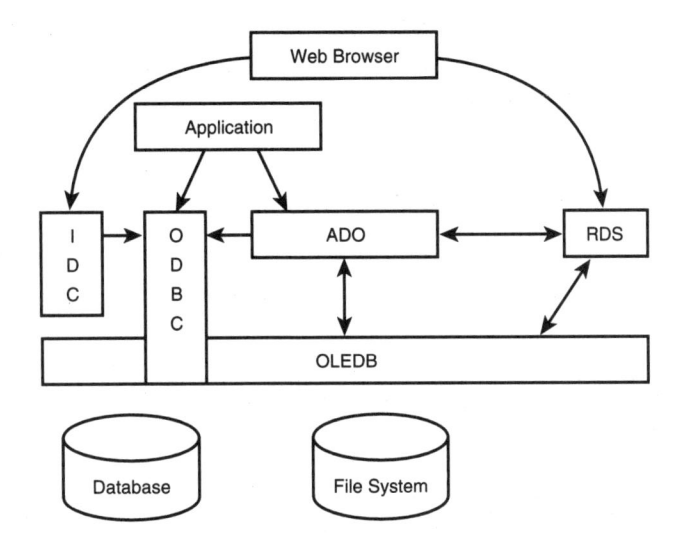

2.3. IIS System Administration

One of the great advantages of the Internet Information Server platform is its ease of administration—an advantage that goes hand in hand with IIS' integration with Windows NT. The graphical tools included with NT Server make it simpler for many people to learn how to configure and administer than do the tools of many competing network operating systems. This is also the case with IIS.

However, as with NT Server, the administration of IIS can be problematic in a complex, centrally administered network environment because many tasks used to be available only in rigid graphical tools. IIS 4.0 greatly improves on the administration functionality of its predecessors, allowing administrators many more options for configuring and administering IIS systems.

In this section, we'll begin by looking at the administration architecture supported by IIS and considering the capabilities this architecture provides. Then we'll examine the various administration features of the platform itself.

2.3.1. IIS Administration Architecture

IIS 4.0 has a powerful, flexible, and extensible administration architecture, which consists of two major components:

- IIS Configuration Store
- IIS Administration Objects

A. IIS Configuration Store

Internet Information Server stores its configuration data in the *IIS Metabase*. This Metabase is a repository for the storage of IIS configuration data and state information.

B. IIS Administration Objects

The IIS Administration Objects (IISAO) are a group of COM objects that provide a simple programmatic interface for managing the underlying Metabase configuration settings for the various IIS services. The IISAO provide developers with a method of managing and configuring IIS without dealing with the complex programmatic interfaces for modifying the Metabase entries that ultimately control the behavior of IIS.

Internet Information Server includes and integrates with a number of tools that use these components to allow administrators a wide range of options for managing IIS, as shown in Figure 2.16.

Figure 2.16.
Internet Information Server's flexible administration tools and architecture provide administrators a number of different ways to manage the product.

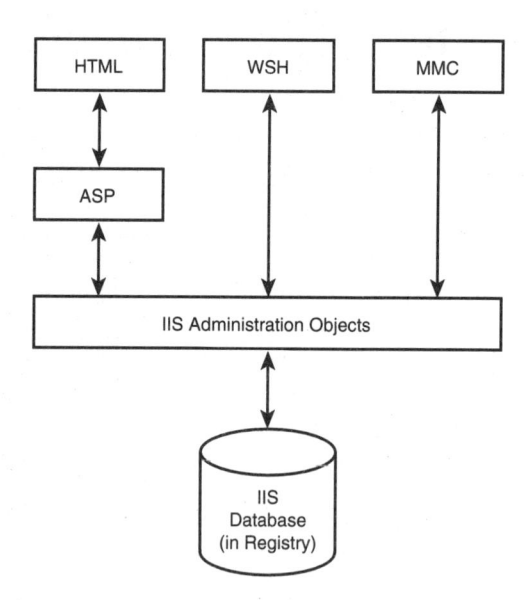

The first, and most common, way for administrators to manage IIS is via the Microsoft Management Console. IIS includes snap-ins and extension snap-ins for performing nearly every important IIS site administration task. The default IIS installation includes an MMC console with all pertinent snap-ins, which can be found on the Start menu, in the IIS 4.0 program group, under the name Internet Service Manager.

> **Note:** For more information on MMC and snap-ins, see Day 1, "Internet Information Server—The Basics."

Another common and powerful tool for administering IIS uses the World Wide Web. IIS 4.0 includes a set of HTML pages that use Active Server Pages and the IIS Administration Objects to provide access to many of IIS' most important configuration tasks.

In addition to these hands-on tools, IIS also provides methods for administrators and third-party solution developers to create administration solutions of their own. First, IIS 4.0 can be administered with scripting languages via the Windows Scripting Host (WSH), a technology that exposes common server administration tasks to common scripting languages like VBScript, JavaScript, and Perl. IIS implements its WSH support via the IIS Administration Objects. Second, the IIS Administration Objects can also be accessed programmatically, either via custom applications (whether standalone administration programs or ISAPI extensions) or by using Active Server Pages to develop custom web front-ends for system administration.

2.3.2. Administration Features

IIS 4.0 includes a number of flexible and powerful features that both ease the burden of administering a large IIS installation and provide features and functionality previously unknown to IIS. Those features and functionality are listed here:

- Tight integration with Windows NT Server
- Support for multiple sites
- Flexible content manipulation features
- Flexible logging support
- Fault tolerance
- Security features
- Performance management

A. Tight Integration with Windows NT Server

Although we've harped on this point often, we must assert once again the importance of IIS' integration with Windows NT. For the administrator, this integration is especially handy because it means that all the following methods for configuring and managing services on Windows NT are available for IIS as well:

- *Microsoft Management Console.* This standard administration tool for Windows NT can be used to perform nearly every IIS administration task.
- *Windows NT Explorer interface.* Not only can this interface be used to manipulate the NTFS rights that impact IIS security, it also provides the ability to manage the IIS security on a directory-by-directory basis.
- *User Manager for Domains.* This NT Server user administration tool manipulates all standard NT users, which can be used to authenticate to an IIS server. In addition, the tool is used to configure the default IIS system users (the IUSR_<COMPUTERNAME> anonymous user context and the WAM* application user context).
- *Performance Monitor.* This enables administrators to monitor all pertinent details of an IIS installation's performance, using the custom performance counters installed during setup. IIS' performance can also be monitored remotely via the SNMP protocol.
- *Event Viewer.* IIS logs many important events that relate to its operation in the System Event Log, which can be viewed and maintained with the Event Viewer utility.

B. Support for Multiple Sites

IIS' support for sites, which we discussed earlier in this chapter, makes supporting multiple Web sites on one server much easier, with its support for sites and virtual directories. In addition, the capability to delegate administration of individual sites is very powerful because it enables administrators to allow their customers or coworkers to administer their own Web sites without giving them the ability to endanger any other sites or the server itself.

> **Test Tip**
> Internet service providers can use the site functionality of IIS to provide multiple customers with their own sites on one IIS server. Each customer can even be given the ability to perform many administrative tasks

> herself, taking the ISP out of the loop for basic functions while still keeping the individual from jeopardizing other sites. With its support for HTTP 1.1 Host Headers, IIS is capable of maintaining all these sites on a system with only one IP address.

In addition, by using the included Site Server Express, administrators (or users) can use HTTP 1.1-compliant browsers or the Web Publishing Wizard to place information on their sites on the IIS server.

C. Flexible Content Manipulation Features

IIS 4.0 provides a number of features that can make the manipulation and management of web site content easier, including:

- The ability to set an expiration date on pages, after which time they will no longer be available to browser clients.
- Support for server-side includes, which allow standard boilerplate text to be easily added to multiple pages while minimizing repetitive text in files. IIS also provides the ability to define HTTP headers and document footers, which are automatically included in served documents.

> **Test Tip:** Although server-side includes save disk space and repetitive data entry, they do increase the CPU load on the server.

- The ability to create redirections on a file or directory basis, which automatically send the browser client to a specified URL.
- The ability to customize the error messages returned to clients, using standard HTML documents (which can include embedded ASP scripts).

In addition, IIS 4.0 includes Microsoft Site Server Express. This tool can analyze the content available through the sites on an IIS server and generate reports detailing that content. In addition, Site Server Express can generate maps that show the layout of pages on the server and show the administrator where objects are missing, where hyperlinks are broken, and where links to offsite content exist. Figure 2.17 shows an example of a Site Server map.

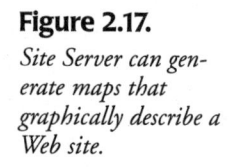

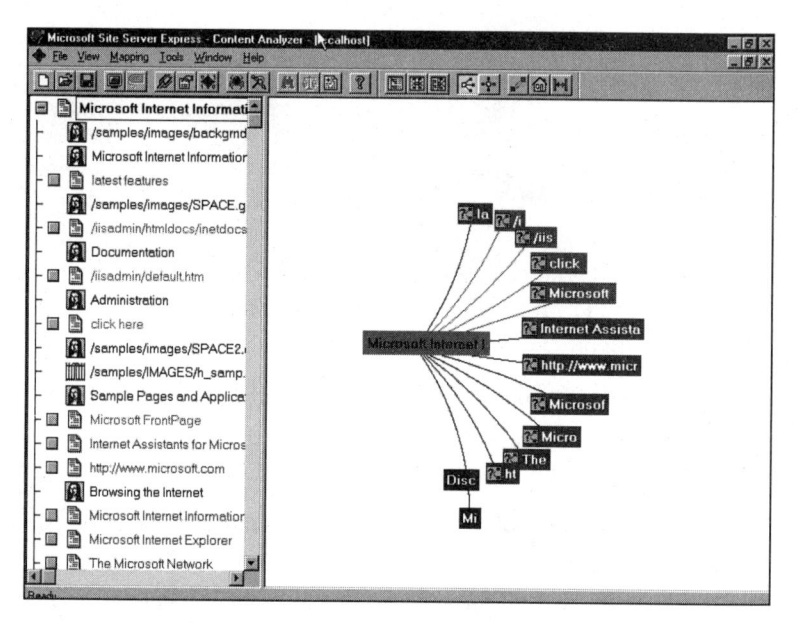

Figure 2.17.
Site Server can generate maps that graphically describe a Web site.

Site Server Express includes a Web Publishing Wizard that can be used to place content on an IIS Web site, as well as a Posting Acceptor, which allows files to be posted via HTTP from any browser that supports the RFC1867 posting protocol.

IIS 4.0 also includes Microsoft Index Server, a powerful tool for automatically generating searchable indices of the objects on one or more of the Web sites on your IIS system. Microsoft Index Server can, by default, generate indices for many different file types, including the following:

- HTML
- Plain ASCII or UNICODE text
- Microsoft Office (Word, Excel, PowerPoint) documents
- Adobe PDF (Portable Document Format) files

Index Server uses an extensible architecture so that developers can easily add file types to the list of objects Index Server can index. Index Server also includes powerful functionality for allowing users to search these indices via the Web, including keyword searches, boolean searches, and natural language queries.

D. Flexible Logging Support

One of the most important tools a Web site administrator has for determining usage requirements and monitoring potential security risks is the Web site access log. IIS 4.0 includes flexible logging on a per-site basis. Logs can be saved in the W3C's advanced Web logging format (known as the "W3C extended log file format"), which allows the administrator to choose which site statistics to monitor. This allows administrators to choose only those statistics that interest them and avoid collecting unnecessary or unwanted data. IIS 4.0 also supports the ability to log to a raw text file or to an ODBC data source, even though database logging increases the performance load on the server. In addition, IIS 4.0 exposes a COM interface for its logging services, allowing developers to write their own custom logging and log analysis services.

E. Fault Tolerance

The ability to prevent loss of Web site data in the event of a system or application failure is critical to managing production Web servers. IIS 4.0 has the ability to easily replicate a content tree from one IIS server to another in order to provide a secondary access source for load balancing as well as to prevent data loss. It also supports Configuration Replication, via which configuration for multiple servers can be performed once on one server and then replicated to multiple IIS systems. IIS 4.0 also allows administrators to back up and restore all the configuration settings. The restoration process is treated as a transaction, and all changes can be rolled-back to a previous state if necessary.

F. Security Features

We've already discussed the basics of IIS security a great deal. In addition to those basics, however, IIS includes a number of additional features for providing security both for the Web server itself and for the clients accessing it:

- *IP- and domain-based security.* The administrator of an IIS 4.0 server can configure the system to accept or reject HTTP requests based on either the IP address of a client or the IP domain from which the client is connecting.
- *ISAPI filters.* As we've already mentioned, developers can use the Internet Service Application Programming Interface not only to create dynamic Web applications, but also to create filters.
- *SSL encryption.* IIS can use the Secure Sockets Layer standard for providing encryption of HTTP data between server and client. This is valuable for sites

that transmit or request private information—such as credit card numbers and Social Security numbers—to or from remote Web clients.

- *Server Gated Cryptography (SGC)*. SGC is an extension to SSL. Designed specifically for banks, SGC gives IIS 4.0 the capability to switch from standard SSL encryption to a stronger 128-bit encryption mechanism for those clients holding SGC certificates. This allows such institutions to use the strongest possible encryption for financial transactions, depending on what encryption is supported by remote clients.

- *Digital certificate services*. IIS 4.0 can authenticate users via *digital certificates*, which are objects issued by trusted authorities that uniquely identify an individual. IIS allows administrators to map certificates to individual users or to map a group of certificates to an individual user context. Authentication can also be performed based on specific fields within a certificate instead of by using the entire certificate; this allows administrators, for instance, to map all certificates granted by a particular authority to a particular user context.

IIS 4.0 also includes Microsoft Certificate Server, which allows organizations to issue and manage their own custom digital certificates. This allows organizations to base their security around their own custom certificate-based scheme instead of relying on traditional certificate providers or standard authentication services.

G. Performance Management

IIS has a number of features that allow the administrator to tune the system's performance. In addition to using the Keep-Alives and pipelining features we've already discussed, administrators can also throttle the amount of network bandwidth used by the server to prevent the server from overloading a network link used by other systems. IIS 4.0 also adds the capability to throttle bandwidth usage on a per-site basis in order to ensure that individual sites on the IIS server do not monopolize the entire bandwidth available to the server.

2.4. Additional Components

In our discussion of IIS's architecture and components, we've discussed nearly every component included with the platform. However, two packages that you should know about haven't fit into any of our discussions: Microsoft SMTP Service and Microsoft NNTP Service.

2.4.1. Microsoft SMTP Service

Microsoft SMTP Service is an implementation of the SMTP (Simple Mail Transfer Protocol) standard used for e-mail transfer over TCP/IP across the Internet. It is not designed, however, to perform the traditional role (often filled by UNIX systems) of serving e-mail to individual users with e-mail clients. It is designed specifically to allow applications running on the server to send outbound mail using SMTP.

Microsoft SMTP Service does not, therefore, support standard client connectivity protocols (such as POP or IMAP), nor does it support the use of mailboxes. In addition, the SMTP Service is configured, by default, not to perform mail relaying to external e-mail addresses, which prevents it from being used by unauthorized users as a relay for unsolicited e-mail (or *spam*, as it's commonly known).

> **Note**
> IIS itself *can* function as an SMTP mail client in order to send messages based on administrative events. In addition, IIS 4.0 supports having a single mailbox on the IIS server itself so that mail can be sent to the site and processed by server administrators.

Microsoft SMTP Service supports the use of Transport Layer Security (or TLS) for encrypting its outbound SMTP transmissions; this provides a higher level of security, particularly when transmitting sensitive data from Web-hosted applications. The SMTP Service can be administered using the standard Microsoft Management Console interface, and it integrates with IIS 4.0's flexible logging architecture.

2.4.2. Microsoft NNTP Service

Microsoft NNTP Service is an implementation of the NNTP (Network News Transprt Protocol) standard used for the creation and maintenance of Internet newsgroups. It's designed to allow for the creation of local discussion groups on the IIS server itself, which allow connections from standard NNTP newsreader clients. It does not, however, support the use of newsfeeds, so it cannot be integrated into the Usenet network of Internet newsgroups.

The NNTP Service implements the latest standards for secure connectivity, including NNTP password encryption to prevent usernames and passwords from being sent in clear-text over the network. Discussion groups can be configured to allow or disallow postings from remote clients, as well as to support moderated discussion groups in which a designated individual must approve postings before they are added to the discussion. The NNTP Service can be administered through the standard MMC interface, and it supports flexible transaction logging.

2.5. Choosing an Implementation Strategy

In the previous chapter, you installed IIS 4.0 on a Windows NT computer—probably your workstation or some development server. That installation didn't require very much planning or a roll-out plan. However, those things come into play when you are going to deploy Web sites on either your company's intranet or the worldwide Internet.

The easiest way to implement an IIS server is to set it up on a stand-alone server, which manages its own user accounts and has all the content and databases loaded on the local hard disks. You use the same setup procedure as with your development machine, whether for intranet or Internet scenarios.

> **Note** You always need to keep security in mind when exposing servers in a network (even if it is only one server located on your intranet). See Day 6, "Internet Information Server Security," to see how to implement IIS and NT security to prevent attacks on your servers.

The most common scenario when implementing IIS on an intranet is that you want to use the existing user accounts to restrict access to areas on your intranet servers (in the Internet case, you most often use a separate user database that is stored on a database server). To facilitate this in either single-domain or multiple-domain environments, you specify the access permissions with NTFS permissions on a file or directory level and then enforce NTLM Challenge/Response for logon to the Web server. The benefit of such an implementation is this: Because in domain environments users need to log on, this information is automatically passed to the IIS server so the user doesn't have to enter his or her password again for the intranet Web server.

Lab

This lab consists of review questions pertaining to this chapter and provides an opportunity for you to use walk-through exercises to apply the knowledge that you've learned.

Questions

1. You've been asked to implement an FTP site on your IIS server that will allow employees all over the country to access important data files via the Internet. Your boss wants those users to be able to use their NT domain usernames and passwords to access the data, and you would like to avoid sending clear-text passwords over the wire. Which of the following authentication mechanisms would enable you to meet all these criteria? (Choose the best answer.)

    A. Anonymous user authentication

    B. Basic user authentication

    C. NTLM user authentication

    D. None of the above

2. One of your Web developers would like to test a new ISAPI extension in correlation with one of the Web pages on your IIS server. However, he cannot guarantee that it will not terminate abnormally. How should you set up this ISAPI extension to execute? (Choose the best answer.)

    A. In-process

    B. Out-of-process

    C. Dynamically threaded

    D. None of the above

3. You're developing an application for IIS that needs to be highly reliable and fault tolerant. In particular, any data it modifies in its data store must always be left in a consistent state, even if the system fails catastrophically. Which technology included with IIS 4.0 will help you to achieve these goals? (Choose the best answer.)

    A. Microsoft Transaction Server

    B. Microsoft Message Queue Server

    C. Microsoft Scalability Manager

    D. Microsoft Certificate Server

Day 2: IIS Architecture and Components

4. Your boss needs you to write an application for IIS that will communicate with applications written by other in-house developers, both on the same server and on some back-end application servers. Which technology included with IIS 4.0 will help you to achieve these goals? (Choose the best answer.)

    A. Microsoft Transaction Server
    B. Microsoft Message Queue Server
    C. Microsoft Management Console
    D. Microsoft Certificate Server

5. You're performing Web administration services for an Internet service provider. One of the your clients is absolutely enthralled with the new corporate Web site your company has developed for them; however, that company's customers would like to be able to search the site for important information. The site includes data in both HTML and Microsoft Word formats. Which technology included with IIS 4.0 can provide this functionality? (Choose the best answer.)

    A. Microsoft SMTP Server
    B. Microsoft Index Server
    C. Microsoft Search Server
    D. None of the above

6. Your company develops software solutions for the defense industry. In the interest of enhancing security, your company's new director of security would like to be able to identify clients via digital certificates instead of via usernames. She is unwilling to trust any other organization's identity verification services and would instead like to be able to issue her own certificates. Which technology included with IIS 4.0 can provide her with this functionality? (Choose the best answer.)

    A. Microsoft Identity Verification Services
    B. Microsoft Index Server
    C. Microsoft Certificate Server
    D. Microsoft Transaction Server

7. Your company's developers are creating an application on IIS that needs to be able to send e-mail to system administrators to notify them of various events. Which technology included with IIS 4.0 will provide this functionality? (Choose the best answer.)

A. Microsoft NNTP Server

B. Microsoft Exchange

C. Microsoft SMTP Server

D. Microsoft Transaction Server

8. Your company provides a large amount of technical support for developers using your products. You'd like to provide the developers with a discussion group where they can share tips and techniques. Which technology included with IIS 4.0 can provide this functionality? (Choose the best answer.)

    A. Microsoft NNTP Server

    B. Microsoft Exchange

    C. Microsoft SMTP Server

    D. Microsoft Transaction Server

In the next two questions, you're presented with a scenario and a proposed solution. Choose the answer that indicates which of the criteria the solution meets.

9. You've been asked to consult for a software development firm called Rhesus Reasoning, Ltd. Their new product is taking off far beyond anyone's expectations, and their support costs are growing faster than they can hire individuals to meet them. They want you to implement a new Internet site that will allow customers to view information about their products, order and register their products online, and contact tech support.

    Required results:

    - The site must use one of Rhesus' proprietary back-end commerce solutions to handle the sales and registration functions (they've allocated a developer to help you implement the solution).

    - The technical support group wants to use a discussion group to make common questions and answers available on the site.

    Desired results:

    - Only the technical support group should be able to post to the discussion group.

    - Customers should be able to download patches to products with a minimum of effort on the part of the system administrator.

Day 2: IIS Architecture and Components

Proposed solution:

Create the site using Internet Information Server 4.0. Create an HTTP site that allows anonymous access. Create an FTP site using anonymous user authentication with Read rights to a directory for patches. Use Microsoft NNTP Server to create a support discussion group. Use Microsoft Message Queue Server to handle messaging between web applications and the Rhesus back-end.

How well does the solution meet the requirements?

A. The proposed solution provides all required and desired results.

B. The proposed solution provides all required results and one desired result.

C. The proposed solution provides all required results but none of the desired results.

D. The proposed solution does not meet all requirements.

10. You've been asked to develop a Web-hosted database front-end for a company called Knowledge Base Solutions, Inc.

    Required results:

    ■ Only those customers who have paid a fee and registered with the company should be able to access the site.

    ■ All queries and modifications to the back-end database must be completely fault-tolerant.

    Desired results:

    ■ Customer usernames and passwords should not be sent in clear-text over the Internet.

    ■ The front-end should be able to email the system administrator in case of an error.

    Proposed solution:

    Implement the front-end using IIS 4.0. Create a site that uses only NTLM user authentication. Do not allow anonymous or basic authentication to the site. Install Microsoft SMTP server.

How does the solution meet the requirements?

A. The proposed solution provides all required and desired results.

B. The proposed solution provides all required results and one desired result.

C. The proposed solution provides all required results but none of the desired results.

D. The proposed solution does not provide all required results.

Answers to Questions

1. **D.** Anonymous authentication does not provide user-specific authentication to the server. Basic user authentication passes usernames and passwords in clear-text. NTLM user authentication is not available with FTP.

2. **B.** The Web Application Manager can run an ISAPI application in its own process; if that application crashes, it cannot affect other applications or IIS itself. If the application were run in-process and it crashed, it could also crash the server or other applications when it went down. There is no "dynamically threaded" startup class for ISAPI applications.

3. **A.** MTS provides applications with the ability to use *transactions*, which either commit data in a consistent state or roll data back to its previous consistent state, even if the system fails. Microsoft Message Queue Server provides messaging services, Microsoft Certificate Server is used for issuing digital certificates, and Microsoft Scalability Manager does not exist.

4. **B.** MSQS provides network- and protocol-independent messaging services for applications. Microsoft Management Console is used to manage IIS and other NT services.

5. **B.** Index Server can generate searchable indices for many types of objects on your web sites, including HTML and Microsoft Office documents. It also provides functionality for searching those indices. Microsoft SMTP Server implements the Simple Mail Transfer Protocol; Microsoft Search Server does not exist.

6. **C.** Microsoft Certificate Server allows organizations to generate their own digital certificates. Microsoft Identity Verification Services does not exist.

7. **C.** SMTP Server implements the Simple Mail Transfer Protocol to allow applications to send outbound e-mail. Microsoft NNTP Server is used for discussion groups, and Microsoft Exchange is not included with IIS.

8. **A.** NNTP Server implements the Network News Transfer Protocol, which is used to create Internet discussion groups (also known as newsgroups).

9. **B.** Microsoft Message Queue Server provides the messaging services needed to communicate with Rhesus' back-end tools, and NNTP Server allows you to create the tech support discussion group. Setting up the FTP site with anonymous user authentication allows people to easily download patches even if they don't have accounts on the server. However, because the discussion group was not set up as a Moderated group, people other than the tech support group can post to it. Thus, all required results but only one of the desired results are provided.

10. **D.** Using NTLM user authentication requires the use of usernames and passwords, and preventing basic authentication prevents those usernames and passwords from being transmitted in the clear. SMTP Server provides the outbound mail functionality required by the application. However, Microsoft Transaction Server is required to provide the required fault-tolerance, and it is not listed in the solution. Thus, even though all desired results are met, one required result is not met.

2

Test Day Fast Facts

Here are a few fast facts about this chapter that you may want to know ahead of time. Don't forget that these facts also provide great last-minute study material.

- The Microsoft Management Console (MMC) provides a common management framework that can be extended by snap-ins.
- You can use stand-alone or extension snap-ins to extend MMC. Additionally, you can add folders, Web links, and ActiveX controls.
- Administration tasks for WWW and FTP services are provided by the Internet Information Server snap-in. It can be extended by the Mail and News extension snap-ins to allow for administration of SMTP and NNTP services.
- All configuration information about sites is stored in the Metabase, a hierarchical database.
- The Metabase can only be restored in its entirety on the machine the backup was created on. You cannot restore the backup on a different machine.
- By default, custom consoles are stored in the My Administrative Tools folder in the Programs group in the Start menu.

Day 3

Configuring IIS 4.0

by Christoph Wille

The way you are configuring IIS—and the amount of what you can configure—has changed very much with Internet Information Server 4. IIS 4's configuration tools are integrated in the Microsoft Management Console (MMC), which will be the common management console for Windows NT 5.0. Furthermore, the configuration information has been moved from the Registry to a high-speed hierarchical information store, the Metabase. With the Metabase, you can now configure your Web sites down to the file level, whereas in IIS 3, you could configure virtual directories only.

This chapter introduces you to using the MMC, creating your own management consoles specific to the tasks you are performing, backing up and restoring the configuration changes you make to IIS, and performing Registry-related tasks. We also take a look at MIME mappings that allow you to define file types on your server.

The IIS exam emphasizes using the MMC to configure your IIS servers, including a simulation of the MMC where you have to perform administrative tasks. It is therefore mandatory that you make yourself familiar with this primary management tool of Internet Information Server.

Objectives

This chapter helps you prepare for the Microsoft Exam by covering the following objectives:

- Configure and save consoles by using Microsoft Management Console.
- Verify server settings by accessing the Metabase.
- Choose the appropriate administration method.
- Manage MIME types.

TEST DAY FAST FACTS

- You can use MMC to administer downlevel Web servers like IIS 3.0.
- MIME mappings are used to describe the file types that are returned from the server to the browser.
- IIS Registry entries are used to configure service startup and are used for backward compatibility.

3.1. Working with the Microsoft Management Console

If you are used to previous versions of Internet Information Server, you will be familiar with its administration tool, the Internet Service Manager (ISM). When you explore the Microsoft Internet Information Server folder in the Windows NT 4.0 Option Pack program group, you'll find a link that is named Internet Service Manager. However, when you start the IIS 4.0 ISM, the Microsoft Management Console opens with a preconfigured console for Internet Information Server (see Figure 3.1).

Figure 3.1.
The Internet Service Manager for IIS 4.0 is an MMC console.

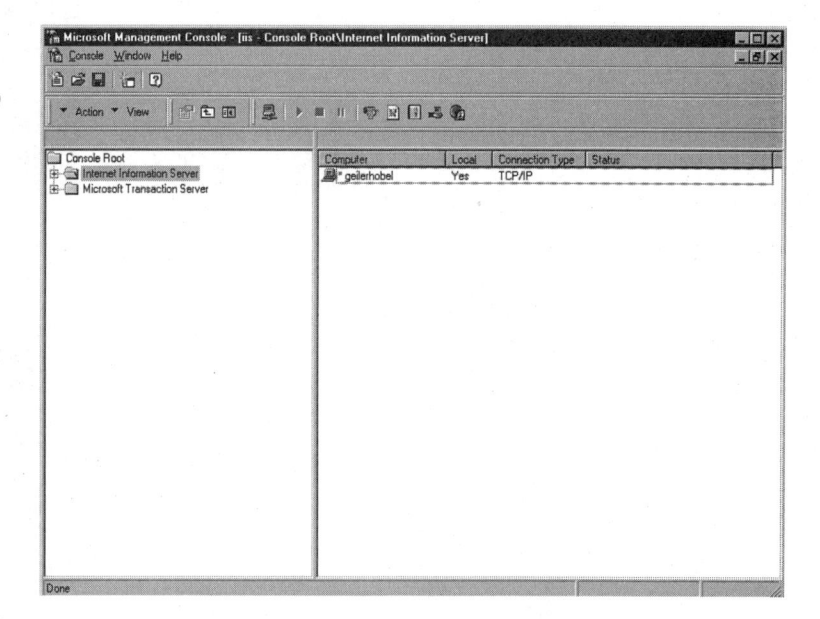

Day 1, "Internet Information Server—The Basics," contained an introduction to MMC; however, today we are focusing on getting actual work done with the MMC. There is one important point that we need to emphasize again before going on: The MMC provides only the user interface for network management tools—the MMC does not imply any network management protocol, nor is it capable of administering any part of the network.

The Microsoft Management Console displays consoles that host programs called snap-ins (more on those in the next section), which are used to actually administer parts of your network. For example, in Figure 3.1, two snap-ins are loaded: the Internet Information Server snap-in and the Microsoft Transaction Server snap-in.

The consoles can include one or more windows, each of which has two panes: the scope pane and the results pane (see Figure 3.1). The scope pane is the left-hand pane of an MMC console, and it displays a tree view of the namespace, which displays all the items that can be managed by MMC at the current time. Each item—also referred to as a node—in the scope pane can be one of a variety of objects, containers, or tasks. If you select a node in the scope pane, the results pane is populated with the results of the current selection. (In Figure 3.2, the results are the components in the ExAir MTS package.)

Figure 3.2.
You view the components of a Transaction Server package in the Microsoft Management Console.

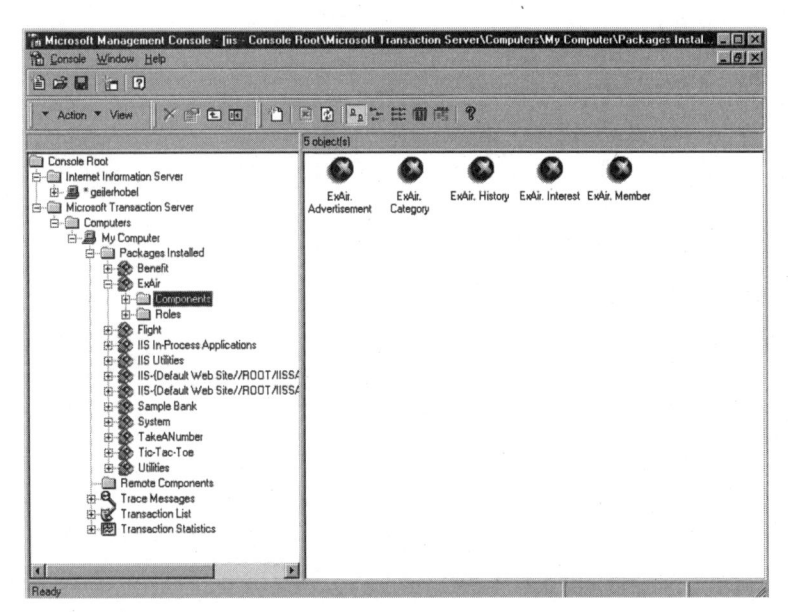

You can add snap-ins, folders, links to Web pages, or even ActiveX controls as items to your namespace. With NT 5.0, the MMC is at the center of network administration, and all management applications (like User Manager, Disk Administrator, and Event Viewer) are available as snap-ins.

In the following section, you are introduced to the various types of snap-ins you can use to create custom consoles. How to create consoles, add snap-ins, and manage folders or HTML items are discussed in later sections.

3.1.1. Snap-Ins

The Microsoft Management Console provides no management behavior by itself, but the snap-ins that extend the console do, by exposing behavior through one or more of these MMC extension mechanisms:

- *Stand-alone snap-in.* Functions autonomously of other snap-ins.
- *Extension snap-in.* Extends the behavior of another snap-in. The extension snap-ins depend on the parent snap-in for contextual data.

The following standalone snap-ins come with Internet Information Server 4.0 in its standard installation:

- Folder
- General Control
- Index Server
- Internet Information Server
- Link to Web Address
- Microsoft Transaction Server
- Monitoring Control

The only snap-in in the preceding list that can be extended is the Internet Information Server snap-in. It provides the following two extension snap-ins:

- Mail - SMTP
- News - NNTP

In the next few sections, you will learn how to create consoles using these snap-ins.

3.1.2. Creating and Using Custom Consoles

Although Internet Service Manager (ISM) already provides a preconfigured console for administering IIS, you need to be able to create, manage, and use custom consoles to pass the IIS exam (however, this is definitely not the only reason, learning it now will help you transition easily to administering NT 5.0). The following sections walk you through the processes of creating, storing, modifying, and using custom consoles.

A. Creating a New Console

As you learned earlier, the MMC doesn't provide any administrative power by itself. You need to add snap-ins to the namespace in order to be able to administer certain parts of your network.

The following steps walk you through the process of creating a new console for administering Internet Information Server:

1. To start the Microsoft Management Console, click on Start, Run and then enter mmc.exe in the resulting Run dialog box. This opens MMC with an empty console (see Figure 3.3).

Figure 3.3.
The MMC opens with an empty console.

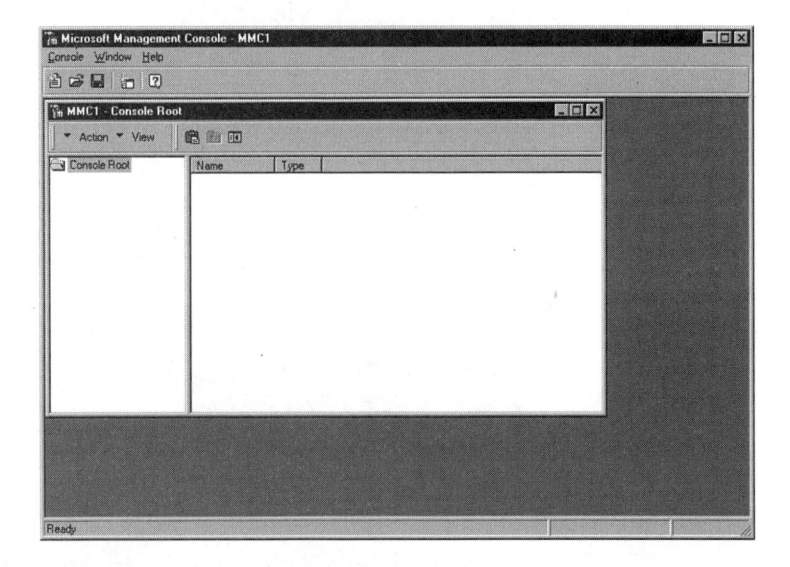

2. To add a new snap-in, choose the Add/Remove Snap-in command from the Console menu. The Add/Remove Snap-in dialog box appears, with the Standalone snap-ins tab activated. Notice that no snap-ins are added at this point (see Figure 3.4).
3. To add a new stand-alone snap-in to the console, click the Add button. In the Add Standalone Snap-in dialog box, select the Internet Information Server snap-in and click OK (see Figure 3.5). The snap-in is added to the list of available snap-ins for the console.

Figure 3.4.
No stand-alone snap-ins have been added so far to this new console.

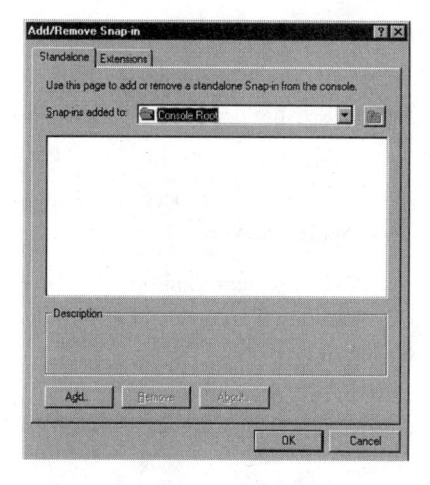

Figure 3.5.
The Internet Information Server snap-in is added to the list of available snap-ins for the console.

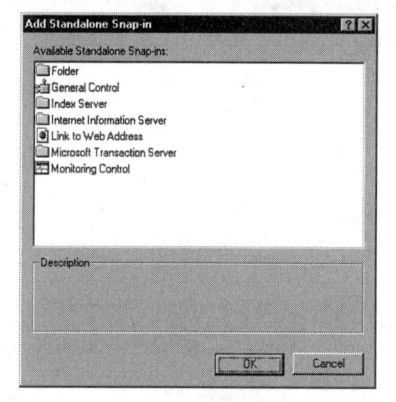

4. Click OK to close the Add/Remove Snap-in dialog box. The snap-in is added to the console. Maximize the console window.

5. Expand the Internet Information Server node. The IIS snap-in searches the local computer for installed IIS services. Your console window should now look similar to Figure 3.6.

6. To save the console, select Save from the Console menu or click the Save button on the toolbar. The Save As dialog box opens, proposing to store the console in the *My Administrative Tools* folder. This folder is a private program group located in the Programs folder of the Start menu. Stick with the suggested storage location and enter `TYS IIS4 Console` as the name. Click Save to store the console. The default file type for consoles is .msc.

3.1. Working with the Microsoft Management Console | 91

Figure 3.6.
The newly created console shows the local computer in the IIS namespace.

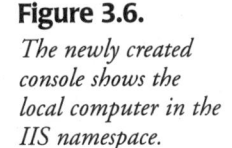

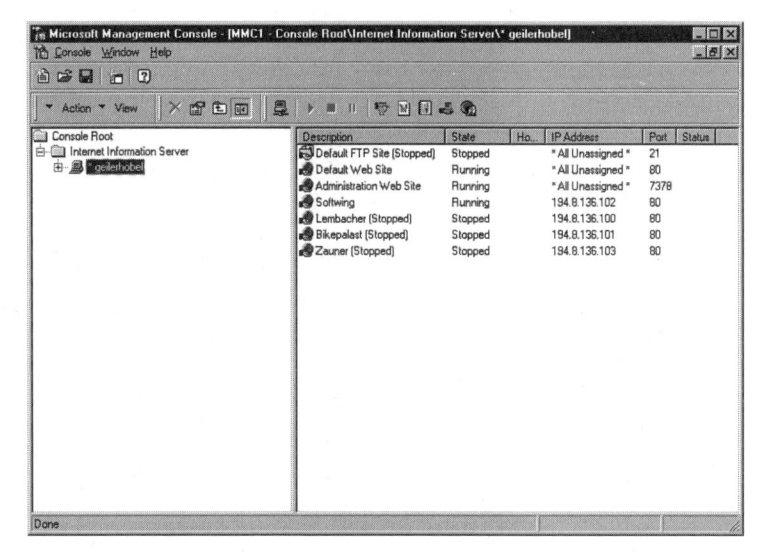

7. Exit MMC by choosing Exit from the Console menu.
8. Reopen the newly created console by selecting the entry TYS IIS4 Console in the My Administrative Tools program group.
9. Start exploring the local computer.

Creating new consoles is a snap. Though you added only the Internet Information Server snap-in, it is equally easy to add the Index Server snap-in or the one for Microsoft Transaction Server.

The next section deals with another snap-in topic: adding extension snap-ins.

B. Adding Extension Snap-Ins

Internet Information Server comes with two extension snap-ins—one for Mail and the other one for News. These extension snap-ins are used to administer the SMTP and NNTP services.

The following steps show you how to modify the console you created in the previous tutorial by adding snap-ins. The snap-ins to be added are Mail and News, which are implemented as extension snap-ins to the Internet Information Server stand-alone snap-in. Perform the following tasks:

1. Open the console that you created in the previous tutorial by clicking on TYS IIS4 Console in the My Administrative Tools program folder.

2. To add the extension snap-ins, select Add/Remove Snap-ins from the Console menu.

3. Switch to the Extensions tab in the Add/Remove Snap-ins dialog box. The Internet Information Server snap-in is already selected as an extendable snap-in with the Mail and News extensions listed (see Figure 3.7).

Figure 3.7.
Use the Extensions tab in the Add/Remove Snap-in dialog box to extend existing snap-ins.

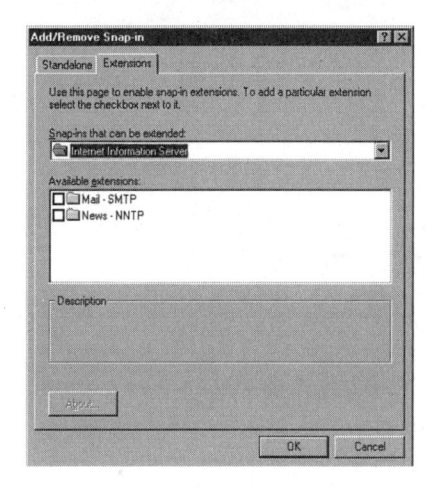

4. To activate the two snap-ins, place check marks in the check boxes next to the items.

5. Click OK to confirm your changes. You are returned to your console.

6. Expand the Internet Information Server tree and your local computer's tree. You are presented with the sites running on your computer. If you have installed NNTP and SMTP, the default sites will show up (see Figure 3.8).

7. Save the console to make your changes permanent.

Extension snap-ins can't live without their parents, which are standalone snap-ins. Internet Information Server comes with two extension snap-ins for administering Mail and News, which you can selectively add to your console.

Snap-ins are at the heart of consoles, but there are two more items you can use to organize and customize your consoles: folders and Web links.

C. Adding Folders and Web Links

You are not limited to adding only snap-ins to your console. In addition to those, you can create folders to modify the hierarchy or you can add links to administration Web pages, test pages, or whatever fits your needs.

Figure 3.8.
Now the SMTP and NNTP extension snap-ins are installed in the console.

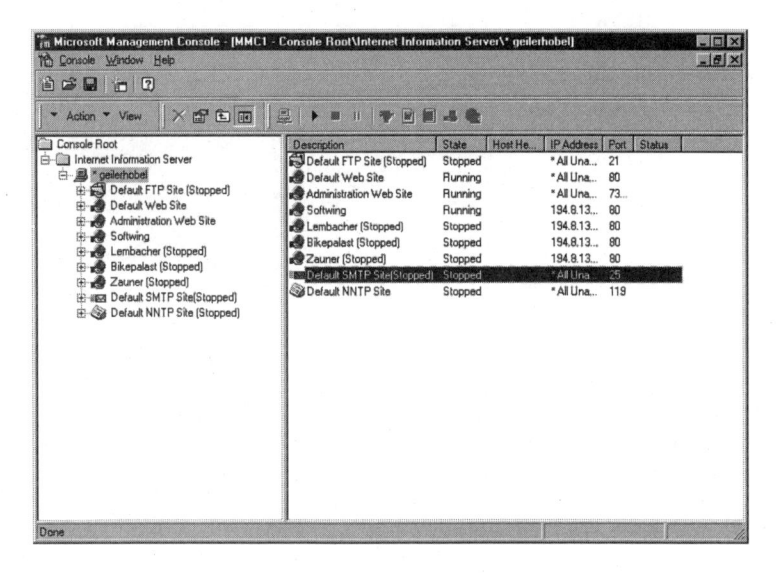

The following steps show you how to extend the TYS IIS4 Console console by using folders and Web links:

1. Open the console that you created in the previous tutorials by clicking on TYS IIS4 Console in the My Administrative Tools program folder.

2. Right-click on Console Root in the scope pane and select New/Folder. (Alternatively, you could click on the Action drop-down arrow and select New, Folder.) A new folder is created with the default name New Folder.

3. Right-click the new folder and select Rename. Change the folder name to Demo.

4. Right-click on the newly created folder and select New, Link To Web Address.

5. You are asked for the URL to the resource. This can be either an Internet address or a file URL. Enter http://localhost to point to the default Web site of IIS. Click Next to continue.

6. Enter the name of the link. You can go with the default, which is the link address, or you can choose to specify a different name. Click Finish when you're done.

7. Test the link by clicking on it. IE opens the page in the results pane (see Figure 3.9).

Figure 3.9.
You can display a Web link in MMC.

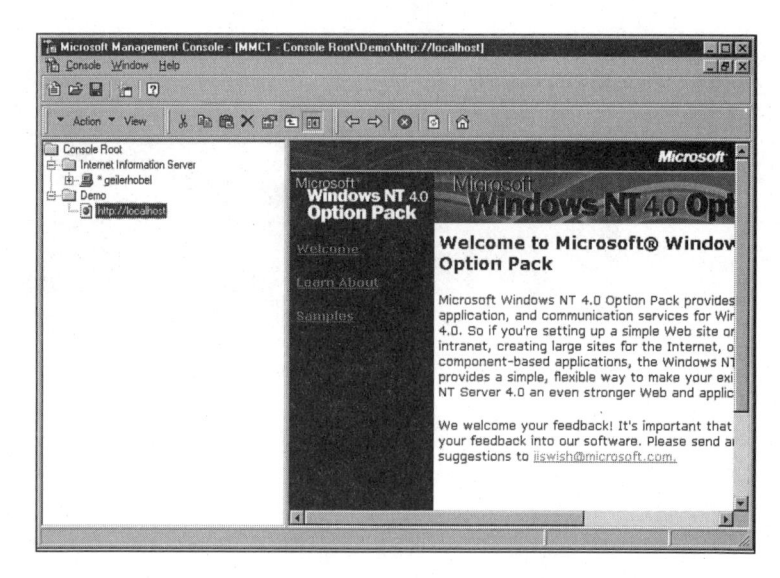

8. Click on the Internet Information Server snap-in and drag and drop it on the Demo folder. Now your IIS snap-in is located below the Demo folder.

9. Save the console.

Folders provide a convenient way to organize Web links or snap-ins. Use them to organize your work. You use the Web links to check the operational status of Web sites.

Now we have finished discussing the elements you can use to create custom consoles. Before going on with managing IIS 4 servers, take a short detour to learn how you can use the Microsoft Management Console to manage older versions of IIS from within the same environment as IIS 4.

3.1.3. Managing Downlevel Web Servers

When you are running multiple Web servers, you probably won't migrate every machine to IIS 4.0 immediately; instead, you'll probably have a mix of IIS 3.0 and IIS 4.0 machines running at the same time. The Microsoft Management Console (MMC) allows you to administer previous versions of IIS. However, this functionality doesn't come out of the box—you have to make some changes manually.

The following steps show you how to manage downlevel Web servers from within MMC. To complete this tutorial, you need the Windows NT Server CD. Perform the following tasks:

3.1. Working with the Microsoft Management Console | 95

1. Insert the Windows NT Server CD in your CD drive.
2. Open Windows NT Explorer and navigate to the \I386\inetsrv\ directory on the Windows NT Server CD (or \Alpha\inetsrv\ if you are working on a Digital Alpha computer).
3. Copy the files Fscfg.dll, Gscfg.dll, and W3scfg.dll to a temporary folder (for example, c:\temp). Then go to the \I386\inetsrv\help directory and copy the Fscfg.hlp, Gscfg.hlp, and W3scfg.hlp help files to the temporary folder as well. (Make sure that the View Options in Explorer are set to view all files.)
4. You need to rename the files in the temporary folder. The following table shows the necessary name changes:

Old Name	Rename To
Fscfg.dll	Fscfg3.dll
Gscfg.dll	Gscfg3.dll
W3scfg.dll	W3scfg3.dll
Fscfg.hlp	Fscfg3.hlp
Gscfg.hlp	Gscfg3.hlp
W3scfg.hlp	W3scfg3.hlp

Notice that you wouldn't need to rename the Gopher files (Gscfg.*) because the Gopher service is no longer supported with IIS 4.0; however, this has been done for consistency.

5. Copy the renamed files to the installation root of your IIS 4.0 installation. Usually this will be the \WINNT\system32\inetsrv directory.
6. Finally, you have to make changes to the Registry for the MMC to use the files for downlevel Web server support. Open the Registry Editor by selecting Run from the Start menu and entering `regedit.exe`.

> **Warning**
> Be careful when editing the Registry because making a wrong setting can cause problems, including failure of Web or FTP sites.

7. Navigate to the `HKEY_LOCAL_MACHINE\SOFTWARE\Microsoft\InetMgr\Parameters\AddOnServices` key.

8. To indicate that the existing files have been superseded, you have to add three values to the Registry (the paths to the files depend on your Windows NT installation):

```
FTP3=c:\winnt\system32\inetsrv\fscfg3.dll::SUPCFG:
c:\winnt\system32\inetsrv\fscfg.dll
GOPHER3=c:\winnt\system32\inetsrv\gscfg3.dll
WWW3=c:\winnt\system32\inetsrv\W3scfg3.dll::SUPCFG:
c:\winnt\system32\inetsrv\W3scfg.dll
```

The `::SUPCFG:<iis4 dll>` indicates that the files have been superseded. Notice that for the Gopher entry, you don't need such an indication because IIS 4.0 doesn't support Gopher services.

To add these three values, repeat the following procedure for each value:

a. Right-click in the right-hand pane of the Registry Editor and select New, String Value.

b. Change the value name to one of the three values shown in the previous list.

c. Double-click on the value name and enter the file locations in the Value Data field (see Figure 3.10).

9. When you finish adding these three values, close the Registry Editor.

Figure 3.10.

Here is where you edit the value data for the WWW3 value.

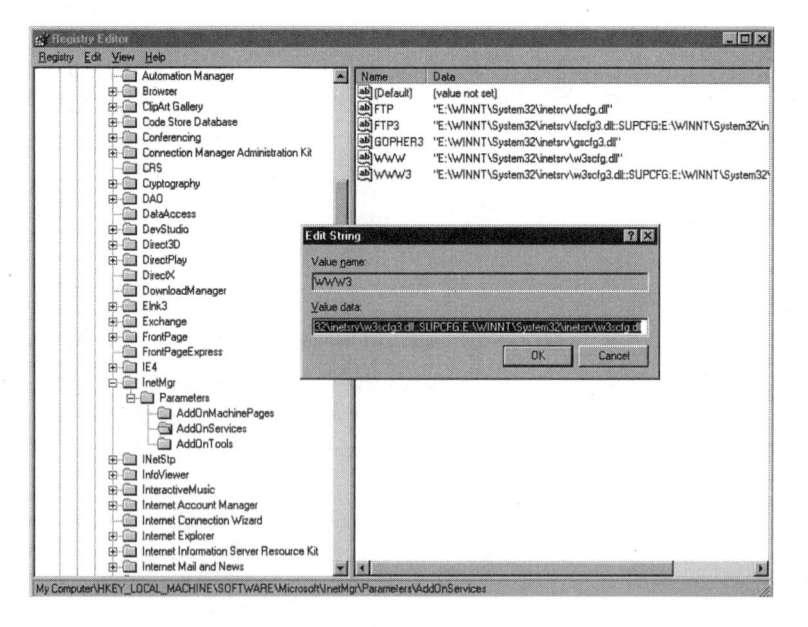

3.1. Working with the Microsoft Management Console

Having prepared the MMC for administering downlevel Web sites, you can now administer both IIS 3.0 and IIS 4.0 machines using MMC on this computer.

Now that you have completed all prerequisites for managing different versions of IIS from MMC, the upcoming tutorial shows you how to actually do it.

The following steps show you how to manage different versions of IIS with MMC. To complete this tutorial, you must have completed the previous one and must have a server that runs IIS 3.0:

1. Open the MMC using the Run command in the Start menu. Enter `mmc.exe` and click OK to open MMC.
2. MMC opens with a new, empty console window. From the Console menu, select Add/Remove Snap-in (or use the shortcut Ctrl+M).
3. Add the Internet Information Server snap-in (see previous tutorials on how to add snap-ins to a console).
4. Right-click the Internet Information Server entry below the Console Root and select Connect. Enter the DNS name or the IP address of the IIS 3.0 server that you want to administer. Click OK to connect to this server.
5. Expand the computer in the left-hand pane of MMC to show the services that are running on the IIS 3.0 server. Notice that the IIS snap-in identifies the services as "downlevel."
6. Right-click the Web service and select Properties from the context menu. This opens the service properties dialog box, which enables you to administer all aspects of an IIS 3.0 Web server (see Figure 3.11).

Figure 3.11.
The MMC allows you to edit an IIS 3.0 server.

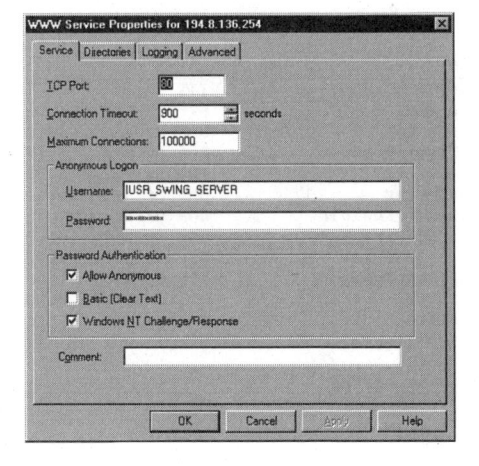

When you are running a mixed environment of IIS 4.0 and older IIS servers, the downlevel support included within MMC makes your life easier for administering the various servers because you have one central administration console.

We turn now to a discussion of the Metabase, the high-speed hierarchical information store that holds the IIS configuration information.

3.2. Overview of the Metabase

With Internet Information Server 3, all settings pertaining to Web sites and virtual directories were stored in the Registry. Some settings had to be modified via the Internet Service Manager (ISM), and some settings had to be added/changed manually in the Registry. As for Web servers, the only thing you really could configure were virtual directories.

IIS 4.0 has changed this picture radically: You can configure nearly everything you have ever dreamed of down to the file level (yes, you can even have different settings for files in the same directory!). This magic is made possible by the new repository for configuration metadata, called the Metabase.

3.2.1. Purpose of the Metabase

The purpose of the Metabase is to replace the Registry as the storage location for configuration data. The Metabase is faster and more flexible than the Registry and stores IIS configuration parameters in a fast-access memory-resident data store. It is a hierarchical datastore that mirrors the structure of IIS, and each node in the Metabase structure is called a key and has multiple configuration values associated with it (see Figure 3.12 for a general hierarchy).

Figure 3.12.
The Metabase offers a general hierarchy of keys.

```
Machine                          IIS running on a machine
  FtpService                     FTP services
    FtpServer                    One or more virtual FTP server
      FtpVirtualDir              One or more FTP virtual directories (*)
  WebService                     Web services
    WebServer                    One or more virtual Web servers
      WebVirtualDir              One or more virtual Web directories (*)
        WebDirectory             One or more Web directories (*)
          WebFile                One or more Web files
    IIsCertMapper                IIS Certification mapper
    Filters                      Filters collection
      Filter                     One or more filters
  MimeMap                        Mime mappings for the server

(*): can be nested
```

One important feature about the Metabase worth noting is that it supports inheritance. When you set inheritable configuration keys for the two services outlined in Figure 3.12 (WebService and FtpService), these affect all servers (WebServer and FtpServer). Values set at the server level affect only the specific servers, but they are still inheritable. For example, you could set Read permissions on a directory branch, and those permissions would promote to all subdirectories until you set specific other permissions for one of those subdirectories.

3.2.2. Editing Tools

Why a section about editing tools for the Metabase? Well, because the Internet Service Manager console is not the only thing you can use to administer your IIS server. Several other tools can do the job:

- *Internet Service Manager (HTML).* This is the HTML-based version of the Internet Service Manager. You can use it to remotely administer your IIS server via any Web browser (see Figure 3.13). To start it, go to the Internet Information Server program group and select Internet Service Manager (HTML). Note that the port number varies from installation to installation.

Figure 3.13.
For Web-based administration of IIS, you can use the Internet Service Manager (HTML).

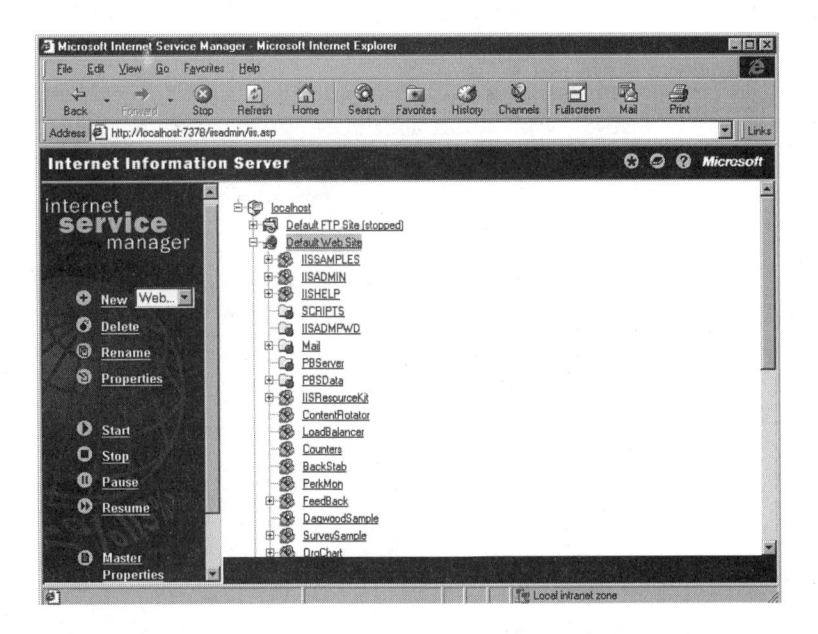

- *Scripts.* Internet Information Server supports ADSI (Active Directory Services Interface) to manipulate its namespace. You can write scripts to automate tasks on your server such as backing up or creating a virtual server. For examples of such scripts, see the Internet Information Server Resource Kit.

- *MetaEdit.* Much like the Windows NT Registry Editor, the MetaEdit tool that comes with the IIS Resource Kit allows low-level access to the Metabase (see Figure 3.14). It also comes with a Metabase consistency checker.

Figure 3.14.
The MetaEdit Metabase editing tool that comes with the IIS Resource Kit allows low-level editing.

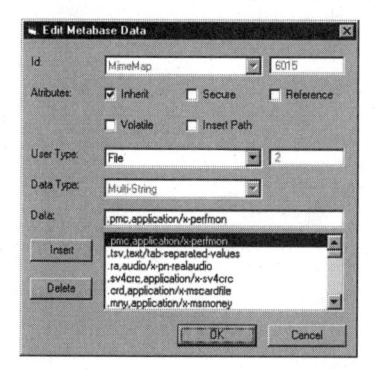

3.2.3. Backing Up and Restoring the Metabase

Anyone who has ever lost data knows how important backups are for getting up and running again as quickly as possible after a crash occurs. Therefore, it is quite natural that you want to back up (and eventually restore) the configuration of an IIS server and all its sites. Because the Metabase is stored in a disk file, you could simply create a copy of it in some location; however, this solution isn't feasible when you are doing remote administration of an IIS machine.

IIS 4.0 includes a mechanism for backing up the entire Metabase (however, it doesn't allow you to back up a single site). Backups are stored in the \WINNT\system32\inetsrv\MetaBack directory by default. A later section shows you how to choose a different directory to store the Metabase backups.

The following steps walk you through the process of backing up the Metabase:

1. Open the Internet Service Manager (ISM) from the IIS program group in the NT Option pack program group.
2. The ISM opens in the state you last saved it. For this tutorial, select the local computer on which you installed IIS 4.
3. Right-click on the computer to get the context menu and select Backup/Restore Configuration.

4. In the Configuration Backup/Restore dialog box, click the Create Backup button to create a new backup.
5. Enter the name of the backup in the Configuration Backup dialog box. For this tutorial, choose TYS IIS4 Backup as the backup name (see Figure 3.15).

Figure 3.15.

Enter the name of the backup in the Configuration Backup dialog box.

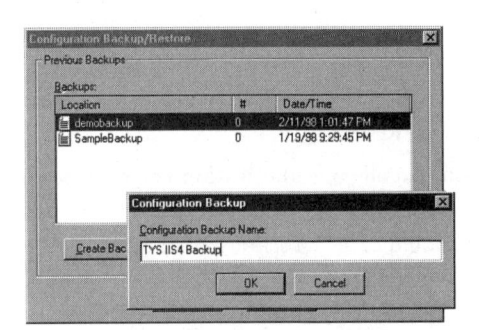

6. Click OK to create the configuration backup. This won't take very long.

Backing up the configuration settings is not very time consuming; nor does it require large amounts of disk storage. Therefore, it is advisable to make backups whenever you make configuration changes to your IIS server.

Here are some important things to keep in mind with the backups you create for IIS servers:

- You cannot use the backup to apply the configuration information to a different machine by restoring the backup on that machine.
- When restoring a backup, you cannot choose to restore only a single site. All configuration information for all sites will be restored, and if you made changes after your last backup, they will be lost. Therefore, you should always create a backup when you make a change to the IIS configuration!

Now that you know the implications of IIS configuration backups, you can move forward to restoring the configuration to the server you backed up.

In the following steps, you will restore the backup named TYS IIS4 Backup that you created in the previous tutorial. To verify that restoring a backup really wipes out all changes applied after the backup was created, make a slight change. For example, rename or delete the default Web site before you start the restore operation (settings are still contained in the backup you created previously). Then perform the following steps:

1. Open the Internet Service Manager.
2. Right-click the computer for which you want to restore the previously created backup.
3. Select Backup/Restore Configuration from the computer's context menu.
4. In the Configuration Backup/Restore dialog box, select the TYS IIS4 Backup backup and click Restore.

    IIS warns you that all your information will be wiped out and the services will be stopped (see Figure 3.16). The warning that the restore operation will be a lengthy one should be taken seriously—it really takes a lot of time!

Figure 3.16.
You are warned that all your information will be wiped out and the services will be stopped.

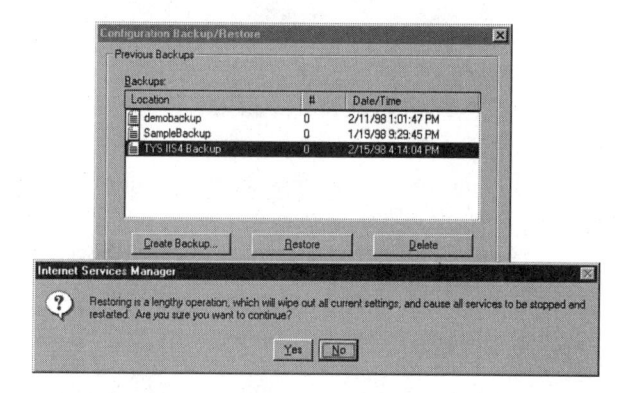

5. Click Yes to continue the restore procedure. You will be notified when the operation has finished.

As with every backup policy, not only should you perform the backups, you also should verify that the backups really work when needed. It is very beneficial to perform a restore operation of your server to have an estimate of how long it takes to restore all configuration data.

3.2.4. Relocating the Metabase and the Backup Folder

The Metabase is stored in a binary file called MetaBase.bin, which is located in the INETSRV directory (which by installation default is located in the SYSTEM32 directory of your Windows NT installation). The file is loaded from disk when IIS starts, saved to disk periodically, and closed when the IIS service is stopped.

3.2. Overview of the Metabase

> **Note:** If you have installed IIS on an NTFS partition—which is definitely the preferred way of installing IIS for security and performance reasons—take the time to examine the permissions that are set for MetaBase.bin: Administrators and SYSTEM have Full Control, but no one else has any permissions on this file. Keep this in mind if you want to run IIS under a user account other than LocalSystem (which shouldn't be necessary anymore with IIS 4.0).

Although for most installations the file location or the filename of the Metabase won't matter, given certain security scenarios (moving the Metabase to a mirrorset partition, for example), you might want to store the file in some other—possibly more central—location. To change the directory where the file resides, you have to change a Registry setting.

The following steps show you how to relocate the MetaBase.bin file to a different directory. This process involves making changes to the Registry that might affect the operation of your Web server. Perform the following steps:

1. You need to stop all IIS services before you can relocate the Metabase. (Stopping the IISADMIN service stops all dependent services, such as FTP and the WWW service.) To stop the IISADMIN service, enter the following command at the command prompt or in the Run dialog box:

```
net stop IISADMIN
```

2. After stopping the IIS services, copy the existing MetaBase.bin file to the new location using NT Explorer (you can even rename it). Check the permissions on the new file. The SYSTEM account must have Full Control for IIS to work properly.

3. Open the Registry Editor. Select Run from the Start menu, and then enter `regedit.exe` in the Run dialog box to start the Registry Editor.

4. Navigate to the `HKEY_LOCAL_MACHINE\SOFTWARE\Microsoft\INetMgr\Parameters` key.

5. Add a new string value named *MetadataFile* and enter the full path to the new file as well as the filename. (You can choose a name other than MetaBase.bin if you want.)

6. Close the Registry Editor.

7. Restart the IIS services. To restart the WWW and the IISADMIN service, open a command prompt and enter the following two command lines:

```
net start W3SVC
net start IISADMIN
```

Now your configuration information is stored in a different place. You might relocate the Metabase for security reasons or simply to separate configuration information from the IIS program files.

Now you know how to relocate the Metabase from its default location. However, there is one thing that might be even more interesting for you to change: the folder in which Metabase backups are stored. By default, configuration backups are stored to %systemroot%\inetsrv\MetaBack directory, which is on the same partition as the Metabase itself. But that could cause trouble if the hard disk were to crash because both the working copy and the backups would be gone. Therefore, moving the backups to a different hard disk would speed up the recovery process in the case of a hard disk crash. You can change the backup location by modifying one setting in the Registry.

The following steps walk you through changing the location for configuration backups. You should be extremely careful when making such changes because the Registry is central to the configuration of a Windows NT system. Perform the following steps:

1. Decide which folder to use for the backups.
2. Open the Registry Editor. Select Run from the Start menu, and then enter `regedit.exe` in the Run dialog box to start the Registry Editor.
3. Navigate to the `HKEY_LOCAL_MACHINE\SOFTWARE\Microsoft\INetStp` key.

   If the *MetaBackup* key does not exist, select New, Key and create it. Then open the newly created key.
4. Add a new string value named *BackupPath*, and then enter the path of the new backup directory.
5. Close the Registry Editor.
6. Stop and restart the IISADMIN service to put the change into effect.

Changing the storage location for Metabase backups enables you to protect your system (in a sense) because the Metabase is then located on one drive and the backups reside on a different drive. (Remember, in the default setup, both the MetaBase.bin file and the backups reside on the same drive.)

Now it is time to actually use the Metabase configuration store to configure IIS.

3.3. IIS Configuration

So far, we have kept a low profile on actual configuration work for the server. And because most configuration work is very service-specific, this section gives only an overview of what is to come.

> **Note:** Configuration for the WWW service is covered in Day 4, "The WWW Server." In-depth coverage on configuration of the FTP service is given in Day 5, "The FTP Service."

The following list outlines a few things you can administer at the computer level:

- *Master properties for the WWW and FTP services.* Defines inheritable properties for newly created Web and FTP sites
- *Bandwidth throttling.* Limits the available bandwidth for the entire Web server. You can set bandwidth limits on specific sites, too.
- *MIME map.* Enables you to configure the MIME types that are sent to a client browser when a file is returned by the server (see the following section, "Configuring MIME Mappings").

You access these settings through the computer's Properties dialog box. To open it, right-click the current IIS server in MMC and select Properties from the context menu. Figure 3.17 shows the computer's Properties dialog box.

The next two chapters address bandwidth throttling and the master properties for Web and FTP sites; the next section deals with configuring MIME maps.

Figure 3.17.
You use the computer's Properties dialog box to set server-wide settings.

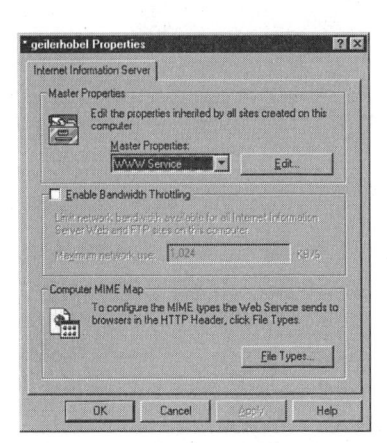

3.4. Configuring MIME Mappings

The Multipurpose Internet Mail Extensions (MIME) mappings are used to describe the file types that are returned from the server to the browser. For example, a file with the extension .htm is mapped to the MIME type text/html, which instructs the Web browser to render it as an HTML file. See Table 3.1 for a list of the most common MIME types.

Table 3.1. Common MIME types.

MIME Type	Extension
text/tab-separated-values	.tsv
audio/x-pn-realaudio	.ra
application/octet-stream	.bin
application/x-dvi	.dvi
application/postscript	.eps
application/msword	.doc
application/postscript	.ps
audio/x-wav	.wav
video/mpeg	.mpeg
text/html	.stm
application/x-director	.dir
audio/x-aiff	.aiff
application/x-mswrite	.wri
application/vnd.ms-excel	.xls
image/x-cmx	.cmx
application/postscript	.ai
application/octet-stream	.*
image/jpeg	.jpeg
application/x-javascript	.js
application/mac-binhex40	.hqx
application/zip	.zip
text/plain	.txt
image/tiff	.tif
text/html	.html
image/x-xbitmap	.xbm

3.4. Configuring MIME Mappings

MIME Type	Extension
application/pdf	.pdf
image/jpeg	.jpg
text/html	.htm
application/x-director	.dcr
application/vnd.ms-powerpoint	.ppt
application/octet-stream	.exe
video/quicktime	.mov
video/mpeg	.mpg
application/rtf	.rtf
image/gif	.gif
application/x-tex	.tex
video/x-msvideo	.avi
image/bmp	.bmp

IIS 4.0 allows you to define MIME mappings at the following levels:

- Computer
- Web site
- Directory

Because MIME mappings can be redefined at the directory level, it is possible to, for example, map the .htm extension to text/html in one directory and to some other MIME type in another directory on the same Web site.

All MIME mappings are listed in the master properties for the computer. The MIME mappings dialog box for Web sites and directories shows not only those mappings that have been changed at this level, but all the mappings that have been defined.

The following steps show you how to add a new mapping to the MIME map for the computer:

1. Open the Internet Service Manager.
2. Right-click the IIS server for which you want to administer the MIME mapping. In the context menu, select Properties to open the properties dialog box.
3. In the computer's Properties dialog box (refer to Figure 3.17), click the File Types button.

4. In the File Types dialog box, you can browse a list of registered file types (see Figure 3.18).

Figure 3.18.
You can add, remove, or change MIME mappings in the File Types dialog box.

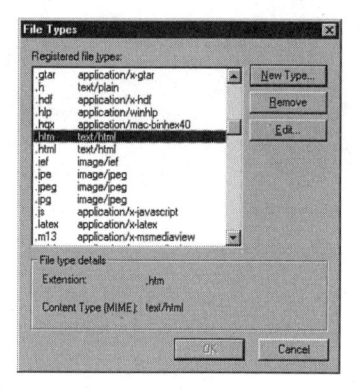

5. To add a new mapping, click the New Type button.
6. Enter the associated extension and content type in the resulting dialog box. For this tutorial, the extension is .adf and the content type is application/x-netscape-autoconfigure-dialer.
7. Click OK to add the new type, and it appears in the list of defined mappings.

The MIME mapping you just created is now available to all Web sites and directories because you defined it at the computer level. Every time the Web server sends a file with the extension .adf, the browser will be informed of its type: application/x-netscape-autoconfigure-dialer.

The changes you made to the MIME map are stored in the Metabase. However, some other important configuration settings must be set manually in the Registry.

3.5. The Windows NT Registry

In previous versions of IIS, all Web site configuration information was stored in the Registry. In IIS 4.0, the Metabase has taken over the job of storing most configuration information; however, some remaining Registry keys are used for backward compatibility and service initializing. Those keys fall into the following groups:

- *Global Registry Entries.* Affect all services.
- *Service-Specific Registry Entries.* Specific to a service; however, this entry is available for all services.

- *WWW Service Registry Entries.* Entries specific to the WWW service.
- *FTP Service Registry Entries.* Entries specific to the FTP service.

Because the global Registry entries affect all services, you must restart all services for these changes to take effect. For the service-specific entries, you must restart only that particular service for the changes to take effect.

> **Warning:** Making changes to the Registry incorrectly may render your system unstable or lead to failures of parts of the system. Therefore, when editing the Registry, be extra cautious!

3.5.1. Global Registry Entries

The Registry entries listed in Table 3.2 affect the entire operation of the IIS server. All these entries are located under the `HKEY_LOCAL_MACHINE\SYSTEM\CurrentControlSet\Services\InetInfo\Parameters` key. (This table is intended for informational purposes only; please refer to the Administrators reference in the IIS documentation for more in-depth information.)

Table 3.2. Global Registry entries.

Entry	Description
CacheSecurityDescriptor	Specifies whether or not to cache the security descriptors for file objects. By default, it is enabled (1).
CheckCertRevocation	Determines whether IIS should check for certificate revocation. By default, IIS does not check for certificate revocation (0).
DisableMemoryCache	Disables server caching. The default is to enable caching (0).
ListenBackLog	Determines the number of active connections to be queued for server attention. The default is 15.
MaxConcurrency	Specifies how many threads per processor should be allowed to run simultaneously if there is a pending I/O operation.
MaxPoolThreads	Determines the number of pool threads to create per processor. The default is 4.
PoolThreadLimit	Determines the maximum number of pool threads that can be created on the system.

continues

Table 3.2. continued

Entry	Description
MinFileKbSec	As part of the timeout calculation, it determines when a transfer should be ended.
ObjectCacheTTL	Determines the amount of time (time to live) an object is cached in memory until it's discarded.
ThreadTimeout	Specifies the idle time before an I/O thread is discarded.
UserTokenTTL	Specifies the amount of time to cache the user credentials.

3.5.2. Service-Specific Registry Entries

The Registry entries listed in Table 3.3 affect the services' operation. The first two entries are located under the HKEY_LOCAL_MACHINE\SYSTEM\CurrentControlSet\Services*ServiceName*\Parameters key (replace *ServiceName* with either W3SVC or MSFTPSVC). The remaining two entries are located under the HKEY_LOCAL_MACHINE\SYSTEM\CurrentControlSet\Services\W3SVC\ASP\Parameters key. (This table is intended for informational purposes only; please refer to the Administrators reference in the IIS documentation for more in-depth information.)

Table 3.3. Service-specific Registry entries.

Entry	Description
AllowGuestAccess	Specifies whether Guest logons are allowed for Internet services.
EnableSvcLoc	Determines whether IIS registers itself with the service locator so it can be discovered by the Internet Service Manager. By default, registration is enabled.
ProcessorThreadMax	Determines the maximum number of worker threads to create per processor.
RequestQueueMax	Determines the maximum number of .asp requests to keep in the request queue for each available worker thread.

3.5.3. WWW Service Registry Entries

The Registry entries listed in Table 3.4 are valid for the WWW service only. All these entries are located under the HKEY_LOCAL_MACHINE\SYSTEM\CurrentControlSet\Services\W3SVC\Parameters key. (This table is intended for informational purposes only; please refer to the Administrators reference in the IIS documentation for more in-depth information.)

Table 3.4. WWW service Registry entries.

Entry	Description
AcceptByteRanges	Determines whether the server will process the byte ranges. By default, it is enabled (1).
AllowSpecialCharsInShell	Determines whether special characters are allowed in batch scripts.
DLCSupport	Specifies whether downlevel client support will be enabled for clients that do *not* support HOST headers. By default, this behavior is not enabled.
DLCCookieNameString	Specifies the name of the HTTP cookie that the server sends to downlevel clients.
DLCHostNameString	Specifies the name of the Web site that contains the downlevel host menu.
DLCCookieMenuDocumentString	Specifies the file name of the host menu for clients that do support cookies, but do not support HOST headers.
DLCMungeMenuDocumentString	Specifies the file name of the host menu for clients that do not support cookies.
DLCMenuString	Specifies the special prefix of URLs that are requested by downlevel clients.
LogErrorRequests	Enabled by default, this determines whether or not to log errors in the log file.
LogSuccessfulRequests	Enabled by default, this setting determines whether or not to log successful requests in the log file.
SSIEnableCmdDirective	Determines whether or not to enable the #exec directive for SSI.
TryExceptDisable	Disables exception handling for the ISAPI extension. Set to 1 when debugging such extensions; in normal operation, it should be disabled.
UploadReadAhead	Specifies the default amount the server will read before passing control to the application.
UsePoolThreadForCGI	Determines whether IIS should use a pool thread for CGI processing.

3.5.4. FTP Service Registry Entries

The Registry entries listed in Table 3.5 are valid for the FTP service only. All these entries are located under the `HKEY_LOCAL_MACHINE\SYSTEM\CurrentControlSet\Services\MSFTPSVC\Parameters` key. (This table is intended for informational purposes only; please refer to the Administrators reference in the IIS documentation for more in-depth information.)

Table 3.5. FTP service Registry entries.

Entry	Description
AnnotateDirectories	Determines whether custom messages are enabled for directories. See Chapter 5 for in-depth coverage of this key.
EnablePortAttack	If you are going to use FTP ports other than the default ones in the range below 1024, you have to enable this flag.
LowercaseFiles	Determines whether to use lowercase filenames or the native case of the file for comparison.

Lab

This lab consists of review questions pertaining to this chapter and provides an opportunity for you to use walk-through exercises to apply the knowledge that you've learned.

Questions

1. Which of the following statements about the MMC is true? (Select the best answer.)

    A. The MMC enables you to administer IIS.

    B. The MMC enforces the use of SNMP as the network management protocol.

    C. The MMC can be extended by snap-ins.

    D. The MMC allows remote administration of Windows NT computers.

2. Which snap-ins can be installed in an MMC console? (Select all that apply.)

    A. Stand-alone snap-ins

    B. Extensible snap-ins

    C. Extension snap-ins

    D. Console Root snap-ins

3. Which of the following snap-ins are available for Internet Information Server? (Select all that apply.)

    A. Web Server snap-in

    B. FTP Server snap-in

    C. Mail snap-in

    D. News snap-in

4. Which of the following is the default extension of MMC consoles?

    A. .mmc

    B. .con

    C. .mcs

    D. .msc

5. Where is the MetaBase.bin file stored by default? (Select the best answer.)
   A. %systemroot%\inetsvr\MetaBase.bin
   B. %systemroot%\inetsrv\MetaBase.bin
   C. c:\InetPub\MetaBase.bin
   D. c:\InetPub\config\MetaBase.bin

6. Which of the following statements is true about restoring the Metabase? (Select all that apply.)
   A. You can restore configuration information on a per-site basis.
   B. The backup can be restored on only the computer where it was created.
   C. To restore the Metabase, you must stop all services.
   D. None of the above statements is true.

7. MIME mappings are used to tell the client browser what? (Select the best answer.)
   A. The extension of the file it is downloading
   B. The type of file it is downloading
   C. How to render the file it is downloading
   D. Which PICS ratings the file has

8. You are creating a new console from scratch, and you want to be able to administer Web sites and Index Server from this console. Which snap-ins do you need to add to the new console? (Select all that apply.)
   A. Web Service snap-in
   B. Index Server snap-in
   C. Internet Information Server snap-in
   D. WWW snap-in

9. At which level can you set MIME mappings? (Select all that apply.)
   A. Web site
   B. Virtual directory
   C. Directory
   D. File

10. Your company's Web server is located in New York. While you are attending a conference in Seattle, you get a call from your boss that the site isn't functioning properly. Which administration tool should you use from an exhibit PC that has only Internet Explorer loaded? (Select the best answer.)

    A. Internet Service Manager

    B. Microsoft Management Console

    C. Remote Web Manager

    D. Internet Service Manager (HTML)

Answers to Questions

1. **C.** The Microsoft Management Console can be extended by snap-ins, which allow you to administer remote NT computers and to administer IIS. MMC doesn't enforce any special network management protocol; it only provides a user interface framework.

2. **A, C.** Stand-alone and extension snap-ins are available for creating consoles.

3. **C, D.** Mail and News are extension snap-ins for the Internet Information Server stand-alone snap-in, which is used to manage WWW and FTP sites. There are no special snap-ins for WWW or FTP.

4. **D.** The default file extension for consoles is .msc. Because it is also registered as a shell file type, you can open consoles by double-clicking on the .msc file.

5. **B.** By installation default, the MetaBase.bin file is located under %systemroot%\inetsrv\. You can change this location by changing the Registry value `HKEY_LOCAL_MACHINE\SOFTWARE\Microsoft\InetMgr\Parameters\MetaDataFile`.

6. **B, C.** In order to restore the Metabase, all services must be stopped. Also, you can restore only the entire server; you cannot selectively restore sites.

7. **B.** MIME mappings tell the client which file type it is downloading. With this information, the client decides how to render the file.

8. **B, C.** To administer WWW, FTP, and Index Server, you need the Internet Information Server snap-in and the Index Server snap-in.

9. **A, B, C.** MIME mappings can be defined at server, Web site, and directory levels. Directory level includes "normal" directories as well as virtual directories.

10. **D.** As only Internet Explorer is loaded on the exhibit PC, the Internet Service Manager (HTML) is the only tool with which you can administer your site remotely.

Exercise
Exercise 3.1.: Verifying Server Settings

This exercise addresses the following Microsoft exam objectives:

- Configure and save consoles by using Microsoft Management Console.
- Verify server settings by accessing the Metabase.

Follow these steps to create a new console to verify the settings for the Default Web Site on your local computer:

1. Click on Start, Run and enter `mmc.exe` in the Run dialog box to open the Microsoft Management Console (MMC).
2. MMC opens a new, empty console at startup. Open the Console menu and select the Add/Remove Snap-in command.
3. In the Add/Remove Snap-in dialog box, click the Add button to open the Add Standalone Snap-in dialog box. Select the Internet Information Server snap-in and click OK.
4. Click OK in the Add/Remove Snap-in dialog box to add the Internet Information Server snap-in to the new console.
5. Expand the Internet Information Server tree. Your local computer should be listed in the results pane. Double-click on it to open the list of sites that are maintained on it.
6. Right-click on Default Web Site and select Properties from the context menu (settings come from the Metabase).
7. In the Web Site Properties dialog box, select the HTTP Headers tab and click on the File Types buttons. This brings up the MIME Mappings dialog box. Because no mappings are defined, the standard mappings from the computer are enforced. Close this dialog box.
8. Explore the other tabs to see what other options are available.

3

TEST DAY FAST FACTS

Here are a few fast facts about this chapter that you may want to know ahead of time. Don't forget that these facts also provide great last-minute study material.

- Only one site can be designated to be administered by downlevel programs.

- Web sites are identified by a three-part identity. Any two Web sites on a given server must differ in at least one part.

- Host header names can be used to differentiate two Web sites with the same IP address.

- Virtual directories can have their content location either on the local computer or on a remote server. Remote resources are always accessed with the account you supply.

- You should disable Log Access for directories that contain files you do not want to log access for (like standard images).

- Process isolation provides additional server robustness; however, the trade-off is a speed penalty.

- You can restrict access to your site with username/password access, by requiring certificates, or by using IP address and domain name restrictions.

Day 4

The WWW Server

by Christoph Wille

One of the most important services that comes with Internet Information Server is definitely the WWW service. It allows you to host multiple Web sites on a single IIS server and comes with rich configuration options. This chapter takes an in-depth look at creating, managing, and adding content to Web sites.

The WWW service also plays a prominent part in the IIS exam. Therefore, it is advisable that you take the time to get familiar with configuring all aspects of Web sites, virtual directories, and files.

In this chapter, you will find information ranging from basic site setup tasks to performance tuning of a site (specifically, the TYS IIS4 Site, which you create, expand, and manage throughout the course of this chapter). In addition to creating a site, you will learn to change IP addresses and port numbers for that site. After having set up the site, you are going to add virtual directories to it and set access permissions. You will also learn about designating site operators for managing site administration, setting security on directories, modifying performance parameters, and more—basically, your everyday needs.

Objectives

This chapter helps you prepare for the Microsoft exam by covering the following objectives:

- Configure IIS to support the WWW service.
    - Set bandwidth and user connections
    - Set user logon requirements and authentication requirements
    - Modify port settings
    - Set default pages
    - Set HTTP 1.1 host header names to host multiple Web sites
    - Enable HTTP Keep-Alives

- Manage the WWW service.
- Create and share local and remote virtual directories with appropriate permissions.
    - Create a virtual directory and assign an alias
    - Set directory-level permissions
    - Set file-level permissions

- Create and share virtual servers with appropriate permissions.
    - Assign IP addresses

TEST DAY
FAST FACTS

- Modify HTTP headers to specify content expiration and content rating.

- Limit the bandwidth for specific sites or the entire server so that your sites don't eat up all your bandwidth.

- Use HTTP Keep-Alives to improve the performance of your Web server.

4.1. Configuration Options for the WWW Service

Before diving right into the processes of creating and managing a site, we are starting with an overview of the configuration options you have at your disposal. This section is intended to show you the big picture of IIS's feature set and where those features are located in which tool.

You can configure the WWW service using different methods, including the Internet Service Manager (ISM), the ISM for HTML, and scripts. Each of these has advantages: ISM provides easy administration; ISM for HTML is ideal for remote administration; and scripts are best for automated tasks. Today, you will exclusively use the ISM because you are going to use it most of the time when you are onsite and because most questions in the exam are targeted at ISM.

4.1.1. Configuration in the ISM

Internet Service Manager provides properties dialog boxes for four main items of the WWW service:

- *WWW master service.* Properties that apply to all Web sites created on the current server.
- *Web site.* Properties that apply to a single Web site.
- *Directory.* Properties that apply to a directory (including virtual directories).
- *File.* Properties that apply to a single file.

Using these four items, you can configure every aspect of an IIS server and its Web sites. The properties dialog boxes have multiple tabs of options, each of which you'll learn about in detail later in this chapter.

4.1.2. Looking at the Configuration Tabs

As you learned in the previous section, you can configure four items, and each of them has different tabs in its properties dialog box. Table 4.1 contains a list of all tabs and where they are located.

4.1. Configuration Options for the WWW Service

Table 4.1. Configuration tabs availability.

Tab/Properties	WWW Service Master Properties	Web Site Properties	Directory Properties	Virtual Directory Properties	File Properties
Web Site	X	X			
Operators	X	X			
Performance	X	X			
ISAPI Filters	X	X			
Home Directory	X	X			
Directory			X		
Virtual Directory				X	
File					X
Documents	X	X	X	X	
Directory Security	X	X	X	X	
File Security					X
HTTP Headers	X	X	X	X	X
Custom Errors	X	X	X	X	X
IIS 3.0 Admin	X				

Now that you have an overview of the tabs that exist, take a look at this quick overview of what each tab can do for you. After that, we'll get on to examining these tabs in live action without further ado.

The tabs presented in the previous table are used as described here:

- *Web Site.* To define site identification.
- *Operators.* To designate users that can administer sites.
- *Performance.* To tune performance of your sites.
- *ISAPI Filters.* To add ISAPI filters to your sites.
- *Home Directory, Directory, Virtual Directory, File.* To specify access permissions and content control for directories and files.
- *Documents.* To assign default documents for directories.
- *Directory Security, File Security.* To define security restrictions for directories and files.

- *HTTP Headers.* To define HTTP headers for content.
- *Custom Errors.* To create custom error messages for server errors.
- *IIS 3.0 Admin.* To specify the site that can be administered by programs that expect to deal with an IIS 3.0 server. Only one site can be administered by programs expecting older versions of IIS.

This section was intended to give you an overview of configuration options you have with the Internet Service Manager. The following sections make heavy use of the configuration tabs you just read about, starting with the one that enables the creation of Web sites.

4.2. Web Sites

Central to the administration of IIS are sites, which come in flavors of Web, FTP, news, and mail sites. This chapter deals with Web sites, which are used to administer, well, your Web sites. To run a Web site, you need an IP address for the server that hosts the site. You can host multiple sites on the same machine. However, if you want to do this, either you need more than one IP address bound to the server computer, or you need to use the host header name feature. Both are described later in this section.

4.2.1. Adding IP Addresses to Windows NT

This section contains a short tutorial on adding IP addresses to a Windows NT computer so you can run multiple Web sites on your IIS server. If you need more information about TCP/IP, refer to the Windows NT Help system.

In the following steps, you are preparing your server for hosting multiple Web sites, each of which uses a distinct IP address by binding additional IP addresses to your server. To complete the following steps, you need administrative privileges as well as unused IP addresses to add (including the subnet masks). Perform the following steps:

1. Open Control Panel and double-click on the Network applet.
2. In the Network applet, switch to the Protocols tab. Select the TCP/IP protocol and click the Properties button. You are presented the Microsoft TCP/IP Properties dialog box.
3. At least one IP address is already assigned. To add more IP addresses, click the Advanced button. The Advanced IP Addressing dialog box appears (see Figure 4.1).

Figure 4.1.
You add additional IP addresses in the Advanced IP Addressing dialog box.

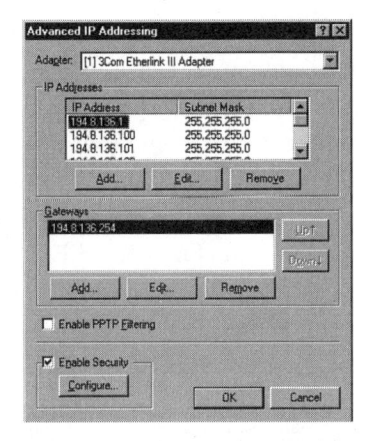

4. Click the Add button in the IP Addresses section to add IP addresses. Then enter both the IP address and the subnet mask in the Add dialog box. Repeat this step for as many IP addresses you want to add.

5. Dismiss all dialog boxes by clicking OK, and then restart the computer when prompted to do so.

On your server, you now can host multiple Web sites, each using a distinct IP address.

> **Note:** In some cases, you might want to install multiple network cards in your server and split the IP address pool across those adapters to improve server performance. That, however, is beyond the scope of this book.

4.2.2. Creating a New Web Site

A default Web site is installed when IIS 4 is set up. However, in most cases, you'll want to serve your own content from the IIS server. Therefore, you must create a new Web site, which is now easily possible because you've added additional IP addresses to your server.

The Web site you create in the following tutorial will be referenced and changed throughout the tutorials in this chapter. Therefore, you must complete the following task in order to be able to complete all others.

The Web site you create in the following steps will serve almost the same content as the default Web site because the home directory of the new site will point to the home directory of the default Web site. The name for the newly created site is TYS IIS4. Perform the following steps:

1. Open the ISM by selecting Internet Service Manager in the Microsoft Internet Information Server subfolder of the Windows NT Option Pack public group.
2. In ISM, open the Internet Information Server folder. You are presented with a list of all the servers you have connected to. Because you haven't connected to any so far, only the local machine is included in the server list.
3. Double-click on the machine name to view all sites that are running on this machine. You should see default sites for Web and FTP, and depending on whether you installed the services, you might also see the SMTP and NNTP sites.
4. Right-click on the machine name and select New, Web Site (see Figure 4.2).

Figure 4.2.
Select New, Web Site from the context menu to create a new Web site.

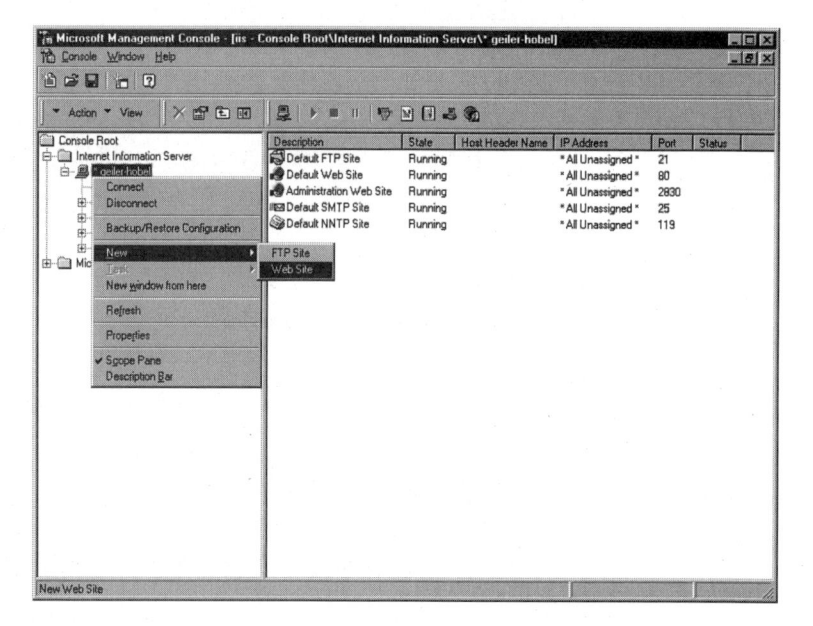

5. The New Web Site wizard opens. Enter the name of the Web site (TYS IIS4) in the Web Site Description edit field in the first step.
6. In the second step, you are asked to enter the IP address for the Web site and the server port (standard port for WWW is 80). Select the IP address you want to use for the new site.
7. In the next step, you provide such information as the directory where the Web site is located on the server and whether anonymous access to this Web site should be allowed. Browse for the directory of the default Web site (which should be c:\InetPub\wwwroot with a standard installation).

8. The last options you need to set are the access permissions for the Web site. Choose from the following options:

   Allow Read Access

   Allow Script Access

   Allow Execute Access (includes Script Access)

   Allow Write Access

   Allow Directory Browsing

   The defaults are to allow Read and Script access, which is sufficient for most cases. You'll learn more about the different access methods in the section entitled "Access Permissions and Content Control."

9. To create the site now, click the Finish button. The site is created in a stopped state, which means it exists but cannot be reached from the outside.
10. Select the newly created site, and then click the Start Item button on the toolbar or right-click and select Start from the context menu. The Web site is started.
11. To verify that your setup is working, open a Web browser and connect to the site using the IP address. If everything went all right, you should get a result similar to the one shown in Figure 4.3. Notice that the images don't show up; you are going to correct that later.

Figure 4.3.
View the newly created site with Internet Explorer.

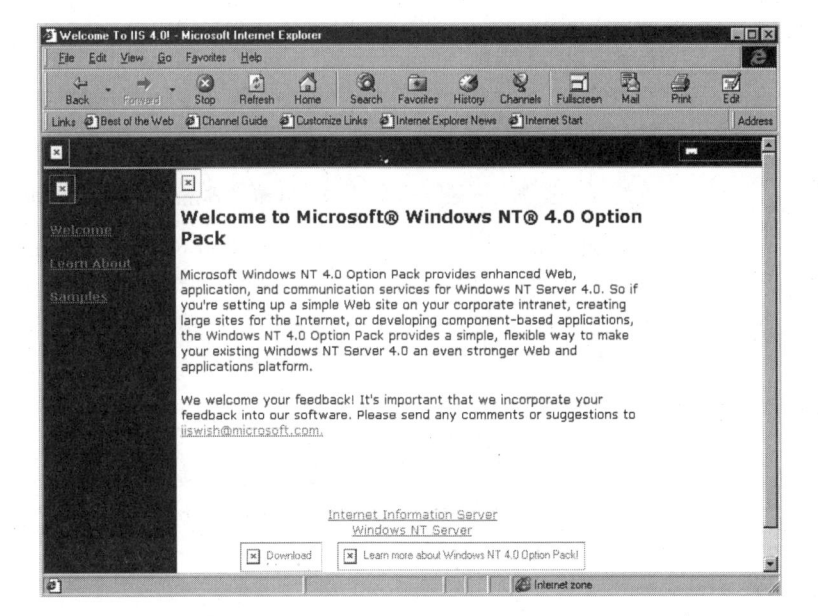

Creating new Web sites is very easy with IIS 4.0. Although right now it is only a very basic site without any of the advanced features that IIS 4 offers, more will come shortly.

4.2.3. Web Sites Using IP Addresses Versus Host Headers

If you are used to versions of IIS prior to 4.0, the only way you could host more than one site on a server was to assign every site a unique IP address. With IIS 4, you can uniquely identify Web sites in three ways:

- IP address
- Port number
- Host header name

You can host as many sites on your server as you like, as long as every site differs in at least one part of this three-part identity. This means that you can have sites that share the same IP address and port number but differ in their host headers. For those of you migrating from other Web server products, the concept of host headers might be familiar to you. However, for most IIS users, this is a new concept for identifying Web sites.

An example might help. Assume you want to host two friends' Web sites on your server, one with the DNS name www.somegirl.nom and the other one www.someboy.nom. The problem is, your server has only one unassigned IP address left. How do you solve this problem? With IIS 4, there is no problem: In the DNS server database, you can assign both sites the same IP address. Then, on the IIS server, you create new sites with the same IP address assigned. Now two parts of the three-part identity are the same. So you need to use the third one to make each site distinct for IIS.

The following steps show you how to use host headers to distinguish two Web sites that use the same IP address and port number. A prerequisite for this tutorial (to get two sites that really work) is that you must have two DNS entries that point to the same IP address. Perform the following steps:

1. Follow the steps outlined in the previous section's tutorial to create the two sites. Use names "Site1" and "Site2" for the sites.
2. Right-click on Site1 in the Sites list and select Properties from the context menu. You are presented the Web Site tab of the site's Properties dialog box.

3. Click the Advanced button in the Web Site Identification frame.
4. In the Advanced Multiple Web Site Identification dialog box, you see a list of three-part identities for the current site. Select the current record (which has only an IP address and port number defined) and click the Edit button to open the Advanced Web Site Identification dialog box.
5. Enter the DNS name for this site in the Host Header Name field. Figure 4.4 shows the Advanced Web Site Identification dialog box with a host header name entered. Click OK to save the changes for this identity.

Figure 4.4.
Use the Advanced Web Site Identification dialog box to change a three-part identity for a site.

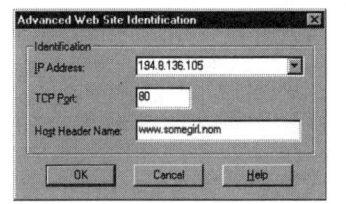

6. Click OK twice, once to close the Advanced Multiple Web Site Identification dialog box and once to close the site's Properties dialog box.
7. Repeat steps 2 through 6 for Site2.

If you have two DNS entries, you can now go ahead and test both sites from a Web browser. The only problem with host headers are the browsers: You need a browser that sends the host header, which allows the server to extract the host name and then decide what content to serve. (Although there is a way to get around this problem and use the host header feature with browsers that don't support them, we are not going to cover that here. That workaround includes making rather sophisticated changes to the Registry, which are described in the online documentation for IIS.)

4.3. Directories

Up to this point, we have dealt with *creating* Web sites only. But now we begin to explore the structure of your Web site: the directories. You have already encountered one kind of directory: the home directory of your site. The various kinds of directories include:

- *Home directory.* The root directory of your site, which is specified during initial creation of the site. It can be changed at any time.

- *Virtual directories.* Directories that are mapped in the directory tree of a site but that physically reside outside of this tree or even on a different server.
- *Redirections.* Redirect clients accessing a resource to a page specified by the site administrator.

If you're wondering what redirections have to do with directories, don't worry. The following sections will show you.

4.3.1. Home Directory

The home directory is the root directory of your Web site, which stores the content that can be accessed by users. This directory can contain any number of subdirectories or files, and you can set properties for those directories and files.

The initial properties that are set for your Web site—and, therefore, for your home directory—are controlled by the WWW master properties for the computer. To modify the WWW master properties, right-click the IIS server for which you want to set master properties and select Properties from the context menu. In the computer's Properties dialog box, select WWW Service from the Master Properties drop-down box and click the Edit button. You will then be able to edit the WWW Service Master Properties (see Figure 4.5).

Figure 4.5.
Use the WWW Service Master Properties dialog box to change properties for all sites.

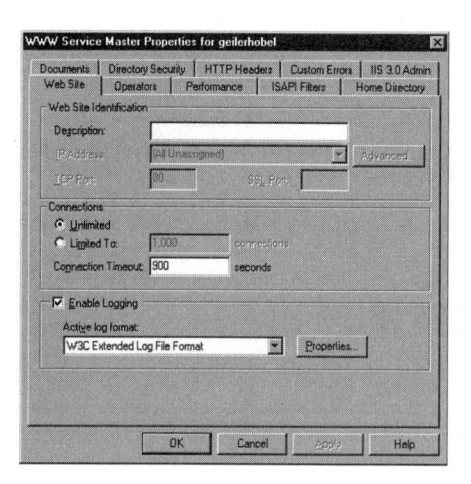

All the settings you define here are inherited by new sites created on this computer. Therefore, if you want any special settings to be inherited by new sites, set them here.

4.3.2. Virtual Directories

When you have created a Web site, users can access only content that physically resides below the root directory. Users cannot access any directories that are not contained in the directory tree below the home directory. To allow access to other directories not contained in this tree, you need to use *virtual directories*—directories that are mapped into the root tree as if they were physically located beneath it.

If you are used to working with virtual directories on IIS 3, note this small difference: If you are creating Web applications for Active Server Pages (ASP), you no longer need virtual directories; now you can activate any directory to contain a Web application. For more information on programming with ASP, see Day 11, "Programmability."

The following two sections describe the usage of two slightly different types of virtual directories: local and remote. The latter one has some implications for security.

A. Creating a Local Virtual Directory

The most common use of virtual directories is to map directories that are local to the server into the Web site directory tree.

The following steps walk you through adding a virtual directory to the Web site you already created. The virtual directory you're going to add is the directory that's needed to view the images that were missing when you initially created the Web site (because that directory is mapped into the directory tree of the Default Web Site). Perform the following steps:

1. Open ISM and locate the TYS IIS4 Web site to which you want to add the virtual directory.
2. Right-click on the site and select New, Virtual Directory. The New Virtual Directory Wizard opens.
3. In the first step, enter the name of the virtual directory (the alias under which the virtual directory will be referenced), which is IISSAMPLES.
4. In the second step, select the directory in which the virtual directory is located. The location of the IISSAMPLES directory for standard installations is c:\InetPub\Iissamples.
5. In the final step, choose the access permissions. Go with the defaults: Read and Script.
6. Click Finish to create the virtual directory.

Notice that the new virtual directory is displayed with a different icon (see Figure 4.6). This icon shows that the directory is a Web application starting point. Start your Web browser and navigate to the TYS IIS4 site. Now all the images show up on the main page.

Figure 4.6.
Notice that the IISSAMPLES directory is displayed with a different icon to indicate it's a virtual directory.

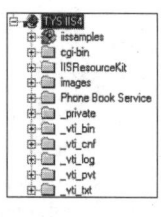

B. Creating a Remote Virtual Directory

You are not limited to adding virtual directories from the local computer only. You can also map network shares to a virtual directory.

The following steps walk you through the process of changing the newly created local virtual directory IISSAMPLES to a remote virtual directory. To complete this task, you must have a network share you can connect to. Perform the following steps:

1. Right-click on the virtual directory you created in the previous tutorial. Select Properties from the context menu. You are presented the Virtual Directory tab of the iissamples Properties dialog box.

2. In the When Connecting To list, select A Share Located on Another Computer. Notice that the caption for the location changes from "Local Path" to "Network Directory."

3. Enter the UNC name for the share in the Network Directory edit box.

4. You need to specify which user account to use to access this resource. To do so, click the Connect As button.

5. In the Network Directory Security Credentials dialog box, enter the username (which you can browse for if necessary) and the password (see Figure 4.7).

Figure 4.7.
Fill in the logon information in the Network Directory Security Credentials dialog box.

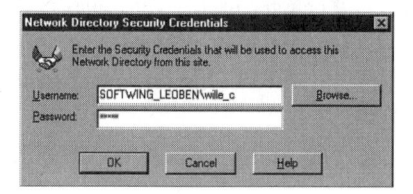

6. Click OK to close this dialog box, and click OK again to close the iissamples Properties dialog box. Now the IISSAMPLES virtual directory's contents comes from a network share.

4.3. Directories

Using network shares as a base location for your virtual directories (this also works for the home directory) is hardly more complicated than using a local directory.

However, one important security consideration needs to be mentioned here: All files that are accessed from the remote location are accessed with the privileges of the user account you supplied in step 5, *not* with the privileges the browsing client has. Keep this in mind when creating remote virtual directories!

4.3.3. Directory Properties

Up to this point, we've yet to talk about the specific properties of the directories we've created. By directory properties, I'm talking specifically in this discussion about access permissions for directories, content control, and application settings. The next couple sections tackle these concepts, starting with directory access permissions and content control.

A. Access Permissions and Content Control

In the previous sections, you created virtual directories pointing to the local and remote machines, always using the standard settings for directory access. If you select the Properties dialog box for the IISSAMPLES directory (see Figure 4.8) and examine the additional options we haven't covered so far, you will see the check boxes that control access permissions and content.

Figure 4.8.
The Properties dialog box offers check boxes for controlling access permissions and content.

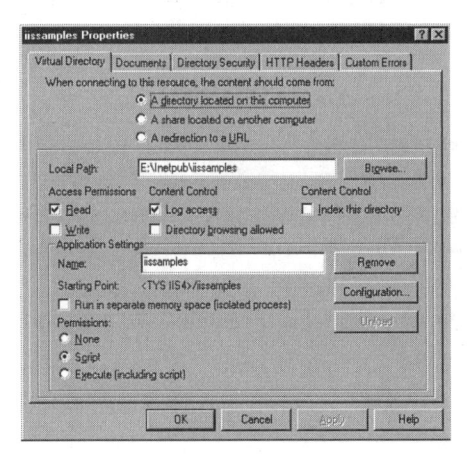

Under Access Permissions, you see only two check boxes: Read and Write. However, there are additional access permissions in the application frame that are not necessarily tied to the application settings. Therefore, the access permissions total five:

- *Read.* Allows clients to read files in a directory.
- *Write.* Allows clients to write to a directory. (Used for directories that allow uploading of files.)
- *None.* No Script or Execute permissions are set.
- *Script.* Allows clients to execute scripts in a directory.
- *Execute.* Allows clients to execute applications (.exe and .dll) in a directory. (This permission also includes Script permission.)

Before moving on to the application settings, take a look at the Content Control options listed in the directory's Properties dialog box:

- *Log Access.* Controls whether you want to log access to files in this directory. For example, you might want to disable logging for directories that contain only images in order to decrease the overall size of your log files.

  Logging for a site is enabled in the Web Site tab, where you can choose between NCSA format, ODBC logging (to a database), and W3C log file formats (the default). For W3C log files, you can choose to create new log files daily, weekly, monthly, never (unlimited size), or when a specific file size is reached. If you set the logging directory and use the W3C extended format, as a bonus, you can also choose which fields you want to include in the log file.

- *Directory Browsing Allowed.* Allows users to browse a directory listing when no default document is located in a directory. If no default document is in a directory and directory browsing is not allowed, users will receive an `Access Denied` message. Therefore, you can consider this content control feature to be an additional access permission.

- *Index This Directory.* Instructs Index Server to index this directory.

B. Web Applications

For every Web site or virtual directory you create, IIS automatically creates an application for you. What are applications used for? First, they are used for creating Web applications with ASP (Active Server Pages). Second—and for today's topic—they can help you to isolate Web sites from one another. (For more information on programming with ASP or programming IIS in general, see Day 11.)

4.3. Directories

> **Note:** Applications are not limited to Web sites or virtual directories. You can also create an application with a "normal" directory that resides below the home directory. This is a major change from IIS 3 to IIS 4, so keep it in mind for the exam!

Process isolation means that IIS creates a new process for this site, which results in poorer performance because process-to-process communication is costly on NT. However, there is one huge advantage to this approach: Should a component crash some other Web site, the process-isolated site won't be affected, and the same holds true the other way around. An additional benefit of a process-isolated site is that if it crashes, the crash will be detected automatically, and a new process will be created when a new request comes in for that site. And the feature is easy to use. Simply check the Run in Separate Memory Space check box in the Properties dialog box (see Figure 4.9).

Figure 4.9.
You can run applications in isolated processes.

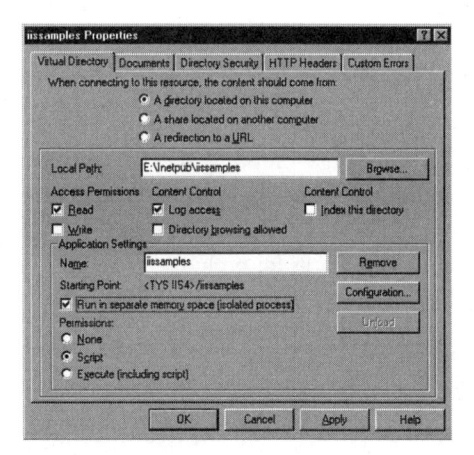

There are some configuration options for applications that you need to be aware of. Click the Configuration button in the Application Settings area to access the following options:

- *App Mappings.* Maps a specific file extension to programs, ISAPI extensions, or scripting engines. You can also limit the allowed HTTP actions for these mappings.
- *App Options.* Contains ASP-specific application options, such as default scripting language, session state, and script timeout.

- *App Debugging*. Enables application debugging for Web applications. You can also specify whether clients should receive the script error message (recommended on development servers) or a standard error message (recommended for production servers).

The one last thing to say about applications is that you can remove them. For example, if you remove the application for the IISSAMPLES virtual directory, it will still be displayed in ISM but with a different icon next to it (see Figure 4.10).

Figure 4.10.
On the left side, IISSAMPLES is an application root; the right side shows the IISSAMPLES directory with the application removed.

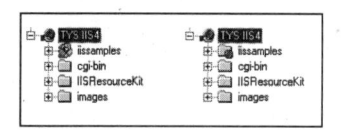

4.3.4. Redirections

Have you ever wanted to take an entire directory tree offline for maintenance and redirect users to some status page informing them about the maintenance work? Or maybe you want to move the contents of one directory to another one, but users still have the old directory bookmarked. Redirecting requests is an important capability. The redirections feature that works for both directories and files can be invoked in the Directory (or File) tab of the respective Properties dialog box.

The following steps show you how to redirect all requests made for the IISSAMPLES directory to the default.asp file in the home directory root of the TYS IIS4 site:

1. Open the Properties dialog box for the IISSAMPLES virtual directory.
2. From the When Connecting To list, select A Redirection to a URL. The current tab will change.
3. In the Redirect To field, enter `/default.asp`.
4. For this example, choose The Exact URL Entered Above from the following options:
    - *The Exact URL Entered Above*. Redirects users to the URL entered above without adding it to the original request URL.

- *A Directory Below This One.* Redirects users to a child directory of the current parent directory.
- *A Permanent Redirection for This Resource.* Sends a message to the client (`301 Permanent Redirect`) so the client can change the bookmarks to the new location. This is in contrast to the message `302 Temporary Redirect`, which won't affect bookmarks because it is not a permanent redirect.

The Properties dialog box should now look like Figure 4.11.

Figure 4.11.
You can create a redirection for the IISSAMPLES virtual directory.

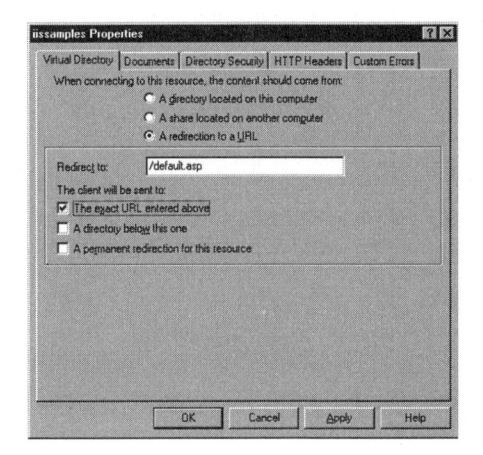

5. You are finished. Use your browser to verify that the redirection works.

If you are (re)moving files or entire directory branches, it's likely that users will have bookmarks to those items on their browsers. To prevent users from receiving error messages when they navigate to the bookmarked item, use the redirection feature to direct the users automatically to a status page or even to the moved content.

4.4. Key Items to Configure

In this section, we take a close look at the important parameters you can set for Web sites, directories, and files that haven't been covered so far. The following topics are covered:

- Configuring Web site identification
- Assigning site operators
- Defining default documents

- Setting directory security
- Modifying HTTP headers
- Configuring ISAPI filters
- Customizing error messages
- Modifying performance parameters

4.4.1. Configuring Web Site Identification

In the earlier section, "Web Sites Using IP Addresses Versus Host Headers," you learned the basics about configuring Web sites. However, because that is a very important topic for the exam, we are going to take a second look at it.

A Web site has a three-part identity that consists of the IP address, port number, and host header name. Any two Web sites that are configured on a server must differ in at least one of the three parts. For example, the IP address and port number can be the same, but the host header names must differ. Or maybe the host headers and IP addresses match, but the port number is different.

Changing the port number can be useful if you want to "hide" your site because Web browsers always try to connect to standard port 80 on a Web server. Also an important port to configure is the SSL port, which is 443 by default (see Figure 4.12). You'll learn more about SSL in Day 6, "Internet Information Server Security."

Figure 4.12.
The Web Site tab in the Properties dialog box for a site offers additional configuration options.

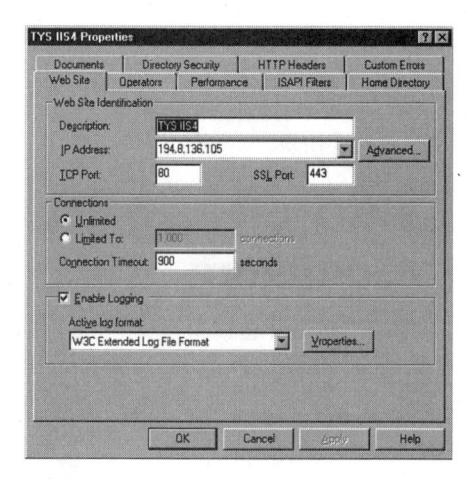

4.4.2. Assigning Site Operators

One of the neat features of IIS 4 for administering Web sites is that you can grant certain users the right to administer a specific Web site. This allows you to delegate administration work for certain sites to other users without having to give them administrative access to all sites on a machine.

In the following steps, you grant a new user the right to administer the TYS IIS4 site. To accomplish this task, you need to be logged on as a user with administrative rights. Perform the following steps:

1. Open User Manager in the Administrative Tools program folder and add a new user named SiteAdmin. (Don't put this user in the Administrators group because those users are automatically allowed to administer all sites.)
2. After creating the new user, go to the Internet Service Manager and open the Properties dialog box for the TYS IIS4 site.
3. Switch to the Operators tab. Notice that currently only the Administrators group has the right to administer the site.
4. Click the Add button, browse for the newly created user account, and add it to the list of operators. The Properties dialog box should now look like Figure 4.13.

Figure 4.13.
The new user called SiteAdmin has been granted the right to administer the TYS IIS4 site.

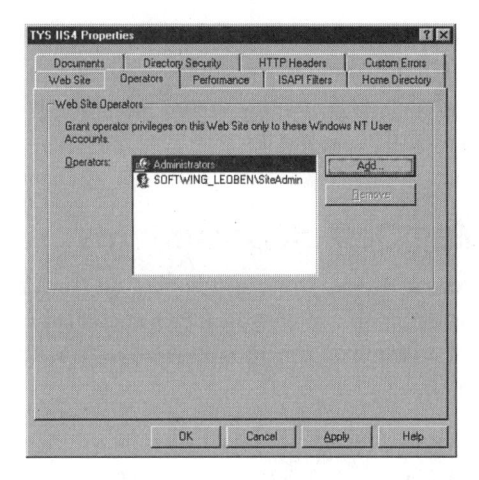

5. Click OK to close the Web site Properties dialog box.
6. Log off the computer.

7. Log on as the new user (SiteAdmin) and open the Internet Service Manager. Notice that for sites the operator is not allowed to administer, the description is not displayed and the status is set to stopped (see Figure 4.14).

Figure 4.14.
This operator is allowed to administer only the TYS IIS4 site.

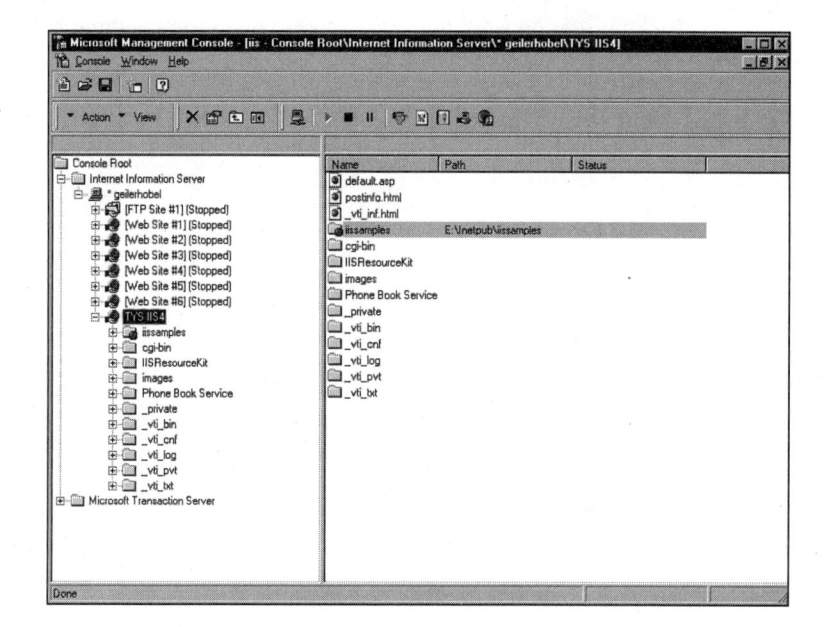

Delegating administration work to other users is a very useful feature because you can limit the operator's rights to specific Web sites. Internet service providers will agree on that.

4.4.3. Defining Default Documents

Whenever you enter a URL to a company's home page (such as http://www.microsoft.com), you don't include a document name to retrieve. However, content from some document is returned to you. That's the content from the default document.

You can define which documents IIS should consider default documents and specify which of these takes priority when more than one default document is located in a directory. The default documents that are enabled by IIS are default.htm and default.asp, but you can change this either for the entire site or at the directory level. To do so, select the Documents tab from the Properties dialog box (see Figure 4.15). There you can add default documents, remove default documents from the list, or rearrange the order in which default documents are evaluated.

Figure 4.15.
You view the existing default documents for the TYS IIS4 site on the Documents tab.

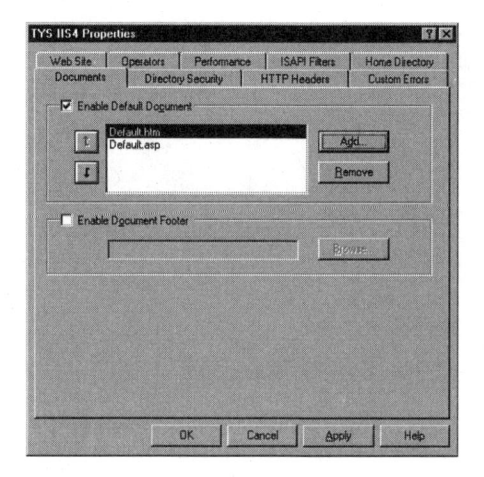

This tab contains another option in addition to the default documents setting: document footers. If you enable this option, IIS will append a document footer to every document it sends to the client. The drawback of this feature is that it uses considerable server power.

4.4.4. Setting Directory Security

Although Day 6 is dedicated to securing your Web server, security needs to be mentioned in the configuration chapters, too. (We can't repeat security topics too often.) An entire tab in the Properties dialog boxes is dedicated to security: the Directory Security tab. It contains the following three security areas:

- *Anonymous Access and Authentication Control.* Allows you to determine how users will be authenticated by your Web site. You can choose from the following three authentication options:

    Allow Anonymous Access

    Basic Authentication

    Windows NT Challenge/Response

- *Secure Communications.* Enables you to set up secure communication with the ability to use client certificates to verify users (see Figure 4.16). For more information on secure communication, see Day 6 for more information on issuing client certificates, see Day 7, "Microsoft Certificate Server."

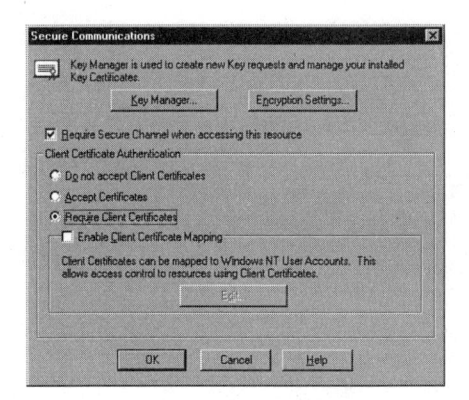

Figure 4.16.
Use the Secure Communications dialog box to manage SSL settings, including the use of client certificates for authentication.

- *IP Address and Domain Name Restrictions.* Restricts access to your Web site by use of either IP addresses or domain names. Either you can grant everyone access to your site except the addresses and domains you specify, or you can deny everyone access to your site except the addresses and domains you specify (see Figure 4.17). You can specify the following allow/deny entries:

    Single Computer. Enter the IP address of the computer you want to include in the allow/deny list.

    Group of Computers. Enter the network ID and the subnet mask of the group of computers you want to include in the allow/deny list.

    Domain Name. Enter the domain name you want to include in the allow/deny list. Notice that the server must perform reverse DNS lookups before it decides whether to grant or deny access to a resource, thereby putting a heavy load on your server and slowing down client access.

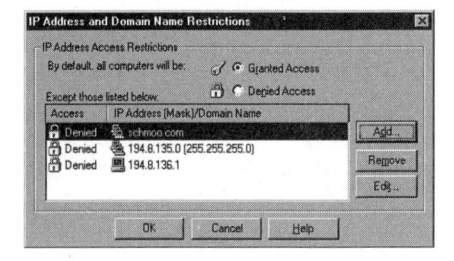

Figure 4.17.
Everyone is granted access to the site except the listed resources.

4.4.5. Modifying HTTP Headers

Another very important tab is the HTTP Headers tab, which is available at all levels from computer to file (see Figure 4.18). HTTP headers allow you to send information to the client before the actual document arrives at the client's browser, including information about the document type, its content, and lifetime.

Figure 4.18.
In the HTTP Headers tab for the TYS IIS4 site, you can add your custom headers.

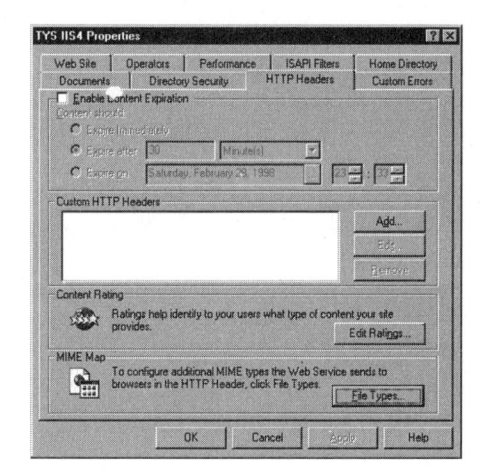

You can set the following HTTP header information:

- *Content Expiration.* Determines when the content will be expired by the client's browser. After a page has expired in the client's cache, a new version is fetched from your server the next time the user wants to view the page. You can set the content to expire immediately, after a set amount of time, or on a given date.

- *Custom HTTP Headers.* Allows you to define and set any HTTP headers you want.

- *Content Rating.* Rates the content using the Recreational Software Advisory Council (RSAC) rating system. Content can be rated for violence, sex, nudity, and language.

- *MIME Map.* Redefines the computer's MIME map. See Day 3, "Configuring IIS 4.0," for more information on MIME maps.

4.4.6. Configuring ISAPI Filters

You can extend Internet Information Server by using ISAPI (Internet Server Application Programming Interface) filters that add additional functionality to your server or site. Examples of such filters are the FrontPage extensions (see Figure 4.19) and custom user authentication filters.

Figure 4.19.
ISAPI filters installed for all Web sites are displayed.

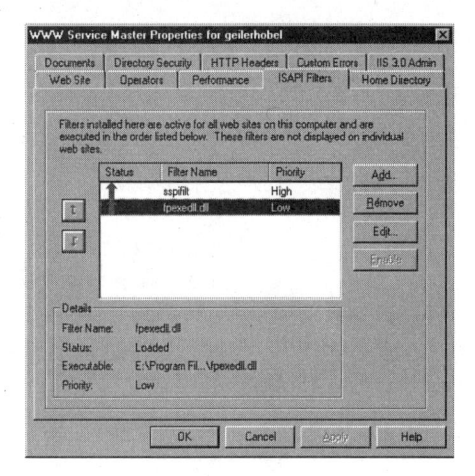

On the ISAPI Filters tab, you can determine the priority of the filters, add or remove filters, and edit existing filters. A nice feature is to be able to enable/disable filters on an as-needed basis.

4.4.7. Customizing Error Messages

You are surely familiar with error messages like `404 not found` when you've tried to retrieve a file that didn't exist. For novice users, this message isn't very informative at all, and for power users who are sure that this resource does exist, it is annoying to search for information on whom to contact about that error. IIS 4 introduces a powerful means of customizing the error messages that are sent to the client. You can assign three message types to server errors:

- *Default.* With this option, only the default error text is sent to the client (such as `404 not found`).
- *File.* Enables you to specify a file (usually an HTML document) that contains extended error information and contact information. By default, most errors on IIS 4 have error description files assigned.
- *URL.* Allows you to direct users to a central error help desk (for example), which allows them to file error reports or to contact the administrator directly.

The following steps show you how to customize the error message for 404 not found. In this case, you are adding the webmaster's e-mail address to the standard error message file. Perform the following steps:

1. Open the Properties dialog box for the TYS IIS4 Web site and go to the Custom Errors tab.
2. Locate the HTTP Error 404. You can see that it is mapped to a file. Open Explorer and make a copy of that file in some other folder (such as c:\custerrors).
3. Open the HTML file you just copied in any HTML Editor (like FrontPage Express or Notepad) and add the webmaster's e-mail address as a hyperlink to the page. Save the modified page.
4. Go back to the Internet Service Manager, select the 404 error, and click Edit Properties.
5. In the Error Mapping Properties dialog box, you can change the error message types; leave that set to File. In the File text box, enter the new location of the 404 error message file you customized in step 3. The dialog box should now look like Figure 4.20.

Figure 4.20.
You can change the default error message file to a customized one.

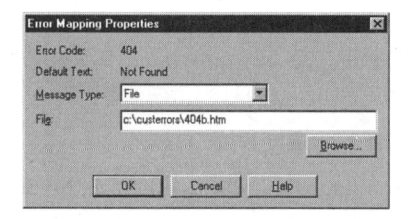

6. Click OK to save your changes.
7. Open your browser and request error.htm (or some other bogus nonexisting file) from the TYS IIS4 site. You are presented with the error message you just customized (see Figure 4.21).

Figure 4.21.
This error message is the one you just customized.

This new feature for customizing error messages is available at the computer, site, directory, and file levels. It allows you to send more detailed error information to the client or even to redirect clients to a central error help desk.

4.4.8. Modifying Performance Parameters

The performance tuning parameters for the Web service and sites are distributed across multiple tabs in properties dialog boxes. This section identifies these settings and shows you how to configure them.

Some settings can be chosen without doing performance analysis; others require that you examine the actual bottlenecks in your system. To learn how to identify bottlenecks and how to get rid of them, see Day 12, "Performance Tuning."

A. User Connection Limits

By default, IIS allows an unlimited number of connections to your Web site. However, if your server has limited resources, you should limit the number of concurrent connections to your site.

The following steps show you how to restrict the maximum number of connections to the TYS IIS4 site to 20 simultaneous users:

1. Open the Properties dialog box for the TYS IIS4 Web site.
2. Select the Web Site tab if necessary. In the Connections area, select the Limited To radio button.
3. The Limited To edit box is activated, and 1,000 connections appears as the default value. Change this value to 20, as shown in Figure 4.22.

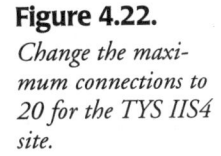

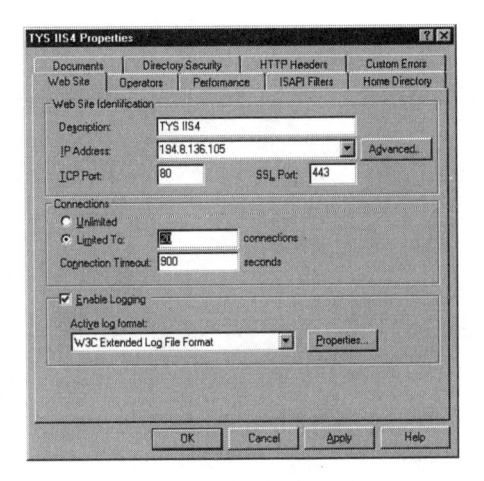

Figure 4.22.
Change the maximum connections to 20 for the TYS IIS4 site.

4. Click OK to close the Properties dialog box. Now only 20 users can connect simultaneously to the TYS IIS4 site. The 21st person who attempts to connect to the site will receive the error message `403.9 Access Forbidden: Too many users are connected`.

Limiting the maximum number of user connections is useful for sites where you have tight hardware resources or simply want to limit the maximum number of concurrent users to guarantee decent performance for those that are connected.

B. Setting Bandwidth Usage

Another important setting for not only server performance but also network performance is bandwidth usage. For example, if you have a T3 line, it is not acceptable for a single Web site to take all bandwidth and leave nothing for other Web sites. You also have to consider that your company uses that line not only for your server, but also for employees retrieving information from the Web. Therefore, unless you have virtually unlimited bandwidth—which is unlikely—you need to set bandwidth limits for your server and consequently all your sites.

Setting Bandwidth Usage for the Entire Server

When you are setting the bandwidth usage for the entire server, all your FTP and WWW sites have to share the bandwidth you are setting forth.

The following steps walk you through the process of limiting the bandwidth for an entire server. Notice that this bandwidth limitation is enforced only for Web and FTP sites; Mail and News sites are not affected. Perform the following steps:

1. Open the Properties dialog box for the server for which you want to limit the bandwidth.

2. Enable bandwidth throttling by checking the Enable Bandwidth Throttling check box.

3. The Maximum Network Use edit box is enabled and displays a default value of 1,024 KB/S bandwidth usage for the entire server. Change this to a value that fits your needs (see Figure 4.23).

Figure 4.23.
Set the maximum bandwidth usage for the entire server to 2,048 KB/S.

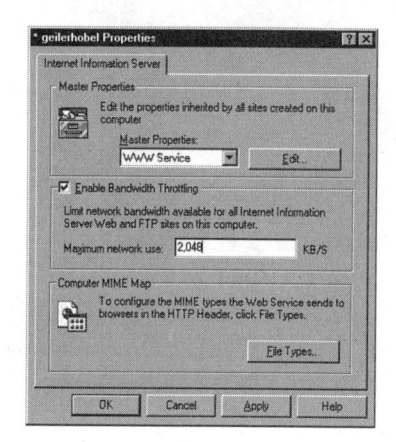

4. Click OK to put your changes into effect.

Setting bandwidth usage is very important because in most Internet cases your bandwidth is not as unlimited as it usually is for intranet scenarios. You can fine-tune bandwidth usage for sites also, as described in the next section.

Setting Bandwidth Usage for a Single Site

To fine-tune the bandwidth usage, you can assign certain bandwidth amounts to specific sites depending on their popularity. There is one very important point you need to know about site-level bandwidth throttling: Site-level bandwidth settings override the computer settings. For example, if you have limited the entire server to 2,048 KB/S and then you set a site to a limit of 4,096 KB/S, the site's bandwidth limit overrides the server limit, resulting in a maximum bandwidth usage of 4 MB/S.

The following steps illustrate how to limit the bandwidth usage for a single site (the TYS IIS4 site):

1. Open the Properties dialog box for the TYS IIS4 site and switch to the Performance tab.

2. Check the Enable Bandwidth Throttling check box.

3. Enter the Maximum Network Usage limit. Figure 4.24 shows the maximum limit set to 1,512 KB/S.

Figure 4.24.

The maximum limit is set to 1,512 KB/S.

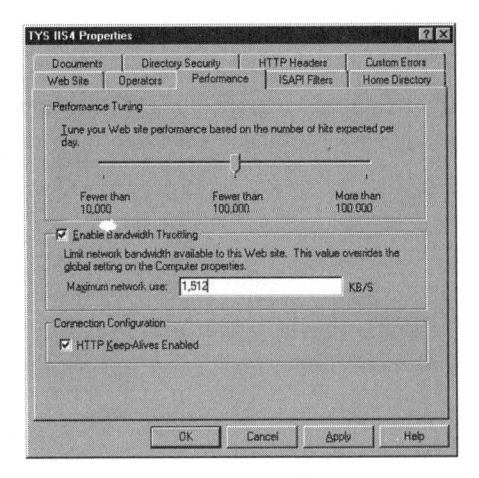

4. Click OK to put your changes into effect.

Although you have chosen a lower bandwidth for this site than for the entire server, it is possible to enter a value greater than the bandwidth for the entire server. As a matter of fact, you aren't even warned if you set a higher bandwidth limit than is allowed for the entire server.

C. HTTP Keep-Alives

You probably noticed that there are two other frames on the Performance tab (refer to Figure 4.24). The Connection Configuration frame allows you to enable or disable HTTP Keep-Alives. This feature is enabled by default because it decreases the server load significantly by allowing clients to keep a connection open to the server, thus eliminating the need to establish a new connection for each file that needs to be retrieved from the server. Just imagine the overhead for an HTML document that contains 20 little graphics if the client had to reopen a connection for every single file instead of using the connection that's already open.

D. Expected Hits

The Performance Tuning area of the Performance tab enables you to tune your Web site for expected hits (refer to Figure 4.24). However, this is feasible only when you do regular analysis of your log files to see how many hits you have on your Web site.

This setting affects server memory usage and connection establishing performance. In general, choose a slightly higher number of hits than you actually receive to help server performance. Choosing a much higher number of hits only wastes server memory and does not help performance. (See Day 13, "Site Analysis," for more information on analyzing the number of hits on your site.)

Lab

This lab consists of review questions pertaining to this chapter and provides an opportunity for you to use walk-through exercises to apply the knowledge that you've learned.

Questions

1. Which of the following sites can be hosted together on a single computer? (Select all that apply.)

   A. IP address: 194.8.136.1
      Port: 80

   B. IP address: 194.8.136.1
      Port: 81

   C. IP address: 194.8.136.1
      Port: 80
      Host Header: www.softwing.com

   D. IP address: 194.8.136.1
      Port: 81
      Host header: www.siteam.com

2. Applications can be enabled for which of the following items? (Select all that apply.)

   A. Home directory
   B. Directories
   C. Virtual directories
   D. Redirections

3. Which access permissions can be set for a directory? (Select all that apply.)

   A. Read
   B. Write
   C. Delete
   D. None

4. Which of the following statements is true about remote virtual directories? (Select the best answer.)

    A. You need to supply a username to connect to that share, and then IIS uses the impersonated user to verify file access.

    B. You need to supply a username to connect to that share, and IIS uses that user's credentials to verify file access.

    C. You need to enable SSL to be able to create remote virtual directories because otherwise no passwords can be transmitted to the share.

    D. You need to supply the username, password, and share name, and you need to require client certificates from the connecting users.

5. A user connects to your site and requests http://www.yoursite.com/testdir. You know the directory exists, but the user receives an access denied message. What is the most likely cause? (Select the best answer.)

    A. You are at fault. The directory doesn't exist.

    B. The directory exists, but it doesn't contain any default documents, and the Disallow Directory Browsing option is enabled.

    C. The directory exists, but it doesn't contain any default documents, and the Directory Browsing Allowed option is disabled.

    D. It is a remote virtual directory, and the user doesn't have access permissions for it.

6. Where can you redirect users to by using the redirection feature? (Select all that apply.)

    A. A relative URL

    B. An exact URL

    C. A directory anywhere on your server

    D. Anywhere on the Internet

7. You are creating a new user account called SiteAdmin that should be able to administer one of your six sites. You put the user in the Administrators and Users groups and assign this user as an operator to the one site you want her to administer. What will happen? (Select the best answer.)

   A. She will be able to administer only this one application.
   B. She will be able to administer all sites.
   C. She won't be able to administer any site.
   D. She will be able to administer all sites except the one she should be able to.

8. Which IP address and domain restrictions can you enforce? (Select all that apply.)

   A. IP address
   B. Any range of IP addresses
   C. Domains
   D. IN-ADDR.ARPA domains

9. Which content expiration options can you set? (Select all that apply.)

   A. Immediately
   B. Never
   C. Time Period
   D. Specific Date

10. You are setting a bandwidth limit on the server with 1,024 KB/S and a bandwidth limit on the TYS IIS4 site with 2,512 KB/S. Which limit will be enforced? (Select the best answer.)

    A. Server limit
    B. Site limit
    C. Site limit – Server limit
    D. None of the above

Answers to Questions

1. **A, B, C, D.** All four sites differ in one part of their three-part identity.
2. **A, B, C.** With the exception of files and redirections, you can create applications for all directories.

3. **A, B, D.** Read and Write are access permissions; None is an execute permission.
4. **B.** The user account you supply is used to access files on the remote share.
5. **C.** The most likely cause for the `access denied` error is that no default document exists and directory browsing is not allowed.
6. **A, B, C, D.** All answers are correct because a relative redirection occurs when you don't check the Exact URL check box. You can redirect users anywhere on your server and even to the Internet.
7. **B.** Because she is member of the Administrators group and the Administrators group by default is allowed to administer all sites, she can do it, too.
8. **A, C.** You can restrict access to a site to specific IP addresses, groups of IP addresses, and domains. The definition for groups means limiting to specific subnets, not to any range you can think of. Also, the IN-ADDR.ARPA domains cannot be excluded because they provide IP addresses to domain mapping.
9. **A, B, C, D.** All four answers are correct for the server side of the story. However, on the client side, the Never answer doesn't hold true because you can set cache expirations for your browser.
10. **B.** The site limit always overrides the server limit.

Exercise

Exercise 4.1.: Creating a New Site

This exercise addresses the following Microsoft exam objectives:

- Manage the WWW service.
- Create and share local and remote virtual directories with appropriate permissions.
- Create and share virtual servers with appropriate permissions.

The purpose of this exercise is to create a new site named ExSite on the local server. The content root is located in c:\ExSite\Root. One directory with the alias /DemoApp located in c:\samples\demo requires an application. A second one that does not require an application is located on \\exserver\exvdir and shall be mapped to /VdirDemo. The user account to be used is ExDomain\exshareuser with the password "exshare." Finally, the bandwidth of the entire server needs to be limited to 2,456 KB/S.

1. Open the Internet Service Manager and connect to the local server.
2. Create a new site named ExSite and point the content root to c:\samples\demo.
3. Add the virtual directory DemoApp to ExSite. The application is generated automatically for you.
4. The remote virtual directory involves more steps. First, create a new virtual directory and point it to some local path. Then change the directory properties to the share and enter the user information. Finally, remove the application.
5. Open the Properties dialog box for the computer and set the bandwidth limit to 2,456 KB/S.
6. Start the site.

4

TEST DAY FAST FACTS

Here are a few fast facts about this chapter that you may want to know ahead of time. Don't forget that these facts also provide great last-minute study material.

- FTP sites can be assigned to only one IP address and port number. Host headers are not supported.

- Usernames and passwords for logging on to an FTP server are sent in clear text across the network.

- You can customize messages for welcome, exit, and maximum connections.

- If someone logs on with the anonymous FTP account, it is mapped by default to the Windows NT IUSR_*machine-name* account.

- You can assign Read and Write permissions for a directory. If you need further granularity, you need to use NTFS permissions.

- You can limit the number of concurrent connections to your FTP site as well as determine the connection timeout. Bandwidth usage is set on a per-server basis.

- For the entire site, you can choose to return either UNIX- or MS-DOS-style directory listings.

Day 5

The FTP Service

by Christoph Wille

Day 4 covered the creation and management of Web sites. This chapter deals with FTP (File Transfer Protocol) sites, which are heavily used for providing reliable heavy-load download sites. You already might have encountered FTP sites before or even when you downloaded your copy of the Windows NT Option Pack.

FTP sites are used most often as download servers for software, upgrades, and patches. FTP servers don't include quite as rich a user experience as Web sites do; however, there are still some important configuration options you need to be aware of—and not just for the exam.

This chapter focuses on creating and managing FTP sites and also addresses directory management. In the tutorials throughout this chapter, you are going to create and then manage an FTP site named FTP for TYS IIS4. Following the tutorials will help you get used to managing the FTP service.

Objectives

This chapter helps you prepare for the Microsoft Exam by covering the following objectives:

- Configure IIS to support the FTP service.
  - Configure virtual directories and servers.
  - Modify port settings.
  - Set user logon requirements and authentication requirements.
  - Set bandwidth and user connections.
  - Set directory listing style.
- Manage the FTP service.

TEST DAY
FAST FACTS

- You can write annotation files for specific directories. To enable annotation files, you have to set the *AnnotationFiles* **registry parameter.**

- **Virtual directories don't show up in the directory listing by default.**

- **You can restrict access to your FTP site using TCP/IP restrictions for single computers, groups of computers, and entire domains.**

5.1. Creating and Managing FTP Sites

This chapter deals with different aspects of creating and managing your FTP site(s). Besides the topics mentioned in the following list, you'll find more information on directory-specific configuration tasks later in the chapter. The topics covered for FTP sites include:

- Creating an FTP site
- Configuring FTP site identification
- Setting FTP messages
- Managing security accounts
- Setting access permissions
- Disconnecting users
- Setting connection limits
- Listing styles

5.1.1. Creating an FTP Site

IIS 4 comes with a preconfigured FTP site you can use to explore the features of the FTP service. Experimenting with the default FTP site might not be the best idea, so you are going to create a new FTP site that uses the same home directory as the default one. You need to follow the upcoming tutorial because all tutorials in this chapter will reference the site that you create here initially.

The following steps show you how to create a new FTP site that uses the standard settings proposed by the New FTP Site Wizard. The site name will be FTP for TYS IIS4. Perform the following steps:

1. Open Internet Service Manager (ISM) and right-click on the server you are administering. Select New, FTP Site to open the New FTP Site Wizard.

2. Enter the description of the FTP site in the first step of the wizard. The description is FTP for TYS IIS4.

3. Select the IP address for the FTP server in the next step. Do not change the port setting.

4. In the next step, you have to enter the directory that serves as the FTP root. Choose Browse and locate the *x*:\inetpub\ftproot directory, where *x* is the drive letter where you chose to install the InetPub directory to during initial setup.

5. Finally, set the access permissions for this FTP server. You can choose between the following access permissions:
   - Allow Read Access
   - Allow Write Access

   By default, the Allow Read Access permission is selected, and the Allow Write Access is deselected. Leave these defaults in place. You'll learn more about directory permissions later in this chapter.

6. Click Finish to create the new FTP site. The FTP site is created in a stopped state.

7. Put some files in the home directory of the FTP site (no files are copied to the \inetpub\ftproot location during IIS setup). Then go back to ISM and start the site (either by right-clicking on the site and selecting Start from the context menu or by clicking the Start Item button on the toolbar).

8. Open a command prompt and run the `ftp` command. Connect to the site and log in as anonymous (using an email address as the password). Issue the `ls` command to view the files in the home directory, and then close the FTP utility with the *bye* command. Figure 5.1 shows the entire FTP session.

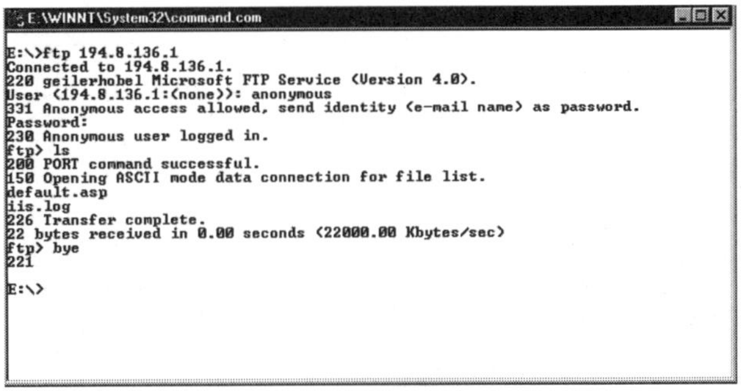

Figure 5.1.

Connect to the newly created FTP site using the `ftp` command, log in as anonymous, get a directory listing, and then disconnect.

```
E:\>ftp 194.8.136.1
Connected to 194.8.136.1.
220 geilerhobel Microsoft FTP Service (Version 4.0).
User (194.8.136.1:(none)): anonymous
331 Anonymous access allowed, send identity (e-mail name) as password.
Password:
230 Anonymous user logged in.
ftp> ls
200 PORT command successful.
150 Opening ASCII mode data connection for file list.
default.asp
iis.log
226 Transfer complete.
22 bytes received in 0.00 seconds (22000.00 Kbytes/sec)
ftp> bye
221
E:\>
```

Every site you create with the New FTP Site Wizard is, by default, installed with Read access, including the anonymous login option. You are going to alter this site several times throughout today's lesson.

5.1.2. Configuring FTP Site Identification

The site you created in the previous tutorial uses the defaults that the New FTP Site Wizard proposed. Contrasting FTP sites to Web sites, you'll find that you don't have as many options when configuring the FTP site identification. For example, you can't use host headers, and you can't add multiple IP addresses for a single site.

However, you still can change the IP address the site is bound to, as well as the server port (see Figure 5.2). (The site description doesn't strictly count as site identification because it isn't visible to the outside world.)

Figure 5.2.
You can change the IP address and port number for an FTP site by accessing the FTP Site tab of the site's Properties dialog box.

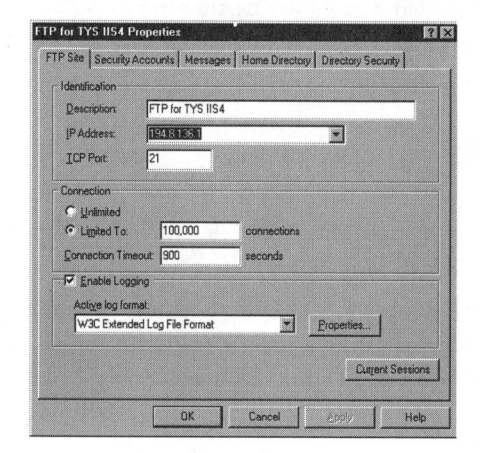

The following steps show you how to change the default port number (21) for the FTP for TYS IIS4 site to 1067 (this is an arbitrary port number; you can choose any port that fits your needs). Under normal circumstances, you won't need to change the port number. However, if you want to hide your FTP site, you should use a port number other than the default.

1. Open the Properties dialog box for the FTP for TYS IIS4 site.
2. Change the TCP port number from 21 to 1067.
3. Click OK to put your change into effect. You do not need to stop the FTP service.
4. Connect to the FTP site using the new port number.

You will seldom need to change the port number for an FTP site. However, keep one thing in mind: If you choose a port number below 1024 (which are mostly reserved), you might need to enable the *EnablePortAttack* registry setting for the FTP service in order to allow passive connections in this port range.

5.1.3. Setting FTP Messages

FTP servers aren't very interactive for the user. You can customize your FTP site in only a couple of ways, the most popular being through the use of FTP site messages. The following message types are supported by the IIS FTP service:

- *Welcome.* The message that is displayed when the user has successfully logged in to the FTP server.
- *Exit.* The message that is displayed when the user has logged off from the FTP server.
- *Maximum Connections.* The message a user receives when the maximum number of users are already logged in to the FTP server.

The following steps show you how to add the welcome, exit, and maximum connections messages to the FTP for TYS IIS4 site:

1. Open the Properties dialog box for the FTP for TYS IIS4 site.
2. Select the Messages tab (see Figure 5.3). Notice that you have multiple lines for the welcome message but only one line for the exit and maximum connections messages.
3. Enter your desired Welcome message. You might want to add information about recent changes to the site or an email address of the site operator (so that users can contact him or her if they have trouble using your site).
4. Add the exit and the maximum connections messages (refer to Figure 5.3 for examples).
5. Click OK to put your changes into effect.

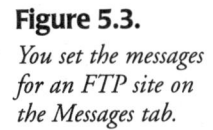

Figure 5.3.
You set the messages for an FTP site on the Messages tab.

The welcome, exit, and maximum connections messages offer a way to add additional information to the response your server gives the user.

5.1.4. Managing Security Accounts

You can set fewer security options (in terms of access permissions) directly in the FTP site Properties dialog box than you can for WWW sites. However, those options are still very important for the security of your server and even your entire network. The following subsections deal with the security accounts-related issues of FTP sites:

- Site access
- Site operators

A. Site Access

When a new FTP site is created, anonymous access is allowed by default (see Figure 5.4). In addition, all users that have an account on the web server's computer can also log on. Anonymous access is handled the same way for FTP as it was for the Web service: by using a standard Windows NT account (IUSR_*machinename* by default) to impersonate the anonymous user. In the Allow Anonymous Connections frame of the Security Accounts tab, the automatic password synchronization feature is also enabled by default, which allows you to change the password for that account; IIS then automatically picks up the new password.

Figure 5.4.
Use the Security Accounts tab to control anonymous access to a site and to manage site operators.

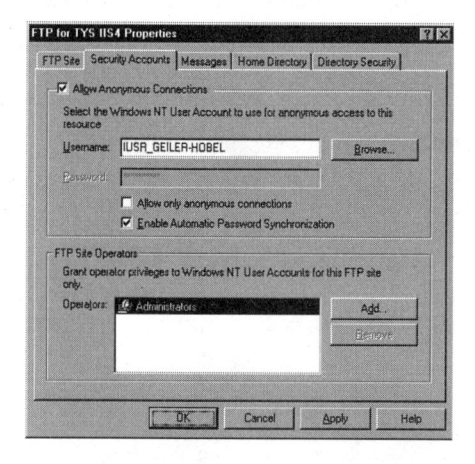

Before you decide whether to allow anonymous access only or to also allow all other users to log on to the FTP server, you have to consider a really big security issue:

Usernames and passwords are always transmitted in clear text over the wire when using FTP. This poses a security threat on your Windows NT accounts because there is no way to secure the connection between the client and the server, and therefore, anyone who can tap the wire between the client and the server can get at valid Windows NT accounts.

The following steps show you how to enable only anonymous access to the FTP for TYS IIS4 site. With this setting enabled, only the anonymous user can log in to the site, and users supplying a valid username and password won't be allowed to log in. Perform the following steps to achieve that end:

1. Open the Properties dialog box for the FTP for TYS IIS4 site.
2. Switch to the Security Accounts tab.
3. Check the Allow Only Anonymous Connections check box.
4. Click OK to put this change into effect. Now only anonymous users can log on to the FTP site.
5. Try to connect to the FTP site and log on using your account. Notice that you are no longer allowed to log on. Try logging on with anonymous, and you are granted access.

If you want to make sure that only anonymous connections to your server are allowed, you need to perform this tutorial. However, setting this restriction doesn't prevent users from *trying* to use their Windows NT accounts to log on to your site. They fail to log on, but their usernames and passwords are still transferred across the wire.

B. Site Operators

As with Web sites, you can also grant the right to administer FTP sites on a per-site basis. You can either grant the right to specific users or to entire groups (like the Administrators group, which by default has the right to administer all sites on an IIS server). This enables you to delegate administration work for certain sites to other users without having to give those users administrative access to all sites on a machine.

The following steps show you how to grant a new user the right to administer the FTP for TYS IIS4 site. To complete this tutorial, you must be logged on as a user with administrative rights.

> **Note** If you have already completed the similar tutorial for the Web site, you can skip this procedure.

Perform the following steps:

1. Open User Manager in the Administrative Tools program folder and add a new user by the name of SiteAdmin. Don't put this user in the Administrators group because administrators are automatically allowed to administer all sites.
2. After creating the new user, go to the Internet Service Manager and open the Properties dialog box for the FTP for TYS IIS4 site.
3. Switch to the Security Accounts tab and take a look at the FTP Site Operators frame. Notice that currently only the Administrators group has the right to administer the site.
4. Click the Add button and browse for the account you created in step 1 (see Figure 5.5). Add it to the list of FTP site operators.

Figure 5.5.

The new SiteAdmin user now has the right to administer the FTP for TYS IIS4 site.

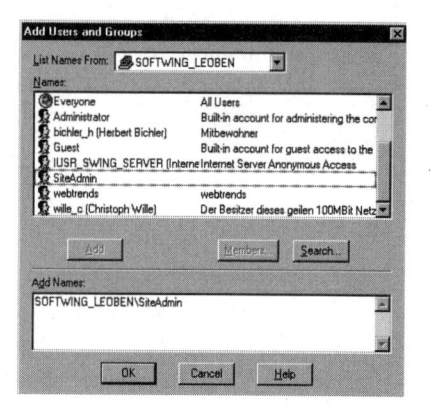

5. Click the OK button in the Properties dialog box to save the changes you made for the FTP site.
6. Log off the computer.
7. Log on as the new user (SiteAdmin) and open the Internet Service Manager. Notice that for all sites the operator is not allowed to administer, the descriptions are not displayed and the status is set to stopped (see Figure 5.6). Take a look, too, at the tabs of property settings for the FTP for TYS IIS4 site.

FTP site operators are not allowed to administer every aspect of an FTP site. For example, they cannot change the IP address or the port of the server; nor can they move the home directory or change security account settings. With these restrictions in place, you can safely allow others to administer sites.

Figure 5.6.

The operator is allowed to administer only the two TYS sites.

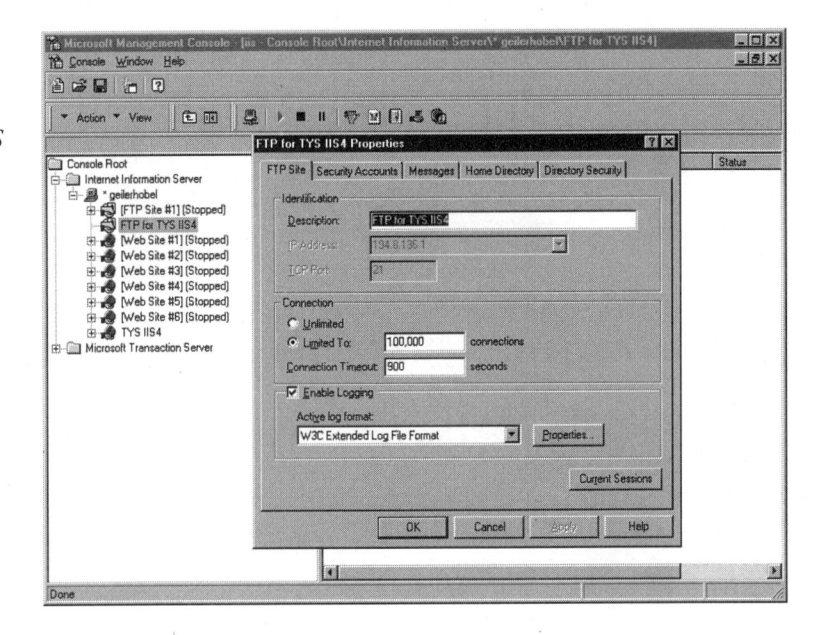

5.1.5. Setting Access Permissions

We touched on the topic of access permissions during the initial creation of the FTP for TYS IIS4 site. As you should remember, you can choose between two access permission types:

- *Read* (the default) allows users to download files from that directory.
- *Write* allows users to upload or delete files from that directory.

When you take a look at the Home Directory tab for the FTP site, shown in Figure 5.7, you will see that those two are the only available access options (Log Access is not an access permission).

Although two access permissions don't seem to be very many, they can be pretty impressive when combined with NTFS permissions. You'll learn more about security and securing content with NTFS in Day 6, "Internet Information Server Security."

As we noted, there is a third option, Log Access, below the two access permissions (refer to Figure 5.7). Logging can be very valuable for determining server traffic, distinguishing the most popular files, or simply monitoring what users are doing on your site. For more information on analyzing log files, see Day 13, "Site Analysis."

Figure 5.7.
You set access permissions on the Home Directory tab for the FTP for TYS IIS4 site.

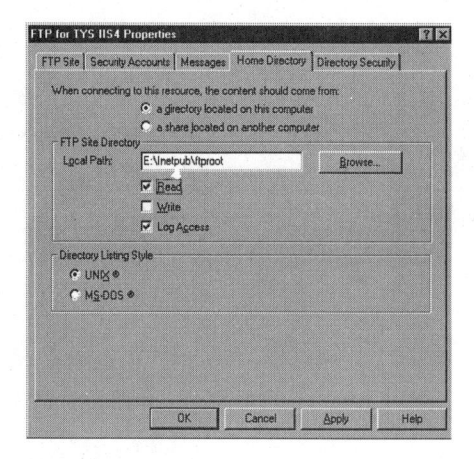

> **Warning**
>
> Although it is not obvious, the Write permission also includes the ability to delete files. If you want to allow users to upload files but not delete files, you have to take a closer look at securing your content with NTFS permissions.

5.1.6. Disconnecting Users

FTP uses a connection that is always kept open between the server and the client. Therefore, it is possible to determine who is logged on to your site at any given time. In addition to showing who is logged on, the FTP service of IIS also allows you to disconnect specific users or to disconnect all users who are currently logged on.

The following steps show you how to display a list of users who are currently logged on and how to disconnect one or all of them:

1. Log on to the FTP for TYS IIS4 site using an FTP client program.
2. Switch to the Internet Service Manager and view the Properties dialog box for the FTP for TYS IIS4 site.
3. On the FTP Site tab, click the Current Sessions button. This brings up the FTP User Sessions dialog box, which shows a list of users who are currently logged on. The session you opened in step 1 should be listed there, too (see Figure 5.8).
4. To disconnect yourself, select your session and click Disconnect. Acknowledge the warning message.

To disconnect everyone connected to the server, click the Disconnect All button.

Figure 5.8.
The FTP User Sessions dialog box displays the session on an FTP server.

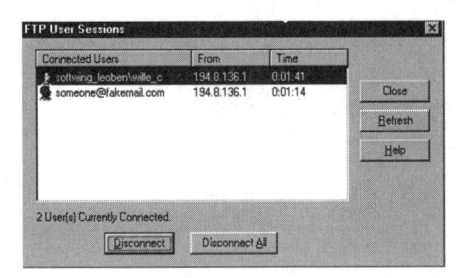

Being able to disconnect users might come in handy if you need to restart your server or want to get rid of a specific user (for whatever reason—perhaps the user tried to hack your site).

5.1.7. Setting Connection Limits

By default, each newly created FTP site allows an unlimited number (100,000 counts as nearly unlimited) of connections to your FTP site. If your server has limited resources, you should limit the number of concurrent connections to your site.

Because it's possible that a user could have an open connection to your site but not perform any actions on your server—maybe because he forgot about the open FTP window or because his dial-up line crashed—there is a timeout value after which a session is automatically abandoned (if there has been no action). The default value is 900 seconds, but you can change it to whatever value fits your needs.

The following steps show you how to restrict the maximum number of connections to the FTP for TYS IIS4 site to 45 simultaneous connections and how to reduce the timeout value from 900 seconds to 600 seconds.

1. Open the Properties dialog box for the FTP for TYS IIS4 site.
2. Click the FTP Site tab if necessary. The settings for limiting connections are located in the Connection frame. By default, connections are limited to 100,000.
3. Click the Limited To radio button and change the value in the edit box to 45.
4. In the Connection Timeout edit box, change the value to 600 seconds. The Properties dialog box should now look like Figure 5.9.
5. Click OK to close the Properties dialog box and put your changes into effect.

Figure 5.9.
You can limit connections for the FTP site by using the controls in the Connection frame of this dialog box.

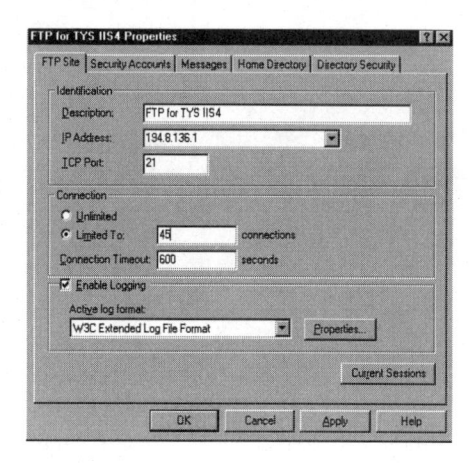

Limiting the maximum number of user connections is useful for sites on which you have limited hardware resources or you simply want to limit the maximum number of concurrent users in order to guarantee decent performance for those that are connected. When the maximum number of users is reached, every user who tries to connect receives the `Maximum Connections` message until someone who is currently logged on disconnects.

5.1.8. Setting Listing Styles

When you do a directory listing on a server, the listing is returned in a specific format. The FTP service that comes with IIS supports two directory listing styles:

- *UNIX.* Returns a UNIX-style directory listing when a user is issues the `dir` command. For example, this is the FTP for TYS IIS4 directory listing in UNIX style:

```
150 Opening ASCII mode data connection for /bin/ls.
dr-xr-xr-x   1 owner    group              0 Feb 26 11:35 AnnotateTest
-r-xr-xr-x   1 owner    group        1193045 Jan 15 22:52 iis.log
dr-xr-xr-x   1 owner    group              0 Feb 26 11:00 WebVirt
226 Transfer complete.
```

- *MS-DOS.* Returns the directory listing in MS-DOS fashion (this is the default). For example, the `dir` command for the FTP for TYS IIS4 site returned the following listing:

```
150 Opening ASCII mode data connection for /bin/ls.
02-26-98  11:35AM       <DIR>          AnnotateTest
01-15-98  10:52PM               1193045 iis.log
02-26-98  11:00AM       <DIR>          WebVirt
226 Transfer complete.
```

Depending on your user base (whether it's mostly UNIX or PC users), you will decide which listing style you want to use. The following steps show you how to change the directory listing style for the FTP for TYS IIS4 site from MS-DOS style (the default) to UNIX style:

1. Open the Properties dialog box for the FTP for TYS IIS4 site.
2. Select the Home Directory tab.
3. In the Directory Listing Style frame, click the radio button to enable UNIX-style directory listing.
4. Click OK to put your changes into effect.

Now when you connect to the FTP for TYS IIS4 site and issue the `dir` command, you get a UNIX-style directory listing. You should configure your site to use the directory listing style your users are more familiar with.

5.2. FTP Directories

Up to this point, we have dealt with creating and managing the actual FTP site only; now we begin to explore the structure of FTP sites: the directories. You have already encountered one kind of directory: the home directory of your site, which is managed as part of the FTP site properties. There is only one other "flavor" of directory for FTP sites, and that is the *virtual directory*. This section begins with a discussion of virtual directories. It then moves on to cover annotating directories and setting TCP/IP restrictions.

5.2.1. Virtual Directories

You use virtual directories for FTP sites for exactly the same reason you use them for Web sites—to add directories that physically reside on another hard disk or another computer to the home directory.

A. Creating a Virtual Directory

Creating virtual directories for FTP sites is as easy as creating them for Web sites. Most often, you will map local directories into the directory tree of your FTP site using virtual directories.

The following steps show you how to add a virtual directory to the FTP site you created earlier in this chapter. The virtual directory you are adding is the root directory of the TYS IIS4 Web site. The description for the new virtual directory is "WebVirt." Perform the following steps:

1. Open ISM and locate the FTP for TYS IIS4 site to which you want to add the virtual directory.
2. Right-click on the site and select New, Virtual Directory. The New Virtual Directory Wizard opens.
3. Enter the name of the virtual directory, WebVirt, in the first step.
4. In the second step, select the directory where this virtual directory is located. The location of the home directory for the TYS IIS4 Web site is *x*:\inetpub\wwwroot, where *x* represents the drive letter where you chose to install the InetPub directory during initial setup of IIS. Select that directory as the virtual directory's physical path.
5. In the final step, you choose the access permissions. Go with the default access permission, Read.
6. Click Finish to create the virtual directory.
7. Open an FTP client program (a graphical one) and connect to the FTP for TYS IIS4 site. Notice that the virtual directory is not displayed in the directory listing (see Figure 5.10).

Figure 5.10.
Virtual directories don't show up in an FTP program.

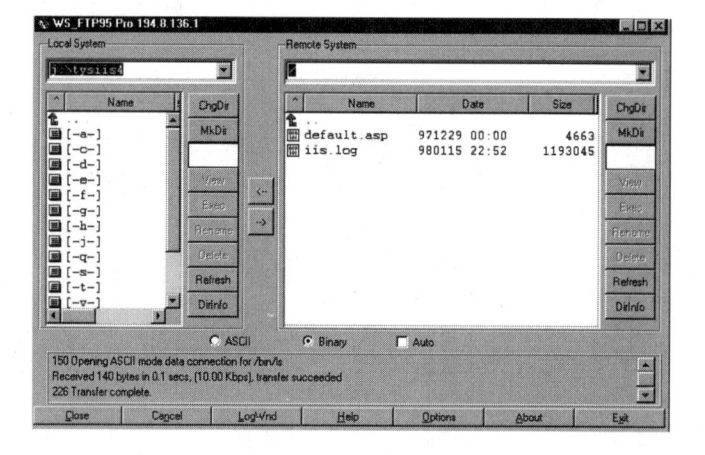

8. Although the virtual directory is not displayed in the directory listing, you can access it by changing to WebVirt using the command `cd WebVirt`. If you do a directory listing now, you can see that the virtual directory points to the correct location.

You can use virtual directories to add directories (or entire branches) to your site that are not actually located below your site's home directory. The drawback is that virtual directories are not shown in directory listings. But we are going to change that with another trick in just a second.

If you are operating a download server and your content is spread across multiple disks (or even located on CDs), the fact that virtual directories don't show up in the home directory listing is very annoying because you don't want to tell users about all your hidden directories. On an intranet, it is relatively easy to train the users of your FTP site to use the virtual directory that's not listed. On the Internet, however, it's more complicated communicating to users about your site structure; users simply expect everything to show up.

There is no official way around this problem. However, there is a very practical workaround that relies on the fact that IIS first looks for a virtual directory match and then for a directory match below the home directory. For example, if you have a /Secret virtual directory as well as a /Secret directory in your home directory and a user changes to /Secret, IIS always directs the user to the virtual directory because a match with a virtual directory is evaluated first.

> **Warning**
> Because virtual directories always take precedence over normal directories, gaining access to a normal directory of the same name is basically impossible. Therefore, be careful when creating a new virtual directory that you don't accidentally choose a name that has already been given to an existing directory.

The following steps show you how to add the virtual directory named WebVirt to the directory listing in the home directory of the FTP for TYS IIS4 site:

1. Open Explorer and go to the *x*:\inetpub\ftproot directory (replace *x* with the appropriate drive letter).
2. Create a new folder named WebVirt.
3. Close Explorer.
4. Open your FTP client program and connect to the FTP for TYS IIS4 site. Notice that now the WebVirt directory that you just created shows up (see Figure 5.11).
5. Now change to the WebVirt directory. Notice that you are taken to the virtual directory instead of the empty one you just created. This happened because IIS evaluates matches for virtual directories first.

This neat trick of creating an empty directory that has the same name as your virtual directory allows you to produce a directory listing that contains all virtual directories and takes users automatically to the correct directory. As with all undocumented tricks, you need to check to see whether new versions of IIS support it.

Figure 5.11.
With the changes you made, the newly created directory shows up.

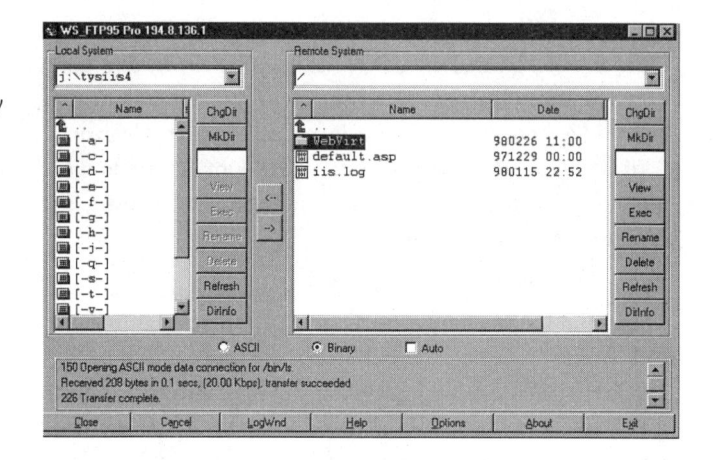

B. Using Server Share

You are not limited to adding virtual directories from the local computer only. You can also map network shares to a virtual directory.

The following steps show you how to change the content location for the WebVirt virtual directory from a physical path to a share on a remote server. In order to perform this tutorial, you must have a network share you can connect to. Perform the following steps:

1. Right-click on the WebVirt virtual directory you created in the previous tutorial. Select Properties from the context menu. The WebVirt Properties dialog box appears, with the Virtual Directory tab displayed.

2. From the When Connecting To… box, select A Share Located on Another Computer. Notice that the caption for the location changes from "Local Path" to "Network Share."

3. In the Network Share edit box, enter the UNC name for the share.

4. You need to specify which user account to use to access this resource. To do so, click the Connect As button.

5. In the Network Directory Security Credentials dialog box, enter the username (which you can browse for) and the password (see Figure 5.12).

6. Click OK, and then click OK again to close the WebVirt Properties dialog box. Now the WebVirt virtual directory's contents comes from the network share you specified in step 3.

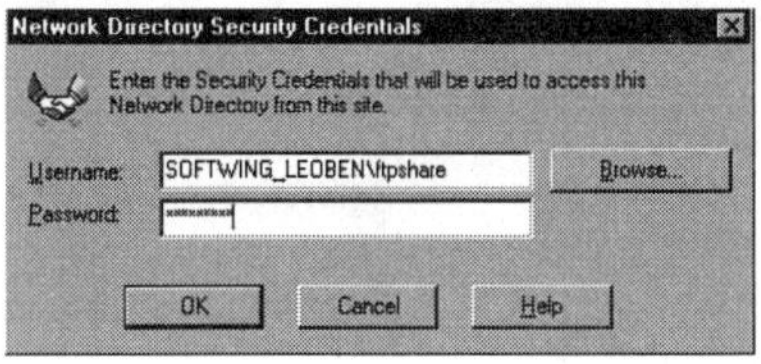

Figure 5.12.
You fill in the logon information in the Network Directory Security Credentials dialog box.

Using network shares as a base location for your virtual directories (which also works for the home directory) is hardly more complicated than using a local directory. However, you need to be aware of one important security consideration: All files that are accessed from the remote location are accessed with the privileges of the user account you supplied in step 5, *not* with the privileges the browsing client has. Keep this in mind when creating remote virtual directories.

5.2.2. Annotating Directories

Users connecting to your FTP server now see only directory listings, which is not very user-friendly. What can you do to automatically provide users with additional information, for example, about special downloads? You can do that by *annotating directories*. To do so, you place a specially named file in the directory you want to annotate. This file contains the information you want sent to the user every time she changes to that annotated directory.

However, there is more to annotating directories than simply placing a file in a directory. The following steps walk you through annotating directories on FTP sites:

1. Open the Registry Editor (regedit.exe).
2. Navigate to the `HKEY_LOCAL_MACHINE\System\CurrentControlSet\Services\MSFTPSVC\Parameters` key.
3. Create the value *AnnotateDirectories* (if it does not already exist) with the type DWORD.
4. Set the value for *AnnotateDirectories* to 1 to enable annotation of directories (see Figure 5.13).
5. Restart the FTP service to put the changes into effect. To restart the FTP service, open a command prompt and issue the following commands:

```
net stop MSFTPSVC
net start MSFTPSVC
```

Figure 5.13.

You enable directory annotations in the Registry.

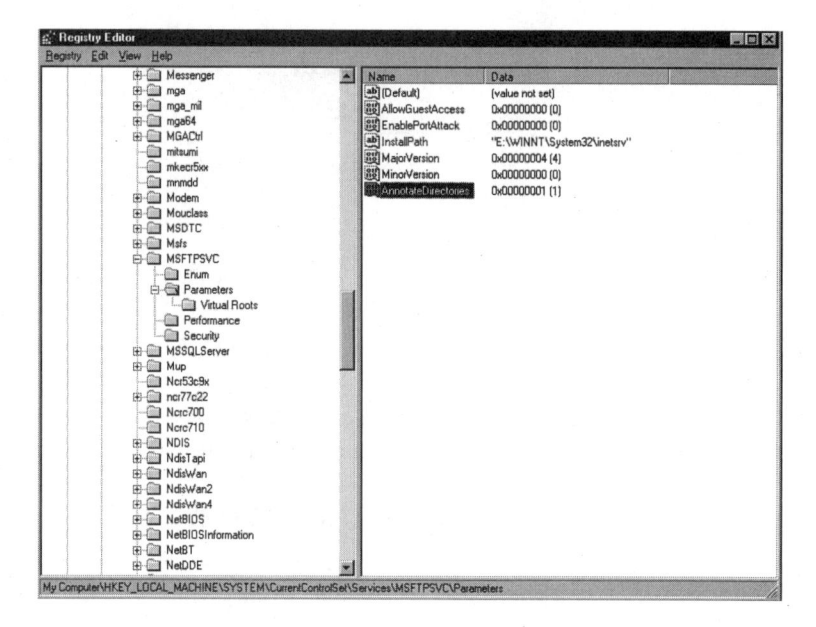

6. Open Explorer and create a folder named AnnotateTest. In this folder, create a file with some text in it and save it with the name *~ftpsvc~.ckm* (which identifies it as an annotation file). Set the Hidden attribute so the file will not appear in normal directory listings.

7. Open an FTP client and navigate to this directory. You are presented the text you just entered in the annotation file (see Figure 5.14).

Figure 5.14.

The annotations are shown as selected text. Notice that the annotation file does not show in the directory listing in the background.

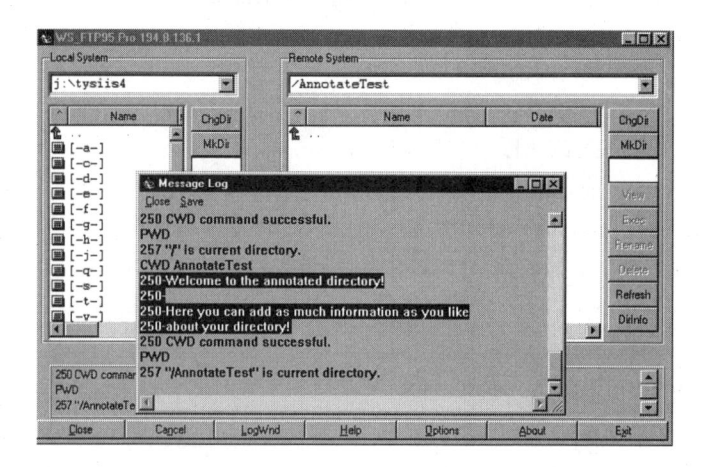

Annotations offer a useful way for you to inform your FTP site's users about important downloads or usage guidelines. This setting can be reached only via the Registry and is enforced for all FTP sites.

5.2.3. Setting TCP/IP Restrictions

You can restrict access to your FTP site not only by using account restrictions; you can also apply TCP/IP access restrictions, which are set at the directory level. Either you can grant everyone access to a directory except the addresses and domains you specify, or you can deny everyone access to a directory except the addresses and domains you specify. Both of these limitations are controlled by settings on the Directory Security tab of the Properties dialog box. You can specify the following allow/deny entries on both site and directory level as described here:

- *Single computer.* Enter the IP address of the computer you want to include in the allow/deny list.
- *Group of computers.* Enter the network ID and the subnet mask of the group of computers you want to include in the allow/deny list.
- *Domain name.* Enter the domain name you want to include in the allow/deny list. Notice that the server must perform reverse DNS lookups before it decides whether to grant or deny access to a resource, thereby putting a heavy load on your server and slowing down client access.

The following steps walk you through the process of establishing all three different kinds of TCP/IP restrictions for the entire FTP for TYS IIS4 site. All computers will be allowed access except the ones that are added to the list in the Directory Security tab. Perform the following steps:

1. Open the ISM and open the Properties dialog box for the FTP for TYS IIS4 site.
2. Select the Directory Security tab.
3. Click Add, leave Single Computer selected, and enter the IP address of the computer for which you want to deny access to the site. Click OK to add it to the deny list.
4. To deny access for an entire group of computers, specify the network ID and subnet mask.
5. Finally, add a domain restriction. Keep in mind that this slows down the server considerably. Your TCP/IP restrictions should now look like Figure 5.15.

Figure 5.15.
TCP/IP restrictions for an FTP site.

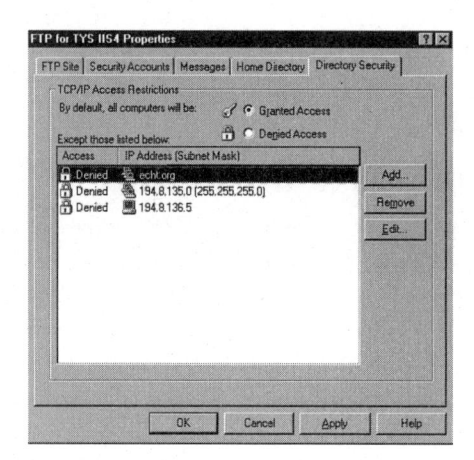

You can use TCP/IP restrictions to restrict access to your FTP server for your intranet only (as an extra protection, for example). Additionally, you can lock out IP addresses from which you know attacks have originated.

Lab

This lab consists of review questions pertaining to this chapter and provides an opportunity for you to use walk-through exercises to apply the knowledge that you've learned.

Questions

1. You are creating a new web site for your company. Because the FTP server doesn't have the content on local hard disks, you need to map it from a remote server. Can you point the home directory of an FTP site to a remote share? (Select the best answer.)

    A. Yes, but you need to change the anonymous account to an account that has access permissions on the remote computer.

    B. Yes, but you need to supply the share name.

    C. Yes, but you need to supply the share name and an account that has permission to access that share.

    D. No, you can't map the home directory to a remote share.

2. Which of the following access permissions can be set for both FTP sites and virtual directories on FTP sites? (Select all that apply.)

    A. Read

    B. Write

    C. Execute

    D. Delete

3. You need to change the port number of your FTP site from standard port 21 to 9876. Where do you change this setting? (Select the best answer.)

    A. In the FTP Service Properties dialog box because port settings are global for all sites.

    B. In the FTP site Properties dialog box, in the Identification frame.

    C. In the FTP site Properties dialog box, and you also need to inherit this property to all virtual directories.

    D. This port can't be used.

4. You are operating an intranet FTP site. You get a call from an angry user that he can't find the SalesInfo directory on your site. You tell him that it is there (even in the root), but he still can't see it in the directory listing. What is the most likely cause? (Select the best answer.)

    A. The user is using an outdated FTP client.

    B. You accidentally renamed the directory.

    C. The SalesInfo directory is a virtual directory.

    D. The user does not have permission to access that directory; therefore, it is hidden.

5. You want to tell your users to send complaints about your new company FTP site to `ftpquestions@mycorp.com`. Where should you put this information? (Select the best answer.)

    A. In the Login message

    B. In the annotation file in the home directory

    C. In the welcome message

    D. In the instructions.txt file

6. You want to limit the connections to your department's FTP site to a maximum of 20 concurrent connections. Where do you find the control for this setting? (Select the best answer.)

    A. In the Connections edit box on the Performance tab of the FTP site Properties dialog box.

    B. In the Limited To edit box on the FTP Site tab of the Properties dialog box for the site.

    C. You have to make this setting in the FTP Service Properties dialog box.

    D. You can't do that.

7. Which of the following listing styles can you choose from for your FTP site? (Select all that apply.)

    A. MS-DOS

    B. OS/2

    C. UNIX

    D. Joliet

8. What is the filename of the annotation file for a directory? (Select the best answer.)

    A. ~ftpsvc.ckm

    B. ftpsvc~.ckm

    C. ~ftpsvc~.ckm

    D. ftpsvc.ckm

9. Which TCP/IP restrictions can you enforce for your FTP site (virtual directory)? (Select all that apply.)

    A. Domain

    B. Subnet

    C. Computer

    D. Mask

10. You want to allow only anonymous connections to your FTP site. Which of the following options must you enable for this to happen? (Select the best answer.)

    A. Allow only anonymous connections

    B. Disallow everyone except anonymous connection

    C. Limit to anonymous connections

    D. You can't do that

Answers to Questions

1. **C.** You can use a server share as the home directory for your FTP site. However, you need to supply a valid Windows NT account for that machine (username/password).

2. **A, B.** You can set only Read and Write permissions for directories of your FTP site. If you need more control, you have to set NTFS permissions in your FTP sites physical directories.

3. **C.** You set the TCP port in the Identification frame.

4. **C.** The most likely cause is that the SalesInfo directory is a virtual directory because these don't show up in a directory listing. Even if the user wouldn't be granted access to a directory, it would still be contained in the directory listing.

5. **C.** The best place to put announcements is the welcome message. However, you could also use the annotation file in the home directory.
6. **B.** Connection limits are set in the Limited To edit box.
7. **A, C.** MS-DOS and UNIX are valid listing styles. MS-DOS is the default.
8. **C.** The valid filename for annotation files is ~ftpsvc~.ckm.
9. **A, B, C.** Although the term subnet hasn't been used to describe a "group of computers" so far, a subnet is identified by the network ID and subnet mask and therefore identical to it.
10. **A.** You set this option in the Security Accounts tab of the FTP site's properties dialog box.

Exercise

Exercise 5.1.: Creating a Public Download Site

This exercise addresses the following Microsoft exam objectives:

- Configure IIS to support the FTP service, specifically...
    - Configure virtual directories and servers.
    - Set user logon requirements and authentication requirements.
    - Set bandwidth and user connections.
    - Set directory listing style.

In this exercise, you are going to create an FTP site for your company that allows customers to download upgrade patches for your company's software. You should allow only anonymous access, and you should limit the maximum number of connections to 150. Because most of the customers are familiar with UNIX, you must provide them with the UNIX listing style. Perform the following steps:

1. Open ISM and right-click on the server you are administering. Select New, FTP Site to open the New FTP Site Wizard.
2. Enter the description of the FTP site in the first step of the wizard. Select the IP address for the FTP server in the next step. Do not change the port setting because 21 is the default port, and users will try to connect to your site using that port. In the next step, you have to enter the directory that is used as the FTP root. Finally, set the access permissions for this FTP server. Because it is a download-only server, restrict the permissions to Read only. Click Finish to create the new FTP site.

3. Open the Properties dialog box for the newly created FTP site and change the maximum connections to 150.
4. Select the Security Accounts tab and check the Allow Only Anonymous Connections check box to satisfy the requirement of anonymous-access only.
5. To meet the last requirement, change to the Home Directory tab and choose the UNIX directory listing style.
6. Click OK to save your changes. To make your site available, start it now.

TEST DAY FAST FACTS

Here are a few fast facts about this chapter that you may want to know ahead of time. Don't forget that these facts also provide great last-minute study material.

- There are three types of authentication that you can use to verify the identity of users connecting to your IIS Web site: anonymous, basic, and NT challenge/response.

- Access can be controlled by IP address or domain name.

- Users can have different types of permissions for different directories, including read and write.

- Applications can have mappings for file types, and settings can be added to control how ASP pages function.

- You should use NTFS to add extra security.

- Each site can have a different account associated with it.

- SSL is implemented as an ISAPI filter and requires extra processing.

Day 6

Internet Information Server Security

by Rob Scrimger

Security is one of the key issues that affects anyone who is setting up an Internet or intranet. Controlling access on your site is one of the key topics on the exam. Therefore, you should make sure that you are very familiar with it.

IIS security is tightly integrated with the Windows NT security model, allowing IIS administrators to control user access on a file-by-file and folder-by-folder basis when IIS folders are stored on NTFS partitions. In order for this to occur, a user must log on using a valid Windows NT account and password. A security token is generated to identify the user, and the token is verified against the ACL (Access Control List) for a specific object (such as an HTML file).

This is where authentication comes into play. If a user has not been authenticated (that is, she has not provided a valid NT username and password), she is considered to be anonymous. Because the NT security model has no way of handling this, an anonymous user account is created when IIS is installed. By default, this account is called IUSR_*computername* (where *computername* is the name of the computer that IIS has been installed on). However you can change that name if you want. So if a user does not give IIS a valid NT username and password, she will be given a security token that identifies her as IUSR_*computername*. When she attempts to access an object, she will have only those permissions that have been assigned to that account.

Of course, sometimes certain users require different levels of access. For example, you might want only members of your IS department to be able to access documents pertaining to your network infrastructure. In such a case, you would need a method of determining who the user accessing your site is in order for Windows NT to verify that the person has permission to access a specific object. This is done through a process called *authentication*. As you learned earlier, IIS offers three levels of authentication: anonymous, basic, and Windows NT challenge/response.

Basic authentication uses clear text. Because clear text can be used with any browser, it can support the widest variety of clients. When a user accesses an IIS site, he is prompted for his username and password, both of which must match the information in the NT security database. However, when the password is transmitted across the network, it is sent as clear text. And someone running a network analyzer (such as the one included with Microsoft's Systems Management Server) could intercept both the username and password and gain access to your resources. (Now imagine the damage that person could cause if she got the password to an administrator's account!)

Therefore, it is recommended that you use either anonymous authentication or Windows NT challenge/response. Anonymous has two major benefits: Users do not have to have a valid Windows NT account, and it will support any browser. Windows NT challenge/response, on the other hand, requires both a valid Windows NT account and the use of a compatible browser (such as Microsoft Internet Explorer).

For the exam, it is important that you understand the available choices and the consequences of those choices. In summary, anonymous does not require users to provide a valid username and password; therefore, anyone can access your sites. Clear text is compatible with many Web browsers, but it could compromise the security of the Windows NT installation. Windows NT challenge/response is very secure but requires a compatible browser.

This chapter takes a look at IIS security in the following main sections:

- Understanding security
- Basic security
- Advanced security
- Adding security from NT

Objectives

This chapter helps you prepare for the Microsoft exam by covering the following objectives:

- Choose a security strategy for various situations.
    - Control anonymous access.
    - Control access to known users and groups.
    - Control access by host or network.
    - Configure SSL to provide encryption and authentication schemes.
    - Identify the appropriate balance between security requirements and performance requirements.
- Create and share directories with appropriate permissions.
    - Set directory-level permissions
    - Set file-level permissions

6.1. Understanding IIS Security

Two of the most important decisions that you will need to make are the amount and type(s) of security that you will add to your Web site. The addition of security comes at the expense of ease of use and raw speed.

You must remember that many different types of security are available, and each of them adds some level of protection to a site. However, no security that's available will ever be able to completely lock out a very determined user. It is always possible that someone might break into your site, but monitoring should be used to protect against this.

On a battlefield, the mine fields and other deterrents serve only to slow down and annoy the enemy; the same is true of security on an Internet site.

The amount of security you will require depends primarily on who can access the site (internal vs. external) and who you are trying to keep out. If the material is extremely sensitive, you may want to consider combining different security methods, such as applying NTFS permissions to your files and restricting access to specific hosts.

Security in any installation must be determined based on the needs of the organization. Having an absolutely secure system is fine, but you must balance security with usability. You need to make it as easy as possible to ensure that your users can access the data they need, while ensuring the integrity of that data. At the very least, you should ensure that you do not allow anonymous users to access critical data by removing the IUSR_*computername* account from the ACL for that object.

6.2. Basic Security

This section takes a look at some of the simplest methods of securing an IIS site (for example, ensuring that anonymous users cannot access confidential data). The security settings that are covered in this section can be applied on two levels: at the server level and at the site level. This section addresses the server-level settings; however, all of these settings can also be applied to the individual sites your server is hosting.

6.2.1. Allowing (and Controlling) Anonymous Access

In most cases, the user will connect to your IIS server as anonymous. When a user connects as anonymous, he will be logged on to the server locally as a user called IUSR_*computername*.

There are couple of things that you should do with the IUSR_*computername* account to ensure that there is at least some security on the server. This primarily involves the following two steps:

1. *Changing the password.* You should change the password on the IUSR_*computername* account because the password is the same by default on every

NT installation, and you would want to ensure that you aren't introducing potential security holes. If you are truly concerned about security, you can use a different account for anonymous access entirely. Once a user knows a valid username and password on your system, it is only a matter of time before he might be able to get past your security checks.

2. *Setting NTFS permissions.* You can set NTFS permissions on the directories that contain the Web site to ensure that the IUSR_*computername* account has the ability only to read directories that contain HTML documents and has the ability to both read and execute directories that have applications associated with them.

> **Note** NTFS permissions are covered in detail later in this chapter, in the section "Adding Security from NT."

Before you change the account's password, you need to make sure you have told IIS that it should coordinate passwords when you change the password in User Manager. It's now possible to do that in synchronized fashion—new to IIS 4.0; in IIS 3.0 and earlier, you were required to change the password yourself, which caused problems with many servers.

To ensure that password synchronization is turned on and to select a different anonymous account, perform the following steps:

1. Open the Internet Service Manager.
2. Expand the Internet Information Service.
3. Right-click on the server to set the options for it (or, if you wish, you can change this on a single site—in which case you right-click on the site).
4. Choose the Directory Security tab, and in the Anonymous Access and Authentication Control area, click on Edit.
5. Make sure that Allow Anonymous Access is checked.
6. Click the Edit button, and the Anonymous User Account dialog box appears (see Figure 6.1).
7. To enter a different account name to use for anonymous logons, click the Browse button and select the account from the list provided.
8. Make sure the Enable Automatic Password Synchronization box is checked. Click OK to exit this dialog box.

Figure 6.1.
In the Anonymous User Account dialog box, you can set the account name, password, and synchronization option.

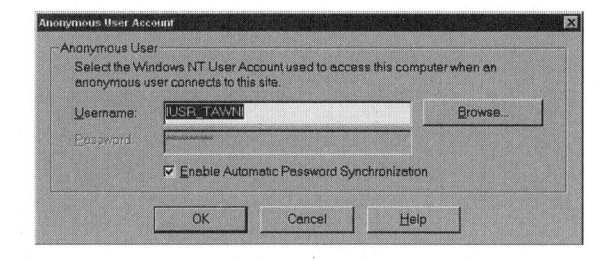

9. Click OK two more times to close the Authentication dialog box and the Properties dialog box.
10. Close the Microsoft Management Console.

With this option set, you can use the User Manager to change the password for the account, and the IIS server will pick up the change automatically.

Anonymous authentication allows a user to connect to your site even if she doesn't have a username and password on your network. Although this is a normal situation for almost all Internet sites and many intranets, you do have other options.

6.2.2. Using Clear Text Authentication

Another choice for allowing users to connect to your Web site is to have them supply a username and password; as you learned earlier, though, this username and password must exist in the Windows NT accounts database. Therefore, an administrator must create accounts manually for every user, which would not be an efficient system for a high-traffic public Internet site. IIS offers two methods for authenticating username/password authentication. The first one is clear text authentication, and the second one is NT Challenge/Response. This section will look quickly at clear text authentication. (The section "NT Challenge/Response" is coming up soon.)

Clear text offers a simple way to allow many users to connect to your site. When prompted for a username and password, the client sends the information as standard text. However, there is a significant risk in using clear text because many users can use network analysis tools to capture packets that are passing through a network. These tools are normally used for diagnostic purposes, such as to inspect data that is being sent over the network; but they can be used maliciously to intercept passwords sent in clear text. Because the Internet consists of many individual connected LANs, the problem increases greatly. Anyone on any of the networks your packets travel through can grab the packet using these freely available programs.

As you already know, clear text enables you to implement simple authentication that is compatible with any Web browser, but it is not very secure. It should be used only on an intranet, which you can be reasonably sure is secure. However, for highly sensitive data, such as employees' human resources files, even this is not recommended.

> **Test Tip**
>
> There is still one way to securely use basic authentication without compromising usernames or passwords: by securing directories or your entire site with SSL. This encrypts all traffic (incoming and outgoing), including the authentication traffic. You'll find more information on SSL later in this chapter.

A. Capturing Passwords Using Network Analysis Tools

Sending your password using clear text means that other users could capture your username and password and then use them to log on to the IIS server you were connecting to. In addition, because the username and password are from NT, the captured information might allow those persons to log into your NT domain or connect to your server's shares from across the Internet.

If this concerns you, you should consider implementing Windows NT challenge/response authentication, which we will discuss shortly.

B. Setting Up Basic Authentication

Clear text authentication should be used only on internal sites and even then only if it's absolutely necessary—based on drawbacks as outlined in previous section(s). To enable clear text authentication, follow these steps:

1. Open the Internet Service Manager.
2. Expand the Internet Information Service.
3. Right-click on the server to set the options for it (or, if you want, you can change this on a single site—in which case you right-click on the site).
4. Choose the Directory Security tab. Then, in the Anonymous Access and Authentication Control area, click on Edit.
5. Check the Basic Authentication check box.
6. A dialog box appears (see Figure 6.2), warning you that passwords could be captured as they cross the network.
7. Click Yes to continue.

6.2. Basic Security

Figure 6.2.
This warning will be displayed if you enable Basic Authentication.

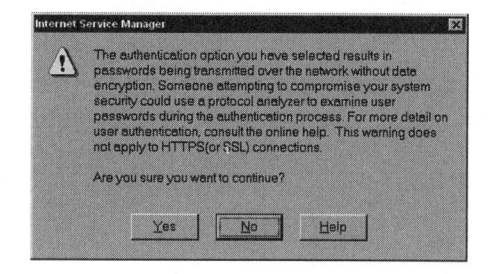

8. By default, the usernames and passwords will be checked against the domain database of the domain that the IIS server belongs to. If you want IIS to verify accounts against a different domain's database, click EDIT and enter the correct domain. You might do this if the IIS server were a member of one domain but all the accounts were stored in a different domain.

9. Click OK two times to close the Authentication dialog box and the Properties dialog box.

10. Close the Microsoft Management Console. Clear text authentication is now enabled.

6.2.3. NT Challenge/Response

If NT Challenge/Response authentication is configured, the server will engage in cryptographic exchange with the client. The NT server sends out a challenge, the client performs a calculation using that challenge in conjunction with the password the user provides, and the client generates a response. The client then sends the response to the NT server, which verifies whether it is the expected response. This entire conversation is used to verify the password, but the password itself is never sent across the network (which makes this method safer than basic authentication). The only problem is that this type of security currently works with only the Internet Explorer. Therefore, some of your users would have to switch to IE or would not be able to use the site.

To turn on NT Challenge/Response, just make sure it is selected in the Authentications Methods dialog box. To facilitate the use of NT challenge/response, the system will use the Security Support Provider Interface, or SSPI. SSPI is an ISAPI filter that is included with IIS 4.0 by default.

To verify that the filter is in place, follow these steps:

1. Open the Internet Service Manager.

2. Expand the Internet Information Service.
3. Right-click on the server to set the options for it (or, if you want, you can change this on a single site—in which case you right-click on the site).
4. Choose the ISAPI Filters tab (see Figure 6.3) and verify that sspifilt is included in the list. If it is not included, click Add, select it from the list, and then click OK. You may be prompted for the location of the IIS source files.
5. Click OK and close the Microsoft Management Console.

Figure 6.3.
Use the ISAPI Filters page to verify that filters are installed or to add or remove them.

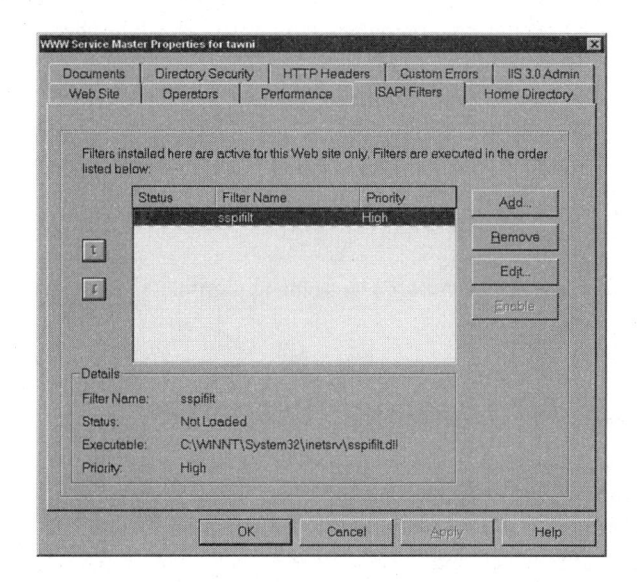

6.2.4. Restricting Access by IP Address/Domain Name

Another option that you have to secure your Web site is to restrict which systems are allowed to connect to your site. In this way, you are restricting access by IP Address/Domain Name. This is very effective if you are setting up an internal site and want to make sure that addresses from outside your organization will not be able to connect to your server. It can also be used to stop certain domains from connecting to your Web site.

To set up restricted access by IP Address/Domain Name, perform the following steps:

1. Open the Internet Service Manager.
2. Expand the Internet Information Service.

3. Right-click on the server to set the options for it (or, if you want, you can change this on a single site—in which case you right-click on the site).
4. Choose the Directory Security tab. Then, in the IP Address and Domain Name Restrictions area, click Edit. The IP Address and Domain Restrictions dialog box appears (see Figure 6.4).

Figure 6.4.
Use the IP Address and Domain Name Restrictions dialog box to limit access by computer IP or domain name.

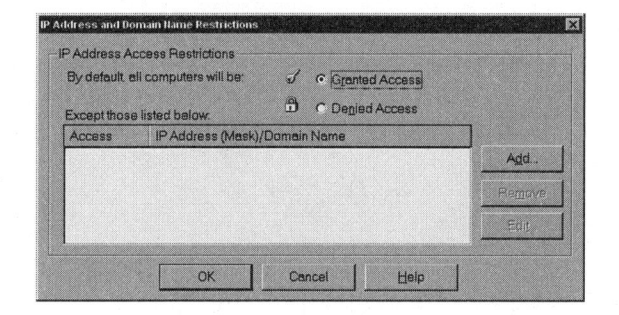

5. Set the By Default... option to either Granted Access (use this if you only want to stop certain groups) or Denied Access (this would normally be used for an internal site, when you will allow only IP addresses from your company). Typically, you would choose Granted Access unless you wanted to limit access to only certain hosts or networks.
6. Click the Add button to start adding exceptions to the default setting. If you chose to deny access by default, you specify the addresses you want to allow; if you granted access by default, you specify which addresses to deny.
7. Choose the type of address to add according to the appropriate instructions given here:
   - If you want to make an exception for a single address, choose Single Computer and enter the IP Address (see Figure 6.5). If you don't know the IP address, click the DNS Lookup button and enter the name (for example: www.microsoft.com) to find the computer's IP address.
   - If you want to make exceptions for a group of computers, choose Group of Computers and enter the Network ID and Subnet Mask (see Figure 6.6).
   - If you want to make an exception for an entire domain, choose Domain Name (see Figure 6.7) and enter the domain name. (If this is the first time you have configured a domain restriction, you will see a dialog box warning you that your DNS server must support reverse lookup for this to be effective.)

Figure 6.5.
You set an exception for a single computer by entering the IP address here.

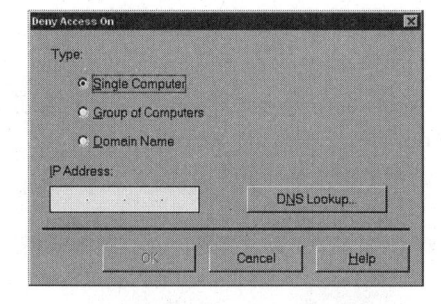

Figure 6.6.
If you want to make exception for a group of computers, choose Group of Computers.

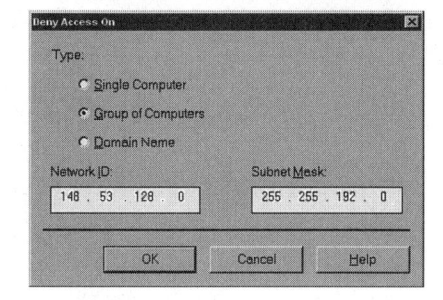

> **Warning:** Applying restrictions by domain name adversely affects server performance because of the overhead of DNS resolution.

> **Note:** Reverse lookup is the process for resolving an IP address to a computer name. For example, if I did a reverse lookup on 207.68.137.59, it would tell me that was the address for www.microsoft.com.

Figure 6.7.
If you want to make an exception for an entire domain, choose Domain Name.

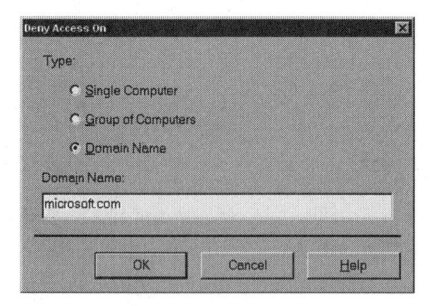

8. Continue to add (or edit or remove) entries until you have completed the exceptions (see Figure 6.8).

Figure 6.8.
The exceptions are displayed in the IP Address and Domain Name Restrictions dialog box.

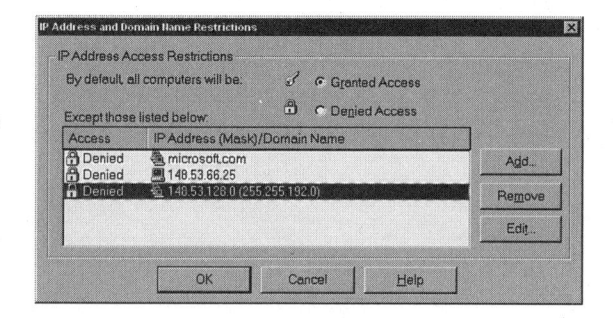

9. Close the dialog boxes and exit the Internet Service Manager.

6.2.5. Configuring Basic Security Using Home Directory Settings

Another way to manipulate security on a basic level is through a few settings on the Home Directory tab. Essentially, the settings fall into three categories:

- Access Permissions
- Application Settings
- Content Control

The next few sections discuss these categories in detail.

A. Access Permissions

The Access Permissions control what a person will be able to do with the directory that you have selected. The controls include two check boxes: Read (the user will be able to read the information) and Write (the user will be able to write information to the directory). If you know that remote users will need to upload content to your site, make sure that they have Write access (in most situations, you would allow only Read access).

B. Application Settings

You can also enter settings for an application in order to control what permissions the users will have when they run the application. As you can see in Figure 6.9, there are several options you can set; additional options can be accessed via the Configuration button.

Figure 6.9.
The Home Directory settings control the access to the directory.

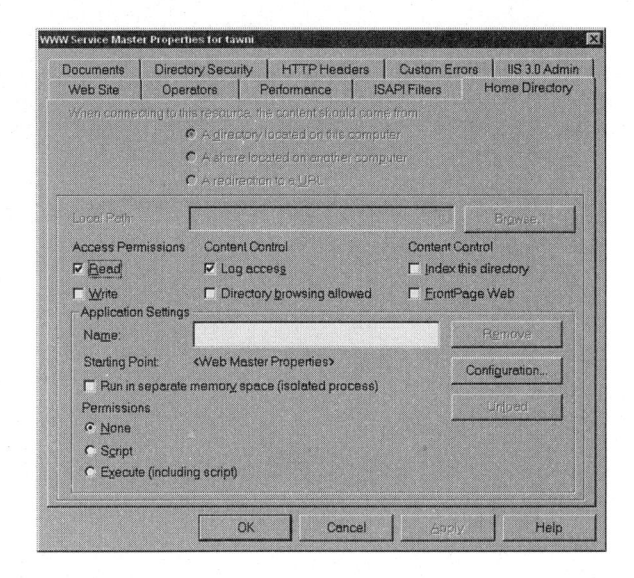

The following list provides a description of the Application Settings:

- *Name.* This is the name of the application for your purposes.
- *Run in Separate Memory Space (Isolated Process).* Normally all applications on the Web site run in the Inetinfo process. If you select this option, the Web site will generate a new process, which decreases the speed but increases the security by isolating the application from the Inetinfo process.
- *Permissions.* You can specify three levels of permission for the specified application:

    None. Doesn't allow the application to run.

    Script. Allows basic scripts to run.

    Execute. Allows all types of applications to be executed.

From the Applications Settings area of the Properties dialog box, you also can enter configuration settings for the application. To do so, click on the Configuration button. You'll be presented with the following three screens of configuration settings:

- App Mappings
- App Options
- App Debugging

6.2. Basic Security | 193

The App Mappings options (see Figure 6.10) enable you to configure which extensions are associated with which applications. Here, you can convert links from different file types into .DLLs. There is also a check box that tells IIS to cache ISAPI applications.

Figure 6.10.
Use the App Mappings dialog box to map a file extension to the application type.

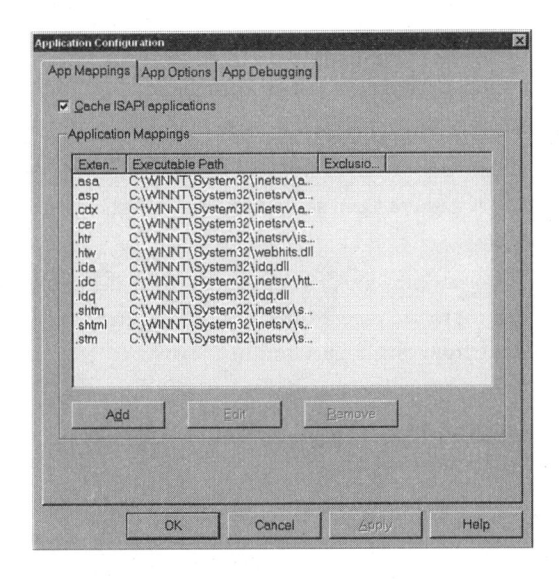

The App Options tab (see Figure 6.11) contains several settings that control the way the application will run.

Figure 6.11.
The App Options tab controls how the ASP pages work.

The following list describes the options on the App Options tab:

- *Enable Session State.* When this option is selected, the Session object is available in ASP programs. It enables the programs to track users as they move around the site. (This is done by way of *cookies*—variables that are stored on the client computer—and requires that the client is using a browser that supports them).
- *Session Timeout.* The number of minutes that can pass before the cookie is dropped if no activity is seen.
- *Enable Buffering.* When this is selected, all output that will be generated by the ASP page is gathered and sent at one time (instead of the application sending it as it goes).
- *Enable Parent Paths.* This will cause the paths that are being used in the pages to be relative to the parent directory of the current site. This enables you to jump users from one application to another.
- *Default ASP Language.* Specifies the default script language for ASP pages. Two scripts engines come with IIS: vbscript (Visual Basic Scripting Edition) and jscript (Microsoft JScript).
- *ASP Script Timeout.* The maximum amount of time that a script can be running on the server. This prevents CPU time from being consumed by a single erring script. To allow the script to continue running forever, enter –1 in this box.

The last tab, App Debugging, contains the debugging options for the server and the client (see Figure 6.12). There are two sections on this tab. The Debugging Flags section turns on client- and/or server-side debugging. The other section controls whether the client will be sent only detailed ASP debugging information or the debugging information along with a simple text message that you enter. You should opt to send a text message when configuring production servers because debugging information might reveal implementation details of your servers (thereby posing a security risk).

Now that you have seen your options for modifying how applications will run on our system, all that remains is to look at how you can modify content control settings in order to meet your needs.

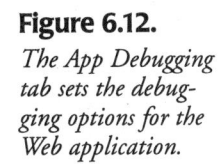

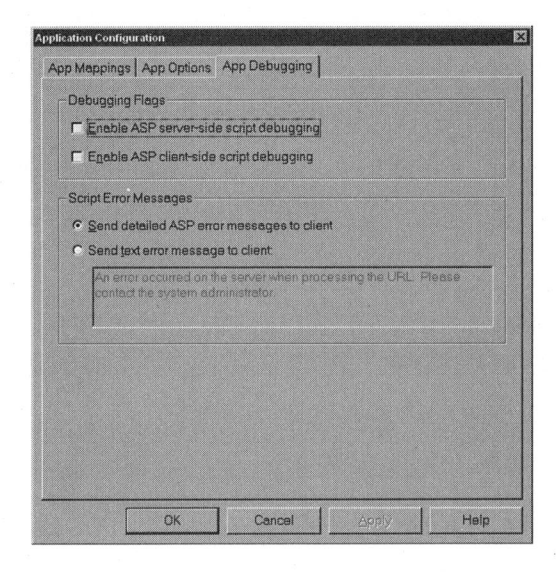

Figure 6.12.
The App Debugging tab sets the debugging options for the Web application.

C. Content Control

The last part of the Home Directory tab that we are going to address is the Content Control area. This area contains the logging and directory access options. Two options that can be set here affect security:

- *Log Access.* This option turns off the logging for a directory so that you can control which of the directories on your server you will log access to. Excessive logging can deteriorate server performance. By moving this option to the individual directories, you have a great deal more control in IIS 4.0 than you did in IIS 3.0. Log files not only enable you to create usage statistics, they also tell you if someone tried to hack your site by supplying bogus query strings to scripts and applications—take a look at the log file!

- *Directory Browsing Allowed.* This option controls whether a user can connect to a directory that does not have a default page. If this is enabled and a client connects to a directory where there is no default page, the client will receive a directory listing. If this is not enabled, the client will receive an error. You will probably disable this feature for most directories because implementation details might be revealed (once again, revealing as little implementation information as possible boosts security).

Here is an example of how you can modify the content control properties. In this exercise, you will disable directory browsing to ensure that if the default document is missing, users will not be presented with the directory contents. Follow these steps:

1. Start the Internet Service Manager and find the server or site for which you want to disable directory browsing.
2. Right-click on the server or site and choose Properties.
3. In the Properties dialog box, choose the Home Directory tab.
4. Select the Access Permissions and Content Control options.
5. Click the Allow Directory Browsing box to remove the check mark.
6. Click OK to disable directory browsing.

6.3. Advanced Security

The Internet Information Server also provides the ability to increase the security by adding ISAPI extensions and filters. ISAPI (Internet Server Application Programming Interface) can be used to add security by including a filter that can be used to encrypt and decrypt packets moving to and from the server. ISAPI can be used for much more than simply security, as you will see when we discuss programmability in IIS.

Encryption must be set up using some method of authentication—this can include public keys and private keys, X.509 certificates, or some physical method of authentication—in order to verify the identities participating in the exchange. For example, X.509 certificates are used to verify that the party in question is who he says he is; a third, real-world entity has verified his identity and generated this certificate as identification.

6.3.1. Encryption Overview

Currently the most common method of encrypting data is to use public key technologies. Generally, there is a *public key* and a *private key*. The public key encrypts data, and the private key decrypts data. When you use a key pair, only the public key is known and can be used to encrypt the data. The private key is then needed to decrypt it.

Public key cryptography works like this: You generate a private/public key pair using your cryptography software. You distribute the public key, which is used to encrypt data, to anyone who wants to send you information. You do not need to be concerned about who has access to your public key. But without the private key (which only you have access to), no one, not even the sender, can decrypt that data. You can send out the public key via many methods, such as on a disk, via e-mail, or on your Web site.

In IIS, Secure Sockets Layer (SSL) is used to create a secure connection across the Internet. We will discuss SSL, along with PCT and SET, which are other security protocols you can use, in the next few sections.

A. Secure Sockets Layer

In order to support electronic commerce over the Internet, it was felt that customers needed a way of ensuring that people were who they said they were. For example, if you were talking to your bank, you'd want to be certain that it was, in fact, your bank. It was also felt, with good reason, that credit card numbers must be able to be transferred across the network without being intercepted.

Thus the SSL (Secure Sockets Layer) was developed. In order to support SSL, you must have a certificate. You obtain this certificate by sending proof of your identity and your public key to a certifying authority such as VeriSign. That authority signs your public with their private key, which forms a certificate, and then sends the certificate back to you for installation on your server. Once the SSL certificate is installed, clients can connect to your Web site and verify the identity of it, as previously mentioned.

Before you can use the Secure Sockets Layer (SSL) for encryption, you must obtain and install the server certificate. The server certificate enables your clients to verify the identity of your server and to set up a secure channel for communication.

The certificate is an X.509 certificate just like the ones you can use with the Certificate Server. Obtaining the certificate is a three-step process:

1. Generate a request.
2. Send the request to the authentication authority.
3. Install the certificate when it comes back.

To generate a request file, perform the following steps:

1. Start the Internet Service Manager and find the server or site for which you want to enable SSL.
2. Right-click on the server and choose Properties.

3. Choose the Directory Security tab and, in the Secure Communications area, click Edit.
4. Choose Key Manager from the Secure Communications dialog box.
5. Open the Key menu and choose Create New Key to start the Create New Key wizard.
6. The first screen (shown in Figure 6.13) asks you to select the name of the file for the request or to choose to send the request online.

Figure 6.13.

The first screen of the Create New Key Wizard allows you to select how the request file should be sent.

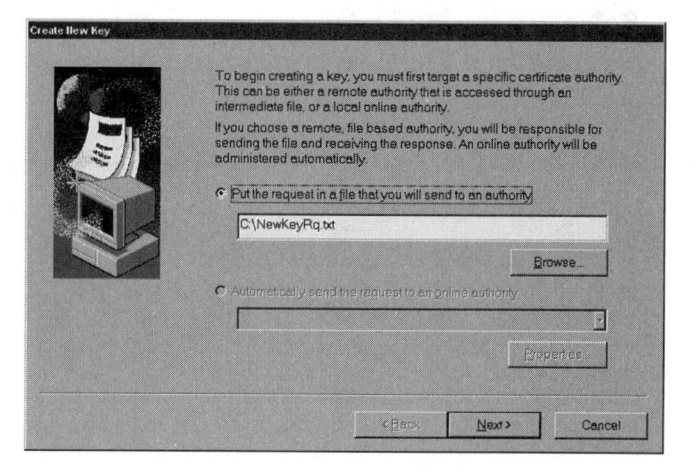

7. Next you will be asked for the key name, password, and encryption length (longer keys are more secure but slower). Figure 6.14 shows this dialog box.

Figure 6.14.

On the second screen of the wizard, you enter the key name and length.

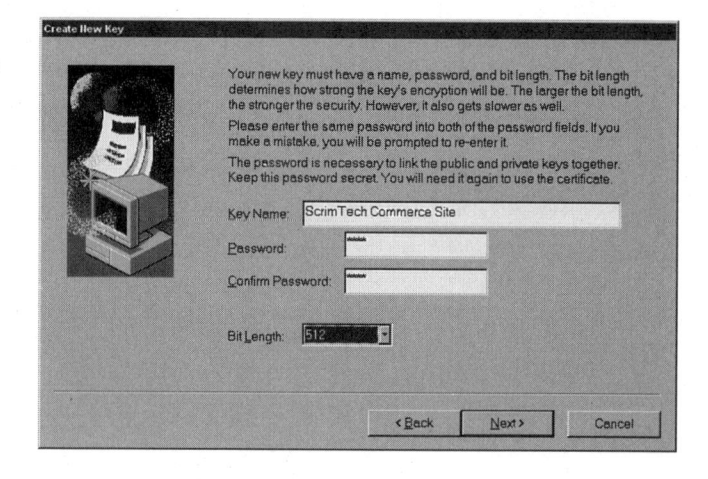

8. Next you need to enter your organization name and the full name of your server. (In Figure 6.15, the name of the server is "scrimtech," which is for an internal site; for an external site, the name would be "www.scrimtech.com").

Figure 6.15.
On this screen, you enter the organization and server name.

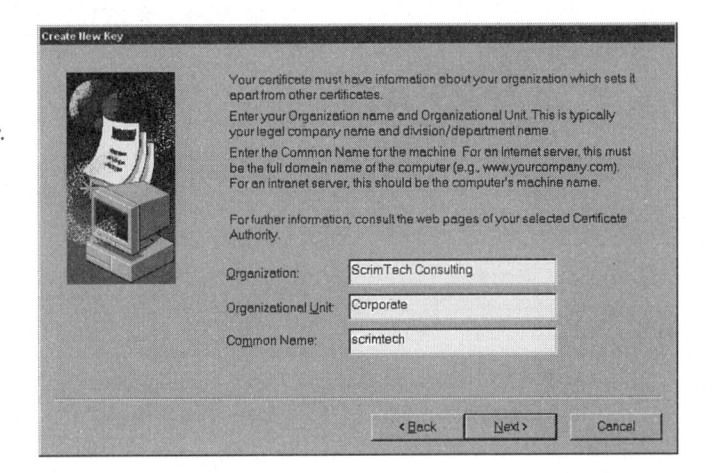

9. On the fourth screen, you enter your location, including the country, the province or state, and the locality (see Figure 6.16).

Figure 6.16.
Enter the locality information on this screen.

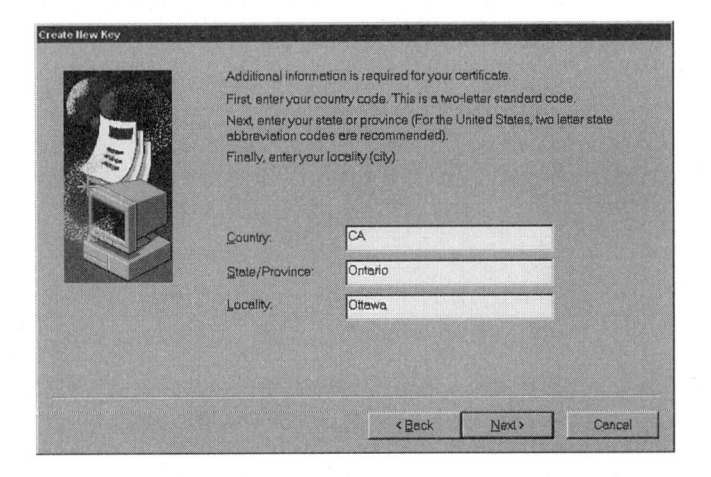

10. The last information you will need to enter is your name, e-mail address, and phone number (see Figure 6.17).

Figure 6.17.

The last information you have to enter is your contact information.

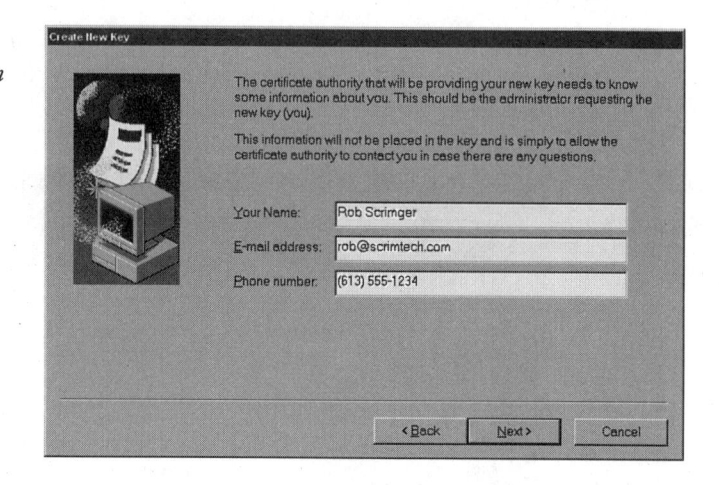

11. On the last screen, click Finish, and a dialog box appears, telling you where the file is located. Click OK to close that dialog box.

Now that you have generated the request file, you need to send the file to the certificate authority. Because procedures change often on the Internet, it is not possible for us to include an absolute example of how to acquire a certificate. In general, you should know that they will require you either to cut and paste the information in the request file or to e-mail the file itself.

The following steps walk you through the process of sending the file to the certificate authority (in this case, VeriSign):

1. Open the VeriSign site in your browser (www.verisign.com).
2. Click the Server IDs box (see Figure 6.18).
3. On the next screen, click the Get Your Secure Server ID Now! link.
4. The next screen asks you to choose the type of ID that you require.
5. The next page asks that you select your server (see Figure 6.19).
6. Next you are presented a page that outlines all the steps that are required to obtain the ID and the requirements. When you have read the information, click Begin.
7. The next screen provides you a dialog box to paste the contents of the request file into; the whole file is copied, not just the key request (see Figure 6.20). When you finish copying and pasting the information, click Continue.

Figure 6.18.
From the VeriSign main screen, click the Server IDs box on the left.

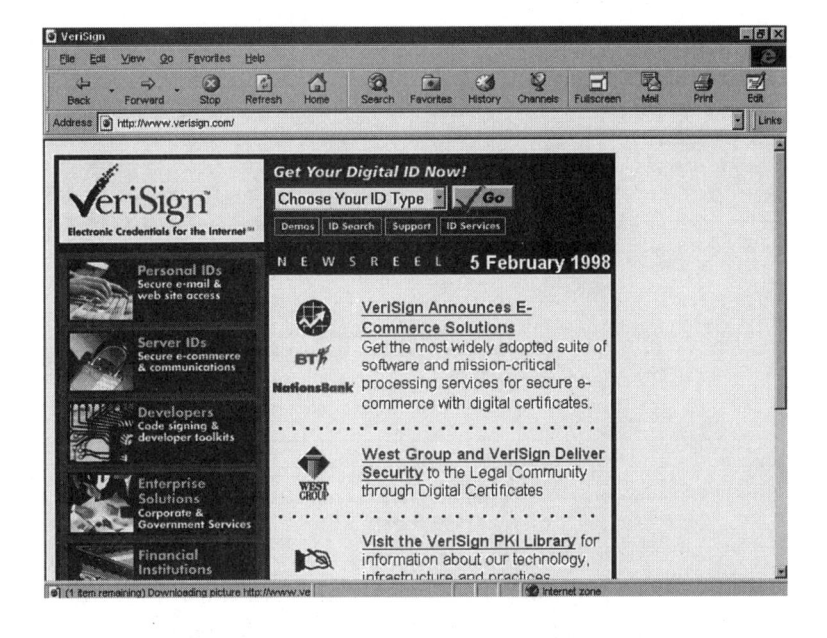

Figure 6.19.
Select the server type from a list box.

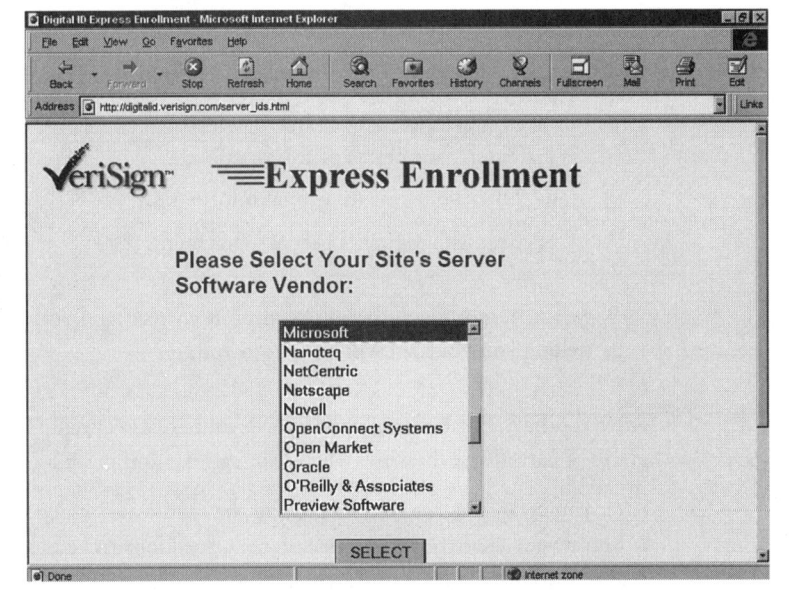

Day 6: Internet Information Server Security

Figure 6.20.
The information from the request file can be pasted straight into the Web site.

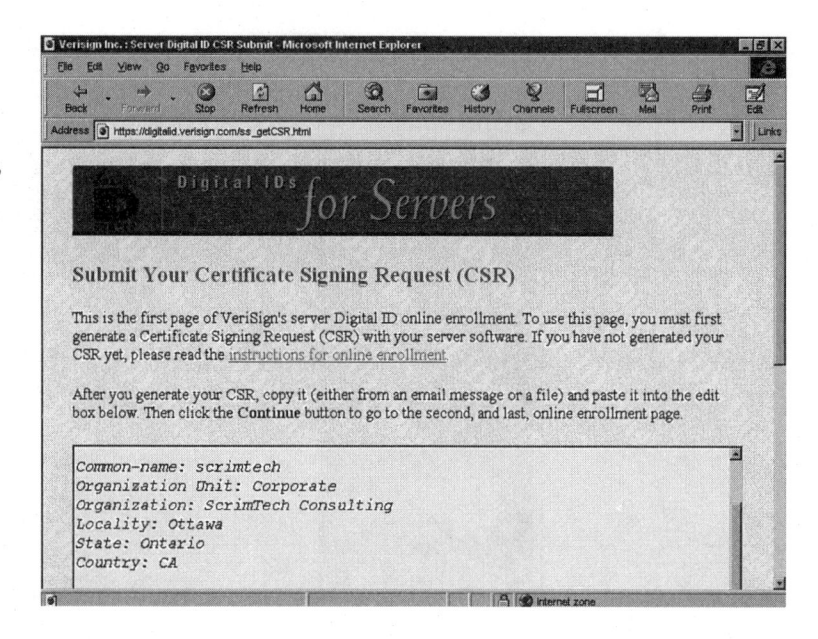

8. The next few steps will confirm all the information that you have provided:
   a. Verify your distinguished name.
   b. Enter your digital ID information.
   c. Enter your payment information.
   d. Enter your organizational information.
   e. Read the digital ID server agreement.

9. Click Accept when the information is correct, and you should receive a screen telling you your ID will be sent to you.

After you have finished, you will receive your ID via e-mail. The certificate will arrive as part of the message, which you can cut and paste to a text file.

After you create the file, you can install the certificate, which will then allow clients to verify your identity and create secure connections to your site. Perform the following steps to install the certificates:

1. Start the Internet Service Manager and find the server or site for which you want to enable SSL.
2. Right-click on the server and choose Properties.

3. Choose the Directory Security tab and, in the Secure Communications area, click Edit.
4. Choose Key Manager from the Secure Communications dialog box.
5. From the Key menu, choose Install Key Certificate.
6. Enter the file location. After you choose the file, you will need to enter the password (see Figure 6.21).

Figure 6.21.
You need to enter the password that was used when you created the key in the first place.

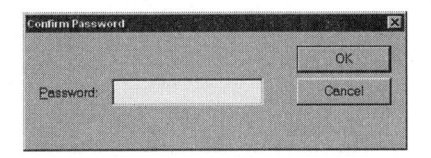

7. The next screen asks you which servers this key will be used for (see Figure 6.22).

Figure 6.22.
The binding screen allows you to bind the key to various servers.

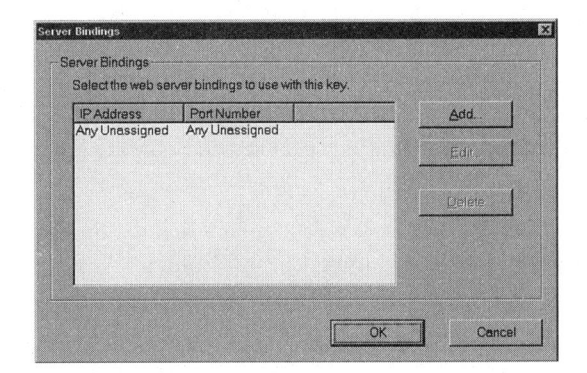

8. You will receive a warning about the certificate file. Read it, and then click OK.
9. Close the Key Manager.

Now that the certificate is installed successfully, you can turn on SSL for the sites that will need secure data transmission. As with anything else that you might add to an Internet site, you will pay a penalty. Setting up a secure channel increases the amount of overhead required to set up the session.

The following list outlines the steps that take place during the SSL handshake:

1. The client requests the page from the server.
2. The server sends its certificate and public key.
3. The client creates a session encryption key that will be used during the session.
4. The client encrypts the session key with the server's public key.
5. The client sends the encrypted session key to the server.
6. The server decrypts the key using its private key.
7. The server returns a message to the client encrypted with the session key.

At this point, the first phase is complete. If the site does not require client certificates, the client and server can communicate using the session key to encrypt the data going back and forth. With SSL enabled on a site, you can require (or only allow) users to provide Client Certificates to authenticate with that site.

> **Note:** If the server does require Client Certificates for authentication, Certificate Server will be used to issue these certificates. See Day 7, "Microsoft Certificate Server," for more information.

To set up your site for requiring client certificates, you need to perform the following steps:

1. Start the Internet Service Manager and find the site for which you want to enable authentication using Client Certificates.
2. Right-click on the site and choose Properties from the context menu.
3. Choose the Directory Security tab and, in the Secure Communications area, click the Edit button.
4. Select the Require Secure Channel When Accessing This Resource box and the Require Client Certificates box to require clients to provide a certificate before accessing this resource.
5. Click OK to close the Properties dialog box.
6. Stop and then restart the Web site.

B. PCT

Although SSL is probably the most common of the secure protocols, there are others. PCT, or Private Communication Technology, is another method of securing site access. In essence, PCT is the same as SSL; however, PCT does offer some advantages:

- PCT turnaround time and message structure is shorter.
- PCT uses extended cryptographic algorithms and format negotiation.
- The keys used for the message are different from the keys used for the session setup.
- PCT provides an authentication verify-prelude, which allows the client and server to verify that identity messages have not been modified.

The reason that PCT has not yet supplanted SSL is that a black box of some nature is required to verify that the server is valid. With SSL, the certificate can be verified with the certificate authority; however, PCT does not rely on (or use) certificates.

C. SET

Another communications technology that should be mentioned is SET or Secure Electronic Transaction. This method of allowing secure transmissions was developed expressly for credit card payments over the Internet. An extension of PCT, SET requires the financial institution to have a server that will become involved to verify the merchant to the client and to process the payment. This means that a black box is not required, but more importantly, the merchant never sees the credit card information.

6.3.2. Considerations

As a last note, the inclusion of any form of security increases the amount of processing that the system will need to perform. This will increase the load on the server and reduce both the number of connections and the speed of connections that the system can handle. Generally, you should include security only if it is required.

6.4. Adding Security from NT

As you have seen, many options in IIS can be used to secure a Web site. In addition, you can do a number of things with Windows NT that will allow you to further secure the information that you will keep on the IIS server.

6.4.1. Setting Directory and File Level Permissions

Because the functions that are available in IIS all rely on the transfer of files, it makes sense that one of the simplest and most effective actions you can take from NT is to use NTFS permissions to secure access to the information.

NTFS security is used because the connection to the IIS server creates a local logon on the IIS server; otherwise share permissions would be used. NTFS (NT's File System) enables you to work with permissions at the file and directory level. When connecting to an NT system via Windows 3.1's File Manager, for example, you can set permissions on the share so that you can control how users access resources over the network without affecting how users access resources locally. However, IIS does not connect through shares the way regular network clients do, so you must set the security on the files and folders directly.

Setting NTFS permissions is fairly easy; the following steps outline the general process:

1. Start NT Explorer.
2. Expand the directory for which you want to set permissions.
3. Right-click on the directory to set directory permissions, or right-click on the file to set file permissions.
4. Choose Properties, and the Properties dialog box appears (see Figure 6.23).

Figure 6.23.

The Properties dialog box leads you to the Security tab.

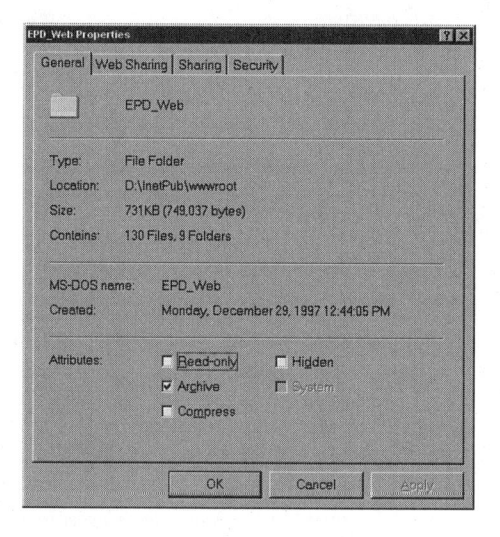

5. Choose the Security tab (see Figure 6.24).
6. Click the Permissions button, and the Directory Permissions (or File Permissions) dialog box appears (see Figure 6.25).

Figure 6.24.

The Security tab allows you to set permissions and auditing.

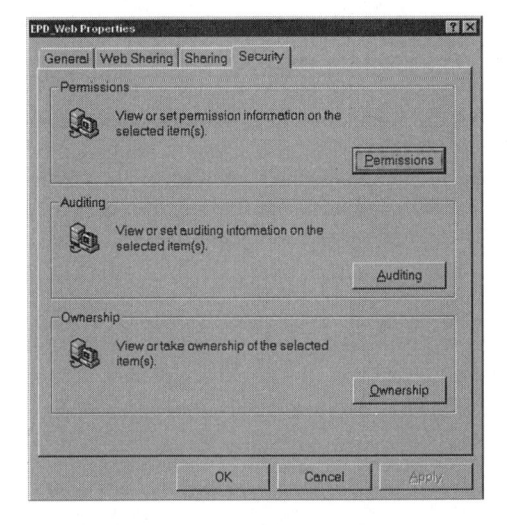

Figure 6.25.

The Directory Permissions dialog box allows you to extend permissions to additional users and groups.

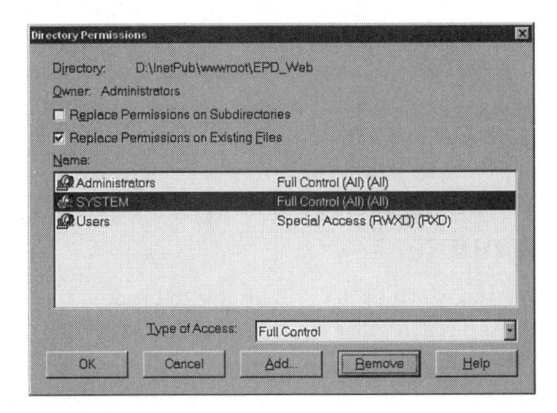

7. Click the Add button, and the Add Users and Groups dialog box appears. Select the user or group that you want to add permissions for and click Add again (to show users, click Show Users). Select the type of access this user or group should have, and then click OK. For example, if you want anonymous users to be able to access this document (but not make changes to it), add IUSR_*computername* and give it the Read permission.

If you are allowing anonymous access, use the IUSR_*computername* account when setting permissions.

> **Note:** You can set these levels of permission: Read, Change, Full Control, and No Access (the most powerful option is Special Access, which allows even more granularity). Read allows users to view your documents but not modify them. Change allows your users to modify and view documents but not modify their permissions. Full Control, as the name implies, allows users to do whatever they choose to these files. No Access prevents all access to these files.

8. Review the permissions in the Directory Permissions dialog box and click OK when they are correct. (In directory permissions, you must note whether you want the permissions to apply to all subdirectories; check the Replace Permissions on Subdirectories option.)

9. Click OK to close the Properties dialog box, and then close NT Explorer.

You have now seen how you can set security at the file and directory level so you can specify which users have access to your resources. It is important to understand that the permissions you set apply not only to IIS, but also to other network clients and users accessing these files locally.

6.4.2. Disabling Other Services Running on the IIS Computer

One of the ways in which people will be able to break into the server that is running IIS is to come in through other services. This can easily be prevented by simply stopping the services that you will not be using on the server. For example, someone running the Client for Microsoft Networks on a Windows 95 machine might be able to log into your NT server through shared folders instead of through IIS. Make sure that you are not leaving potential holes in your security system.

Several services run on NT systems that are not required for IIS to run; some may be needed if you want to be able to authenticate users; others are not needed at all. The following list covers the basic services that are loaded on an NT system, which you could consider disabling:

- *Alerter.* This service handles sending alerts on the network for the system. It will not be necessary on an IIS server in most cases. However, you may want to enable it so that NT can send messages to your workstation in case of errors.

- *Computer Browser.* To allow computers to know what servers are available on a network, you use the Computer Browser service. This broadcasts the existence of a server periodically so that it can be added to the browse list that is seen in Network Neighborhood. This service can be stopped.
- *Event Log.* This service handles the logging of information to the Event Log. If this service is disabled, no event will be written in the case of error. This service can be disabled; however, there will be no information available in case of system crashes, and auditing will not be available.
- *Remote Procedure Call (RPC) Locator.* This is used to connect to RPC servers on the network. Many of the server products coming from Microsoft these days use RPC. This can be disabled; however, integration with Exchange and other BackOffice servers could be affected.
- *Remote Procedure Call (RPC) Service.* This is the system's RPC server. This portion will allow other systems to connect to this one. If you are using the system for more than IIS, this should not be disabled.
- *Server.* This is the NetBIOS server service that allows other systems to connect to the system using Microsoft networking tools. Generally this is not required by IIS and can be disabled. In a previous example, we showed how someone using the Microsoft Client for Networks may be able to bypass your IIS security by accessing your server through this service. Therefore, unless you absolutely need to service non-IIS clients, this service should be stopped.
- *Spooler.* This service handles printing for the local system and can be disabled.
- *TCP/IP NetBIOS Helper.* NetBIOS, which is used for Microsoft networking, cannot work directly with TCP/IP. This service acts as the interface to Windows Sockets and provides all of Microsoft networking components with the ability to connect over TCP/IP. If you are using the system only for IIS, this can be disabled.
- *Workstation.* Finally, this service is used to connect to other systems across the network. Generally, this can be disabled.

A great deal of consideration should be given to disabling services. The impact on the system can be great: At the very least, the ability to control the server remotely is normally affected. Always test the affect of disabling a service in a lab environment before putting it into production so you know what the restrictions will be.

To disable a service, follow these simple steps:

1. Open the Control Panel and go to the Services applet (see Figure 6.26).

Figure 6.26.
The Services dialog box lists the services on your system.

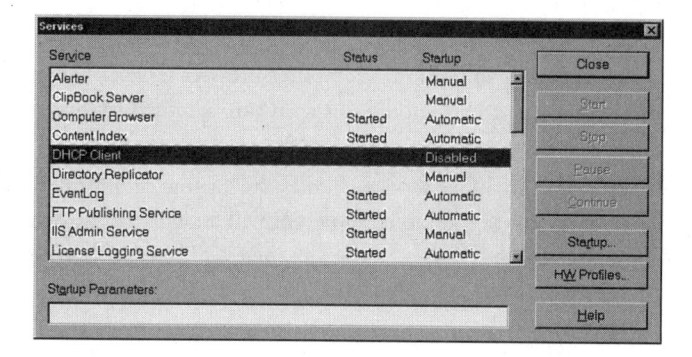

2. Click on the service in the list and choose Startup; the Service dialog box appears (see Figure 6.27).

Figure 6.27.
The Service dialog box shows the startup type and account information for a service.

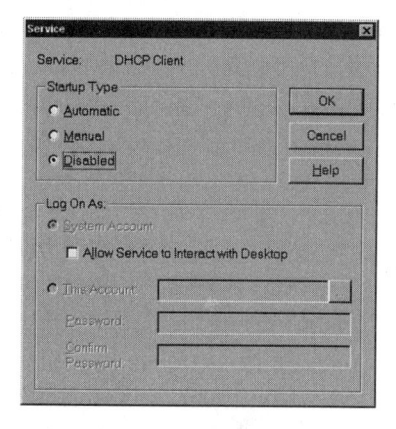

3. Choose Disabled (or Manual) as the Startup type, and then click OK to close the dialog box.
4. Close the Services dialog box and the Control Panel.
5. Restart the system. (Note that you can just start the service; however, restarting the system will verify that any other services this service relies on are also started.)

6.4.3. TCP/IP Advanced Security

Another way in which you can secure the server that is running IIS is to implement NT advanced TCP/IP security. This can be used to restrict access to a computer. If you choose to use it for security, there is a very good chance that you will have to administer the system locally instead of across the network.

To access the TCP/IP security settings, perform these steps:

1. Right-click Network Neighborhood and choose Properties.
2. Choose the Protocol tab and double-click on TCP/IP.
3. Click the Advanced button; the Advanced IP Address dialog box appears.
4. Click the Enable Security check box, and then you can click the Configure button. The configuration dialog box appears.
5. For each of the three protocols, choose either Permit All or Permit Only.
6. If you choose Permit Only, click Add and enter the port number to allow (for example, port 80 under TCP is the default for HTTP communications).
7. Continue to add ports until all the ports that you want to allow are entered (such as 443 for SSL connections).
8. Close the Advanced Security dialog box and the TCP/IP Settings box. Then close the Network Settings dialog box and restart the computer.

6.4.4. User Account Issues

If the server that is running IIS is used for other purposes (where possible it should be on a server of its own) or if you will use NT Challenge/Response, you need to ensure that the user accounts the system will use are sufficiently secure. The following are general rules about accounts. These concepts are just as crucial when dealing with IIS security as they are when planning NT networks, if not more.

- *Do not enable the guest account.* Users from the Web will use the IUSR_*computername* account, so the guest account is not required.
- *Choose difficult passwords.* Ensure that passwords are not simple. Generally, passwords should be eight or more characters and should contain special characters or numbers, preferably in the middle.
- *Don't use basic authentication.* This sends your passwords as clear text. If you use the TRACERT utility, you can see the path that packets will take across the Internet. Between each pair of routers listed is a network on which a protocol analyzer could be located—and could be used to capture passwords.
- *Manage strict account policies.* Creating a program that guesses a password is simple. Use account lock out to ensure that the unlimited number of guesses

required for this type of program to work is not available. You should also use account policies to ensure that users change their passwords from time to time.

- *Limit membership in the Administrators group.* Administrators have complete control of a server (or the entire domain or multiple domains). Make sure that only the users who need to belong to the Administrators group. Also, be careful with the Operator groups because these also have many extra rights.

- *Don't use the Everyone group.* The Everyone group includes all the users that can attach to the system. This includes the IUSR_*computername* account and any other account—local or global—that can attach to the server.

- *Change the host name.* Because the NetBIOS computer name and the host name are normally the same, users could try to attack the NetBIOS side after finding the host name. Changing the host name adds another variable that can frustrate hackers.

- *Restrict traffic to IP ports 20, 21, and 80.* This limits users to connecting to only the FTP ports (20 and 21) and the HTTP port (80). If you limit the number of potential entry points into your system, you can focus your attention on securing only the ports that your clients will actually be using.

Lab

This lab consists of review questions pertaining to this chapter and provides an opportunity for you to use walk-through exercises to apply the knowledge that you've learned.

Questions

1. You are in charge of an Internet server. Your server receives several thousand hits a day, and you are concerned that your competitors at DB Engineering are using your Web site to answer questions from their customers. You want to stop this.

   As a solution, you enable basic authentication and disable the anonymous account. You will log access to your site and will search the log for any of the users from your competitor company.

   How well does this solution work?

   A. This is the optimum solution and accomplishes the goal.

   B. This is a good solution and will accomplish the goal.

   C. This solution works, but another solution would be better.

   D. This solution appears to work but does not.

   E. This solution does not meet the goal.

2. You are in charge of an Internet server. Your server receives several thousand hits a day, and you are concerned that your competitors at DB Engineering are using your Web site to answer questions from their customers. You want to stop this.

   You enable the restrictions by IP address. Based on the information you found from the InterNIC, you deny access to the blocks of addresses that have been assigned to your competitors.

   How well does this solution work?

   A. This is the optimum solution and accomplishes the goal.

   B. This is a good solution and will accomplish the goal.

   C. This solution works, but another solution would be better.

   D. This solution appears to work but does not.

   E. This solution does not meet the goal.

3. What is the primary difference between SSL and PCT?

    A. SSL is more advanced than PCT because of the verify prelude.

    B. PCT provides certificates, and SSL does not.

    C. SSL does not require a black box to verify the server; PCT does.

    D. PCT is only a transport for SET and does not perform encryption.

4. Which of the following are access permissions for a directory?

    A. Connect

    B. Read

    C. Write

    D. Execute

5. Your organization is connected to the Internet, and all the desktop computers have valid IP addresses and access. You are establishing an internal Web site that will contain information to be used for quotes that should be considered sensitive. You must provide security for this site.

    You create the site and disable anonymous connections, and the site is placed on a FAT partition with all the other sites. You enable NT Challenge/Response and disable basic authentication.

    How well does this meet the requirements?

    A. This is the optimum solution and accomplishes the goal.

    B. This is a good solution and will accomplish the goal.

    C. This solution works, but another solution would be better.

    D. This solution appears to work but does not.

    E. This solution does not meet the goal.

6. Your organization is connected to the Internet, and all the desktop computers have valid IP addresses and access. You are establishing an internal Web site that will contain information to be used for quotes that should be considered sensitive. You must provide security for this site.

    You ensure that the site is on an NTFS partition and that the user ISUR_*computername* does not have access. Then you restrict access by IP address, denying access to all addresses except those within your company.

How well does this meet the requirements?

A. This is the optimum solution and accomplishes the goal.

B. This is a good solution and will accomplish the goal.

C. This solution works, but another solution would be better.

D. This solution appears to work but does not.

E. This solution does not meet the goal.

7. Which of the following actions will stop network connections for all services except the basic HTTP and FTP services?

A. Stop all the NT services and set them to start up disabled.

B. Set the TCP/IP advanced security to only accept TCP ports 20, 21, and 80.

C. Set the IIS server to use 100% of the bandwidth.

D. This is not possible.

8. What consideration(s) are valid if you are setting up SSL?

A. Bandwidth requirements

B. System overhead

C. Memory overhead

D. SSL will require NTFS

9. Which of the following statements are true?

A. FAT is significantly more secure than NTFS.

B. The Everyone group should be used to manage site security.

C. NTFS provides file- and directory-level permissions.

D. Certificate server must be used before any security added to a site can be used.

10. Which tools can be used to add security to a site?

A. Key Manager

B. Security Manager

C. NT Explorer

D. Internet Service Manager

Answers to Questions

1. **E.** This solution will not stop the DB Engineers from using your site; it only provides you with a list of users and where they connected from (which can easily be hidden).

2. **A.** This is probably the best option that you have. Using the domain name works only if all their systems are registered with the DNS server's reverse lookup zone. Users from DB Engineering can still call from home service providers (although that would be inconvenient). In addition, the block of addresses is often assigned to the service provider, so this may not be readily available.

3. **C.** The main difference is that PCT requires a black box to verify the server, whereas the client can use the certificate that SSL provides to verify the server with the certificate authority.

4. **B, C.** Although connections can be entered as restrictions, they are not permissions. The execute permission is associated with the application settings. Therefore, the only directory permissions are Read and Write.

5. **B.** This is a good solution and will accomplish the goal. However, because the site is housed on a FAT partition, it is possible that an external user will be able to access the information.

6. **A.** This solution is a good solution and provides solid access control without the overhead of SSL and certificates.

7. **B.** The FTP ports are ports 21 (control) and 20 (data); HTTP uses port 80. If only those are enabled, no other ports will allow access over TCP/IP.

8. **A, B, C.** Because the system will have to perform more functions, it will need more bandwidth to handle the extra communications, as well as more system resources (including memory) to handle encryption, decryption, and buffering.

9. **C.** FAT does not provide any security; only NTFS does. The Everyone group includes any user that can connect to a site and should never be used for security purposes. The Certificate server is only needed to work with certificates from the client (and mapping those to NT accounts, as described in Day 7, "Microsoft Certificate Server").

10. **A, C, D.** The Key Manager will let you enable the SSL layer. NT Explorer lets you set NTFS permissions on files, and the Internet Service Manager allows you to set the type of authentication and access to the site and servers. There is no Security Manager.

Exercises

This lab assumes that you have IIS 4.0 installed and running correctly and that you installed the sample Web sites. (If you did not install those sites, you can create a site and substitute it in the exercises.)

Exercise 6.1.: Adding IP Address Restrictions

This exercise addresses the following Microsoft exam objective:

- Choose a security strategy for various situations (more specifically, this subobjective: Control access by host or network).

This exercise shows you how to restrict access to a site based on the IP address of a client.

1. Start the Internet Service Manager.
2. Expand your server and right-click the samples directory.
3. Start the Internet Explorer (but don't close the Internet Service Manager).
4. Load your default site (choose File, Open, select your computer name, and click OK). Make sure that you can open this site and that it works before proceeding to the next step.
5. Open the samples site (*computer_name*/samples) to make sure that it is working.
6. Switch to the Internet Service Manager, right-click the samples directory, and choose Properties.
7. Choose the Directory Services tab and, in the IP Address and Domain Name Restrictions section, click Edit.
8. Make sure that Granted is selected and click the Add button. In the dialog box that appears, make sure that Single Computer is selected.
9. Enter your system's IP address as the restricted address (you can find this by running IPCONFIG from a command prompt). Click OK to add the entry. Notice your IP address is in the list of those denied.
10. Click OK to return to the directory properties.
11. Click OK to close the Properties dialog box.
12. Switch back to the Internet Explorer and click the Refresh button. You should get an error message (`403.6 Forbidden: IP address rejected`).
13. Switch back to the Internet Service Manager, right-click the samples directory, and choose Properties.

14. On the Directory Security tab, edit the IP Address and Domain Name Restrictions settings.
15. Select your computer, and then click Remove.
16. Click OK to close the restrictions dialog box, and then click OK to close the Properties dialog box.
17. Switch to the Internet Explorer and try the Refresh button. The site should appear.

Exercise 6.2.: Creating a Certificate Request File

This exercise addresses the following Microsoft exam objectives:

- Choose a security strategy for various situations (more specifically, this subobjective: Configure SSL to provide encryption and authentication schemes).

In this exercise, you create a certificate request file (which is required to set up SSL on your site). Please *do not* send the request to VeriSign unless you intend to pay for a certificate.

1. Start the Internet Service Manager. Expand your server and locate the samples directory.
2. Right-click the samples directory and click the Directory Security tab.
3. If it's available, click the Edit button in the Secure Communications area.
4. Click the Key Manager button.
5. Under your computer name, select the WWW service.
6. From the menu choose Key, Create New Key. The Create New Key Wizard should appear.
7. On the first screen, change the file name to C:\TestKeyRq.txt. Then click Next.
8. For the key name, enter Test Key. Then enter and confirm the password as "password" and click Next.
9. Enter your own information for the Organization and Organizational Unit. Enter your computer name as the common name. Then click Next.
10. Enter your country code, state, and city on the next screen, and then click Next.
11. Enter your identification on the next screen and click Next.

12. Read the information on the last screen and click Finish.
13. When the dialog box appears telling where the file is, click OK to close it.
14. From the menu, choose Computers, Commit Changes Now. A key symbol and the name should appear beside your server.
15. Close the Key Manager.
16. From the Start menu, choose Run and enter `C:\TestKeyRq.txt`. Look at the file, and then close it.

You can now transmit this key request file to a certifying authority (such as VeriSign) so they can certify your key and generate a certificate for you. After they return the certificate and you install it, you will be able to support SSL on your sites.

TEST DAY FAST FACTS

Here are a few fast facts about this chapter that you may want to know ahead of time. Don't forget that these facts also provide great last-minute study material.

- Certificate Server can be used to issue X.509-compatible client and server certificates. In addition, you can issue S/MIME certificates and—by extending Certificate Server—your own brand of certificates.

- Symmetric cryptography is used for bulk encryption. Public cryptography is used for encrypting smaller amounts of data, such as session keys or message digests for signed documents.

- The information contained in a certificate is signed by a trusted third party called a Certificate Authority (CA). It confirms the validity of the information by its signature.

- In the current release, you can install Certificate Server only as a Root Certificate Authority. Certificate hierarchies needed to implement Non-Root CAs are not supported.

- You can enroll (issue) server certificates either by pasting the certificate request file in the Web Server Enrollment page or by creating the certificate online with Key Manager.

Day 7

Microsoft Certificate Server

by Christoph Wille and David Gulbransen

You got your feet wet with certificates in Day 6, "Internet Information Server Security." However, you dealt with the server side of certificates only—using certificates to establish SSL connections and identifying clients with their client certificates.

This chapter introduces you to Certificate Server, which lets you issue certificates yourself (client, server, and more) that can be used for the tasks described in Day 6. In this chapter, you will learn how to install and configure Certificate Server, create new server and client certificates, and master everyday administration.

Certificates are becoming more and more important to prove identity. They are at the heart of secure transactions on the Internet. Therefore, knowing about certificates is not only mandatory for the exam, but it also boosts your everyday administrator performance.

Objectives

This chapter helps you prepare for the Microsoft exam by covering the following objectives:

- Install and configure Certificate Server
- Configure Certificate Server to issue certificates

TEST DAY FAST FACTS

- Use the Administration Log Utility to revoke certificates.
- Use `CertUtil-crl-` to publish Certificate Revocation Lists (CRLs).
- To run the Certificate Authority service in stand-alone mode, issue the `CertSrv-z` command.

7.1. Certificate Basics

Before starting with Certificate Server, we will take a look at what certificates are and how they fit in with topics such as encryption and signatures.

Day 6 discussed these topics. However, because security and certificates are one of the most important topics today, a little bit of repetition won't hurt. We'll start with a section on encryption, go on to a short explanation of digital signatures, and finally see how certificates fit into that picture.

7.1.1. Encryption

Encryption is the process of turning plain text into ciphertext. The reversal of this process is called *decryption*. The two main things you need for both are a cryptographic algorithm and a key. Two main "cipher" types are in use: symmetric and public key.

A. Symmetric Cryptography

The encryption and the decryption key are the same. Therefore, this key is referred to as a "shared secret" between the two parties participating in the data transfer. The advantage of symmetric algorithms is that they are very fast. Examples of such algorithms include DES (Data Encryption Standard) and IDEA (International Data Encryption Algorithm). The disadvantage is that if one party discloses the shared secret, everyone can listen on the encrypted conversation between the two parties.

B. Public Key Cryptography

With public key cryptography, there is no shared secret. Instead of having one key, two keys are created at the same time: a private key and a public key. Both are mathematically related; it is infeasible to determine one without knowing the other. Algorithms for public key cryptography include RSA (named after the inventors Ron Rivest, Adi Shamir, and Leonard Adleman) and Diffie-Hellmann.

Usually, the public key is made public (on a key server, for example) and the private key is kept private. If the private key is used to encrypt data, only the public key can be used to decrypt the data. If the public key is used to encrypt data, only the private key can be used to decrypt it.

There is a downside to public cryptography algorithms. They are much slower than symmetric algorithms, so you wouldn't want to use them for bulk encryption.

7.1.2. Digital Signatures

The problem of encrypting data is solved. However, in today's electronic world, you also have to (for example) prove that it was you who sent a message, as well as prove that the message you sent wasn't tampered with.

Both of these problems can be solved using digital signatures. First you'll see how to ensure that no one can change a message. Then you'll see how to prove that the message is from you and that it hasn't been changed.

A. One-Way Hash

One-way hashes are generally used to determine whether a message has been tampered with. The way this works is by generating a "message digest" that is usually 120 to 160 bits long. It would be virtually impossible to produce two documents that have the very same digest. A nice characteristic of hash algorithms is that a single-bit change in a document affects about half the bits in the digest—which makes quite a difference. Algorithms that you will find in wide use include MD5 (Message Digest) and SHA-1 (Secure Hash Algorithm).

So how does this work in the real world? Assume that I want to send you a message and I want to prove that it wasn't changed by anyone. I will generate a message digest and add it to the message. You as the recipient take the digest off the message, apply the digest algorithm to the message, and compare the two digests. If they match, you know that the message hasn't been tampered with (or at least that it was changed by someone who knew the digest algorithm). However, how do you know that I (and not someone else) sent you the message?

B. Authentication

Here is where public cryptography comes into play again. If I want to prove to you that I sent you the message, I use my private key to encrypt the message digest. You as the recipient use my public key to decrypt the message digest and then perform the same steps to verify the digest. If the digests match, you know that I was the sender and that no one could have tampered with the message.

There is still one problem: Unless I personally handed you my public key, you won't know that the public key you have is actually mine. This is where certificates take over.

7.1.3. Certificates

A certificate contains information about the certificate holder and the certificate issuer, the certificate holder's public key(s), and an expiration date. The certificate also contains a digest that is signed by a Certificate Authority's (CA) private key.

If I want to send you my public key, I will send you a certificate that contains my public key. You can verify my certificate's authenticity if you trust the CA that signed my certificate. Certificate Authorities that are already very established on the Internet include VeriSign, GTE, and many others. CAs themselves use so-called self-signed certificates to verify their public keys.

So how can I apply for a certificate? First, I need to generate a public/private key pair. Next, I need to send a certificate request containing my public key to a certificate authority, which will issue a certificate to me when the CA can positively validate that it is really I who is applying for a certificate. The certificate I'll receive upon approval from the CA can then be used to verify my public key.

Who can apply for certificates, and which kinds of certificates are commonly used? The following list describes common uses of certificates:

- *Server certificates.* These are used for SSL connections between Web servers and browsers. First, the client verifies the server certificate it is presented with. Upon successful verification, it generates a session key, encrypts it with the server's public key contained in the certificate, and sends it back to the server. The server decrypts the session key with its private key, and all further SSL traffic is encrypted using a symmetric algorithm with the generated key. Server certificates are X.509 version 3 SSL-compatible.

- *Client certificates.* This kind of certificate is used to prove the identity of a client to (for example) a Web server. IIS 4.0 supports mapping client certificates to NT user accounts (even with wildcard mapping). Client certificates are X.509 version 1 and version 3 SSL-compatible.

- *S/MIME (secure/MIME) certificates.* These are used to secure e-mail traffic by encrypting and signing messages.

- *Custom certificates.* You need to write a custom policy module to issue certificates other than the previous three. An example is certificates for SET (Secure Electronic Transaction).

7.2. Usage Scenarios for Certificate Server

The preceding section gave you a quick rundown on cryptography relevant to the topic of certificates. Certificates let you authenticate clients (client certificates) and secure connections (server certificates). One important point about certificates is that the information contained in the certificate (whether only personal information or a number of public keys) is signed by a trustworthy third party, which is referred to as a Certificate Authority.

This is where Certificate Server can take over for you. It lets you play the role of a Certificate Authority and issue any kind of certificates yourself for any use you can think of. Microsoft Certificate Server is used in various scenarios. You'll read about the following scenarios in this section:

- Enterprise-level internetworking
- Partner internetworking
- Customer registration

7.2.1. Enterprise-Level Internetworking

As large organizations with regional or branch offices are faced with the problem of connecting different geographic locations, the Internet represents a cost-effective means of connecting users. Large organizations can make use of the Certificate Server to

- Provide access to corporate IS resources from different locations, ensuring that communication between offices is secure.
- Offer strategic partners or vendors access to corporate intranet resources.

Additionally, by customizing the CA's policies, you can add extra security. This includes verifying the organization or organizational unit fields of the client certificate with the server configuration before issuing it.

7.2.2. Partner Internetworking

The Certificate Server can also be used by end-users within your organization to achieve similar virtual WAN connectivity throughout the organization.

For example, employees may access corporate data from remote offices or home offices by using certificates to access corporate resources. This not only expands the capability of a virtual WAN but also gives your staff a high degree of remote, secure access to valuable business resources.

Similarly, users from partner organizations, suppliers, or sales channels can be given access to strategic information and resources on a very restricted and limited level, to ensure that they have the information they need without having unlimited access to your information service's resources.

7.2.3. Customer Registration

Finally, Certificate Server offers an excellent way to register users for services on the Internet. Because Certificate Server receives certificate requests and issues certificates over HTTP, your customers can access resources using secure browser technology, such as that found in Internet Explorer or Netscape Communicator.

Certificate Server can also be configured to check customer information against an external database before issuing a certificate. And for situations in which absolute verification is paramount, the Certificate Server can be configured to defer pending transactions until the customer can be contacted for verbal or physical verification.

By combining these features of the Certificate Server, it is possible to create a very secure, high-confidence environment in which to conduct business.

7.3. Certificate Server Features

The Microsoft Certificate Server is designed to provide for the data security needs of a wide range of organizations. With data security being an increasingly important topic among information providers and corporate entities, the Certificate Server becomes an integral part of a security system within organizations.

The Certificate Server is specifically designed to provide a means to issue, revoke, renew, and manage certificates within an organization. Although the functionality of the Certificate Server could be used for external data security, it is also focused on providing complete certificate services within an organization, without relying on an outside Certificate Authority. The following sections cover the key features of the Certificate Server and how they affect organizational use.

7.3.1. Policy Independence

When considering a request for a certificate, the Certificate Authority considers the policy established for issuing a certificate. Different policies might reflect the various concerns of the organization toward the level of security necessary and the type of data that will be affected by issuing a certificate.

For example, suppose you have three types of data consumers at your organization: leads, current customers, and vendors. You have various levels of security for each: Leads have access to publicly available information, customers have access to product documentation, and vendors have access to your inventory. Obviously the requirements for authorizing each type of consumer will vary. You may authorize leads with a simple e-mail and customers through their purchases. You might require vendors to present your Certificate Authority with physical identification. These varying authentication methods are your certificate policies.

Policies are likely to vary widely. For example, it's easier to get a grocery store frequent-customer card than it is to obtain a passport. That is why the Certificate Server supports policy independence.

The Certificate Server supports policy modules that can be written in Java, Visual Basic, or C/C++. These modules allow application developers and Certificate Authority administrators to write policies for authentication that are not married to the current version or implementation of the Certificate Server. This allows your policy to be portable to other applications and saves you time when upgrading server versions to ensure compatibility.

7.3.2. Transport Independence

Just as there are many choices for policy implementation, there are also a number of ways in which a client might want to apply for a certificate. The application requesting a certificate might be a Web browser, a mail client, or a custom-developed application at your organization. Keeping in mind the diversity of the protocols used by networking software, the Certificate Server utilizes transport independence for maximum compatibility.

The Certificate Server utilizes intermediary applications and exit module DLLs to isolate the Certificate Server functions from the protocols used by clients to request certificates. The flexibility of using intermediary applications means that you can code a customized transport for virtually any kind of client and the Certificate Server. In addition to creating a custom transport, the Certificate Server natively supports the following transports: HTTP, RPC, and disk file.

7.3.3. Standards

Microsoft Certificate Server adheres to industry-standard PKCS #10 (Public Key Cryptography Standards) requests and issues X.509 version 1.0 and 3.0 certificates to ensure maximum compatibility. Additionally, through the use of custom exit modules, the Certificate Server can be extended and modified to write certificates to virtually any database or directory service.

7.3.4. Key Management

At the heart of any certificate system is key management. Any certificates issued by a Certificate Authority are only as secure as the CA's encryption keys. Therefore, it is essential that the CA's private keys remain just that.

The Certificate Server enacts several safeguards to ensure that the private keys are not compromised by anyone, well-meaning or not. The Certificate Server makes use of the Microsoft CryptoAPI to separate key management from certificate management, removing the Certificate Server from a position in which it could compromise keys. Additionally, due to the extensibility of the CryptoAPI, external software modules or encryption engines can be used to fortify the strength of key management. This allows the Certificate Server to be customized for a variety of applications, depending on the key management strength needed by an organization.

7.3.5. Reliability

The Certificate Server builds on many features of Windows NT to achieve a high level of reliability. By relying on the NTFS file system and the Windows NT memory model, the Certificate Server is prevented from being corrupted by other Windows applications. Windows NT is also United States Government C2 certified for security.

7.3.6. Scalability

The Certificate Server relies on the Windows NT architecture for a great deal of flexibility and scalability in implementation from small to very large organizations. By making use of the Certificate Authority hierarchy, it is possible to deploy a very complex and large structure of Certificate Servers on an enterprise level.

7.4. Installing and Configuring Certificate Server

Certificate Server is installed as part of the Windows NT Option Pack. You can install two different kinds of Certificate Authorities with Certificate Server:

- Root CA
- Non-Root CA

Which installation option you choose depends on whether you want to integrate in an existing certification hierarchy. If you want to provide certificates for your company's purposes only, the Root CA option is the way to go during installation and configuration. If you need to be integrated in a certification hierarchy, your choice will be Non-Root CA.

All of the important configuration choices are set during initial installation. These are covered in the appropriate sections.

> **Note:** The current release of Certificate Server doesn't let you install on a Backup Domain Controller.

Right after you have finished installation, you should test your server configuration. However, because your CA is new, no one knows how to trust you and your certificates. To achieve that trust, the clients need to install your CA's certificate that was generated during the initial configuration process. This installation step repeats for every client that needs to verify certificates issued by your CA. Although this is not an installation or configuration step for the Certificate Server itself, it is a mandatory installation step for every client—it is an important client-side configuration step.

7.4.1. Installing (and Configuring) a Root CA

If you don't want to participate in a CA hierarchy—which is most likely the case if you use certificates only for your organization's purposes—you will want to install Certificate Server as a Root CA.

The following steps show you how to install a Root CA, which is the default installation choice of Certificate Server:

1. Launch the Option Pack Setup from the Option Pack CD-ROM. When the installer is running, choose a custom installation. If you have already installed portions of the IIS Server, click Add/Remove.

2. From the Subcomponents list, select Certificate Server and mark it for installation. You can choose from several subcomponents, as shown in Figure 7.1.

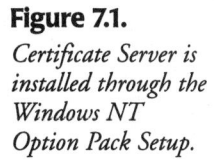

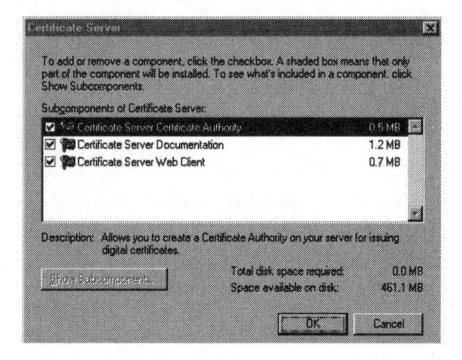

Figure 7.1.
Certificate Server is installed through the Windows NT Option Pack Setup.

Day 7: Microsoft Certificate Server

3. Click Next to continue. You will see a couple of screens with options for IIS and the Transaction Server. If you don't have any special configurations for IIS or the transaction server, just accept the defaults for these screens.

> **Note:** If you have already installed IIS, you won't see the IIS screens or the Transaction Server screens. You can simply proceed with the Certificate Server installation.

4. In the first Certificate Server Setup screen, shown in Figure 7.2, you are asked to provide various directory locations. These include the shared folder (hosts the configuration file CertSrv.txt, the CA signature, and key exchange certificates, as well as the CA certificate list Web page), the database, and the log. The Shared Folder location is initially left blank, so you need to specify it. I recommend creating a folder named CertShare in the %systemroot% directory, because by default the database and the log directory are contained in the same location. This will help you locate all important information quickly and easily.

Figure 7.2.

In the first Certificate Server Setup screen, you specify the shared folder, as well as the log and database directories.

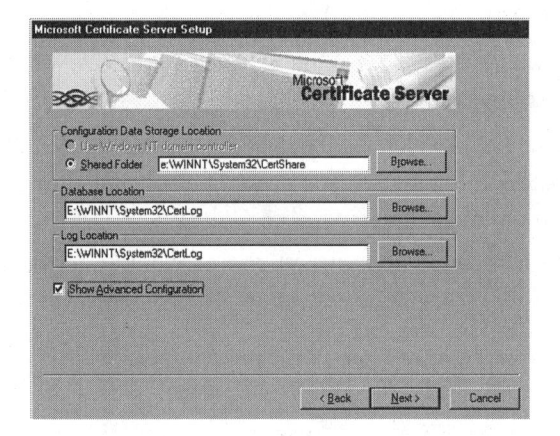

> **Note:** In this release of Certificate Server, the shared folder must reside on the local machine. You can't use network shares.

7.4. Installing and Configuring Certificate Server 231

If you check the Show Advanced Configuration checkbox, you will see an additional setup screen. If you decide not to perform any advanced configuration, you can skip to step 6.

5. In the advanced configuration dialog box, shown in Figure 7.3, you can choose which cryptographic service provider (CSP) you want to use. In addition, you can choose a different hashing algorithm and decide if you want to use existing keys. In the Certificate Authority Hierarchy frame, you can choose whether you want to install a Root CA or a Non-Root CA. The default is Root CA.

Figure 7.3.
Certificate Server offers advanced configuration settings.

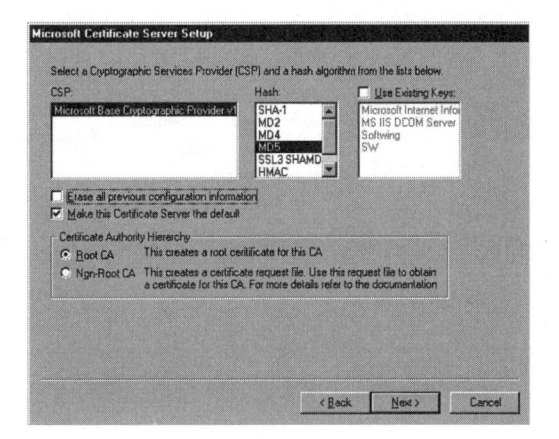

6. The final step of Certificate Server setup is to create the certificate for the Root CA, for which you must enter identifying information (see Figure 7.4). The Configuration Wizard takes care of all the other necessary steps, such as creating a private/public key pair, creating the self-signed root certificate, and writing the configuration file, CA signature, and key exchange files to the shared folder.

> **Note**
> Certificate Server requires that the Subject Common Name specified in this step be limited to the following characters:
>
> a to z
> A to Z
> 0 to 9
> {space}
> \ ( ) + - . / : = ?

continues

> It is generally recommended for maximum compatibility that you use only the following characters in a certificate request, an issued certificate, and the Certificate Server itself:
>
> a to z
> A to Z
> 0 to 9
> {space}
> ( ) + - . / : = ?

Figure 7.4.
The final step of Certificate Server setup calls for identification information.

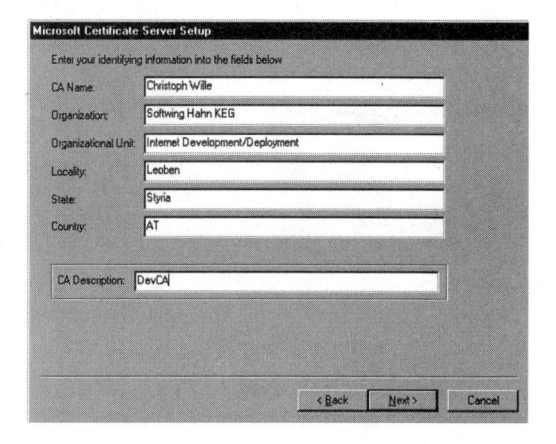

7. Internet Information Server setup will end with the copying of files and the configuration of your server.

Installing and configuring a Root CA is very straightforward. After installation is complete, you can immediately start issuing certificates. This topic is discussed later.

7.4.2. Installing a Non-Root CA

The main difference in the installation process between a Root CA and a Non-Root CA is that Setup doesn't create a self-signed certificate for your server. Instead, a certificate request file is generated, and you have to send it to a CA to have it signed. The final step is then installing this certificate so that you can start issuing certificates yourself. With this certificate, you are then embedded in a certificate hierarchy. For example, if your CA certificate is signed by VeriSign, you are located in the CA hierarchy below VeriSign.

> **Note:** Installing a Non-Root CA requires that you install a certificate authority hierarchy, which is not supported in the current release of Certificate Server. Therefore, you can't install Non-Root CAs with the current version.

7.4.3. Installing the Certificate Authority Certificate

If you start issuing certificates right now, no one can verify that the certificates are in fact valid—your CA is not trusted. To verify certificates and the digital signature of your CA on a certificate, users must obtain your CA's certificate, which contains (among other things) your CA's public key. With this public key, the digital signatures on certificates created with your CA's private key can be verified.

You need to install the CA certificate on both client computers and servers where you will verify certificates issued by your CA. For the client side, the CA's certificate is needed to verify a server certificate for establishing an SSL connection. On the server side, you need the CA's certificate to verify client certificates presented as logon credentials.

The following steps show you how to install the newly created CA's certificate on a computer that needs to trust the new CA (such as a client computer that connects to an SSL-enabled site that uses a certificate from this CA):

1. Open Internet Explorer and navigate to `http://caserver/CertSrv/CertEnroll`. (Replace *caserver* with the fully qualified domain name (FQDN) of your certificate server.) You see the Certificate Enrollment Tools page, shown in Figure 7.5.

2. Follow the link Install Certificate Authority Certificates. You see a list of certificates that are available on this server, as shown in Figure 7.6.

3. To install the certificate, click Certificate for.... The File Download dialog box appears. Choose to open the file from the current location rather than downloading it.

4. The New Site Certificate dialog box, shown in Figure 7.7, appears. By default, the certificate is enabled and can be used for network client authentication, network server authentication, secure e-mail, and software publishing. Click the View Certificate button to see details about the certificate.

Figure 7.5.
You install and request certificates using the Certificate Enrollment Tools page.

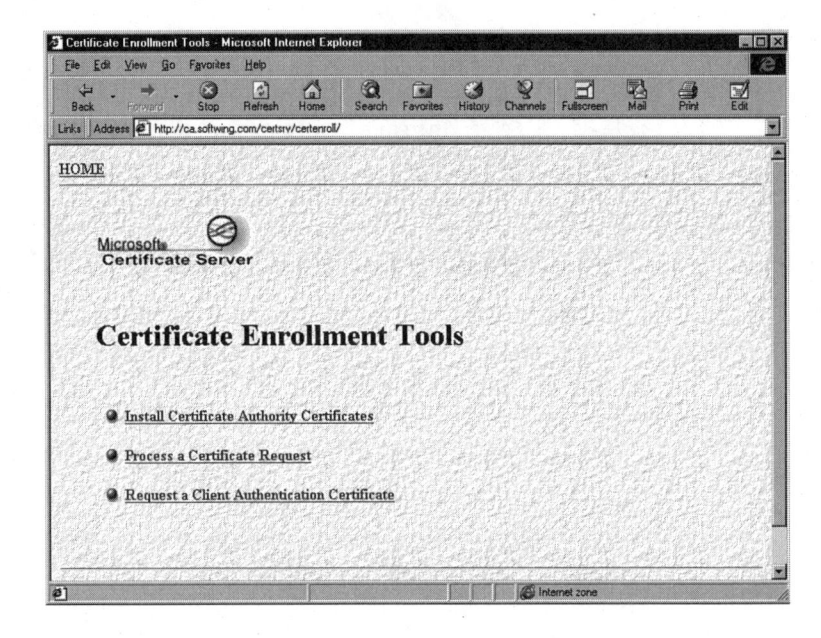

Figure 7.6.
You install the CA certificate by clicking the Certificate for... link.

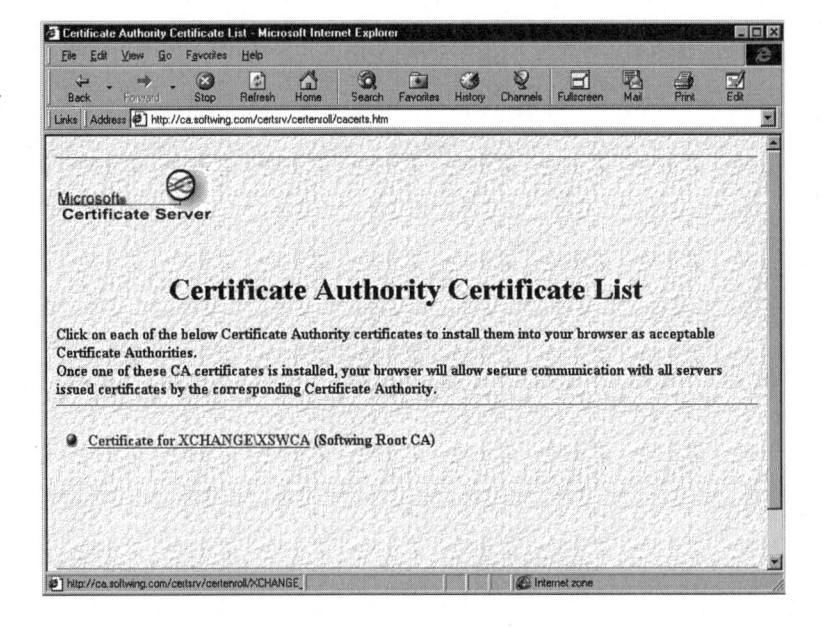

7.4. Installing and Configuring Certificate Server

Figure 7.7.
You specify certificate usage in the New Site Certificate dialog box.

5. Click OK to install the certificate. As shown in Figure 7.8, you are asked whether you really want to add the new certificate to the root store. Click Yes.

Figure 7.8.
Before IE installs the certificate, you are asked again if you really want to do so.

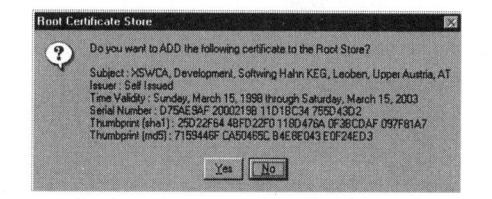

6. Now the CA's certificate is installed and ready to use. If you need to view installed CA certificates, select View | Internet Options. Choose the Content tab. In the Certificates frame, click the Authorities button. You see a list of certificates arranged by usage type, as shown in Figure 7.9. You can disable a CA by simply removing the check mark next to its name.

Figure 7.9.
You use Internet Explorer to view installed certificates.

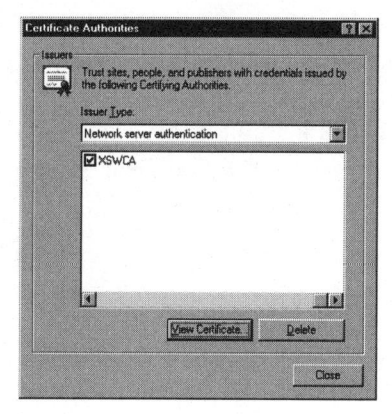

7. To be able to use the new certificate for the Web server, you need to stop and restart the Web service.

Before you can use any certificates issued by a CA, you need to install the CA certificate in order to be able to verify the certificates issued by that CA (remember, certificates are signed documents). An important point to remember is that both Internet Explorer and IIS use the same storage location for CA certificates.

7.5. Enrolling Certificates

You have finished all the preliminary steps of installing and configuring Certificate Server, as well as installing the CA certificate. Now you can start issuing your own certificates with Certificate Server. The following sections deal with different ways to enroll certificates, on both the server and the client side:

- Web Server Enrollment Page
- Web Server Enrollment via Key Manager
- Client Enrollment

> **Note:** The terms *issue* and *enroll* are used interchangeably in this discussion.

7.5.1. Web Server Enrollment Page

Web server certificates are used to set up SSL connections with clients to ensure encrypted traffic across the Internet. Essentially, the certificate contains the same information you entered for the CA certificate, as well as the server's public key, which is used by the client to send the session encryption key back to the server.

If you completed the CA certificate installation tutorial in Day 6, "Internet Information Server Security," you are already familiar with obtaining a certificate from a CA such as VeriSign. In this section, you will obtain the certificate from your newly created CA using the same mechanism: a request file and a Web enrollment form.

The following steps show you how to create a new certificate for your Web server that you can use to SSL-secure a Web site. You will create a certificate request and then use the Web Server Enrollment Page to acquire the new certificate.

7.5. Enrolling Certificates 237

1. Open Internet Service Manager, and then open the Key Manager using its toolbar button.
2. Select the WWW subtree and then select Key | Create New Key. You see the first dialog box of the Create New Key wizard, as shown in Figure 7.10. If you have already installed the CA certificate, the online authority option will be selected by default. Choose to put the key request in a file instead. Click Next to start the information-gathering process.

Figure 7.10.

Choose to put the request in a file.

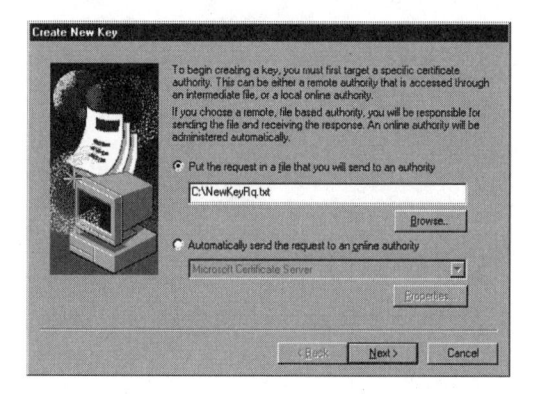

3. In the second step, you are asked for the key name, password, and key length, as shown in Figure 7.11. Remember the password, because you will need it for installing the certificate as well as restoring the server. Click Next to continue.

Figure 7.11.

You enter the key name, password, and key length in the second step.

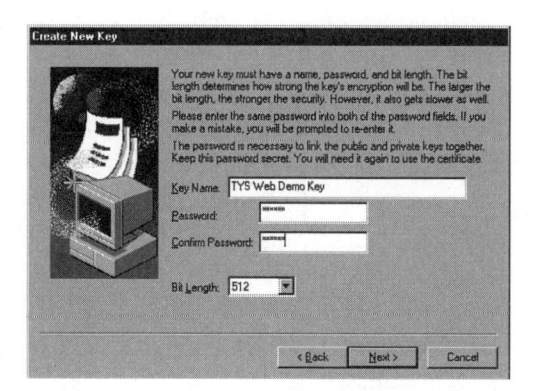

4. As shown in Figure 7.12, you need to enter some information about your company (the organization name and the organizational unit). You also need to enter the common name of your server that will be using the key certificate.

Day 7: Microsoft Certificate Server

The common name is the fully qualified domain name (FQDN) of your server when a DNS lookup is performed. This information is used by clients to verify the identity of your site.

Figure 7.12.
When providing the common name, keep in mind that clients use it to identify the site.

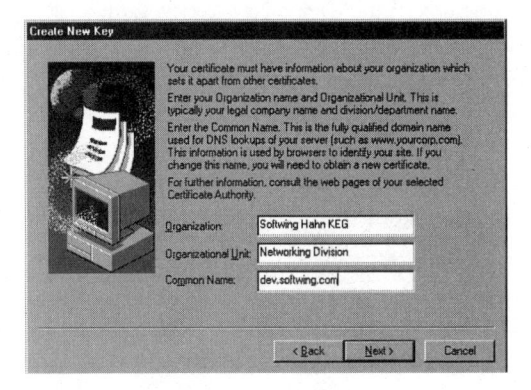

> **Warning**
>
> If you change the common name of your server, you will also need to obtain a new certificate.

5. Click Next to proceed to step 4. Here you enter the country code, state/province, and city/locality. You need to use the two-letter ISO country codes. Click Next to continue.

6. The final information-gathering screen asks you for some information about the administrator (you) in case the certificate authority needs to contact you.

7. Click Next to reach the final screen. It tells you what steps you need to take next. Click Finish to generate the key request file. After the file has been generated, the new (invalid) key is added to the WWW tree, as shown in Figure 7.13.

8. To obtain the certificate for the key you just generated, open Internet Explorer on the server computer you are running Key Manager on and navigate to `http://caserver/certsrv/certenroll`. (Replace *caserver* with the FQDN of your certificate server.)

9. On the Certificate Enrollment Tools page, select Process a Certificate Request. You see the Web Server Enrollment page, shown in Figure 7.14. It consists of a text field and a Submit Request button. Open the key request file (the one you created in step 2) and copy the contents to the Clipboard. Switch to Internet

7.5 Enrolling Certificates | 239

Explorer and paste the request into the text field. When done, click the Submit Request button so that Certificate Server can process your request.

Figure 7.13.
You can't use the key immediately, because it isn't valid. A CA must sign it, and then it becomes a certificate.

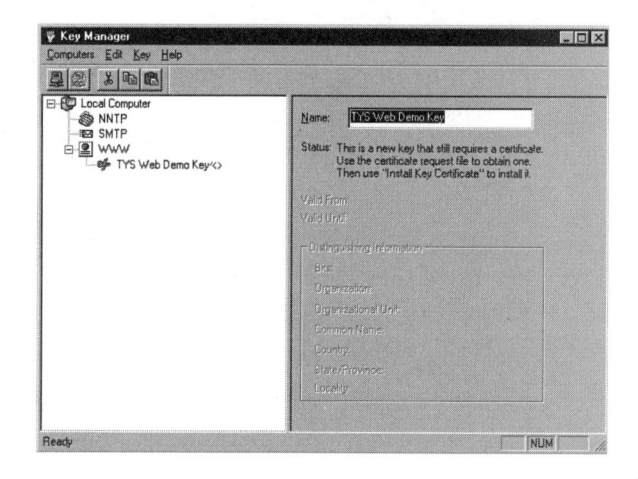

Figure 7.14.
You use the Web Server Enrollment page to request a server certificate.

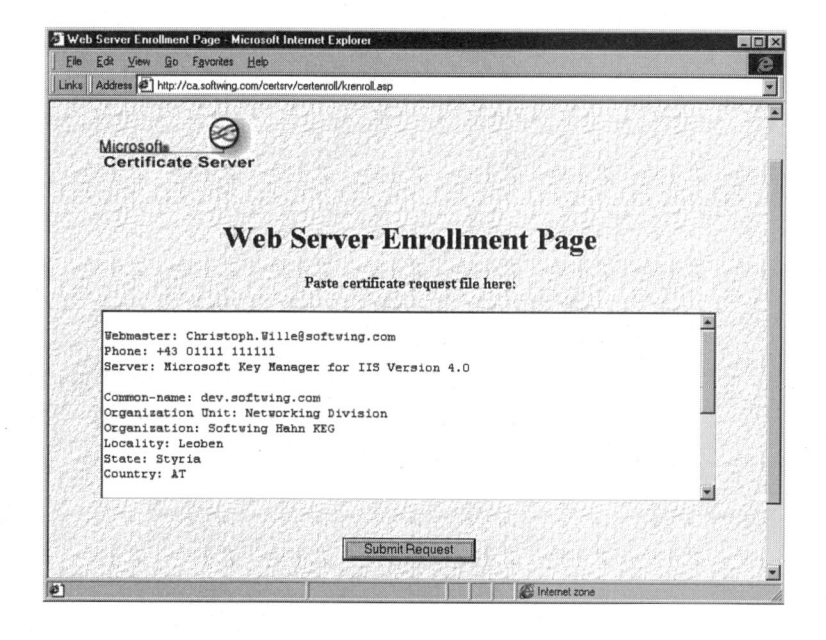

10. After your certificate request has been processed, you see the Certificate Download page, as shown in Figure 7.15. Instead of downloading the CA's certificate, choose to save the certificate to a file.

Figure 7.15.

After your certificate request has been processed, you see the Certificate Download page.

11. Now you have your certificate. The last thing left to do is install this certificate for use on your server. Switch back to Key Manager, right-click the key name, and select Install Key Certificate.

12. You are prompted for the filename of the certificate. Browse to the file you downloaded in step 10.

13. Before installing the certificate, you are prompted for the password used to create the request. Enter the password and continue.

14. Another mandatory step before the certificate is activated is that you specify the server bindings (see Figure 7.16). Enter the IP address (the one for the common name you entered) and port number (for SSL, this is 443) that the certificate is bound to.

Figure 7.16.

Specifying the server bindings.

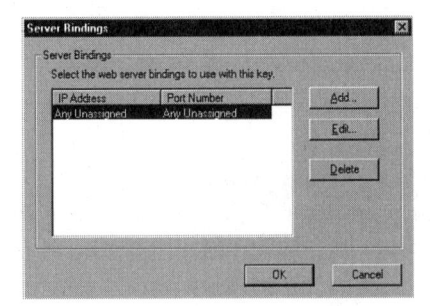

15. Now the key is complete and usable (see Figure 7.17). Commit the changes you made by selecting Computers | Commit Changes Now.

Figure 7.17.
Commit the changes to the server keys so that you can start using the new key.

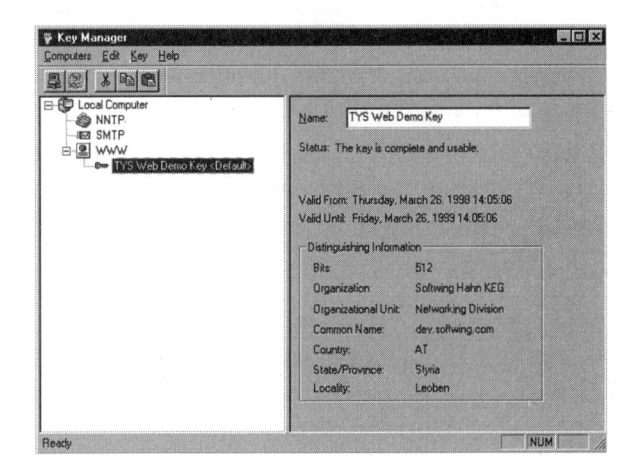

You have walked through all the steps needed to create and activate a key that can be used for SSL encryption. The steps listed here apply not only to Certificate Server, but also to applying for a certificate at other authorities (although differences are likely in steps 8, 9, and 10). The next section deals with creating a certificate automatically with Certificate Server.

7.5.2. Web Server Enrollment Via Key Manager

If you want to shorten the process of acquiring a certificate with your CA, you can use Key Manager to communicate directly with online authorities to apply for and acquire a new certificate. Certificate Server implements the functionality of an online authority that Key Manager can communicate with. This will shorten the process of obtaining a server certificate substantially. However, there are times when you still might want to restrict the process of obtaining a certificate to the use of request files. For example, CAs that are heavily secured behind a firewall or some kind of enrollment process might not be supported by the standard online authority mechanism.

The following steps show you how to create a new certificate for your Web server that you can use to SSL-secure a Web site. In contrast to the preceding tutorial, you will use Certificate Server as an online authority to apply for a certificate.

1. Open Internet Service Manager, and then open the Key Manager by using its toolbar button.
2. Select the WWW subtree and then select Key | Create New Key. You see the first dialog box of the Create New Key wizard. If you have already installed the CA certificate, the online authority option will be selected by default. Stick with this setting and click Next.
3. In the second step, you are asked for the key name, password, and key length. Be sure to remember the password! Click Next to continue.
4. Now you need to enter your organization name and organizational unit. You also need to enter the common name of your server that will be using the key certificate. The common name is the fully qualified domain name (FQDN) of your server when a DNS lookup is performed. This information is used by clients to verify the identity of your site.

> **Warning**
> Again, if you change the common name of your server, you will also need to obtain a new certificate.

5. Click Next to proceed. Here you enter the country code, state/province, and city/locality. You need to use the two-letter ISO country codes.
6. Click Finish to start creating the key.
7. The new key is generated automatically (Key Manager contacts the Certificate Server) and added to the WWW tree.
8. The last step before the certificate is activated is to specify the server bindings. Enter the IP address (the one for the common name you entered) and port number (for SSL, this is 443) that the certificate is bound to.
9. Now the key is complete and usable. Commit the changes you made by selecting Computers | Commit Changes Now.

This tutorial walked you through all the steps needed to create and activate a key that can be used for SSL encryption using an online authority—which in this case was Certificate Server. However, the steps described here apply not only to Certificate Server, but also to applying for a certificate at other online authorities (except for a difference in step 6).

7.5.3. Client Enrollment

So far, we have covered only the ways in which you enroll a server certificate. Now we will switch gears and learn about issuing client certificates. Because there are differences in procedures for enrolling certificates depending on browser type, two sections are dedicated to the two big players:

- Microsoft Internet Explorer
- Netscape Navigator

A. Using Microsoft Internet Explorer

This section looks at using Internet Explorer to generate a client certificate and store it for later use on the client computer. The newly generated client certificate can then be used for Web sites that require you to have a client certificate for authentication.

To obtain a client certificate using Internet Explorer 4, follow these steps on a client computer (you need to have installed the CA's certificate up front):

1. Open Internet Explorer on the client computer that you want to use the client certificate for that you are creating in this tutorial. Navigate to `http://caserver/CertSrv/CertEnroll`. (Replace *caserver* with the FQDN of your certificate server.) You see the Certificate Enrollment Tools page.

2. Follow the link Request a Client Authentication Certificate. You see the Certificate Enrollment form, shown in Figure 7.18. You must enter information that is contained in the client certificate, including the individual's name, department, organization, city, state, country, and e-mail address. For this tutorial, enter information about yourself. (When you use Certificate Server in the real world, clients will enter their personal information here.)

3. Click the Submit Request button to process the new certificate request. You can use the Advanced button to open the Advanced Settings page, shown in Figure 7.19. Here you can change the hash algorithm, the cryptography service provider (CSP), the usage of the certificate, and other properties.

4. When the certificate has been generated successfully, you see the Certificate Download page, shown in Figure 7.20. Click the Download button to install the client certificate.

5. Verify the client certificate by selecting View | Internet Options. Choose the Content tab and click the Personal button in the Certificates frame. You see a list of installed client certificates. Click View Certificate to get more information about a certificate, as shown in Figure 7.21.

Figure 7.18.
You enroll a new client certificate on the Certificate Enrollment form.

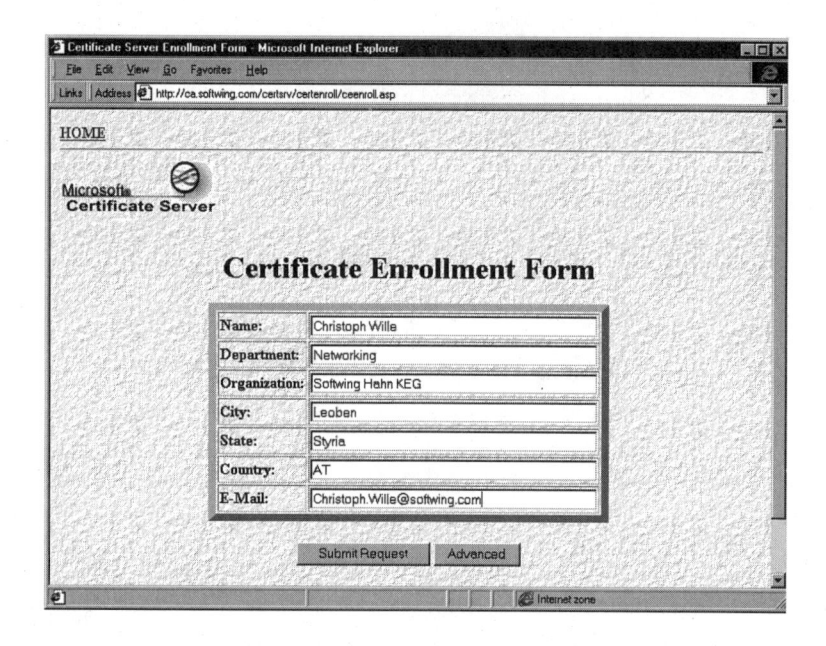

Figure 7.19.
You can set advanced settings for a certificate.

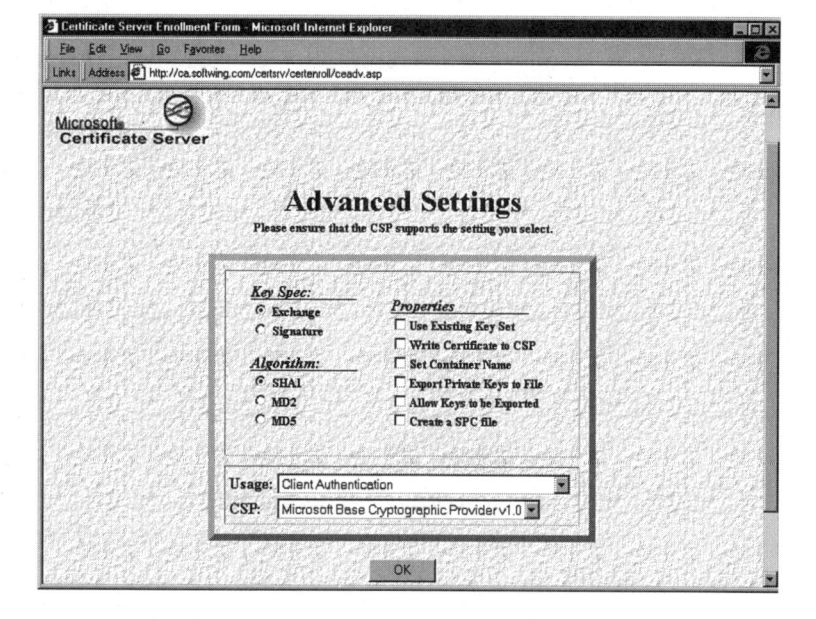

Figure 7.20.
The client certificate has been successfully installed.

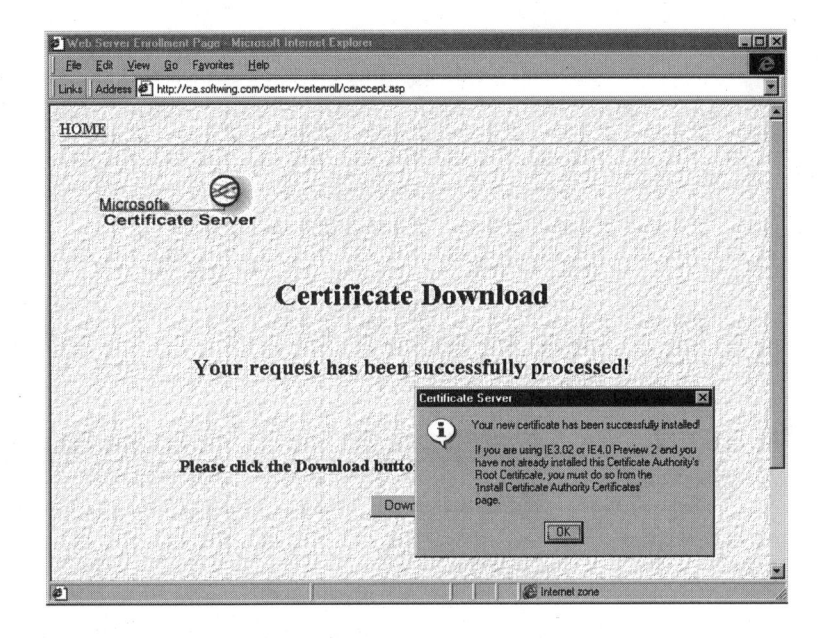

Figure 7.21.
The Properties dialog box lets you view information about an installed client certificate.

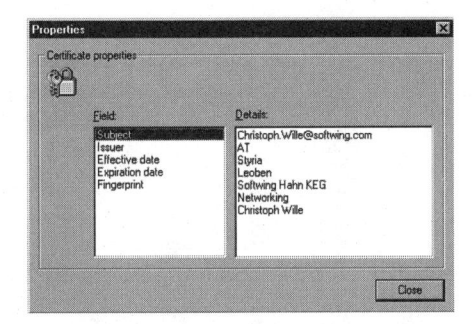

Creating and installing a client certificate is easy. You might be wondering if you are the only one who can access your certificate. You are, because all certificates are encrypted and can be accessed only by the owner, even if several users share a single computer.

B. Using Netscape Navigator

Client certificates are used with Netscape Navigator the same way they are used with Internet Explorer. I've devoted an entire section to Navigator because certificate enrollment is handled differently.

Day 7: Microsoft Certificate Server

To enroll a certificate for yourself (clients will use the same procedure or one that you customize for them) using Netscape Navigator 3 on a client computer, follow these steps:

1. Open Netscape Navigator and navigate to `http://caserver/CertSrv/CertEnroll`. (Replace *caserver* with the FQDN of your certificate server.) You see the Certificate Enrollment Tools page.
2. Follow the link Request a Client Authentication Certificate. You see the Certificate Enrollment form, shown in Figure 7.22. Enter your name, department, organization, city, state, country, and e-mail address. You are also asked to define the key length for your private key.

Figure 7.22.
Netscape Navigator can also be used to enroll a client certificate.

3. You see a screen informing you that Navigator is about to create a private key for you. Click OK.
4. In the next step, Navigator informs you that you are about to download a certificate from the certificate server. Click Next to proceed.
5. You see information about the certificate that was generated. You can click the More Info button to show all fields in the certificate. Click Next.
6. Navigator proposes a display name for the certificate that is composed of the name and the organization. Change the name as needed, and click Next.

7. The last step informs you of the successful installation of the certificate. Click Finish to return to the browser window.

8. Verify the installed certificate by selecting Options | Security Settings. Choose the Personal Certificates tab, shown in Figure 7.23, and select the certificate you want to view. If you want to view more information about the certificate, click the More Info button.

Figure 7.23.
Netscape Navigator displays the installed certificates.

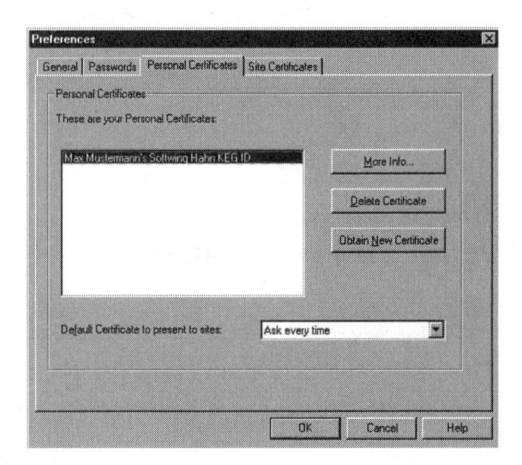

You perform more steps (client-side) when installing a client certificate when using Netscape Navigator. However, it is equally easy and straightforward.

7.6. Administering Certificate Server

In this section we'll take a tour of the most important HTML-based administration screens, server maintenance procedures, and command-line utilities used to manage the Certificate Server. The following topics are covered:

- The Certificate Log Administration utility
- The Certificate Server Queue Administration utility
- Revoking certificates
- Backing up and restoring configuration
- Replacing damaged or missing CA certificates
- Command-line utilities

7.6.1. The Certificate Log Administration Utility

The Certificate Log Administration utility, shown in Figure 7.24, lets you view all the certificates that were issued on that server. The information presented is retrieved from the certsrv.mdb database, which is located in the %systemroot%\CertLog directory. You can view the Log Administration utility page by pointing your browser to http://caserver/CertSrv/ (replace *caserver* with your CA's FQDN) and following the link to the Log Administration utility page.

Figure 7.24.

The Certificate Log Administration Utility lets you view all the certificates that were issued on that server.

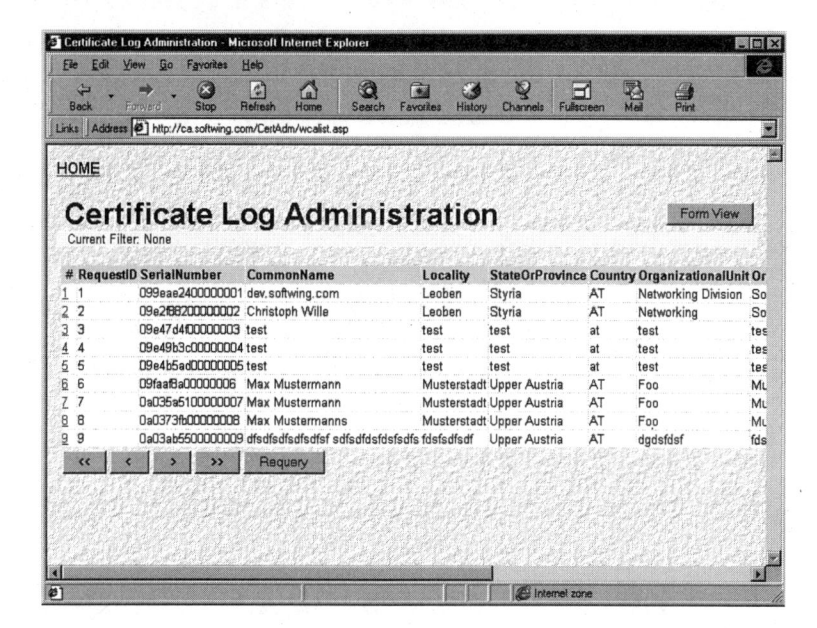

You are not limited to viewing the information in list view only. You can also view each certificate in form view, as shown in Figure 7.25. One way to narrow down the number of certificates viewed is to use filters. You can reach the Filter feature only from Form view, not from List view.

Note that you can only view information here—you can't edit it (because these certificates have already been issued). Although it might seem that with this utility you are only allowed to administer Certificate Server in the capacity of gathering information, this utility also lets you revoke certificates. (This topic is covered in section 7.6.3.)

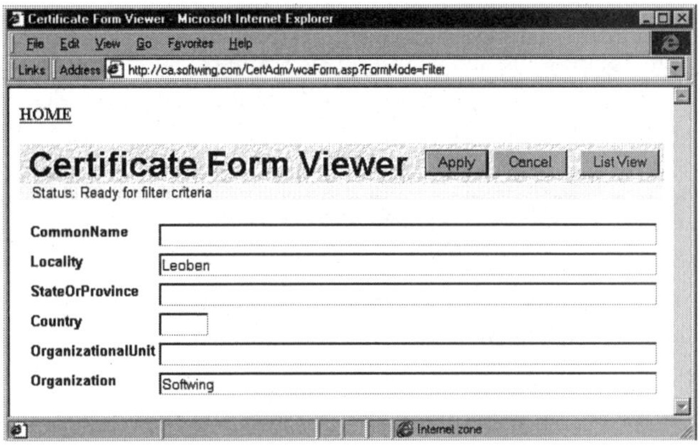

Figure 7.25.
Use filters to narrow down the number of certificates viewed.

7.6.2. The Certificate Server Queue Administration Utility

If you need to manage requests in the server queue, the Certificate Server Queue Administration utility is your single stop (see Figure 7.26). To view the Queue Administration Utility page, point your browser to `http://caserver/CertSrv/` (replace *caserver* with your CA's FQDN) and follow the link to the Administration Queue Utility page.

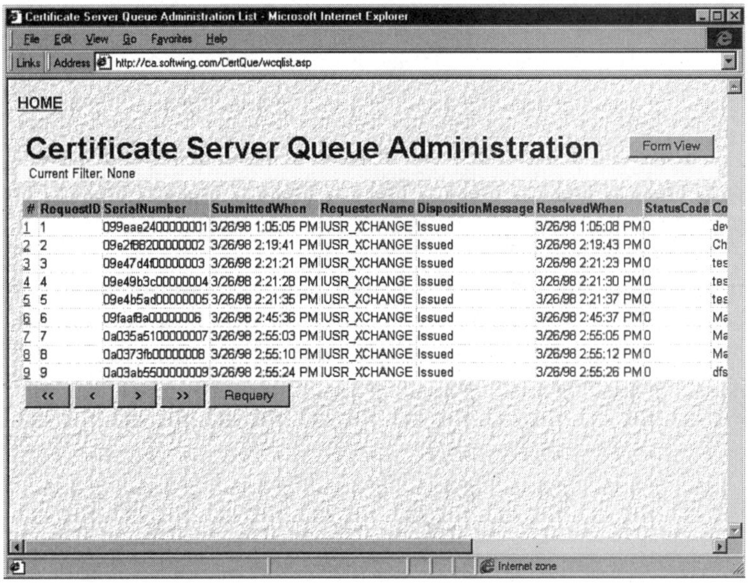

Figure 7.26.
Use the Queue Administration utility to manage requests in the server queue.

The sixth column shows the disposition message, which tells you whether a certificate is already issued or still queued. You can also view the queue on a per-request basis, as well as apply filtering to the queue. You are allowed to administer Certificate Server with this utility only in the capacity of gathering information.

7.6.3. Revoking Certificates

Certificate Server itself does not perform any user validation or certificate verification. However, many servers and clients rely on the validity of certificates issued by that server. The question is how to invalidate a certificate and prohibit further use of it. Certainly it is not possible to simply delete the certificate on the Certificate Server as you would with user accounts. No one would know that the certificate is no longer valid, because it would still have a valid digital signature from your CA.

The way to achieve the invalidation of a certificate is to revoke it on the server and then publish a list of revoked certificates—the certificate revocation list (CRL). This list can then be used by clients that rely on certificates issued by your CA to check for invalid certificates.

The following steps show you how to revoke a certificate and then publish the CRL. To complete these steps, you must be logged on locally to your certificate server.

1. Open Internet Explorer and navigate to http://caserver/certsrv. (Change *caserver* to the FQDN of your certificate server.) Open the Certificate Log Administration utility.

2. You see a list view of certificates issued by that certificate server. Select the one you want to revoke, and click the # link to open it in form view, as shown in Figure 7.27.

3. To revoke the certificate, click the Revoke button. If the RevokedWhen date (the last item in the form) doesn't display a date, requery the form to see all database updates.

4. The next step is to create the certificate revocation list. From the Certificate Server program group, choose Generate New Certificate Revocation List, or give the following command:

```
CertUtil -crl
```

5. You need to publish the CRL. Because step 4 generated the CRL in the default Web location, users relying on your CA certificates can now easily download the CRL from http://caserver/certsrv/certenroll/caname.crl (replace *caserver* with the FQDN of your certificate server and replace *caname* with your CA's name).

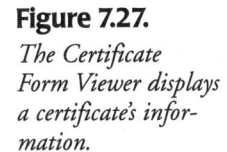

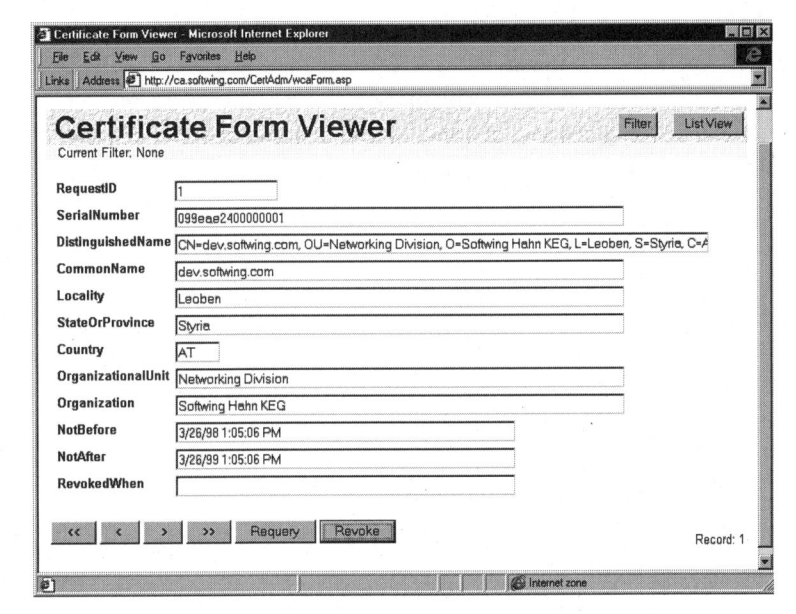

Figure 7.27.
The Certificate Form Viewer displays a certificate's information.

Because certificates are valid until they expire, the only way to invalidate them is by revoking them at the CA and publishing a CRL. Everyone relying on certificates from that CA for user validation must regularly obtain the CRL to be able to identify revoked certificates when presented with one.

7.6.4. Backing Up and Restoring Configuration

As with any application that your organization relies on, the Certificate Server can and should be backed up so that in the event of an accident you can recover your configuration information and installed certificates. The process of backing up the Certificate Server is quite simple. You will need four components to back up and correctly recover your Certificate Server installation:

- *The shared folder and its contents.* The shared folder that you specified during the initial configuration will contain the CertSrv.txt configuration file, your CA certificates, and some other miscellaneous HTML/GIF support files. Since this folder contains your CA certificates and the CertSrv.txt file, it is essential that you back up the entire folder.

- *The CertLog directory.* This directory should be located in C:\WINNT\System32. It contains the Certificate Server's main database file, CertSrv.mdb.

- *The CertSrv directory.* This should also be located in C:\WINNT\System32. It contains the Active Server Pages and HTML files that are used to administer, configure, and manage your Certificate Server.
- *The Registry.* It's not a bad idea to have a backup of your Registry regardless, but you will need the current Registry entries in order to recover your installation.

With those files and directories backed up, you should have the information you need to recover your current Certificate Server in the event that something goes wrong, such as a hard disk failure or some other hardware incident. Keep in mind, though, that if you install new certificates, revoke certificates, and so on, you will need to update the backup files for your server. You might want to institute a policy of backing up the Certificate Server nightly, or at another regular interval that fits your organizational needs.

Recovering your Certificate Server is a very straightforward process:

1. Upon recovering your system or correcting the problem that caused your Certificate Server to fail, reinstall the Certificate Server using the Windows NT 4.0 Option Pack media. You need to cancel the Configuration Wizard during the installation.
2. Once the Certificate Server has been installed, reinstall the Registry, the shared folder files, and the CertLog directory.

That's it. Now the original configuration of your Certificate Server is restored.

7.6.5. Replacing Damaged or Missing CA Certificates

The Certificate Authority certificates for your Certificate Server are located in the shared folder that you specified during the initial installation of the Certificate Server. Although these files can be backed up, simply reinstalling old copies of the CA certificates will cause the Certificate Server to malfunction.

However, you can use the Certificate Server command-line program CertUtil to restore your certificates from the certificate store. Here is the syntax:

```
CertUtil -config Configuration -ca.ExchangeFile.crt
```

Two files are associated with the CA certificate: the Exchange File and the Signature. Both of these files need to be recovered in order to correctly restore your CA certificate. Therefore, you will need to use CertUtil twice: once for the Exchange file, and once for the Signature:

```
CertUtil -config Configuration -ca.exchange ExchangeFile.crt
CertUtil -config Configuration -ca.signature SignatureFile.crt
```

`Configuration` is the server name followed by the Certificate Authority name. You can use the CertUtil command

```
CertUtil -getconfig
```

to obtain the configuration for your server. The Exchange file and Signature filenames need to be the same as the names of your original .crt files.

7.6.6. Command-Line Utilities

Three primary command-line executables control the Certificate Servers features:

- CertUtil
- CertReq
- CertHier

Each of these executables can be accessed via the command line, although the functionality of several of them can also be achieved through the Web interface. Access via a command line allows easier access to scripting and automated control of the Certificate Server and can prove useful for emergency recovery as well.

In addition to these three command-line utilities, the service itself can be run in debugging mode to determine problems through the use of CertSrv.

A. CertUtil

Of all the command-line utilities designed to be used with the Certificate Server, CertUtil is one of the most useful and powerful. The certutil.exe file can be used to

- Dump Certificate Server configuration information:

```
CertUtil -dump
```

- Revoke certificates:

```
CertUtil -revoke Serialnumber
```

- Publish CRLs:

```
CertUtil -crl -
```

- Get the CA configuration string:

```
CertUtil -getconfig
```

- Resubmit or deny pending requests:

```
CertUtil -resubmit RequestId
```

- Dump a KeyGen file:

```
CertUtil -keygen KeyGenFile
```

> **Note:** The usage scenarios presented here are the most common ones. There are more command-line parameters and command options that you can use with CertUtil. Refer to the Command Line Summary topic in the NT Option Pack documentation for exhaustive coverage of these.

B. CertReq

The CertReq utility is used to submit certificate requests to Certificate Server. CertReq can handle three tasks:

- Submitting a certificate request file to Certificate Server
- Submitting a KeyGen input file to Certificate Server
- Resubmitting a pending certificate request to Certificate Server

There are two ways to invoke CertReq: via the Process Certificate Request File command in the Certificate Server program group, or via the command line. If you choose the first way, you will be prompted for the request file (source) location and the certificate file (destination) location. From the command line, you would issue the following command to process a certificate request:

```
CertReq ReqFile CertFile
```

> **Note:** There are more command-line parameters and command options that you can use with CertReq. Refer to the Command Line Summary topic in the NT Option Pack documentation for exhaustive coverage of these.

C. CertHier

This utility is used to complete installation of Non-Root CAs. It takes no command-line parameters and must be run after you have applied for and received the server certificate.

7.6. Administering Certificate Server | 255

> **Note:** In this release of Certificate Server, certificate hierarchies aren't supported, so you can't create Non-Root CAs.

D. CertSrv

The server engine that is executed when the Certificate Authority service is run is located in the CertSrv.exe executable. This executable should generally be set to start automatically as a service through the Services application in Control Panel.

However, you can either start (or stop) the Certificate Authority service through Control Panel or through the command line with the following syntax:

```
net start "Certificate Authority"
```

or

```
net start CertSvc
```

Both commands will start the Certificate Authority service.

Another option is offered with the certsrv.exe executable. It lets you start the service manually to run within a console window. This capability lets you debug possible installation and configuration problems by sending all the logging and error information to the console window rather than a log file. To invoke the Certificate Authority service in debugging mode, use the -z flag:

```
certsrv -z
```

This causes the service to run in stand-alone mode, for troubleshooting your Certificate Server.

Day 7: Microsoft Certificate Server

Lab

This lab consists of review questions pertaining to this chapter and provides an opportunity for you to use walk-through exercises to apply the knowledge that you've gained.

Questions

1. Which of the following statements about public key cryptography are correct?
   A. Public key cryptography uses a symmetric algorithm.
   B. Public key cryptography is fast.
   C. Public key cryptography uses a public/private key pair.
   D. Public key cryptography is slower than symmetric ciphers.

2. Which of the following certificates can be issued by Certificate Server?
   A. X.509 version 1-compatible server certificates
   B. X.509 version 3-compatible server certificates
   C. X.509 version 1-compatible client certificates
   D. X.509 version 3-compatible client certificates

3. Which kind of certificate is best used to identify Root CAs?
   A. Root-signed certificate
   B. Self-signed certificate
   C. Signed certificate
   D. No certificate is needed.

4. You need to revoke a certificate that was issued a month ago. Which steps do you need to take?
   A. In the Queue Administration utility, revoke the certificate. Next, to publish the revocation list, issue the `CertUtil -crl -` command.
   B. In the Queue Administration utility, revoke the certificate. Next, to publish the revocation list, issue the `CertUtil -getcrl` command.
   C. In the Log Administration utility, revoke the certificate. Next, to publish the revocation list, issue the `CertUtil -getcrl` command.
   D. In the Log Administration utility, revoke the certificate. Next, to publish the revocation list, issue the `CertUtil -crl -` command.

5. To recover a damaged Certificate Authority certificate, you use which command-line utility?

    A. CertHier

    B. CertReq

    C. CertUtil

    D. CertSrv

6. What information is stored in the shared folder? Select all that apply.

    A. The CA's certificate

    B. The CertSrv.txt configuration file

    C. The Certificate Server log files

    D. Installed certificates

7. You want to enable SSL on your server shop.megacorp.com. However, the existing certificate was issued for the common name www.megacorp.com. What course of action would be best?

    A. Apply for a new certificate.

    B. Use the existing certificate but add new bindings.

    C. Use the existing certificate.

    D. Install the CA's certificate.

8. What items should you back up in order to be able to restore operation of your Certificate Server?

    A. Shared folder, CertSvr directory, CertLog directory, Registry

    B. Shared folder, CertSrv directory, CertShare directory, metabase

    C. Shared folder, CertSrv directory, CertLog directory, metabase

    D. Shared folder, CertSrv directory, CertLog directory, Registry

9. When is the only time the Certificate Authority service should be run from the command line using the -z parameter?

    A. When you are manually starting the service.

    B. When you are running the service in the stand-alone configuration for debugging.

    C. When you are recovering a failed installation.

    D. When your Certificate Authority certificates have been corrupted.

Day 7: Microsoft Certificate Server

10. What is the format of certificate requests?

    A. PKCS #10

    B. X.509 version 3

    C. PCS 5

    D. X.400

Answers to Questions

1. **C, D.** Public cryptography algorithms use a public/private pair of keys that are generated at the same time. Both are mathematically related, but you can't compute the private key given the public key. Also, symmetric encryption algorithms are faster than public key algorithms.

2. **B, C, D.** You can use Certificate Server to issue X.509 version 3-compatible server certificates as well as X.509 version 1 and 3-compatible client certificates. You can also generate S/MIME certificates out of the box.

3. **D.** Root CAs use self-signed certificates.

4. **D.** First you have to revoke the certificate in question using the Log Administration utility, and then you need to use CertUtil -crl - to publish the certificate revocation list in the default Web directory.

5. **C.** CertUtil is the tool you need to use. However, you would need to run it twice, to recover the Signature file and the Exchange file.

6. **A, B, D.** The shared folder contains the CA's certificate, the CertSrv.txt configuration file, and the installed certificates.

7. **A.** The only solution is to apply for a new certificate, because the old one is bound to www.megacorp.com. Clients verify the common name in the certificate.

8. **D.** In order to be able to restore a Certificate Server, you need to back up the shared folder, CertSrv directory, CertLog directory, and the Registry.

9. **B.** You run the Certificate Authority server engine in stand-alone mode when you need to debug server operation.

10. **A.** Certificate Server processes PKCS #10 certificate requests.

Exercise

Exercise 7.1.: Setting Up a New Root-CA

This exercise addresses the following Microsoft exam objectives:

- Install and configure Certificate Server
- Configure Certificate Server to issue certificates

In this exercise, you install a new Root CA on a server of your choice. After having finished the installation of the CA, install the new CA's certificate on a development server and create a new server certificate by using Key Manager. The certificate is created using the online authority feature of Key Manager. Follow these steps:

1. Launch the Option Pack Setup from the NT Option Pack program group. Select Add/Remove.

2. From the subcomponents list, select the Certificate Server option and mark it for installation.

3. In the first Certificate Server Setup screen, you are asked to provide various directory locations. These include the location of the shared folder, the database, and the log.

4. In the second and final step, you need to supply information about the CA you are creating (for the self-signed certificate). After that, Internet Information Server setup will conclude with copying files and configuring your Certificate Server.

5. Install the CA's certificate on the server you want to create the server certificate for. Restart the WWW service to make the change take effect.

6. In Key Manager, create the new server key using the online authority feature.

7. Commit the changes in Key Manager. You can start using the certificate for SSL connections immediately.

TEST DAY FAST FACTS

Here are a few fast facts about this chapter that you may want to know ahead of time. Don't forget that these facts also provide great last-minute study material.

- Microsoft's SMTP Service is built on the Simple Mail Transfer Protocol, the Internet standard for e-mail exchange.

- The SMTP Service is administered graphically through the SMTP extension snap-in in Internet Service Manager or through the HTML-based SMTP Service Manager.

- SMTP Service configuration and folders are stored in the mailroot directory specified during installation.

- The Badmail folder contains messages that could not be delivered.

- The Drop folder contains messages that have been delivered to the local system.

- Clients and users can deposit outgoing messages for delivery in the Pickup folder.

- The SMTP Service stores outgoing mail messages in the Queue folder while it is in the process of delivering them.

- Each configurable aspect of the SMTP Server has a properties sheet in the ISM that contains its configuration information.

Day 8

The SMTP Server

by David Gulbransen

Microsoft has expanded the functionality of the Internet Information Server to include many of the most commonly used applications of the Internet, including the transfer of electronic mail. The mechanism that is used to transport e-mail from server to server over the Internet is known as the Simple Mail Transfer Protocol, or SMTP.

Version 4.0 of the Internet Information Server allows administrators of Windows NT 4.0 Servers to install the SMTP Service and then to use their servers as a mail server for their organization.

The SMTP Service provides an important new capability to IIS. Therefore, administrators should be familiar with the functionality that it provides and how to perform the basic configuration of the SMTP Service. Although it is a fairly small portion of the exam, familiarity with the functions of the SMTP Service, including when to use it and its basic configuration, is important.

In this chapter, we will take a look at the process of installing, configuring, and managing IIS with the SMTP Service. Although this is not a comprehensive manual for mail administration, you should still be able to install, configure, and begin sending and receiving mail with the SMTP Service by the time you complete this chapter. You should also be familiar with the tools that are available to help you diagnose trouble with mail services and some performance metrics that can show you how your SMTP Service is performing. A mastery of these goals will prepare you well for any questions concerning the SMTP Service that might be on the exam.

Objectives

This chapter helps you prepare for the Microsoft Exam by covering the following objectives:

- Install and configure Microsoft SMTP Service.
- Configure Microsoft SMTP Service to host personal mailboxes.
- Optimize performance of Microsoft SMTP Service.

TEST DAY
FAST FACTS

- The SMTP Server can service multiple mail delivery for multiple domains through local domain aliases.

- Message size and properties can be limited to conserve space and prevent abuse.

- SMTP Service supports user authentication and Transport Layer Security (TLS) for added security and message encryption.

- The SMTP Service logs all errors to the standard Windows NT Event Log.

- The standard Windows NT Performance Monitor can be used with SMTP Counters to provide real-time performance feedback.

8.1. SMTP Overview

One of the more common applications for computer networks is the sending and receiving of electronic mail. Many organizations still rely on complex UNIX systems for delivery of Internet e-mail. Many others rely on proprietary systems for delivering interoffice e-mail and lack the capability to transfer e-mail to other systems via the Internet.

For many years, Internet e-mail has been transmitted using a single protocol, designed to transfer e-mail from system to system regardless of the operating systems or mail clients and servers being used by any particular organization. This protocol is known as the Simple Mail Transfer Protocol (SMTP).

Many types of mail servers and clients use SMTP for sending mail, and those clients run on UNIX systems, Windows systems, and Macintosh systems. Some hand-held devices even handle e-mail that is sent using SMTP.

Microsoft's SMTP Service for IIS 4.0 adds the capability to send and receive Internet SMTP-based e-mail to your IIS Server. By using the SMTP Service, you can provide a gateway to the Internet for a proprietary e-mail system, or you can simply use an SMTP mail client to use SMTP Service for your sole mail provider. Microsoft's SMTP Server offers the following features:

- *SMTP standard mail compatibility.* The Microsoft SMTP Service for IIS 4.0 is compatible with the SMTP Internet standard (RFC 821) and is compatible with other servers and clients that support SMTP.
- *Scalability.* In conjunction with Windows NT Server 4.0 and IIS 4.0, the SMTP Service is designed for high scalability and reliability. It is capable of providing services to hundreds of connections and multiple domains, and it can be clustered with other servers to provide enterprise solutions.
- *SMTP Service Manager (HTML) administration.* The SMTP Service for IIS 4.0 is administered through the SMTP Service Manager, which provides an HTML-based graphical administrative user interface that makes the installation, configuration, and administration of SMTP Service easier than ever. Additionally, the SMTP Service can take advantage of the Simple Network Management Protocol (SNMP) for even more administrative flexibility.

> **Note:** The Simple Network Management Protocol (SNMP) provides a standard mechanism that enables networking hardware and monitoring software to communicate. By using the features of SNMP, software vendors can provide monitoring applications that can automatically configure, manage, and monitor various vendors' networking hardware solutions.

- *Microsoft Management Console.* The latest innovation to the Internet Service Manager comes in the form of the Microsoft Management Console, or MMC. The MMC provides a unified graphical interface for administration, but does so through extensible snap-ins that can be used to control the various IIS Services offered.

> **Note:** The administrative functionality provided by the HTML-based ISM and the MMC-based ISM is virtually identical. Similarly, administering the SMTP Service is very similar to administering the NNTP Service. For that reason, we will cover the use of the HTML-based ISM in this chapter and concentrate on the MMC-based ISM in Chapter 9. This should expose you to both management formats and prepare you to manage services through either mechanism.

- *Security.* Microsoft SMTP Service supports the use of Transport Layer Security (TLS) to provide encrypted data transmissions with compatible applications.
- *Directed mail delivery and pickup.* SMTP Service supports the use of a Mail Drop directory that holds all incoming messages for the default domain, allowing other applications access to incoming mail (this is similar to a post office box). It also supports the use of a Pickup directory, which can act as a clearing house for other applications' mail delivery needs. When outgoing messages are placed in the Pickup directory, the Microsoft SMTP Service picks the messages up and delivers them appropriately.

In the upcoming sections, we will take a look at how SMTP delivers mail, what is involved in transferring mail files to the local machine, and relaying messages to other machines on the network.

8.1.1. Processing Messages

Processing mail messages is very straightforward. The SMTP Service operates on TCP port 25, which is the standard TCP port for SMTP mail servers. Incoming messages are sent to the SMTP Service via this port, and the SMTP Service uses this port on other servers to connect for outside mail delivery.

8.1.2. Delivering Local Messages

The delivery of a local mail message takes place in one of two ways. In the first scenario, the mail message originates from within your organization on the local server. The mail message is placed in the Queue directory and slated for delivery. When the SMTP Service determines that the message is to be delivered to a local user, the mail message is moved to the Drop directory, and the SMTP Server cycle is finished. The local user can access the message in the Drop directory.

In the second scenario, an incoming message request is received on TCP port 25, and the SMTP Service checks the request to see that the intended recipient is a user on the local system. If that is confirmed, the SMTP Server routes the incoming message from the remote server into the Drop directory, where it awaits delivery to the local user's mail client.

8.1.3. Delivering Remote Messages

Of course, the SMTP Service is also capable of delivering mail messages that are routed outside of your organization. The SMTP Service follows this procedure for delivering messages that are addressed to recipients outside your organization:

1. *Queuing.* Messages that are placed in the Pickup directory are first sorted and then placed in the Queue directory, where they await delivery. During the sorting process, the SMTP Service groups messages that are addressed to the same organization so that when the SMTP Service contacts the remote mail server, all the messages can be sent in one batch (instead of each message being sent separately). Sorting the messages this way is more efficient for both your SMTP Server and the remote server to which you are connecting.

2. *Determining server availability.* Once the messages from the Pickup directory have been moved into the Queue directory, the SMTP Service contacts the servers to which the mail is being delivered to make sure they are available. Because temporary outages often occur on the Internet and performance is sometimes sluggish, checking for server availability increases the reliability of message delivery. If the remote server is not available for some reason, the message (or batch) is re-queued. That is, those messages are set aside, and the SMTP Service attempts to deliver them again at a later time. You can

configure the number of attempts and the interval between attempts to maximize delivery potential while limiting the impact on your server.

3. *Delivering the message.* Upon contacting the remote server and verifying that the message is addressed to a local user on that remote system, the SMTP Service transfers the message to the remote site. Once the remote server verifies that it has received the message, the message is removed from the Queue directory, and the process is complete.

In the next section, you will take a look at installing the SMTP Service for Internet Information Server 4.0. This will take you through the installation process so you can get SMTP set up and can begin configuring your mail delivery system.

8.2. Installing SMTP Service

The SMTP Service for Internet Information Server 4.0 is a part of the Windows NT 4.0 Option Pack and can be found on the Option Pack CD. It is installed using the same mechanism as other optional packages, and it shares the hard disk and memory requirements of IIS. The SMTP Service also requires the Windows NT Server 4.0 operating system and a working installation of Internet Information Server 4.0.

The installation process is quite simple:

1. Launch the Option Pack Setup from the Option Pack CD-ROM. Then, from the Components List, select the Internet Information Server option and click on Show Subcomponents (see Figure 8.1).

Figure 8.1.
The SMTP Service is installed through the Windows NT Option Pack Setup.

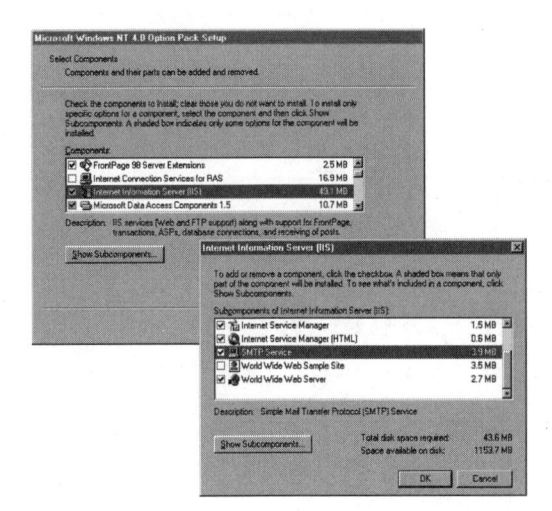

2. Select the SMTP Service, click OK, and then click Next to continue.

3. You will be presented with a couple of screens offering options for IIS and the Transaction Server. To enter a location where you would like each of the components installed, you can either accept the defaults or enter different disk volumes. Click Next through each of these screens.

> **Note** The precise option screens for the IIS Options and Transaction Server options may vary if you installed these components previously.

4. Next you will be presented with the option screen for the SMTP Service, shown in Figure 8.2. Here you will be asked to enter the Mailroot Directory for your SMTP Service. The Mailroot directory is the directory that contains your Drop directory, Pickup directory, and Queue directory. You can use the default directory, or you can specify another existing directory.

   Keep in mind that this directory will contain the subdirectories for incoming and outgoing mail. So if you intend to do a very high volume of mail traffic, make sure the disk volume that contains this directory has adequate space available.

5. Click Next, and the installation is complete.

Figure 8.2.
The SMTP Service Setup options screen allows you to enter the Mailroot Directory for the SMTP Service.

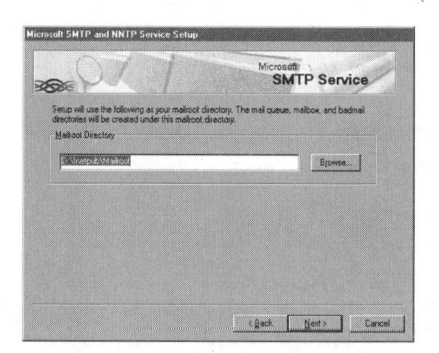

8.3. Configuring SMTP Service

After you have installed the SMTP Service, you will want to configure the service for your organization. Because of the nature of mail delivery and users' reliance on mail, many of the SMTP configuration options have the potential for seriously affecting mail delivery and SMTP Service performance.

While the configuration of the SMTP Service is not complex, it is essential that configuration be accurate because mail delivery is generally one of the most mission-critical net applications at any organization. The slightest misconfiguration can result in mail being rejected or, worse, mail being delivered incorrectly.

The SMTP Service has seven major areas of administration:

- The SMTP site
- Local domain
- Remote domains
- Messages
- Delivery
- Security

Each of these options can be managed through the SMTP Service Manager, which offers a user-friendly HTML-based interface. They can also be controlled via the Microsoft Management Console, which provides a unified, extensible management interface.

In the following sections, we will take a look at the various options for configuring the SMTP Service and how to establish the configuration using the management tools.

8.3.1. Using the SMTP Service Manager (HTML)

The Internet Service Manager (HTML) for Internet Information Server 4.0 is a Web-based graphical administration tool that allows you to configure and administer the features of IIS and the SMTP Service. Follow these steps to configure SMTP via the Service Manager:

1. Launch the ISM for the SMTP Service by choosing Windows NT 4.0 Option Pack from the Start menu.
2. Select Microsoft Information Server from the submenu.
3. From the Microsoft SMTP Service submenu, select SMTP Service Manager (HTML). This launches the Internet Service Manager for SMTP.

8.3.2. Components

The main ISM screen contains several icons, which represent the various areas of your SMTP Service that are available for configuration, as shown in Figure 8.3.

Figure 8.3.
The SMTP Service Manager allows administrators to edit the performance parameters for the service.

The components of the SMTP Server control the various elements of functionality for mail delivery and message handling. Proper configuration of these components is essential to a correctly functioning SMTP Service.

As you can see, three main components appear on the initial ISM page:

- *Default SMTP Site.* This is your main SMTP site, which contains information about the domains that you have configured, the site's property sheets, and the current sessions for the SMTP Service.

- *Domains.* These are the various domains for which you have configured your SMTP Service to accept mail. While you can configure your SMTP Service to accept mail for multiple domains, for external mail to be deliverable to those domains, they must be registered Internet domains.

- *Current Sessions.* This displays the current mail sessions that are utilizing SMTP Service. This might include information about both outgoing and incoming connections or information about the messages delivered and the duration of the connection. This feature can be very useful for monitoring the performance of your SMTP Service, for troubleshooting, for investigating violations of your mail policy, or for blocking spam e-mail from your site.

8.3.3. Directories

SMTP uses the Windows directory structure to store and transport mail messages on the local system before sending them on their way across the Internet, as well as for local delivery.

Five directories are created by default within the Mailroot directory that you established during the installation. Each of these directories plays a vital role in the function of your SMTP Service. The five directories are:

- *SortTemp.* The SortTemp directory is a temporary directory that is created as a temporary scratch space for the SMTP Service to use when it is sorting and arranging messages in the Pickup folder to be queued.
- *Badmail.* The Badmail directory is the electronic equivalent of the Dead Letter Office. When a mail message cannot be delivered to the recipient for some reason and the SMTP Service is unable to return the message to the original sender, the message is placed here. As the administrator, you should keep an eye on this directory. If it gets full often, it might be an indicator of a serious misconfiguration.
- *Drop.* The Drop directory is where incoming mail messages are delivered. It functions as an electronic post office box. Client applications can access the Drop directory to access their mail.
- *Pickup.* The Pickup directory functions as an electronic post box. Users and applications can place messages that are to be delivered by SMTP Service in the Pickup directory. Periodically, the SMTP Service polls the directory and sorts the messages stored there before placing them in the queue for delivery.
- *Queue.* The Queue directory contains all the outgoing mail that has been sorted and is slated for delivery. Once messages are in the queue, the SMTP Service attempts to deliver the messages at a regular interval. When the messages have been successfully delivered, SMTP removes them from this folder.

8.3.4. Configuring the SMTP Site

The first properties sheet you come to when using the ISM is the SMTP Site properties sheet shown in Figure 8.4. You access this properties sheet by selecting the Properties link from the SMTP Service Manager (HTML) main screen.

Figure 8.4.
Administrators alter configuration information for the SMTP Service at the SMTP Site Properties sheet.

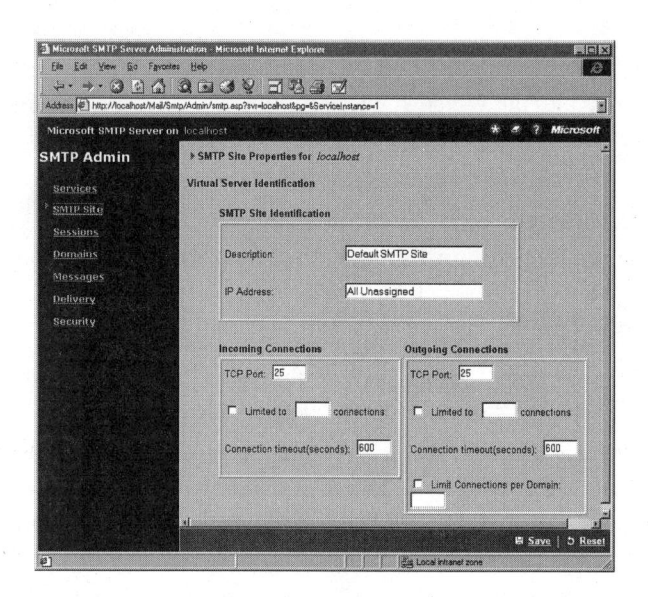

From this sheet, you can configure three main areas of your SMTP Service:

- *SMTP Site Identification.* Here you can enter a description and the IP address for your site. If you intend to use your SMTP Service for external mail on the Internet, you should have the IP number and domain name registered with the InterNIC. You should also make sure that your Internet service provider has your Domain Name Service records (particularly your mail exchange or MX records) configured to point to this machine for your domain. You might also consider naming or creating an aliased domain name such as mail.mycompany.com to help users easily point their systems to the machine that is the organizational mail server.

- *Incoming Connections.* Here you can configure how your SMTP Server responds to incoming connections. You can specify the TCP port, and you can control how many concurrent connections your machine will accept. Limiting the number of connections can help keep your machine from becoming bogged down with mail delivery during peak usage periods. Finally, you can also set the time limit (in seconds) before your server breaks a connection.

- *Outgoing Connections.* For Outgoing Connections, you can establish similar restrictions. You can alter the port, the number of connections that can be made, and the timeout. You can also limit the number of connections that are allowed per domain (which can be used to keep traffic to a minimum) by limiting the number of times your server connects to any individual domain. However, that can also lead to delivery problems for high-traffic domains.

> **Warning:** Although you can alter the TCP Connection Port on the SMTP Site Properties sheet, if you intend to use the SMTP Server for Internet mail, you might want to refrain from doing so. Your site might suffer delivery problems if you alter the port number.

8.3.5. Configuring Domains

From the Domains section of the ISM, you can edit the properties of the current local domain, or you can add domains to be handled by your SMTP Service.

To access the Domains section, click Domains in the left pane of the main screen. Then double-click on the domain you want to edit, and you'll see the properties sheet for that domain. You can also use the Add, Remove, and Edit Properties options at the bottom of the console to edit domains for SMTP. Figure 8.5 shows the Edit Domain Properties sheet.

Figure 8.5.
The Edit Domain Properties sheet for SMTP Service.

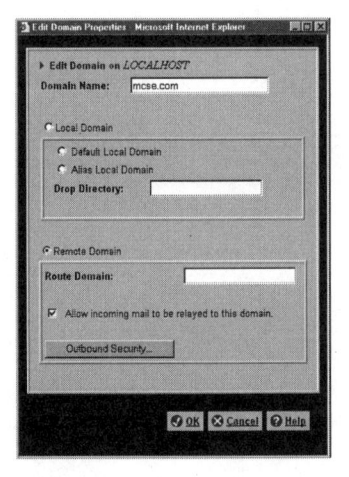

You cannot edit the active default domain. However, you can create a new local domain and then select the Default Local Domain option on the style sheet to make the new domain the default domain.

When you add a new domain, you can choose whether to make the new domain a local domain. If so, you can specify whether you want to create a Drop directory specifically for the new domain.

Alternatively, you can choose to add a new remote domain to your SMTP Service, which allows you to configure a direct route for delivery to a remote server or to have local mail rerouted to an outside domain. If you choose to add an outside domain for local delivery, you can also set Outbound Security options, which allow you to require that the outside mail hosts use Account Authentication or TLS Encryption for mail delivery. This option works to your advantage if you're configuring a mail server for the entire organization that then routes mail to different local domains for various workgroups or branch offices.

8.3.6. Managing Messages

The Message Properties sheet is one of the most powerful configuration tools for your SMTP Service. As the prevalence of Internet e-mail grows, so does the potential for abuse. Already in many organizations, users are fighting battles against electronic junk mail, or *spam*, which clogs SMTP resources and annoys users.

Figure 8.6 shows the Message Properties sheet, which allows you to configure message options to reduce e-mail abuse (among other things).

Figure 8.6.

The SMTP Message Properties sheet can be used to specify limits for messages, which will increase performance and limit abuse.

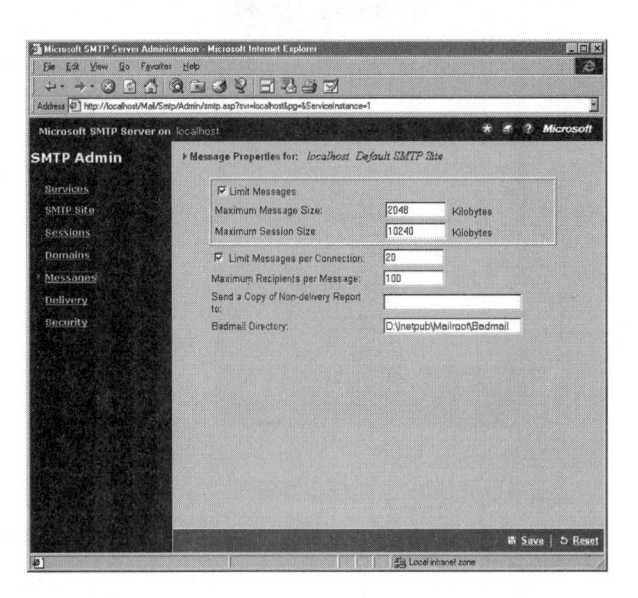

By checking the Limit Messages option, for example, you can prevent both attackers and well-meaning but uninformed users from crashing your mail server.

For example, suppose your Drop directory is on a partition with 500 MB of free space, and you have 50 users on your system. One day, a hacker sends a 25 MB file to each of the users on your system via SMTP. That's more than 1,250 MB worth of information. If you didn't have the Maximum Message Size option set, your Drop directory would fill up, and no mail could be delivered to your entire site. This kind of attack is called a "denial of service" attack. But the same thing could happen if a user on your system decided to mail everyone in the company a huge report. By limiting the message size, you protect your server and your users' ability to get the mail they depend on.

Limit Messages per Connection is also a very important feature. For example, if you have 500 users on your system, and an e-mail junk mailer wants to send mail to all of them, a limit of 25 messages per connection would make the process much more difficult—and the person might be inclined to remove your site from his or her spam list. The Maximum Recipients per Message option has a similar effect: It prevents potential abusers from addressing a single mail message to everyone in your organization.

The Send a Copy of Non-Delivery Report To option and the Badmail directory option also serve an administrative purpose. As an SMTP administrator, you should receive a copy of messages regarding non-deliverable mail, and you should periodically check the Badmail directory for non-deliverables so you can use them as troubleshooting guides for your SMTP installation.

8.3.7. Configuring Delivery

The Delivery Properties sheet allows you to configure how your SMTP Service functions when delivering e-mail messages. Figure 8.7 shows the Delivery Properties sheet.

The most important settings for delivery are the Maximum Retries setting and the Retry Interval setting for both local and remote delivery. These settings determine how long a message will remain in the queue until it is considered undeliverable. The default for both is to attempt delivery every 60 minutes for 48 tries. This amounts to a queue time of two days. Generally, 60 minutes is a good retry interval because it accounts for minor outages of 5–10 minutes, which are frequent on the Internet. However, some sites might want to lower or raise the number of maximum retries, as two days might be too long for mission-critical mail to sit.

Day 8: The SMTP Server

Figure 8.7.
The Delivery Properties sheet allows you to customize mail delivery.

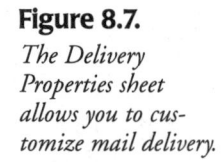

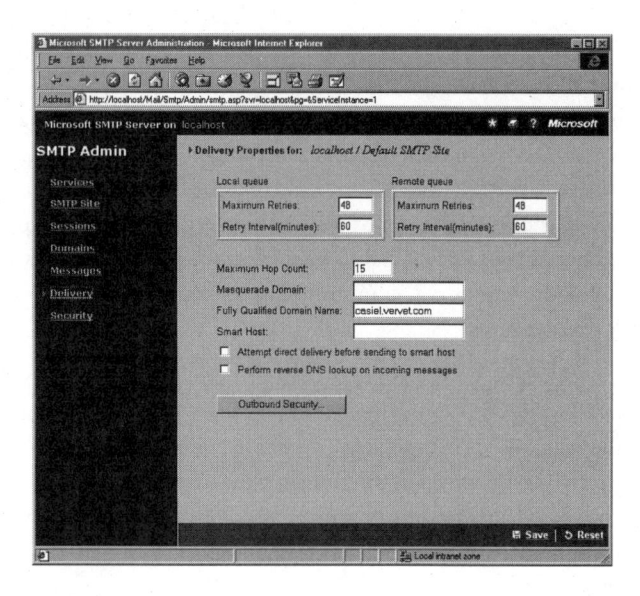

Other delivery options include the following:

- *Maximum Hop Count.* Each server a mail message passes through en-route to the recipient is considered a "hop." Here you can set the maximum number of hops that can occur before a message is delivered.

- *Masquerade Domain.* Because your server might be operating as the SMTP Server for a whole organization, you may want your outgoing mail to be addressed as @mycompany.com instead of @mymachine.mycompany.com. The Masquerade Domain is the shortened version of your domain name that you can have appear on all outgoing messages.

- *Fully Qualified Domain Name.* The Fully Qualified Domain Name is the complete DNS name for your server, in the form of mymachine.myorganization.mytopdomain. For example, for a machine called "chimp" at a company called "NewTech," the FQDN would be chimp.newtech.com. Because the FQDN will be the name for your machine that is registered with an Internet service provider, you need to enter it here if you are routing mail to your SMTP Server from outside organizations because what you enter here will correspond to the name that is indicated in the Mail Exchange (MX) records with your service provider's Domain Name Server.

- *Smart Host.* The Smart Host is simply another machine that serves as a relay host for your outgoing messages. For example, if you were configuring your

SMTP Server for a remote office but you wanted to route all outgoing mail through the home office's corporate server, you could enter that server's name here as a smart host. You can also use the Smart Host feature to protect the identity of your internal mail servers behind a firewall.

- *Attempt Direct Delivery Before Sending to Smart Host.* Selecting this option tells your server to attempt to contact the remote server directly first and then, if the mail is undeliverable, to relay the message to the smart host. This could be useful for making the most efficient use of your server's resources. If the SMTP Server can't deliver the message immediately, you can relay it to the smart host so that your server is not taxed by repeatedly trying to deliver the message.

- *Perform Reverse DNS Lookup on Incoming Messages.* Selecting this option tells your SMTP Server to look up the domain names for incoming messages and to verify that the IP number for the incoming server connection matches the domain in the From header of the message. While this procedure can cut down on fraudulent mail, it cannot eliminate forged mail, and it can be a very drastic performance drain against your mail server.

8.3.8. Configuring Security

The SMTP Service offers two primary areas for security configuration. To access these settings, access the Directory Security Properties sheet through the Internet Service Manager. The two areas for security are:

- Anonymous Access and Authentication Control
- Secure Communications

The Anonymous Access and Authentication Control setting allows you to configure whether you will allow anonymous connections to your SMTP Server. The default is to allow anonymous access because Internet mail depends on it. However, if you are configuring your SMTP Server as an internal mail relay or for internal use only, you may want to configure it for Basic Authentication or for Windows NT Challenge/Response. The latter provides the highest level of security and prevents outside servers from gaining unauthorized access to your SMTP Server.

Using the Secure Communications properties, you can require that your SMTP server make a secure connection when transferring e-mail. A secure connection means that you're connecting to another server that supports an encryption protocol (such as SSL or TLS) and then encrypting messages en-route between the servers. Once again, for external e-mail, this option can adversely affect mail delivery. Internally, however, it can provide a robust security solution. Figure 8.8 shows the Secure Communications Properties sheet.

Figure 8.8.
The Secure Communications property allows you to boost the level of security provided by SMTP Service.

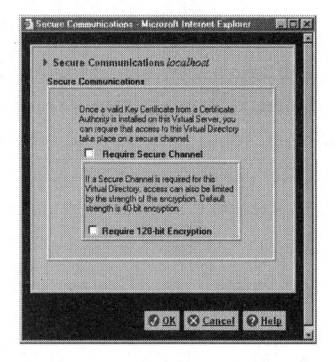

If you choose the Require Secure Channel option, your server will only be able to connect to other servers that support TLS for secure transmission. Also, by default, the level of data encryption for secure transmissions is 40-bit. You can boost the level of encryption to 128-bit for secure applications.

> **Note:** 40-bit encryption is intended for international use. 128-bit encryption is intended for domestic use only. United States law forbids the exportation of 128-bit encryption.

8.4. Monitoring and Performance Tuning

Because mail service is often considered a mission-critical application, it is often necessary to fine-tune the performance of your mail server. In addition, you must keep a close eye on how your server is performing transactions so that the delivery of mail is never impeded.

A number of tools for monitoring the performance of your SMTP Server are at your disposal. This section offers an overview of the available tools, their functions, and the information they can provide about your SMTP Server.

8.4.1. Monitoring System Processes

Because the SMTP Service is run as a Windows NT System Service, you can make use of the same tools that are provided to monitor the performance of your

8.4. Monitoring and Performance Tuning

Windows NT Server. For example, the Windows NT Event Logs are a resource you can use to check for errors that are being generated by your SMTP Server.

In particular, you should check these three logs regularly for indications of problems with the SMTP Service:

- System log
- Application log
- Security log

If, in any of these logs, you encounter errors that have been generated by the SMTP Service, you may want to conduct some delivery tests to make sure mail is still being routed properly. In addition, you should look for configuration parameters that might be related to the errors to make sure the configuration of your SMTP Service is functional. Both of these things can be viewed using the Event Viewer, shown in Figure 8.9.

Figure 8.9.
SMTP errors and messages are logged to the Windows NT Event Log, which is accessible through the Event Viewer.

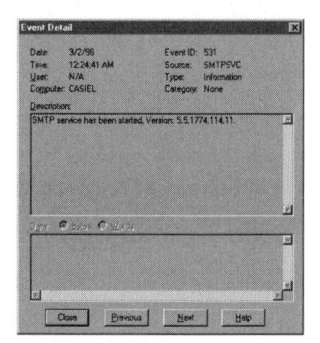

Events generated by the SMTP Service will be identifiable by the "SMTPSVC" label in the Source column. Periodic review of the Event Log and the errors listed there can help alleviate problems with the SMTP Service. In scanning the Event Log, if you notice events generated by the SMTPSVC, you should make sure that they are just notices of the service starting up, and not errors that indicate problems. For example, you may encounter errors indicating that messages cannot be delivered due to permissions problems. If so, you would want to check the permissions on the SMTP folders, such as the Drop directory and the Queue directory.

8.4.2. Monitoring Message Transactions

Using the ISM, you can also monitor the currently active SMTP sessions, and you can take the necessary actions to eliminate problem connections.

The Sessions panel for ISM is shown in Figure 8.10 (click on the Current Sessions link from within the Internet Services Manager to access it).

Figure 8.10.
Through the ISM, you can monitor current SMTP sessions.

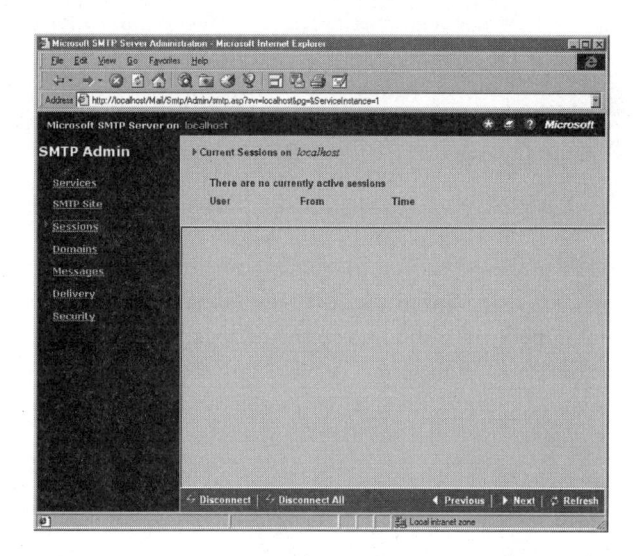

This panel allows you to view any current connections, incoming or outgoing, which are currently engaging your SMTP Server. Using the options at the bottom of the panel, you can select a session and disconnect it, or you can choose Disconnect All to stop all the currently active sessions.

If you notice that a connection seems to be hung or if you are currently receiving unsolicited spam e-mail, you can use the sessions monitor to disconnect the offending site. Similarly, if you are under attack or are being bombarded with spam, you can simply disconnect all the connections for now, and then reconfigure your server or bring it up later when you feel the threat has dissipated.

8.4.3. Monitoring SMTP Performance

Perhaps the most valuable performance monitoring tool is the Windows NT Performance Monitor shown in Figure 8.11. The same performance monitor that can be used to monitor your Windows NT Server can be used to monitor the performance of your SMTP Service, and it can provide you with real-time updates on the status and performance of the service.

Figure 8.11.
The Windows NT Performance Monitor can also monitor SMTP counters to provide performance stats specifically for your SMTP Service.

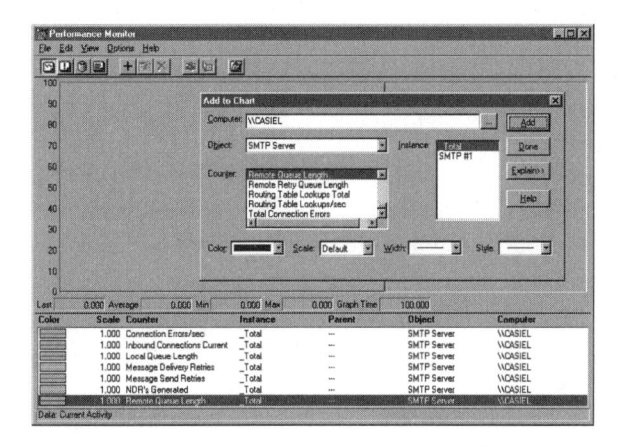

By adding performance counters for SMTP Services, you can chart the performance of your SMTP Server in real-time, and you can identify performance problems as they happen. Here are some of the more important counters that you can use to gather information that can help customize your SMTP Server:

- *% Recipients Local.* This performance metric can provide you with data about how users are utilizing the mail server; a higher percentage of local recipients should indicate that users are relying on your server for local mail delivery.

- *% Recipients Remote.* Similar to the % Recipients Local parameter, this can help you identify if users are relying on your server for Internet mail.

- *Messages Delivered/sec.* This reading can serve as a performance benchmark to indicate how efficient your server is at delivering messages, and it can also help call your attention to a peak server usage (such as incoming spam) or a general delivery bottleneck.

- *Message Delivery Retries.* The number of Message Delivery Retries can be useful for identifying mail delivery problems. If the number of retries increases dramatically, it can indicate another potentially serious problem with the delivery to local users.

- *NDR's Generated.* The number of Non-Delivery Reports (NDR) generated can also indicate delivery problems. If your server is generating a high number of NDR's, you might contact the administrator of the server generating the errors to see if he or she is experiencing a problem. Keep in mind that when another server is malfunctioning and hitting your server, it can affect your server's performance.

- *Local Queue Length.* This counter should normally be 0. If it exceeds zero, the SMTP Server is processing more messages that it can handle. While occasional spikes during peak periods might be normal, a recurring pattern could indicate the need for a server upgrade.
- *Remote Queue Length.* The Remote Queue Length counter should also be 0. A higher number might indicate slow network connectivity or an unreachable site, or it could indicate a more serious connectivity problem. Again, occasional spikes during peak usage should be considered normal; however, recurring patterns should be investigated.
- *Local Retry Queue Length.* This counter indicates the number of messages that are currently being queued for a delivery retry. If the number of retries queued increases steadily, it can indicate a delivery problem on the local system, such as a full disk.
- *Remote Retry Queue Length.* The Remote Retry Queue Length is also an indicator of potential delivery bottlenecks. If the remote queue increases dramatically, there may be a problem delivering to a particular site, or more importantly, there may be a problem with your Internet connectivity.

To add counters to your Performance Monitor, follow these steps:

1. Select the Add to Chart option from the Edit menu.
2. From the Object list, select SMTP Service. A list of the available SMTP Counters appears in the Counters selection box.
3. Select the counter you want to add by highlighting it and clicking the Add button.

Repeat this process for as many counters as you want to review. Note, however, that the more counters you add, the more confusing the Performance Monitor display will become.

> **Note**
> For more information on monitoring and optimizing your IIS system, see Day 12, "Performance Tuning."

8.5. Troubleshooting SMTP

With a service as complex and demanding as SMTP, a number of problems can arise and prevent your users from sending and receiving mail as intended. In this section, we'll review some of the most common problems that are experienced with SMTP Services and how those problems can be corrected.

The best way to troubleshoot problems with SMTP is through regular checkups. As the system's administrator, you should routinely visit the Event Log to watch for errors, and you should keep an eye on the performance meter to make sure that performance is progressing as it should. Here are a few other things you can do to keep an eye on the system and your SMTP Service:

- *Check Non-Delivery Reports.* Although you cannot create mailboxes on your SMTP Server, you can configure the server to deliver Non-Delivery Reports to a mailbox on another server so that you can regularly review problem reports and act immediately when there is an indication of trouble.

  You can accomplish this by entering the e-mail address of that server in the Send a Copy of Non-Delivery Report To field on the Message Properties sheet.

- *Review queue transcripts.* The Queue directory contains two transcripts: an .ltr and an .rtr. These files are transcripts of mail delivery problems, indicating why a message has not been delivered and why it remains in the queue. Using the information from these transcripts, you can get a better idea of where a delivery problem originates—whether on your system or on the remote system.

In addition, a few other areas can cause trouble with SMTP.

8.5.1. System Troubleshooting

If there is a problem with delivery and a number of messages begin to back up in the mail queue, you run the risk of generating an `Out of Memory` error. This error occurs when too many messages are in the local and remote queue, and the total number of messages exceeds 100,000. This can occur as the result of a mail loop or because of a connectivity problem that is preventing mail from being delivered. When this occurs, you should review the queue transcripts to see what the nature of the problem is, and then remove any offending messages from the queue to establish normal delivery service.

8.5.2. Troubleshooting SMTP Services

The two most common problems with the SMTP service itself are:

- Clients unable to connect
- .bad files in queue

If a user complains that her client is generating errors because it is unable to connect to your SMTP Server, you should review the security setup information. Remember that if you enable security on your server, you will need to make sure that clients connecting to your server support both the security features and the level of security you have enabled.

When the Badmail directory becomes full, messages in the queue that are undeliverable remain in the queue with a .bad extension. If this occurs, you may want to investigate why you are generating so many .bad letters, and then clear the Badmail directory. The queue should then be clear.

8.5.3. Troubleshooting Delivery

Nothing is more frustrating than experiencing e-mail delivery problems when you are expecting an important message. Here are some of the common errors that impede delivery (and what you can do):

- *Drop directory contains no messages.* Check first to make sure that the path to the Drop directory is valid. If it is, check to make sure the disk volume where the Drop directory is located is not full. Because incoming messages consume disk space, you need to make sure the mailroot directory is located on a volume with lots of space.

- *Remote Site is not receiving messages.* The remote server might be temporarily down and not accepting incoming messages. However, you should also double-check to see if the name for the remote server is correct in the message headers. This is one of the most common problems that cause undeliverable messages. Finally, if you have a direct route configured for the remote site, you should also check to make sure that the direct route is valid and contains no typos.

- *Messages are not properly routing through the smart host.* If messages are supposed to be routed through a smart host and are not, make sure there is not a direct route configured for the remote host in question. If there is, keep in mind that a direct route configuration will bypass the smart host. If there is not, you might check your security settings to make sure that the smart host and your server share similar security configurations.

Lab

This lab consists of review questions pertaining to this chapter and provides an opportunity for you to use walk-through exercises to apply the knowledge that you've learned.

Questions

1. SMTP Service provides what functionality to Internet Information Server?
   A. Standard Mail Transfer Protocol, a Microsoft Mail format
   B. Standard Mail Trusted Path, a secure messaging context
   C. Simple Mail Transfer Protocol, an Internet e-mail protocol
   D. Simple Mail Trusted Protocol, an encrypted e-mail format

2. What Performance Meter counter could be used to monitor for possible connectivity or networking problems?
   A. Local Retry Queue Length
   B. % Recipients Remote
   C. Remote Retry Queue Length
   D. Local Queue Length

3. Users are complaining that they are not receiving mail, and you notice that the Local Retry Queue has increased drastically. What potential problem is the most likely cause of the trouble?
   A. The hard disk hosting the Drop directory is full.
   B. The number of message objects has exceeded 100,000.
   C. The Badmail folder is full.
   D. Security has been enabled and requires a Windows NT Challenge/Response.

4. The standard TCP port for connections between SMTP Servers is:
   A. 119
   B. 25
   C. 80
   D. 23

Day 8: The SMTP Server

5. What purpose is served by the SMTP Service's support of TLS?

    A. An Internet e-mail delivery standard

    B. Data-encrypted connections for increased security

    C. An advanced graphics-based management console

    D. Scalability for enterprise deployment and support

6. When a mail message is not deliverable within the established retry time, what happens to the message file?

    A. An NDR is generated.

    B. The message is deleted.

    C. An NDR is generated, and the file is moved to the Badmail directory.

    D. An NDR is generated, and the message is returned to the sender.

7. Limiting the size of incoming mail messages can help prevent what kind of SMTP problem?

    A. Mail bypassing the smart host for remote delivery

    B. Mail exceeding the maximum number of hops

    C. A "denial of service" attack

    D. Anonymous connections to the server

8. A smart host can be used to improve SMTP Service functionality in what way? (Select all that apply.)

    A. To relieve the primary SMTP Server load

    B. To increase the delivery efficiency

    C. For returning undeliverable mail

    D. To configure the SMTP site automatically

9. John is configuring e-mail for his company. What function can the Masquerade Domain property provide?

    A. To establish a direct path to remote delivery domains

    B. To configure additional local domains for message delivery

    C. To provide DNS lookup for incoming connection requests

    D. To mask the Fully Qualified Domain Name of the SMTP Server

10. What are the five default folders created by the SMTP Service and located in the mailroot directory?

   A. SortTemp, Badmail, Drop, Pickup, and Queue
   B. Temp, Deadletter, Delivery, POBox, and Queue
   C. SortTemp, Deadletter, Drop, POBox, and Queue
   D. Temp, Badmail, Dropbox, Pickup, and Queue

Answers to Questions

1. **C.** SMTP stands for Simple Mail Transfer Protocol, which is an Internet e-mail protocol that provides a simple mechanism for transferring mail messages between servers.

2. **C.** If the Remote Retry Queue Length rises over a significant period of time, it indicates that remote messages are not being delivered. This could point to a problem with an individual remote site or an overall network connectivity problem. The other listed performance counters do not specifically address networking issues.

3. **A.** One of the most common problems with local mail delivery is a full Drop directory. Make sure that the disk that hosts the Drop directory has an adequate amount of free space. Although it is conceivable that messaging objects might exceed 100,000, it's not likely, and security and the Badmail folder should not inhibit delivery of all mail.

4. **B.** The standard TCP port for SMTP Service is 25.

5. **B.** The Transport Layer Security (TLS) provides a mechanism for providing a secure encrypted channel for mail message exchange. It is not an Internet standard, and it has no impact on management or user interface issues.

6. **D.** An NDR is generated, and the message is returned to the original sender. Only messages that cannot be returned are stored in the Badmail directory.

7. **C.** A "denial of service" attack. Limiting the size of incoming messages prevents users and attackers from filling the disk containing the Drop directory. The smart host is used for outgoing mail, not incoming mail.

8. **A, B.** The use of a Smart Host can increase mail delivery efficiency by reducing the load on the primary server and delivering the message at a later time when direct delivery is not possible. The smart host, however, does not serve any management functions.

9. **D.** The Masquerade Domain is used to shield the host name of the SMTP Server from outside mail recipients. It causes the Fully Qualified Domain Name for the server to be truncated in the From header so that it contains only the top-level domain information.

10. **A.** SortTemp, Badmail, Drop, Pickup, and Queue are the default SMTP directories created and used by the SMTP Service and located in the mailroot directory.

Exercises

Exercise 8.1.: Configuring a Remote Domain

This exercise addresses the following Microsoft exam objective:

■ Install and configure Microsoft SMTP Service

In this exercise, you will add a remote domain configuration for direct mail delivery.

1. Launch the Internet Services Manager for SMTP.
2. Double-click on the Default SMTP Site.
3. Select the Domains option from the SMTP Admin panel.
4. Click on Add at the bottom of the panel to add a new domain.
5. Enter the Fully Qualified Domain Name for the new domain in the Domain Name field.
6. Click on the Remote Domain radio button.
7. Click OK.

Exercise 8.2.: Configuring a Local Alias

This exercise addresses the following Microsoft exam objective:

■ Install and configure Microsoft SMTP Service

In this exercise, you will add an alias for a local domain that your server is receiving mail for.

1. Launch the Internet Services Manager for SMTP.
2. Double-click on the Default SMTP Site.
3. Select the Domains option from the SMTP Admin panel.
4. Click on Add at the bottom of the panel to add a new domain.

5. Enter the Fully Qualified Domain Name for the new domain in the Domain Name field.
6. Click on the Local Domain radio button.
7. Click on the Alias Local Domain radio button.
8. Specify the location of the aliased domain's Drop directory.
9. Click OK.

Exercise 8.3.: Stopping and Restarting SMTP Service

This exercise addresses the following Microsoft exam objective:

- Install and configure Microsoft SMTP Service

In this exercise, you will stop and restart the SMTP Service.

1. From the Start menu, open the Control Panel.
2. Select the Services Control Panel and open it.
3. From the Services list, select Microsoft SMTP Service.
4. Click on the Stop button.
5. Wait until you have system confirmation that the service has stopped. Then click on the Start button.
6. Wait until you have confirmation that the service has started. Then click Close.

Exercise 8.4.: Limiting the Size of Incoming Messages

This exercise addresses the following Microsoft exam objective:

- Optimize performance of Microsoft SMTP Service

In this exercise, you will limit the size of incoming messages to 5 MB.

1. Launch the Internet Services Manager for SMTP.
2. Double-click on the Default SMTP Site.
3. Select the Messages option from the SMTP Admin panel.
4. Make sure the Limit Messages check box is checked.
5. Enter **5120** in the Maximum Message Size field (1024 Kilobytes = 1 Megabyte).
6. Click Save.

TEST DAY FAST FACTS

Here are a few fast facts about this chapter that you may want to know ahead of time. Don't forget that these facts also provide great last-minute study material.

- NNTP stands for Network News Transport Protocol.
- The Microsoft NNTP Service supports MIME, HTML, GIF, and JPEG standards.
- The NNTP Server supports secure communications through the Secure Sockets Layer (SSL).
- The NNTP Service is administered through the Internet Services Manager, providing an easy-to-use graphical user interface.
- NNTP Service supports anonymous connections, Basic Authentication, and Windows NT Challenge and Response.
- Discussion forums are called newsgroups, and they are organized into hierarchies based on subject matter.
- The NNTP Server stores newsgroup articles in a unique directory for each group.
- The \inetpub\nntpfile directory contains the NNTP Service files used to track article information (.hsh, .hdr, .lst, .txt). These files should not be edited by hand.

Day 9

The NNTP Server

by David Gulbransen

A number of different protocols are now being used on the Internet to communicate information. In the last chapter, we looked at the most common protocol used for messaging, the Simple Mail Transfer Protocol, or SMTP. Another messaging protocol is also in widespread use on the Internet: the Network News Transport Protocol, or NNTP.

You might already be familiar with the practical side of NNTP. If you have ever read or posted an article on a newsgroup, you have already used NNTP. This protocol is used by news servers and news clients to communicate articles back and forth over the Internet.

Because News is such a popular service, many organizations are turning to newsgroups to provide support for their products or to provide forums on a topic so that users can communicate with each other. The Internet Information Server features support of Network News through an add-on module similar to the SMTP Service. However, this service—the NNTP Service—is built just for News.

In this chapter, we will look at all facets of the NNTP Service for IIS 4.0. We will look at the benefits of News and see where it's an appropriate tool. We'll also look at how the NNTP Service functions. Finally, we'll cover installing and administering your own NNTP Service under IIS so that you will have the tools you need to start running your own NNTP Server.

Objectives

This chapter helps you prepare for the Microsoft exam by covering the following objectives:

- Install and configure the Microsoft NNTP Service.
- Configure the NNTP Service to host a newsgroup.
- Optimize the performance of the NNTP Service.

Test Day Fast Facts

- The NNTP Server can be used to communicate between groups within your organization and can also be used to communicate with outside users.
- Access to newsgroups can be restricted to username/password authentication.
- Access to newsgroups can be restricted based on IP numbers or domain names.
- Administrators can configure various expiration policies for each group, to clear out old messages and conserve disk space.
- Control messages can be sent to the server via special control groups to provide for remote administration.
- NNTP Service can be monitored through standard Windows NT system tools, such as the Event Log and the Performance Monitor.
- Rebuilding the NNTP Service can correct problems with delivery and article management.

9.1. Introducing Microsoft NNTP Service

In the earliest days of the Internet, many users saw a need for a public message forum that could be shared by a number of users, each of whom would have access to the same information resources and the ability to respond to all the message participants as a whole. Although e-mail is very effective as a one-to-one medium or as a one-to-many format, it is limited for many-to-many communications.

The Usenet News standard (now commonly referred to as NNTP News or just Internet News) was developed to allow individuals with a common interest to share messages in a discussion format, like a public bulletin board where anyone could post a message. Then the members of the group could read the messages and respond to them.

Today, Internet News encompasses literally thousands of discussion groups, ranging from sports and hobbies to science and business. These subject matters are categorized into "newsgroups" that people can subscribe to using a newsreader. If you have an interest, there is probably a newsgroup that is organized around that interest. All you need in order to participate is a newsreader, such as the Internet News client that ships with Internet Explorer.

With all the momentum behind discussion groups of this nature, your organization might want to take advantage of News to provide a forum for the staff or to interact with clients. Many organizations host news servers where their customer support personnel can interact with clients from around the globe. How you use the news server is up to you and your organization, but the Microsoft NNTP Service provides a robust, easy-to-administer solution for providing Internet News Service.

The following sections cover the NNTP features that are provided by the NNTP Service for IIS.

9.1.1. Standards Support

The Microsoft NNTP Service supports all of the common protocols currently in use for Internet News Service. The NNTP Service fully supports the Network News Transport Protocol (NNTP) for connectivity from News Client to News Server; however, newsfeeds (connectivity between servers for news propagation) are not supported. In addition to the NNTP protocol, the Microsoft NNTP Service also supports the following:

- MIME (Multipurpose Internet Mail Extension)
- HTML (Hypertext Markup Language)
- GIF (Graphics Interchange Format)
- JPEG (Joint Photographic Experts Group)

Support of the MIME and HTML formats means that users of NNTP Service can post articles in a variety of multimedia formats, including Web pages that have images and links embedded in the actual article. Full support of images comes through GIF and JPEG support, allowing posters to illustrate articles or post images to groups using Internet standard graphic files.

9.1.2. Ease of Administration

The Microsoft NNTP Service is a fully integrated Windows NT service. Because it functions as a service under the Windows NT Server operating system, it can make full use of Windows NT's administrative features, such as the Event Log and the Performance Monitor.

In addition, the NNTP Service also supports the use of a graphical user interface through the Internet Service Manager, providing a means of administering the NNTP Server from any machine on the local network quickly and easily. The ISM is available through the Microsoft Management Console or as an HTML site. However, Microsoft is currently transitioning administrative interfaces to use the MMC version of the ISM, so that is what we will cover primarily in this chapter.

9.1.3. Security Features

The Microsoft News Server offers a flexible security implementation that supports the following:

- *Anonymous connectivity.* The standard mode for news servers, anonymous connectivity allows anyone to access newsgroups hosted on your server without providing a username and password.
- *NNTP Security Extension.* The NNTP Security Extensions (AUTHINFO USER/PASS) give news server administrators the flexibility to require a username/password pair in order to access the newsgroups and articles on your server. This can be a useful feature for establishing an NNTP Server that is accessible only to your organization or for creating a private support group for your customers.

- *Windows NT Challenge/Response.* Because the NNTP Service is closely integrated with Windows NT, you can also configure the server to issue a Windows NT Challenge and Response for maximum data security by using a secure connection to verify a user's credentials. With Windows NT Challenge/Response, the actual username and password are not sent across the network unless authentication fails, in which case the user will be prompted for his or her ID and password.

The Microsoft NNTP Service also supports the Secure Socket Layer protocol for encrypting data transmissions between the server and the news client.

9.2. Understanding the Basics of Microsoft NNTP Service

In order to best understand the functionality and features of the NNTP Service, it helps to have a firm grasp of the basics of Internet News Service. Internet News has a great deal of myth and folklore surrounding the available groups and the people who use them. However, understanding the mechanisms of News is half the battle of using it effectively. The upcoming sections look at some of these issues.

9.2.1. Subscribing to Groups

NNTP discussion forums are called newsgroups or groups. To participate in a group—that is, to read and post articles—you need a newsreader (such as Internet Explorer 4 or Netscape). Next, you can instruct your browser to "subscribe" to a particular discussion group that has a topic you're interested in. Newsgroups are named according to their subject matter. For example:

`rec.sports.basketball`

would be a recreational sports group for basketball players. It might also have some discussion about the sport, but there might also be a group called

`rec.sports.basketball.ncaa`

that focuses even more narrowly on college basketball. How do you know what the primary subject matter of the group is? The best way is to subscribe and read messages from the group for a while, but not post your own messages until you feel comfortable.

The newsgroups themselves are broken down into different hierarchical categories to help people find the groups that interest them. There are seven main categories of newsgroups:

- *alt.* These groups are alternatives. NNTP Servers aren't required to carry them.
- *rec.* These groups are on topics related to recreational activities.
- *biz.* These groups are business-related.
- *misc.* The miscellaneous groups. Includes groups such as `misc.forsale`, a group similar to newspaper classifieds.
- *comp.* Computer-related groups.
- *sci.* Science-related groups.
- *soc.* Social groups, for meeting and chatting.

As the popularity of News has skyrocketed, there are many, many other hierarchies, such as uk for groups originating in the United Kingdom. Generally speaking, there is a group for every activity you can think of. And if there isn't one, with NNTP Service you can always create one.

9.2.2. Posting Articles

To post an article to a newsgroup, you must first subscribe to the newsgroup and then compose your article using a newsreader, such as the Microsoft Internet News client. Once you have composed your message, the newsreader will connect to the NNTP Server via TCP port 119 (or port 563 for secure connections). Once connected, the news client will transfer the content of the message to the NNTP Server, where the message will be stored for a preestablished period of time so that other users can access the message with their news clients and respond if they choose.

9.2.3. Reading Articles

Reading articles is much like posting articles, with the client and server exchanging information about the groups and articles. First, the user connects to the NNTP Server using her newsreader. The NNTP Server then sends the newsreader a list of newsgroups that are available on the server. Once the user has reviewed the list of available groups and subscribed to a few, she can choose to read a specific group.

Once the user has selected a group to read, the news client obtains a list of available articles from the NNTP Server. The user can then read over the subjects of these articles and choose which articles to read and which to ignore. When the user selects an article she wants to read, the client contacts the NNTP Server again.

This time, the NNTP Server delivers the actual content of the message to the newsreader. The user can then read the article and move on, or post a reply if she has something to add or comment on. The process can be repeated for as many articles and groups as the user has time for.

One important aspect of the relationship between NNTP Server and client is that the newsreader keeps track of whether or not a user has seen a particular article. The news server only stores the articles and sends them out when requested. It can be configured to store a certain number of articles or to keep an article for a certain period of time, but it doesn't keep track of each user's preferences or read articles.

9.2.4. Data Structures

By default, the Microsoft NNTP Service creates a news root directory located in C:\Inetpub\nntproot. This directory is sometimes referred to as the spool directory, because this is also where all of the articles that are stored on the server will be located.

Within this directory, each newsgroup has its own directory structure based on the group hierarchy. For example, the group `rec.pets.rabbits` would store its articles in C:\Inetpub\nntproot\rec\pets\rabbits. The pets directory might contain several folders, such as cats and dogs, each corresponding to a different group in the `rec.pets.*` hierarchy.

The articles stored in each directory are simply plain-text files with an .nws extension, indicating that they are NNTP News articles. Each directory also has an index file, which has an .xix extension. A new index file is created for each 128 messages within a group.

The \inetpub\nntpfile\ directory also contains a number of files with extensions such as .hsh, .hdr, .lst, and .txt. These configuration files help the server keep track of how old each article is and when it should be deleted. Files within this hierarchy *should never be edited by hand,* because doing so could destroy the server's record of which articles are old and whether or not they should be deleted. Sometimes these index files will become corrupted, and it will be necessary to rebuild them. We will discuss the methodology for doing so later in this chapter, in the section "Rebuilding NNTP Service."

9.3. When to Use NNTP Service

An NNTP Server can be a useful resource in a variety of situations, ranging from an internal message forum for a branch office to a public bulletin board at a university. Literally anywhere you want to provide a service for users to exchange messages, you can take advantage of NNTP Server to provide discussion group services. The following sections offer a couple of examples of prime uses for the NNTP Services for Windows NT.

9.3.1. A Private News Server

Hosting an internal private news server is a very straightforward task. Upon installing the news server on your Windows NT Server, you can simply configure your news server so that only users who have the correct username and password can access it.

Next, you can easily create a newsgroup or two to discuss issues facing your company, and that's it. Now you have a password-protected server that can be accessed only from inside your organization. If you are operating a small server like this, with very limited access, the NNTP Service will do very nicely. Serving a small number of groups is not a very resource-intensive activity and should be possible on almost any server.

Another way you might host a semi-private newsgroup would be to make the group available outside your organization, but only to a selected group of people. For example, you might create a news server for technical support on your products. You can then distribute a password to your clients, and they can utilize the server as well as your technical support staff. Again, as long as the group doesn't have tons of traffic, this is not an especially resource-intensive application.

9.3.2. A Public News Server

Now let's look at the opposite extreme. Let's say that you are an administrator at a small community college and you want to offer newsgroups to your students so that they can communicate with each other and with users all over the world.

Because you are establishing a public server that in theory will carry a large number of groups to a large number of people, you will need to be more careful about the server configuration. News can be very popular. For example, for public news servers carrying a "full feed" of available newsgroups, a number of newsgroups have a very high volume of messages. And with far more than 10,000 groups to choose from, operating a full-fledged news server can quickly become very resource-intensive. A full public news server today needs to have anywhere from 20 to 40 gigabytes of disk storage space in order to keep articles on the server for a decent period of time while still carrying a large number of groups and updating them frequently.

Fortunately, you currently don't have to deal with this headache. In order to maintain a full public server, the current version of Microsoft's NNTP Service doesn't let you accept newsfeeds from other sites. You can host publicly available groups, but they will still be limited to your server. But even public groups on a single server can become very large. So always keep this performance limitation in mind for your server.

Of course, even if you're running a public news server for your organization, you can still control what groups you create on your server. This flexibility can give you a great deal of control when it comes to configuring your server and managing your resources.

Now that you have a full understanding of what NNTP Service is and what it does, let's look at the mechanisms employed in setting up and managing the service. In the next section, we will discuss the installation of the NNTP Service. Then we'll move on to the administrative tasks you can use to configure and manage NNTP Service.

9.4. Installing NNTP Service

The NNTP Service for Internet Information Server 4.0 is a part of the Windows NT 4.0 Option Pack. It requires a machine that has Windows NT Server 4.0 and Internet Information Server 4.0.

The installation process is quite simple:

1. Launch the Option Pack Setup from the Option Pack CD-ROM. When the installer is running, choose a custom installation. If you have already installed portions of the IIS Server, select Add/Remove.

2. From the Components list, select Internet Information Server (IIS) and click the Show Subcomponents button (see Figure 9.1).

3. Select the NNTP Service and click OK. Click Next to continue. You will see a couple of screens with options for IIS and the transaction server. If you don't have any special configurations for IIS or the transaction server, just accept the defaults for these screens.

4. You see the option screen for NNTP Service, as shown in Figure 9.2.

> **Note:** If you have already installed IIS, you won't see the IIS or Transaction Server screens. You can simply proceed with the NNTP installation.

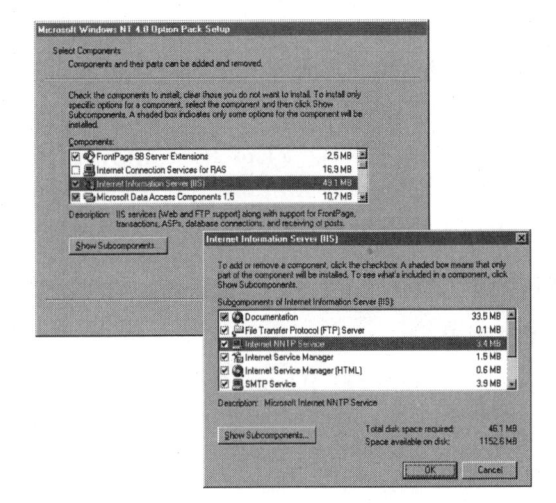

Figure 9.1.
The NNTP Service is installed through the Windows NT Option Pack Setup.

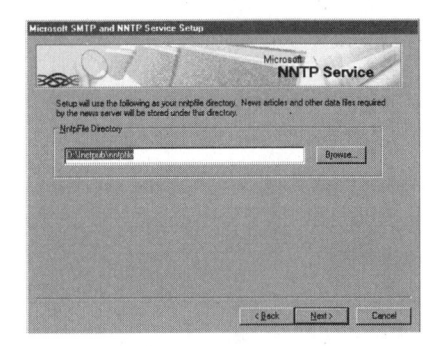

Figure 9.2.
The NNTP Service setup options screen lets you configure which NNTP Service components are installed.

Here you enter the newsroot directory for your NNTP Service. This is where your news datafiles and articles will be stored. It's important that this directory be publicly readable and on a volume with significant space to hold the amount of news you intend to carry. You can use the default directory or specify an existing directory depending on your needs.

5. Once you have selected the directory, click Next, and the installation will be completed.

9.5. Configuring NNTP Service

The Windows NNTP Service offers a very flexible, easy-to-configure, easy-to-manage solution for Windows NT News Service. Through a combination of tight integration with the Windows NT operating system and the ease of the Internet Service Manager administrative console, configuring the Windows NT NNTP Service is very straightforward.

In the following sections, we'll take a look at the Internet Service Manager, the tool used to configure NNTP Service. We'll also cover some of the initial restrictions you can make regarding the ability to connect to your news server.

9.5.1. Using Internet Service Manager for NNTP Service

Much like the SMTP Service for Internet Information Server, the NNTP Service can be configured and managed through the Internet Service Manager (ISM). Two versions of the ISM can be used to manage NNTP Service:

- HTML-based interface
- Microsoft Management Console

The HTML-based interface can be accessed through the Web. This is similar to the interface that you used to access and manage SMTP Services in the last chapter.

The Internet Service Manager also supports a more modular approach by using the Microsoft Management Console (MMC), which consolidates all of the Web interface functionality into a standalone application that can be extended with snap-in modules.

The functionality of both the Web and the MMC versions of the Internet Service Managers are the same. However, since Microsoft will be moving most of the services to use the MMC exclusively, we will go ahead and use the MMC version of the ISM for this chapter. It's a good idea to become familiar with both mechanisms, which isn't too time-consuming considering the functionality is the same.

To launch the Microsoft Management Console version of the Internet Service Manager, do the following:

1. Select Start | Windows NT 4.0 Option Pack | Microsoft Internet Information Server | Internet Service Manager.
2. You will be presented with a management console that functions much like Windows Explorer. You should see a folder icon that represents the console root and another folder for the Internet Information Server. Click the IIS Folder to expand it, and you should see an icon for your server.

3. Expand your server by clicking it. This reveals the services installed, including the NNTP Service, as shown in Figure 9.3.

Figure 9.3.
The NNTP Service is installed on the Internet Service Manager console.

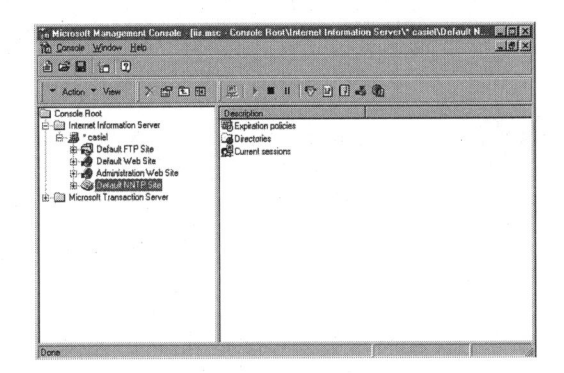

4. From here you can configure all the operating parameters of the server by editing the various property sheets for the NNTP Service configuration.

Now that you are up and running in the Internet Service Manager, let's take a look at configuring the main properties page for the NNTP Service:

1. Right-click Default NNTP Site and select Properties. This will bring up your NNTP site's main properties sheet.
2. The first section contains information to identify your NNTP site. For the description, enter the name of your site.
3. If you want a specific path header to appear in the postings on your site, enter it under Path Header.
4. The IP address represents the IP address that your machine is using. However, if your server is using multiple IP numbers, you can use this setting to specify which IP number your NNTP site will respond to.
5. The TCP port and SSL port numbers represent the port that your news server will use to communicate with clients. Unless you are prepared to deal with setting clients up to contact your server on a special port, it's best to leave these as the defaults.
6. In the Connections settings, you can choose to allow unlimited connections to your NNTP Server, or you can select a limit. If you want to set a limit, enter a number to represent the maximum number of connections allowed. You can also enter a number for the connection timeout, which is how many seconds a client can remain connected and idle before your server kicks it off.

7. Finally, you can enable logging by clicking Enable Logging. You have the option of selecting the style of your log format as well. The default of Microsoft IIS Log File Format is fine. If you're using tools to analyze your logs, you might also consider using the NCSA Common Log File Format.

That's all there is to it. With that information entered, the basic setup of your server is complete. Of course, there are still many more configuration options at your disposal, so let's take a look at some of them and how they can help you fine-tune NNTP Services.

9.5.2. Restricting Operator Access

You can configure the accounts that you want to let access your NNTP site as administrators via the Internet Service Manager. Restricting operator access gives you tighter control over who can create, delete, and edit newsgroups hosted by your site. Here's how you can restrict the operators of your NNTP site:

1. Launch the ISM.
2. Right-click Default NNTP Site and choose Properties. This will bring up the properties sheet for the NNTP Site.
3. Select the Security Accounts tab so that you can add and remove operators, as shown in Figure 9.4.

Figure 9.4.
The Security Accounts tab in the Default NNTP Site Properties dialog box can configure authorized news site operators.

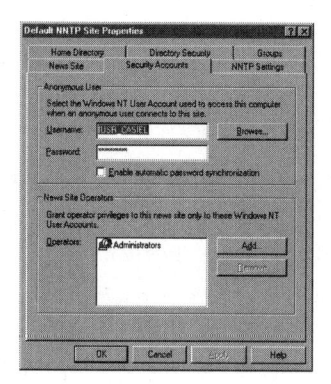

4. To add a user, simply click the Add button.
5. You will see a list of the groups and accounts that are available on your NT Server. Select the group you want to add and click Add. When you're finished adding users and/or groups, click OK.

> **Note:** From this dialog box you can also alter the account that is used to run requests when users connect to your site using standard newsreader software. You should be careful when altering the account that the NNTP Service runs requests under, because granting users access under an account other than the default can compromise system security. For example, if you were to run all requests as the Administrator for your NT Server, you could be opening a very troublesome security hole.

6. Your new user/group should be added to the list of operators. To remove an operator, simply select it from the list and click Remove.

Using this property, you can configure any authorized user on your NT Server as an administrator for your NNTP Service. You can do this to give different users the ability to share management responsibilities if your news site requires multiple administrators.

9.5.3. Restricting Access to Newsgroups

In addition to configuring which users can connect to your server as administrators, you might also want to restrict which users can connect to your site. There are two different methods to control user access to your newsgroups:

- Authentication
- IP/DNS restrictions

The NNTP Service supports several different methods of authenticating users. To configure how users may connect, right-click Default NNTP Site. From the Properties dialog box, choose Authentication Methods (see Figure 9.5).

Figure 9.5.
The Authentication Methods dialog box lets you configure secure methods for users to connect to your server.

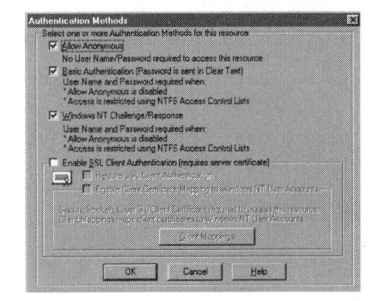

From this dialog box you can select the Directory Security properties sheet, which contains the Password Authentication Method and IP Address and Domain Name Restrictions properties sheets. Simply click the Edit button for either option to edit its properties.

Four different options are available for controlling user access:

- *Allow Anonymous.* This option lets anyone connect to the news server without entering any username/password information.
- *Basic Authentication.* This requires that the user enter a username and password, which are based on NTFS Access Control List settings in the newsgroup directories. Password information is sent as clear text.
- *Windows NT Challenge/Response.* With NT Challenge/Response, the client and the server "handshake" using an encrypted protocol, so the username and password are not passed directly over the Internet. This method also uses NTFS Access Control Lists, but it does so using Windows NT account-level security; if the initial verification fails, the user is prompted for username/password information.
- *Enable SSL Client Authentication.* When you have installed a server certificate from a valid certificate authority, you can enable a Secure Sockets Layer connection to your news server, which allows a secure data-encrypted channel to be opened between the server and the news client for secure news sites. It's important to note that the client connecting to your site must also have an installed client certificate in order for SSL to function properly.

In addition to restricting access to your news server through username/password pairs, you can also configure your news server to reject connections from certain domain names or IP numbers. This feature can let you restrict access to your news server from trusted domains or eliminate access from IPs or domains that have caused problems with your server.

The IP Address and Domain Name Restrictions dialog box, shown in Figure 9.6, can be accessed from the Default Site properties sheet under the Directory Security tab.

Figure 9.6.
The IP Address and Domain Name Restrictions dialog box lets you configure who may and may not connect to your server.

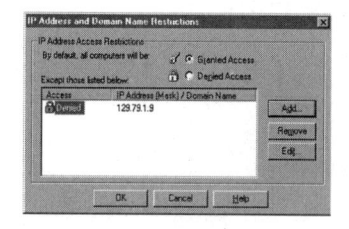

Using this dialog box, you can enter the IP numbers or domain names of individual machines, sites, or groups of machines that you want to ban from your site or grant access to your site. You can use wildcards here to exclude/include ranges of machines.

Suppose you wanted to restrict all access to your site from educational institutions (those with an .edu domain name). Here's how this would be done:

1. Launch the ISM, right-click Default NNTP Site, and choose Properties.
2. Select the Directory Security tab.
3. Click the Edit button to see the IP Address and Domain Name Restrictions dialog box.
4. Confirm that the default, Granted Access, is selected (as shown in Figure 9.6), because you will grant access to all computers except those you're going to enter. Click Add.
5. In the next dialog box, select Domain Name.
6. In the Domain Name text field, enter `*.edu`. This is the wildcard to specify all .edu domains.
7. Click OK on all the open dialog boxes. Now you have restricted access to your NNTP Server from any machine that has an .edu address.

9.6. Managing NNTP Service

The tasks necessary to correctly manage an NNTP site are individually very simple. However, when applied collectively to possibly thousands of groups, their importance is significantly increased. None of the management tasks outlined in the following sections are complicated. However, they do need to be followed up on regularly to make sure that the NNTP Service hasn't encountered any problems. A small problem with one group can quickly blossom into a nightmare for all the groups available on a server.

9.6.1. Creating Newsgroups

Creating new groups on your server is a very simple process. From the NNTP Default properties sheet, select the Group tab. You will have the option of creating a new group.

Once you have chosen to create a new group, you will be prompted to enter the group information in the Newsgroup Properties dialog box, shown in Figure 9.7.

Figure 9.7.
The Newsgroup Properties dialog box allows you to create new newsgroups on your server.

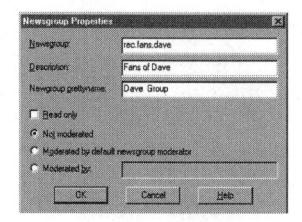

Here are the options for configuring your new group:

- *Newsgroup.* This is the name of your new group, in the format of `hierarchy.name.category`.
- *Description.* A description of the group's purpose.
- *Newsgroup Prettyname.* A descriptive name for your group. This option is not supported by all newsreaders.
- *Read Only.* Check this option if you want to prevent readers from posting articles to the group.
- *Not Moderated.* By default, newsgroups are not moderated. A moderated group is one in which one individual (or collective group) must approve all posts to the newsgroup, usually in an effort to keep postings relevant.
- *Moderated by Default Newsgroup Moderator.* By default, the moderator is `newsgroup@yourdomain`.
- *Moderated By.* If you want to appoint a specific moderator, you can enter his e-mail address here.

Once you have selected your options and entered the new group information, click OK to create your group. It should then be available from any newsreader that connects to your server.

Now let's perform the steps to actually create a newsgroup. Suppose you're working for ACME Widgets, and you want to start a newsgroup on your site called `acme.widgets.service`. Here's how you would set up the group:

1. Launch the ISM and select the Default News Site. Right-click to bring up the Default NNTP Site properties.
2. Select the Groups tab.
3. Click Create New Newsgroup.
4. In the first text box, enter the name of the group you are creating—in this case, `acme.widgets.service`.

5. Enter a description for the group—for example, `Service information for owners of ACME Widgets`.
6. Enter a "prettyname" for clients that support the Prettyname feature, such as `Widgets Help`.
7. Select Not Moderated, because you want this to be a publicly accessible group.
8. Click OK.

The newsgroup is created! Users can now connect to your server and begin posting messages on `acme.widgets.service`.

9.6.2. Editing and Deleting Newsgroups

Once a newsgroup is created and living on your server, you can edit the group properties at any time through the Groups tab in the ISM. You can also delete groups from your site through this tab.

To edit a group, select the group you want to edit from the Matching Newsgroups list and click the Edit button. This brings up the newsgroup properties for the group, allowing you to make changes to the group name or prettyname, for example.

Removing a group is even simpler. Select the group you want to delete from the Matching Newsgroups list, and click Delete. After you confirm that you want to delete the group, it is removed.

9.6.3. Defining Newsgroup Limits

Because newsgroups can be a very resource-intensive service, it is often necessary to put limits on the amount of information that can be exchanged via the newsgroups installed on your system. The most common means of limiting newsgroups is through the use of expiration policies.

Articles are usually posted in a group for a specific topic, and they remain in that group until the article is purged from the system. When the article is purged is at the discretion of the NNTP site administrator. Expiration times can be set based on a length of time or when the group directory reaches a certain size. You use the Expiration Policy Wizard, shown in Figure 9.8, to configure how articles are expunged from the system.

Figure 9.8.
The Expiration Policy Wizard lets you create separate policies for each group as to when articles should be thrown away.

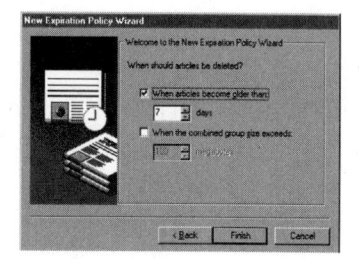

You can choose to apply an expiration policy to your entire server, to a limited selection of groups, or even to individual groups. Once you have selected which groups the expiration policies apply to, you need to specify how the expiration is to be carried out.

Here you have two options. You can purge articles from the group after they are a certain number of days old, or you can purge articles when the directory for the group reaches a predetermined size limit. Either way works well, and both result in the oldest articles being purged first.

Let's look at how to set up an expiration policy. Let's give our group `acme.widgets.service` a 14-day expiration policy:

1. Launch the ISM, and click Default NNTP Site to expand the options available.
2. Right-click Expiration Policies, click New, and click Expiration Policy.
3. This should launch the Expiration Policy Wizard. Now you can name the policy to keep track of it. We'll call this one Service. Click Next.
4. Select Only Selected Newsgroups on This Site and click Next.
5. Enter the group name `acme.widgets.service` and click Add to add it to the list of groups the expiration applies to. Click Next.
6. Enter 14 in the When Articles Become Older Than *xx* Days field. Click Finish.

Now your expiration policy is in place. Any articles that are posted to `acme.widgets.service` will remain on the site for 14 days before they are erased.

9.6.4. Using Virtual Directories

Because disk space management is such a problem, it is sometimes necessary to add additional disk space to handle new groups or old groups that are just too popular.

To compensate for spreading your NNTP articles over multiple disks, the NNTP Service allows for virtual directories. You can configure these through the Virtual Directory Wizard, shown in Figure 9.9.

Figure 9.9.
The Virtual Directory Wizard allows you to specify a virtual directory for groups to improve disk space utilization.

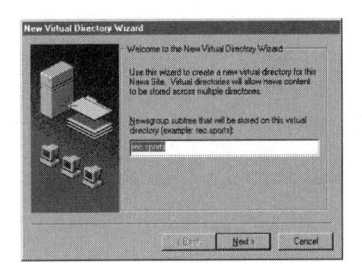

To configure a virtual directory, select the new directory on the new volume you want to use for a group or hierarchy, and then assign a group to the directory. The NNTP Service will then place articles for the group you selected in the virtual directory, hopefully freeing up some of your disk resources. As far as the NNTP Service is concerned, there is no difference between a physical group directory under the NNTP root and a virtual directory.

Let's turn again to a real example. Suppose you want to add a group called `acme.customer.feedback`, and you anticipate that it will receive a large amount of traffic. You might want to place it on another disk partition using a virtual directory. Here's how:

1. Launch the ISM, and click Default NNTP Site to expand the options available.
2. Right-click Directories, click New, and click Virtual Directory.
3. This should launch the Virtual Directory wizard. Now you can enter the name of the newsgroup that will be using the virtual directory—in this case, `acme.customer.feedback`. Click Next.
4. Enter the physical path to the new drive—for example, `D:\`. (This will vary, depending on your system configuration.)
5. Click Finish.

Now the virtual directory has been created for the NNTP Service, and all articles for your new group `acme.customer.feedback` will be stored in a new location, giving you more control over your disk resources.

9.6.5. Generating Control Messages

Control messages are specially formatted messages that are posted to the `control.*` newsgroup hierarchy and can perform administrative tasks on your NNTP Server. For example, the Microsoft NNTP Service supports the following control commands:

- *Cancel.* This command lets a user or administrator cancel the posting of an article.
- *Newgroup.* This command creates a new newsgroup on your server.
- *Rmgroup.* This command removes an existing newsgroup from your server.

The cancel command is usually generated by newsreaders, while the newgroup and rmgroup commands are usually generated by servers. Because there is such a strong potential for abuse of these commands, you will probably want to restrict who you allow to execute commands on your NNTP Server.

9.6.6. Restricting Control Messages

Because of the power of control messages, you might want to restrict access to the `control.*` newsgroups on your server. This will prevent general users from abusing the ability to cancel messages and create groups, and will also prevent users from accidentally removing important groups.

The easiest way to limit control messages is to have the `control.*` hierarchy of groups be moderated by the administrator. That way, the administrator will have to approve any control messages before they are executed by NNTP Service.

Now that you know how to add and remove groups as well as control the access that users have to your NNTP Server, let's take a look at some of the tools you can use to monitor your NNTP Service's performance. These tools can help you decide if your server is functioning up to par, and if not, what hardware might be needed to make your news server run more smoothly.

9.7. Optimizing Performance

The NNTP Service can really tax your resources. If your site hosts a large number of groups, and those groups are heavily trafficked, you can consume large amounts of memory and disk space. Optimizing your NNTP Server for your usage can be one of the most critical tasks with administering an NNTP site. Improperly configured and unwatched news servers can be slow and annoying for readers and can cause real resource-management problems on the server.

The following sections offer a few techniques that you can use to maximize the efficiency of your NNTP site while still providing the widest range of service to your end users.

9.7.1. System Monitoring Tools

Like the SMTP Service, the NNTP Service also makes use of Windows NT built-in performance monitors to keep track of performance. Errors and notices for the NNTP Service are logged as Windows NT events and can be accessed through the Windows Administration tools such as Event Viewer.

Additionally, the system Performance Monitor can be used to monitor the performance of the NNTP Service. With the NNTP Service, it is particularly useful to keep track of the following:

- *Articles Posted.* This counter can give you an indication as to how many articles are being posted to the groups hosted on your server.
- *Articles Sent.* This counter can give you an indication as to how many articles are being read in the groups hosted on your server.
- *Control Messages Failed.* This counter can give you an indication as to how many incoming control requests are failing on your server. If the number is increasing dramatically or in a pattern, this can indicate a server misconfiguration.
- *Current Connections.* This counter can help you determine what times of day are peak usage and when lulls occur. Additionally, it can help you track the usage demographics for your server so that you can expand along with your user base.
- *% Total Processor Time.* This counter can give you an indication as to how the NNTP Service is affecting your system's processing abilities.
- *% Free Space.* This counter is very important. Since news delivery depends on adequate disk drive space being available, this counter helps you monitor your disk utilization. If you're consistently running into disk problems, you can shorten the expiration time for articles to clear them off the server faster, or you can limit the number of groups that your site carries.
- *Available Bytes.* This counter is useful to keep track of the available memory on your server. As more people connect, memory usage increases. If people are

having trouble connecting, and the Available Bytes counter indicates that memory is scarce, it might be time to add more memory to your system.

9.7.2. Rebuilding NNTP Service

Because of the high-volume nature of many news sites, your NNTP site might sometimes have trouble keeping track of messages accurately, particularly if there are problems with corrupted articles or disk space.

If problems like this occur, it might become necessary to rebuild your NNTP site. If you are recovering from a crash, you see articles disappearing, or you notice other odd behavior, try rebuilding the site.

Rebuilding is easy. Simply stop the NNTP service right-click the default NNTP site, and select Tasks | Rebuild. The Rebuild Wizard will then step you through the rebuild process, as shown in Figure 9.10.

Figure 9.10.
The NNTP Service Rebuild Wizard can be used to restore the proper article and group settings.

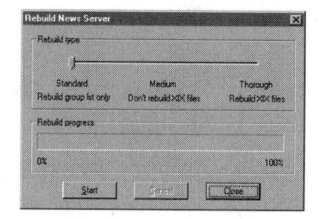

The NNTP Service can perform three levels of rebuilding:

- *Standard.* The standard rebuild is the quickest, but it doesn't rebuild all the articles and indexes on your server.
- *Medium.* The medium rebuild is slower. It rebuilds any articles or indexes that it detects are corrupt. This is generally a nice balance for rebuilds.
- *Thorough.* The thorough rebuild option rebuilds every article and index on the entire server. This option is best when you're recovering from a catastrophic disk crash. However, it is extremely slow, and on slower machines operating large sites, it can literally take days.

9.7.3. Verifying Connectivity

Once your server is configured and running, you can verify connectivity to the server using a telnet application (such as Microsoft Telnet) to access the server on port 119, which is the default NNTP TCP port. Figure 9.11 shows the results.

Figure 9.11.

Verifying that NNTP Server is accepting connections using telnet.

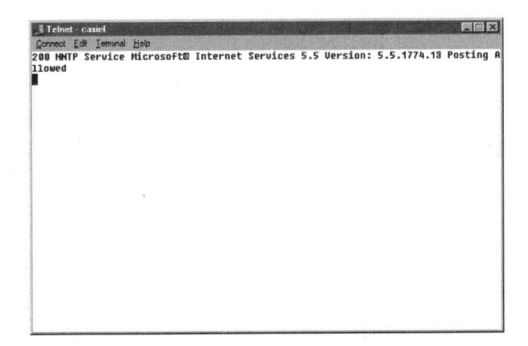

You can launch telnet to check your server by selecting Start | Run and entering `telnet` *myhost* `119`, where *myhost* is the name of your machine. This should connect you to your news server, and you should be greeted with a message such as

```
200 NNTP Service Microsoft Internet Services 5.5 Version: 5.5.1774.13
Posting Allowed
```

If you do, your service is running correctly. If you don't, you should begin troubleshooting with the Internet Service Manager to make sure that the NNTP Service is running (see Day 14, "Troubleshooting"). If it is, the next step is to examine your Windows NT networking configuration.

Lab

This lab consists of review questions pertaining to this chapter and provides an opportunity for you to use walk-through exercises to apply the knowledge that you've gained.

Questions

1. You are creating a group for technical support personnel to post answers to customers' e-mail questions as a resource. You want to review questions before they're posted. You would select a moderated group over a standard group because

   A. Standard groups do not have a predetermined expiration time.

   B. Moderated groups are limited in the size of articles that can be posted.

   C. Standard groups do not require usernames and passwords.

   D. The group moderator must approve all articles that are posted to the newsgroup.

2. Articles for the group `soc.talk.radio` would be stored in which directory structure?

   A. \inetpub\nntproot\soc

   B. \inetpub\nntproot\soc\talk\radio

   C. \inetpub\nntproot\

   D. \inetpub\nntproot\soc.talk.radio

3. A user has been trying to issue commands to create a group on your server. The best way to stop his control messages is to

   A. Block the IP numbers and domains of users who attempt to send control messages.

   B. Configure the newsgroups in the `control.*` hierarchy to be moderated groups.

   C. Establish an expiration policy that clears the `control.*` groups instantly.

   D. Configure access to the `control.*` groups to require authentication.

4. Telnet can be used as a diagnostic tool to see if your NNTP site is

   A. Out of disk space.

   B. Configured for authentication.

   C. Correctly responding to network requests.

   D. Currently running a newsgroup expiration.

5. The default TCP port for the NNTP protocol is
    A. 119
    B. 80
    C. 21
    D. 25

6. If your nntproot directory keeps filling to capacity, what are some measures you can take to better manage disk resources? (Select all that apply.)
    A. Configure some groups to be moderated.
    B. Install a new disk volume and establish virtual directories.
    C. Limit access to your NNTP site by enabling authentication.
    D. Increase the frequency of the site expiration.

7. Users are complaining that articles are not being posted, and they are receiving bad message errors. What action would likely correct the problem?
    A. Increase the site's expiration period.
    B. Enable anonymous access to the NNTP site.
    C. Rebuild the NNTP site.
    D. Stop and restart the NNTP Service.

8. The default authentication scheme for the NNTP Service is
    A. Allow Anonymous
    B. Windows NT Challenge/Response
    C. Basic Authentication
    D. Enable SSL Client Authentication

9. What Windows NT system tool can provide real-time feedback for NNTP Service performance?
    A. Event Log
    B. Windows Explorer
    C. Task Manager
    D. Performance Monitor

10. Which of the following are valid NNTP control commands?
    A. Cancel, Create, Destroy
    B. Cancel, Newgroup, Rmgroup
    C. Cancel, Add, Remove
    D. Cancel, Addgroup, Delgroup

Answers to Questions

1. **D.** Articles may be posted to moderated groups only after they have been approved by the moderator. This lets your technical support staff review the questions and prepare adequate answers before the messages are posted for the public.

2. **B.** Articles are stored in a directory hierarchy that follows the structure of the group name, where each element in the name is represented by a new folder level.

3. **B.** If you configure the `control.*` hierarchy to be moderated, no messages can be posted to the group without the approval of the moderator. Therefore, if you moderate the control groups, none of the user's messages will be processed by your server until they are approved by an administrator.

4. **C.** By telneting to port 119, you can test to see if the NNTP server is responding to network requests.

5. **A.** NNTP News operates on port 119 for standard news. Port 563 is utilized for secure NNTP connections with SSL.

6. **B, D.** Installing virtual directories is an efficient way to increase disk space by distributing articles over multiple volumes. Increasing the frequency of the expiration can also help keep new articles coming in, in spite of a full disk.

7. **C.** Rebuilding the NNTP site can correct many delivery problems by reindexing the articles currently posted in groups.

8. **A.** Allow Anonymous lets any newsreader connect to the NNTP Service. It is the default NNTP configuration.

9. **D.** The Windows NT Performance Monitor includes counters to track performance of the NNTP Service. Using these counters, you can track memory usage and disk usage and then add the appropriate hardware to increase performance when necessary.

10. **B.** Cancel, Newgroup, and Rmgroup are valid NNTP control commands.

Exercises

Exercise 9.1.: Creating a New Newsgroup

This exercise addresses the following Microsoft exam objectives:

- Install and configure the Microsoft NNTP Service
- Configure the NNTP Service to host a newsgroup

In this exercise you will create a new newsgroup to be hosted on your NNTP server. Follow these steps:

1. Launch the Internet Service Manager.
2. Right-click the Default NNTP Site.
3. Select Properties from the pop-up menu.
4. Select the Groups tab.
5. Click the Create New Newsgroup button.
6. Enter the group name—for example, mycompany.mygroup.announce.
7. Enter a description for the newsgroup—for example, An announcement group for my department.
8. Enter a newsgroup prettyname, such as My Group's Announcements.
9. Click OK.

Exercise 9.2.: Creating a Moderated Newsgroup

This exercise addresses the following Microsoft exam objectives:

- Install and configure the Microsoft NNTP Service
- Configure the NNTP Service to host a newsgroup

In this exercise you will create a moderated newsgroup. Follow these steps:

1. Launch the Internet Service Manager.
2. Right-click the Default NNTP Site.
3. Select Properties from the pop-up menu.
4. Select the Groups tab.
5. Click the Create New Newsgroup button.
6. Enter the group name—for example, mycompany.managers.moderated.
7. Enter a description for the newsgroup—for example, A moderated management group.
8. Enter a newsgroup prettyname, such as Executive Management Forum.
9. Click the Moderated By: radio button.
10. Enter the e-mail address of the designated moderator, such as moderator@mycompany.com.
11. Click OK.

Exercise 9.3.: Deleting a Newsgroup

This exercise addresses the following Microsoft exam objectives:

- Install and configure the Microsoft NNTP Service
- Configure the NNTP Service to host a newsgroup

In this exercise you will delete an existing newsgroup from your NNTP server. Do the following:

1. Launch the Internet Service Manager.
2. Right-click the Default NNTP Site.
3. Select Properties from the pop-up menu.
4. Select the Groups tab.
5. Highlight the group to be deleted in the Matching Newsgroups list box.
6. Click the Delete button.
7. Click OK.

Exercise 9.4.: Establishing a Newsgroup Expiration Time

This exercise addresses the following Microsoft exam objective:

- Optimize the performance of the NNTP Service

In this exercise you will establish the time period for articles to expire within a newsgroup. Perform the following tasks:

1. Launch the Internet Service Manager.
2. Select the Default NNTP Site, and click it to expand the administrative modules.
3. Right-click Expiration Policies and select New Expiration Policy from the pop-up menu.
4. Enter the name of your new policy, such as `Site Expire Policy`. Click Next.
5. Select the All Newsgroups on This Site radio button. Click Next.
6. Choose your expiration policy. For example, for When Should Articles Be Deleted?, enter 3 in the When Articles Become Older Than *xx* Days field.
7. Click Finish.

Exercise 9.5.: Rebuilding NNTP Service

This exercise addresses the following Microsoft exam objective:

- Optimize performance of the NNTP Service

In this exercise you will rebuild your NTTP Service to restore the article histories for all your groups. Follow these steps:

1. Launch the Internet Service Manager.
2. Stop the NNTP Service by selecting the Default Site and pressing the Stop button.
3. Right-click the Default NNTP Site.
4. Select Task | Rebuild Server.
5. Choose the level of rebuild—for example, Thorough.
6. Click Close.

TEST DAY FAST FACTS

Here are a few fast facts about this chapter that you may want to know ahead of time. Don't forget that these facts also provide great last-minute study material.

- The Index Server runs as a service called Content Indexer.
- The Index Server can index many different types of files by using filters that can be added for different file types.
- Indexing can work with several different languages because word breakers (which separate words in a document) and the normalizer (which removes words such as "the" and "and") both have language modules.
- The Index Server generally doesn't require much in the way of administration.
- Administration can be handled through the HTML administration tool or the Microsoft Management Console.
- Multiple catalogs can index different parts of a Web page or document directories.
- Word lists are created and kept in RAM until they are merged to shadow indexes.
- Shadow indexes are merged by a master merge into the master index.

Day 10

Microsoft Index Server

by Rob Scrimger and Glen Martin

One of the biggest challenges users face with the Internet or with an intranet is finding information. Having to click through an endless series of links to get to the desired information is time-consuming and frustrating.

The best way to avoid this problem is to provide some method whereby the user will be able to search an entire site for a series of key words. Providing this ability can be complicated because of the number of different document formats and languages that could exist not only on the Internet but even in your intranet.

The Index Server gives you a powerful tool to overcome these problems. It also lets you provide the ability to search your site. The nice part is that setting up the Index Server is incredibly simple. Because the Index Server was designed from the ground up to be very simple to install and administer, the exam includes only a few questions on it. They primarily test your knowledge of managing indexes and understanding which files are used to interact with the Index Server. We will discuss these topics later in this chapter.

Objectives

This chapter helps you prepare for the Microsoft exam by covering the following objectives:

- Configure the Index Server to index a Web site
- Configure IIS to integrate with the Index Server
    - Specify query parameters by creating the .idq file
    - Specify how the query results are formatted and displayed to the user by creating the .htx file
- Optimize the performance of the Index Server

Test Day Fast Facts

- The master index has the highest compression, making files small and faster to search.

- Query pages can be built quickly using .idq files and basic .asp pages. ActiveX Data Objects (ADO) can also be used to access the Index Servers database.

10.1. Roles for the Index Server

The Index Server provides a wonderful tool to add search capabilities to your Web site and can also be used to perform other functions. The following sections discuss in detail the two roles of the Index Server.

10.1.1. Indexing Web Sites

One of the key areas that has driven the growth of the Internet is the ability to make information available to a large number of people in a simple cross-platform medium. The Internet is not about technology or computers; it is about information. And the ability to find that information requires indexing.

Imagine walking into a library and looking for a book on Thai cooking. Now imagine that there is no index in the library and the books are placed on the selves in alphabetical order rather than by category. You would probably go to the T section and hope to find a book called *Thai Cooking*—and you might succeed.

However, you will have missed any books on the subject that don't start with the word Thai. You also will have searched through a whole series of books that started with the word Thai but had nothing to do with cooking.

Without indexing, the same situation occurs every time you connect to a site on the Internet (or an intranet). There are several general indexes on the Internet (Yahoo!, Webcrawler, and Alta Vista, to name a few) that will get people to your site. Index Server will help users locate specific information on your site.

This indexing capability is even more criticial for your internal site, because the Internet search engine will not be available. Simple sites are made easier with search capabilities. When a site is more complex or contains many documents, indexing becomes even more important.

10.1.2. Document Warehousing

Most large organizations have thousands, perhaps millions, of documents that they need to maintain. The sheer number of documents produced internally in a year is staggering. These documents need to be stored and kept for various reasons (legal requirements, reference, and so on), and this is what document warehousing is all about—storing and cataloging documents. How many times have you tried to locate a document that you wrote six months ago and ended up losing half a day in the process?

10.2. Installing the Index Server

Normally you will install the Index Server with the rest of the IIS package. You can, however, choose to install it separately. This section covers the steps that are required to do this.

In order to add the Index Server after other components are already in place, you need to start the Setup program again. To do this, select Start | Programs | Windows NT 4.0 Option Pack | Windows NT Option Pack Setup. You will see the introduction screen. Click Next to move to the next screen, and follow these steps:

1. In the installation options dialog box, shown in Figure 10.1, click Add/Remove. You see the dialog box shown in Figure 10.2.

Figure 10.1.
The installation options screen from NT Option Pack setup allows you to change the installed options.

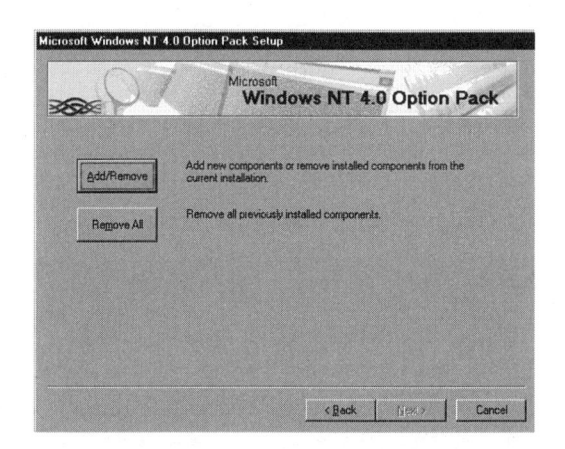

Figure 10.2.
Select Index Server from the component list so that it can be added to the installed components.

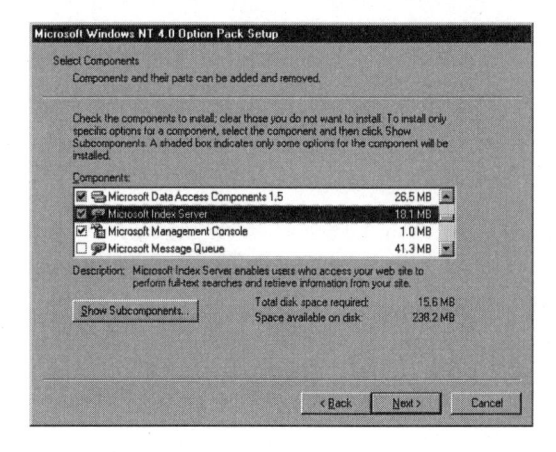

2. Check the box beside Microsoft Index Server and click Next.
3. When the files are finished copying, click Finish.

10.3. Configuration Options for the Index Server

In general, the Index Server can be left to its own devices. Once the server has been installed and you restart the system, you should expect that there will be a period of high CPU usage. This occurs as the Index does the initial indexing of the *corpus* (this is the term Microsoft uses to describe the body of information that will be indexed).

You can change some settings for the Index Server. The next two sections look at the two methods you can use to control the index:

- The HTML Administration tool
- Configuration in Microsoft Management Console

A section within this configuration discussion takes a look at the configuration tabs.

10.3.1. The HTML Administration Tool

The HTML Administration tool lets you control the index process and see the current status of the server from Internet Explorer 4.0. To access the page, select Start | Programs | Windows NT 4.0 Option Pack | Microsoft Index Server | Index Server Administration.

From outside your organization, you can use `http://host_name/iisadmin/isadmin/admin.htm` (where *host_name* is the name or IP address of your server). Either of these will take you to the main administration screen, shown in Figure 10.3.

Four options are available from this screen:

- *Index Statistics*. From here you can see the current index statistics and check how the server is running. The first part of the page tells you about the cache statistics, and the second part tells you about the server statistics.
- *Unfiltered Documents*. This allows you to see a list of documents that have not yet been filtered on the server. If any are listed, the server is in the process of indexing (see Figure 10.4).

10.3. Configuration Options for the Index Server | 323

Figure 10.3.
The main HTML administration screen for the Index Server lets you control the Index Server from any system that has a browser.

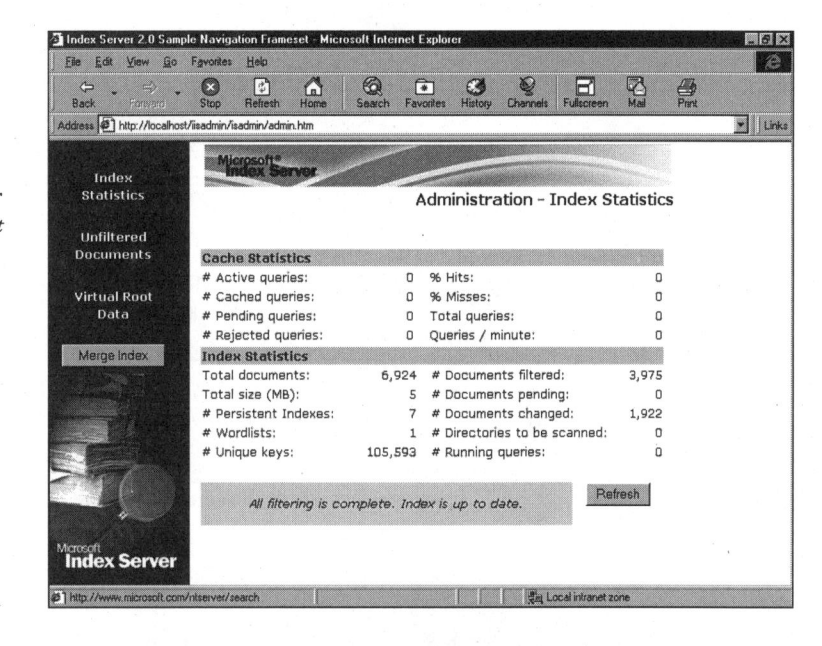

Figure 10.4.
The Unfiltered Documents screen shows you the documents that need to be filtered on the server. In this case, no documents are waiting to be filtered.

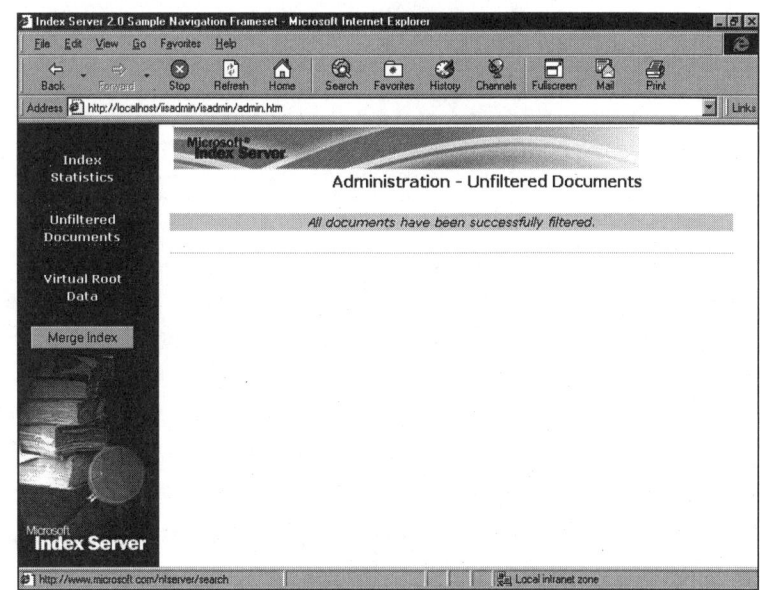

- *Virtual Root Data.* If you have a directory that is not on an NT partition (virtual roots can be anywhere on your system or across the network—anywhere except under the \INETPUB\WWWROOT directory), the server will have to actively scan these areas for new documents that need to be indexed. This normally happens automatically, but you can force the system to scan a virtual root using this page (see Figure 10.5).

Figure 10.5.
Selecting virtual roots to scan forces the system to search for documents that need to be indexed on non-NTFS partitions.

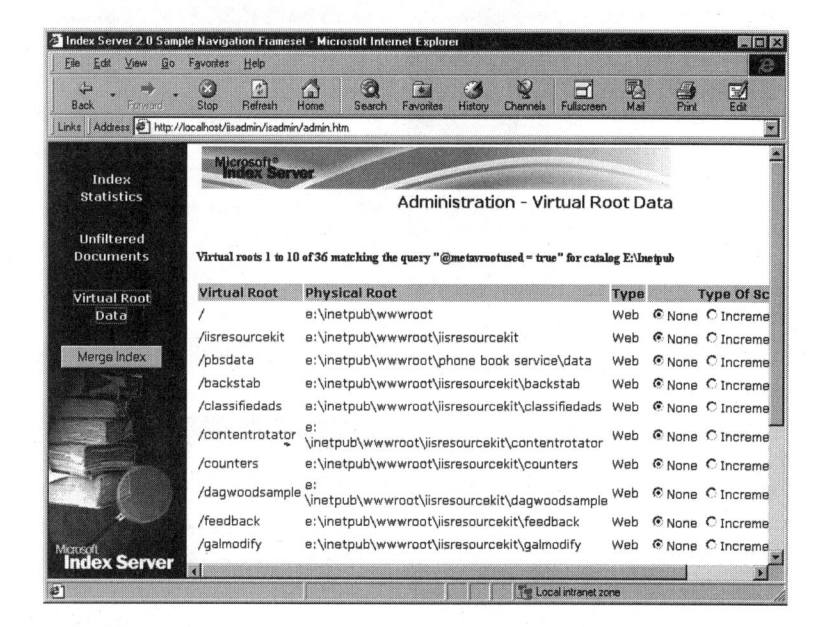

- *Merge Index.* This forces a merge that combines all the indexes and lists that the server has created into a single index (see the "Merges" section). You can also do this from the Index Statistics page by clicking the Merge Index button.

The HTML administration pages provide you with most of the functionality you require. However, you also need to know what options you can set in the Microsoft Management Console.

10.3.2. Configuration in the Microsoft Management Console

The Microsoft Management Console (MMC) is a centralized administration shell. In other words, it doesn't do any adminstration itself; instead, it lets you snap in

10.3. Configuration Options for the Index Server

standard administration modules (this was covered in Day 3, "Configuring IIS 4.0"). When you first start to use the MMC, the Index Server snap-in is not loaded. To load the Index Server snap-in, follow these steps:

1. Start the MMC by choosing Start | Programs | Windows NT 4.0 Option Pack | Microsoft Internet Information Server | Internet Service Manager.

2. Select Console | Add/Remove Snap-in. You see the dialog box shown in Figure 10.6.

Figure 10.6.
The Add/Remove Snap-in dialog box for the MMC lets you add the Index Server snap-in.

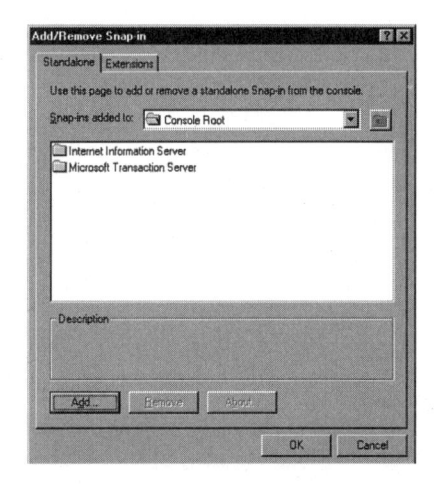

3. Click the Add button. From the Add Standalone Snap-in dialog box, shown in Figure 10.7, choose Index Server and click OK.

Figure 10.7.
Adding the Index Server standalone snap-in to the current console.

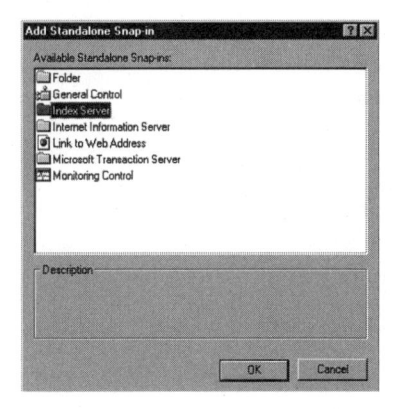

4. Choose the computer that you will manage (either local or remote), and click Finish.

5. Click the OK button to return to the MMC. You should see the Index Server list for the machine you chose, as shown in Figure 10.8.

Figure 10.8.
The MMC with the Index Server snap-in added.

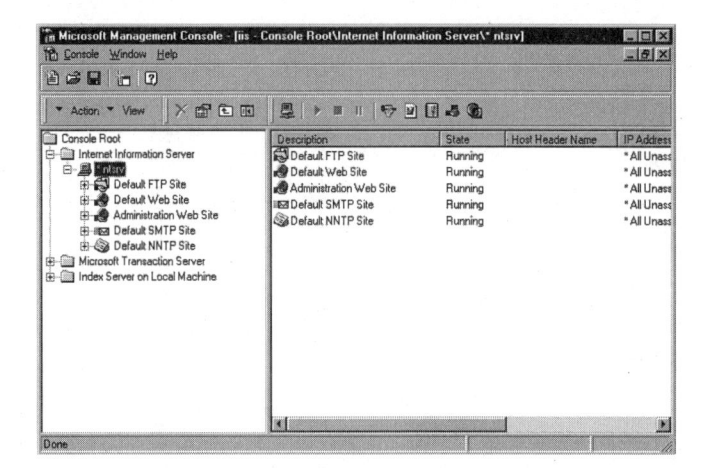

When you expand the Index Server using the + sign, you will see the catalogs that the server is taking care of. (The section called "The Indexing Process" has information on catalogs. For now, you should think of a catalog as being one index.) Each catalog has two tabs:

- *Directories*. This lists the directories that are being handled by this catalog.
- *Properties*. This lists various properties of the catalog.

You will perform several functions in the MMC:

- Forcing a rescan
- Stopping and starting the server
- Adding a catalog
- Adding directories to the catalog
- Adding virtual directories to the catalog
- Removing a directory

The following sections describe these topics in more detail.

A. Forcing a Rescan

When you force a directory rescan, you are basically rebuilding the entire index. This can be very time-consuming and should be done only if the index is returning incorrect results or you have added new filters to the server (files that will read the documents).

To force a rescan, follow these steps:

1. Choose the catalog and select the Directories item (the virtual roots should be listed in the right pane).
2. Choose the roots to rescan, and right-click.
3. From the context menu, select Rescan, as shown in Figure 10.9.

Figure 10.9.
The context menu shows the rescan option and the other available options.

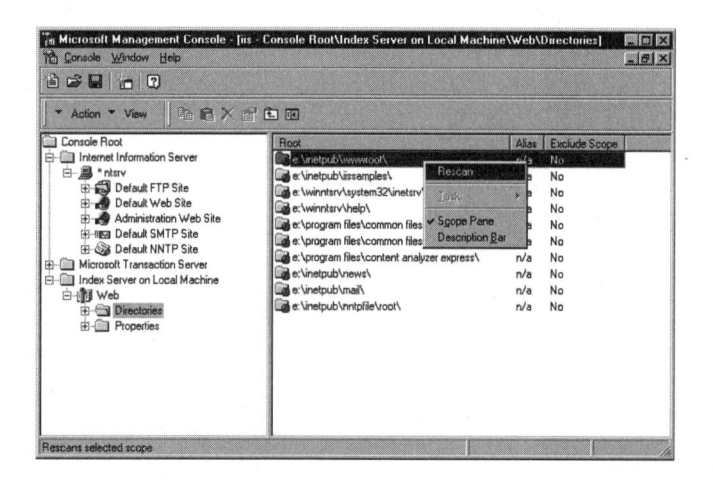

4. A dialog box will appear, asking you to confirm the action. Click Yes.

B. Stopping and Starting the Server

Occasionally you will need to stop and start the Index Server. In IIS 4.0, the Index Server runs under its own process, not in the Inetinfo process as it did under IIS 3.0. (This service is called Content Indexer, and it will actually index the sites and respond to queries.) The upshot of this is that you can actually stop and start it separately.

You will need to stop and start the service when you add new filters or languages or if you add another catalog. This can be done using all the normal methods (Control Panel, Services, or the Server Manager), but it is useful to have the service in the

MMC as well. To stop or start the Content Indexer Service, select the Index Server, right-click it, and then click Stop or Start.

C. Adding a Catalog

Sometimes you will want to add another catalog to the Index Server. This will allow you to put certain virtual roots or directories (which are treated as the same thing) into a separate corpus. This means that each corpus will be small and, therefore, so will the index, making searches faster. You also can control what information users will find by allowing them to search only certain areas of the site.

The down side is that you will only be able to search for information in one corpus with a single query. This means that, to search an entire site, you might need to search two or more times.

To add a catalog, follow these steps:

1. Right-click the Index Server heading and choose New.
2. From the New menu, choose Catalog. You see the dialog box shown in Figure 10.10.

Figure 10.10.

Adding a catalog in the MMC lets you split the body of information to be indexed between two (or more) catalogs.

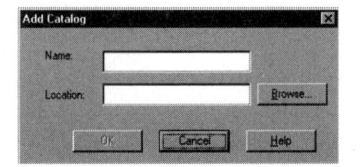

3. Enter the name of the catalog and the location where the catalog information will be stored. Click OK.
4. A dialog box will appear, indicating that the catalog will remain off-line until the Index Server is restarted.
5. Click OK, and stop and start the server.

D. Adding Directories to a Catalog

Now that you have another catalog, you will want to add the directories that this catalog will index. This is simply a matter of adding entries to the Directory tab of the new catalog:

1. Expand the catalog that you want to add a directory to.
2. Right-click the Directories object and choose New | Directory.

10.3. Configuration Options for the Index Server

3. In the Add Directory dialog box, enter the information for the new directory.
4. Click OK.

E. Adding Virtual Directories to a Catalog

If the catalog you are working with is for a Web site on the same server, you can also control how the site is indexed from the WWW settings (directories are covered on Day 4, "The WWW Server"). To control whether a virtual directory is included, do the following:

1. Expand the Internet Information Server object, and then expand the computer name you are working on. Choose the virtual directory that you want to control, and right-click.
2. Choose Properties. The Properties dialog box should appear with the Home Directory tab already selected, as shown in Figure 10.11. If not, select it.

Figure 10.11.

The properties page for a virtual directory allows you to control whether the directory will be indexed or not.

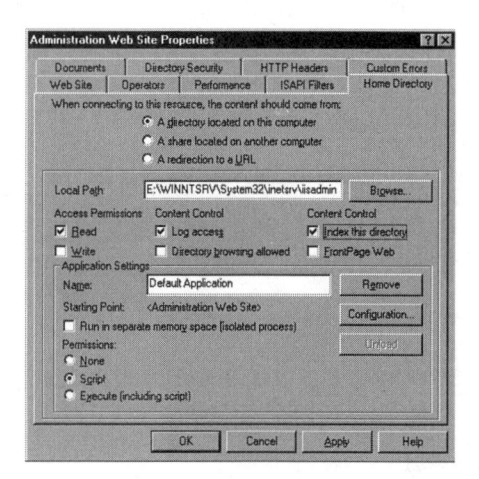

3. To include the directory in the index, be sure that the Index this directory check box is checked.

F. Removing a Directory

After you create a new catalog, you might want to move some of the directories from one catalog to another. Or perhaps you want to stop publishing a section of your Web site. In either case, you will need to remove the directory from the catalog that it is currently in.

To remove a directory from a catalog, follow these steps:

1. Expand the catalog and the directories objects in the MMC.
2. Right-click the directory you want to remove.
3. Choose Remove Directory from the context menu.
4. Confirm that you want to remove the directory by clicking Yes in the confirmation dialog box.

10.3.3. Looking at the Properties

You will need to configure very few properties after you have added the various directories to a catalog. This configuration can be done on one of two levels—for the entire Index Server or for the individual catalogs. On the server, only a couple of properties can be configured.

A. Setting Options on the Server

If you set the options on the server, they will apply to all the catalogs that you don't set individual options for. Only three settings are available in the Index Server Properties dialog box.

To configure the server options, do the following:

1. Right-click the Index Server and choose Properties. The Index Server properties sheet, shown in Figure 10.12, appears.

Figure 10.12.
The Index Server properties dialog box lets you set the options that affect the server itself.

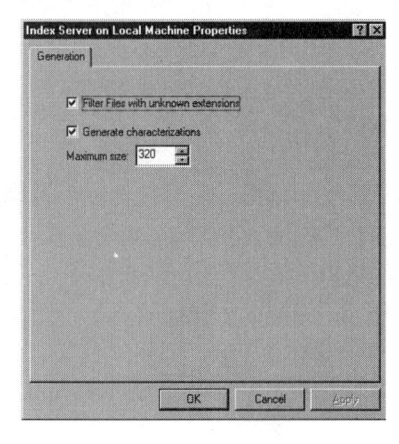

2. Enter the configuration information. Here are your options:
   - *Filter Files with unknown extensions.* This tells the Index Server to try to filter all files that are in the directory (and subdirectories), even if the file type is unknown.
   - *Generate characterizations.* If this option is enabled, the Index Server will keep a characterization (brief description) of the document. This is the first part of the document.
   - *Maximum size.* The number of characters to keep as the characterization for the document.

3. Click OK.

B. Setting Options on Catalogs

As with most of the other components that make up IIS 4.0, you have the option of setting the properties of the individual items within any of the servers. This gives you increased flexibility. For example, if you are indexing a Web site, you may only want to provide a short description of the documents. If you use the Index Server to warehouse documents, you might want to provide a longer characterization of the document.

To set options for a single catalog, follow these steps:

1. Right-click the catalog that you want to set the options for.
2. Choose Properties. A dialog box will appear that provides basic information about the catalog (see Figure 10.13). It can't be edited.

Figure 10.13.
The first page of properties for a catalog can't be edited, because it is for informative purposes only.

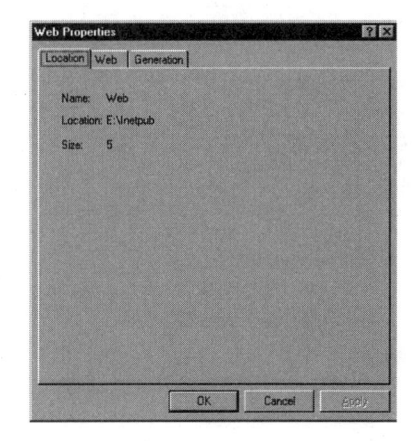

3. On the Web tab, shown in Figure 10.14, you can specify whether this catalog is specifically for one of the WWW or NNTP sites on this server. Here are your options:

- *Track Virtual Roots.* Indicates that this catalog will be for a virtual site on the WWW server.
- *Virtual Server.* The name of the WWW virtual server that this catalog will track.
- *Track NNTP Roots.* Tells the server that this catalog will index the articles in an NNTP server on this site.
- *NNTP Server.* The name of the news server on this site to index.

Figure 10.14.
The Web settings for a catalog let you set which part of the server is contained in this catalog.

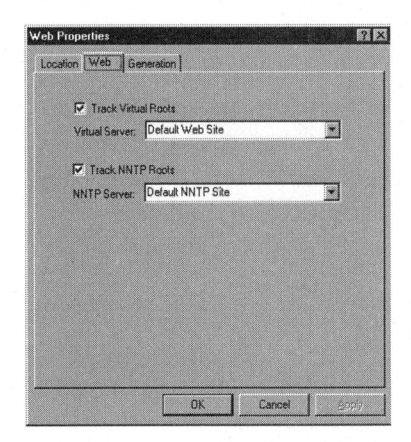

4. On the Generation tab, shown in Figure 10.15, you can set the characterization options for the catalog (these options are the same as the server options).

Figure 10.15.
The Generation options for a catalog are the same as the options for the server.

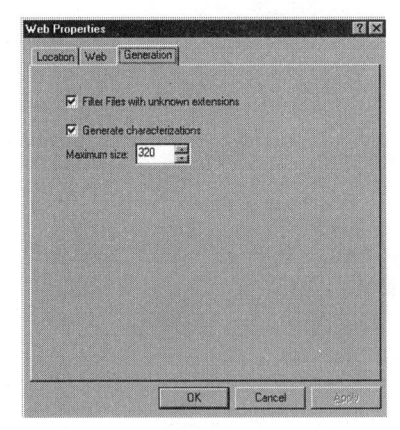

5. Click OK to set the options.

10.4. The Indexing Process

Now that you have seen how to configure the Index Server, the next sections will explain a little about how the server actually performs the indexing. This will help you as you learn how to create search pages (which you will do in the section "Querying the Index Server") and start to work with the index that is created.

10.4.1. Working with the File System

Since the Index Server will index your documents, it needs to read the files. It also needs to be able to read the properties (because these are also included in the index), and it needs to know when a document changes.

This means that the Index Server needs to be able to work with your file system. Because the Index Server is built on NT, it has no problems reading NT file systems. In fact, NT will even tell the Index Server if a document changes so that the index can be updated.

However, virtual directories can be set up to point to other servers, including Netware, UNIX, Banyan, and any other system that NT can talk to. These file systems present a different problem, because they don't let the Index Server know when files are updated. To facilitate this process, the Index Server periodically needs to scan these directories for new files (you can also force this to happen, as you saw earlier).

The Index Server also uses part of the disk to hold the index. There will be a catalog directory for each catalog you create; this directory is normally called catalog.wci (Web Content Indexer). Several files are located in this directory. The following list summarizes them:

- *.prp. This is the property information cache. It lets users search by date or size or other properties of the document.
- *.ci. This is the indexes. There may be several different indexes.
- *.dir. This is the index key. Each index has an index key that allows the index to be searched quickly.
- cicat.hsh. This is used to convert (hash) path information into an identifier that will be used throughout the index.

- *CiCL0001.*.* This contains the list of documents that still need to be indexed.
- *CiFL*.*.* This is the mapping between the documents and the most current index.
- *CiPS0000.*.* These files are used to describe the record format of the property cache.
- *CiPT0000.*.* These files map ActiveX property descriptors to an internal identifier.
- *CiSL0001.*.* This maintains a list of files that couldn't be filtered because they were in use. These files will be filtered later.
- *CiSP0000.*.* This keeps the list of directories that are contained in this index.
- *CiST0000.*.* This maps the NTFS security information to internal identifiers. This allows Index Server to display only documents a user is allowed to access.
- *CiVP0000.*.* This maps the virtual directory names to the physcial path.
- *index.*.* This maintains the list of all indexes that are present.

10.4.2. Filters

After Index Server has found the files it will index, it needs to read them. You will see many different file formats on the Internet. This makes it difficult for a single product to be able to read all the files as they are, let alone continue to provide this service as formats change.

With this in mind, the designers of the Index Server decided to use *filter files* (*DLLs*). These are small files that can be called on by the Index Server to read a file (such as an Excel spreadsheet or a Word document) and produce the stream of characters that will be indexed.

Index Server comes with filters that let you read most Microsoft files, as well as the basic file types that you encounter on the Internet. Other manufacturers (such as Corel's WordPerfect) may also provide the filters that are required to allow Index Server to read there file formats, and Microsoft continues to add filters as time goes on.

The filters are responsible for the first part of the indexing process. They read the file and extract the text that will be indexed. Filters also need to be able to handle other jobs related to the documents, including finding shifts in languages and dealing with embedded objects (such as an Excel spreadsheet embedded in a Word document).

If embedded documents are encountered, a filter can be loaded to deal with the file format of the embedded object. When this is completed, the initial filter takes over again. This means that not only will the main document be indexed, but all the embedded objects (for which there are filters) will be indexed at the same time.

If the language changes, the filter must note this so that the correct word breaker (see the next section) can be used.

10.4.3. Word Breakers

After the filters have extracted the text, the word breakers take the resulting stream of characters and break it into words. Because different languages have different ways of spacing words, the word breakers need to understand the language you're working with.

The Index Server comes with word breakers for several languages:

- Dutch
- French
- German
- Italian
- Japanese
- Spanish Modern
- Swedish
- UK English
- US English

What comes out of this process is a list of words (that is built in RAM); it contains all the words in the document. This list will include the word "and" several thousand times. Words such as "and," "the," and so on are considered "noise words" that would clutter the index with useless information. To combat this clutter, the Index server utilizes the normalizer.

10.4.4. Normalizer

The server removes from the word list all the noise words, which helps reduce the overall size of the index and makes it easier to search for information. This process is handled by the normalizer, which uses a list of "junk" words for each of the languages that is installed.

The word list that is in memory now contains only the key words from the document. Word lists are the first structure that is used for searching. Once a word list exists, you can search the document. However, word lists are not an efficent way to keep the index, because they are not compressed and, as they exist in RAM, they are not permanent.

10.4.5. Merges

To solve the problems associated with word lists, the server creates different structures that will be saved to disk. This makes the index permanent and gives the server the ability to compress the lists, making the searches faster and using less space on the server.

The process that creates these structures (called *shadow indexes* and the *master index*) is called a *merge*. There are three types of merges:

- Shadow merge
- Annealing merge
- Master merge

The merging process takes the information from a word list or shadow index and "hashes" it; that is, it converts it to a code rather than using the actual word. This reduces the size of the word and makes it easier to store. This hashing process uses different algorithms, depending on what type of merge is being done.

A. Building Shadow Indexes

A shadow merge creates a shadow index. A *shadow index* is a permanent structure that is stored on the disk. A shadow index uses only light hashing and takes up more space than a master index. However, the process of creating a shadow index is less CPU-intensive than creating a master index and is preferable if users will be online when merges are done.

A shadow merge takes the word lists that are in memory and puts them into a shadow index. This frees up RAM and makes the word lists permanent (so that they don't have to be recreated). Several conditions can trigger a shadow merge; the settings for these conditions are kept in the Registry. The following are the entries that affect shadow merges (they are under HKEY_LOCAL_MACHINE\System\CurrentControlSet\Control\ContentIndex):

- *MaxIndexes*. The total number of word lists, shadow indexes, and the master index allowed on the system.
- *MaxWordLists*. The maximum number of word lists that can be in RAM.

- *MinSizeMergeWordlists*. The total memory used to hold word lists can't exceed this value.
- *MaxWordLists*. The most word lists that can be in RAM.

Shadow merges are performed if any of these values are exceeded. A shadow merge also will be performed if a master merge is about to happen or if CPU idle time is high.

B. Annealing Merge

An annealing merge is essentially a shadow merge but is triggered by CPU idle time. Two settings in the Registry affect whether an annealing merge will be performed. They are located under HKEY_LOCAL_MACHINE\System\CurrentControlSet\Control\ContentIndex:

- *MinMergeIdleTime*. This is the minimum CPU idle percentage required before the merge will occur.
- *MaxIdealIndexes*. There must be more than this number of indexes before the merge will occur.

C. Building the Master Index

A master merge creates a new master index. This is a combination of the current master index and all shadow indexes and word lists that are on the system. The master index uses a stronger hashing algorithm (much like a compression utility can use fast compression with larger file sizes or work slower for smaller file sizes), which makes the master index smaller than the other indexes. This makes searching faster and saves on disk space and RAM used by the Index Server.

By default, a master merge is performed once a day at midnight. You can also force a master merge by using the administration tools discussed earlier. Several entries in the Registry affect master merges. They are located under HKEY_LOCAL_MACHINE\System\CurrentControlSet\Control\ContentIndex:

- *MasterMergeTime*. This is where you set the time of the daily master merge. The entry is the number of minutes past midnight.
- *MaxFreshCount*. This is the most documents that can change before the Index Server will force a master merge.
- *MinDiskFreeForceMerge*. If there is less than this amount of disk space free, a master merge will be forced.

- *MaxShadowFreeForceMerge*. This is the maximum number of shadow indexes that can be present before a master merge is forced.
- *MaxShadowIndexSize*. This is the maximum amount of disk space that shadow indexes can occupy before a master merge is forced.

As you can see, much configuration is possible, but the default settings are sufficent for most operations.

10.5. Querying the Index Server

Now that you have seen the administration and configuration of the Index server and the different types of merges, it's time to look at what you can get from the Index Server. The purpose of the Index Server is to give your users a method of finding information. To do this, a user needs to be able to query the server.

10.5.1. Types of Queries

There are two different types of information you can query: the data itself and the properties of the documents. Both types of information are stored in the index.

Getting at the index is simple, and you can perform different types of queries. The simplest and fastest involve .idq files. However, you can add a great deal of functionality using ActiveX and .asp pages, which allow you to use Server Side Objects, and SQL extensions for your queries. The next sections look at each of these in detail.

A. Using Basic .idq Files

The simplest way to query the database is to use an .idq file. Using .idq files actually involves using a series of files. First, a regular .htm file is used to get the query from the user. When you create this file, you need to include some extra information so that IIS knows to send the information to the Index Server.

The following is an example of a basic .htm document that can be used:

```
<HTML>

<HEAD>
<TITLE>Index Server Basic Query</TITLE>
</HEAD>

<H2>Basic Query Form</H2>

<FORM ACTION="/BasicSearch/basic.idq" METHOD="GET">
    Enter your query below:
<INPUT TYPE="TEXT" NAME="CiRestriction" SIZE="60" MAXLENGTH="100" VALUE="">
```

10.5. Querying the Index Server

```
<INPUT TYPE="SUBMIT" VALUE="Execute Query">
<INPUT TYPE="RESET" VALUE="Clear">
<INPUT TYPE="HIDDEN" NAME="CiMaxRecordsPerPage" VALUE="10">
        <INPUT TYPE="HIDDEN" NAME="CiScope" VALUE="/">
        <INPUT TYPE="HIDDEN" NAME="TemplateName" VALUE="queryhit">
        <INPUT TYPE="HIDDEN" NAME="CiSort" VALUE="rank[d]">
        <INPUT TYPE="HIDDEN" NAME="HTMLQueryForm" VALUE="/samples/search/
➥queryhit.htm">

</FORM>

<BR>

</BODY>
</HTML>
```

Several special codes are listed on this page:

- *CiRestriction*. This is the variable that will pass the actual query to the .idq file.
- *CiMaxRecordsPerPage*. This is the number of records that will be matched.
- *CiScope*. Using this variable lets you specify the scope (starting directory) for the search.
- *TemplateName*. The name of the template that will be used for the search results.
- *CiSort*. How the output should be sorted (here the sort is by the index ranking in descending order).

The other piece of information is in the FORM tag, where the ACTION pointing to the .idq file is what actually does the search. When this form is displayed, it looks like Figure 10.16.

When the query is executed, the .idq file is used to describe how the search should take place. The following is an example of such a file:

```
[Query]
CiColumns=filename,size,rank,characterization,vpath,DocTitle,write
CiFlags=DEEP
CiRestriction=%CiRestriction%
CiMaxRecordsInResultSet=300
CiMaxRecordsPerPage=%CiMaxRecordsPerPage%
CiScope=%CiScope%
CiTemplate=/BasicSearch/%TemplateName%.htx
CiSort=%CiSort%
```

Figure 10.16.

The query form as it appears in the browser.

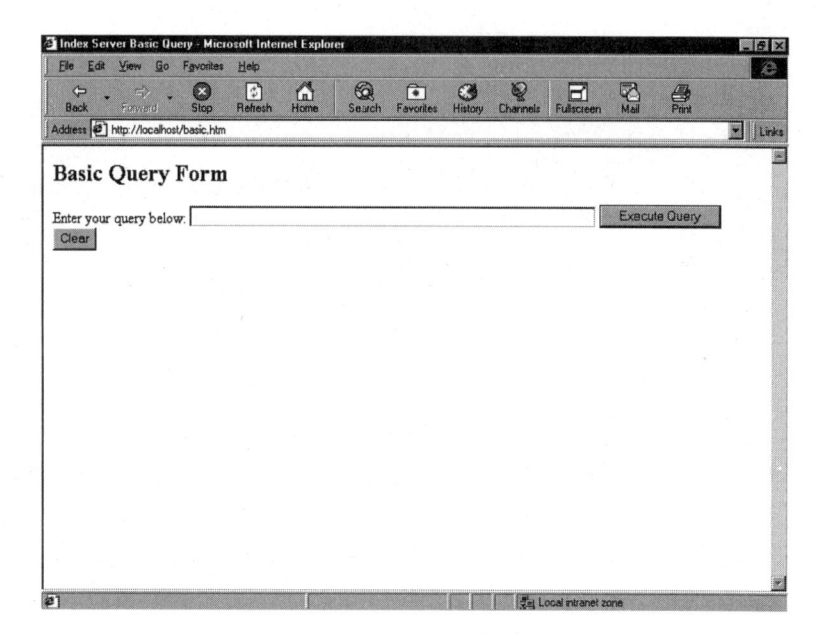

There are couple of new variables in this file:

- *CiColumns*. This is the columns to return from the index.
- *CiFlags*. This determines if all the subdirectories can be searched. DEEP means that the directory and all subdirectories will be searched, whereas SHALLOW searches only the directory.
- *CiMaxRecordsInResultSet*. This is the most hits that can be returned.

> **Note**
> The %variable% statements are used to retrieve the values from the form fields that were passed from the HTML form.

The .htx file is then used to format the output. The following is a sample of this type of file that has been annotated, beginning with the head section:

```
<HTML>
<HEAD>
<%if CiMatchedRecordCount eq 0%>
  <TITLE><%CiRestriction%> - no documents matched.</TITLE>
<%else%>
  <TITLE><%CiRestriction%> - documents <%CiFirstRecordNumber%> to
  <%CiLastRecordNumber%></TITLE>
<%endif%>
</HEAD>
```

This code first checks to see if any records were returned and puts the appropriate page header on the page. `%CiRestriction%` will be replaced by your query (the % signs call this information from memory variables that are defined when the query is run).

```
<h2>Search Results - "<%CiRestriction%>"</h2>
<H5>
<%if CiMatchedRecordCount eq 0%>
  No documents matched the query "<%CiRestriction%>".
<%else%>
  Documents <%CiFirstRecordNumber%> to <%CiLastRecordNumber%> of
<%CiMatchedRecordCount%>
<%endif%>
</H5>
```

This section of code displays your query on the results page (the first line) and then tells the user which set of records is being displayed.

```
<%begindetail%>
<p>
    <dt>
        <%CiCurrentRecordNumber%>.
        <%if DocTitle isempty%>
            <b><a href="<%EscapeURL vpath%>"><%filename%></a></b>
        <%else%>
            <b><a href="<%EscapeURL vpath%>"><%DocTitle%></a></b>
        <%endif%>
    <dd>
        <b><i>Abstract:   </i></b><%characterization%>
        <br>
        <cite>
            <a href="<%EscapeURL vpath%>">http://<%server_name%><%vpath%></a>
            <font size=-1> - <%if size eq ""%>(size and time unknown)
            <%else%>size <%size%> bytes - <%write%> GMT<%endif%></font>
            <BR>
        </cite>
<%enddetail%>
```

This code displays information about documents that matched the query and were returned by Index Server. This section of code is enclosed in `<%begindetail%>` and `<%enddetail%>` to mark it as the section that repeats. The record number is shown, and then the document title is checked. If there is a title, it is displayed. Otherwise, the filename will be shown. The characterization (abstract) is then included (this is generally the first 300 characters of the document). Finally, the server and virtual path are displayed on the next line, along with the file data and time.

When this file is used, the output from a query for TCP/IP would look like Figure 10.17.

Figure 10.17.
The output of the simple query shows search results.

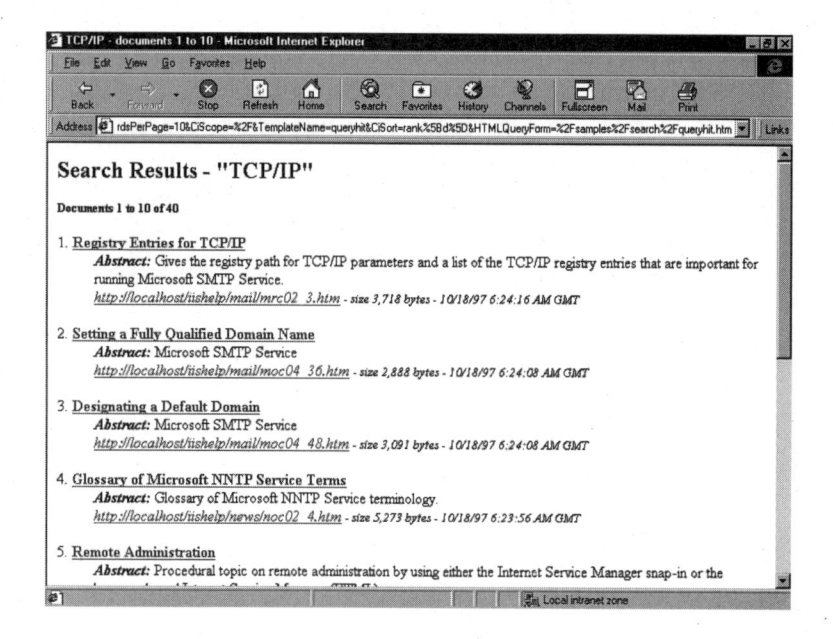

There are many variables you can use in the files. A list of them can be found in the online documentation for the NT 4.0 Option Pack 3.

B. Using Server-Side Objects (SSO) in ASP Pages

Another option you have when building query forms is to use server-side objects for Index Server in conjunction with Active Server Page scripts (.asp files). Queries created this way can include scripting in Visual Basic Script (VBScript) and/or JScript to add flexibility in displaying query results.

Two kinds of objects help you access and format Index Server queries:

- Query objects
- Utility objects

Although this approach nicely integrates with sites that use ASP extensively, Microsoft explicitly recommends not using the server-side objects approach when the site receives a large number of simultaneous queries.

C. Using ActiveX Database Objects

The third option when querying Index Server indexes is to access the index via ActiveX data objects in ASP scripts. This is possible because Index Server supplies an OLE-DB provider, which offers almost the same functionality as the OLE-DB provider for ODBC (except writing, of course).

Again, you start with an .htm file to gather the information that the user is looking for. To call an ASP page instead of an IDQ file from the query form, use the following line:

```
<FORM ACTION="response.asp" METHOD="GET">
```

The file response.asp contains the code needed to access the index and format the results.

The following piece of code from response.asp demonstrates how to connect to the Index Server provider (second line) using an ADO database connection object. Notice that the code is very similar to connecting to other databases, such as a Microsoft SQL Server database, via ODBC data sources.

```
Set Conn = Server.CreateObject("ADODB.Connection")
Conn.ConnectionString = "provider=msidxs;"
Conn.Open
Set AdoCommand = Server.CreateObject("ADODB.Command")
Set AdoCommand.ActiveConnection = Conn
```

You can then define the query by assigning the command object an SQL query string. (If you want to, you can use an SQL query string as your selection criteria when specifying the record set to select from the database.) The following sample shows a query being assigned based on the information in the .htm file.

```
strCommand = "SELECT " & Request.QueryString("CiColumns") & " FROM "
strCommand = strCommand & Request.QueryString("CiScope") & " WHERE " &
strCommand = strCommand & Request.QueryString("CiRestriction") & " ORDER BY "
strCommand = strCommand & Request.QueryString("CiOrderBy")
AdoCommand.CommandText = strCommand
```

Finally, you can create a record set by running the query. The following code will execute the query and initialize the recordset:

```
Set RS = Server.CreateObject("ADODB.RecordSet")
AdoCommand.Properties("Bookmarkable") = True
RS.Open AdoCommand
```

The data is now available in the record set and can be massaged or displayed. For more details on ASP and ADO, see Day 11, "Programmability."

10.6. Performance Issues

The Index Server is fairly robust; very little needs to be tuned. However, there are a couple of factors you should keep in mind:

- Using .idq files is faster than using .asp files. It is recommended that you use .idq files when your site receives large numbers of simultaneous queries.
- Index Server requires more memory, especially if the server has many document changes (and therefore word lists) or ActiveX technology is used (to track the user processes).

10.6.1. Monitoring Performance

You can monitor performance remotely by creating an .htx file that includes performance variables. This will require you to run an .ida file, which is the administrative form of an .idq file. The following is a simple example of an .ida file:

```
[Admin]
CiCatalog=
CiTemplate=/Scripts/srchadm/state.htx
CiAdminOperation=GetState
```

The .htx file can then contain any of several variables that can return a value that reports on the server's status. See Table 10.1.

Table 10.1. Administrative variables.

Variable	Description
CiAdminCacheActive	Number of executed queries.
CiAdminCacheCount	Number of cached queries.
CiAdminCacheHits	Percentage of HTTP requests that use an existing cached query.
CiAdminCacheMisses	Percentage of HTTP requests that generate a new query.
CiAdminCachePending	Number of queries waiting for execution.
CiAdminCacheRejected	Number of queries that have been rejected because the server is too busy.
CiAdminCacheTotal	Number of queries that have been executed since the server was started.

10.6. Performance Issues

Variable	Description
`CiAdminIndexCountDeltas`	Number of documents that have changed (been indexed) or have been deleted since the last master merge.
`CiAdminIndexCountFiltered`	Total documents filtered since the server was started.
`CiAdminIndexCountPersIndex`	The total number of persistent indexes on the server.
`CiAdminIndexCountQueries`	Number of queries currently accessing the Index database.
`CiAdminIndexCountToFilter`	Number of documents that need to be filtered.
`CiAdminIndexCountTotal`	Total number of documents in the catalog.
`CiAdminIndexCountUnique`	Number of unique words in the index.
`CiAdminIndexCountWordlists`	Current number of word lists in use on the server.
`CiAdminIndexMergeProcess`	Status of the current merge. Returns the percentage completed.
`CiAdminIndexSize`	The size of the index in megabytes.
`CiAdminIndexStateAnnealingMerge`	Returns true if there is an annealing merge in progress.
`CiAdminIndexStateMasterMerge`	Returns true if there is a master merge in progress.
`CiAdminIndexStateScanRequired`	Returns true if the index needs to be rebuilt.
`CiAdminIndexStateShadowMerge`	Returns true if there is a shadow merge in process.

Lab

This lab consists of review questions pertaining to this chapter and provides an opportunity for you to use walk-through exercises to apply the knowledge that you've gained.

Questions

1. What is the directory name for a catalog?

    A. catalog.wci

    B. index.wci

    C. index

    D. catalog.ind

2. What kind of files are involved in a normal query?

    A. .htx

    B. .htm

    C. .ida

    D. .idq

3. Which of the following are types of merges?

    A. Annealing

    B. Master

    C. List

    D. Automatic

4. You have recently added new documents to your Web site, and you want them to be indexed by Index Server. What should you do to make sure this takes place?

    A. Use the HTML Administration tool and click the Reindex button.

    B. Use the Microsoft Management Console.

    C. Use the rescan option in the HTML Administration tool.

    D. Nothing. This process is automatic.

5. What term is used to describe all the files and directories that are indexed in a catalog?

    A. Index base

    B. Corpus

    C. Information base

    D. Virtual directory

6. You recently added a large number of Corel WordPerfect documents to your site, and Index Server doesn't seem to be indexing them correctly. What might be causing the problem?

    A. Index Server can't index third-party documents.

    B. The word breaker for WordPerfect documents is corrupted.

    C. You don't have the WordPerfect filter installed.

    D. You need to force a merge before these documents can be indexed.

7. Where do you create a new catalog?

    A. In the Microsoft Management Console.

    B. Using the HTML Administration tool.

    C. In the Registry.

    D. This is not possible.

8. What do you need to do in order for Index Server to index new documents placed on a virtual directory on a NetWare server?

    A. Use the HTML Administration tool and click the Reindex button.

    B. Use the Microsoft Management Console.

    C. Use the rescan option in the HTML Administration tool.

    D. Nothing. This is automatic.

9. Which of the following can you query on?

    A. A word that might appear in any document, such as "the"

    B. A word that should be unique and that appears in few documents

    C. A property of a document

    D. Only by keywords that appear in the word list

10. Index Server has a large number of shadow indexes, and you suspect that this is affecting the performance of user queries. What should you do to solve this problem?

   A. Reduce the number of HTML documents on your site.

   B. Remove unnecessary filters.

   C. Force an index merge.

   D. This does not affect performance, so no action is required.

Answers to Questions

1. **A.** The index is stored in files located in the catalog.wci directory by default.

2. **A, B, D.** The .htm file reads the information and points to the .idq. The .idq runs the query and uses the .htx to format the output. An .ida file is the administrative form of an .idq file.

3. **A, B.** There are three types of merges. The shadow merge builds word lists into shadow indexes. The annealing merge also merges word lists to shadow indexes (depending on CPU idle time). The master merge brings all the indexes together.

4. **D.** On an NT system, the operating system will inform the Index Server when new documents are added or existing files are updated or deleted. If you were to click the Reindex button in the HTML Administration tool, it would reindex every document on the site—a rather lengthy and unnecessary process.

5. **B.** The information being indexed is the body of information, or the corpus. A virtual directory has nothing to do with indexing.

6. **C.** Index Server can index many different types of files through the use of filters. Any vendor can create filter files for their file types if they choose. Once these filters are installed, indexing is automatic. Word breakers are used after a document has been filtered to determine where one word stops and the next begins.

7. **A.** Although you can also create a new catalog in the Registry, it is much easier to do so in the MMC.

8. **B, C.** Although Index Server will occasionally scan these directories, you can force it to rescan the directory in the MMC or on the HTML Administration page. Again, clicking Reindex would reindex *all* documents, which wouldn't be desirable. This process is only automatic on NT volumes, not NetWare volumes.

9. **B, C.** Junk words such as "the" are removed in the normalization process. More-unique words and properties are both stored in the index so that they can be searched.

10. **C.** Although Index Server will do this eventually on its own, if this problem is affecting performance or consuming a large amount of disk space, you can force Index Server to merge immediately. Note that performance will temporarily degrade while the merge is occurring.

Exercises

Exercise 10.1.: Installing the Index Server

This exercise addresses the following Microsoft exam objective:

- Configure the Index Server to index a Web site

If you have already installed the Index Server, move on to Exercise 2. This exercise walks you through the installation of the Index Server.

1. Select Start | Programs | Windows NT 4.0 Option Pack | Windows NT 4.0 Option Pack Setup.
2. On the welcome screen, click Next.
3. Click Add/Remove for the installation option.
4. From the list of options, choose Microsoft Index Server.
5. Ensure that the box is checked, and then click Show Subcomponents.
6. There are four parts to the server installation. Select Language Resources and click Show Subcomponents.
7. Select both UK English and US English.
8. Click OK to return to the Index Server subcomponents.
9. Click OK to return to the setup dialog box, and then click Next.
10. Click Next on the directory screen to accept the default directory.
11. When the file copy is finished, click Finish.

Exercise 10.2.: Looking at the Administration Pages

This exercise addresses the following Microsoft exam objectives:

- Configure the Index Server to index a Web site
- Configure IIS to integrate with the Index Server

In this exercise, you will see how you can use the HTML-based administrative pages to look at the status of the Index Server. You will also see how you can use these pages to carry out administrative tasks such as forcing an index merge.

1. Start your browser and open the site
   `http://127.0.0.1/iisadmin/isadmin/admin.htm`.
2. Click the Index statistics button.
3. Scroll down and note the number of persistent indexes and word lists.
4. Click the Back button on your browser.
5. Click the Force merge now button.
6. Check that the merge has occurred. Go back to the index statistics.
7. If the number of persistent indexes is larger than 1, try refreshing the page.

Exercise 10.3.: Creating a Sample Query

This exercise addresses the following Microsoft exam objective:

- Configure IIS to integrate with the Index Server

This exercise steps you through the creation of a basic query page.

1. Using NT Explorer, create a directory called BasicSearch under your WWW root folder (for example, c:\inetpub\wwwroot by default).
2. Create the .htm file by entering the following in Notepad and saving it as basic.htm:

```
<HTML>
<HEAD>
<TITLE>Index Server Search Form</TITLE>
</HEAD>
<H2>Basic Query Form</H2>
<FORM ACTION="/BasicSearch/basic.idq" METHOD="GET">
    Enter your query below:
<INPUT TYPE="TEXT" NAME="CiRestriction" SIZE="60" MAXLENGTH="100"
➥VALUE="">
<INPUT TYPE="SUBMIT" VALUE="Execute Query">
<INPUT TYPE="RESET" VALUE="Clear">
<INPUT TYPE="HIDDEN" NAME="CiMaxRecordsPerPage" VALUE="10">
        <INPUT TYPE="HIDDEN" NAME="CiScope" VALUE="/">
        <INPUT TYPE="HIDDEN" NAME="TemplateName" VALUE="basic">
        <INPUT TYPE="HIDDEN" NAME="CiSort" VALUE="rank[d]">
        <INPUT TYPE="HIDDEN" NAME="HTMLQueryForm" VALUE="/BasicSearch/
➥basic.htm">
</FORM>
</BODY>
</HTML>
```

3. Create the .idq file by entering the following in Notepad and saving the file as basic.idq:

```
[Query]
CiColumns=filename,size,rank,characterization,vpath,DocTitle,write
CiFlags=DEEP
CiRestriction=%CiRestriction%
CiMaxRecordsInResultSet=300
CiMaxRecordsPerPage=%CiMaxRecordsPerPage%
CiScope=%CiScope%
CiTemplate=/BasicSearch/%TemplateName%.htx
CiSort=%CiSort%
```

4. Finally, enter the following into Notepad and save it as basic.htx:

```
<HTML>
<HEAD>
<%if CiMatchedRecordCount eq 0%>
  <TITLE><%CiRestriction%> - no documents matched.</TITLE>
<%else%>
  <TITLE><%CiRestriction%> - documents <%CiFirstRecordNumber%> to
➥<%CiLastRecordNumber%></TITLE>
<%endif%>
</HEAD>

<h2>Search Results - "<%CiRestriction%>"</h2>

<H5>
<%if CiMatchedRecordCount eq 0%>
  No documents matched the query "<%CiRestriction%>".
<%else%>
  Documents <%CiFirstRecordNumber%> to <%CiLastRecordNumber%> of
➥<%CiMatchedRecordCount%>
<%endif%>
</H5>

<dl>

<%begindetail%>

<p>
    <dt>
        <%CiCurrentRecordNumber%>.
        <%if DocTitle isempty%>
            <b><a href="<%EscapeURL vpath%>"><%filename%></a></b>
        <%else%>
            <b><a href="<%EscapeURL vpath%>"><%DocTitle%></a></b>
        <%endif%>
    <dd>
        <b><i>Abstract:   </i></b><%characterization%>
        <br>
        <cite>
            <a href="<%EscapeURL vpath%>">http://<%server_name%>
➥<%vpath%></a>
```

Day 10: Microsoft Index Server

```
            <font size=-1> - <%if size eq ""%>(size and time unknown)
            ↪<%else%>size <%size%> bytes - <%write%> GMT
            ↪<%endif%></font>
            <BR>

    </cite>

<%enddetail%>

</dl>
<P><BR>
</HTML>
```

5. Start your browser and open http://localhost/BasicSearch/basic.htm. Enter a query and click Execute query.

6. View the results. If you receive an error, double-check the code you entered.

10

TEST DAY FAST FACTS

Here are a few fast facts about this chapter that you may want to know ahead of time. Don't forget that these facts also provide great last-minute study material.

- Internet Information Server comes with built-in programming support for Active Server Pages, CGI, ISAPI, and Internet Database Connector.

- Microsoft JScript and VBScript scripting languages are provided with IIS. Microsoft JScript is 100 percent ECMAScript-compliant.

- Windows Scripting Host can be used as a batch file replacement for MS-DOS batch files.

- Custom programs can completely administer IIS via the IIS Admin objects (IISAO).

- ActiveX Data Objects (ADO) in conjunction with Active Server Pages let you create dynamic, database-driven Web sites.

- Internet Information Server comes with an Active Directory Services Interface provider.

Day 11

Programmability

by Gerry High

The last few chapters have covered the architecture and variety of services that come with IIS. In this chapter you'll see how to tie some of these services together and leverage them optimally using the programming features of IIS. We'll discuss each of the ways you can program IIS, with an emphasis on Active Server Pages. We'll also cover scripting languages and Windows Scripting Host. Finally, we'll cover the Active Directory Services Interface, with an emphasis on the metabase and the IIS Admin Objects. With the release of IIS 4.0, Microsoft has done an excellent job of making IIS extensible and manageable; now much of the product is exposed through programming interfaces.

You will need at least a basic understanding of programming concepts. To master the exam, pay particular attention to the following:

- Using Open Database Connectivity in conjunction with ActiveX Data Objects, and the types of errors that can occur

- Understanding Active Directory Services Interface (ADSI) and how IIS implements ADSI

Objectives

This chapter helps you prepare for the Microsoft exam by covering the following objectives:

- Configure IIS to run ISAPI applications.
- Configure IIS to support server-side scripting.
- Configure IIS to connect to a database (includes configuring ODBC).
- Write scripts to manage the FTP service or the WWW service.

11.1. Server-Side Programming

Server-side programming refers to programming activities associated with creating Web sites that involve more than just static HTML pages. The ability to augment a Web site with server-side programming is becoming more and more important as companies recognize that they need to provide Web sites that have live, dynamic data.

IIS provides built-in support for server-side programming via Active Server Pages (ASP), Internet Server Application Programming Interface (ISAPI), Common Gateway Interface (CGI), and Internet Database Connector (IDC). The following sections briefly describe each of these methods. Later in this chapter, we'll go into more depth with Active Server Pages, since it is Microsoft's primary technology for creating Web sites.

11.1.1. Active Server Pages

Active Server Pages (ASP) is a server-side scripting environment that makes it easy to create dynamic, database-driven Web pages. Active Server Pages 1.0 was introduced with IIS 3.0 in December of 1996. (You might remember its beta name, "Denali.") ASP 1.0 was essentially an add-on to IIS 3.0. Active Server Pages 2.0 is built into IIS 4.0.

Active Server Pages let you combine HTML, scripts, and COM (Component Object Model) components.

> **Note:** Component Object Model is Microsoft's binary standard for how objects communicate and interact. The COM plumbing is built into all current versions of Microsoft operating systems. The Distributed version of COM (DCOM) is designed to allow objects to run on remote systems. Since COM is a binary standard, you need not be concerned about the language in which the component was built. In fact, COM objects can be built in a variety of languages, including Java, C++, and Visual Basic.

The resulting output that gets sent to the client Web browser can be standard HTML or can include scripts or other content that is targeted to a particular browser.

To better understand Active Server Pages, consider the following:

1. A user requests a Web page with an .asp extension.
2. IIS "sends" the page to the ASP component; the ASP component processes the page for any scripts.
3. The scripts are executed by the appropriate script engine. ASP checks for any installed script engines, such as Microsoft JScript and VBScript. Scripts may connect to a database or call other business objects, and so on.
4. The resulting HTML is sent back to the client.

An ASP application consists of the grouping of .asp files underneath a particular directory structure (including subdirectories) and an optional global.asa file. If an application has a global.asa file, it must be in the root of the application. global.asa files are commonly used to initialize session- and application-level variables based on events such as the startup of the session.

Application starting points are defined using a tool such as the Internet Service Manager. An application ends when another starting point is found for another application. To run an ASP application, the directories containing the ASP files must be marked with script permission.

After we cover the other supported server-side programming technologies, we'll come back to ASP. In section 11.2, we'll discuss scripting languages, the various objects that come with ASP, and how to connect to a database using ASP.

11.1.2. ISAPI

ISAPI (Internet Server Application Programming Interface) was introduced by Microsoft as a high-performance alternative to CGI. ISAPI, unlike Common Gateway Interface (CGI) executables, consists of dynamic link libraries (DLLs), which means that they run in the same process as the Web server. As a result, ISAPI has reduced resource overhead, is fast-loading, and performs better and is more scalable than CGI applications. Most of the other Web server vendors also support ISAPI (such as O'Reilly, Purveyor, and Spyglass).

When Microsoft designed ISAPI, it specified two forms of ISAPI components:

- *Extensions*. ISAPI extensions are applications packaged in DLLs that implement the ISAPI programming interfaces. ISAPI extensions are loaded when an URL is requested that references the ISAPI extension (for example, http://mydomain.com/scripts/foo.dll?param1). IIS may unload an extension when it is no longer needed.

■ *Filters.* ISAPI filters can be used to customize the behavior of IIS (for example, custom authentication, encryption, and logging). Filters are triggered by events, as opposed to ISAPI extensions, which are triggered by a user's request for the extension. Filters are loaded at server startup time and are kept in memory until IIS is shut down.

To configure IIS to run ISAPI extensions, the directory containing the ISAPI extension must be given execute permission. For example, the Scripts directory (\inetpub\scripts) comes preconfigured with execute permission. If you don't want to place your ISAPI extensions in the Scripts directory, you can perform the following steps to configure another directory with execute permission:

1. Using the Internet Service Manager, right-click the directory containing the ISAPI extension.
2. Select Properties from the pop-up menu. The dialog box shown in Figure 11.1 appears.

Figure 11.1.
The properties dialog box for a directory containing an ISAPI extension is used to set execute permissions.

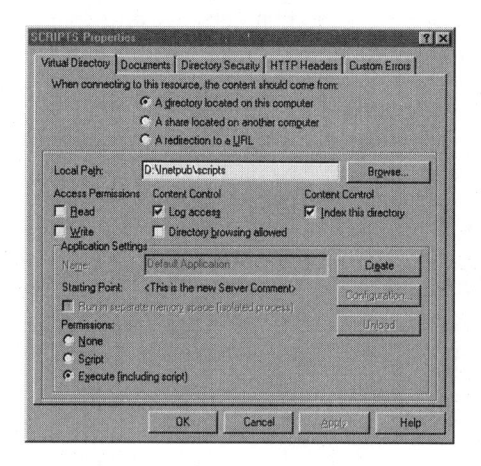

3. Click the Execute (Including Script) radio button.
4. Click OK to dismiss the dialog box.

At this point, you may test your extension.

IIS lets you create mappings of file types to ISAPI extensions. For example, an association of .asp is mapped to the file asp.dll as follows:

1. Using the Internet Service Manager, right-click the application directory.
2. Select Properties from the pop-up menu.
3. Choose the Home Directory, Virtual Directory, or Directory tab.
4. Click the Configuration button. The dialog box shown in Figure 11.2 appears.

Figure 11.2.
The Application Configuration dialog box lets you configure application mappings, options such as the default scripting language, and debugging options.

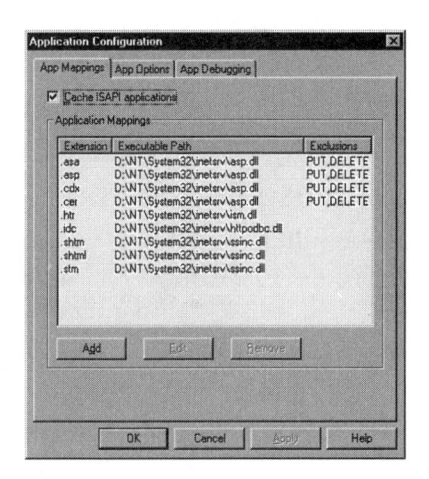

5. Click the Add button. Type in the path to the ISAPI extension and also the file extension to be associated with the extension.
6. Click OK to dismiss the dialog box.
7. Verify that your directory containing the ISAPI extension is marked with execute permissions and that the directories containing your script files are marked with script permissions.

At this point, you may test your mapping. For example, if you created a mapping of .irq and had a file named test.irq in the root directory, you could type `http://localhost/test.irq` to launch your ISAPI extension.

11.1.3. CGI

Common Gateway Interface (CGI) is a standard for programs to interface with Web servers. Although IIS 4.0 provides full support for CGI programs, Microsoft recommends using other methods, such as ASP or ISAPI, for new Web application development. This is because CGI, in contrast to ISAPI and other method a separate process for each CGI request. Although this has the benefit of isolation from the Web server, it has the added overhead and performance problems of a separate process. For more information about CGI, see http://hoohoo.ncsa.uiuc.edu/cgi.

To run a CGI executable application, the directory containing the CGI application must be marked with execute permissions. If the CGI program is a script (for example, a Perl script), the directory must have script permissions. By default, IIS comes configured with a CGI-BIN directory that already has the execute permission set. For security reasons, it is recommended that you use a separate directory for your CGI programs.

11.1.4. Internet Database Connector

The Internet Database Connector (IDC) first shipped with IIS in version 1.0. IDC is used to render database queries in HTML pages. Although most data-driven Web sites today use Active Server Pages, IDC is still important since many sites still have some pages that use it.

The Internet Database Connector is implemented as an ISAPI extension with a file mapping of IDC. If a URL containing .idc is sent to IIS, it passes the information to the IDC ISAPI extension (httpodbc.dll). By default, this mapping is already set up when IIS is installed.

Here is a sample IDC file:

```
Datasource: IISDSN
Username: sa
Password: pwd
SQLStatement: select *
+ from invmas
Template: sample.htx
```

IDC files minimally contain the following:

- *Datasource.* The ODBC system-level DSN.
- *Template.* The name of an .htx file that contains the formatting for the results of the SQL query.
- *SQLStatement.* The SQL query.

The .htx file is an HTML file with additional tags that is used to process the resulting output from the IDC file. These pages are contained within <% and %>, much like Active Server Pages. However, an .htx file has only six keywords (begindetail, enddetail, if, else, endif, and %z) and is very limited compared to ASP. Microsoft also distributes a program to convert IDC files to ASP. (You can find more information at http://www.microsoft.com/iis.)

11.2. Server-Side Scripting with Active Server Pages

The preceding sections introduced Active Server Pages as Microsoft's primary technology used to create dynamic Web sites. In the next sections, we'll go deeper into Active Server Pages. First, we'll discuss scripting languages, because they are fundamental to using ASP. Next, you'll see how to create more-functional scripts using built-in and installable objects. Last, we'll focus on one of the objects (ActiveX Data Objects, or ADO) and see how to hook up ASP to a database.

Scripting languages are high-level languages that are designed to be used to glue together objects in the system. In the case of IIS, the objects are Microsoft COM objects.

Besides acting as the glue, scripting languages are typically runtime-interpreted (versus compiled languages such as C, C++, and COBOL) and don't have all the bells and whistles that full-blown programming languages have.

IIS comes with three environments for hosting scripting:

- *Active Server Pages* provides a server-side environment for hosting scripting languages. Scripts that run in ASP are typically used to generate and render HTML from a variety of sources (such as business objects and databases).
- *Internet Explorer (IE) 4.01* provides a client-side environment for hosting scripting languages. Scripts that run in IE 4.01 are usually in response to a user's interaction with a Web page (such as validation handlers for forms, and so on).
- *Windows Scripting Host (WSH)* provides a lightweight scripting engine that can be used for either server- or client-side scripts. WSH will be discussed in detail later in this chapter.

Although all three environments are quite similar, there are differences in how scripts are identified. Within an Active Server Page, scripts are denoted by the script delimiters `<%` and `%>` or by a `<SCRIPT RUNAT=SERVER LANGUAGE=...>` tag. The language of a script is determined by one of the following:

- An ASP processing directive `<%@ LANGUAGE = ScriptingLanguage%>`, where `ScriptingLanguage` is VBScript, JScript, and so on. This directive sets the default scripting language for a page. This directive must be the first line in the ASP file.

- A `<SCRIPT RUNAT=SERVER LANGUAGE=`*`ScriptingLanguage`*`>` tag, where *ScriptingLanguage* is VBScript, JScript, and so on. This tag is used when you want to specify that a script is of a different language than the default scripting language.
- An application level setting specified via the Internet Service Manager (or some other tool) to modify the metabase.

In the following steps, you'll use the Internet Service Manager to set the default scripting language for an application:

1. Open the Internet Service Manager.
2. Right-click the application directory and select Properties.
3. Choose the Home Directory tab of the Properties dialog box.
4. Click the Configuration button, and then choose the App Options tab. You should see the dialog box shown in Figure 11.3.

Figure 11.3.
The Options tab of the Application Configuration dialog box is used to specify such things as the default scripting language and the session timeout.

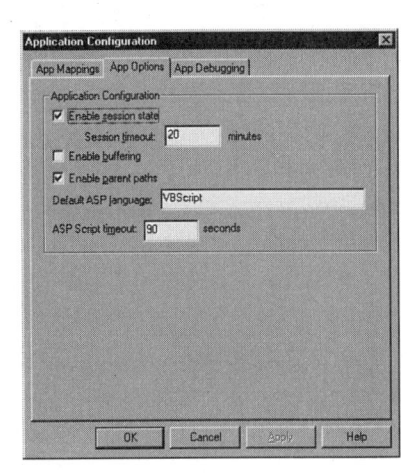

5. In the Default ASP Language field, enter the name of a valid scripting language, such as VBScript or JScript.
6. Click OK to save your changes.

Let's turn now to a discussion of the supported scripting languages under ASP.

11.2.1. Supported Scripting Languages

Active Server Pages comes with out-of-the-box support for Microsoft's JScript and VBScript scripting languages. However, Microsoft has made the scripting architecture extensible so that third parties can easily hook in their scripting engines. For example, a Perl scripting engine is available from a third party.

A. Visual Basic Script (VBScript)

VBScript is a trimmed-down version of Microsoft's popular Visual Basic language. VBScript was designed to be portable to other platforms. As a result, VBScript doesn't include support for the Clipboard, Dynamic Data Exchange, or other non-portable elements.

Visual Basic programmers can easily transition to VBScript. However, be aware that if you use VBScript on the client side (that is, in scripts that run on the client browser), Microsoft's Internet Explorer browsers (versions 3.0 or later) are the only browsers that support VBScript today.

The following is an example of VBScript in which the doSum procedure increments a variable to 10:

```
Sub doSum()
    dim i,j
    i = 0
    for i= 1 to 10
       i = i + 1
    next
End Sub
```

B. JScript

JScript 3.0 is Microsoft's implementation of the ECMA (European Computer Manufacturers Association) 262 specification (also known as ECMAScript). The ECMA 262 standard is based on submissions by Microsoft, Netscape, IBM, SUN, Borland, and other companies. You can view the specification at http://www.ecma.ch/stand/ecma-262.htm.

JScript is quite similar to Netscape's JavaScript. JScript (and JavaScript) often get mistaken for Java, which is incorrect. JScript is an object-based scripting language, while Java is a true object-oriented language. In other words, although JScript lets you create your own simple objects, you can't create objects that support inheritance or interfaces or any of the other features of object-oriented languages such as Java.

JScript has an advantage over VBScript in that it runs on both Netscape and Internet Explorer browsers. If cross-platform browser support is important, JScript really is your only option.

JScript's syntax is very "C-like," so if you are a C, C++, or Java programmer, you'll feel right at home using JScript. JScript, like C, is case sensitive. (VBScript, like Visual Basic, is not case sensitive.) If you are porting script from VBScript to JScript, make sure that you specify the case correctly.

Here is the previous VBScript example in its JScript form:

```
function doSum()
{
    var i,j = 0;
    for(i=0; i<10; i++)
    {
        j = j + 1;
    }
}
```

In the next sections we'll discuss some of the available objects for ASP and how to access them from scripts.

11.2.2. Available Objects

Although scripting languages let you do a lot more than you could with traditional HTML, the real power of scripting comes when you add objects (the objects we're talking about now are based on Microsoft COM, which we discussed earlier). Active Scripting Engines (such as JScript and VBScript) let you access objects built outside of the scripting engines. By recognizing and utilizing these objects, you can significantly enhance and extend your Web site.

Microsoft has included a set of built-in objects in ASP as well as a set of installable component objects. The built-in objects are listed in Table 11.1.

Table 11.1. ASP built-in objects.

Object	Description
Application	Can be used to store global variables that are shared among all users of an application.
ObjectContext	Used by transactional Web pages to commit or abort a transaction.
Request	Contains information about the type of request that the client's browser is making, header information, cookies, and other information.
Response	Controls output sent to the client browser. Can also be used to set cookies and redirect the browser to another page.
Server	Contains information about the Web server. Is also used to create COM objects.
Session	Container for information that exists for a user's session.

11.2. Server-Side Scripting with Active Server Pages

The built-in objects can be used to get information from a user, control output sent to the browser, and store per-session and per-application information. Built-in objects don't need to be explicitly created and can be used by just referencing the object. Here is an example that utilizes each of the built-in objects:

```
<%@ LANGUAGE=JSCRIPT TRANSACTION=REQUIRED%>
<%
    var sInput, sPath;
// get the input from the query
    sInput = Request.querystring("input");
    sPath = Server.MapPath("/");
    Response.write("IIS 4.0 Query String: " + sInput + "<BR>");
    Response.write("IIS 4.0 Server Path: " + sPath + "<BR>");
// store the input string in the Session
    Session("sInput") = "Another input value";
// store the path in the Application
    Application("sPath") = sPath
// complete the transaction
    if(sInput == "Complete")
        ObjectContext.SetComplete();
    else
        ObjectContext.SetAbort();

    function OnTransactionAbort()
    {
        Response.write("Abort");
    }
%>
```

In this example, the Request object is used to get an input parameter from the URL. The Response object is used to write output to the page. The Session and Application objects are used to store variables. The Server object is used to get the path to the root. Finally, the ObjectContext object is used to commit or roll back the transaction. (In this case, we aren't calling any objects that use transaction, so there isn't really anything to roll back.)

Besides the built-in objects, ASP also comes with quite a few installable components. These components can be used to create dynamic Web sites.

Table 11.2 lists the set of installable components that come with Active Server Pages.

Table 11.2. ASP installable objects.

Object	Description
Ad Rotator	Used to display a series of advertisement images on a Web page.
Browser Capabilities	Used to describe the client's Web browser so that you can tailor a page to a specific browser.

continues

Table 11.2. continued

Object	Description
ADO	ActiveX Data Objects let you access and manipulate data in a database.
Collaborative Data Objects for NTS	Collaborative Data Objects allow you to send and receive e-mail.
Content Linking	Used to create a Nextlink object that can be used to manage a list of URLs for navigation.
File Access	Used to access the file system to check for file existence, create files, and so on.
Content Rotator	Used to automatically rotate content strings on a Web page.
Page Counter	Provides a persistent count and display of visits to a Web page.
Permission Checker	Used to check if a user has access to a particular file.
MyInfo	Can be used to track personal information such as name and address.
Status	Used to keep track of site information such as the number of visitors and the number of HTTP connections.
Tools	Used to check for the existence of plug-ins and files, to generate random numbers, and to carry out other utility-like functions.

These objects, unlike the built-in objects, must be explicitly created using the CreateObject method of the built-in Server object. For example, to create and use the Browser Capabilities object, you could use the following VBScript code:

```
Set oBrowser = Server.CreateObject("MSWC.BrowserType")
```

Besides the list of installable objects, many other objects are available from third-party component developers. You can also easily build your own objects using a variety of tools (such as Visual Basic, Visual C++, and Visual J++).

In the next section, we'll discuss how you can use the ActiveX Data Object (ADO) to connect to a database.

11.2.3. Connecting to a Database

We have discussed how you can use scripting coupled with Microsoft COM objects to do some really neat things. One of the more common needs that companies have today is connecting live data from a database to their Web sites. For example, a company offering training might want to post its course listings and class schedules if they are in a database.

Web servers and database servers are typically on different servers (in many cases this is for performance reasons). Even if they run on the same machine, they might be in different processes. In either case, the Web server needs some mechanism to connect to the database. With IIS 1.0, the primary way to connect to a database was via the Internet Database Connector. With the release of IIS 3.0, ASP 1.0 in conjunction with ADO 1.0 became the preferred way of connecting to a database. Now, with IIS 4.0, the preferred way is with ASP 2.0 and ADO 1.5.

If you've used other Microsoft data access technologies, such as DAO (Data Access Objects) and RDO (Remote Data Objects), you might be wondering why we need another acronym. Microsoft felt there were too many competing ways to get to data. As a result, Microsoft's DAO and RDO teams joined forces to merge the two models into ADO. ADO is now part of Microsoft's Data Access Components. For more information, visit Microsoft's data access Web page at http://www.microsoft.com/data.

> **Note:** Although ActiveX Data Objects are most commonly used for accessing databases via the OLE DB Provider for ODBC, ADO can also be used to access other data providers. For example, you can also use the OLE DB Provider for Microsoft Index Server and the OLE DB Provider for Active Directory Services. The advantage of using ADO is that the same programming model can be used to access a variety of data providers.

To use ADO to connect to your database, you will need ODBC (Open Database Connectivity) drivers for your particular database. ODBC is a standard for connecting to heterogeneous SQL databases. One of the great advantages of ODBC is that as a Web developer, you can easily change your ASP pages to use a different database by just changing the ODBC drivers that your pages refer to.

In the next few sections we'll cover configuring ODBC and learn a little about AADO; we'll finish this section with a discussion of performance considerations.

A. Configuring the ODBC Connection

Microsoft has made the process of configuring an ODBC connection pretty easy and also very flexible. You can build a connection using a graphical interface and completely specify it in an ASP page.

To configure the ODBC connection to your database, you need to first make sure you have the appropriate database drivers installed on your system. Out of the box, IIS comes with ODBC drivers for Microsoft Access, Microsoft SQL Server, and Oracle.

In the following steps, you will determine which ODBC drivers are installed on your system:

1. Open the Control Panel.
2. Double-click the ODBC icon.
3. Choose the ODBC Drivers tab. Note the list of drivers, version numbers, and dates (see Figure 11.4).

Figure 11.4.
The ODBC Drivers tab of the ODBC Data Source Administrator dialog box lists the ODBC drivers that are installed on your system.

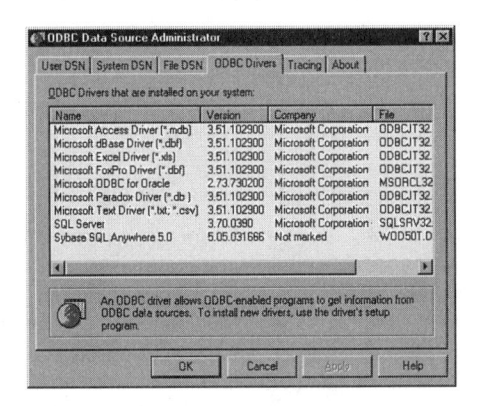

If your database driver isn't listed, you need to contact your database vendor to obtain 32-bit ODBC drivers.

Once you have the appropriate ODBC drivers installed, you are ready to create your Data Source Name (DSN). DSNs contain information about how to connect to a data source and are referenced by their unique names (per machine). DSNs can be of several types:

- *User DSN.* User DSNs are used by the interactive user, not by Active Server Pages. User DSNs are stored in the Registry under `HKEY_CURRENT_USER\SOFTWARE\ODBC\odbc.ini`.

11.2. Server-Side Scripting with Active Server Pages

- *System DSN.* System DSNs are accessible by system processes, such as IIS and other NT services. System DSNs are stored in the Registry under `HKEY_LOCAL_MACHINE\SOFTWARE\ODBC\odbc.ini`.
- *File DSN.* File DSNs are stored in files that have an extension of .dsn. By default, file DSNs are stored in \Program Files\Common Files\ODBC\Data Sources.

DSNs minimally contain the following:

- Information about the database driver (such as Microsoft Access or SQL Server).
- Where the database is located. If it is a Microsoft Access database, the location might be the file path. If the database is SQL Server, the location is the name of the server.
- The name of the database.

The following steps show you how to create a system DSN to Microsoft SQL Server. You will need a server running Microsoft SQL Server and a SQL Server login.

1. Select Start | Settings | Control Panel.
2. Double-click the ODBC icon.
3. Choose the System DSN tab. Click the Add button.
4. In the Create New Data Source dialog box, select SQL Server and click the Finish button. You should then see the Create a New Data Source to SQL Server dialog box, shown in Figure 11.5.

Figure 11.5.
The Create a New Data Source to SQL Server dialog box is a wizard that walks you through the steps of creating a DSN to a SQL Server database.

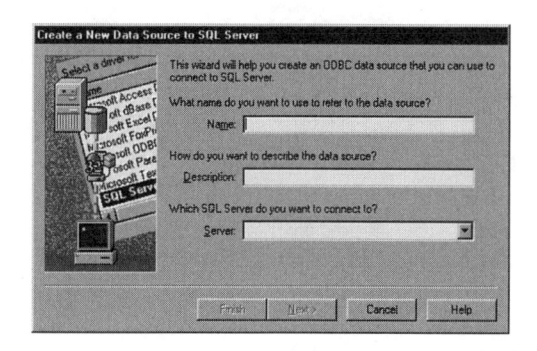

5. In the Name field, enter `TestDSN`. In the Description field, enter `A test DSN`. In the Server field, enter the name of your server that is running SQL Server. Click the Next button when you have filled out these three fields.

6. Click the With SQL Server Authentication radio button. Type in the login ID and password for the server.

7. Click the Client Configuration button. Verify that the listed protocol (TCP/IP, Named Pipes, and so on) is a valid network protocol for your SQL Server. Click OK.

8. Click the Next button. The ODBC installer will try to connect to the SQL Server. If the connection is unsuccessful, you will see an ODBC dialog box with a description of the error.

9. If the connection was successful, you will be able to specify the default database. Click Change the Default Database To: and then select the pubs database from the drop-down list. Click the Next button and then the Finish button.

10. The ODBC SQL Server Setup dialog box appears. You can click the Test Data Source button if you want to test the DSN. Click the OK button to save the DSN.

11. You should see the DSN displayed in the list of System DSNs. Click the OK button to dismiss the ODBC Data Source Administrator dialog box.

At this point, the DSN is completely configured and may be used from an ASP page on your Web site. The next section discusses ADO, and then you'll see how to use your ODBC connection from ASP.

B. Using Active Data Objects

ADO lets you easily access data from database servers. (You can use ADO to access data in other forms, such as Index Server using other data providers, but this isn't discussed here because it isn't relevant to the exam.) Because ADO is based on Microsoft COM, it can also easily be used inside ASP. Because ADO and connecting to databases is such a large subject, we'll only touch the surface of ADO. However, you should complete this section with at least a basic understanding of ADO. You should also be aware of the basic objects that make up ADO and be able to use an ODBC DSN with ADO.

Table 11.3 lists the seven ADO objects.

11.2. Server-Side Scripting with Active Server Pages

Table 11.3. ADO objects.

Object	Description
Command	Contains the SQL query to be sent to the server.
Connection	Used to make a connection to the database.
Error	Contains information about an error condition.
Field	Contains information about a single column in a recordset.
Parameter	Contains a single parameter to be used by the Command object.
Property	Contains a single characteristic of an ADO object.
Recordset	Contains the result of the SQL query.

Of the seven ADO objects, the Connection, Command, and Recordset objects will be used the most. These three objects are typically used together to produce a Web page with content from a database.

The Connection object's Open method is used to connect to a database, as shown in Listing 11.1.

Listing 11.1. Using the Connection and Recordset ADO objects.

```
<%@ LANGUAGE=JScript %>
<%
var conTest, rsTest;
conTest = Server.CreateObject("ADODB.Connection");
conTest.Open ("DSN=Pubs","sa","");
rsTest = conTest.Execute("select * from authors");
%>
```

In this example, a connection is made to a database using a system DSN of the name Pub with a username of sa and a null password.

Besides using a system DSN, you can use a file DSN in the connect string by changing `DSN=` to `FILEDSN=`. Here's an example:

```
conTest.Open("FileDSN="pubs.dsn","sa","");
```

If you don't want to use a DSN, you can specify the complete connection information in the connect string. Here's an example of connecting to a SQL Server database:

```
conTest.Open("Driver={SQL Server};Database=pubs;uid=sa;pwd=;
➥Server=NTSQLServer");
```

The advantage of using a connection without a DSN is that you can easily copy the Web page to another server and not worry about setting up the DSN on the other machine.

C. Performance Considerations

This section discusses a few tips on optimally configuring IIS for database access:

- Connection pooling
- Configuring remote SQL Server connections
- Configuring ADO for SQL Server-only systems

Connection Pooling

If you have many Web pages that are opening and closing connections to the database, your database performance might degrade. Fortunately, ODBC 3.5 supports connection pooling. Connection pooling optimally reuses database connections to provide for more efficient resource allocation. When an ODBC connection is terminated, ODBC will keep it in a connection pool for a specified amount of time before releasing it. By keeping a connection in a pool, if an application wants to reopen a database connection, it can be reopened much quicker if it is already in the pool and ready to be used.

Connection pooling is enabled by default. You can customize the amount of time a connection stays in the connection pool using the Registry.

To configure connection pooling, you need to use the Registry Editor. In the following steps, you will modify the SQL Server connection pooling timeout to 90 seconds. The SQL Server timeout value is 60 seconds by default.

1. Select Start | Run. Type `regedit` in the text box and click OK.
2. Navigate to the `HKEY_LOCAL_MACHINE\Software\ODBC\ODBCINST.INI\SQL SERVER` tree, as shown in Figure 11.6.
3. In the right pane you should see several parameters. Double-click CPTimeout. The default value is 60 seconds. Change it to 90 and click OK.
4. Exit the Registry Editor.

Figure 11.6.
By default, the CPTimeout is set to 60 seconds for the SQL Server driver.

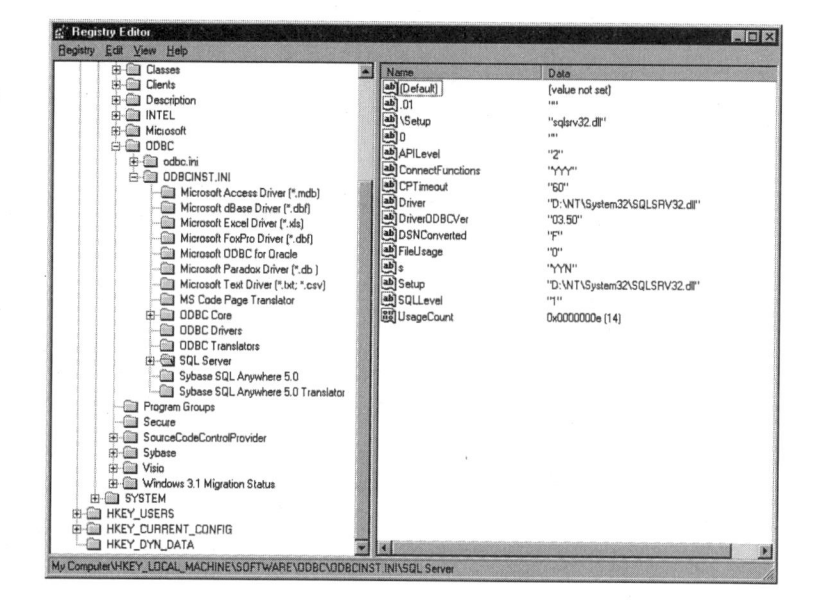

Configuring Remote SQL Server Connections

If you are using IIS to connect to a remote SQL Server, you should be aware that how you configure your connection can affect performance. To make remote SQL Server connections, you may choose either TCP/IP Sockets or Named Pipes. Of the two, TCP/IP Sockets is more efficient because it doesn't require an authentication by Windows NT before connecting.

You can configure your ODBC connection to use TCP/IP Sockets by clicking the Client Configuration button during the setup of your ODBC Data Source Name. Make sure that you've installed TCP/IP Sockets support on the SQL Server machine to which you're connecting.

Configuring ADO for SQL Server-Only Systems

If the only database that you access from ADO is Microsoft SQL Server, you can improve the performance of ADO by changing the threading model of ADO. By default, ADO is marked for Apartment model threading, which means that all accesses to ADO are via a single thread. By switching from Apartment model threading to Both, you allow ADO to run in a multithreaded apartment. This means that ADO may be accessed concurrently. (For more details on threading models, read the SDK documentation titled "Creating Components for ASP.")

To change the threading model, there are two batch files in the ADO directory (\program files\common files\system\ado). To switch to Both, run makfre15.bat; to switch back to Apartment model threading, run makapt15.bat.

11.3. Windows Scripting Host

As mentioned earlier, Windows Scripting Host (WSH) is one of the three scripting environments you can install with IIS (the other two are Internet Explorer and Active Server Pages). One of the main advantages of WSH is that it can be used for batch processing since it has a command-line interface. Using the `at` command on Windows NT means that you can write WSH scripts that get executed automatically and periodically.

WSH also has a much smaller memory footprint than either IIS or Internet Explorer. However, WSH scripts can't be executed remotely (at least not without some other tool to handle the remoting of the WSH scripts). This means you'll still create ASP pages for administrative tasks that you need to run remotely.

WSH, like ASP and IE, supports the scripting languages JScript and VBScript. However, WSH uses the filename extension to determine the language of the script; unlike IE and ASP, WSH doesn't use the `<SCRIPT>` tag or Language attribute. JScript files have an extension of .js, and VBScript files have a .vbs extension.

In the following sections I'll explain how to run scripts using WSH, describe the WSH objects, and tell you where you can go to find other sample scripts.

11.3.1. Running Scripts

WSH scripts can be run in a couple different ways:

- Using the command-based host cscript.exe. To run a script from a command prompt, you may simply type `cscript` followed by the script's filename.
- By double-clicking the .vbs or .js file. This will launch wscript and run the script.
- By using the Windows-based host wscript.exe. For example, select Start | Run and type `WSCRIPT` followed by the script's filename.

11.3.2. Available Objects

WSH comes with several built-in objects to help you write scripts. They are listed in Table 11.4.

Table 11.4. WSH objects.

Object	Description
Wscript	Used for parsing input parameters, printing output, creating objects, and so on.
WshArguments	Collection object obtained from the Wscript Arguments property.
WshCollection	Collection object obtained from the WshNetwork object.
WshEnvironment	Contains environment variables. Collection object obtained from the WshShell Environment property.
WshNetwork	Provides access to network devices such as printers and network drives.
WshShell	Provides access to the Windows shell environment (such as folders and the desktop).
WshShortcut	Used to create a shortcut. Obtained from the WshShell object.
WshSpecialFolders	Contains a collection of special folders (Desktop, Recent, and so on). Obtained from the WshShell object.
WshUrlShortcut	Used to create an URL shortcut. Obtained from the WshShell object.

11.3.3. Available Sample Scripts

WSH comes with quite a few scripts that you will want to use to build your own scripts. They are stored in the \inetpub\iissamples\sdk\admin directory and the %WINDIR%\system32\inetsrv\adminsamples directory.

11.4. Active Directory Services Interface

Microsoft created the Active Directory Services Interface (ADSI) to allow client applications to use just one interface to access a variety of different directory services. Examples of directory services include NDS, NetWare 3.x, LDAP, and Windows NT.

ADSI also makes it easier for software vendors to directory-enable their applications. IIS is one such application that comes with an ADSI namespace provider. (If you'd like to install other ADSI namespace providers, go to http://www.microsoft.com/msdn/sdk to install ADSI.)

Objects within a particular namespace are uniquely identified by a case-sensitive string called an ADsPath. The ADsPath always begins with the programmatic id of the ADSI provider (Ads, IIS, WinNT, LDAP) followed by ://. The rest of the syntax is provider-dependent. For example, to name a computer using the Windows NT ADSI provider, you would use the following:

`WinNT://SomeDomain/SomeComputer`

For IIS, the AdsPath would be

`IIS://LM/Service/WebSite/Root/Virtual Directory/Dir/File`

- *LM* is the name of the local machine. You can use localhost.
- *Service* is either W3SVC or MSFTPSVC.
- *WebSite* is the instance of the site (such as 1 or 2).
- *Root* is the virtual directory root.
- *Virtual Directory* is the name of the virtual directory.
- *Dir* is the name of a directory.
- *File* is the name of a file.

To make this easier to understand, here are several examples:

- IIS://localhost/W3SVC specifies the IIS Web service.
- IIS://localhost/W3SVC/1 specifies the IIS Web server.
- IIS://localhost/MSFTPSVC/1 specifies the IIS FTP server.
- IIS://localhost/W3SVC/1/Root specifies the IIS Web root virtual directory.

The next two sections discuss the relationship between ADSI and the metabase. Then you'll see how to programmatically modify the metabase.

11.4.1. Metabase

The metabase is a hierarchical in-memory database that is used to store configuration information about IIS. The metabase is loaded from disk when IIS is started and is periodically written to disk. The metabase provides better performance and more granularity than just accessing the Registry; the metabase is also optimized for read performance. In addition to these features, the metabase supports inheritance.

You might be wondering what the connection between ADSI and the metabase is. The metabase hierarchy is what is exposed in the ADSI namespace. As you'll see in the next section, you can use a few different methods to modify the metabase.

11.4.2. IIS Admin Objects

There are two sets of interfaces you can use to programmatically modify the metabase:

- *IIS Admin Base object.* This object implements the IMSAdminBase interface. The IIS Admin Base object is intended to be used by lower-level programmers using C++. The Internet Service Manager snap-in to the MMC also utilizes the IIS Admin Base object.
- *IIS Admin objects (IISAO).* The IISAO is used by the HTML administration pages in IIS. The IISAO consists of 17 different objects that parallel the ADSI namespace. They are listed in Table 11.5.

Table 11.5. IIS Admin objects.

Object	Description
IIsCertMapper	Manages the mapping of NT user accounts to client certificates.
IIsComputer	Used to specify global metabase properties. These properties (such as MaxBandwidth and Mimemap) specify how IIS operates.
IIsFilter	Used to specify ISAPI filter properties.
IIsFilters	Container of IIsFilter objects.
IIsFtpInfo	Used to set metabase properties for the info subkey of the MSFTPSVC key.
IIsFtpServer	Properties of a specific FTP server. May contain IIsFtpVirtualDir objects.
IIsFtpService	Properties of FTP virtual servers and directories. May contain IIsFtpServer and IIsFtpInfo objects.
IIsFtpVirtualDir	Properties of an FTP virtual directory.
IIsLogModule	Properties that pertain to IIS logging.
IIsLogModules	Container of IIsLogModule objects.
IIsMimeMap	Properties of MIME mappings used by the W3SVC service.
IIsWebDirectory	Properties of Web directories for a Web server.
IIsWebFile	Properties of a file in a Web directory.
IIsWebInfo	Used to set metabase properties for the info subkey of the W3SVC key.
IIsWebServer	Properties of a specific Web server. May contain IIsCertMapper, IIsFilters, and IIsWebVirtualDir objects.

continues

Table 11.5. continued

Object	Description
IIsWebService	Properties of Web virtual servers and directories. May contain IIsFilters, IIsWebInfo, and IIsWebServer objects.
IIsWebVirtualDir	Properties of a specific Web virtual directory.

Of these two methods, the IISAO is more commonly used. To better understand how to use these, we'll go through an example using the IISAO. The following steps cover how to use the IIS Admin Objects to create an FTP virtual directory:

1. Open Notepad and enter the following code:

```
On Error Resume Next
set oRoot = GetObject("IIS://localhost/MSFTPSVC/1/Root")
if err <> 0 Then
     wscript.echo "Error getting Root object"
     wscript.quit
end if
set oVDir = oRoot.Create("IIsFtpVirtualDir","MCSE")
if err <> 0 Then
     wscript.echo "Error creating Virtual Directory"
     wscript.quit(1)
end if
oVDir.Path = "d:\inetpub\ftproot"
if err <> 0 then
     wscript.echo "Error setting path"
     wscript.quit(1)
end if
oVDir.EnableDirBrowsing = False
oVDir.AccessScript = True
oVDir.AccessRead = True
oVDir.SetInfo
if err <> 0 then
     wscript.echo "Error " & err.description
else
     wscript.echo "MCSE FTP Virtual Directory created."
end if
```

2. Save the file as vdirftp.vbs.

3. Locate this file in Windows Explorer and double-click it. This will launch Wscript.

4. If the script is successful, it should display the message MCSE FTP Virtual Directory created.

Lab

This lab consists of review questions pertaining to this chapter and provides an opportunity for you to use walk-through exercises to apply the knowledge that you've gained.

Questions

1. You receive the following error when connecting to a page on your Web site:

```
Microsoft OLE DB Provider for ODBC Drivers error '80004005'
[Microsoft][ODBC Driver Manager] Data source name not found and no
➥default driver specified
/default.asp, line 5
```

What is the most likely cause of this error?

A. The DSN is incorrectly specified in the ASP file, or the DSN isn't set up on the server.

B. Active Server Pages is not installed.

C. The specified database doesn't exist.

D. OLE DB is not installed on the server.

2. You receive the following error when connecting to a page on your Web site:

```
Microsoft OLE DB Provider for ODBC Drivers error '80004005'
[Microsoft][ODBC Driver Manager] Data source name not found and no
➥default driver specified
/default.asp, line 5
```

Default.asp contains

```
Set conTest = Server.CreateObject("ADODB.Connection")
conTest.Open Session("Test_ConnectionString"),
➥Session("Test_RuntimeUserName"), Session("Test_RuntimePassword")
```

and your global.asa contains

```
Sub Session_OnStart
Session("test_connectionString")="DSN=Test;"
Session("test_runtimeuserName")="sa"
Session("test_runtimepassword")=""
End Sub
```

You have confirmed that the connection information is correct and that the DSN named Test exists. What is the most likely cause of the error?

A. The global.asa is incorrect. The Session variables need to be moved to the Application_OnStart method.

B. The global.asa file is in the wrong directory or is not getting executed.

Day 11: Programmability

C. ASP 2.0 doesn't use the global.asa file.

D. The session variables are incorrectly specified since they are case sensitive.

3. You need to create a script to manage your Web site. You would like to be able to run the script from a batch file. What technology should you use?

   A. Active Server Pages
   B. Windows Scripting Host
   C. CGI
   D. ISAPI

4. Which statement will return the list of ISAPI filters for a Web server?

   A. `GetObject("IIsFilters")`
   B. `GetObject("IIS:/localhost/W3SVC/1/Filters")`
   C. `GetObject("http://localhost/w3svc/filters")`
   D. `GetObject("\\localhost\w3svc\filters")`

5. Which scripting languages are installed with IIS? Select all correct answers.

   A. JScript
   B. VBScript
   C. Perl
   D. JavaScript

6. Which programming methods are supported by IIS? Select all correct answers.

   A. ASP
   B. CGI
   C. ISAPI
   D. NSAPI

7. You would like to connect IIS to a SQL Server database running on another machine. You get the following error when configuring the DSN:

```
Connection failed:
SQLState: '08001'
SQL Server Error: 6
[Microsoft][ODBC SQL Server Driver][Named Pipes]Specified SQL server
➥not found.
Connection failed.
SQLState:'01000'
SQL Server Error:2
[Microsoft][ODBC SQL Server Driver][Named Pipes]ConnectionOpen
➥(CreateFile()).
```

Select all possible causes of the problem.

A. The specified SQL Server is not running.

B. The specified SQL Server is unreachable from the IIS server.

C. The database doesn't exist on the server.

D. All of the above.

8. You get the following error when trying to run an ISAPI extension:

```
HTTP Error 403
403.2 Forbidden: Read Access Forbidden
```

What is the most likely cause of the problem?

A. The directory containing the ISAPI extension has read permission but needs script permission.

B. The directory containing the ISAPI extension has script permission but needs execute permission.

C. The ISAPI extension needs to be registered using regsvr32.exe.

D. The directory containing the ISAPI extension has execute permission but needs script permission.

9. You have recently copied the files for an ASP application to a new server. However, users notice that they get an error when they access the page. The page accesses a database using ADO. However, other webs on the server that use ADO work fine. What is the most likely cause of the problem?

A. The DSN needs to be re-created on the new machine.

B. ADO needs to be installed on the new server.

C. ADO needs to be installed on the new application.

D. The application needs to be registered on the new server.

10. You are trying to connect to a database via a file DSN from an ASP page. However, you receive an error with the following connect string to the ADO connection object:

```
Conn.open("File Data Source=MyDSN")
```

What should you do to correct the problem?

A. The correct syntax is "FileDSN=MyDSN".

B. The file DSN MyDSn.dsn needs to be placed in the system32 directory.

C. ADO doesn't support file DSNs. Convert the file DSN to a System DSN.

D. ASP doesn't support file DSNs. Convert the file DSN to a System DSN.

Answers to Questions

1. **A.** Of the possible causes, only A could be true. B is not possible: It's obvious that ASP is already installed, because the page being executed (default.asp) is an ASP page. C can't be true, because the error happens before a connection is made to a database. D also can't be true, because the error is being generated by OLE DB, which implies that OLE DB is already installed.

2. **B.** Only B is correct. ASP uses the global.asa file. It is possible that the global.asa is in the wrong directory—it must be in the root directory of the application. Session variables are not case-sensitive. Session variables should be placed in the Session_OnStart method.

3. **B.** Active Server Pages, CGI, and ISAPI are all run in IIS. Only Windows Scripting Host allows you to run scripts from a command-line interface.

4. **B.** IIS uses the Active Directory Services Interface to enumerate its objects. Only B uses the correct ADSI syntax, where IIS denotes the namespace provider, localhost is the name of the machine, W3SVC is the service, 1 is the first Web server, and Filters refers to the filters collection.

5. **A, B.** IIS comes with the Microsoft JScript and VBScript Active Scripting Engines. Perl is a popular scripting language that can be added onto IIS via third-party software. JavaScript, although similar to JScript, is Netscape's implementation of the ECMA 252 standard.

6. **A, B, C.** IIS supports ASP, CGI, and ISAPI programming methods. NSAPI is supported by Netscape on its Web server.

7. **A, B.** A is correct because if for some reason the SQL Server is not running, you will get this error. B is also correct and could be due to network problems or mismatched network protocols, for example.

8. **B.** ISAPI extensions require execute permission on a directory containing the extension. D is incorrect because having execute permission also includes script permission. A is incorrect because script permission is not sufficient. C is incorrect because this is a permissions problem and also because ISAPI extensions can't be registered via the regsvr32.exe program.

9. **A.** Copying an application can be as easy as moving the files from one server to another. However, if the application uses ADO connect strings that reference a DSN, the DSN must be re-created. This is the most common problem in moving Web applications.

10. **A.** A is correct since you specify a file DSN in a connect string using `FileDSN=""`. Both ADO and ASP support file DSNs, so C and D are wrong.

B is wrong because the default location for File DSNs is \program files\common files\odbc\data sources.

Exercise

Exercise 11.1.: Writing an ASP Script to Display and Modify the Server Comment for the W3SVC Service

This exercise addresses the following Microsoft exam objective:

- Write scripts to manage the FTP service or the WWW service.

In this exercise you will create an Active Server Page script that uses the IIS Admin objects. The script you write must display and modify the server comment for the W3SVC service.

1. Before writing your script, start up the Internet Service Manager and view the comment for the default Web site. The comment is listed in the tree control on the left. You can also view the comment by right-clicking the site and selecting Properties from the pop-up menu.

2. Open Notepad and enter the following code.

```
<%@ LANGUAGE=JScript %>
<%
// Grab the node object
var oIIsWebServer;
oIIsWebServer = GetObject("IIS://localhost/W3SVC/1");
Response.write ("Server Comment: " + oIIsWebServer.ServerComment
↪+ "<BR>");
oIIsWebServer.ServerComment = "This is the new Server Comment";
Response.write ("New Server Comment: " + oIIsWebServer.ServerComment
↪+ "<BR>");
oIIsWebServer.SetInfo();
%>
```

The script is written in JScript. The IISAO IIsWebServer object is obtained via the call to GetObject. The ServerComment property is printed, updated, printed again, and then saved to the metabase via the SetInfo method.

3. Save the file in the IIS Admin directory (by default, this is \winnt\system32\inetsrv\iisadmin) as serverComment.asp. You can save this in another directory, but you will have to make sure that it is in a directory that requires authentication (that is, nonanonymous).

4. Select Start | Windows NT 4.0 Option Pack | Microsoft Internet Information Server | Internet Service Manager (HTML). In the address bar,

Day 11: Programmability

you should see the URL to the IIS Admin directory (`http://localhost:3659/iisadmin/iis.asp`). Note that the URL includes the port number, which is different with every installation of IIS. Modify the URL by changing iis.asp to serverComment.asp. The page should display the current server comment and the updated server comment.

5. Launch the Internet Service Manager to display the server comment. You should now see that it displays `This is the new Server Comment`.

TEST DAY FAST FACTS

Here are a few fast facts about this chapter that you may want to know ahead of time. Don't forget that these facts also provide great last-minute study material.

- IIS can always use more memory.
- Network Monitor can show network utilization levels for the local subnet and display traffic that is sent from or to the local machine.
- NETSTAT is used for viewing protocol-related statistics.
- The four main areas of concern when dealing with system performance are memory, processor, network, and disk.
- Use Performance Monitor's Log function to track data over long periods of time.
- Use Performance Monitor's Chart view to see what is currently happening in your system.
- Performance monitoring with regard to IIS is very closely tied into Windows NT performance. IIS is basically self-tuning.
- The more features you implement, the higher your hardware requirements will be.

Day 12

Performance Tuning

by Rob Scrimger and Glen Martin

In this chapter, we will discuss how you can ensure that your IIS systems are running as smoothly as possible, as well as how you can detect what might be causing problems if things aren't running as well as they could be.

It's important that as an administrator you be able to identify performance problems. In the vast majority of cases, these are caused by insufficient hardware resources, and you will need to decide whether to upgrade or possibly remove some of the extra features from your site.

We'll also discuss some ways to improve IIS performance after you have isolated your bottlenecks. For purposes of the exam, you really only need to concern yourself with what tools are available and which would be used for a specific situation. IIS is primarily self-tuning, so performance optimization really focuses on isolating performance problems to the bottleneck and then eliminating that bottleneck by upgrading the subsystem in question.

Objectives

This chapter helps you prepare for the Microsoft exam by covering the following objectives:

- Monitor the performance of various functions by using Performance Monitor. Functions include HTTP and FTP sessions.
- Interpret performance data.
- Analyze performance. Tasks include identifying bottlenecks, network-related performance issues, disk-related performance issues, and CPU-related performance issues.
- Optimize a Web site by using Content Analyzer.

12.1. IIS Performance Issues

Factors that affect IIS performance are typically hardware-related, such as not having a sufficient amount of RAM in your server. Although it's easy to upgrade the system, it's important to be able to identify where bottlenecks reside. (A *bottleneck* is the factor most affecting performance. Think of it as the weakest link in the performance chain. For example, in a high-end Pentium system with only 16 MB of RAM, the memory would most likely be the bottleneck, not the CPU.)

In order to identify these bottlenecks and make informed decisions about the best path to resolving performance issues, you need to understand the tools available and know which tool to use in a given situation. This chapter discusses these tools, as well as how to use them.

However, you must also remember that through proper planning, you might be able to avoid some of these performance issues to begin with. We'll discuss this in the next section.

12.1.1. Balancing Performance and Function

IIS is an excellent package that was designed to meet the needs of as broad a user base as possible. As such, it includes many advanced features that can greatly enhance a user's visit to your site. These features are wonderful, and you can do lots of great things with them, but it's important to remember that any extra features you deploy on your site will require more hardware resources in order to perform optimally. (For example, if you're using Active Server Pages, you might require a faster CPU in order to ensure that your clients receive their pages as quickly as possible.) It is therefore important to take a good look at exactly what features you need versus what features you would like and then to decide whether you can justify the extra load that these features might generate on your server. Remember, for every feature you implement, there will always be a trade-off in performance.

For example, if you use Netshow On-Demand, you can provide real-time audio and video to your users whenever they ask for it. This would be great for letting employees and customers listen to the speech that your CEO recently made to the shareholders, but if you don't have the resources in place (such as sufficient memory in your server or bandwidth to service all your users) to support these high-end functions, not only will you *not* improve your users' experience on your site, they might get turned off by the poor performance and have a negative experience.

In summary, it is always best to analyze what impact rolling out a new feature might have on your system and decide if your users really need to see all those fancy features when all they want to do is see when the next city bus will arrive.

Next let's look at some factors that affect performance on IIS.

12.1.2. Factors That Limit Performance

One of the primary factors affecting performance in IIS is simply system memory. IIS, like Windows NT itself, will always run much better if you give it more memory to work with.

Many of the other factors that affect Windows NT performance also affect IIS, such as CPU load, disk speed and the amount of data being transferred to and from the disks, and network utilization. This typically isn't an issue with Windows NT, because LAN bandwidth is relatively cheap, and many organizations are deploying Ethernet networks capable of more than 100 megabits per second.

On the Internet, however, one other primary concern must always be bandwidth, because the cost of Internet links is exponentially more than local networks. You must ensure that you provide a large-enough pipe for data to flow from your site and to your users. If your IIS site is connected to the Internet by a T1 that runs at 1.5 megabits per second, you can support about 60 users at a time running at 28.8 kilobits per second if they are all transferring large files. This number will go up if you have a large number of smaller files, but it's a good example of how planning can help you avoid bottlenecks. If you needed to support thousands of users at 56.6 kilobits per second and all are transferring large files, you would need a huge amount of bandwidth!

Next we'll look at some of the tools available for analyzing how your network connection is performing.

12.2. Tools for Analyzing Network Performance

This chapter focuses primarily on the Performance Monitor tool. But first, let's see some of the other tools available for analyzing performance.

12.2.1. NETSTAT

NETSTAT is a utility provided with Windows NT that is used to analyze TCP/IP connections and statistics. NETSTAT has a large number of options, most of which are outside the scope of this book. This section gives you an overview of what NETSTAT can do and how it can be used. For the purposes of the exam, all you need to know is that it is used for displaying statistics related to TCP/IP and your Ethernet network (such as the total number of bytes transferred and the number of errors that have occurred).

NETSTAT can be run from a command line in order to analyze how TCP/IP and your network are performing. With it you can see a wide variety of statistics, such as connected networks, the number of packets sent and received, the number of errors, and so on. It doesn't have some of the advanced features of a full-blown graphical program like Network Monitor or Performance Monitor, but it can be very useful for isolating problems with TCP/IP.

To run NETSTAT, simply type NETSTAT at a command prompt. You will see a list of all the connections currently being made on your system. Typing NETSTAT -? shows a list of command-line options, such as Ethernet statistics. Figure 12.1 shows NETSTAT displaying transfer statistics. This was generated by typing NETSTAT -E at the NT command prompt.

Figure 12.1.
NETSTAT can be used to display transfer statistics.

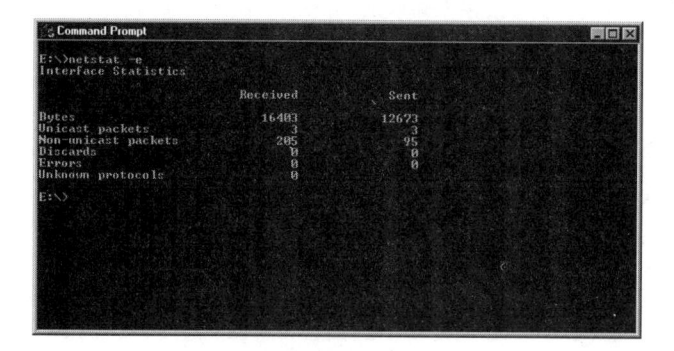

In the following steps, you will do this yourself in order to become familiar with NETSTAT. (Note that this probably won't be on the exam, but it's good knowledge to have.)

1. Open an NT command prompt by selecting Start | Programs | Command Prompt.

2. Type NETSTAT -?. This will display the options available to you.
3. In order to display TCP/IP statistics, type NETSTAT-S | MORE. This will pause NETSTAT after each screen so that you can read it.

The data displayed by running NETSTAT-S lets you see how much data is being transferred and how many errors are occurring. From a performance point of view, if your users are complaining of slow response, a high number of errors could indicate faulty network hardware. A large amount of data being transferred would also result in reduced performance for your users. Unfortunately, that is the price we must pay. If it is consistently very high, you would either have to start limiting the number of connections or consider upgrading to a faster Internet connection.

Although NETSTAT operates at the protocol level, Network Monitor is more concerned with monitoring at the network level. In the next section, we will take a more in-depth look at Network Monitor.

12.2.2. Network Monitor

The Windows NT Network Monitor is provided in order to analyze the performance of your networks, as well as act as a diagnostic tool for identifying very low-level problems. Because the focus of this chapter is performance, we will only touch briefly on the packet analysis functions. Most of the time will be spent becoming familiar with using Network Monitor to analyze network utilization. For purposes of the exam, you should be familiar with Network Monitor's purpose (analyzing the performance of the network rather than the specific protocols).

Network Monitor can be used for two purposes:

- Analyzing usage levels
- Capturing and displaying packets

We will look at how you can work with packets in the next section. Network Monitor is limited to monitoring traffic originating from or destined for the machine where it is running, and you must install it as a network service.

When Network Monitor is capturing data, it will operate your network interface in promiscuous mode: Rather than looking only at its own traffic, it processes all traffic being sent on the wire. Figure 12.2 shows an example of capturing data using Network Monitor.

Figure 12.2.
Network Monitor captures data being sent to and from a workstation.

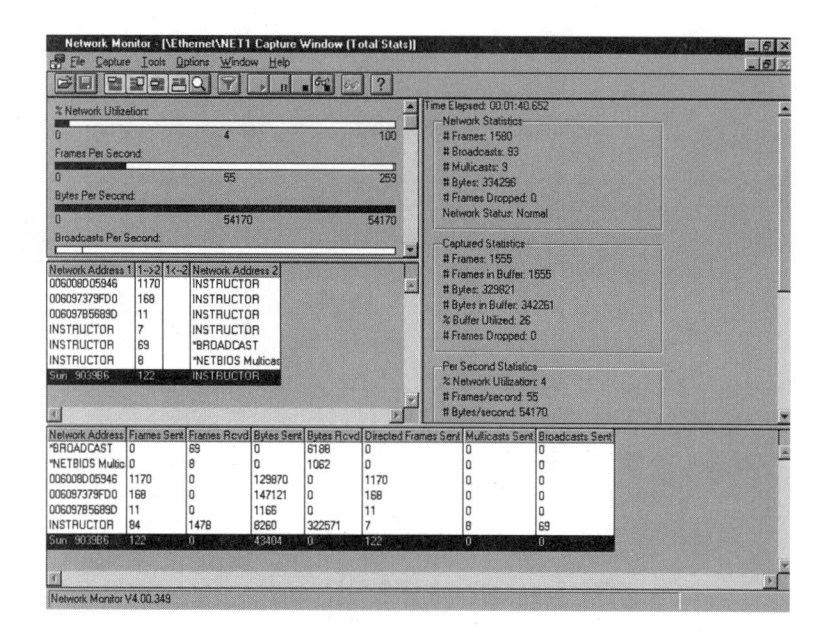

> **Note:** For security reasons, Network Monitor doesn't display the data but uses it to calculate network utilization. If you need to capture all the data, this feature is available in an upgraded version of Network Monitor that comes with Microsoft Systems Management Server.

In order to display this type of information, you first need to install Network Monitor (the tool that is used to view the data) and Network Monitor Agent (which is responsible for placing the Network Adapter in promiscuous mode and retrieving the data from the network). Follow these steps:

1. Right-click the Network Neighborhood icon on your desktop and select Properties.
2. Choose the Services tab, and then click the Add button.
3. From the services list, select Network Monitor Tools and Agent.
4. Click OK to return to the Network Control Panel. Click OK to close the Network Control Panel.
5. Restart your computer. You now have Network Monitor and Network Monitor Agent installed.

In order to use Network Monitor to display the type of data shown in Figure 12.2, you need to become familiar with how it is used. When you first open Network Monitor, you see a screen with no activity on it. In order to display information, you must first start capturing data:

1. Start Network Monitor by selecting Start | Programs | Administrative Tools | Network Monitor. You will see a screen similar to Figure 12.3.

Figure 12.3.
The screen that is first displayed when you start Network Monitor.

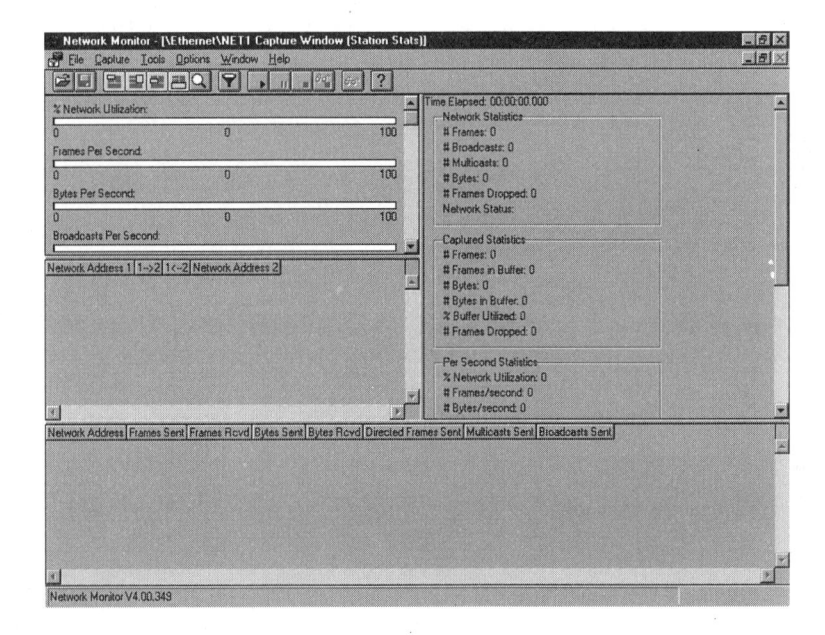

2. Select Capture | Start Capture. (While Network Monitor is capturing data, you will experience a decrease in system performance.)
3. Network Monitor will display performance statistics. When you're done, select Capture | Stop. (You will see how to view packets a little later in this chapter.)
4. Select File | Exit to close Network Monitor. When prompted to save captured data, click No.

The most important thing to note on the Network Monitor screen is the gauge in the upper-left corner, which displays network utilization levels. If this number is consistently very high (50 percent on Ethernet networks and 80 percent on Token Ring networks), you should consider upgrading to a faster network or moving to a subnet with less traffic.

Although Performance Monitor has many other functions, they are outside the scope of this book and have no bearing on the exam. However, in order to give you more insight into what the product is capable of, the following sections discuss looking at the captured data.

A. Looking at Packets

As mentioned earlier, Network Monitor has the capability not only to capture data, but also to display it. This can be useful if you need to directly examine data being sent to and from your server. This doesn't need to be done under normal circumstances, and it isn't covered on the exam, but you should be aware of how to do this if you ever need to. Follow these steps:

1. Start Network Monitor and begin capturing data.
2. When you have captured all the data you want to view, select Capture | Stop and View. You will see a screen similar to Figure 12.4.

Figure 12.4.

Network Monitor displays captured packets.

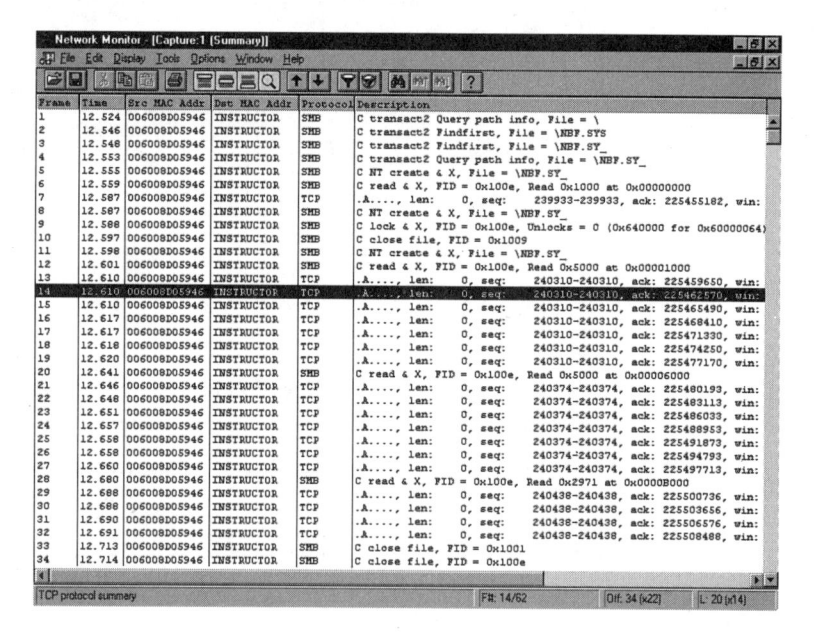

3. To view a specific packet, double-click it.
4. To move through the captured packets, use the up and down arrow keys to go to the previous or next packet.
5. When you're done, select File | Exit. When prompted to save the data, click No.

B. Finding Performance Problems: Utilization Rate

Network Monitor isn't necessarily the best tool for isolating performance problems, but it is useful for looking at the utilization rate of your network segment as well as the number of broadcasts on your segment, which can adversely affect performance.

If you're seeing a large number of broadcasts on your system, they are probably being caused by clients running protocols such as NetBEUI on your network. Although it is normal to see broadcasts when running strictly TCP/IP, high numbers here can suggest either the use of other protocols or excessive name-resolution broadcasts. To reduce name-resolution broadcasts, you should consider a solution such as WINS, in which a client can send requests to a name server rather than generating broadcasts that need to be processed by all the machines on your subnet.

The most important thing to note here is the percent of network utilization. Again, if it is consistently above 50 percent on an Ethernet network and consistently above 80 percent on a Token Ring network, you should consider upgrading or moving your server to a different subnet with less traffic.

Once you have eliminated the network as the source of performance problems, you need a way to determine if other factors might be at fault. You can determine this using the Windows NT Performance Monitor, which gives you the ability to analyze a wide variety of data from many different sources. We will discuss Performance Monitor in the next section.

12.3. Performance Monitor

Windows NT includes a great little utility called Performance Monitor, which can be used to track dozens of counters to monitor performance. (*Counters* are objects that NT automatically keeps track of, such as the CPU utilization rate or the amount of free memory.)

Although other tools let you track what is occuring on your network, Performance Monitor is the main tool you will use in order to determine which other hardware subsystems might be causing bottlenecks in your system. (Note that Performance Monitor provides a huge array of information, but for purposes of the exam, all you need to know is how to isolate problems in specific subsystems, such as memory.)

When Microsoft developed this utility, it also gave other packages the ability to register their counters with Performance Monitor, so it allows you to access a single source for looking at most of the performance-related data in your system. IIS adds a

Day 12: Performance Tuning

large number of counters to Performance Monitor; however, most of them, like many of the counters in Windows NT itself, are rarely used and rather obscure.

In the rest of this chapter we'll take a look at how to use Performance Monitor, as well as learn about the most useful counters to track in order to easily monitor IIS's performance.

First, let's take a look at Performance Monitor, shown in Figure 12.5, and get familiar with its interface.

Figure 12.5.
Windows NT's Performance Monitor utility lets you easily monitor the performance of IIS.

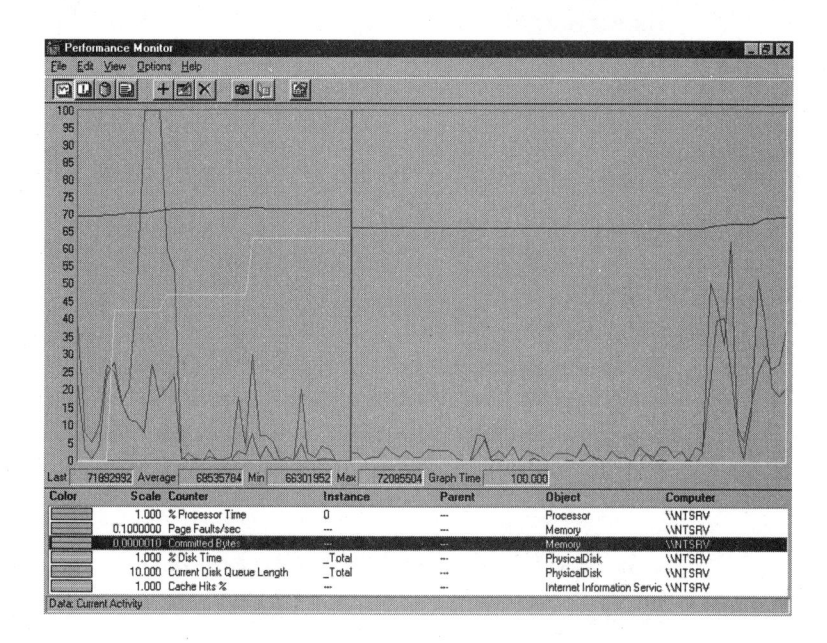

12.3.1. How to Use Performance Monitor

The first four toolbar buttons are used to set the Performance Monitor view:

- Chart
- Alert
- Log
- Report

We'll discuss these views in more detail in the next section.

12.3. Performance Monitor

The next three buttons let you do the following:

- Add a counter
- Modify the selected counter (if you have multiple counters displayed, you can select a different one by clicking its name in the list of counters at the bottom of the window)
- Delete the selected counter so that it is no longer displayed

The remaining buttons let you do the following:

- Manually update the counters (rather than waiting for the next update to occur)
- Insert a bookmark in the current log file (this is available only in Log view)
- Set options for the current view

As you will see, you can track a staggering number of objects and counters. Normally, most of these won't be necessary. Later in this chapter I'll highlight some of the most important ones for you. The following steps show you how to view performance data using Performance Monitor's Chart view:

1. Start Performance Monitor by selecting Start | Programs | Administrative Tools | Performance Monitor. You should see a screen that looks like Figure 12.6.

Figure 12.6.
The Windows NT Performance Monitor after being started.

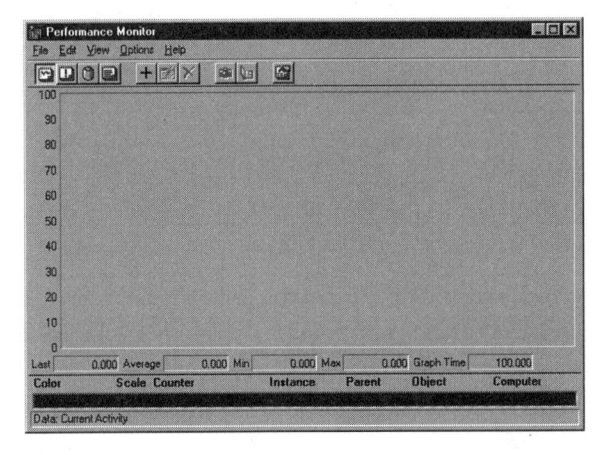

2. Add counters to the Chart view by clicking the + button on the toolbar. Select the object you would like to monitor (for example, Processor) by choosing it from the Object drop-down list. Select the specific counter you would like to track (for example, % Processor Time) by choosing it from the Counter list.

3. Click the + button.

4. Repeat steps 2 and 3 for every counter you want to track. Rather than listing all the counters here, Microsoft has provided a very handy feature in Performance Monitor: To get an explanation of what each counter does when you click it, click the Explain button. You can add any number of different counters to your Performance Monitor view from any number of different objects—but don't select so many that you will have trouble keeping track of them all!

5. Click Done.

6. When you're done, if you would like to save your current chart settings so that you can easily track these same counters later, select File | Save Chart Settings, provide a filename when prompted, and click OK. (To use these settings again, start Performance Monitor and select File | Open, and then select the file you previously saved.)

7. Select File | Exit to close Performance Monitor.

A. Views

The Chart view gives you a graphical view of what's happening in your system. Other views are also available, and we'll discuss them here.

We've already seen the Chart view and how it can be used to display counter data graphically over a period of time. The Alert view lets you set thresholds to trigger alerts. For example, if your network utilization or connection limit per second gets to a certain preset point, you can have Performance Monitor notify you or run a program. This is called an *alert*. The Alert view also lets you see what alerts have been set on this server and modify those alerts if required.

The Log view lets you output counter data to a file rather than to the screen. You can then import this log into another program later in order to analyze the data you have accumulated. We'll take a more in-depth look at logging in the next section.

Finally, the Report view lets you see the current value of counters without displaying them graphically over time, as with the Chart view. The Report view is useful if you need to take a snapshot of system performance to include in a presentation or to assist in troubleshooting. It's also useful to generate a report when your system is working nominally under normal usage conditions in order to generate a baseline. Once you have a baseline, you can use it to anticipate the value of your counters, thereby giving you the ability to easily isolate abnormal activity. In order to diagnose problems, you must be able to determine what is normal and what is not. By comparing your baseline data and your current data, you can easily spot the differences and address them.

Now, let's take a more in-depth look at the process of creating logs, because this will help you track performance over long periods of time.

B. Creating Logs

The logging process in Performance Monitor is intended to output counter values to a file rather than to the screen. This log file could then be used to view the data in another package, such as a spreadsheet or a data analysis package, which could then, for example, be used to generate a monthly report of system performance for display at departmental meetings. Alternatively, you can also view the log files in one of the other Performance Monitor views in order to see historical data (for example, comparing this month's data to last month's).

The Log view in Performance Monitor doesn't let you see what is actually happening on your system. It simply gives you the logging process's operating state. It shows you the file it is logging to, the size of the log, whether or not it is currently logging, its update interval, and a list of objects it will be logging. Once you have accumulated enough data in your log, you can export it to a text file and then import it into another package, such as Microsoft Excel for analysis, or view the data in one of Performance Monitor's other views, such as Chart view. We will dicuss this in the next section.

In the following steps, you will create a log file using Performance Monitor:

1. Start Performance Monitor.
2. Select View | Log.
3. Click the + button and add the objects you want to track. (Unlike with Chart view, you can't select specific counters. Performance Monitor will log *all* counters for that object.)
4. When you have added all your counters, select Options | Log.
5. Specify a filename for your log.
6. Specify an update interval.
7. Click Start Log. You will see a display similar to Figure 12.7.

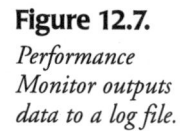

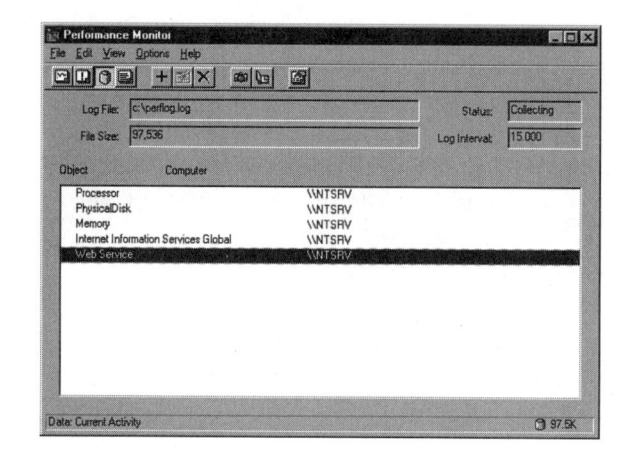

Figure 12.7.
Performance Monitor outputs data to a log file.

8. When you finish generating a log, select Options | Log and click Stop Log.

Once you have created a log, you need to tell Performance Monitor to extract its data from that log or to export it so you will be able to view the data you have collected in a third-party package such as Excel. We will look at both of these processes in depth in the following section.

C. Exporting Data for Analysis

In this section, you will see how you can work with the data that you created in the preceding section. You will look at exporting data so that you can import it into a third-party package. It's important to understand the logging process so that you can easily keep track of system performance over time and compare historical data to present data in order to spot trends. For example, if you see a large increase in traffic every month, you can start planning for a network upgrade, because you will be forewarned that eventually you will saturate your network connection.

Exporting data from log files is quite simple. Performance Monitor simply outputs its data into a text file that can easily be read by almost any software package, thereby allowing you to use whatever spreadsheet or charting software you are most familiar with. You can then include that information in your documents—for example, generating a monthly report for tracking system usage over time.

When exporting, you have the choice of using .tsv files, which are text files in which the columns are separated by tab stops, or .csv files, which are text files whose columns are separated by commas.

In the next section, we'll discuss which objects are most important to track and which counters give you the data you need to identify performance problems.

12.3.2. Key Areas of Concern

Once you have installed IIS, it will add many counters to Performance Monitor. However, most of these counters, although very helpful in determining what sort of activity is occurring on your site, don't give you much insight into what components might be causing bottlenecks.

In order to determine that, you need to look at how much use you're getting out of your primary hardware subsystems. In this section, you will see how you can do that by identifying those subsystems and associating them with their respective objects in Performance Monitor. You will also look at which counters will give you the best measurement of system performance. As stated earlier, four major hardware subsystems affect Windows NT and IIS performance: memory, disk subsystem, network subsystem, and processor. The next sections discuss these. First, we'll take a look at the most important hardware consideration in any Windows NT solution: memory.

A. Memory

The best investment you can make in improving system performance is memory. At today's prices, it has never been less expensive to buy additional RAM for your servers. With the standard desktops now shipping with 64 MB of RAM, there is no excuse for running into memory problems. But you may already have enough memory, so adding more memory might not help. There are a few easy ways to tell.

Table 12.1 shows you what counters you should be tracking from the Memory object in Performance Monitor, as well as what values are acceptable.

Table 12.1. Tracking counters from the Memory object.

Counter to Track	Acceptable Value
Page Faults/sec	Less than 5
Pages/sec	Less than 20
Available Bytes	Greater than 4 MB
Committed Bytes	Less than the amount of RAM (ideally)

Although ideally Committed Bytes should be less than the amount of RAM in your server, this can be ignored as long as the other indicators are in their acceptable ranges. If more than one of these counters is outside the acceptable limit over an extended period of time, you will definitely see a performance increase by adding memory.

Next we'll look at the disk subsystem and see how you can isolate problems occuring within it.

B. Disk Subsystem

The disk subsystem, although not as crucial as some of the other hardware subsystems, should not be overlooked—particularly if you are deploying very high-bandwidth services such as Netshow On-Demand. Isolating problems within this subsystem is easiest when done in conjunction with other objects, such as the memory and processor. However, before you can track these counters, you must run the command `diskperf -y` from an NT command prompt and then restart your system.

Once this has been done, you should track Avg. Disk Queue Length, the number of commands waiting to be processed per second, and % Disk Time, which tells you how much of the disk's time is busy servicing requests. Both of these should closely approximate the % Processor Time counter, which you will soon see. However, if these counters are high without corresponding activity from the other counters in your system, you should consider getting faster hard drives or a higher throughput controller.

% Disk Time and % Processor Time should match fairly closely. If % Disk Time is high without corresponding Processor activity, you should consider moving some data or applications to another drive or upgrading to a faster drive or controller. In order to verify that this is the case, track both these counters. They should be similar. (For example, when % Processor Time is low, % Disk Time should also be low.)

Next let's look at the network subsystem and what information we can gain from its counters.

C. Network Subsystem

Unfortunately, the counters for the Network Segment option are far more useful in a LAN environment than in a WAN/Internet environment. The main reason for this is that the % Network Utilization counter will only give you the utilization rate of the segment the server is directly attached to, which would typically be a high-speed Ethernet connection that then connects over a relatively low-speed WAN connection to get to the Internet. So while your local Ethernet utilization might be fairly low, your WAN connection might be entirely bogged down!

However, % Network Utilization should not be over 50 percent on an Ethernet network and 80 percent on a Token Ring network.

You should also be concerned with your processor subsystem. As CPU vendors continually release new products, it can be tempting to upgrade often, but this won't always improve performance as much as you might like. In the next section, you will see how you can determine if your processor or processors are causing a bottleneck. Based on this information, you can decide if it's worth your while to upgrade.

D. Processor

A slow processor is probably the easiest thing to diagnose in IIS. You should monitor the % Processor Time counter under the Processor object for each CPU in your system. If they are consistently over 80 percent, your system could benefit from faster or additional CPUs.

You are now armed with enough knowledge to be able to identify hardware bottlenecks. Although there is a huge number of counters and objects in Performance Monitor, you can isolate which ones are most important. However, you should also spend some time becoming familiar with some of the other counters, because they might be able to give you more background information on what is going on in your system. In the next section, we will look at the counters that IIS adds to Performance Monitor. For more information on Performance Monitor and for an in-depth description of all the counters, see the Windows NT Resource Kit.

12.3.3. IIS Counters

The previous sections discussed NT Performance Monitor counters in depth. To review, every subsystem and most services in NT (such as memory or the DNS service) are represented by objects. These objects have various counters, which are used to track specific criteria within these subsystems (such as the total amount of memory in use in the system). Microsoft also provided other programs so that any vendor can register its counter with Performance Monitor, which means that one tool can be used for most of your performance analysis.

IIS adds a large number of counters to Performance Monitor. Although the counters we have discussed give you the ability to see which subsystems are performing poorly, the following counters can give you insight into what is causing those subsystems to perform poorly. Therefore, if you see that one system is experiencing very heavy usage, such as the FTP service, you can consider moving that service to another system or reducing the number of users who can connect at any given time. Rather than going into depth about each counter, this section gives you an overview of those counters as they apply to the various IIS components.

You will not need to know these counters or how to use them for the exam. They are provided here as a reference so that you can easily look up what each counter does. IIS is basically self-tuning, so improving performance is usually a case of upgrading your hardware or removing certain features or services. (For example, if you are running the WWW, FTP, NNTP, SMTP, and Index Server all on the same server and are experiencing heavy usage, there is really nothing you can do except to remove some services or upgrade your hardware.)

A. Active Server Pages

Active Server Pages normally affect the processor and memory on a system, due to the overhead of having the server actually build HTML documents on-the-fly. By monitoring the ASP counters, you can get a handle on how the use of ASP in your system affects performance.

Sluggish performance from ASP will result in taking much longer for IIS to rebuild documents, meaning longer wait times for your users' requests, so it's important to ensure prompt response.

Table 12.2 lists Active Server Pages counters in Performance Monitor.

Table 12.2. Active Server Pages counters in Performance Monitor.

Counter	Description
Debugging Requests	The number of debugging document requests.
Errors During Script Runtime	The number of requests that failed due to runtime errors.
Errors From ASP Preprocessor	The number of requests that failed due to preprocessor errors.
Errors From Script Compilers	The number of requests that failed due to script compilation errors.
Errors/sec	The number of errors per second.
Memory Allocated	The total amount of memory, in bytes, currently allocated by Active Server Pages.
Request Bytes In Total	The total size, in bytes, of all requests.
Request Bytes Out Total	The total size, in bytes, of responses sent to clients. This does not include standard HTTP response headers.
Request Execution Time	The number of milliseconds it took to execute the most recent request.
Request Wait Time	The number of milliseconds the most recent request was waiting in the queue.

Counter	Description
Requests Disconnected	The number of requests that were disconnected due to communication failure.
Requests Executing	The number of requests currently executing.
Requests Failed Total	The total number of requests that failed due to errors, authorization failure, and rejections.
Requests Not Authorized	The number of requests that failed due to insufficient access rights.
Requests Not Found	The number of requests for files that were not found.
Requests Queued	The number of requests waiting for service from the queue.
Requests Rejected	The total number of requests not executed because there were insufficient resources to process them.
Requests Succeeded	The number of requests that executed successfully.
Requests Timed Out	The number of requests that timed out.
Requests Total	The total number of requests since the service was started.
Requests/sec	The number of requests executed per second.
Script Engines Cached	The number of script engines in cache.
Session Duration	The number of milliseconds that the most recent session persisted.
Sessions Current	The current number of sessions being serviced.
Sessions Timed Out	The number of sessions that timed out.
Sessions Total	The total number of sessions since the service was started.
Template Cache Hit Rate	The percentage of requests found in template cache.
Template Notifications	The number of templates invalidated in the cache due to change notification.
Templates Cached	The number of templates currently cached.
Transactions Aborted	The number of transactions aborted.
Transactions Committed	The number of transactions committed.
Transactions Pending	The number of transactions in progress.
Transactions Total	The total number of transactions since the service was started.
Transactions/sec	The transactions started per second.

B. Content Index

The Content Index (also known as the Index Server) also primarily requires memory (for storing word lists and indexes) and processor time (for merging indexes).

Poor performance will manifest itself in slow queries, which can cause undue stress for your users.

Table 12.3 lists Content Index counters in Performance Monitor.

Table 12.3. Content Index counters in Performance Monitor.

Counter	Description
# Documents Filtered	The number of documents filtered since the index was mounted.
Files to Be Filtered	The files to be filtered and added to the index.
Index Size (Mbytes)	The size of the Content Index in megabytes.
Merge Progress	The percentage of the current merge that is complete.
Persistent Indexes	The number of persistent indexes.
Running Queries	The number of running queries.
Total # Documents	The total number of documents in the index.
Unique Keys	The number of unique keys (such as words) in the index.
Wordlists	The number of wordlists.

C. Content Index Filter

Content Index Filter shows you the performance of adding new documents to the Index Server corpus.

This will primarily take processor time but may also require large amounts of memory for very large files or for a large number of different filters.

Poor performance here would cause new documents to take a long time to be added to the index, which could result in your users not getting timely results for their queries. For mission-critical data, in which time is of the essence, it is vital for the filtering process to occur as quickly as possible.

Table 12.4 lists Content Index Filter counters in Performance Monitor.

Table 12.4. Content Index Filter counters in Performance Monitor.

Counter	Description
Binding Time (msec)	The average time spent binding to indexing filters.
Filter Speed (Mbytes/hr)	The speed of filtering contents of files, measured in megabytes per hour.
Total Filter Speed (Mbytes/hr)	The speed of filtering file contents and properties, measured in megabytes per hour.

D. FTP Service

The FTP Service object lets you monitor the performance of transferring files to and from your FTP server and assess its performance.

The FTP Service primarily requires bandwidth. Therefore, it is closely tied to network utilization.

Table 12.5 lists FTP Service counters in Performance Monitor.

Table 12.5. FTP Service counters in Performance Monitor.

Counter	Description
Bytes Received/sec	The rate that data bytes are received by the FTP Service.
Bytes Sent/sec	The rate that data bytes are sent by the FTP Service.
Bytes Total/sec	The sum of Bytes Sent/sec and Bytes Received/sec. This is the total rate of bytes transferred by the FTP Service.
Current Anonymous Users	The number of users who currently have an anonymous connection using the FTP Service.
Current Blocked Async I/O Requests	The number of current requests temporarily blocked due to bandwidth throttling settings.
Current Connections	The current number of connections established with the FTP Service.
Current NonAnonymous Users	The number of users who currently have a nonanonymous connection using the FTP Service.
Maximum Anonymous Users	The maximum number of users who have established concurrent anonymous connections using the FTP Service since service startup.

continues

Table 12.5. continued

Counter	Description
Maximum Connections	The maximum number of simultaneous connections established with the FTP Service.
Maximum NonAnonymous Users	The maximum number of users who have established concurrent nonanonymous connections using the FTP Service since service startup.
Measured Async I/O Bandwidth Usage	The measured bandwidth of asynchronous I/O averaged over a minute.
Total Allowed Async I/O Requests	The total number of requests allowed by bandwidth throttling settings (counted since service startup).
Total Anonymous Users	The total number of users who have established an anonymous connection with the FTP Service since service startup.
Total Blocked Async I/O Requests	The total number of requests temporarily blocked due to bandwidth throttling settings (counted since service startup).
Total Connection Attempts	The number of connections that have been attempted using the FTP Service since service startup.
Total Files Received	The total number of files received by the FTP Service.
Total Files Sent	The total number of files sent by the FTP Service since service startup.
Total Files Transferred	The sum of Total Files Sent and Total Files Received. This is the total number of files transferred by the FTP Service since service startup.
Total Logon Attempts	The number of logons that have been attempted using the FTP Service since service startup.
Total NonAnonymous Users	The total number of users who have established a nonanonymous connection with the FTP Service since service startup.
Total Rejected Async I/O Requests	The total number of requests rejected due to bandwidth throttling settings (counted since service startup).

E. HTTP Content Index

The HTTP Content Index object shows you how Content Indexer is performing with regards to searching on your HTTP content. It primarily tells you how many queries can be answered from the memory cache, rather than having to retrieve them off the disk.

This is affected primarily by the memory in the system. The more memory available to the cache, the better your performance will be when users submit similar queries.

Slow performance here will result in taking longer for users to be able to find the documents they are looking for.

Table 12.6 lists HTTP Content Index counters in Performance Monitor.

Table 12.6. HTTP Content Index counters in Performance Monitor.

Counter	Description
% Cache Hits	The percentage of queries found in the query cache.
% Cache Misses	The percentage of queries not found in the query cache.
Active Queries	The current number of running queries.
Cache Items	The number of completed queries in the cache.
Current Requests Queued	The current number of query requests queued.
Queries Per Minute	The number of queries per minute.
Total Queries	The total number of queries run since the start of service.
Total Requests Rejected	The total number of query requests rejected.

F. Internet Information Services Global

The IIS Global counters give you an overview of what is happening to the IIS system as a sum of its parts rather than on a service-by-service basis. This lets you easily see how the system is performing, especially with regards to other NT services.

As you look at IIS as a whole, as opposed to each individual service, you will not be focused as much on specific hardware subsystems, but you can get an idea of whether the performance problem might be related to IIS. For example, if you are running IIS and SQL Server on the same server, and you receive hundreds of database queries per second, but only a few IIS users per hour, the performance problem clearly lies with SQL as opposed to IIS.

Table 12.7 lists Internet Information Services Global counters in Performance Monitor.

Table 12.7. Internet Information Services Global counters in Performance Monitor.

Counter	Description
Cache Flushes	The number of times a portion of the memory cache has expired due to file or directory changes in an Internet Information Services directory tree.
Cache Hits	The total number of times a file open, directory listing, or service-specific object request was found in the cache.
Cache Hits %	The ratio of cache hits to all cache requests.
Cache Misses	The total number of times a file open, directory listing, or service-specific object request was not found in the cache.
Cached File Handles	The number of open file handles cached by all the Internet Information Services.
Current Blocked Async I/O Requests	The number of current requests temporarily blocked due to bandwidth throttling settings.
Directory Listings	The number of directory listings cached by all the Internet Information Services.
Measured Async I/O Bandwidth Usage	The measured bandwidth of asynchronous I/O averaged over a minute.
Objects	The number of objects cached by all the Internet Information Services. These objects include file handle tracking objects, directory listing objects, and service-specific objects.
Total Allowed Async I/O Requests	The total number of requests allowed by bandwidth throttling settings (counted since service startup).
Total Blocked Async I/O Requests	The total number of requests temporarily blocked due to bandwidth throttling settings (counted since service startup).
Total Rejected Async I/O Requests	The total number of requests rejected due to bandwidth throttling settings (counted since service startup).

G. NNTP Commands

The NNTP Commands object lets you track what commands are being executed on your news server.

The NNTP Service primarily makes use of the processor and memory subsystems, so these are the areas in which the NNTP Service is most likely to cause performance problems.

Table 12.8 lists NNTP Commands counters in Performance Monitor.

Table 12.8. NNTP Commands counters in Performance Monitor.

Counter	Description
Article Commands	The number of ARTICLE commands received by the NNTP server since it was started.
Article Commands/sec	The number of ARTICLE commands per second received by the NNTP server since it was started.
Check Commands	The number of CHECK commands received by the NNTP server since it was started.
Check Commands/sec	The number of CHECK commands per second received by the NNTP server since it was started.
Group Commands	The number of GROUP commands received by the NNTP server since it was started.
Group Commands/sec	The number of GROUP commands per second received by the NNTP server since it was started.
Help Commands	The number of HELP commands received by the NNTP server since it was started.
Help Commands/sec	The number of HELP commands per second received by the NNTP server since it was started.
IHave Commands	The number of IHAVE commands received by the NNTP server since it was started.
IHave Commands/sec	The number of IHAVE commands per second received by the NNTP server since it was started.
Last Commands	The number of LAST commands received by the NNTP server since it was started.
Last Commands/sec	The number of LAST commands per second received by the NNTP server since it was started.
List Commands	The number of LIST commands received by the NNTP server since it was started.

Table 12.8. continued

Counter	Description
List Commands/sec	The number of LIST commands per second received by the NNTP server since it was started.
Logon Attempts	The number of logon attempts that have been made to the NNTP server.
Logon Attempts/sec	The number of logon attempts per second that have been made to the NNTP server.
Logon Failures	The number of logons that have failed.
Logon Failures/sec	The number of logons per second that have failed.
Mode Commands	The number of MODE commands received by the NNTP server since it was started.
Mode Commands/sec	The number of MODE commands per second received by the NNTP server since it was started.
Newgroups Commands	The number of NEWGROUPS commands received by the NNTP server since it was started.
Newgroups Commands/sec	The number of NEWGROUPS commands per second received by the NNTP server since it was started.
Newnews Commands	The number of NEWNEWS commands received by the NNTP server since it was started.
Newnews Commands/sec	The number of NEWNEWS commands per second received by the NNTP server since it was started.
Next Commands	The number of NEXT commands received by the NNTP server since it was started.
Next Commands/sec	The number of NEXT commands per second received by the NNTP server since it was started.
Post Commands	The number of POST commands received by the NNTP server since it was started.
Post Commands/sec	The number of POST commands per second received by the NNTP server since it was started.
Quit Commands	The number of QUIT commands received by the NNTP server since it was started.
Quit Commands/sec	The number of QUIT commands per second received by the NNTP server since it was started.
Search Commands	The number of SEARCH commands received by the NNTP server since it was started.

Counter	Description
Search Commands/sec	The number of SEARCH commands per second received by the NNTP server since it was started.
Stat Commands	The number of STAT commands received by the NNTP server since it was started.
Stat Commands/sec	The number of STAT commands per second received by the NNTP server since it was started.
Takethis Commands	The number of TAKETHIS commands received by the NNTP server since it was started.
Takethis Commands/sec	The number of TAKETHIS commands per second received by the NNTP server since it was started.
XHdr Commands	The number of XHDR commands received by the NNTP server since it was started.
XHdr Commands/sec	The number of XHDR commands per second received by the NNTP server since it was started.
XOver Commands	The number of XOVER commands received by the NNTP server since it was started.
XOver Commands/sec	The number of XOVER commands per second received by the NNTP server since it was started.
XPat Commands	The number of XPAT commands received by the NNTP server since it was started.
XPat Commands/sec	The number of XPAT commands per second received by the NNTP server since it was started.
XReplic Commands	The number of XREPLIC commands received by the NNTP server since it was started.
XReplic Commands/sec	The number of XREPLIC commands per second received by the NNTP server since it was started.

H. NNTP Server

The NNTP Server object lets you see the performance of transferring articles to and from your clients.

The main areas of concern here are network bandwidth and disk transfer rates.

Table 12.9 lists NNTP Server counters in Performance Monitor.

Table 12.9. NNTP Server counters in Performance Monitor.

Counter	Description
Article Map Entries	The number of entries inserted into the article mapping table of the NNTP server.
Article Map Entries/sec	The number of entries inserted per second into the article mapping table of the NNTP server.
Articles Deleted	The number of articles deleted on the NNTP server since it was started.
Articles Deleted/sec	The number of articles deleted per second on the NNTP server since it was started.
Articles Posted	The number of articles posted to the NNTP server.
Articles Posted/sec	The number of articles posted per second to the NNTP server.
Articles Received	The total number of files received by the NNTP server.
Articles Received/sec	The total number of files received per second by the NNTP server.
Articles Sent	The total number of files sent by the NNTP server.
Articles Sent/sec	The total number of files sent per second by the NNTP server.
Articles Total	The sum of Articles Sent and Articles Received. This is the total number of files transferred by the NNTP server.
Bytes Received/sec	The rate that data bytes are received by the NNTP server.
Bytes Sent/sec	The rate that data bytes are sent by the NNTP server.
Bytes Total/sec	The sum of Bytes Sent/sec and Bytes Received/sec. This is the total rate of bytes transferred by the NNTP server.
Control Messages Failed	The total number of control messages that failed or that weren't applied by the NNTP server.
Control Messages Received	The total number of control messages received by the NNTP server.
Current Anonymous Users	The number of anonymous users currently connected to the NNTP server.

12.3. Performance Monitor

Counter	Description
Current Connections	The current number of connections to the NNTP server.
Current NonAnonymous Users	The number of nonanonymous users currently connected to the NNTP server.
Current Outbound Connections	The number of current outbound connections being made by the NNTP server.
Failed Outbound Logons	The number of failed outbound logons made by the NNTP server.
History Map Entries	The entries inserted into the history mapping table of the NNTP server.
History Map Entries/sec	The entries inserted per second into the history mapping table of the NNTP server.
Maximum Anonymous Users	The maximum number of anonymous users simultaneously connected to the NNTP server.
Maximum Connections	The maximum number of simultaneous connections to the NNTP server.
Maximum NonAnonymous Users	The maximum number of nonanonymous users simultaneously connected to the NNTP server.
Moderated Posting Failed	The total number of moderated postings that the NNTP server fails to send to an SMTP server.
Moderated Posting Sent	The total number of moderated postings that the NNTP server attempts to send to an SMTP server.
Sessions Flow Controlled	The number of client sessions currently in a flow-controlled state in the NNTP server.
Total Anonymous Users	The total number of anonymous users who have ever connected to the NNTP server.
Total Connections	The number of connections that have been made to the NNTP server.
Total NonAnonymous Users	The total number of nonanonymous users who have ever connected to the NNTP server.
Total Outbound Connections	The number of outbound connections that have been made by the NNTP server.
Total Outbound Connections Failed	The number of unsuccessful outbound connections that have been made by the NNTP server.
Total Passive Feeds	The number of passive feeds accepted by the NNTP server.

continues

Table 12.9. continued

Counter	Description
Total Pull Feeds	The number of pull feeds made by the NNTP server.
Total Push Feeds	The number of push feeds made by the NNTP server.
Total SSL Connections	The number of SSL connections that have been made to the NNTP server.
XOver Entries	The number of XOver entries in the XOver table of the NNTP server.
XOver Entries/sec	The number of XOver entries inserted per second in the XOver table of the NNTP server.

I. SMTP Server

The SMTP Server object lets you track the flow of Internet e-mail through your system.

Here you should concern yourself primarily with memory and network bandwidth.

Table 12.10 lists SMTP Server counters in Performance Monitor.

Table 12.10. SMTP Server counters in Performance Monitor.

Counter	Description
% Recipients Local	The percentage of recipients who will be delivered locally.
% Recipients Remote	The percentage of recipients who will be delivered remotely.
Avg Recipients/msg Received	The average number of recipients per inbound messages received.
Avg Recipients/msg Sent	The average number of recipients per outbound messages sent.
Avg Retries/msg Delivered	The average number of retries per local delivery.
Avg Retries/msg Sent	The average number of retries per outbound message sent.
Bytes Received Total	The total number of bytes received.
Bytes Received/sec	The rate that bytes are received.
Bytes Sent Total	The total number of bytes sent.

Counter	Description
Bytes Sent/sec	The rate that bytes are sent.
Bytes Total	The total number of bytes sent and received.
Bytes Total/sec	The rate that bytes are sent and received.
Connection Errors/sec	The number of connection errors per second.
Directory Drops Total	The total number of messages placed in a drop directory.
Directory Drops/sec	The number of messages placed in a drop directory per second.
Directory Pickup Queue Length	The number of messages in the directory pickup queue.
DNS Queries Total	The total number of DNS lookups.
DNS Queries/sec	The rate of DNS lookups.
ETRN Messages Total	The total number of ETRN messages received by the server.
ETRN Messages/sec	The number of ETRN messages per second.
Inbound Connections Current	The total number of connections currently inbound.
Inbound Connections Total	The total number of inbound connections received.
Local Queue Length	The number of messages in the local queue.
Local Retry Queue Length	The number of messages in the local retry queue.
Message Bytes Received Total	The total number of bytes received in messages.
Message Bytes Received/sec	The rate that bytes are received in messages.
Message Bytes Sent Total	The total number of bytes sent in messages.
Message Bytes Sent/sec	The rate that bytes are sent in messages.
Message Bytes Total	The total number of bytes sent and received in messages.
Message Bytes Total/sec	The rate that bytes are sent and received in messages.
Message Delivery Retries	The total number of local deliveries that were retried.
Message Received/sec	The rate that inbound messages are being received.

continues

Table 12.10. continued

Counter	Description
Message Send Retries	The total number of outbound message sends that were retried.
Messages Delivered Total	The total number of messages delivered to local mailboxes.
Messages Delivered/sec	The rate that messages are delivered to local mailboxes.
Messages Received Total	The total number of inbound messages accepted.
Messages Refused for Address Objects	The total number of messages refused due to no address objects.
Messages Refused for Mail Objects	The total number of messages refused due to no mail objects.
Messages Refused for Size	The total number of messages rejected because they were too big.
Messages Retrieved Total	The total number of messages retrieved from the mail pick-up directory.
Messages Retrieved/sec	The rate that messages are being retrieved from the mail pick-up directory.
Messages Sent Total	The total number of outbound messages sent.
Messages Sent/sec	The rate that outbound messages are being sent.
NDRs Generated	The number of nondelivery reports that have been generated.
Number of MailFiles Open	The number of handles to open mail files.
Number of QueueFiles Open	The number of handles to open queue files.
Outbound Connections Current	The number of connections currently outbound.
Outbound Connections Refused	The number of outbound connection attempts refused by remote sites.
Outbound Connections Total	The total number of outbound connections attempted.
Remote Queue Length	The number of messages in the remote queue.
Remote Retry Queue Length	The number of messages in the retry queue for remote delivery.

Counter	Description
Routing Table Lookups Total	The total number of routing table lookups.
Routing Table Lookups/sec	The number of routing table lookups per second.
Total Connection Errors	The total number of connection errors.

J. Web Service

The Web Service counters let you monitor what is occurring with regards to HTTP requests from Web-based clients.

Here your primary concern is network bandwidth, followed by memory.

Table 12.11 lists Web Service counters in Performance Monitor.

Table 12.11. Web Service counters in Performance Monitor.

Counter	Description
Anonymous Users/sec	The rate that users are making anonymous connections using the Web service.
Bytes Received/sec	The rate that data bytes are received by the Web service.
Bytes Sent/sec	The rate that data bytes are sent by the Web service.
Bytes Total/sec	The sum of Bytes Sent/sec and Bytes Received/sec. This is the total rate of bytes transferred by the Web service.
CGI Requests/sec	The rate of CGI requests that are simultaneously being processed by the Web service.
Connection Attempts/sec	The rate that connections using the Web service are being attempted.
Current Anonymous Users	The number of users who currently have an anonymous connection using the Web service.
Current Blocked Async I/O Requests	Current requests temporarily blocked due to bandwidth throttling settings.
Current CGI Requests	The current number of CGI requests that are simultaneously being processed by the Web service.

continues

Table 12.11. continued

Counter	Description
Current Connections	The current number of connections established with the Web service.
Current ISAPI Extension Requests	The current number of extension requests that are simultaneously being processed by the Web service.
Current NonAnonymous Users	The number of users who currently have a nonanonymous connection using the Web service.
Delete Requests/sec	The rate that HTTP requests using the DELETE method are made. Delete requests are generally used for file removals.
Files Received/sec	The rate that files are received by the Web service.
Files Sent/sec	The rate that files are sent by the Web service.
Files/sec	The rate that files are transferred—that is, sent and received by the Web service.
Get Requests/sec	The rate that HTTP requests using the GET method are made. Get requests are generally used for basic file retrievals or image maps, although they can be used with forms.
Head Requests/sec	The rate that HTTP requests using the HEAD method are made. Head requests generally indicate that a client is querying the state of a document it already has to see if it needs to be refreshed.
ISAPI Extension Requests/sec	The rate of ISAPI extension requests that are simultaneously being processed by the Web service.
Logon Attempts/sec	The rate that logons using the Web service are being attempted.
Maximum Anonymous Users	The maximum number of users who have established concurrent anonymous connections using the Web service since service startup.
Maximum CGI Requests	The maximum number of CGI requests simultaneously processed by the Web service.
Maximum Connections	The maximum number of simultaneous connections established with the Web service.

Counter	Description
Maximum ISAPI Extension Requests	The maximum number of extension requests simultaneously processed by the Web service.
Maximum NonAnonymous Users	The maximum number of users who have established concurrent nonanonymous connections using the Web service since service startup.
Measured Async I/O Bandwidth Usage	The measured bandwidth of asynchronous I/O averaged over a minute.
NonAnonymous Users/sec	The rate that users are making nonanonymous connections using the Web service.
Not Found Errors/sec	The rate of errors due to requests that couldn't be satisfied by the server because the requested document couldn't be found. These are generally reported as an HTTP 404 error code to the client.
Other Request Methods/sec	The rate that HTTP requests are made that don't use the GET, POST, PUT, DELETE, TRACE, or HEAD methods. These may include LINK or other methods supported by gateway applications.
Post Requests/sec	The rate that HTTP requests using the POST method are made. Post requests are generally used for forms or gateway requests.
Put Requests/sec	The rate that HTTP requests by using the PUT method are made.
Total Allowed Async I/O Requests	The total requests allowed by bandwidth throttling settings (counted since service startup).
Total Anonymous Users	The total number of users who have established an anonymous connection with the Web service since service startup.
Total Blocked Async I/O Requests	The total requests temporarily blocked due to bandwidth throttling settings (counted since service startup).
Total CGI Requests	Custom gateway executables (.exe) that the administrator can install to add forms processing or other dynamic data sources. CGI requests spawn a process on the server that can be a large drain on server resources. The count is the total since service startup.

continues

Table 12.11. continued

Counter	Description
Total Connection Attempts	The number of connections that have been attempted using the Web service since service startup.
Total Delete Requests	The number of HTTP requests using the DELETE method since service startup. Delete requests are generally used for file removals.
Total Files Received	The total number of files received by the Web service since service startup.
Total Files Sent	The total number of files sent by the Web service since service startup.
Total Files Transferred	The sum of Total Files Sent and Total Files Received. This is the total number of files transferred by the Web service since service startup.
Total Get Requests	The number of HTTP requests using the GET method since service startup. Get requests are generally used for basic file retrievals or image maps, although they can be used with forms.
Total Head Requests	The number of HTTP requests using the HEAD method (counted since service startup). Head requests generally indicate that a client is querying the state of a document it already has to see if it needs to be refreshed.
Total ISAPI Extension Requests	Custom gateway Dynamic Link Libraries (.dll) that the administrator can install to add forms processing or other dynamic data sources. Unlike CGI requests, ISAPI requests are simple calls to a DLL library routine, so they are better suited to high-performance gateway applications. The count is the total since service startup.
Total Logon Attempts	The number of logons that have been attempted using the Web service (counted since service startup).
Total Method Requests	The number of HTTP GET, POST, PUT, DELETE, TRACE, HEAD, and other method requests (counted since service startup).

Counter	Description
Total Method Requests/sec	The rate that HTTP requests using GET, POST, PUT, DELETE, TRACE, or HEAD methods are made.
Total NonAnonymous Users	The total number of users who have established a nonanonymous connection with the Web service since service startup.
Total Not Found Errors	The number of requests that couldn't be satisfied by the server because the requested document couldn't be found. These are generally reported as an HTTP 404 error code to the client. The count is the total since service startup.
Total Other Request Methods	The number of HTTP requests that are not GET, POST, PUT, DELETE, TRACE, or HEAD methods (counted since service startup). These may include LINK or other methods supported by gateway applications.
Total Post Requests	The number of HTTP requests using the POST method (counted since service startup). Post requests are generally used for forms or gateway requests.
Total Put Requests	The number of HTTP requests using the PUT method (counted since service startup).
Total Rejected Async I/O Requests	The total number of requests rejected due to bandwidth throttling settings (counted since service startup).
Total Trace Requests	The number of HTTP requests using the TRACE method (counted since service startup). Trace requests allow the client to see what is being received at the end of the request chain and use the information for diagnostic purposes.

You are now able to use Performance Monitor to identify hardware bottlenecks in your system and determine which IIS services are making the most use of your system. The next section shows you how to use Site Server Express's Content Analyzer to analyze your Web sites to help track what features you might have implemented that are consuming resources on your system. (For example, it will tell you how many Java applets you have implemented.)

12.4. Using Content Analyzer to Analyze a Web Site

IIS ships with a group of programs called Site Server Express, which is a scaled-down version of Microsoft's Site Server. It can't really be used for performance monitoring the way some of the other utilities can, but it is very useful for getting a feel for what has been implemented on your site, especially if you have a number of different developers. (For example, one of your site authors might have deployed a large number of very complex images that cause a lot of traffic on your system.)

In this section, you will see how you can use one component of Site Server Express, Content Analyzer, to analyze a Web site. Content Analyzer can be used for a wide variety of purposes, such as graphically exploring the layout of a site as a WebMap, as well as generating site reports that display data about your site, such as the number of graphics or the number of hyperlinks to other sites.

In this section we will concern ourselves only with generating and interpreting site reports. Figure 12.8 is an example of a site report. It was generated by running Content Analyzer on the sample site included with IIS.

Figure 12.8.

The Content Analyzer generates a site report for the IIS sample site.

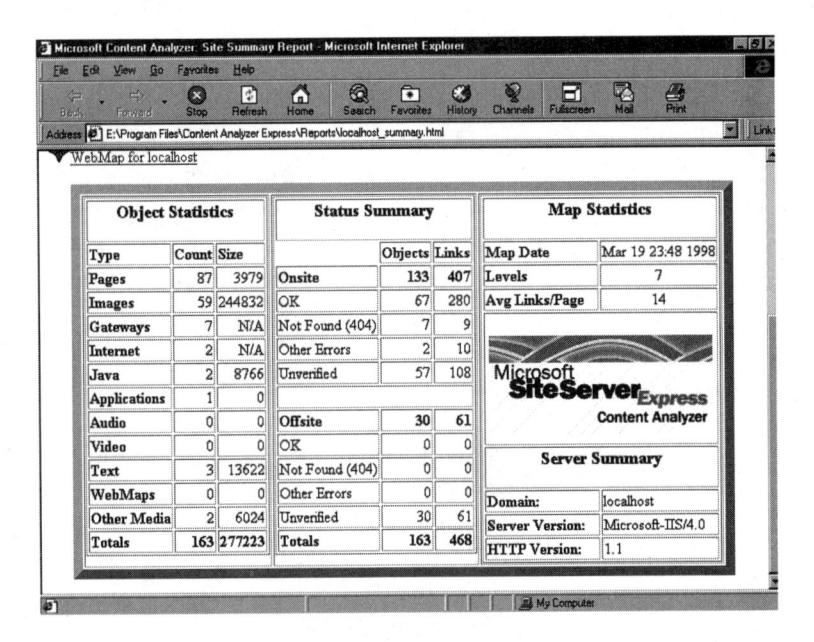

To generate a WebMap for a site, do the following:

1. Start Content Analyzer by selecting Start | Programs | Windows NT 4.0 Option Pack | Microsoft Site Server Express 2.0 | Content Analyzer.
2. When prompted, click the New WebMap button.
3. You will be prompted to create a map from a file or URL. Choose URL and click OK.
4. Enter the URL for your site. (If you are running Content Analyzer on your IIS server, you can type `localhost`.)
5. Make sure that Explore Entire Site and Generate Site Reports are checked.
6. Click OK.
7. Content Analyzer will create a map for your site. (This can take quite a while for a large site.)
8. Select a directory and prefix for your reports. (For this exercise, you can leave the defaults as is.)
9. Click OK. A site report will then be generated for your site, and Content Analyzer will automatically launch your Web browser to display it.

You can now get a report of exactly what you have deployed on your site. You will also see the number of errors on your site, which can be useful for ensuring that your site is running in top shape.

Lab

This lab consists of review questions pertaining to this chapter and provides an opportunity for you to use walk-through exercises to apply the knowledge that you've gained.

Questions

1. You suspect that you have implemented too many features in your Active Server Pages and that they are placing too much of a burden on your system. Which subsystem or subsystems would most likely be affected?

    A. Network

    B. Processor

    C. Disk

    D. Memory

2. You want to monitor performance on your IIS system over a period of two weeks. Which Performance Monitor view would best suit your needs?

    A. Chart

    B. Report

    C. Log

    D. Alert

3. Your IIS system is experiencing performance problems. After using Performance Monitor, you see that there is a rather high number of page faults per second. Which component would be causing this?

    A. CPU

    B. Cache

    C. System RAM

    D. Network Interface Card

4. You are trying to monitor the performance of your disk subsystem, but you can't track any of the counters. A coworker proposes converting all the partitions to NTFS in order to enable those counters. He says NT can't monitor those counters on FAT partitions. How would you rate this solution?

    A. This solution is excellent.

    B. This solution is fair.

    C. This is only part of the solution.

    D. This solution will not work at all.

5. What tool would you use to monitor the performance of TCP/IP on your system?

    A. Windows NT diagnostics
    B. Network Monitor
    C. NETSTAT
    D. IPCONFIG

6. Network Monitor can be used to capture which of the following?

    A. Traffic destined to any host, no matter where it originates.
    B. Traffic from any host destined to the machine running Network Monitor.
    C. Traffic originating anywhere on the local subnet and destined to any host.
    D. Traffic from the machine running Network Monitor and destined to any host.

7. Your organization has deployed IIS. You are currently supporting several dozen users in the Graphic Design group who are constantly transferring very large files between offices. They are using the FTP service over a 56 Kbps dial-up modem. They are not satisfied with the performance. What is most likely the bottleneck in this case?

    A. Processor
    B. Memory
    C. Network
    D. Disk

8. What must you do before you can track physical disk counters in Performance Monitor?

    A. Run `diskperf -y` from a command prompt and reboot.
    B. Install the correct service in NT.
    C. Run `diskcount -y` from a command prompt.
    D. None of the above.

9. You have been monitoring the % Processor Time counter in Performance Monitor. At what point should you consider upgrading your system's CPU?

    A. When it is consistently above 50 percent.
    B. When it is consistently below 90 percent.
    C. When it is consistently above 80 percent.
    D. If it ever reaches 100 percent.

10. Your manager has recently read that a large number of graphics files can cause slow response for your users. She asks you for a report on the number and size of the graphics on your site. What tool would you use to get this information for her?

    A. Performance Monitor

    B. NETSTAT

    C. Internet Service Manager

    D. Content Analyzer

Answers to Questions

1. **B, D.** As you have seen, implementing many ASP files typically requires extra processor power and memory. They are not much more disk-intensive than regular HTML files and make no more use of network bandwidth than regular HTML files.

2. **C.** Log view should be used. It will let you track data over a long period of time and review the data at any time in the future. Chart is more suitable for viewing these log files or for viewing near-real-time data. Report will only show the current value of your counters. Alert is used to trigger events when a certain criteria is met.

3. **C.** Excessive page faults indicate that the system is constantly having to access the paging file because the information it is looking for is not available in physical RAM.

4. **D.** Performance Monitor can track physical disk counters on any partition, regardless of the type. In order to enable this, you must run `diskperf -y` from a command prompt and restart your system.

5. **C.** You would use NETSTAT. Network Monitor lets you see statistics for the network connection as a whole, but not TCP/IP specifically. IPCONFIG is used to view your TCP/IP information and release/renew DHCP leases. Performance Monitor doesn't include counters for TCP/IP.

6. **B, D.** The Network Monitor included with Windows NT only allows you to view data destined to or originating from the machine where it is running. To see other data traveling on the network, you would require the version of Network Monitor that ships with Systems Management Server.

7. **C.** In this case, a 56 Kbps modem would be the limiting factor, regardless of the other subsystems. The FTP service can consume a large amount of bandwidth easily.

8. **A.** You must run `diskperf -y` and restart your system. NT can track physical disk counters without any additional software.
9. **C.** You should consider upgrading if your % Processor Time counter is consistently above 80 percent.
10. **D.** Only Content Analyzer will scan your IIS sites and generate this type of report. The Internet Service Manager is used to configure and manage IIS, but it doesn't provide this sort of data.

Exercises

Exercise 12.1.: Using Performance Monitor to Track Performance Data

This exercise addresses the following Microsoft exam objective:

- Monitor the performance of various functions by using Performance Monitor

This exercise shows how you can track counters in Performance Monitor:

1. Select Start | Programs | Administrative Tools | Performance Monitor.
2. You will see a screen similar to Figure 12.1. Click the + button on the toolbar to add a counter.
3. In the screen that appears, select the object that you want to track by clicking the drop-down list beside the object and then selecting the object you want (for example, Processor or Memory). These objects are collections of counters. Once you have selected an object, you will see the list of counters change to display the counters available for that object.
4. Once you have selected the object you want to monitor, you must select the counters you want to track. Click the counter you want to track, and then click Add. Before adding it, you can also set options such as what color to use on the chart. If you like, you can repeat this process to select multiple counters from multiple objects in order to get a better feel for what is happening in your system.
5. Once you have added all the counters you need, click Done to get back to the Chart view.

Exercise 12.2.: Exporting Performance Monitor Data

This exercise addresses the following Microsoft exam objective:

- Monitor the performance of various functions by using Performance Monitor

In this exercise, you will create a log and export it to a text file to prepare for importing it into a spreadsheet or data-analysis package.

1. Open Performance Monitor by selecting Start | Programs | Administrative Tools | Performance Monitor.
2. Switch to Log view by selecting View | Log.
3. Click the + button to begin adding objects to your log.
4. Select the objects you want to log (for example, HTTP service and FTP server) by selecting the object you want and clicking the Add button. (Note that you don't have to choose specific counters. Performance Monitor will always log *all* counters associated with that object.)
5. When you have added all the objects you need, click Done. You will see a list of all the objects you have selected.
6. To set logging options, such as the filename and update frequency, select Options | Log.
7. In the filename box, type the name of the file you want to log to. You can also specify an alternative path for the file if you want to.
8. Set the update interval by choosing Periodic Update and setting the update time (the default is 15 seconds) or by choosing Manual Update. (If you choose Manual Update, Performance Monitor will require you to manually tell it when to update, so this isn't practical for long-term logging.)
9. Click Start Log.

To export your data, do the following:

1. From Performance Monitor's Log view, select File | Export Log.
2. Select a path and filename to export to, and then select whether you will export to a .tsv or .csv file.
3. Click Save.
4. You have now exported your data to a text file. For more information on importing that data into your spreadsheet software, consult your software documentation.

Exercise 12.3.: Using Network Monitor to Capture and View Data

This exercise addresses the following Microsoft exam objective:

- Analyze performance

In this exercise, you will use Network Monitor to analyze your network and look at the data that was captured.

1. Start Network Monitor by selecting Start | Programs | Administrative Tools | Network Monitor.
2. Select Capture | Start.
3. Network Monitor will display statistics for your network. Note the % Network Utilization and number of Broadcasts.
4. Select Capture | Stop and View.
5. You will see all the frames that were transferred. You can view them by double-clicking them.
6. Close Network Monitor. It will ask if you want to save this capture. If you need to store it for future reference, click Yes and save it like any other file. For the purposes of this exercise, click No.

TEST DAY FAST FACTS

Here are a few fast facts about this chapter that you may want to know ahead of time. Don't forget that these facts also provide great last-minute study material.

- Internet Information Server comes with Site Server Express 2.0, a set of tools that helps you analyze your Web and FTP sites.
- Usage Import is used to import log files into a Microsoft Access database.
- Report Writer is used to generate reports from log files that were imported using Usage Import.
- Both Usage Import and Report Writer support a command-line interface, which means you can automate the import of data and generation of reports.
- Content Analyzer lets you create, customize, and navigate WebMaps.
- Content Analyzer lets you check for broken links and output a summary report.
- IIS lets you configure four different types of logging for Web sites and three different types for FTP sites.
- Logging may be configured to output ASCII text files or to log to an ODBC-compliant database.
- Of the different log file formats that IIS supports, only the W3C Extended Log File format is customizable.

Day 13

Site Analysis

by Gerry High

As you near the end of this book, you might be wondering what site analysis is and why it is important. Site analysis involves analyzing both site usage and Web content. Site analysis is tremendously important because it tells you the following:

■ How your site is being used (frequency, duration, volume, bandwidth utilization, most frequently accessed pages, referrers to your site, and so forth)

■ Information about your Web content (if you have any broken links, pages that are over a certain size, unreachable hosts)

Site usage information is obtained by logging activity on your site. Understanding Web site activity is difficult, however, because Web usage is stateless. In other words, when a user connects to a Web site to retrieve a page, there is no persistent state or connection (at least not without HTTP keep-alives enabled). Hence, understanding how long a user was accessing your site, his path through the site, and so on must be *inferred* from the log files.

Another fact that complicates calculating site activity is that many hits on a Web site may be done through a proxy server of some sort. Proxy servers act as a go-between for a user and your Web site. They cache pages for efficiency purposes, which means that users accessing your site may actually be accessing pages from their proxy server's cache. As a result, the page hits in the log files are conservative estimates of real page views.

Analysis of Web content will tell you if your content (Web pages, applets, controls, and so on) has errors or other problems. As Web sites have grown and become more complex, it has become increasingly difficult to test all the pages and links on a Web site. By analyzing your Web's content, you will quickly be able to get a grasp of your site's topology and be able to determine if you need to repair any links or perform maintenance.

In this chapter we'll discuss two aspects of site analysis—usage analysis and content analysis. Since usage analysis requires usage data, we'll spend quite a bit of time discussing IIS logging. Next we'll cover the two usage analysis tools, Usage Import and Report Writer. Last, we'll focus on content analysis (using Content Analyzer) to help you better understand your site.

To master the exam, pay particular attention to the following:

- Automation of Usage Import and Report Writer via the command-line interface
- Internet Information Server log file formats

Objectives

This chapter helps you prepare for the Microsoft Exam by covering the following objectives:

- Customize the installation of Site Server Express Analysis Content Analyzer
- Customize the installation of Site Server Express Analysis Report Writer and Usage Import
- Manage a Web site by using Content Analyzer

- Create, customize, and navigate WebMaps
- Examine a Web site by using the various reports provided by Content Analyzer
- Track links by using a WebMap
■ Maintain a log for fine-tuning and auditing purposes
    - Import log files into a Report Writer and Usage Import database
    - Configure the logging features of the WWW service
    - Configure the logging features of the FTP service
    - Configure Report Writer and Usage Import to analyze logs created by the WWW service or the FTP service
    - Automate the use of Report Writer and Usage Import
■ Use a WebMap to find and repair broken links, hyperlink texts, headings, and titles

13.1. Introduction to Microsoft Site Server Express

Internet Information Server comes with a set of site analysis tools called Site Server Express 2.0. These tools provide a subset of the functionality of Microsoft Site Server 2.0. For example, the Express version of these tools provides a more limited set of import options or output reports. However, the versions of these tools that are included with Site Server Express are sufficient to perform most site analysis tasks. For more information on the full-featured versions of these tools, visit `http://www.microsoft.com/siteserver`.

The following two sections describe the components that make up Site Server Express and explain how to install them.

13.1.1. Components Included in Site Server Express 2.0

The components that make up Site Server Express 2.0 are as follows:

- Content Analyzer is used to analyze site content and perform site visualization.
- Usage Import loads Web and FTP log files into a Microsoft Access database.

13.1. Introduction to Microsoft Site Server Express | 435

- Report Writer is used to generate reports from the data imported by Usage Import.
- Web Publishing Wizard is a client-side application that makes it easy to upload content to Web servers.
- Posting Acceptor is used to receive files uploaded to a Web server via the Web Publishing Wizard (or other clients).

The Posting Acceptor and Web Publishing Wizard aren't covered on the exam, so they aren't discussed in this chapter.

13.1.2. Installing Site Server Components

If you haven't yet installed the Windows NT 4.0 Option Pack, you need to do a custom installation to get the Site Server Express components installed. After the installation finishes, the components will be installed in the \Program Files\UA Express directory.

To perform a custom installation, do the following:

1. Select Start | Settings | Control Panel. Click the Add/Remove Programs icon.
2. Select Windows NT 4.0 Option Pack from the list of programs and then click the Add/Remove button.
3. After the Setup program launches, click the Add/Remove button.
4. In the components list, select Microsoft Site Server Express 2.0 and then click the Show Subcomponents button. You should see the dialog shown in Figure 13.1.

Figure 13.1.

The subcomponents dialog lets you specify which Site Server Express components you would like to install.

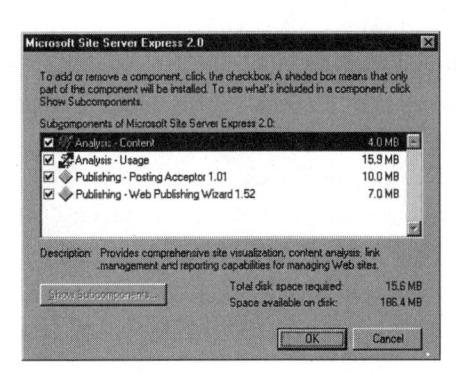

5. Select Analysis - Content and Analysis - Usage from the subcomponents list. Click OK and then Next to begin the installation.

After the installation completes, you will see the Site Server Express program group listed under the Windows NT 4.0 Option Pack program group on the menu.

Now that you've installed Site Server Express, we'll cover logging, because you'll need usage data in order to use some of the Site Server Express components.

13.2. Logging Site Activity

Before you can begin to analyze user activity, you need to configure IIS to log activity on your site. In this section you will learn about the different log formats supported by IIS and how to configure logging for the Web and FTP services.

Log information may be stored in either ASCII text files or in an ODBC-compliant database. Regardless of the type of logging you configure, logs can tell you

- Who is accessing your server (for example, their computer names or IP addresses)
- What content they are accessing (for example, files or directories)
- When they accessed it (date and time)

Log information is written whenever a user accesses content on a Web or FTP site that has logging enabled. Logging may be enabled or disabled at the site level. In addition, Web sites may have logging enabled or disabled on individual directories.

The following steps show you how to enable logging on the default Web site and disable logging for a particular directory:

1. Start the Internet Service Manager.
2. Click the Default Web site. Select Action | Properties. You see a dialog showing the properties for the site, as shown in Figure 13.2.
3. Check to make sure that the Enable Logging check box is checked. If it isn't, click it to enable logging. Choose the desired log format by selecting one of the four log formats from the Active log format list (we'll discuss these log formats in the next section).
4. Click OK to dismiss the dialog.
5. Click the IISHELP directory. Select Action | Properties. The dialog shown in Figure 13.3 appears.

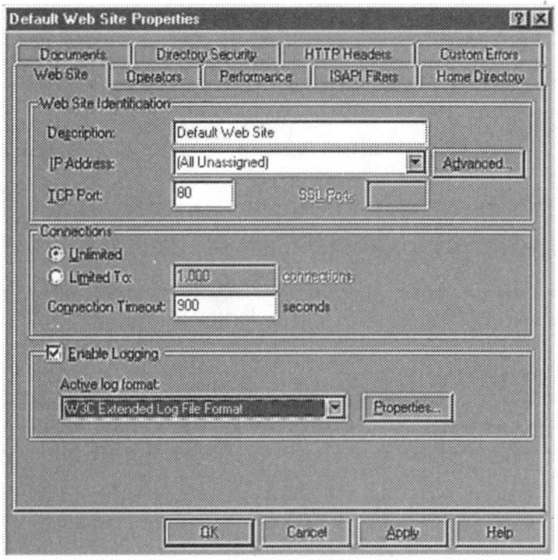

Figure 13.2.
The properties dialog for a site is used to enable logging.

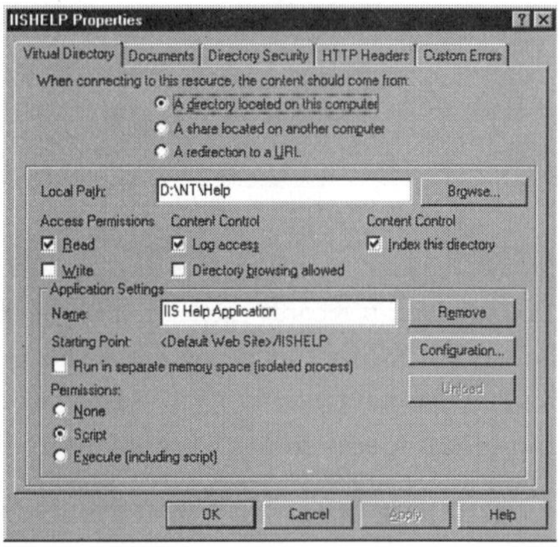

Figure 13.3.
In the properties dialog for the IISHELP virtual directory, you may enable or disable logging.

6. By default, Log access is checked. Click Log access to remove the check mark. Click OK to dismiss the dialog.

You've now enabled logging on the default Web site and disabled logging for the IISHELP virtual directory. Now when you access IIS help, you won't generate entries in the log files.

In the next few sections you'll examine the different IIS log formats, see where and when log files are generated, and learn how to convert log files from one format to another.

13.2.1. Log Formats

IIS supports four different types of log file formats. They are outlined in Table 13.1.

> **Note:** The Delimited column in Table 13.1 refers to how fields are separated. The fields in IIS log formats are separated by either spaces or commas.

Table 13.1. Log formats supported by IIS.

Name	Customizable?	Delimited	Time Zone	Services
NCSA Common Log File format	No	Spaces	Local	Web, NNTP, SMTP
Microsoft IIS Log File format	No	Commas	Local	Web, FTP, NNTP, SMTP
W3C Extended Log File format	Yes	Spaces	Greenwich Mean Time	Web, FTP, NNTP, SMTP
ODBC Logging	No	N/A	Local	Web, FTP, NNTP, SMTP

Of these formats, the NCSA Common Log File format is the oldest and is supported by most Web servers. However, it records the least amount of information of the four log formats. Only the W3C Extended Log File format lets you customize what information is logged; this format is also the default logging format used by IIS. The following four sections describe each format in more detail.

A. The NCSA Common Log File Format

The NCSA Common Log File format records eight data items. They are listed in Table 13.2.

Table 13.2. Description of NCSA Common Log File format.

Name	Description	Example
Remote Host Name	IP address of the client computer.	199.217.211.65
rfc931	Remote logname of the user.	-
User Name	The name of the user accessing your site.	MICHIGAN\smith

Name	Description	Example
Date	The date that the user accessed your server.	01/Mar/1998
Time and GMT offset	Specifies the time and the offset from Greenwich Mean Time.	12:39:01 -0600
Request	The action and resource specified in the HTTP request.	GET /default.asp, HTTP/1.0
Service Status Code	The HTTP status code.	200
Bytes Sent	The number of bytes that were returned to the user.	2001

The primary advantage of using the NCSA Common Log File format is that it is universally supported by Web servers and site analysis tools. Here's an example:

```
199.217.211.65 - MICHIGAN\smith [08/Mar/1998:12:39:04 -0800]
➥"GET /default.asp, HTTP/1.0" 200 2001
```

B. The Microsoft IIS Log File Format

The Microsoft IIS Log File format is a comma-delimited format in which blank items are indicated by a hyphen. One of the advantages of using the IIS format is that it is the only format that is comma-delimited, which means that it can be imported (parsed) more easily than the other formats.

The information contained in the IIS Log File format is a superset of the NCSA Log File format. This format's 14 data items are listed in Table 13.3.

Table 13.3. Description of Microsoft IIS log File format.

Name	Description	Example
Client IP	The IP address of the client computer.	199.217.211.65
User Name	The name of the user accessing your site.	-
Date	The date that the user accessed your server.	2/16/98
Time	The time that the user accessed your server.	1:18:12

continues

Day 13: Site Analysis

Table 13.3. continued

Name	Description	Example
Service	The name of the service (such as MSFTPSVC or W3SVC).	W3SVC
Computer Name	The name of the server.	FINANCE
IP Address of Server	The IP address of the server.	206.4.70.99
Elapsed Time	The elapsed time of the request (in milliseconds).	2883
Bytes Received	The number of bytes that were received from the client computer.	430
Bytes Sent	The number of bytes that were returned to the user.	2001
Service Status Code	The HTTP status code.	200
Windows NT status code	The Windows NT status of the request.	0
Method	The name of the HTTP method.	GET
Target	The name of the resource specified in the HTTP request.	/default.asp

Here's an example of the IIS Log File format:

```
199.217.211.65, -, 2/17/98, 7:45:56, W3SVC1, DENALI, 206.4.70.99, 2883, 430,
➥2001, 200, 0, GET, /Default.htm, -,
```

C. The W3C Extended Log File Format

The W3C Extended Log File format is the only format that can be customized to specify which fields you would like to log. In addition, this format is the only one that captures the user agent (for example, the type of browser) and referrer information (for example, which URL a client was referred from).

The information contained in the W3C Extended Log File format is a superset of the NCSA Log File and IIS Log File formats. The 20 data elements of the format are listed in Table 13.4.

Table 13.4. Description of W3C Extended Log File format.

Name	Description	Example
Time	The time that the user accessed your server.	23:03:41
Client IP	The IP address of the client computer.	198.248.24.210
Method	The name of the method.	GET
URI Stem	The name of the resource specified in the request.	/default.asp
Date	The date that the user accessed your server.	1998-02-17
User Name	The name of the user accessing your site.	Anonymous
Service	The name of the service (such as MSFTPSVC or W3SVC).	MSFTPSVC1
Computer Name	The name of the server.	FINANCE
Server IP	The IP address of the server.	153.35.217.120
URI Query	The search strings that a user was performing.	-
Http Status	The HTTP status code.	401
Win32 Status	The Windows NT status of the request.	5
Bytes Sent	The number of bytes that were returned to the user.	812
Bytes Received	The number of bytes that were received from the client computer.	325
Server Port	The number of the port used by the user.	80
Time Taken	The elapsed time of the request (in milliseconds).	30
Protocol Version	The version of the protocol used.	HTTP/1.1 or HTTP/1.0

continues

Table 13.4. continued

Name	Description	Example
User Agent	The type of browser used by the client.	Mozilla/4.0+ (compatible; +MSIE+4.01; +Windows+NT)
Cookie	Contains the cookie (either sent or received).	ASPSESSION-IDGGGGGQBT=LKGNDF
Referrer	The URL of the page that the user was on before coming to your site	`http://www.microsoft.com/default.asp`

Here's an example of the W3C Extended Log File format:

```
#Software: Microsoft Internet Information Server 4.0
#Version: 1.0
#Date: 1998-02-21 23:11:04
#Fields: time c-ip cs-method cs-uri-stem sc-status
23:11:04 127.0.0.1 GET /Default.htm 304
```

The following steps show you how to customize the information that is logged using the W3C Extended Log File format:

1. Start the Internet Service Manager.
2. Click the Default Web site. Select Action | Properties. A dialog showing the properties for the site should appear.
3. Check to make sure that the Enable Logging check box is checked. In the Active log format list, select W3C Extended Log File Format. Then click the Properties button.
4. Select the Extended Properties tab. The dialog shown in Figure 13.4 appears.
5. By default, Time, Client IP Address, Method, and URI Stem are selected. Select the User Name, User Agent, and Referrer fields. Click OK twice to dismiss the dialog.

Now that you've customized logging, you'll need to access your site to generate some hits. After doing this, you can examine the log files to see what information was logged.

Figure 13.4.
From the Extended Logging Properties dialog for the W3C Extended Log File Format, you may customize the fields to be logged.

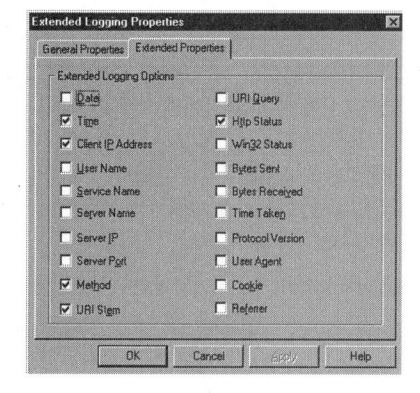

D. The ODBC Log Format

ODBC (Open Database Connectivity) logging is used when you want to log information to a database. One advantage of ODBC logging is that once the data is stored in a database, it can be analyzed with any number of tools that work with relational databases.

ODBC logging requires an ODBC-compliant database, such as Microsoft Access or Microsoft SQL Server. Table 13.5 describes the ODBC Log format.

Table 13.5. Description of the ODBC Log format.

Column Name	Description	Example
ClientHost	The IP address of the client computer.	159.140.10.3
Username	The name of the user accessing your site.	REDMOND\Ed
LogTime	The date and time that the user accessed your server.	3/1/98 3:45:12PM
Service	The name of the service (such as MSFTPSVC or W3SVC).	MSFTPSVC1
Machine	The name of the server.	FINANCE
ServerIP	The IP address of the server.	153.35.217.120
ProcessingTime	The elapsed time of the request (in milliseconds).	1001
BytesRecvd	The number of bytes that were received from the client computer.	235

continues

Table 13.5. continued

Column Name	Description	Example
BytesSent	The number of bytes that were returned to the user.	900
ServiceStatus	The HTTP status code.	401
Win32Status	The Windows NT status of the request.	5
Operation	The name of the HTTP method.	GET
Target	The name of the resource specified in the request.	/default.asp
Parameters	Not used.	-

If you want to use the ODBC Log format, you should be aware that it isn't supported by the Site Server Express tools (such as Report Writer and Usage Import). To use ODBC logging with these tools, you'll need to upgrade Site Server Express to Site Server.

Now that I've described log formats, I'll cover where log files are stored and when log files get created.

13.2.2. Log Storage and Generation Scheduling

Log files are stored in subdirectories underneath the log files directory; there is a separate subdirectory for each service. The following table lists these subdirectories:

Service	Directory	Example
Web	W3SVC	W3SVC1
FTP	MSFTPSVC	MSFTPSVC1
News	NNTPSVC	NNTPSVC1
Mail	SMTPSVC	SMTPSVC1

The default location of the log file directory is %WINDIR%\System32\LogFiles. This directory can be changed via the General Properties tab of the Logging Properties dialog (we'll discuss this in a moment).

Log files can be generated on a daily, weekly, or monthly basis or when a log file reaches a certain size. Log files can also be of unlimited size. Log files are created with a prefix that depends on the type of log format. The following table lists the respective prefixes for each log type:

Format	Prefix	Example
NCSA	nc	nc980216.log
Microsoft IIS	in	in9802.log
W3C Extended	ex	ex980311.log

The following steps show you how to change when and where log files are generated:

1. Start the Internet Service Manager.
2. Click the Default Web site. Select Action | Properties. A dialog showing the properties for the site should be displayed.
3. Click the Properties button. You should see a dialog similar to the one shown in Figure 13.5.

Figure 13.5.
The General Properties tab lets you configure the log time period and the location of log files.

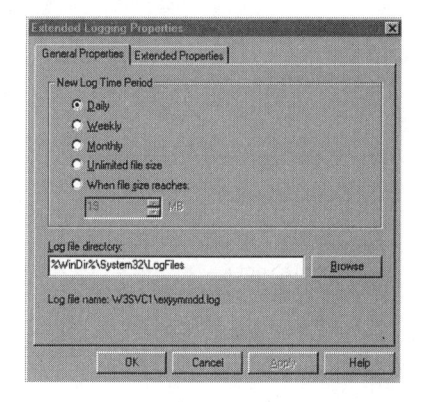

4. By default, the Daily log time period is selected. You may select another time period if you wish.
5. Notice that by default the log file directory is set to %WinDir%\System32\LogFiles. You can modify this location by typing in a new path or by browsing to find a new directory.
6. Click OK twice to dismiss the dialog.

You are now finished configuring the log time period. Look in the W3SVC log file directory (such as %windir%\system32\logfiles\w3svc1\) to see what files now exist.

13.2.3. Converting Log Files to NCSA Format

If you are using a program that doesn't support the Microsoft IIS Log File format or the W3C Extended Log File format, you may use the CONVLOG program. CONVLOG is used to convert log files to NCSA Common Log file format. It may also be used to convert TCP/IP addresses into DNS names.

The CONVLOG program is a console application that runs in a command prompt window. To run it, you open a command prompt window and type `convlog` with several parameters. Typing `convlog` without parameters provides usage information. The output from running CONVLOG with no parameters is shown in Listing 13.1.

Listing 13.1. Output from the CONVLOG program.

```
Microsoft Internet Log Converter
Converts Microsoft Internet Services log files
to the NCSA Common LogFile format
Copyright (C) 1997 Microsoft Corporation

Usage: convlog [options] LogFile
Options:
-i<i¦n¦e> = input logfile type
    i - MS Internet Standard Log File Format
    n - NCSA Common Log File format
    e - W3C Extended Log File Format
-t <ncsa[:GMTOffset] ¦ none> default is ncsa
-o <output directory> default = current directory
-x save non-www entries to a .dmp logfile
-d = convert IP addresses to DNS
-l<0¦1¦2> = Date locale format for MS Internet Standard
    0 - MM/DD/YY (default e.g. US)
    1 - YY/MM/DD (e.g. Japan)
    2 - DD.MM.YY (e.g. Germany)

Examples:
convlog -ii in*.log -d -t ncsa:+0800
convlog -in ncsa*.log -d
convlog -ii jra*.log -t none
```

Now that we've covered logging, we can move on to the Site Server Express tools that utilize log information (Usage Import and Report Writer).

13.3. Usage Import and Report Writer

Microsoft Usage Import and Report Writer are used to analyze log files from IIS. In this section you'll learn how to use Usage Import to import log files and how to generate reports using Report Writer.

13.3.1. Importing Log Files

Usage Import imports log files into a Microsoft Access database. By default, this database is located in \Program Files\UA Express\msusage.mdb.

Usage Import supports four different log file formats (the version of Usage Import that comes with the Enterprise version of Site Server 2.0 supports many other formats):

- Microsoft IIS Log File Format
- NCSA Common Log File Format
- W3C Extended Log File Format
- Site Server Log File Format

> **Note:** Of these formats, only the Site Server Log File format hasn't been discussed in this chapter. Because the IIS Web and FTP services don't output this format, it won't be discussed here. You should also note (again) that the ODBC Log File format isn't supported by the Express version of Usage Import.

Usage Import will import logs for either a Web server or an FTP server. However, if you select the NCSA Common Log File format, you will only be able to import logs for Web servers, because the NCSA format isn't supported for FTP servers.

The following steps show you how to select a log format and import log files into Usage Import:

1. Select Start | Programs | Windows NT 4.0 Option Pack | Microsoft Site Server Express 2.0 | Usage Import. After Usage Import starts, you should see a message that there are no Internet sites configured in this database.
2. The Server Manager window appears, followed by a Log Data Source dialog. In this dialog you must select one of the four log file formats discussed in this chapter. Select the format that matches your site, and click OK.
3. The Server Properties dialog appears, as shown in Figure 13.6.
4. In this dialog, the required fields are the server type (either World Wide Web or Ftp), time zone, and domain name (such as www.mydomain.com). Click OK when you're finished.
5. The Site Properties dialog appears, as shown in Figure 13.7.

Figure 13.6.
The Server Properties dialog in Usage Import lets you specify information such as the server type and domain name.

Figure 13.7.
The Site Properties dialog lets you specify URLs to your home page and also any hosts you want to exclude from the import.

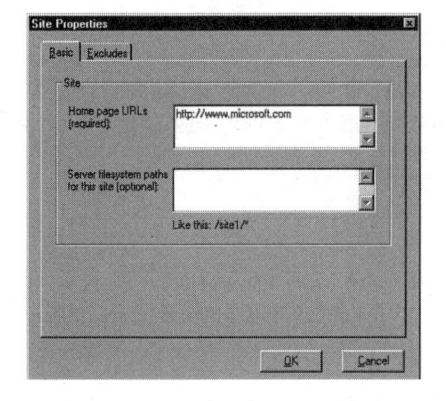

6. In this dialog, the home page URLs are the only required input. If your site has multiple URLs, make sure that you enter each one (for example, http://www.mycompany.com, http://mycompany.com). Click OK when you're done.

7. Now that the site is defined, you may open the Log File Manager. Select File | Log File Manager. You will see the window shown in Figure 13.8.

8. Click the Browse button. Locate the log files for your Web server; by default, this directory is %WINDIR%\system32\LogFiles\W3SVC1. Select several log files and then click Open.

9. Now select File | Start Import. You will see several dialogs displaying the progress during the import, including a dialog that indicates that the import is complete and how long the import took. Finally, you should see the Usage Import Statistics dialog, shown in Figure 13.9.

13.3. Usage Import and Report Writer   449

Figure 13.8.
The Log File Manager window lets you specify which files you want to import.

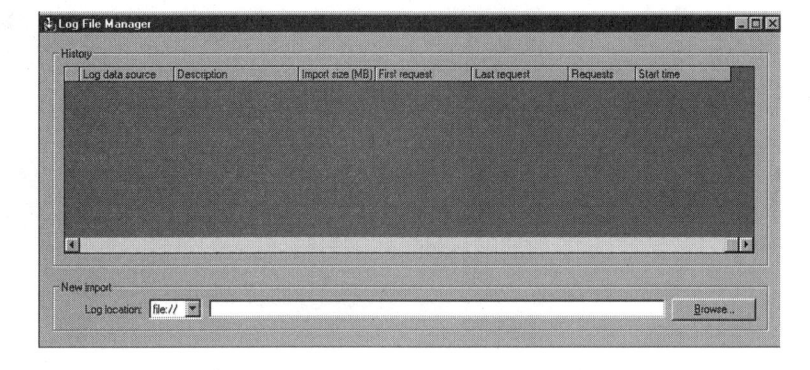

Figure 13.9.
The Usage Import Statistics dialog displays summary information after you import log files.

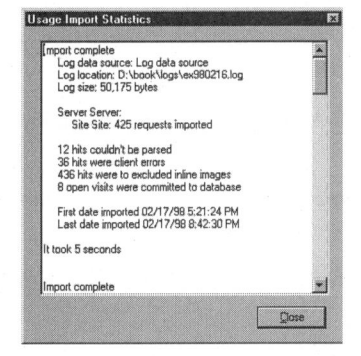

10. This dialog contains information for each log file that Usage Import processed, such as the number of requests that were imported, the number of hits, and the number of visits. If you want to save this information, you need to select it and copy it to the Clipboard so that you can paste it into another program, such as Notepad. There is no other way to save the information.

You have now finished importing log files into Usage Import.

After completing these steps, you will see an entry in the Log File Manager window for each log file you imported. Figure 13.10 shows a sample Log File Manager window with a populated history table.

If for some reason you need to delete a log file from your database (for example, if the data is old or you imported a log file more than once), you may delete log files by using the Log File Manager window. To delete a log file, select a row in the history table and press Shift+Delete or select Edit | Delete Import.

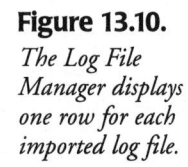

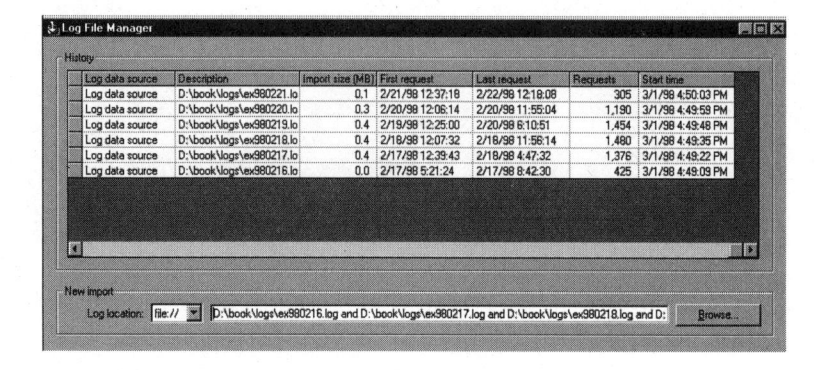

Figure 13.10.
The Log File Manager displays one row for each imported log file.

Besides importing log files into the Microsoft Access database, you can also use Usage Import to perform other tasks that are necessary from a maintenance standpoint or else needed for some of the different reports:

- Select Tools | Resolve IP Addresses to resolve any unidentified IP addresses in the database.
- Select Tools | Whois Organizations to resolve any unknown organization names in the database.
- Use Delete Requests to clean up the database by specifying a filter on what you want deleted.
- You can compact the database using the Database menu. (Compacting the database is necessary periodically to clean up the database and allow it to run optimally.)

This completes our focused coverage of Usage Import. At this point, you should have imported your log files into the database. Now you are ready to run some reports on the database. In the next section, I'll show you how to do that using Report Writer.

13.3.2. Analyzing Log Files

Report Writer works in conjunction with Usage Import. After you have imported log files into the Microsoft Access database using Usage Import, you may use Report Writer to analyze the log information.

Report Writer comes with a set of prebuilt reports; they are either summary or detailed. These reports are described in Table 13.6.

Table 13.6. Description of Report Writer reports.

Name	Description
Bandwidth	Reports bandwidth (in MB) on a hourly, daily, and weekly basis.
Browser and operating system	Reports the user's browser and operating systems.
Executive Summary	Provides a high-level view of Web site usage (available only as a summary report).
Geography	Provides a geographical breakdown (cities, states, regions, countries) of people using your Web site.
Hits	Provides hits by the hour of the day, day of the week, weekly trends, and so on.
Organization	Reports the top 15 and 25 organizations (U.S., Canadian, and international).
Path	Displays the path throughout the site (top five requests, five previous, five next).
Referrer	Provides the top 10 and 25 referring organizations.
Request	Details top and bottom requests (10 percent, top five, top 10).
User	Reports the number of users, average visits per user, average visits per organization, average duration, and average number of requests per user.
Visits	Reports when users visit your site (daily, hourly, weekly).

The following steps show you how to generate a report using Report Writer:

1. Select Start | Programs | Windows NT 4.0 Option Pack | Microsoft Site Server Express 2.0 | Report Writer. After Report Writer starts, click OK on the Report Writer dialog. The Report Writer catalog dialog, shown in Figure 13.11, appears.
2. Expand the Summary reports node. Select the Organization summary report. Click the Finish button.
3. The Organization Summary window appears.
4. Select File | Create Report Document. The Report document dialog, shown in Figure 13.12, appears.

Figure 13.11.
The Report Writer catalog dialog displays a list of summary and detail reports that you may generate.

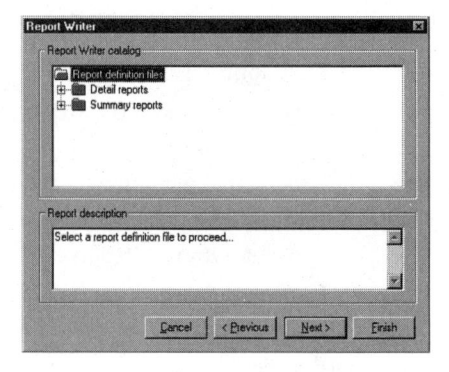

Figure 13.12.
The Report document dialog is displayed when you are ready to create a report.

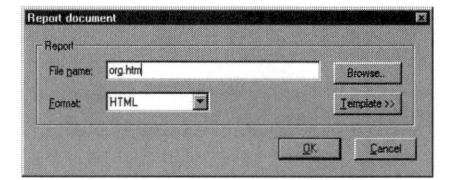

5. In the File name field, enter a name for the report (such as org.htm). Leave the file format set to HTML (you may also select Microsoft Word and Excel as formats). Click OK to generate the report.

6. After the report is generated, it will be displayed in the browser, as shown in Figure 13.13. The organization summary report is used to see the major organizations that are visiting your site.

As you can see, generating reports with Report Writer is quite easy. You can experiment with the other reports to generate other information, such as browser usage or referrer information.

In the next section, I'll show you how to automate this process of importing data and generating reports.

13.3.3. Automating Usage Import and Report Writer

In the previous sections, you learned how to import logs and run reports on the log data. Since log data changes constantly, it is necessary to run these tasks on a daily basis. Fortunately, both Usage Import and Report Writer support a command-line interface that allows for automated scheduling of these tasks.

13.3. Usage Import and Report Writer | 453

Figure 13.13.
The organization summary report displays the number of organizations (U.S., Canadian, international, and unknown) that have visited your site.

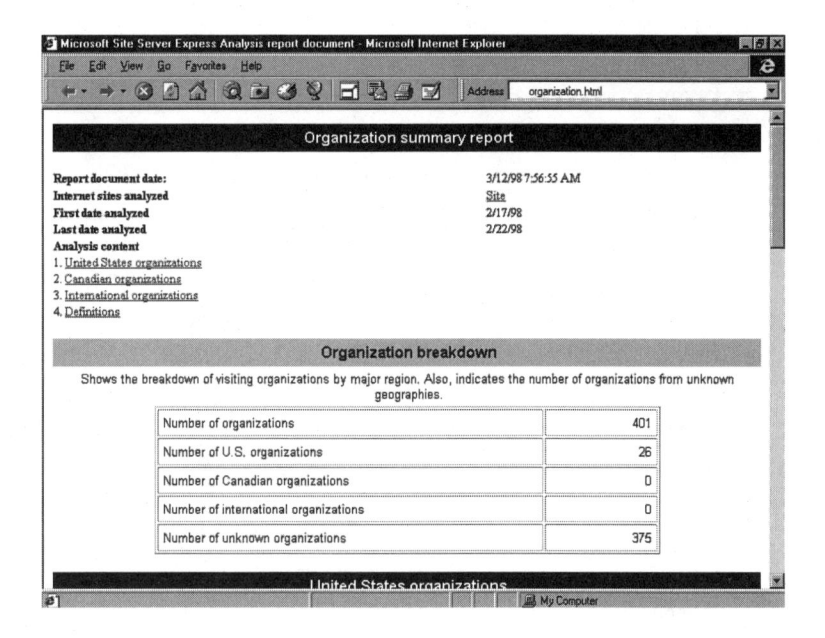

Table 13.7 lists the automated tasks that are supported by Usage Import and Report Writer.

Table 13.7. Automated tasks.

Task	Description
Run a report	You can choose any of the 12 summary or 9 detail reports.
Compact database	Compacts and rebuilds the Access database.
Delete requests	Cleans up the database by deleting requests using various filters.
Import log file	Imports log data.
Resolve Ips	Converts unresolved IP addresses in the database to DNS names.
Lookup HTML titles	Associates a title with every HTML file in the database.
Whois query	Converts any unknown organization names.

Of these tasks, only the Run a report task is run using Report Writer; the rest of the tasks are run through the Usage Import program.

The executable for Usage Import is import.exe. It is located in the \Program Files\ UA Express directory. (Command-line parameters are arguments you pass to the import.exe program.) Table 13.8 lists the parameters for Usage Import.

Table 13.8. Command-line parameters for Usage Import.

Parameter	Description
-help	Displays command-line help.
-silence	Runs the command silently (with no output to the screen).
action="Whois"	Runs the Whois query. (This is the same as selecting Tools | Whois query.)
action="IP resolution"	Runs the IP resolution tool. (This is the same as selecting Tools | Resolve IP addresses.)
db=	The name of the Microsoft Access database to be used with this task.
delete=	The filter to be applied to a delete request.
destdb=	Used in conjunction with sourcedb to compact the database. Destdb is the name of a new database to be created after the sourcedb is compacted.
log=	The name of the log file to be imported.
logsource=	The name of the log data source.
message log=	The name of a file that will contain information about the success of the particular task.
sourcedb=	The name of the Microsoft Access database to be compacted.
Title=	Performs a title search.

The executable for Report Writer is analysis.exe. It is located in the \Program Files\ UA Express directory. Table 13.9 lists the command-line interface for Report Writer.

Table 13.9. Command-line parameters for Report Writer.

Parameter	Description
-help	Displays command-line help.
-silence	Runs the command silently (with no output to the screen).
analysis=	The filename of the catalog report to be run.
db=	The name of the Microsoft Access database to be used with this task.
message log=	The name of a file that will contain information about the success of the particular task.
report=	The output filename for the report (such as myreport.htm).

13.3. Usage Import and Report Writer 455

These command-line parameters can be used in conjunction with the Windows NT AT command to automate various tasks. For more information on the AT command, type AT /? at a command prompt on a machine running Windows NT.

> **Note:** The Schedule service must be running in order for the AT command to work.

Both Usage Import and Report Writer have a graphical interface that can be used to schedule tasks. The following steps show you how to use the graphical interface to automate the import of log data and the generation of a report:

1. From Report Writer or Usage Import, select Tools | Scheduler. The window shown in Figure 13.14 appears.

Figure 13.14.
The Scheduler window is used to create jobs and tasks.

2. Right-click All jobs and select New Job from the pop-up menu. The Job Properties dialog, shown in Figure 13.15, appears.

Figure 13.15.
The Job Properties dialog lets you specify when and how often you want a particular job to run.

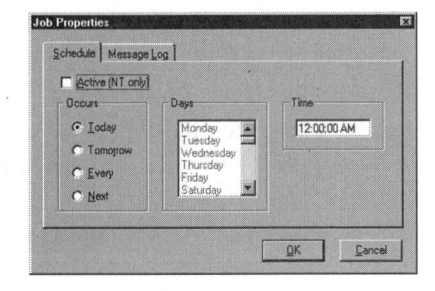

3. Select Active (NT only) to use the schedule service in NT. Click OK.
4. You should see a job called New Job listed under All Jobs. Right-click New Job and select New Task from the pop-up menu. The Task Properties dialog appears, as shown in Figure 13.16.

Figure 13.16.
The Task Properties dialog lets you modify the task type and the appropriate properties for the task.

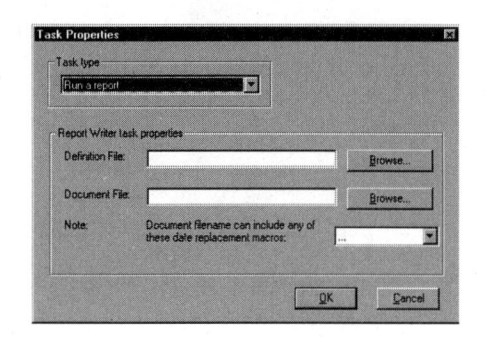

5. From the Task type drop-down list, select Import log file. From the Log data source drop-down list, select Log data source. For the Log location, specify the path to your log files (for example, \winnt\system32\logfiles\w3svc1\) and the appropriate filename (such as ex980212.log). You can also use macros to substitute dates so that when the task is run it will substitute the current date. For example, ex$1.log will substitute the current date (980212, for example).
6. Click OK to dismiss the dialog. You should see New Task listed under New job.
7. Right-click the import task you've created and select New Task from the pop-up menu to insert a new task after the current one.
8. In the Task type drop-down list, select Run a report. For the report definition file, browse to locate the Executive Summary report. (The path to this file is in the Catalog\Summary directory under the UA Express directory.)
9. For the document file, browse to locate the Reports subdirectory under the UA Express directory. Append execSummary$1.htm to the filename (this will substitute the current date for $1).
10. Click OK to dismiss the dialog. You should see New Task.1 listed under New job. Close the Schedule window. This will write the new job to the Schedule directory.

13.3. Usage Import and Report Writer

You may view the contents of the job you just created. Listing 13.2 shows the contents of new job.bat in the Schedule directory.

Listing 13.2. The contents of new job.bat.

```
REM USAGE ANALYST START DO NOT MODIFY
REM USAGE ANALYST SCHEDULER BATCH FILE-- DO NOT MODIFY IN
REM USAGE ANALYST BETWEEN COMMENTS
REM USAGE ANALYST CREATED 1/21/98 5:00:49 PM
REM USAGE ANALYST ACTIVE True
REM USAGE ANALYST JOBID 2
REM USAGE ANALYST OCCURS 0
REM USAGE ANALYST DAYS
REM USAGE ANALYST TIME 12:00:00 AM
SET IMPORT="D:\PROGRA~1\UA Express\IMPORT.EXE"
SET ANALYSIS="D:\PROGRA~1\UA Express\ANALYSIS.EXE"
SET METADATA="D:\PROGRA~1\UA Express\METADATA.EXE"
SET MAIL="D:\PROGRA~1\UA Express\UTILITY\MAIL.EXE"
REM USAGE ANALYST END DO NOT MODIFY

REM USAGE ANALYST START DO NOT MODIFY
REM USAGE ANALYST TASK "New Task"
%IMPORT% -silence message log="D:\PROGRA~1\UA Express\Message\
➥New job.log" db="D:\Program Files\UA Express\MSUsage.mdb" log="D:\NT\
➥system32\LogFiles\W3SVC1\ex$1.log" logsource="Log data source"
REM USAGE ANALYST END DO NOT MODIFY

REM USAGE ANALYST START DO NOT MODIFY
REM USAGE ANALYST TASK "New Task.1"
%ANALYSIS% -silence message log="D:\PROGRA~1\UA Express\Message\
➥New job.log" db="D:\Program Files\UA Express\
➥MSUsage.mdb" report=" D:\PROGRA~1\UA Express\Reports\
➥execSummary$1.htm" analysis="D:\Program Files\UA Express\
➥Catalog\Summary\executive summary.mfa"
REM USAGE ANALYST END DO NOT MODIFY
```

You may run the batch file at a command prompt to test it. After the batch file finishes running, you will have two log files in the \Program Files\UA Express\Message directory:

- Analysis.log will contain the results from the generation of the Executive Summary report.
- New job.log will contain the results of the import.

In the reports directory will be an HTML file containing the Executive summary report. The filename will be based on the current date (for example, execSummary980101.htm).

You've now completed your study of Usage Import and Report Writer. These tools have helped you analyze how your site is being used. In the next section, we'll turn our attention to making sure that the content we've placed on our site works (no broken links, not too large, and so on).

13.4. Content Analyzer

Microsoft Content Analyzer provides site visualization, content analysis, link management, and reports. Content Analyzer lets you do the following:

- View your Web site in tree view and cyberbolic view (both views are available at the same time)
- Analyze your Web site for broken links
- Generate a Site Summary report

The following sections cover two aspects of content analysis:

- WebMaps, a graphical representation of your Web site
- Site Summary report, an HTML report that contains Web site statistics

13.4.1. WebMaps

Content Analyzer creates WebMaps, which are graphical maps of your entire Web site. In this section I'll introduce you to WebMaps and then show you how to navigate a WebMap. I'll also describe the built-in quick searches.

WebMaps may be created by specifying either a URL or a file path. The file path is useful if you're running Content Analyzer on the same machine as the Web server. For example, this file path could be c:\inetpub\wwwroot\default.htm.

The following steps show you how to create and view a WebMap:

1. Start Content Analyzer by selecting Start | Programs | Windows NT 4.0 Option Pack | Microsoft Site Server Express 2.0 | Content Analyzer. Then select File | New | Map from a URL. The New Map from URL dialog box appears, as shown in Figure 13.17.

Figure 13.17.

The New Map from URL dialog is used to create a WebMap from a URL.

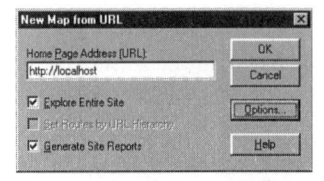

2. Enter the home page address (URL) of the site you want to map. You may click Options to specify mapping options if you wish.
3. Click OK when you're done. The WebMap will be generated and displayed, as shown in Figure 13.18.

Figure 13.18.
A WebMap is a graphical image of your Web site.

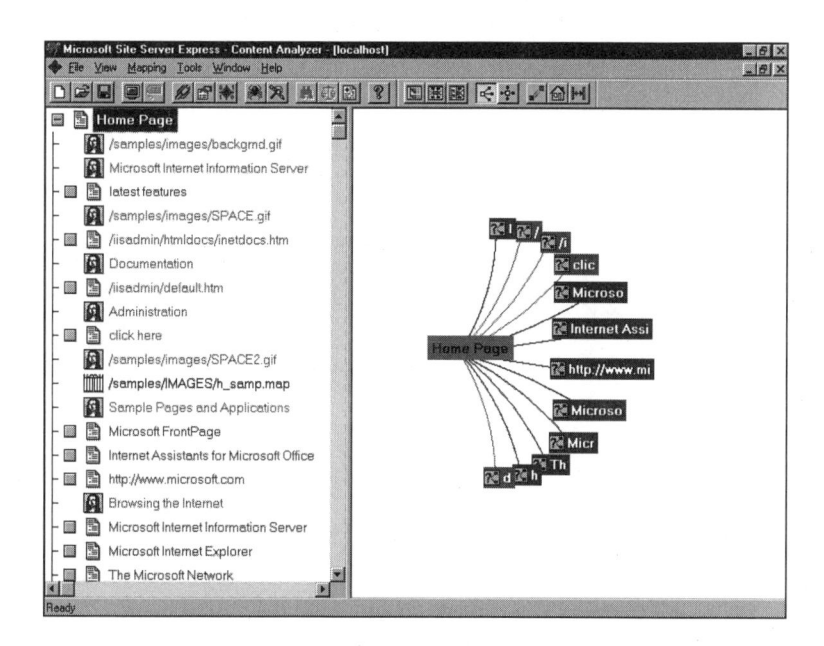

At this point, you are done creating the WebMap. The Generate Site Reports dialog will be displayed, but you can dismiss it for now. (We'll discuss generating site reports in the next section.)

> **Test Tip**
> If you're using ASP scripts or server-side includes extensively on a site you want to examine using Content Analyzer, you need to create a WebMap from a URL. This option also lets you specify the User Agent that should be emulated by Content Analyzer, thus allowing you to check the consistency of your site for specific Web browsers.

The WebMap shown in Figure 13.18 has both a tree view (left pane) and a cyberbolic view (right pane). The tree view contains a hierarchy of objects. If you've used Windows Explorer, the tree view will be very familiar. By default, the tree view displays all objects (such as images, text, video, and Web pages). The tree view is also color-coded. For example, broken links or unavailable servers are shown in red.

The cyberbolic view represents a dynamic nonlinear view of your site. By default, the cyberbolic view contains only Web pages. Like the tree view, the cyberbolic view is color-coded.

After creating a WebMap, you might want to save it. By default, WebMaps are stored in \Program Files\Content Analyzer Express\WebMaps. WebMaps have an extension of .wmp.

> **Test Tip**
> If you have multiple Web administrators for a site, it makes sense to have just one person generate a WebMap for your site. Generating WebMaps can be CPU- and time-intensive for large sites. The WebMap can be saved, and then the other administrators can open it in Content Analyzer.

WebMaps may be printed by selecting File | Print. If you'd like to export WebMaps to other formats, such as HTML, you won't be able to do so with the Express version of Content Analyzer (another reason to buy the Site Server version).

WebMaps may also be customized. You can change the display options for either the tree or cyberbolic view. Select View | Display Options. The Display Options dialog lets you select which objects you want to see. For example, you might want to turn off images to simplify the tree view.

WebMaps may also be used to determine problems with your site. If an object is unavailable (because of a broken hyperlink, unavailable server, and so on), it is shown in red. You can inspect your WebMap for broken links by locating any red objects.

A. Navigating WebMaps

WebMaps provide a graphical view of your Web site that let you easily see the layout of your Web site. WebMaps can save you time since you don't have to use a browser to load each page to view the content. With a WebMap, you can just navigate the tree or cyberbolic view to get to an object you want to view.

You can navigate WebMaps by clicking elements in either the tree view or the cyberbolic view. To view an object, just double-click it; the object will be loaded into your Web browser.

You may also navigate links in a WebMap by selecting View | Object Links. The Link Info dialog appears, as shown in Figure 13.19.

Figure 13.19.
The Link Info dialog lets you navigate links in a WebMap.

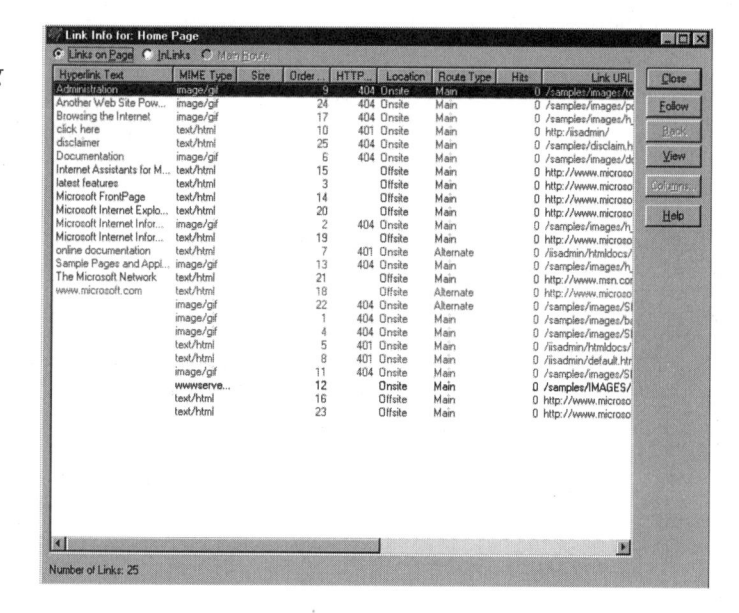

From the Link Info dialog you may follow links forward and backward by clicking the Follow and Back buttons.

B. Searching WebMaps

WebMaps may also be searched to find problems with your site or to just gain more information. Content Analyzer comes with several prebuilt searches ("quick searches"). (The Express version doesn't let you perform custom searches.) The eight quick searches are listed in Table 13.10.

Table 13.10. Preconfigured quick searches.

Name	Description
Broken Links	Generates a table showing broken links.
Home Site Objects	Generates a table showing objects that share the same domain as the home page.
Images without ALT	Generates a table showing images that don't have an ALT tag.
Load Size over 32K	Generates a table showing all pages that have a load size of more than 32 KB.

continues

Table 13.10. continued

Name	Description
Non-Home Site Objects	Generates a table showing objects that don't share the same domain as the home page.
Not Found Objects (404)	Generates a table showing all objects that were not found.
Unavailable Objects	Generates a table showing all unavailable objects (they could not be located or could not be accessed when located).
Unverified Objects	Generates a table showing all objects that have not been verified yet.

You run quick searches by selecting Tools | Quick Search and then selecting the appropriate search. When you run any of the quick searches, a table is generated that contains rows with each object listed. You may double-click a row to launch the listed object.

One of the other useful features of Content Analyzer is the ability to generate reports. In the next section, we'll discuss the Site Summary report.

13.4.2. Reports

The Site Server 2.0 Express edition of Content Analyzer comes with only one report—a Site Summary report. If you want other reports, you'll have to buy the full version of Site Server. The Site Summary report is an HTML report that contains statistics about your Web site.

The following steps generate a Site Summary report (using Content Analyzer):

1. In Content Analyzer, select Tools | Generate Site Reports. The Generate Site Reports dialog appears.

2. In the Report Directory field, enter the path to the directory in which you want to store the report; the default path is \Program Files\Content Analyzer Express\Reports. In the Report Prefix field, enter the name to be prefixed to the summary output file. For example, if your domain is www.mydomain.com, an output filename of www.mydomain.com summary.html will be generated.

3. Click OK to generate the report. The report will be generated and displayed in the browser, as shown in Figure 13.20.

Figure 13.20.

A Site Summary report for a default Web site contains object statistics, a status summary, map statistics, and a server summary.

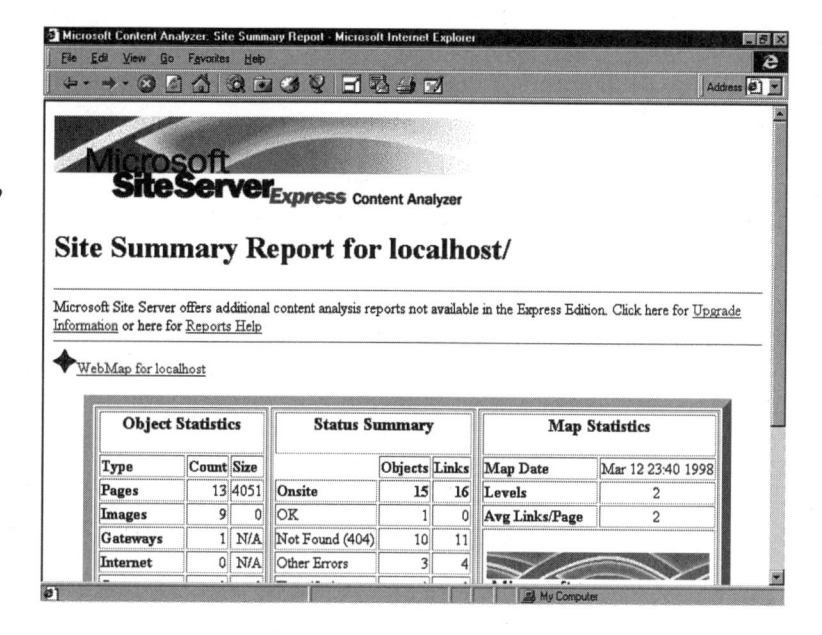

The Site Summary report contains the following information:

- The Object Statistics section contains information such as the number of pages, images and their sizes, and so on.
- The Status Summary lists the number of Not Found (404) and other errors.
- Map Statistics lists the date of the map, the number of levels (number of clicks to navigate through the site), and the average number of links per page.
- The Server Summary lists the domain name, the Web server version, and the HTTP version.

Lab

This lab consists of review questions pertaining to this chapter and provides an opportunity for you to use walk-through exercises to apply the knowledge that you've gained.

Questions

1. Select all log file formats supported by Internet Information Server.

    A. NCSA Common Log File format

    B. Microsoft IIS Log File format

    C. W3C Extended Log File format

    D. All of the above

2. Your Web site uses the W3C Extended Log file format. However, you have a site analysis tool that only supports the NCSA Common Log file format. What can you use to convert your log files to NCSA format?

    A. The convert.exe program.

    B. The convlog.exe program.

    C. The Log File Manager window in Usage Import to export a log file.

    D. You can't convert the log files. You must change the log file format to NCSA Common Log File format and recapture the log information.

3. You have noticed that visits to a set of pages in your Web site are not getting recorded in the log file. What could be the problem? Select all possible answers.

    A. Logging is not performed on Active Server Pages.

    B. Logging is disabled in the directory containing the files.

    C. Logging is not enabled on the site containing the directory.

    D. Logging is not installed.

4. You have used the scheduler in Usage Import to schedule daily imports. However, you notice that no new log data is being added to the database. Furthermore, no message log files are being generated. What is the most likely cause of the problem?

A. The Windows NT schedule service is not running.

B. Usage Import doesn't have the correct NT permissions to run as a batch job.

C. You're using the wrong program to do imports. You should be using Content Analyzer.

D. You specified the incorrect path to the log files.

5. You have generated a WebMap using Content Analyzer. You would like to save it so that other administrators can view it. What filename should you give it so that they can view it in Content Analyzer?

    A. default.asp

    B. default.wmp

    C. Webmap.log

    D. Webmap.idc

6. You need to compact your Usage Import and Report Writer database. Which is the correct command-line syntax to achieve this?

    A. `import.exe sourcedb=msusage.mdb destdb=msusageCompact.mdb`

    B. `import.exe /compact sourcedb=msusage.mdb`

    C. `analysis.exe sourcedb=msuage.mdb destdb=msusageCompact.mdb`

    D. `compact.exe msusage.mdb`

7. You would like to capture which browsers are being used by users of your Web site, along with referrer information. Which log format should you use?

    A. NCSA Common Log File format

    B. W3C Extended Log File format

    C. Microsoft IIS Log File format

    D. ODBC Log File format

8. You installed IIS using a typical installation. However, you can't find the Site Server Express program group on your machine. What must you do to get Site Server Express installed?

A. You must run a separate Site Server Express setup program from the CD.

B. Site Server Express is installed correctly. Use the Internet Service Manager to use the Site Server Express snap-ins.

C. Use the Add/Remove Programs icon in Control Panel to add the Site Server Express component to the Windows NT 4.0 Option Pack.

D. You must remove IIS, reinstall it, and perform a custom installation. During the custom installation, select the Site Server Express component.

9. Users of your Web site have reported that some of the links on your site are broken. How can you find the broken links? Select all correct answers.

    A. View the history window in Usage Import.

    B. Use Report Writer and run the Broken Links report.

    C. Use Content Analysis to perform a Broken Links quick search.

    D. The Site Server Express version doesn't include this tool, so you must manually click links in your site to find the broken ones.

10. You want to make sure that your site is optimized for viewing over a phone line. What tool(s) can you use to help? Select all correct answers.

    A. Run the Load Size over 32K quick search in Content Analyzer.

    B. Run the Site Summary report in Content Analyzer.

    C. Run the Bandwidth Detail report in Report Writer.

    D. Create a custom search in Content Analyzer to tell you which pages are over 32 KB.

Answers to Questions

1. **D.** IIS supports all three of these formats. IIS also supports ODBC logging.

2. **B.** convlog.exe is a command-line tool that converts log files to NCSA Common Log File format. Usage Import is used to import log files; it doesn't support exporting log files. convert.exe is a utility to convert FAT volumes to NTFS.

3. **B, C.** A is incorrect because logging is supported for pages that use Active Server Pages. D is incorrect because logging is automatically installed with IIS. B and C are correct because it is possible to turn off logging on a Web site on a per-directory basis and for the whole site.

4. **A.** The schedule service must be running in order for automated tasks to occur. D is incorrect because even if the path to the log files were incorrect, a log file would still be created for the message log argument. C is incorrect because Content Analyzer is used to analyze Web content, not to import log files.

5. **B.** Content Analyzer stores WebMaps in files that have the extension .wmp. default.asp is an Active Server Page. Webmap.idc is a query file for the Internet Database Connector.

6. **A.** The Usage Import program is import.exe, and it is used to compact the database. Thus, answers C and D are wrong. To compact the database, you give the `sourcedb` and `destdb` parameters. For more information, see section 13.3.3.

7. **B.** Only the W3C Extended Log File format lets you capture the browser (User Agent) and referrer information. The other formats do not include this information. See section 13.2.1 for details on log formats.

8. **C.** Site Server Express components are not installed during a Typical installation. However, you may add them later using the Add/Remove Programs icon in Control Panel. There is no separate installation program, so A is wrong. Although it would be nice to have a snap-in for the Site Server Express components, this is no snap-in, so B is wrong. Although D would work, it is not necessary to remove IIS and perform a reinstallation.

9. **C.** C is correct because Content Analyzer provides a quick search on broken links. B is wrong because Report Writer is used for reports on usage analysis, not content analysis. A is wrong because Usage Import's log file manager window gives you information on logs that have been imported into the system. D is also incorrect. Although many features are missing from the Express version of Site Server, this is one feature that was left in.

10. **A.** The Load Size over 32K quick search will help you find any pages that are too large for quick download. D is wrong because you can't create custom searches in the Express version of Site Server Content Analyzer. B is incorrect because the Site Summary report doesn't tell you if you have any pages over 32 KB. C is also incorrect, because the Bandwidth Detail report gives you information about byte transfers on an hourly, daily, or weekly basis.

Exercise

Exercise 13.1.: Configuring FTP Logging

This exercise addresses the following Microsoft exam objective:

- Maintain a log for fine-tuning and auditing purposes (subobjective: configure the logging features of the FTP Service)

In this exercise, you will configure logging for the FTP server. You will need to have the FTP service installed in order to complete this exercise.

1. Start the Internet Service Manager and click the Default FTP Site.
2. Select Action | Properties. The Properties dialog appears.
3. Be sure that the Enable Logging check box is checked. If it isn't, click it to enable logging. You can also change the log format by selecting one of the three log formats (W3C Extended, ODBC, or Microsoft IIS) from the Active log format list.
4. By default, the W3C Extended Log File format is selected. You should note that the NCSA Common Log File format is not listed because it doesn't support FTP logging.
5. Click OK to dismiss the dialog and apply your changes.

13

TEST DAY FAST FACTS

Here are a few fast facts about this chapter that you may want to know ahead of time. Don't forget that these facts also provide great last-minute study material.

- Don't guess at the source of a problem. Always carefully investigate exactly what caused a problem.
- Use PING and TRACERT to find connectivity problems and NSLOOKUP to investigate name server entries.
- The most likely causes of installation problems are files that are in use, improper user rights configuration, and file-level security settings.
- User accounts are at the heart of IIS security. Check that a given user account has access to a file at NT, IIS, and NTFS level.
- Index Server relies on correctly supplied accounts for indexing data that resides on remote servers.
- When using the Host Headers feature, you still need to assign an IP address to the host name in either the HOSTS file or the DNS server.

Day 14

Troubleshooting

by James F. Causey

This book has given you a great deal of information that will help you understand and implement solutions using Internet Information Server. These chapters have focused on the right ways to install, configure, and implement IIS 4.0 to provide services. However, there's one thing we haven't talked about very much: what to do when things go wrong.

Even if there are no other truths in the systems administration business, all experienced systems administrators will agree with Murphy's Law: "Anything that can go wrong, will." Successful administrators know how to plan for these problems, prevent them as much as possible, and quickly resolve them when they pop up.

My goals in this chapter are twofold. First, I want to give you the information you'll need to succeed with the troubleshooting questions on the IIS 4.0 exam. I also want to give you the information you need to be prepared for many of the most common issues found with IIS 4.0, and even to prevent many of these issues from coming up.

We'll begin by looking at some common strategies and techniques you can use during troubleshooting that will make your life easier. We'll also review some basic TCP/IP troubleshooting techniques that apply to common IIS problems. Then we'll begin looking at

IIS-specific issues, including installation problems, security issues, and problems with remote resource connectivity. We'll also examine issues surrounding virtual servers and host headers, as well as problems with Microsoft Index Server. We'll conclude with some questions and exercises that will firm up your knowledge and help you practice your newly found skills before you hit the test itself.

Objectives

This chapter helps you prepare for the Microsoft exam by covering the following objectives:

- Resolve setup issues when installing IIS on a Windows NT Server 4.0 computer
- Resolve IIS configuration problems
- Resolve WWW service problems
- Resolve FTP service problems
- Resolve security problems
- Resolve resource access problems
- Resolve Index Server query problems
- Choose an implementation strategy for an Internet site or an intranet site for stand-alone servers, single-domain environments, and multiple-domain environments. Includes resolving host header name issues by using a HOSTS file or DNS or both.

14.1. Principles of Troubleshooting

Troubleshooting network problems is something we all dread, to one degree or another. As network administrators, our dream is to take the cool technology we have access to and produce a solution for our users. We'd like for this solution to be quick, robust, and reliable. No one likes their users to be inconvenienced, and no one likes to see the solution they've taken so much time to produce and implement fail in some way or another.

However, no matter what you do or say to the contrary, these failures will happen. Users tend to make changes to system settings inadvertently, therefore causing you problems. Unknown software bugs rear their heads, taking down services or whole systems. Hardware fails. Random acts beyond your control (sometimes called "acts of God" by insurance companies) wreak havoc on your network. This is a fact of life for the network administrator, and one that must be overcome.

New and/or inexperienced technical staff are often amazed by the way more-experienced network and systems administrators rapidly diagnose and solve problems. Often, the junior staff doesn't even know where to begin to figure out the problem, but the experienced staff zeroes in on the problem and solves it almost instantly. This can be disheartening. "How long will it take *me* to know everything that can go wrong like that?" the new staffer thinks. This is the wrong attitude, and one that doesn't accurately reflect the situation. The more-senior staff member does *not* know everything (although he will have seen some common problems crop up many, many times). He has simply practiced successful troubleshooting techniques enough that problems no longer rattle him, and the repetition of these successful techniques through the years has allowed him to quickly, almost intuitively, run through those processes in his head until a likely solution comes up.

> **Test Tip**
>
> I mentioned that thinking that senior staffers know everything is the wrong attitude, and I meant it. Many people in this industry believe that being a successful administrator or support provider means accumulating as much trivia as possible: knowing this switch or that switch to a command-line utility, keeping up with the latest additions to technical support errata, staying on top of rumors and gossip about products. Although understanding facts and figures is an important part of what makes a successful technical person, the ability to pinpoint a problem's cause and then apply intelligent troubleshooting procedures and techniques is far more important.

> Why is this the case? Because no one can know everything, and a person who relies on knowledge of facts, figures, and trivia will be completely lost when something catastrophic that he has no experience with occurs. And believe me, new problems that you have no experience with come up all the time when you're administering a network.
>
> The essence of this tip? On your quest to become a solid, experienced technical person, focus on building a solid knowledge of how things really work under the hood and on developing the ability to work steadily and intelligently through a problem. Don't worry quite as much about the details. Don't completely ignore the details, though (and keep in mind that the Microsoft certification tests often rely almost as much on knowledge of details as of procedures!).

With this in mind, let's look at some successful statements about troubleshooting that can make you more successful.

14.1.1. Information Is Your (Only) Ally

When a problem comes up, the tendency is to make a snap judgment about where the problem lies and begin probing in that direction for a solution. With problems you've experienced before, this isn't such a bad plan; however, with new problems, you will often waste a lot of time this way.

Keep this mantra (or one like it) with you at all times: Information is your best, and sometimes only, ally in solving technical problems. When a problem comes up, you need to collect all the information you can about it. In a tight spot, this information is the only thing you have to help you think through the problem and try new avenues of attack.

What information, then, should you collect? Basically, everything you can. But some knowledge is more valuable than others. When initially diagnosing a problem, successful troubleshooters ask a list of questions like the following:

- *What exactly is the problem?* Normally, this question isn't the kind you just come right out and ask. Usually you have to determine the problem through a series of pointed questions. For example, having an HTML developer tell you "My page isn't working" isn't particularly illuminating; you need to pin down the exact symptoms of the problem. Ask the user for the steps necessary to reproduce the problem and whether this problem occurs every time or only occasionally. Then find out if the problem seems to be affecting just one user or multiple users. Most users will have no idea what the real problem is; they'll just know the symptoms they've experienced. By working with them, you can pin down what is and isn't going on, to get a picture of what exactly is happening.

- *Who is affected by the problem?* Once you know what's going on, it's important to determine the scope of the issue. Is the problem affecting just this page, or is it a problem for the entire IIS installation? Is the problem localized to one site, or is your whole server affected? This will help you isolate the problem as being a configuration issue on one or a few sites or a centralized problem affecting all your users.

- *How much of a problem is there?* This is another method for determining the scope of the problem. It allows you to determine the priority of this issue as compared to any other problems you may be dealing with, and it helps you to further pinpoint the source of the issue. For example, if a number of users can't access a Web page on a particular server, you should determine the status of the server as a whole. Is the server up? Is the server responding to PINGs? Are other services on the server still working?

Armed with information from questions like these, you can better approach the issue and get closer to solving it.

14.1.2. Visualize the Points of Failure

This is a little like saying "Understand how your IIS sites work." When a problem occurs, visualize the process and try to picture at which points that process could fail. Obviously this requires a thorough understanding of how IIS works. It might even seem to violate the last tip. It doesn't, though. For example, you don't need to know the trivia of file system ACL (access control list) modification to understand that improper security configuration can be a major point of failure in any IIS installation.

14.1.3. Changes Are Your Enemy

By saying "changes are your enemy," I don't mean that you should resist and avoid change; I simply mean that if something used to work, and now it doesn't, something probably changed somewhere to cause the failure. In a complicated network environment, changes can often cause a "ripple effect," in which the effects of the change spread across the network to affect other things in subtle, often unexpected, ways.

Changes that can affect IIS sites can be almost anything, from a DNS server reconfiguration to a patch release applied to the server on which IIS is running. If at all possible, try to reverse any changes that have been made that you believe could be causing the problem (sort of retrace your steps), and see if doing so clears things up.

> **Test Tip**
>
> All this talk of changes brings up an important tip that you might already know: Never implement wide-scale changes without testing them first (if at all possible). Try to maintain test workstations and servers (and even domains, if possible) on which you can apply a proposed configuration change or modification. This will allow you to test system functionality without affecting your production environment. If this isn't feasible (or even if it is), try to make changes only during off-hours (usually nights and weekends) so that you will have time to test those changes and fix any problems that come up before they directly affect your users. Doing so leads to happier users and better job security.

14.1.4. Commercial Software Bugs Don't Cause *That* Many Problems

Less-experienced troubleshooters (and sometimes people who are not always willing to take that extra step) are often quick to blame a problem that they don't understand on the operating system or on IIS itself. However, modern network operating systems and server software are generally developed in stringent environments and thoroughly tested before release.

Blaming a problem on bugs as a last resort helps you be sure that you've tried every possible configuration avenue (changing configurations is normally easier than getting a company to upgrade or fix its software). Besides, most problems *aren't* software failure-related, so exploring other avenues first is advantageous and usually brings more success.

Sometimes, however, it *is* the software that fails.

14.1.5. Don't Rule Out Software Bugs

If you're proceeding according to instructions, and exploration of every possible configuration (as well as configuration options that might not seem related) doesn't resolve the issue, it's very possible that your problem might be a bug in the product or products you're using on the site. Keep in mind that IIS is not the only software product in question. The development environment used for your Web applications, the operating system itself, additional OS services on which your product relies, Web browser problems, upgrades to the product or the underlying OS, and many other potential points of failure can all affect your IIS installation. If you can't figure out how to fix the problem, search online resources such as newsgroups, FAQs, and knowledge bases for similar problems. If you still can't find a resolution (or if the problem is mission-critical), contact the software vendor (with problems related to or affecting IIS, this often is Microsoft).

> **Note**
>
> Now that I've acted as the Voice of Reason, I'd like to go into the darker side of software bugs. The current ferociously competitive nature of the software industry, particularly in regards to Internet software, has driven the development and release of Internet server software and Web browsers to a fever pitch. As a result, quality and testing have suffered, and many bugs have appeared.
>
> It's still wise to always explore other solutions before concluding that a bug is to blame. However, once you've exhausted your resources, don't be afraid to call the product vendor and ask for some assistance. If you've found a bug, they'll normally be grateful for the assistance. If not, they should still be able to help you.

14.1.6. Don't Be Afraid to Ask for Help

Being willing to ask for help is one of the most important troubleshooting skills. Having a too-prideful attitude about solving a problem doesn't help your users and just makes your life harder.

Asking for help doesn't just mean talking to other people. It can also involve checking World Wide Web support sites, scanning Usenet for information, looking in books or other reference materials, or even reading the documentation. In fact, I suggest that you exhaust all possible avenues of information before asking your busy colleagues for suggestions. This will avoid wasting their time and give you both more information with which to tackle the problem.

> **Test Tip**
>
> Use the Microsoft Knowledge Base. This resource, available both on the Internet at Microsoft's support site (`http://www.microsoft.com/support/`) and on Microsoft's TechNet product, is an invaluable resource filled with frequently updated information on bugs, misunderstood features, and other frequently asked questions about Microsoft software and hardware products.

14.2. Troubleshooting TCP/IP

Because IIS (like all Internet/intranet servers) relies on TCP/IP to deliver information to remote clients, it's important for you to understand how to diagnose and resolve TCP/IP communication problems. Many problems that users will have trying to connect to your site might stem from improper TCP/IP configuration or network outages rather than problems with your IIS system.

As you might guess, the ability to establish communication between the client workstation and the IIS server is crucial for successful access to your IIS system. A number of factors can contribute to connectivity failure, ranging from misconfigured TCP/IP stacks on either the server or the client to misconfigured hardware to network outages between the two systems. The upcoming sections look at the following tools included with Windows NT that you can use to help troubleshoot these TCP/IP connectivity issues:

- PING
- TRACERT
- NSLOOKUP
- IPCONFIG
- NETSTAT
- ARP

After that, we'll look at the best ways in which to use these tools to help localize problems.

14.2.1. PING

PING (Packet Internet Groper) is the old workhorse of diagnostic tools. The PING utility uses Internet Control Message Protocol (ICMP) Echo Request and Reply packets to verify whether an IP address or canonical name (you might also know this as a fully qualified domain name) is responding to communications, as shown in Figure 14.1.

Figure 14.1.
PING sends Echo Request packets to a destination host. If that host is alive, it responds with Reply packets.

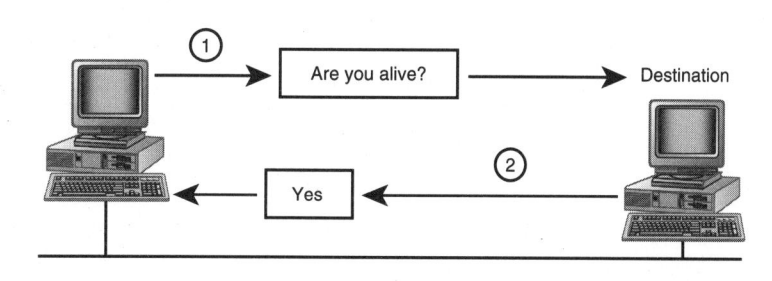

If the remote host that you're PINGing replies, you know that the system is running (or, at least, that its TCP/IP stack is running). PING responses also include data about the amount of elapsed time between the Request and the Reply; this can help you determine whether the network connection between the two systems is acting as a bottleneck.

As I mentioned, you can PING a computer using either its IP address or the canonical host name. For example, if a remote host answers when you PING its IP address, but PINGing the remote host using its canonical host name doesn't work, you know that your computer's DNS setup is wrong (or your DNS server isn't functioning properly).

You can use PING to thoroughly diagnose the condition of your network connectivity by going through the following steps, continuing until one doesn't work properly:

1. PING the localhost address (127.0.0.1). This will tell you whether your TCP/IP stack is functioning at all.
2. PING the actual IP address assigned to your network adapter. If the localhost PING worked, but this one doesn't, you know that your network configuration is incorrect.
3. PING a local IP address. If this works, you know that you can at least see systems on your subnet. However, if the previous steps worked but this one doesn't, you probably have an address configuration problem or a hardware problem between you and the network (often a cable or hub port failure) or possibly a corrupted ARP cache.
4. PING your default gateway address. If you can PING local IP addresses but your gateway doesn't respond, you probably have an incorrect gateway address, a bad port on your gateway, or a gateway that's down or misconfigured.
5. PING a remote IP address. If you were able to PING the gateway but not a remote address, your gateway device is probably misconfigured or not functioning properly, or your subnet mask is improperly configured.
6. PING a canonical IP host name. This will help you determine if TCP/IP name resolution is functioning properly.

Now that you have verified that your network connectivity is working properly, you go a step further and use PING to test whether a remote system is up and responding properly.

14.2. Troubleshooting TCP/IP | 479

If you need to get a quick overview of the parameters offered by PING, simply run PING without parameters, as shown in Figure 14.2. In-depth coverage of all the PING parameters is beyond the scope of this book, but you can refer to a book on TCP/IP for more information. Figure 14.2 also shows a PING command line that can be used to check a host's availability using its IP address and resolving this IP address to a hostname (using the -a parameter).

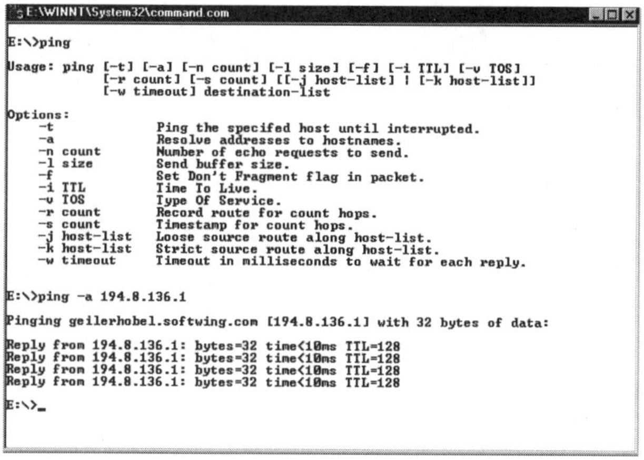

Figure 14.2.
Viewing parameters first, you then issue a PING command with hostname resolution enabled.

14.2.2. TRACERT

TRACERT is another important tool for testing connectivity in an internetwork. TRACERT, which is short for "trace route," essentially lets you PING every gateway device between yourself and a destination IP address. TRACERT comes in handy when you have connectivity on your local network but not to a remote one. By showing you which devices don't respond, it helps you nail down the point of failure in an internetworking issue. Another neat feature of TRACERT is that you can use it to diagnose communications slowdowns, because it lists the amount of time required to receive responses from each gateway device (larger numbers indicate slower links). Figure 14.3 shows sample output generated by TRACERT during tracing for host www.kiva.net. (Note that this route will differ when you perform the TRACERT command from your computer.)

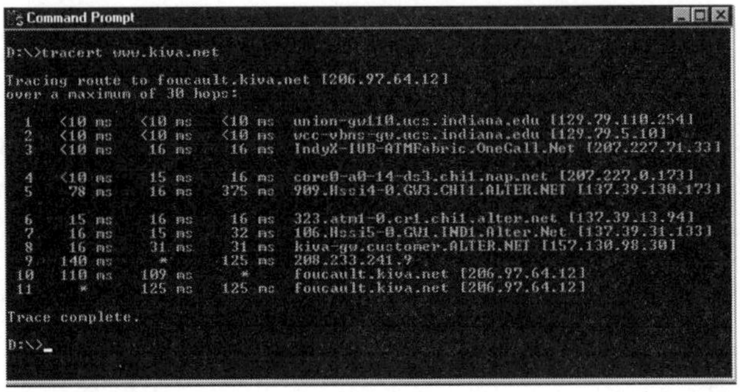

Figure 14.3.

Using TRACERT to identify the route that data packets take from your computer to a remote host.

14.2.3. NSLOOKUP

Usually, the lookup of IP addresses for host names is performed automatically by programs such as Internet Explorer using a DNS server. For example, if you enter www.microsoft.com in the address edit field in Internet Explorer, IE will ask the DNS server for the IP address for www.microsoft.com so that it can contact the Web server. (Note that host names are used for humans; computers use only IP addresses.)

If this lookup doesn't work, you receive an error stating that no entry could be found for the given hostname. In this case, you need the NSLOOKUP tool, which lets you query a DNS nameserver manually. This can be either your local (default) server or any other server. You can perform lookups based on IP addresses (which will return the canonical name or names associated with that address, if any) or based on canonical names (which returns IP addresses). This allows you to diagnose the status of the DNS without having to administer the appropriate DNS server.

14.2.4. IPCONFIG

IPCONFIG gives you a handy shortcut for checking the configuration of your TCP/IP stack, whether configured manually or via Dynamic Host Configuration Protocol (DHCP). In addition to letting you view IP configuration, IPCONFIG also lets you release and renew IP address leases with the DHCP server on computers that use DHCP for IP address and IP configuration assignment. To view the current IP settings on a computer, issue the `IPCONFIG /ALL` command, as shown in Figure 14.4.

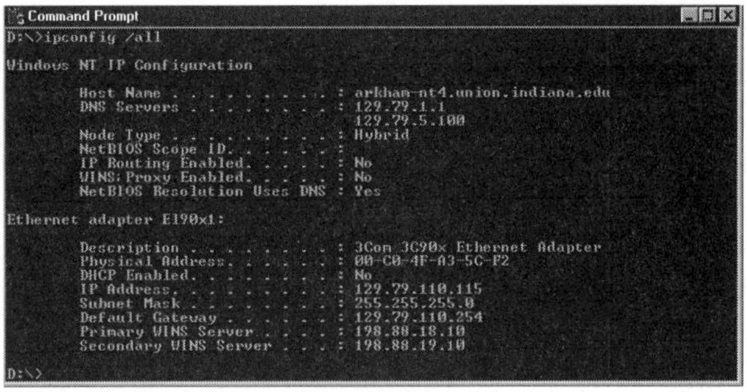

Figure 14.4.
Executing `IPCONFIG /all` *lets you verify the configuration of your TCP/IP stack.*

14.2.5. NETSTAT

NETSTAT is used to display protocol statistics and TCP/IP connections in general. You can use it to display detailed statistics for TCP (Transmission Control Protocol), UDP (User Datagram Protocol), ICMP (Internet Control Message Protocol), and IP (Internet Protocol), as well as summary statistics for all together. In addition to all that, it also lets you verify which ports on your system are listening and lets you examine the status of currently established TCP connections.

There are parameters for NETSTAT that allow you to filter for protocols and control the display of results. For example, in Figure 14.5, `NETSTAT /?` is used to display a short help screen. Again, it is beyond the scope of this book to go in-depth with all the parameters. However, Figure 14.5 shows a command line you can use to view TCP connections in an abbreviated way (`NETSTAT -n -p TCP`).

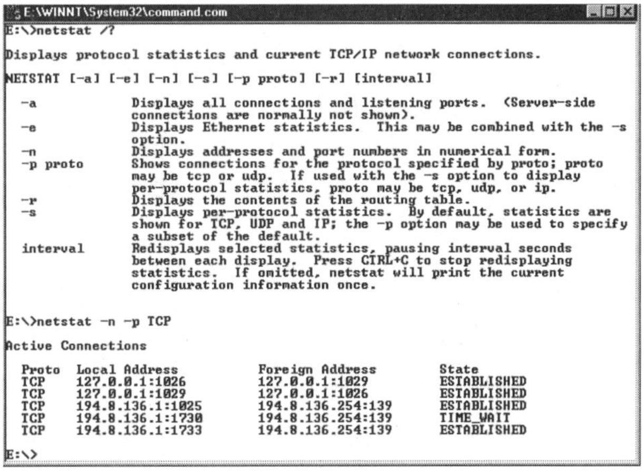

Figure 14.5.
First view NETSTAT parameters, and then execute NETSTAT to show the results in numerical form for the TCP protocol.

14.2.6. ARP

The ARP tool allows you to view, modify, and clear the cache of IP-address-to-MAC-address entries determined by the ARP (Address Resolution Protocol). Sometimes, when IP addresses are switched from machine to machine, the information in your local ARP cache can become inaccurate, preventing proper IP connectivity. ARP lets you determine if the ARP cache entries are, in fact, corrupt, and clear the cache if necessary.

By default, if you run the ARP command without parameters, as shown in the upper part of Figure 14.6, a help screen is displayed. If you want to view the current ARP entries in the cache, issue the command arp -a, as shown in the lower part of Figure 14.6.

Figure 14.6.

First view ARP parameters, and then execute ARP -a *to view current ARP entries.*

```
E:\>arp
Displays and modifies the IP-to-Physical address translation tables used by
address resolution protocol (ARP).

ARP -s inet_addr eth_addr [if_addr]
ARP -d inet_addr [if_addr]
ARP -a [inet_addr] [-N if_addr]

  -a            Displays current ARP entries by interrogating the current
                protocol data. If inet_addr is specified, the IP and Physical
                addresses for only the specified computer are displayed. If
                more than one network interface uses ARP, entries for each ARP
                table are displayed.
  -g            Same as -a.
  inet_addr     Specifies an internet address.
  -N if_addr    Displays the ARP entries for the network interface specified
                by if_addr.
  -d            Deletes the host specified by inet_addr.
  -s            Adds the host and associates the Internet address inet_addr
                with the Physical address eth_addr. The Physical address is
                given as 6 hexadecimal bytes separated by hyphens. The entry
                is permanent.
  eth_addr      Specifies a physical address.
  if_addr       If present, this specifies the Internet address of the
                interface whose address translation table should be modified.
                If not present, the first applicable interface will be used.

E:\>arp -a

Interface: 194.8.136.1 on Interface 2
  Internet Address      Physical Address      Type
  194.8.136.254         00-a0-24-29-f5-16     dynamic

E:\>_
```

14.2.7. TCP/IP Troubleshooting Methodology

When a problem appears while you're attempting to connect to an IIS server (or any TCP/IP host, for that matter), a methodical approach can generally isolate the problem or at least help you rule out TCP/IP connectivity problems.

> **Test Tip**
>
> How can you tell whether a problem is a connectivity problem or something entirely different? Normally you have a TCP/IP connectivity problem if you can't connect to the desired TCP/IP host at all. However, if you can connect but you receive error messages from the server or see unexpected behavior, it's less likely to be a connectivity issue. This doesn't mean that the problem isn't caused by misconfigured networking information; it just means that standard, basic TCP/IP connectivity is probably working okay.

Begin by troubleshooting basic connectivity using PING. If you can't connect to the remote system by name but can by IP address, you know that name resolution has somehow failed. Double-check that the IIS server is functioning properly by testing a Web page or FTP site via the appropriate clients, using an IP address rather than a name. You can then use NSLOOKUP to determine whether the problem is merely misconfiguration of the DNS server.

However, if you can't connect either by IP address or domain name, the problem might be an actual connectivity failure of some sort. PING the localhost address to see if IP works at all on your local workstation. TRACERT between the client and server to see if there's a network failure along the route to the destination system. Use IPCONFIG to check the configuration of your local IP stack and verify that it's configured properly.

14.3. Troubleshooting the IIS Installation Process

One of the first places in which you can have problems with an Internet Information Server installation is during the installation procedure itself. Normally, an IIS installation should go smoothly and seamlessly (but slowly, particularly if you're installing the Option Pack over the Internet). However, the IIS installation program can often run into trouble because of two things:

- Improper configuration of rights or access permissions on the destination server prevents Setup from installing files or making configuration changes.
- More commonly, Setup can't install files or modify server configuration due to files being in use.

The first problem is quite rare, particularly if you have administrative rights on the system to which you're installing the Option Pack.

> **Test Tip** Always make sure you have administrative rights on the system to which you're installing the NT Option Pack. It's terribly difficult to properly install it otherwise.

The second problem is much more likely, particularly if you have previous versions of Internet Information Server running, or applications are running that utilize services that IIS needs to modify (such as applications that use the services of ODBC).

Make certain that any previous installations of IIS are removed (if they're beta versions of IIS) or that their services are stopped (with production versions of IIS) in order to prevent these problems. If you still receive an error message during installation, you can resolve the situation by closing applications or stopping services that are accessing the file in question. For instance, if you receive a message that ODBC files can't be installed, stop the SQL Executive service and retry installing the file.

14.4. IIS Security Problems

One of the most common areas of difficulty that plagues IIS administrators is dealing with security. Although the integration of IIS with Windows NT's standard security model makes its security features both powerful and flexible, it also makes IIS's security rather complex. If you're not entirely familiar with the interactions and interdependencies between IIS and Windows NT's security, it's not unlikely that you'll stumble around a bit trying to get things to work properly at first.

The next sections explore the most common security problems administrators run into.

14.4.1. Problems with Anonymous Access

This is a simple problem that many first-time IIS administrators (particularly those who haven't read the documentation) run into. They don't understand the interaction between the anonymous user context (`IUSR_machinename`) and anonymous access. They often assume that anonymous users have to log in using that username and password, they don't give the anonymous user sufficient rights to connect and access resources, or they give the anonymous user more control than they intended.

Remember that the `IUSR_machinename` account only provides a *context* for anonymous HTTP and FTP access. In other words, anonymous clients connect as normal (using the username ANONYMOUS via FTP, or without logging in at all via HTTP), but their accesses are represented via the context of the `IUSR_machinename` account. Any attempt to access files will be verified against the rights granted to `IUSR_machinename`. Be sure to provide that user with only the minimum required rights in order to reduce the risk of unauthorized access.

14.4.2. Users Can't Access Resources

There are often problems with users not being able to access resources they should have access to (including anonymous users). This is also a common IIS security problem, arising from misconfiguration of the various layers of security that protect your IIS installation. In order to perform the requested task via IIS, a remote user (whether in the anonymous context or that of a specific user) must pass the following tests:

- Is the requested authentication mechanism supported? For example, in order for anonymous access to work at all, the site must allow anonymous connections.

- Did the user authenticate properly? For anonymous access, this isn't a concern. However, users authenticating with clear-text (Basic) authentication or NTLM authentication must have their usernames and passwords authenticated by the Windows NT Security Accounts Manager.

- Does the directory of the site in question allow the requested type of access? For remote users, IIS lets you restrict or give permission to read, write, and execute at the site level, as shown in Figure 14.7. In addition, child directories might have different read and write permissions.

Figure 14.7.

IIS lets you restrict users to reading, writing, or executing files at the site level.

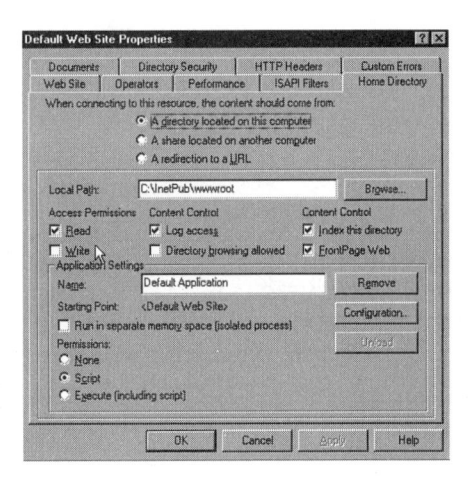

- Does the user have the required Internet access at the file or directory level? When IIS has been installed, the Properties dialog for files and directories in Windows NT Explorer receives the additional ability to set access rights over IIS, as shown in Figure 14.8.

Figure 14.8.

IIS also allows Internet access to be secured at the file or directory level.

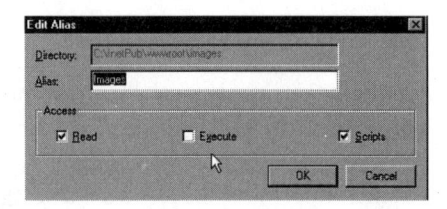

- Does the user have the required file system access at the file or directory level? The final stage of security checking occurs when IIS attempts to perform the requested action to a file or directory on an NTFS file system. The file system operation is authenticated by the Windows NT SAM using standard ACLs and NTFS permission attributes. Even if the user has permission via IIS and the Internet properties to access the file, access can still be prevented if the user has insufficient NTFS file or directory rights to perform the requested action.

Figure 14.9 illustrates the interactions between these various security mechanisms.

Figure 14.9.

A requested operation must run the gauntlet of several security layers before being granted access.

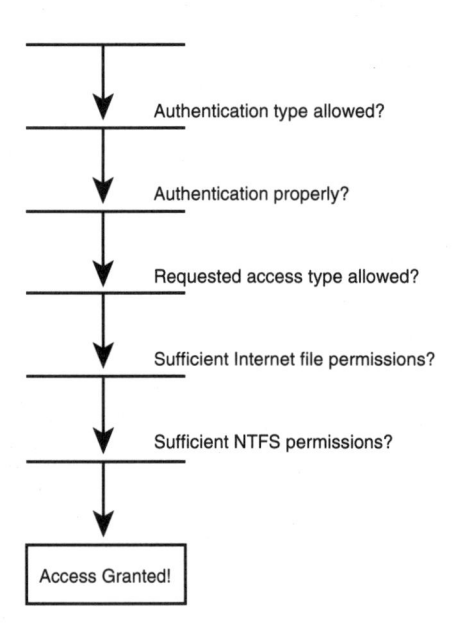

Authentication type allowed?

Authentication properly?

Requested access type allowed?

Sufficient Internet file permissions?

Sufficient NTFS permissions?

Access Granted!

You can think of these interactions as a series of cascading funnels. The only accesses available via IIS are those that are not restricted by any layer of the security process. If any one of the layers rejects the request, the entire request fails. In addition, each layer defines the *highest possible level of access available via that layer;* it doesn't guarantee that access will be provided.

14.4. IIS Security Problems

For instance, if a client is allowed to authenticate to IIS and is given the ability to perform any type of access via IIS, those requests will still be denied if the user's context doesn't have sufficient file system rights. As a consequence, a user who has no restrictions on his file system rights can't perform any actions via IIS that are limited at a higher level by IIS itself.

If users don't have appropriate access to a given resource, the server will return a 403 (Forbidden) error to the Web browser. This error code is subdivided into more-specific error codes. These are described in Table 14.1.

Table 14.1. The different 403 (Forbidden) errors.

Error	Description
403.1 Forbidden: Execute Access Forbidden	This error can be caused if a user tries to execute a CGI, ISAPI, or other executable program from a directory that does not allow programs to be executed.
403.2 Forbidden: Read Access Forbidden	This error can be caused if no default page is available and directory browsing has not been enabled for the directory, or if a user is trying to display an HTML page that resides in a directory marked for Execute or Script permissions only.
403.3 Forbidden: Write Access Forbidden	This error can be caused if a user attempts to upload to, or modify a file in, a directory that does not allow Write access.
403.4 Forbidden: SSL required	This error indicates that the page a user is trying to access is secured with Secure Sockets Layer (SSL). In order to view it, the user needs to enable SSL by typing https:// at the beginning of the address.
403.5 Forbidden: SSL 128 required	This error indicates that the resource a user is trying to access is secured with a 128-bit version of Secure Sockets Layer (SSL). In order to view this resource, the user needs to obtain a browser that supports this level of SSL.
403.6 Forbidden: IP address rejected	This error is caused when the server has a list of IP addresses that are not allowed to access the site, and the IP address the user is using is in this list.

continues

Table 14.1. continued

Error	Description
403.7 Forbidden: Client certificate required	This error occurs when the resource a user is attempting to access requires the browser to have a client Secure Sockets Layer (SSL) certificate that the server recognizes.
403.8 Forbidden: Site access denied	This error can be caused if the Web server is not servicing requests or if the user doesn't have permission to connect to the site.
403.9 Access Forbidden: Too many users are connected	This error can be caused if the Web server is busy and can't process a user's request due to heavy traffic.
403.10 Access Forbidden: Invalid Configuration	This error indicates a more general configuration problem on the Web server.
403.11 Access Forbidden: Password Change	This error can be caused if the user enters the wrong password during authentication.
403.12 Access Forbidden: Mapper Denied Access	The client certificate map for the user has been denied access to this Web site.
403.14 Forbidden: Directory Listing Denied	This error can be caused when directory browsing is disabled and there is no default document in the current directory.

14.4.3. Anonymous Users Have the Same Rights as Local or Domain Users

By installation default, the IUSR_*machinename* anonymous account is placed in the USERS or DOMAIN USERS group (depending on whether you installed on a stand-alone server or a domain controller). This results in a security problem when you want to provide public and private information on your Web server, because most often the local USERS or DOMAIN USERS group is used to provide a simple mechanism for configuring access to secured resources to authenticated users.

If you still want to do this, in order to secure content by using these groups, you need to remove that anonymous user from the appropriate groups using User Manager.

> **Test Tip**
>
> If you need to remove the anonymous user from USERS or DOMAIN USERS, make sure you give that account the Log On Locally user right in User Manager. If you don't, anonymous user accesses will be denied by the Windows NT Security Accounts Manager. If the attempt is made via HTTP, the server will return an error code of 500 (Logon failure: the user has not been granted the requested logon type at this computer). FTP users will simply receive the logon failure message.

14.4.4. Applications Do Not Execute Properly

In order for remote clients to utilize an application installed on your IIS server, those clients' authentication contexts need only be granted the Execute right to the appropriate files. If they are granted Read rather than Execute permission, the client will attempt to download the application, and the application will not be executed by the server. This can also happen if the Read right is given in addition to Execute.

If users are receiving 403 errors when attempting to access pages containing applications, make certain that the required user context has Execute rights to those applications. Do not grant them Read or Write rights, however.

14.4.5. Access to Remote Content Directories Is Denied

When you are adding virtual directories to your site, where the actual content is located on remote servers, you need to supply a user account for that remote resource to access it. The IIS server must be provided with a username and password that have the desired rights on that remote resource. If that username and password are not given, or are given incorrectly, or that user doesn't have sufficient share-level or file system-level rights to the resource, an "Access Denied" error will appear when configuring the remote content directory for a particular IIS site.

> **Test Tip**
>
> When you enter the username for the remote content directory, be sure to use the following syntax:
>
> `domain or computer name\username`
>
> In *domain or computer name*, put in the name of the domain or computer that contains the user. For example, to use the user BOB on server RAIDEN, you would enter
>
> `RAIDEN\BOB`
>
> For the user FRANK in domain BLAH, however, you would use
>
> `BLAH\FRANK`

14.5. Troubleshooting Database Access Problems

Many of the services commonly provided by Internet/intranet servers involve interacting with databases of information. Whether providing a Web-hosted front-end to a corporate database, storing customer transaction data in an orders database, or using a database for another purpose entirely, it's critical that you be able to troubleshoot the common problems that crop up when integrating IIS with back-end database applications. The next sections explore some of the most common problems.

14.5.1. The Browser Client Receives a 502 (Bad Gateway) Error

This error is generated by IIS when the Internet Database Connector can't properly connect to a remote data source. It's usually caused by using a data source name that doesn't exist in the .IDC file. You can resolve this problem by verifying that the DSN supplied in the .IDC actually exists and is mapped to a working ODBC driver. You can verify ODBC datasources and settings in the ODBC applet, which can be launched from Control Panel.

14.5.2. An Attempt to Access SQL Server Results in a `Not defined as a valid user of a trusted SQL Server Connection` Response

When Internet Information Server attempts to perform a specified query against a SQL Server running on a remote system that is using either integrated or mixed security, it must attempt to authenticate to that system when connecting. If a username and password are not provided in the .IDC file, and you're using NTLM authentication, IIS will not pass the client's username and password on to the SQL Server. Instead, it will pass blank data to the SQL Server. This will result in a logon failure.

In order to work around this problem, you need to either install SQL Server on the same system as IIS or use Basic (clear-text) authentication so that IIS can pass the username and password on to SQL Server.

14.5.3. Insufficient Connections on SQL Server

If clients receive error messages stating that the SQL Server is busy or out of connections (`Pipe busy`, `Connection is busy`, `Time-out expired`), you need to increase the number of maximum open connections to SQL Server in the SQL Server's configuration (see Figure 14.10).

Figure 14.10.
Change the user connections to allow for more concurrent connections to SQL Server.

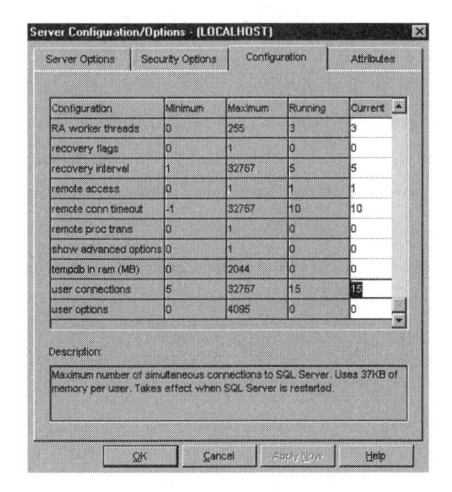

14.5.4. IIS Is Unable to Log to the Remote SQL Server Database

If you're attempting to save logging information to a SQL Server database that is configured to use integrated security, the SQL Server will ignore the username and password configured in the Logging parameters for IIS, and the logging attempts will probably fail. To avoid this problem, be sure to always use mixed security on the logging destination SQL Server.

14.6. Troubleshooting Index Server Query Problems

Microsoft Index Server is a powerful tool for generating searchable indexes of Web content. Although Index Server can be left alone most of the time, some problems still might crop up from time to time. The next sections look at some of the most common problems that come up with Index Server queries.

14.6.1. Queries Don't Return Documents That Exist and Match Criteria

There are a number of reasons why Index Server might not return a document from a query, even if that document exists and matches the query criteria:

- If large amounts of indexed content are being modified, or the server is simply busy for other reasons, there can be a delay between when documents are modified and when they are indexed. If the number of pending pages to be filtered (available through Performance Monitor or an administrative Index Server query) is greater than zero, the document might not have been filtered yet. In addition, if an error occurred during the filtering process, the document might not have been filtered. To determine if this is the case, check the Event Log on the system running Index Server, or run an administrative query.

- If a document meets the query criteria, but the requesting client user doesn't have sufficient permission to read that file, it will not be returned from a query. Check the security for the document and rerun the query.

- Index Server can be configured to restrict the amount of CPU time that can be devoted to a single query, and queries can also be configured (using the `CiForceUseCi` parameter in the .IDQ file) to prevent queries of a certain complexity level. If the specified query is too complex or takes too much CPU time to complete, Index Server will not return documents and might return a `Query too expensive` error message. To determine if this is the case, run an administrative query.

- If a document was filtered using one locale, and the query was issued using a different locale (via the `CiLocale` parameter in the .IDQ file, the default locale of the IIS server, or the locale of the requesting browser), the document might not be returned by the query.

14.6.2. Queries Return Documents from Unwanted Directories

Often you might not want to have certain directories in a site indexed, or (more likely) you don't want to have documents from other sites on the same server returned by a query. You can prevent directories from being indexed entirely by clearing the Index this directory check box on the directory's properties sheet, as shown in Figure 14.11.

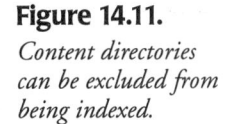

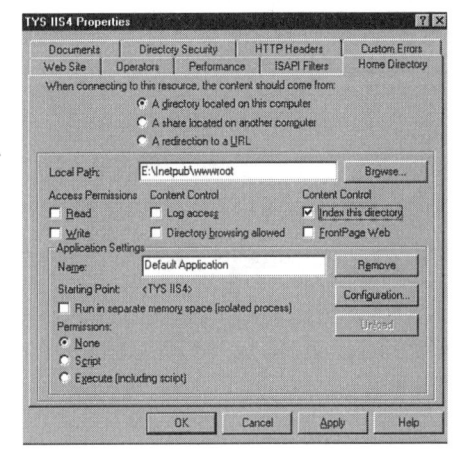

Figure 14.11.
Content directories can be excluded from being indexed.

You can also use query restrictions (with the `CiRestriction` parameter in a query's .IDQ file) to prevent queries from returning data from specific subdirectories or remote site scopes.

14.6.3. Queries Aren't Returning Documents from Remote Virtual Directory Roots

Index Server will not index documents on remote virtual roots if you don't give it a valid user account for the remote directory. When adding directories to the index, use the following syntax to specify the user account:

```
<domain or computer name>\<username>
```

You can specify this information in Index Server Manager for each remote directory you want to index. Figure 14.12 shows you how.

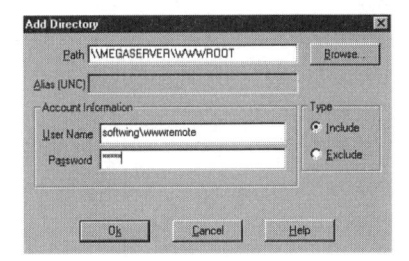

Figure 14.12.
Specifying user account information for a remote directory to be indexed.

14.7. Troubleshooting Host Headers

Internet Information Server uses HTTP 1.1 Host Headers as a way to provide multiple site names on one IP address. A couple of potential problems can crop up with Host Headers. (You can find more information on using Host Headers for your Web sites in Day 4, "The WWW Service.")

14.7.1. Older Web Browsers Don't Support Host Header Names

Due to the relatively recent nature of the HTTP 1.1 Host Header specification, many older browsers don't support Host Header functionality. This prevents those browsers from being able to reach sites on your server that rely on that functionality.

You can implement a workaround for older browsers using Active Server Pages, which uses cookies stored on the remote browser to determine which local host is being requested. For more information on this workaround, check the IIS documentation, under the topic "Supporting Host Header Names in Older Browsers."

14.7.2. Host Header Names Can't Be Resolved

Even though you don't have to have individual IP addresses for each host name when you use Host Header names to identify Web sites, the client must still be able to resolve the host name to the server's IP address. In order for the name resolution to be successful, you (or your DNS administrator) must ensure that the host name entries are mapped to the appropriate IP address.

> **Test Tip:** One important distinction to make is that RAS on Windows NT Server allows for 256 simultaneous dial-in connections, but Windows NT Workstation allows for only one dial-in connection at a time.

Lab

This lab consists of review questions pertaining to this chapter and provides an opportunity for you to use walk-through exercises to apply the knowledge that you've gained.

Questions

1. During an installation of the NT Option Pack on a Windows NT Server, you receive the following message:

```
Cannot install file c:\winnt\system32\odbc32.dll. It might be in use.
Close all applications and click Retry. Click Ignore if you want to skip this
file.
```

    How can you resolve this problem? (Select the best answer.)

    A. Go ahead and click Ignore; this isn't a serious problem.

    B. Cancel the installation, reboot the server, and start the installation over.

    C. Make sure Microsoft Access isn't running, and then click Retry.

    D. Go to the command prompt and type `net stop "SQL Executive"`. When the service has successfully stopped, go back to the NT Option Pack installation and click Retry.

2. One of your customers walks into your office and says his Web browser can't connect to \\KANO, the departmental intranet server. You go to his workstation, and you see that his Web browser is giving him the error `Could not find server: KANO`. What is the problem? (Select the best answer.)

    A. KANO has initiated a broadcast storm that is preventing browser clients from locating it.

    B. Anti-Microsoft hackers have attacked your network and successfully committed a denial-of-service attack on your IIS server.

    C. The workstation can't resolve the name KANO to an IP address.

    D. All of the above

3. Siobhan is in the machine room working on \\KANO. She receives a phone call telling her that the department's manager can't communicate with \\KANO, which isn't responding to PINGs from his workstation. She can see that KANO is up, and since she's downloading files from Microsoft's FTP site, she knows that its network connectivity is good as well. Which of the following steps would be the most appropriate to localize the problem?

A. Use TRACERT to trace the network path between \\KANO and her boss's workstation.

B. Use PING to see if her boss's workstation is alive.

C. Fire up a protocol analyzer and watch traffic patterns on the network.

D. Get out a network media tester to examine the integrity of KANO's connection.

4. Siobhan now receives a call informing her that clients can connect to BRUCE, another IIS server, via IP address but not via host name. The DNS server is alive and functioning. The problem is affecting multiple workstations, which have no trouble resolving other names. What's the best way for her to isolate this problem?

A. PING the DNS server with increasingly larger packet sizes.

B. See if individual workstations are configured properly to connect to the DNS server.

C. Go to BRUCE and run IPCONFIG to determine if its IP stack is configured properly.

D. Use NSLOOKUP to see if BRUCE's entries in the DNS server are configured properly.

5. Your company's IIS server uses Microsoft Index Server to allow customers to search the contents of the site. However, one of your customers has noticed that Index Server is not returning a document that's frequently updated by an ISAPI application. What is the most likely cause of this problem?

A. Index Server never completes the filtering process for the document, because the document is continuously being updated before Index Server has a chance to filter it.

B. Index Server has been configured to ignore the document.

C. Index Server was improperly installed.

D. The document contains only noise words and therefore is not being included in the indices.

6. By observing the access logs on your IIS server named \\CORPIIS, you notice that anonymous clients are accessing files that are intended only for the use of authenticated domain users on your system. What is the most likely cause of this problem?

A. Someone has hacked your domain's security.

B. The IUSR_CORPIIS user has not been removed from the DOMAIN USERS group.

C. IUSR_CORPIIS has been specifically granted NTFS rights to the requested files.

7. You install IIS on a Windows NT server named \\HIGHLANDER. You find that user CMCLEOD can't access files to which you had thought you had granted him access. At which potential points might the security be configured incorrectly? (Choose all correct answers.)

   A. General IIS access rights to the site

   B. IIS access rights to the files themselves

   C. NTFS access rights to the files themselves

   D. NT SAM rights to the site subdirectories

8. Clients are having trouble connecting to one of the Host Header names for a virtual site on your server. You believe the problem is due to a name resolution failure on the client side. The site needs to be accessible to clients across the Internet. How can you make sure the name resolution works properly? (Choose all correct answers.)

   A. Make certain that the mapping of the server's IP address to the Host Header name is in the HOSTS file on each client system.

   B. Make certain that the mapping of the server's IP address to the Host Header name is in your DNS server's tables and that your DNS server is configured properly to participate in Internet DNS queries.

   C. There's nothing you can do to resolve this problem.

   D. Use DHCP to distribute the IP address across the Internet.

9. You're trying to use a script on your IIS server that uses IDC to execute a query against an Oracle database. When you run the query, however, you receive a 502 error. What does this indicate? (Choose all correct answers.)

   A. You're using the wrong ODBC driver for the Oracle DSN.

   B. The DSN referenced in the .IDC file does not exist.

   C. The DSN referenced in the .IDC file is misconfigured.

   D. You can't use Oracle databases for these tasks.

10. Your FTP site has a virtual directory that is connected to a remote share. Users can't access that directory. What is the most likely cause?

    A. The users don't have sufficient rights to access the resources in the virtual directory.

    B. You can't connect FTP virtual directories to remote shares.

    C. The network security account is misconfigured.

    D. To access resources on remote shares, you need to enable NTLM authentication, because otherwise, passwords can't be passed on.

Answers to Questions

1. **D.** You need to stop services that have open ODBC connections in order to allow IIS to properly update the ODBC DLL. You don't want to ignore this problem, because IIS relies on ODBC to perform most forms of database access. You don't need to start the installation over, and the problem is caused by the SQL Executive itself, not Microsoft Access.

2. **C.** The workstation can't resolve the canonical name KANO to an IP address, so the Web browser can't establish communication with the server. A broadcast storm would not cause these specific symptoms—nor would a denial-of-service attack (unless it was on your DNS server).

3. **A** Using TRACERT will allow Siobhan to better pinpoint where the network failure is occurring, since it obviously isn't at KANO's network connection. PING won't do any good, because you won't know if it's the boss's workstation or an intermediate connection that's down. A protocol analyzer won't give you any information on this problem, because it's probably an outage, and a network media tester won't diagnose problems on remote networks.

4. **D.** You know that other workstations are using DNS just fine, so option B is unnecessary, and since the problem is name resolution, a misconfigured network stack on BRUCE won't be the cause. PINGing the DNS server won't do any good, because you know it's up. NSLOOKUP will let you determine exactly what's going on with BRUCE's records.

5. **A.** Since the document is being updated frequently, Index Server never gets to complete the indexing process for it. It's unlikely that a document would contain only noise words. An improper installation would cause much more significant symptoms than this. It's far more likely that the filtering process is simply never taking place than it is that Index Server is ignoring the document.

6. **B.** If the anonymous context user is not removed from DOMAIN USERS, any rights granted to that group will apply to it as well.
7. **A, B, C.** IIS uses its own site-level security, its file-level security, and the NTFS file permissions supported by Windows NT to secure files. Option D is nonsense.
8. **B.** Make certain that the Host Header name is listed in DNS, because this will allow any client supporting Host Headers across the Internet to resolve the name. DHCP isn't used for this purpose, and it's impractical to configure the HOSTS file for all your potential Internet clients.
9. **A, B, C.** The 502 (Bad Gateway) error indicates a problem with ODBC connectivity, caused either by an incorrect DSN reference, a DSN that's misconfigured, or a problem with the DSN's ODBC driver. D is incorrect.
10. **C.** Access permissions on remote shares are controlled by the network security account only. Logged-on users' credentials are not used to verify resource access. Therefore, if the network security account is misconfigured, users can't access resources on the remote share.

Exercises

Exercise 14.1.: Resolving Access Problems on Remote Virtual Directories

This exercise addresses the following Microsoft exam objectives:

- Resolve resource access problems
- Resolve WWW service problems
- Resolve FTP service problems
- Resolve security problems

One of the most common access problems that is closely related to a security problem is the inability of users to access resources that are located on a remote share that is accessed via a virtual directory.

In this exercise you will resolve the problem of misconfigured security credentials for network directories using Internet Service Manager. This exercise applies to both Web and FTP sites, although the figures show the issues resolved for a Web site.

1. Open Internet Service Manager. Open the directory tree for the site where the directory is located that users can't access. When there is a misconfiguration of the security credentials, the directory will have a stop sign, as shown in Figure 14.13.

Figure 14.13.
You can easily identify misconfigured security for remote virtual directories by the stop sign that is shown for that directory.

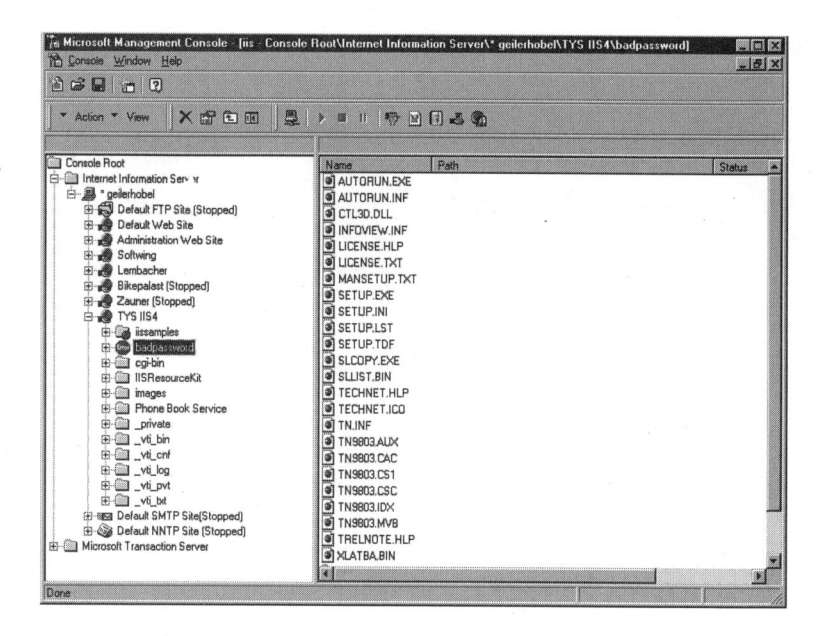

2. Open the Properties dialog box. You will see the share name that this virtual directory is connected to. To view the security account assigned to access that resource, click the Connect As button.

3. Verify that the account is valid (using User Manager) and that it is granted access to the remote share (using Windows NT Explorer). If the account is incorrect, you can browse for a new one, as shown in Figure 14.14.

Figure 14.14.
Change the user account that is used to access the remote resources.

4. You can't verify the password (only asterisks are displayed). When you are sure that the username is correct and has sufficient rights, reenter the password. On exiting the Network Directory Security Credentials dialog box, verify the new password. There is no automatic password synchronization for these security credentials.

5. Close the Properties dialog box. If you have supplied a valid security account, the stop sign should have disappeared. The user can now access resources on the remote share.

Exercise 14.2.: Resolving Host Header Problems

This exercise addresses the following Microsoft exam objectives:

- Resolve WWW service problems
- Choose an implementation strategy for an Internet site or an intranet site for stand-alone servers, single-domain environments, and multiple-domain environments

In this exercise, you will resolve the most common problems related to host headers. The assumption is that your IIS server has two sites configured using host headers, www.mygirl.nom and www.echt.org. Your server has only one IP address (192.168.1.100). Clients can connect to www.mygirl.nom but can't connect to www.echt.org.

1. Open a command prompt window. PING your server's IP address to check that it is up and running.

2. PING www.mygirl.nom. This should work as people receive content from that site. The host name should be resolved to your server's IP address.

3. PING www.echt.org, which users can't seem to connect to. If PING can't resolve the host name to the server's IP address, your DNS server's setup is incorrect, and you need to change it.

4. If step 3 succeeded, you need to check the host name you entered in Internet Service Manager for the www.echt.org site. Open the Properties dialog box for this site, and then open the Advanced Multiple Web Site Identification dialog box. Check the host header you've entered. Most likely, one character is wrong.

5. Make changes to the host header and close the Properties dialog box. The www.echt.org site should now be operational.

Appendix A

Practice Exam

by Gerry High

The following questions are representative of the type and number of questions you will see on the exam. However, since this exam uses Computer Adaptive Testing, the number of questions on the actual exam may vary. The actual exam also includes simulations that imitate the actual product. All simulation questions involve using the Microsoft Management Console (MMC) to perform actual tasks with IIS, so you should be very comfortable in using the MMC.

Questions

1. Which of the following applications is used to manage Internet Information Server 4.0?
    A. User Manager for Domains
    B. Internet Administration Wizard
    C. Internet Service Manager
    D. None of the above

2. What different sources are available for installing the Windows NT Option Pack?
    A. Internet installation from Microsoft's Web site
    B. CD-ROM
    C. Installation from previously downloaded files
    D. Floppy

3. One of your customers would like you to make the same information you're currently serving via HTTP available via Gopher. How would you do this?

    A. You can't. IIS 4 does not support Gopher.
    B. Reinstall IIS 4 and select the Gopher Server option.
    C. From Control Panel, select Add/Remove Programs and choose to add the Gopher Server.
    D. None of the above.

4. Using IIS 4, you're developing a Web site that contains the complete texts of every major work in the English language. What is the easiest way for you to allow customers to search for particular words or phrases in these volumes?

    A. Use Microsoft Index Server.
    B. Generate an index in Microsoft Word.
    C. Write an ISAPI application that indexes the data on your Web server.
    D. None of the above.

5. You would like to ensure that no one can connect to your Web server with a clear-text password. Some of your data is available to anyone, and the rest of it is restricted to company employees. Which authentication methods should you enable?

    A. Basic authentication
    B. Allow anonymous access
    C. Windows NT Challenge/Response authentication
    D. SSL

6. You need to provide multiple Web sites to your customers using one IIS 4 server. You would like to allow each customer to administer his or her own site without being able to modify the other sites. Which feature of IIS 4 enables this functionality?

    A. Web sites
    B. Virtual servers
    C. Internet Service Manager
    D. ISAPI filters

7. Which snap-ins can be installed in an MMC console?

    A. Stand-alone snap-in

    B. Extensible snap-in

    C. Extension snap-in

    D. Console Root snap-in

8. What is the default extension of MMC consoles?

    A. .mmc

    B. .con

    C. .mcs

    D. .msc

9. Where is the metabase.bin file stored by default?

    A. %systemroot%\inetsvr\metabase.bin

    B. %systemroot%\inetsrv\metabase.bin

    C. C:\InetPub\metabase.bin

    D. C:\InetPub\config\metabase.bin

10. You are creating a new console from scratch. You want to be able to administer Web sites and Index Server from this console. Which snap-ins do you need to add to the new console?

    A. Web service snap-in

    B. Index Server snap-in

    C. Internet Information Server snap-in

    D. WWW snap-in

11. At which level(s) can you set MIME mappings?

    A. Web site

    B. Virtual directory

    C. Directory

    D. File

12. Applications can be enabled for which of the following items?

    A. Home directory

    B. Directories

    C. Virtual directories

    D. Redirections

13. Using the redirection feature, where can you redirect users to?
    A. A relative URL
    B. An exact URL
    C. A directory anywhere on your server
    D. Anywhere on the Internet
14. You are creating a new user account, SiteAdmin, that should be able to administer one of your six sites. You put a user in the Administrators and Users group and assign him as an operator to the one site you want him to administer. What will happen?
    A. He will be able to administer only this one site.
    B. He will be able to administer all sites.
    C. He won't be able to administer any site.
    D. He will be able to administer all sites except the one he should be able to administer.
15. Which IP address and domain restrictions can you enforce?
    A. IP address
    B. Any range of IP addresses
    C. Domains
    D. IN-ADDR.ARPA domains
16. You are setting a bandwidth limit on the server with 1.024 KB/s and a bandwidth limit on site TYS IIS45 with 2.512 KB/s. Which limit will be enforced?
    A. Server limit
    B. Site limit
    C. Site limit - Server limit
    D. None of the above
17. You are creating a new Web site for your company. The FTP server doesn't have the content on local hard disks; you need to map it from a remote server. Can you point the home directory of an FTP site to a remote share?
    A. Yes, but you need to change the anonymous account to one that has access permissions on the remote computer.
    B. Yes, but you need to supply the share name.
    C. Yes, but you need to supply the share name and an account that has permission to access that share.
    D. No. You can't map the home directory to a remote share.

18. Which of the following access permissions can be set for both FTP sites and virtual directories on FTP sites?

    A. Read

    B. Write

    C. Execute

    D. Delete

19. You need to change the port number of your FTP site from standard port 21 to 9876. Where do you change this setting?

    A. In the FTP Service Properties dialog box (because port settings are global for all sites).

    B. In the FTP Site Properties dialog box (in the Identification frame).

    C. In the FTP Site Properties dialog box (in the Identification frame). You must also inherit this property to all virtual directories.

    D. This port (9876) can't be used.

20. You want to limit the connections to your department's FTP site to a maximum of 20 concurrent connections. Where do you need to add this setting?

    A. In the Connections edit box in the Performance tab of the FTP site.

    B. In the Limited to edit box of the FTP site tab in the properties dialog box for the site.

    C. In the FTP Service Properties dialog box.

    D. You can't limit connections.

21. What is the filename of annotation files for directories?

    A. ~ftpsvc.ckm

    B. ftpsvc~.ckm

    C. ~ftpsvc~.ckm

    D. ftpsvc.ckm

22. Users are unable to process scripts on your site. Your scripts are stored in a directory called scripts. Your HTML documents are in your WWW root directory. You have allowed read and execute access to your WWW root directory. It still doesn't work. Why?

    A. You must give users execute access to both your WWW root directory and scripts directory.

    B. You must allow script execution permission on your scripts folder, not your WWW root folder.

C. You must give the NTFS permission Full Control.

D. The Anonymous Internet User account must be a member of the script operators group in Windows NT.

23. You want to secure your confidential Web documents residing in a specific directory. You want all users to be denied access—except those from the accounting department. You set the NTFS permission No Access for the Everyone group on these files and give the Accounting group full control. Now no one can access these documents. What should you do to correct the problem?

    A. Set the NTFS permission No Access for every group except the Accounting group. Assign the Accounting group the NTFS permission Full Control.

    B. Remove all users and groups except for the Accounting group from the ACL for the files. Assign the Accounting group Full Control.

    C. Disable the Anonymous Internet user account.

    D. The only thing to do is to restrict access to the directory based on IP address. Tell IIS to deny all users, and then add each member of the accounting department's IP address to the exception list.

24. You want to authenticate users connecting to your IIS-based Intranet Web server. You support a large number of client platforms: Windows 95, NT Workstation, UNIX, and Macintosh. Your manager has assigned you to decide the best method of accomplishing this. The requirements are as follows: You *must* authenticate all users. It would be *desirable* to not allow clear-text passwords to be sent over the network and to keep administrative overhead to a minimum. The proposed solution is to use client-side certificates, authenticate using SSL, and disable the Internet Anonymous User account. How well does this solution meet the requirements?

    A. It meets the required outcome and both desired outcomes.

    B. It meets the required outcome but only one of the desired outcomes.

    C. It meets the required outcome but neither of the desired outcomes.

    D. This solution does not meet the required or desired outcomes.

25. You want to authenticate users connecting to your IIS-based Intranet Web server. You support a large number of client platforms: Windows 95, NT Workstation, UNIX, and Macintosh. Your manager has assigned you to decide the best method of accomplishing this. The requirements are as follows: You *must* authenticate all users so that accesses can be logged. It would be *desirable*

to not allow clear-text passwords to be sent over the network and to keep administrative overhead to a minimum. The proposed solution is to install Internet Explorer on your clients and allow only Windows NT Challenge/Response as an authentication method. How well does this solution meet the requirements?

    A. It meets the required outcome and both desired outcomes.

    B. It meets the required outcome but only one of the desired outcomes.

    C. It meets the required outcome but neither of the desired outcomes.

    D. This solution does not meet the required or desired outcomes.

26. If you specify both IIS permissions and NTFS permissions, which take precedence?

    A. IIS permissions

    B. NTFS permissions

    C. Whichever permissions are most-restrictive

    D. Whichever permissions are least-restrictive

27. How could public-key encryption best be defined?

    A. An encryption algorithm using two keys—one public and one private

    B. A proposed standard for government access to keys

    C. Not currently supported by Microsoft Certificate Server

    D. A mechanism for securing file indexes

28. What feature of the Certificate Server would you use to implement a series of departmental Certificate Servers that all authenticated to a central Certificate Authority?

    A. Key management

    B. Transport independence

    C. Certificate Authority hierarchy

    D. Policy modules

29. Microsoft Certificate Server supports what protocols for certificates and certificate requests?

    A. PKCS #10, X.509 (versions 1.0 and 3.0)

    B. PKCS v4.0, X.509 (versions 1.0 and 3.0)

    C. PICS #10, X.501 (version 4.0)

    D. PKCS, X.905 (versions 1.0 and 3.0)

30. The Microsoft SMTP Service does not support which of the following features?

    A. Internet Mail

    B. Variable queue times

    C. Multiple user mailboxes

    D. Mail drop box

31. Which SMTP Service feature increases delivery reliability by attempting multiple deliveries?

    A. The message Queue directory

    B. The message Drop Box directory

    C. The SMTP Service Smart Host

    D. The Maximum Hop Count

32. You are hosting two separate domains on your NT Server, and you want to receive mail for each. To accomplish this, what would you do?

    A. Configure a mailbox for a local domain delivery.

    B. Configure a smart host for remote delivery.

    C. Configure a mailbox for remote domain delivery.

    D. Configure multiple Fully Qualified Domain Names.

33. Which of the following folders is the SMTP Service equivalent of the "Dead Letter Office"?

    A. Queue

    B. Deadletter

    C. Badmail

    D. DropBox

34. Unsolicited (spam) e-mail can be controlled using what features of the SMTP Service?

    A. SMTP Smart Host

    B. Limit Messages per Connection

    C. Maximum Hop Count

    D. Masquerade Domain

35. News articles are stored using what file extension and in which format?

    A. .nws, plaintext

    B. .txt, plaintext

    C. .nnt, plaintext

    D. .nws, mdb

36. Which of the following would be the correct directory for the newsgroup `rec.hobbies.painting`?

    A. C:\Inetpub\nntpfile\root\rec.hobbies.painting

    B. C:\Inetpub\nntpfile\root\rec\hobbies\painting

    C. //nntp/rec/hobbies/painting

    D. //nntpservice/rec.hobbies.painting

37. You would like to create a newsgroup for your organization, and you want to restrict posts so that they are always related to your product. To do this, you should create what type of newsgroup?

    A. A monitored group

    B. An authorized group

    C. A moderated group

    D. A selected topic group

38. Control messages sent to your NNTP Service can perform all but which of the following administrative functions?

    A. Creating new newsgroups

    B. Authorizing a new user account

    C. Canceling a post to a group

    D. Deleting an existing group

39. The server running NNTP Service has limited disk space, and you want to make sure there is room for new posts. What is the best mechanism for controlling timeliness in conjunction with disk space?

    A. Authorization Access Control

    B. Moderated groups

    C. Message limits

    D. Expire times

40. Your Internet Service Manager doesn't have an item for Index Server. What should you do?

    A. You must add an Index Server snap-in by running the NT Option Pack setup.

    B. You must add Index Server as a stand-alone snap-in to the Internet Service Manager.

    C. You must add Index Server as an extension snap-in to the Web service in the Internet Service Manager.

    D. You can't manage Index server from the Internet Service Manager. You must do it from the HTML administrator.

41. You have recently installed some new filters for different document types. What must you do to activate them?

    A. Stop and restart the Index Server Filter service.

    B. Stop and restart the Content Indexer service.

    C. Force a rescan of the index.

    D. You don't need to do anything.

42. Two users are querying your Web site using the same search terms but are getting different results. What could be causing this?

    A. An error in your .idq file

    B. Too many word lists

    C. A corrupt index

    D. NTFS permissions

43. When running queries, some documents are being returned that are in a directory that you don't want included in the index. What must you do to prevent these documents from being displayed?

    A. Manually add restrictions to your .idq files.

    B. Clear the Index this directory checkbox from the directory properties in the Internet Service Manager.

    C. Add exceptions for these directories from the catalog properties in the Internet Service Manager.

    D. None of the above.

44. The following ASP script:

```
<%
set oConn = Server.CreateObject("ADODB.Connection")
%>
```

generates the following error:

```
Microsoft JScript compilation error '800a03ec'
Expected ';'
/book/js.asp, line 2
set oConn = Server.CreateObject("ADODB.Connection")
```

What is the cause of the error?

A. The default scripting language for the application is set to JScript. You should include the `<@ LANGUAGE=VBScript>` directive in the file.

B. `set` is not a valid VBScript statement. Change `set` to `dim`.

C. You should use `CreateObject`, not `Server.CreateObject`.

D. The statement needs a semicolon at the end to be a valid JScript statement.

45. You have created an ASP page to administer your Web site; the page uses the IISAO. You have placed the file in the default Web directory (\inetpub\wwwroot). However, when you run it, you get the following error:

```
Microsoft JScript runtime error '800a0046'
Permission denied
/admin.asp, line 5
```

What is the cause of the error?

A. IISAO doesn't work in ASP pages. It only works with Windows Scripting Host.

B. The directory needs to be given execute permissions.

C. The directory needs to be given script permissions.

D. To use the IISAO from a Web page, you must be logged in with administrator permissions.

46. You have written the following script to modify the metabase using the IISAO:

```
<%@ LANGUAGE=Jscript %>
<%
var oAdmin;
oAdmin = GetObject("IIS://localhost/W3SVC/1");
oAdmin.ServerComment = Request.querystring("comment");
%>
```

However, you notice that although the script seems to run fine, it doesn't save the changes to the metabase. What is the problem?

A. You must stop and restart the Web service for the changes to take effect.

B. You must stop and restart the site for the changes to take effect.

C. The script is missing a call to the `SetInfo` method on the `IIsWebServer` object.

D. The script is missing a call to the `Commit` method on the `IIsWebServer` object.

47. The following ASP script:

```
<%@ LANGUAGE=JSCRIPT%>
<%
var oConn;
oConn = server.createobject("ADODB.Connection");
%>
```

generates the following error:

```
Microsoft JScript runtime error '800a1391'
'server' is undefined
/book/case.asp, line 4
```

What is the cause of the error?

A. `createobject` is not a method of the server object.

B. `ADODB.Connection` is not a valid Program ID. Use `ADO.Connection`.

C. JScript is case-sensitive. Change `server` to `Server`.

D. The statement needs a `set` added to the start of the line (set oConn = ...).

48. What is Microsoft's recommended data access technology for accessing databases from Web pages?

A. DAO (Data Access Objects)

B. RDO (Remote Data Objects)

C. CGI (Common Gateway Interface)

D. ADO (ActiveX Data Objects)

49. You have been noticing sluggish performance on your Web site. Using Performance Monitor, you have determined that you need to upgrade to a faster Internet connection. Your manager has asked you to make a presentation at the next operations meeting, and you'd like to display your findings in a Microsoft Excel chart. From which view can you export your data to Excel?

A. Chart

B. Log

C. Report

D. All of the above

50. In order to track performance data related to IIS in Performance Monitor, what must you do?

    A. Install an updated version of Performance Monitor from the NT Option Pack.

    B. Install the objects and counters into Performance Monitor.

    C. This is done automatically when you install IIS.

    D. Add the counters as an Internet Service Manager snap-in.

51. Which tools could be used to monitor network utilization levels?

    A. NETSTAT

    B. Internet Service Manager

    C. Performance Monitor

    D. Network Monitor

52. Which hardware subsystem is most likely to affect performance in IIS?

    A. Processor

    B. Network

    C. Memory

    D. Disk

53. What is an acceptable range for the number of page faults per second?

    A. 0 to 5

    B. 0 to 10

    C. 0 to 25

    D. 0 to 50

54. You have been logging date, time, client IP address, user agent, and referrer information to a W3C Extended Log file format. You must convert the log to the NCSA Common Log file format. Which of these fields are supported by the NCSA Common Log File format?

    A. Date, Time

    B. Date, Time, Client IP Address

    C. Date, Time, Client IP Address, User Agent

    D. All fields

55. You are using the W3C Extended Log File format. You notice that your log files are being generated with a time stamp that is six hours ahead of your time zone (CST). What must you configure to cause the W3C logs to be written with times in the CST time zone?

    A. Use the Logging Properties button in the Site Properties dialog to configure the time zone for the format.

    B. Check the time zone setting in Control Panel and correct it.

    C. Use the convlog.exe program to convert the time zone in the W3C format to the CST W3C Extended format.

    D. None of the above. You can't change the W3C Extended Log format to output to any other time zone.

56. You want to use Usage Import and Report Writer to analyze the logs on multiple Web servers in different time zones. You plan on importing the logs into one database. Which is the best log file format to use?

    A. W3C Extended Log File format

    B. NCSA Common Log File format

    C. ODBC Log File format

    D. Microsoft IIS Log File format

57. You want to save your Report Writer reports in different formats. In which formats can you save them?

    A. HTML and Word

    B. HTML, Word, and Excel

    C. HTML and text

    D. HTML only

58. Your users are complaining that your departmental Web server is down. How can you quickly determine if it's responding to network requests?

    A. PING its hostname and/or IP address.

    B. TRACERT to the system's IP address.

    C. Use IPCONFIG.

    D. Use a network protocol analyzer.

59. You want anyone to be able to access your IIS server's Web pages, so you enable anonymous access and grant Read access to anonymous users in the Internet Service Manager. However, users receive "Document forbidden" errors when they try to connect. What is the problem?

A. They're using the wrong anonymous password.

B. Their Web browser doesn't support anonymous access.

C. The files on your server are not set to provide Read access to the `IUSR_computername` user.

D. None of the above.

60. Which right should be given to users who need to be able to run CGI or ISAPI applications on your IIS server?

    A. Read

    B. Write

    C. Execute

    D. Full Control

Answers

1. **C.** The Internet Service Manager is used to manage IIS 4.0. User Manager for Domains is used to create user accounts and so on.

2. **A, B, C.** IIS 4.0 can be installed directly from Microsoft's Web site, from CD-ROM, and from downloaded files.

3. **A.** With the release of IIS 4, Microsoft no longer supports Gopher.

4. **A.** Microsoft Index Server is used to search Web pages and documents on a Web site.

5. **B, C.** Basic authentication transmits passwords in clear text. Anonymous access and Windows NT Challenge/Response authentication do not pass the password in clear-text form. SSL is typically used to encrypt data but is not used to authenticate users.

6. **A.** IIS 4 uses Web sites to distinguish separate Web environments (unlike IIS 3, which used virtual servers for a similar function). Internet Service Manager is the tool used to manage a Web site.

7. **A, C.** Stand-alone and extension snap-ins are available for creating consoles.

8. **D.** The default file extension for consoles is .msc, which is also registered as a shell file type that lets you open consoles by double-clicking the .msc file.

9. **B.** By installation default, the metabase.bin file is located under %systemroot%\inetsrv\. You can change this location by setting the Registry value `HKEY_LOCAL_MACHINE\SOFTWARE\Microsoft\InetMgr\Parameters\MetaDataFile`.

10. **B, C.** To administer WWW, FTP, and Index Server, you need the Internet Information Server snap-in and the Index Server snap-in.

11. **A, B, C, D.** MIME mappings can be defined at all levels, from server level to file level. Directory level includes "normal" directories as well as virtual directories.

12. **A, B, C.** With the exception of files and redirections, you can create applications for all directories.

13. **A, B, C, D.** All answers are correct, because a relative redirection occurs when you don't check the Exact URL checkbox on the Home directory tab. You can redirect users anywhere on your server or on the Internet.

14. **B.** The user can do this because he is a member of the Administrators group, and the Administrators group by default is allowed to administer all sites.

15. **A, C.** You can restrict access to a site to specific IP addresses, groups of IP addresses, and domains. The definition for groups means limiting to specific subnets, not to any range you can think of. The IN-ADDR.ARPA domains can't be used because they provide IP address-to-domain mapping.

16. **B.** The site limit always overrides the server limit.

17. **C.** You can use a server share as the home directory for your FTP site. However, you need to supply a valid NT account for that machine (username/password).

18. **A, B.** You can set only Read and Write permissions for directories of your FTP site. If you need more control, you have to set NTFS permissions in your FTP site's physical directories.

19. **C.** You set the TCP port in the Identification frame.

20. **B.** Connection limits are set in the Limited to edit box.

21. **C.** The valid filename for annotation files is ~ftpsvc~.ckm.

22. **B.** You must allow script execute permission on your scripts directory. Execute permission is not required on the WWW root directory unless it contains scripts.

23. **B.** By removing all other users and groups from the ACL, you will effectively be denying them access. "No access" always take precedence over other permissions you might have set.

24. **B.** This solution meets the required outcome and also meets the desired outcome of not passing clear-text passwords over the network. Because managing certificates for each user creates a lot of administrative overhead, the solution doesn't meet the second desired objective.

25. **A.** Because Internet Explorer supports NT Challenge/Response on any platform, this is the easiest (and cheapest) solution.
26. **C.** IIS will apply whichever permissions are most-restrictive.
27. **A.** Public-key encryption uses two keys, allowing features such as digital signatures and digital envelopes.
28. **C.** Certificate Authority hierarchies allow you to link individual Certificate Servers for scalability, security, and reliability.
29. **A.** The Certificate Server supports PKCS #10 formatted certificate requests and issues X.509 versions 1.0 and 3.0-compatible certificates.
30. **C.** The current version of SMTP Service does not support individual mailboxes based on NT usernames.
31. **A.** The message Queue directory allows the SMTP Service to attempt delivery for a specified period of time to compensate for temporary Internet outages or server downtimes.
32. **C.** You can configure additional mailboxes that are assigned to domain aliases to provide mail delivery for additional locally hosted domains.
33. **C.** The Badmail folder is used by the SMTP Service to store mail that can't be delivered.
34. **B.** Limiting the number of messages per connection to your SMTP Service can help reduce the odds of your host's being used as a spam relay.
35. **A.** News articles are plaintext files with an .nws extension.
36. **B.** The file structure for newsgroups is a series of folders for each hierarchy level, contained within the nntproot directory.
37. **C.** Moderated group posts must be approved by a moderator, so the moderator can keep the group on topic.
38. **B.** Control messages can manipulate group information and posts, but they don't allow access to server administrative features such as account management.
39. **D.** Expire times allow you to purge your NNTP site of messages that are no longer relevant, freeing up space for new articles.
40. **B.** You must add it as a stand-alone snap-in.
41. **C.** You must force a rescan of the index so that Index Server will rescan all your directories for these new file types.

42. **D.** Index Server will always verify the ACL for a document before including it in the query results so that users can't see documents that they don't have permission to access.

43. **B.** You must clear the Index this directory checkbox from the directory properties in the MMC.

44. **A.** The script is valid VBScript, so you need to add a `LANGUAGE` directive. B is incorrect because `set` is a valid VBScript statement. C is also incorrect because you should use `Server.CreateObject` to create any objects so that IIS can track which objects have been created. D is only partially correct. The `set =` portion of the statement would also need to be removed to make it a valid JScript statement.

45. **D.** For security reasons, the IISAO requires an administrator account. The default Web directory is set up for anonymous access, not administrator access. A is incorrect because IISAO works with both ASP and WSH. Both B and C are incorrect because the script is executing.

46. **C.** C is correct because the `SetInfo` method is used to commit changes to the metabase. Both A and B are incorrect because changes to the metabase do not require restarting the Web or the site. D is incorrect because `Commit` is not a member of any of the IISAO objects.

47. **C.** JScript is case-sensitive (like C and Java), so all objects must be spelled correctly in name and case.

48. **D.** ADO is Microsoft's latest data access technology that combines the best of DAO and RDO. ADO is an installable object that comes with IIS.

49. **B.** Log is the only view that gives you the option of exporting to a text file. You can then import the text file into any third-party program.

50. **C.** This is done automatically.

51. **C, D.** Both Network Monitor and Performance Monitor have the ability to display network utilization levels. NETSTAT will only show statistics for TCP/IP.

52. **C.** IIS, like NT, will almost always benefit from additional memory. However, all of these are valid areas of concern.

53. **A.** Anything higher than five page faults per second indicates heavy paging activity, and you should consider adding more memory to your system.

54. **B.** B is correct because NCSA supports the Date, Time, and Client IP fields. The NCSA format doesn't have User Agent or Referrer fields.
55. **D.** The W3C Extended Log File format always outputs time in GMT and can't be changed.
56. **A.** The W3C Extended Log File format is the best format because it logs time in GMT format. This means that when you import logs from your different servers, they will all be normalized to GMT already and won't need to be converted by another program to the same time zone.
57. **B.** Report Writer supports saving reports in HTML, Word, and Excel formats.
58. **A.** PINGing a server is usually the first step in troubleshooting a server.
59. **C.** The anonymous account (`IUSER_computername`) must have at least Read access.
60. **C.** CGI and ISAPI applications must be given Execute permission on the directory containing the CGI or ISAPI application.

Index

A

ActiveX Data Objects, *see* **ADO**
ActiveX database objects, querying Index Server, 343
Add Users and Groups dialog box, 207
Add/Remove Snap-in dialog box, 90
adding
    folders to custom consoles, 92-94
    snap-ins to MMC (Microsoft Management Console), 89, 91-92
    virtual directories to FTP sites, 167-171
addresses (IP), changing for FTP sites, 158
administration, 67
    architecture, 68-69
    FTP sites, 161-162
        security, 163-165
        setting TCP/IP restrictions, 173-174
    Microsoft Certificate Server, utilities, 247
        Certificate Log Administration, 248-249
        Certificate Server Queue Administration, 249-251
        command-line, 253-255
    public news groups, 295-296
    Web-based, Internet Service Manager (HTML), 99-100
Administration Objects, *see* **IISAO**
ADO (ActiveX Data Objects), 66
    ASP connections (Active Server Pages), 366, 370-372
    database connections, 367

ADSI (Active Directory Services Interface), 375-376
    metabase, 376
    objects, 377-378
Advanced Web Site Identification dialog box, 127
Alert View (Performance Monitor), 398
Alerter (Windows NT), 208
algorithms
    encryption, 222-223
    SHA-1 (Secure Hash Algorithm), 223
allowing
    anonymous access for FTP, 161-162
    passive connections for FTP sites, 158
analysis, site, *see* **site analysis**
analyzing
    log files, 450-457
    performance, *see* monitoring, performance
    Web content, 71-73
Anderson, Marc, 5
annealing merges (Index Server), 337
annotating
    directories on FTP sites, 171-173
    FTP (File Transfer Protocol), 61-62
anonymous
    access, 160-162, 183-185, 484-489
        SMTP (Simple Mail Transfer Protocol), 275
        WWW services, 139
    connectivity, 291
    identities, establishing, 48
Anonymous User Account dialog box, 184

Anonymous Users/sec (Performance Monitor counter), 419
Apache Web server, 5
APIs (Application Programming Interfaces),
    CGIs (Common Gateway Interfaces), 52-55
    Microsoft CryptoAPI, 228
application object, ASPs (Active Server Pages), 364
applications
    ASPs (Active Server Pages), 357
    databases
        accessing information, 66
        troubleshooting, 490-491
    debugging, WWW services, 134
    ISAPI, 53-55
    mapping
        security, home directories, 191-193
        WWW service directories, 133-134
    services provided by IIS, 6-7
    transactions, 63-65
    troubleshooting errors, 489
    utilities
        NETSTAT, 390-391
        Network Monitor (Windows NT), 391-395
        Performance Monitor, *see* Performance Monitor
    WWW service directories, 133-134
architecture
    administration, 67-69
    ASP(Active Server Pages), 56-57
    content delivery, 57-59
        dynamic, 51
        static, 45-48
    IIS4 (Internet Information Server 4.0), 44
ARP (Address Resolution Protocol), 482
Article Commands (Performance Monitor counter), 411
Article Commands/Sec (Performance Monitor counter), 411
Article Map Entries (Performance Monitor counter), 414
Article Map Entries/Sec (Performance Monitor counter), 414
articles, newsgroup
    posting, 293
    reading, 293-294
    storing in virtual directories, 307
Articles Deleted (Performance Monitor counter), 414
Articles Deleted/Sec (Performance Monitor counter), 414
Articles Posted (Performance Monitor counter), 414
Articles Posted/Sec (Performance Monitor counter), 414
Articles Received (Performance Monitor counter), 414
Articles Received/Sec (Performance Monitor counter), 414
Articles Sent (Performance Monitor counter), 414
Articles Sent/Sec (Performance Monitor counter), 414
Articles Total (Performance Monitor counter), 414
ASPs (Active Server Pages), 55-57, 132-134, 356-357
    ADO (ActiveX Data Objects), 370-372
    database connections, 367
    objects, 364-366
    ODBC (Open Database Connectivity), 368-370
    Performance Monitor counters, 404-405
    performance optimization, 372-374
    scripting
        debugging, 65
        JScript, 363-364
        VBScript, 363
    security, home directories, 194
atomicity (transactions), 64-65

authentication, 181, 223
   Basic, 49-51
   clear text, 185-187
   digital certificates, 74
   dynamic content, 52-55
   file system, 50-51
   NT Challenge/Response, 187-188
   restricting outside access, 188-191
   SMTP, 275
   user-specific, 49-51
   Windows NT Challenge Response, 49-51
   WWW services, 139
Authentication dialog box, 185
Authentication Methods dialog box, 187, 301
automating Usage Import utility, 452-457
Avg Recipients/msg Received (Performance Monitor counter), 416
Avg Recipients/msg Sent (Performance Monitor counter), 416
Avg Retries/msg Delivered (Performance Monitor counter), 416
Avg Retries/msg Sent (Performance Monitor counter), 416
Avg. Disk Queue Length counter (Performance Monitor), 402

B

backing up
   fault tolerance, 73
   Metadatabase, 100-104
   Microsoft Certificate Server configuration, 251-252
badmail directory, SMTP (Simple Mail Transfer Protocol), 269
bandwidth
   bottlenecks, 10
   reports, analyzing, 451-457
   throttling, configuration, 105
   WWW services, 145-147

Basic Authentication, 49-51
batch files, new job.bat, 457
binding time (msec) (Performance Monitor counter), 407
bottlenecks, 388
   CPU-induced, 11
   network connection induced, 10
   RAM induced, 10
Browser Capabilities object, ASPs (Active Server Pages), 365
Browser Only Installation (IE4.01), 8
browsers
   content expiration dates, 141
   pipelining, 62
   reports, analyzing, 451-457
   Web, 4
      IE4.01, Browser Only Installation, 8
      Netscape Navigator, client certificate enrollment, 245-247
browsing
   content controls, WWW service directories, 132
   home directories, 195-196
buffering home directories, security, 194
bugs (software), troubleshooting, 475-476
building master index, 337-338
built-in objects (ASP), 364-365
Bytes Received Total (Performance Monitor counter), 416
Bytes Received/sec (Performance Monitor counter), 407, 414, 416, 419
Bytes Sent Total (Performance Monitor counter), 416
Bytes Sent/sec (Performance Monitor counter), 407, 414, 417, 419
Bytes Total (Performance Monitor counter), 417
Bytes Total/sec (Performance Monitor counter), 407, 414, 417, 419

C

Cache Flushes (Performance Monitor counter, 410
Cache Hits % (Performance Monitor counter), 410
Cache Hits (Performance Monitor counter), 410
Cache items (Performance Monitor counter), 409
Cache Misses (Performance Monitor counter), 410
Cached File Handles (Performance Monitor counter), 410
Cancel (control command), 308
capturing data, Network Monitor, 393-394
CAs (Certificate Authorities)
    certificates
        installing, 233-236
        replacing, 252-253
    key management, 227-228
    root, Microsoft Certificate Server installation, 229-231
catalogs (Index Server)
    adding, 328-329
    configuration, 331-332
    directories, adding, 328-329
    removing, 329
CertHier (command-line utility), 254-255
Certificate Authorities, *see* CAs
Certificate Server (Microsoft)
    administration, utilities, 247
        Certificate Log Administration utility, 248-249
        Certificate Server Queue Administration utility, 249-251
        command-line utilities, 253-255
    CA certificates
        enrolling, 236-242
        installing, 233-242
        replacing, 252-253
        revoking, 250-251
    client enrollment, 243-247
    configuration, backing up, 251-252
    non-root CA, installing, 232-233
    policy independence, 226
    reliability, 228
    Root CA, installing, 229-231
    scalability, 228
    standards, 227
    transport independence, 227
Certificate Server Queue Administration utility, 249-251
certificates, 222-223
    CA (Certificate Authorities)
        enrolling, 236-242
        installation, 233-236
        replacing, 252-253
        revoking, 250-251
    client, issuing, 243-247
    digital, 74
    PCT (Private Communication Technology), 204-205
    SSL (Secure Sockets Layer), 197-204
CertReq (command-line utility), 254
CertSrv (command-line utility), 255
CertUtil, 253
CGI (Common Gateway Interfaces), 52-55, 359-360
CGI Requests/sec (Performance Monitor counter), 419
Chart View (Performance Monitor), viewing data, 397-398
Check Commands (Performance Monitor counter), 411
Check Commands/sec (Performance Monitor counter), 411
clear text authentication, 181, 185-187
clients
    certificates, issuing, 224, 243-247
    user-specific access, 49-51
Collaborative Data Objects (ASP), 366
COM (Component Object Model), 53-55

combining static and dynamic file delivery, 57-59
command-line utilities
    CertHier, 254-255
    CertReq, 254
    CertSrv, 255
    CertUtil, 253-254
Common Gateway Interfaces, *see* **CGI**
communications, securing, 275-276
compatibility
    Index Server and file systems, 333-334
    server-side Java, 57
    SMTP (Simple Mail Transfer Protocol), 262
components
    DCOM (Distributed Object Model), 53-55
    Microsoft Site Server Express, 434-436
Computer Browser (Windows NT), security, 209
configuration
    error messages, WWW services, 142-144
    FTP (File Transfer Protocol)
        creating directory annotations, 171-173
        messages, 159-160
        session timeout, 165-166
        sites, setting access permissions, 163-165
    IIS, 105
    Index Server, 322-332
    Microsoft Certificate Server, 228
        backing up, 251-252
        non-root CA, 232-233
        Root CA, 229-231
    MIME maps, 106-109
    MMC (Microsoft Management Console), 86-88
    NNTP Service (Network News Transport Protocol), 297
        main properties page, 299-300
        see also Metadatabase
    Registry, 95, 108-112

SMTP (Simple Mail Transfer Protocol)
    domains, 271-272
    sites, 269-270
    WWW services, 120-122, 136
Configuration Replication, 73
Connection Attempts/sec (Performance Monitor counter), 419
connections
    anonymous (FTP), allowing, 161-162
    enterprise-level internetworks, security, 225
    establishing, 45-48
    FTP sites
        disconnecting, 164-165
        setting TCP/IP restrictions, 173-174
    network, bottlenecks, 10
    NNTP sites, restricting, 301
    partner internetworking, security, 225-226
    passive, permitting on FTP sites, 158
    SMTP sites, 270
    pooling, 372
Connections Errors/sec (Performance Monitor counter), 417
connectivity
    anonymous, 291
    NNTP Service, verifying, 311
    TCP/IP, troubleshooting, 477-479, 482-484
consistency of transactions, 64-65
consoles (MMC)
    extension snap-ins, adding, 91-92
    folders, adding, 92-94
    snap-ins, 86-87
    Web links, adding, 92-94
content (Web)
    analysis, 433
    control
        home directories, 195-196
        service directories, 132
    delivery architecture, 57-59

dynamic, 51
  generating, 56-57
  combining with static, 57-59
 manipulation, 71-73
Content Analyzer, 424-425, 458-463
Content Index (Performance Monitor counter) 406-407
Content Linking object (ASPs), 366
Content Rotator object (ASPs), 366
control messages, 308
Control Messages Failed (Performance Monitor counter), 414
Control Messages Received (Performance Monitor counter), 414
converting log files to NCSA format, 446
CONVLOG utility, 446
counters, Performance Monitor, 395-397, 403-404
  ASPs (Active Server Pages), 404-405
  Content Index, 406-407
  FTP Service object, 407-408
  HTTP Content Index object, 409
  Internet Information Services global, 409-410
  NNTP Commands object, 411-413
  NNTP Server object, 413-416
  SMTP, 279-280
  SMTP Server object, 416-419
  viewing data, 397-398
  Web service, 419-423
CPUs (Central Processing Units), bottlenecks, 11
crashes
  fault tolerance, 73
  ISAPI, 54-55
  protection, 54-55
  recovery, 54-55
creating
  custom consoles, 88-91
  FTP sites, 156-157
  newsgroups, 303-304
  public news servers, 295-296

  virtual directories, 167-170
  WebMaps, 458-460
CryptoAPI (Microsoft), 228
cryptography, managing keys, 228
  see also encryption
Current Anonymous Users (Performance Monitor counter), 407, 414, 419
Current Blocked Async I/O Requests (Performance Monitor counter), 407, 410, 419
Current CGI Requests (Performance Monitor counter), 419
Current Connections (Performance Monitor counter), 407, 415, 420
Current ISAPI Extension Requests (Performance Monitor counter), 420
Current NonAnonymous Users (Performance Monitor counter), 407, 415, 420
Current Outbound Connections (Performance Monitor counter), 415
Current requests queued (Performance Monitor counter), 409
custom
  certificates, 224
  consoles, creating, 88-91
  extension snap-ins, adding, 91-92
  folders, adding, 92-94
  HTTP headers, 141
  installation, Microsoft Site Server Express, 435-436
  messages
    error, WWW services, 142-144
    FTP sites, 159-160
  Web links, adding, 92-94
  WebMaps, 460

D

DAO (Data Access Objects), 367
Data Source Names (DSNs), 368-370

databases
- ASP connections (Active Server Pages), 367
  - ADO (Active Data Objects), 370-372
  - ODBC, 368-370
  - performance optimization, 372-374
- metabase, ADSI (Active Directory Services Interface), 376
- Microsoft Access, 66, 447-450
- troubleshooting, 490-491
- *see also* Metadatabase

DCOM (Distributed COM), 53-55

debugging
- home directories, 194
- scripts, Microsoft Script Debugger, 65
- WWW services, 134

Debugging Requests (Performance Monitor counter), 404

decryption, 222-223

default documents, WWW service Web sites, 138-139

Default NNTPSite Properties dialog box, 300-301

DELETE instructions (HTTP), 62

Delete Requests/sec (Performance Monitor counter), 420

deleting
- files (FTP), 164
- newsgroups, 305

Deliveries Properties sheet (SMTP), 273-275

delivering
- dynamic content, 51
- static content
  - establishing connection, 45-48
  - merging with dynamic, 57-59

denying certificates, 250-251

deploying public news servers, 295-296

development
- ASP (Active Server Pages), 56-57
- IIS, 4
- Web servers, 5

diagnosing network problems, 472-476

dialog boxes
- Add Users and Groups, 207
- Add/Remote Snap-in, 90
- Advanced Web Site Identification, 127
- Anonymous User Account, 184
- Authentication, 185
- Authentication Methods, 301
- Authentications Methods, 187-188
- Default NNTP Site Properties, 300-301
- Directory Permissions, 208
- Error Mapping Properties, 143
- IP Address and Domain Name Restrictions, 302
- Job Properties, 455
- Logging Properties, 444-445
- Network Directory Security Credentials, 170-171
- Newsgroup Properties, 303
- Properties, 105, 158-159, 166-167, 245-247
- Report Document, 451-457
- Secure Communications, 198
- Server Properties, 447-449
- Site Properties, 447-449
- Task Properties, 456
- Usage Import Statistics, 449
- WebVirt Properties, 170-171
- WWW Service Master Properties, 128

Diffie-Hellmann (public-key cryptography), 222-223

digital
- certificates, 74
- signatures, 223

directories
- adding to catalogs (Index Server), 328-329
- FTP (File Transfer Protocol) sites
  - annotation, 171-173
  - style selection, 166-167
- home, security, 191-196
- logging, disabling, 436-437
- Metadatabase, relocating, 102-104
- NTFS permissions, 205-208

remote content, troubleshooting, 489
rescans, forcing, 327
SMTP (Simple Mail Transfer Protocol), 263, 269
virtual, 60, 306-307
WWW services, 120-122, 127-131
    access permissions, 131-132
    applications, 133-134
    redirections, 134-135
    security, 139-140
see also virtual directories

Directory Drops Total (Performance Monitor counter), 417
Directory Drops/sec (Performance Monitor counter), 417
Directory Listings (Performance Monitor counter), 410
Directory Permissions dialog box, 208
Directory Pickup Queue Length (Performance Monitor counter), 417
Directory Security Properties sheet (SMTP), 275-276
disabling directory-level logging, 436-437
disconnecting FTP, 164-165
disks
    Performance Monitor, 402
    space management, virtual directories, 306-307
displaying
    current FTP users, 164-165
    Index Server properties, 330-331
    Web site properties, 436
    WebMaps, 459
DLLs (Dynamic Link Library), Index Server, 334-335
DNS (Domain Name Service)
    host headers, 127
    lookup, SMTP services, 275
DNS Queries Total (Performance Monitor counter), 417
DNS Queries/sec (Performance Monitor counter), 417

documents (Web)
    indexing, 333-338
    static and dynamic content, routing, 58-59
    warehousing, 320
    word breakers, 335
    WWW services, 121-122, 138-139
Domain Names, access restrictions, 140, 188-191
domains, SMTP (Simple Mail Transfer Protocol)
    configuring, 271-272
    services, 274-275
    sites, 268
drop directory (SMTP), 269
DSNs (Data Source Names), 368-370
durability, 64-65
dynamic content
    delivery, 51
    receiving, 52-55

E

ECMA (European Computer Manufacturers Association), 363
editing
    Metadatabase, 99-100
    newsgroups, 305
    Windows NT Registry, 95, 108-112
enabling
    Host Headers, 63
    site activity logging, 436-437
encryption, 196-197, 222-223
enhancing IIS performance, 9-11
enrolling certificates, 236-242
enterprise-level internetworking, securing connections, 225
entries (Windows NT Registry)
    global, 109-112
    service-specific, 110-112

Error (ADO object), 371
Error Mapping Properties dialog box, 143
error messages
    403 (Forbidden Error), 487-488
    WWW services, 122, 142-144
Errors During Script Runtime (Performance Monitor counter), 404
Errors From ASP Preprocessor (Performance Monitor counter), 404
Errors From Script Compilers (Performance Monitor counter), 404
Errors/sec (Performance Monitor counter), 404
establishing
    anonymous identities, 48
    connections, 45-48
    public news servers, 295-296
    user-specific identities, 49-51
ETRN Messages Total (Performance Monitor counter), 417
ETRN Messages/sec (Performance Monitor counter), 417
Event Logs (Windows NT)
    SMTP (Simple Mail Transfer Protocol), 277
    security, 209
Event Viewer, viewing SMTP logs, 277
exams, *see* practice exam
execute access permissions, WWW service directories, 132
executing ISAPI applications, 54-55
Executive Summary reports, analyzing, 451-457
Exit messages (FTP), 159-160
expected hits, WWW services, 147
expiration
    dates (Web sites), 141
    policies, creating for newsgroups, 305
Expiration Policy Wizard, 305
exporting log files, Performance Monitor, 400
extensions
    snap-ins, adding to custom consoles, 88, 91-92
    ISAPI (Internet Server Application Programming Interface), 55, 357-359

F

Failed Outbound Logons (Performance Monitor counter), 415
FAT (File Allocation Table), authentication, 50-51
fault tolerance, 73
Field (ADO object), 371
File Access object (Active Server Pages), 366
file system
    authentication, 50-51
    compability with Index Server, 333-334
    see also files
files
    articles, storing, 294
    .asp (Active Server Pages), building query forms, 342
    batch, new job.bat, 457
    deleting, 164
    .htx, creating, 344-345
    .idq, 338-342
    Index Server DLLs (Dynamic Link Library), 334-335
    log
        converting to NCSA format, 446
        importing, 447-450
        Microsoft IIS Log File, 439-440
        NCSA Common Log File format, 438-439
        ODBC (Open Database Connectivity), 443-444
        storage, 444-445
        W3C Extended Log File, 440-443
    Metadatabase.bin, relocating, 103-104
    NTFS permissions, 205-208
    WWW services, 120-122

Files Received/sec (Performance Monitor counter), 420
Files Sent/sec (Performance Monitor counter), 420
Files to be filtered (Performance Monitor counter), 406
Files/sec (Performance Monitor counter), 420
Filter speed (Mbytes/hr) (Performance Monitor counter), 407
filters
　Index Server, 334-335
　ISAPI (Internet Server Application Programming Interface), 55, 142, 358-359
flexible access logging (HTTP), 62
Folder (stand-alone snap-in), 88
folders, Metadatabase, 102-104
Forbidden (403) errors, 487-488
forcing directory rescans (Index Server), 327
formats (logging)
　converting to NCSA format, 446
　Microsoft IIS Log File, 439-440
　NCSA Common Log File, 438-439
　ODBC (Open Database Connectivity), 443-444
　W3C Extended Log File, 440-443
FTP (File Transfer Protocol), 5
　creating sites, 156
　integrated security, 59
　master properties, configuration, 105
　messages, configuration, 60, 159-160
　servers, directory listing styles, 166-167
　session timeout configuration, 165-166
　sites, 60-62
　　access permissions, 163-165
　　annotating directories, 171-173
　　changing IP address, 158
　　changing port number, 158
　　creating, 157
　　disconnecting from, 164-165
　　logging, 436
　　management, 156
　　naming virtual directories, 169
　　restricting maximum number of users, 165-166
　　security, 160-162
　　TCP/IP restrictions, 173-174
　　virtual directories, 60, 167-170
FTP Service object (Performance Monitor counter), 407-408

G

generating
　control messages, 308
　dynamic content (Active Server Pages), 56-57
　page content, 52-55
　site analysis reports, 451-457
　WebMaps, 458-460
geography reports, analyzing, 451-457
Get Requests/sec (Performance Monitor counter), 420
global entries, Windows NT Registry, 109-112
Gopher services, 5
granting user access (FTP sites), 161-162
Group Commands (Performance Monitor counter), 411
Group Commands/Sec (Performance Monitor counter), 411

H

Head Requests/sec (Performance Monitor counter), 420
headers (HTTP), WWW services, 122, 141
Help Commands (Performance Monitor counter), 411

Help Commands/sec (Performance Monitor counter), 411
hiding FTP sites, 158
history of IIS, 4-5
History Map Entries (Performance Monitor counter), 415
History Map Entries/sec (Performance Monitor counter), 415
hits
   reports, analyzing, 451-457
   WWW services, 147
home directories
   security, 191-196
   WWW services, 127-128
hop counts, limiting on SMTP services, 274
Host Headers
   HTTP (Hypertext Transfer Protocol), 63
   troubleshooting, 494
   WWW services, 126-127
hosts, WSH (Windows Scripting Host), 374-375
HTML (Hypertext Markup Language), 4
   documents, routing with static and dynamic content, 58-59
   hyperlinks, 4
   IDC (Internet Database Connector), 360
   ISM (Internet Service Manager), 99-100
   SMTP Service Manager, 267-268
HTTP (Hypertext Transfer Protocol), 4
   flexible access logging, 62
   headers, WWW services, 122, 141
   Host Headers, 63
   instructions, 62
   integrated security, 61-62
   Keep-Alives, 147
   pipelining, 62
   transfer chunk encoding, 62
   user-specific access, 49-51
HTTP Content Index object (Performance Monitor counter), 409
hyperlinks, 4
Hypertext Markup Language, *see* HTML
Hypertext Transfer Protocol, *see* HTTP

I

IDC (Internet Database Connector), 360
IDEA (International Data Encryption Algorithm), 222-223
identification configurations
   SMTP sites, 270
   WWW services, 136
identities, establishing
   anonymous, 48
   user-specific, 49-51
IE4.01 (Internet Explorer 4.01), Browser Only Installation, 8
IHave Commands (Performance Monitor counter), 411
IHave Commands/sec (Performance Monitor counter), 411
IIS (Internet Information Server)
   administration, 68-69
   architecture, 44
   configuration, 105
   history, 4
   Host Headers, troubleshooting, 494
   installation, 12-38
      performance considerations, 10-11
   integration with WindowsNT, 70
   JVM (Java Virtual Machine), 57
   Metadatabase, 68
   MIME maps, configuring, 106-109
   performance, enhancing, 9-11
   services provided, 6-7
   snap-in, 87
   WAM (Web Application Manager), 55
IISAO (IIS Administration Objects), 68-69
IIsCertMapper object (ADSI), 377
IIsFilter object (ADSI), 377
IIsFtpInfo object (ADSI), 377
IIsFtpServer object (ADSI), 377
IIsFtpService object (ADSI), 377
IIsFtpVirtualDir object (ADSI), 377
IIsLogModule object (ADSI), 377

IIsMimeMap object, (ADSI), 377
IIsWebDirectory object (ADSI), 377
IIsWebFile object, (ADSI), 377
IIsWebInfo object (ADSI), 377
IIsWebServer object (ADSI), 377
IIsWebService object (ADSI), 378
IIsWebVirtualDir object (ADSI), 378
implementing IIS
    selecting strategy, 76
    widescale changes, affects on server, 475-476
importing log files, 447-450
improving IIS performance, 9-11
Inbound Connections Current (Performance Monitor counter), 417
Inbound Connections Total (Performance Monitor counter), 417
incoming connections, SMTP sites, 270
Index Server, 320
    bottlenecks, 10
    catalogs
        adding, 328-329
        removing directories, 329
    configuration, 322-332
    content controls, 132
    directory rescans, forcing, 327
    filters, 334-335
    installing, 321-322
    merges, 336-338
    normalizer, 335
    performance, 344-345
    properties, viewing, 330-331
    querying, 338-343
        starting and stopping, 327-328
        troubleshooting, 491-493
    stand-alone snap-in, 88
    word breakers, 335
Index Size (Mbytes) (Performance Monitor counter), 406
indexing Web sites, 320
instability, ISAPI (Internet Server Application Programming Interface), 54-55

installation
    Certificate Server (Microsoft), 228, 232-236
        non-root CA, 232-233
        Root CA, 229-231
    IE4.01 (Internet Explorer 4.01), 12-38
        Browser Only Installation, 8
    IIS, performance considerations, 10-11
    Index Server, 321-322
    Microsoft Site Server Express, 435-436
    Network Monitor, 392
    NNTP (Network News Transfer Protocol) Service, 296-297
    NT Option Pack, minimum hardware requirements, 8-9
    objects, (ASPs), 365-366
    SMTP (Simple Mail Transfer Protocol) services, 265-267
    system requirements, 7-9
    TCP/IP, troubleshooting, 483-484
integrated security, 61-62
    FTP (File Transfer Protocol), 59-60
International Data Encryption Algorithm, *see* IDEA
Internet Database Connector, *see* IDC
Internet Explorer, 5
Internet Information Services Global (Performance Monitor counters), 409-410
Internet Server Application Programming Interface, *see* ISAPI
Internet Service Manager, *see* ISM
Internetworking, securing connections
    enterprise-level, 225
    partner, 225-226
invalidating certificates, 250-251
IP Address and Domain Name Restrictions dialog box, 302
IP addresses
    access restrictions, 188-191
    changing for FTP sites, 158
    WWW services, 122-123, 126-127, 140
IPCONFIG, 480

ISAPI (Internet Server Application Programming Interface), 53-55, 142, 357-359
- extensions, 55
- filters, 55, 121-122, 142
- instability, 54-55
- *see also* WAM

ISAPI Extension Requests/sec (Performance Monitor counter), 420

ISM (Internet Service Manager), 86-87, 120-122, 267
- ASPs (Active Server Pages), 362
- configuring, 120-122
- HTML (Hypertext Markup Language), 99-100
- MMC (Microsoft Management Console), launching, 298-299
- SMTP (Simple Mail Transfer Protocol)
  - Deliveries Properties sheet, 273-275
  - directories, 269
  - domains, 271-272
  - message monitoring, 277-278
  - Message Properties sheet, 272-273
  - performance monitoring, 278-280
  - security, 275-276
  - Service Manager, 267-268
  - site configuration, 269-270
  - system monitoring, 276-277
  - troubleshooting, 281-282

isolation, multiple transactions, 64-65

issuing client certificates (Microsoft Certificate Server), 243-247

J-K

Java, compatibility, 57

JavaScript, 363
- ASPs (Active Server Pages), 363-364

Job Properties dialog box, 455

Keep-Alives (HTTP), 147

Key Manager, enrolling CA certificates, 241-242

keys, 222-223
- encryption, 196-197
- managing, 227-228

L

languages supported by ASP (Active ServerPages), 56-57

Last Commands (Performance Monitor counter), 411

Last Commands/sec (Performance Monitor counter), 411

launching MMC (Microsoft Management Console), 298-299

links (Web), adding to custom consoles, 92-94

List Commands (Performance Monitor counter), 411

List Commands/sec (Performance Monitor counter), 412

Listing 13.1, Output from the CONVLOG program, 446

local messages (SMTP), delivering, 264

Local Queue Length (Performance Monitor counter), 280, 417

Local Retry Queue Length (Performance Monitor counter), 280, 417

Log Access, 163

Log File Manager, opening, 448

Log View (Performance Monitor), 398-399

logging
- analyzing files, 450-457
- directory-level, disabling, 436-437
- Event Log (Windows NT), security, 209
- file storage, 444-445
- files, converting to NCSA format, 446
- flexible support, 73

formats
    Microsoft IIS Log File, 439-440
    NCSA Common Log File, 438-439
    ODBC (Open Database
        Connectivity), 443
    ODBC (Open Database Connectivity)
        logging file format, 444
    W3C Extended Log File, 440-443
home directories, access, 195
HTTP (Hypertext Transfer Protocol), 62
importing files, 447-450
Performance Monitor, 399-400
site activity, 436-437
site analysis, 432-433
WWW service directories, 132
see also Report Writer
Logging Properties dialog box, 444-445
Logon Attempts (Performance Monitor counter), 412
Logon Attempts/sec (Performance Monitor counter), 412, 420
Logon Failures (Performance Monitor counter), 412

M

mail, SMTP services (Simple Mail Transfer Protocol), 260-263
    Deliveries Properties sheet, 273-275
    directories, 269
    domains, 271-272
    installing, 265-267
    message monitoring, 277-278
    Message Properties sheet, 272-273
    messages, processing, 264-265
    performance monitoring, 278-280
    security, 275-276
    Service Manager, 267-268
    site configurations, 269-270
    system monitoring, 276-277
    troubleshooting, 281-282

main properties page (NNTP Service), configuration, 299-300
managing
    ASP scripts, 56-57
    disk space with virtual directories, 306-307
    downlevel Web servers, 94-98
    FTP sites, 156
    keys, 227-228
    NNTP service, 303-304
manipulating Web site content, 71-73
mapping network shares to virtual directories, 170-171
maps, MIME (Multipurpose Internet Multimedia Extensions), 141
Masquerade Domain, 274
master
    index, building, 337-338
    service (WWW), 120-122
Maximum Anonymous Users (Performance Monitor counter), 407, 415, 420
Maximum CGI Requests (Performance Monitor counter), 420
Maximum Connections (Performance Monitor counter), 408, 415, 420
Maximum Connections messages (FTP), 159-160
Maximum ISAPI Extension Requests (Performance Monitor counter), 421
Maximum NonAnonymous Users (Performance Monitor counter), 408, 415, 421
MD5 (Message Digest), 223
Measured Async I/O Bandwidth Usage (Performance Monitor counter), 408, 410
Measured Async I/O Bandwidth Usage (Performance Monitor counter), 421
medium rebuilding (NNTP Service), 310
memory, affect on performance, 389, 401-402
Memory Allocated (Performance Monitor counter), 404
Merge progress (Performance Monitor counter), 406

merges (Index Server)
   annealing, 337
   master, 338
   shadow, 336
   Web page content, static and dynamic, 57-59

Message Bytes Received Total (Performance Monitor counter), 417

Message Bytes Received/sec (Performance Monitor counter), 417

Message Bytes Sent Total (Performance Monitor counter), 417

Message Bytes Sent/sec (Performance Monitor counter), 417

Message Bytes Total (Performance Monitor counter), 417

Message Bytes Total/sec (Performance Monitor counter), 417

Message Delivery Retries (Performance Monitor counter), 417

Message Delivery Retries counter (Performance Monitor), 279

Message Properties sheet (SMTP), 272-273

Message Received/sec (Performance Monitor counter), 417

Message Send Retries (Performance Monitor counter), 418

messages
   control, generating, 308
   error, customizing, 142-144
   FTP (File Transfer Protocol), 61-62, 159-160
   one-way hashes, 223
   SMTP (Simple Mail Transfer Protocol), 264
      monitoring, 277-278
      processing, 264-265

Messages Delivered Total (Performance Monitor counter), 418

Messages Delivered/sec (Performance Monitor counter), 418

Messages Delivered/sec counter (Performance Monitor), 279

Messages Received Total (Performance Monitor counter), 418

Messages Refused for Address Objects (Performance Monitor counter), 418

Messages Refused for Mail Objects (Performance Monitor counter), 418

Messages Refused for Size (Performance Monitor counter), 418

Messages Retrieved Total (Performance Monitor counter), 418

Messages Retrieved/sec (Performance Monitor counter), 418

Messages Sent Total (Performance Monitor counter), 418

Messages Sent/sec (Performance Monitor counter), 418

Metadatabase, 68, 98
   backing up, 100-104
   editing tools, 99-100
   folder, relocating, 102-104
   restoring, 100-104

MetaEdit tool, 100

methodologies of TCP/IP troubleshooting, 482-484

Microsoft Access, importing log files into database, 447-450

Microsoft BackOffice, Web site, 7

Microsoft Certificate Server, 74
   administration, utilities, 247
      Certificate Log Administration utility, 248-249
      Certificate Server Queue Administration utility, 249-251
      command-line utilities, 253-255
   CA certificates
      enrolling, 236-242
      installing, 233-242
      replacing, 252-253
   certificates, revoking, 250-251
   client enrollment, 243-247
   installing, 228
   non-root CA, installing, 232-233

policy independence, 226
reliability, 228
Root CA, installing, 229-231
scalability, 228
standards, 227
Microsoft CryptoAPI, 228
Microsoft IIS Log Files, 439-440
analyzing, 450-457
importing, 447-450
Microsoft Knowledge Base, 476
Microsoft Management Console, *see* **MMC**
Microsoft Message Queue Server, *see* **MSMQ**
Microsoft NNTP (Network News Transfer Protocol) service
anonymous connectivity, 291
articles, posting, 293
configuration, 297
control messages, restricting, 308
directory structure, 294
installing, 296-297
newsgroups
  reading articles, 294
  subscribing, 292
performance, optimizing, 308-309
rebuilding, 310
standards, 290
virtual directories, 306-307
Microsoft Script Debugger, 65
Microsoft Site Server Express
components, 434-436
installation, 435-436
log formats
  Microsoft IIS Log File, 439-440
  NCSA Common Log File, 438-439
  ODBC (Open Database Connectivity), 443-444
  W3C Extended Log File, 440-443
log storage, 444-445
Web site, 434
Microsoft Transaction Server, *see* **MTS**
Microsoft Usage Import, importing log files, 447-450

MIME (Multipurpose Internet Multimedia Extensions)
map configuration, 105-109
WWW services, 141
minimum hardware requirements, NT Option Pack, 8-9
MMC (Microsoft Management Console), 86-87
custom consoles
  adding extension snap-ins, 91-92
  adding folders, 92-94
  adding Web links, 92-94
  creating, 88-91
IIS administration, 68
launching, 298-299
snap-ins, configuration, 88, 324-332
WSH (Windows Scripting Host), 69
Mode Commands (Performance Monitor counter), 412
Mode Commands/sec (Performance Monitor counter), 412
Moderated Posting Failed (Performance Monitor counter), 415
Moderated Posting Sent (Performance Monitor counter), 415
monitoring
Network Monitor (Windows NT), 391-394
  capturing data, 393
  displaying data, 394
  utilization rates, 395
performance, 386, 389
  Content Analyzer, 424-425
  Index Server, 344-345
  NETSTAT, 390-391
  see also logging
SMTP (Simple Mail Transfer Protocol)
  messages, 277-278
  performance, 278-280
  system monitoring, 276-277
system performance, 309

MS-DOS (Microsoft Disk-Operating System), selecting directory listing style for FTP server, 166-167
MSMQ (Microsoft Message Queue Server), 65
MTS (Microsoft Transaction Server), 63-65
    snap-in, 87
    transactions, 63-65
multiple site support, 70-71
MyInfo object (ASP), 366

N

naming
    applications, security, 192
    virtual directories, 169
National Center for Supercomputing, *see* NCSA
NCSA (National Center for Supercomputing Applications, 5
    Common Log Files, 438-439
        analyzing, 450-457
        importing, 447-450
NDRs Generated (Performance Monitor counter), 279, 418
Netscape Navigator, client certificate enrollment, 245-247
NETSTAT, 390-391, 481
Network Directory Security Credentials dialog box, 170-171
Network Monitor (Windows NT), 391-394
    capturing data, 393
    displaying data, 394
    utilization rates, 395
Network News Transfer Protocol, *see* NNTP
networks
    connections
        bottlenecks, 10
        establishing, 45-48
    Performance Monitor, 402-403
    security, 484-489

shares, mapping to virtual directories, 170-171
troubleshooting, 472-476
see also internetworking
New Site Certificate dialog box, 233
Newgroups Commands (Performance Monitor counter), 412
Newgroups Commands/sec (Performance Monitor counter), 412
Newnews Commands (Performance Monitor counter), 412
Newnews Commands/sec (Performance Monitor counter), 412
news servers
    private, 295
    public, 295-296
    restricting access, 302
newsgroup (control command), 308
Newsgroup Properties dialog box, 303
newsgroups, 290
    creating, 303-304
    expiration policies, creating, 305
    posting, 293
    reading, 294
    removing, 305
    restricting access, 301
    storing, 294
    storing in virtual directories, 307
    subscribing to, 292
Next Commands (Performance Monitor counter), 412
Next Commands/sec (Performance Monitor counter), 412
NNTP Commands object (Performance Monitor counter), 411-413
NNTP Server object (Performance Monitor counter), 413-416
NNTP Service (Network News Transfer Protocol), 75
    anonymous connectivity, 291
    articles
        posting, 293
        reading, 294

configuration, 297
control messages, restricting, 308
directory structure, 294
installing, 296-297
ISM Internet Service Manager), 298-300
main properties page, configuration, 299-300
managing, 303-304
newsgroups
    creating, 303-304
    removing, 305
    subscribing, 292
rebuilding, 310
Security Extensions, 291
sites, restricting access, 300-302
standards, 290
virtual directories, 306-307
NNTP Service Rebuild Wizard, 310
nodes, MMC (Microsoft Management Console), 87
Non-Deliverable Reports (SMTP), 281
Non-Root CA (Microsoft Certificate Server), installation, 232-233
NonAnonymous Users/sec (Performance Monitor counter), 421
none access permissions, WWW service directories, 132
Normalizer (Index Server), 335
Not Found Errors/sec (Performance Monitor counter), 421
NSLOOKUP, 480
NT Challenge/Response authentication, 187-188
NT Option Pack, 7-9
NTFS (New Technology File Systems), permissions, 163-164
anonymous access, 184-185
security, 180-181
NTLM (NT/LAN Manager), 49-51
Number of MailFiles Open (Performance Monitor counter), 418
Number of QueueFiles Open (Performance Monitor counter), 418

O

objects
    ADSI (Active Directory Services Interface), 377-378
    ASPs (Active Server Pages), 364-366
    IISAO (IIS Administration Objects), 68-69
    Performanc Monitor, *see* Performance Monitor
    server-side (ASP pages), 342
    viewing on WebMaps, 460
    WSH (Windows Scripting Host), 374-375
Objects (Performance Monitor counter), 410
obtaining client certificates, 243-247
ODBC (Open Database Connectivity), 444
    ASP connections (Active Server Pages), 368-370
    logging file format, 443
one-way hashes, 223
opening Log File Manager, 448
operators
    NNTP news sites, removing, 301
    WWW services, 121
    see also site operators
optimizing performance, 386
    ASP connections (Active Server Pages), 372-374
    NNTP Service, 308-309
organization reports, analyzing, 451-457
Other Request Methods/sec (Performance Monitor counter), 421
Outbound Connections Current (Performance Monitor counter), 418
Outbound Connections Refused (Performance Monitor counter), 418
Outbound Connections Total (Performance Monitor counter), 418
outgoing connections, SMTP sites, 270
output, CONVLOG program, Listing 13.1, 446

P

Page Counter object (ASP), 366
pages
    ASP (Active Server Pages), server-side objects, 342
    Web
        generating content, 52-57
        indexing, 333-338
panes, MMC (Microsoft Management Console), 87
parameters, configuring
    Report Writer command-line, 454-455, 457
    IIS, 105
    master merges, 337-338
parent paths, 194
partitions, security, 180-181
partner internetworking, securing connections, 225-226
passive connections, permitting on FTP sites, 158
passwords
    anonymous access, 183-185
    authentication, 50-51
    clear text authentication, 186-187
    FTP (File Transfer Protocol), 161-162
    security, 180-181
path reports, analyzing, 451-457
PCT (Private Communication Technology), 204-205
performance, 386, 388
    ASP connections (Active Server Pages), 372-374
    bottlenecks, 388
    content analysis, 433
    IIS, enhancing, 9-11
    Index Server, 344-345
    memory, 389
    monitoring, 389
        capturing data, 393
        Content Analyzer, 424-425
        displaying data, 394
        NETSTAT, 390-391
        Network Monitor (Windows NT), 391-394
        Performance Monitor, 395-400
        SMTP (Simple Mail Transfer Protocol), 278-280
        utilization rates, 395
        viewing data, 397-398
        see also Performance Monitor
    NNTP service, optimizing, 308-309
    parameters, WWW services
        bandwidth, 145-147
        expected hits, 147
        HTTP Keep-Alives, 147
        user connection limitations, 144-145
    see also bottlenecks
    site analysis, 432-433
        automating tasks, 452-457
        generating reports, 451-457
        log file storage, 444-445
        Microsoft IIS Log File format, 439-440
        NCSA Common Log File format, 438-439
        ODBC (Open Database Connectivity), 443-444
        Report Writer utility, 450-457
        Usage Import utility, 447-450
        W3C Extended Log File format, 440-443
    speed, 389
    usage analysis, 433
    WWW services, 121-122
Performance Monitor, 309, 395-397
    counters, 403-404
        ASPs (Active Server Pages), 404-405
        Content Index, 406-407
        FTP Service object, 407-408
        HTTP Content Index object, 409
        Internet Information Services Global, 409-410
        NNTP Commands object, 411-413
        NNTP server object, 413-416

SMTP Server object, 416-419
    Web service, 419-423
disks, 402
exporting data, 400
logs, 399-400
memory, 401-402
networks, 402-403
processors, 403
SMTP, 278-279
viewing data, 397-398
views, 398-399

performing quick searches on WebMaps, 461-462

Permission Checker object (ASP), 366

permissions, 181
access, 163-165
home directories, 191-192
NTFS (New Technology File System), 205-208
    anonymous access, 184-185
    write permissions, 163
    see also read
WWW service directories, 131

permitting
anonymous access, 161-162
passive connections, 158

persistent
connections, 62
indexes (Performance Monitor counter), 406
storage, bottlenecks, 10-11

pickup directories, SMTP (Simple Mail Transfer Protocol), 269

PING (Packet Internet Groper), 477-479

pipelining (HTTP), 62

PKCS (Public Key Cryptography Standards), 227

platform
administration, 67-69
architecture
    static content delivery, 45-48

policies
expiration, creating for newsgroups, 305
independence, Microsoft Certificate Server, 226

pooling connections (ASPs), 372

port number, changing for FTP sites, 158

Post Commands (Performance Monitor counter), 412

Post Commands/sec (Performance Monitor counter), 412

Post Requests/sec (Performance Monitor counter), 421

posting articles, 293

practice exam, 502-520

preconfigured quick searches (WebMaps), 461-462

prerequisites, IIS installation, 7-9

printing WebMaps, 460

private
keys (encryption), 196-197, 222-223
news servers, 295

process isolation, WWW service directories, 133-134

processing client requests, 50-51

programmatic intervention, 58-60

programming, 354
ADSI (Active Directory Services Interface), 375-376
    metabase, 376
    objects, 377-378
ASP (Active Server Pages), 56-57, 356-357
    database connections, 367-374
    objects, 364-366
    scripting languages, 361-364
CGIs (Common Gateway Interfaces), 359-360
IDC (Internet Database Connector), 360
ISAPI (Internet Server Application Programming Interface), 357-359
transactions, 63-65
WSH (Windows Scripting Host), 374-375

programs, *see* **applications**

properties
   of transactions, 64-65
   viewing
      Index Server, 330-331
      Web sites, 436
Properties dialog box, 105, 158-159, 166-167, 245-247
Properties sheets (SMTP)
   Deliveries, 273-275
   Directory Security, 275-276
   messages, 272-273
Property (ADO object), 371
public key cryptography, 196-197, 222-223
public news servers, 295-296
PUT instructions (HTTP), 62
Put Requests/sec (Performance Monitor counter), 421
PWS (Peer Web Services), installing on Windows NT Workstation 4.0, 7

Q

queries per minute (Performance Monitor counter), 409
query objects, 342
querying
   databases, 66
   Index Server, 338-343, 491-493
queue directory (SMTP), 269
queuing SMTP (Simple Mail Transfer Protocol)
   messages, 264
   troubleshooting, 281
quick searches (WebMaps), 461-462
Quit Commands (Performance Monitor counter), 412
Quit Commands/sec (Performance Monitor counter), 412

R

RAM (Random Access Memory), bottlenecks, 10
rating Web site content, 141
RDO (Remote Data Objects), 367
RDS (Remote Data Service), 66
read (access permission), 132, 163
reading newsgroup articles, 293-294
rebuilding NNTP Service (Network News Transfer Protocol), 310
receiving dynamic content, 51-55
recognizing points of failure, 474-476
Recordset (ADO object), 371
Recreational Software Advisory Council, *see* **RSAC**
redirections, WWW service directories, 134-135
referrer reports, analyzing, 451-457
Registry (Windows NT)
   configuration, 108-112
   editing, 95
   FTP (File Transfer Protocol) configuration, creating directory annotations, 171-173
   global entries, 109-112
   master merges (Index Server), parameters, 337-338
   service-specific entries, 110-112
reliability, Microsoft Certificate Server, 228
relocating Metadatabase folder, 102-104
Remote Data Service, *see* **RDS**
remote
   messages (SMTP), delivering, 264-265
   SQL Server connections, 373
   virtual directories, creating, 130
Remote Procedure Call, *see* **RPC**
Remote Queue Length (Performance Monitor counter), 418
Remote Retry Queue Length (Performance Monitor counter), 418

removing
    directories from catalogs (Index Server), 329
    newsgroups, 305
    NNTP site operators, 301-302
replacing CA certificates, 252-253
Report Document dialog box, 451-457
Report view (Performance Monitor), 398
Report Writer, 433, 450-457
    automating, 452-457
    command-line parameters, 454-455, 457
reports
    site analysis, generating, 451-457
    Site Summary, generating, 462-463
request
    object (ASP), 364
    reports, analyzing, 451-457
Request Bytes In Total (Performance Monitor counter), 404
Request Execution Time (Performance Monitor counter), 404
Request Wait Time (Performance Monitor counter), 404
requests, client processing, 50-51
Requests Disconnected (Performance Monitor counter), 405
Requests Executing (Performance Monitor counter), 405
Requests Failed Total (Performance Monitor counter), 405
Requests Not Authorized (Performance Monitor counter), 405
Requests Not Found (Performance Monitor counter), 405
Requests Queued (Performance Monitor counter), 405
Requests Rejected (Performance Monitor counter), 405
Requests Succeeded (Performance Monitor counter), 405
Requests Timed Out (Performance Monitor counter), 405
Requests Total (Performance Monitor counter), 405

Requests/sec (Performance Monitor counter), 405
requirements, IIS installation, 7-9
rescans (directory), forcing, 327
resources (network), accessing, 485-489
Responce object (ASP), 364
restoring
    Metadatabase, 100-104
    Microsoft Certificate Server configuraton, 251-252
restricting
    access to newsgroups, 301
    control messages, 308
    IP addresses/Domain Names, 188-191
    NNTP sites, operator access, 300-301
    user access (FTP), TCP/IP restrictions, 173-174
    Web site access, 62
    WWW services, 140
retrieving database information, 66
reverse DNS lookup, SMTP services, 275
revoking certificates, 250-251
ringroup (control command), 308
Root CA (Microsoft Certificate Server), installation, 229-231
routing HTML document content, 58-59
Routing Table Lookups Total (Performance Monitor counter), 419
Routing Table Lookups/sec (Performance Monitor counter), 419
RPC (Remote Procedure Call), security, 209
RSA (public-key cryptography), 222-223
RSAC (Recreational Software Advisory Council), 141
Run in Separate Memory Space, application security, 192
running queries (Performance Monitor counter), 406

S

S/MIME certificates (Secure Multipurpose Internet Multimedia Extensions), 224
scalability
    Microsoft Certificate Server, 228
    SMTP (Simple Mail Transfer Protocol), 262
script access permissions, WWW service directories, 132
Script Engines Cached (Performance Monitor counter), 405
scripting languages
    ASPs (Active Server Pages), 56-57, 361-362
        ActiveX objects, querying Index Server, 343
        debugging, 65
    JScript, 363-364
    VBScript, 363
    WSH (Windows Scripting Host), 374-375
Search Commands (Performance Monitor counter), 412
Search Commands/sec (Performance Monitor counter), 413
searching WebMaps, 461
Secure Communications dialog box, 198
Secure Sockets Layer, *see* **SSL**
security, 73, 180-183, 484-489
    anonymous access, 183-185
    authentication, 181
        Basic, 49-51
        clear text, 185-187
        NT Challenge/Response, 187-188
        receiving dynamic content, 52-55
        restricting outside access, 188-191
    certificates, 222-223, 250-251
    communications, SMTP (Simple Mail Transfer Protocol), 275-276
    connections
        enterprise-level, 225
        partner, 225-226
    digital certificates, 74
    encryption, 196-197, 222-223
    FTP sites, 160-162, 173-174
    home directories, 191-196
    HTTP (Hypertext Transfer Protocol), 61-62
    integrated, FTP (File Transfer Protocol), 59-60
    ISAPI (Internet Server Application Programming Interface), crash protection, 54-55
    NTFS permissions, 205-208
    one-way hashes, 223
    PCT (Private Communication Technology), 204-205
    permissions, 163-165
        restricting per site maximum (FTP), 165-166
    SMTP (Simple Mail Transfer Protocol), 263, 275-276
    SSL (Secure Sockets Layer), 197-204
    TLS (Transport Layer Security), 75
    Windows NT
        disabling services, 208-210
        TCP/IP, 210-211
        user accounts, 211-212
    WWW service directories, 139-140
selecting
    FTP directory listing style, 166-167
    implementation strategy, 76
semi-private newsgroups, 295
Server Gated Cryptography, *see* **SGC**
Server Properties dialog box, 447-449
server-side programming
    ADSI (Active Directory Services Interface), 375-376
        metabase, 376
        objects, 377-378
    ASPs (Active Server Pages), 356-357
        database connections, 367-374
        objects, 364-366
        scripting languages, 361-364
    CGIs (Common Gateway Interfaces), 359-360

IDC (Internet Database Connector), 360
ISAPI (Internet Server Application
  Programming Interface), 357-359
WSH (Windows Scripting Host), 374-375
servers
  certificates, *see* certificates
  FTP (File Transfer Protocol)
    annotating directories, 171-173
    creating virtual directories, 167-170
    restricting site access, 165-166
    security, 160-162
    setting directory listing styles, 166-167
  IIS 3.0, editing Registry, 97-98
  news
    private, 295
    restricting access, 302
  SMTP (Simple Mail Transfer Protocol), 260-262
  Web, 4-5
    Apache, 5
    downlevel, managing, 94-98
  Windows NT, security, 209
  see also Certificate Server, 226
Service Manager (SMTP), 262, 267-268
service-specific entries, Windows NT Registry, 110-112
services
  FTP (File Transfer Protocol), configuring master properties, 105
  provided by IIS, 6-7
  SMTP (Simple Mail Transfer Protocol), 260-263
    Deliveries Properties sheet, 273-275
    directories, 269
    domains, 271-272
    installing, 265-267
    message monitoring, 277-278
    Message Properties sheet, 272-273
    messages, processing, 264-265
    performance monitoring, 278-280
    security, 275-276
    Service Manager, 267-268

site configurations, 269-270
system monitoring, 276-277
troubleshooting, 281-282
WWW (World Wide Web), 118
  bandwidth, 145-147
  configuring, 120-122
  configuring master properties, 105
  error messages, 142-144
  expected hits, 147
  HTTP headers, 141
  HTTP Keep-Alives, 147
  ISAPI filters, 142
  user connection limitations, 144-145
  Web sites, 122-140
Session Duration (Performance Monitor counter), 405
session object (ASP), 364
sessions
  FTP (File Transfer Protocol), timeout, 165-166
  SMTP (Simple Mail Transfer Protocol), 268
Sessions Current (Performance Monitor counter), 405
Sessions Flow Controlled (Performance Monitor counter), 415
Sessions panel (ISM), 278
Sessions Timed Out (Performance Monitor counter), 405
Sessions Total (Performance Monitor counter), 405
SGC (Server Gated Cryptography), 74
SHA-1 (Secure Hash Algorithm), 223
shadow merges (Index Server), 336
shared secrets, 222-223
shares (network), mapping to virtual directories, 170-171
Simple Mail Transfer Protocol, *see* SMTP
site analysis, 432-433
  automating tasks, 452-457
  logging
    file storage, 444-445
    Microsoft IIS Log File format, 439-440

NCSA Common Log File format, 438-439
ODBC (Open Database Connectivity), 443-444
W3C Extended Log File format, 440-443
reports, generating, 451-457
utilities
Content Analyser, 458-463
Microsoft Usage Import, 447-450
Report Writer, analyzing log files, 450-457
see also content, analysis; site operators; sites
site operators (FTP), administration, 162
Site Properties dialog box, 447-449
Site Server Express, 71-73, 424
components, 434-436
installation, 435-436
log formats
Microsoft IIS Log File, 439-440
NCSA Common Log File, 438-439
ODBC (Open Database Connectivity), 443-444
W3C Extended Log File, 440-443
storing log files, 444-445
Site Server Log Files
analyzing, 450-457
importing, 447-450
Site Summary reports, generating, 462-463
sites
Content Analyzer, 424-425
FTP (File Transfer Protocol), 60-62
annotating directories, 171-173
changing IPaddress, 158
changing port number, 158
creating, 156-157
creating virtual directories, 167-170
customizing messages, 159-160
disconnecting from, 164-165
managing, 156
message configuration, 159-160
naming virtual directories, 169

permitting passive connections, 158
restricting maximum number of users, 165-166
security, 160-162
setting access permissions, 163-165
setting FTP restrictions, 173-174
virtual directories, 60
Internet, static and dynamic content delivery, 57-59
NNTP (Network News Transfer Protocol)
creating newsgroups, 303-304
managing, 303-304
restricting access, 300-302
SMTP (Simple Mail Transfer Protocol)
configuring, 269-270
domains, 268
Web
analyzing content, 458-463
creating WebMaps, 458-460
disabling directory-level logging, 436-437
displaying properties, 436
flexible logging, 73
Host Headers, 63
indexing, 320, 333-338
logging, 436-437
Microsoft BackOffice, 7
Microsoft Knowledge Base, 476
Microsoft Site Server Express, 434
support for multiple, 70-71
troubleshooting, 460
WebMaps, creating, 424-425
WWW service
bandwidth, 145-147
creating, 123-126
default documents, 138-139
directories, 127-135
directory security, 139-140
error messages, 142-144
expected hits, 147
host headers, 126-127
HTTP headers, 141

HTTP Keep-Alives, 147
identification configurations, 136
IP addresses, 122-123
ISAPI filters, 142
user administration, delegating, 137-138
user connection limitations, 144-145
Smart Host, 274-275
SMTP (Simple Mail Transfer Protocol), 75, 260-263
    Deliveries Properties sheet, 273-275
    directories, 269
    domains, 271-272
    installing, 265-267
    messages
        monitoring, 277-278
        processing, 264-265
    Message Properties sheet, 272-273
    performance monitoring, 278-280
    security, 275-276
    Service Manager, 267-268
    site configurations, 269-270
    system monitoring, 276-277
    troubleshooting, 281-282
SMTP Server object (Performance Monitor counter), 416-419
snap-ins (MMC), 86-88
    adding, 89
    Index Server, 324-332
    extensions, adding, 91-92
software bugs, troubleshooting, 475-476
SortTemp directory (SMTP), 269
speed (performance), 389
spooler (Windows NT), security, 209
SQL Server (Structured Query Language)
    accessing, 490-491
    connections, ASPs (Active Server Pages), 373
SSL (Secure Sockets Layer), 197-204
stand-alone snap-in, 88
standard rebuilding (NNTP Service), 310

standards
    Microsoft Certificate Server, 227
    NNTP Service, 290
starting
    Index Server, 327-328
    MMC (Microsoft Management Console), 89
Stat Commands (Performance Monitor counter), 413
Stat Commands/sec (Performance Monitor counter), 413
static content, 44
    delivery process, establishing connections, 45-48
    see also dynamic content
Status object (ASP), 366
stopping Index Server, 327-328
storing
    articles, directory structure, 294
    log files, 444-445
strategies of implementation, selecting, 76
structure, NNTP Service directories, 294
styles, FTP directory listings, 166-167
subdirectories, log file storage, 444-445
subscribing to newsgroups, 292
symmetric cryptography, 222-223

T

tabs, WWW services, 121-122
Takethis Commands (Performance Monitor counter), 413
Takethis Commands/sec (Performance Monitor counter), 413
Task Properties dialog box, 456
tasks, automating site analysis, 452-457
TCP/IP (Transport Control Protocol/Internet Protocol)
    HTTP (Hypertext Transfer Protocol), 4
    NetBIOSHelper, 209

setting restrictions on FTP sites, 173-174
troubleshooting, 477-479
Windows NT, security, 210-211
technologies
  ASP (Active Server Pages), 56-57
  RDS (Remote Data Service), 66
telnet, verifying NNTP Service connectivity, 311
Template Cache Hit Rate (Performance Monitor counter), 405
Template Notifications (Performance Monitor counter), 405
Templates Cached (Performance Monitor counter), 405
test, *see* practice exam
text
  authentication, 185-186
  word breakers (Index Server), 335
thorough rebuilding (NNTP Service), 310
timeout
  FTP sessions, configuration, 165-166
  home directories, security, 194
TLS (Transport Layer Security, 75
tokens, 180-181
tools
  Metadatabase editing, 99-100
  troubleshooting
    ARP, 482
    IPCONFIG, 480
    NETSTAT, 481
    NSLOOKUP, 480
    PING (Packet Internet Groper), 477-479
    TRACERT, 479-480
Tools object (ASP), 366
Total # documents (Performance Monitor counter), 406
Total Allowed Async I/O Requests (Performance Monitor counter), 408, 410, 421
Total Anonymous Users (Performance Monitor counter), 408, 415, 421

Total Blocked Async I/O Requests (Performance Monitor counter), 408, 410, 421
Total CGI Requests (Performance Monitor counter), 421
Total Connection Attempts (Performance Monitor counter), 408, 422
Total Connection Errors (Performance Monitor counter), 419
Total Connections (Performance Monitor counter), 415
Total Delete Requests (Performance Monitor counter), 422
Total Files Received (Performance Monitor counter), 408, 422
Total Files Sent (Performance Monitor counter), 408, 422
Total Files Transferred (Performance Monitor counter), 408, 422
Total filter speed (Mbytes/hr) (Performance Monitor counter), 407
Total Get Requests (Performance Monitor counter), 422
Total Head Requests (Performance Monitor counter), 422
Total ISAPI Extension Requests (Performance Monitor counter), 422
Total Logon Attempts (Performance Monitor counter), 408, 422
Total Method Requests (Performance Monitor counter), 422
Total Method Requests/sec (Performance Monitor counter), 423
Total NonAnonymous Users (Performance Monitor counter), 408, 415, 423
Total Not Found Errors (Performance Monitor counter), 423
Total Other Request Methods (Performance Monitor counter), 423
Total Outbound Connections (Performance Monitor counter), 415

Total Outbound Connections Failed (Performance Monitor counter), 415
Total Passive Feeds (Performance Monitor counter), 415
Total Post Requests (Performance Monitor counter), 423
Total Pull Feeds (Performance Monitor counter), 416
Total Push Feeds (Performance Monitor counter), 416
Total Put Requests (Performance Monitor counter), 423
Total queries (Performance Monitor counter), 409
Total Rejected Async I/O Requests (Performance Monitor counter), 408, 410, 423
Total requests rejected (Performance Monitor counter), 409
Total SSL Connections (Performance Monitor counter), 416
Total Trace Requests (Performance Monitor counter), 423
TRACERT, 479-480
traffic (Web sites), logging, 436-437
transactions, 63-65
Transactions Aborted (Performance Monitor counter), 405
Transactions Committed (Performance Monitor counter), 405
Transactions Pending (Performance Monitor counter), 405
Transactions Total (Performance Monitor counter), 405
Transactions/sec (Performance Monitor counter), 405
transfer chunk encoding, 62
troubleshooting
    403 (Forbidden) errors, 487-488
    bottlenecks, RAM induced, 10
    databases, 490-491
    Host Headers, 494
    Index Server, queries, 491-493
    NNTP Service, connectivity, 311
    principles, 472-476
    remote directory access, 489
    SMTP, 281-282
    software bugs, 475-476
    TCP/IP, 477-479, 483-484
    tools, 476-481
    WebMaps, 460
    see also debugging
tuning performance, Index Server, 344-345

U

Unique keys (Performance Monitor counter), 406
University of Illinois, NCSA (National Center for Supercomputing), 5
UNIX, 5, 166-167
updating FTP site IP address, 158
usage analysis, 433
Usage Import utility, 433
    automating, 452-457
    importing log files, 447-450
Usage Import Statistics dialog box, 449
Usenet, 290, 476
user accounts
    FTP (File Transfer Protocol)
        anonymous access, 160-162
            restricting maximum number per site, 165-166
    NNTP (Network News Transfer Protocol) sites, restricting access, 300-302
    permissions, 163-165
    Windows NT, security, 211-212
    see also user reports
User Manager, FTP site administration, 162
user reports, analyzing, 451-457
user-specific access, 49-51

usernames
    authentication, 50-51
    securtiy, 180-181
utilities
    Certificate Log Administration utility, 248-249
    Certificate Server Queue Administration utility, 249-251
    command-line
        CertHier, 254-255
        CertReql, 254
        CertSrv, 255
        CertUtil, 253-254
    Content Analyzer, 458-463
    CONVLOG, 446
    Key Manager (Microsoft Certificate Server), CA certificate enrollment, 241-242
    Log File Manager, 448
    MetaEdit, 99-100
    Microsoft Usage Import, importing log files, 447-450
    NETSTAT, 390-391
    Network Monitor (Windows NT), 391-394
        capturing data, 393
        displaying data, 394
        utilization rates, 395
    Performance Monitor, 309, 395-397
        counters, 403-423
        disks, 402
        exporting data, 400
        logs, 399-400
        memory, 401-402
        networks, 402-403
        processors, 403
        viewing data, 397-398
        views, 398-399
    Report Writer, 433, 450-457
        automating, 452-457
        command-line parameters, 454-455, 457
    troubleshooting
        ARP, 482
        IPCONFIG, 480
        NETSTAT, 481
        NSLOOKUP, 480
        PING (Packet Internet Groper), 477-479
        TRACERT, 479-480
    Usage Import, 433, 452-457
    User Manager, FTP site administration, 162
utility objects, 342-343
utilization rates, Network Monitor (Windows NT), 395

V

variables, .idq files (Index Server), 340
VBScript, ASPs (Active Server Pages), 363
verifying NNTP Service connectivity, 311
VeriSign, 201
    see also certificates
viewing
    current FTP users, 164-165
    Index Server properties, 330-331
    MMC (Microsoft Management Console), nodes, 87
    objects on WebMaps, 460
    Performance Monitor data, 397-398
    Web site properties, 436
views
    Performance Monitor, 398-399
    WebMaps, 459
virtual directories, 60, 306-307
    adding to catalogs (Index Server), 329
    creating, 167-170
    mapping network shares, 170-171
    naming, 169
    WWW services, 128-131
visits reports, analyzing, 451-457

W

W3C (World Wide Web Committee), 5
   Extended Log Files, 440-443
      analyzing, 450-457
      importing, 447-450
WAM (Web Application Manager), 54-57
warehousing documents, 320
Web
   browsers, 4, 62
      IE4.01, Browser Only Installation, 8
      Netscape Navigator, client certificate enrollment, 245-247
   links, adding to custom consoles, 92-94
   pages
      generating dynamic content, 56-57
      language support, 56-57
      generating page content, 52-55
   servers, 4-5
      anonymous access, security, 484-489
      Apache, 5
      downlevel, managing, 94-98
   sites
      analysis, *see* site analysis
      analyzing content, 458-463
      content manipulation, 71-73
      disabling directory-level logging, 436-437
      displaying properties, 436
      indexing, 320, 333-338
      logging activity, 436-437
      Microsoft BackOffice, 7
      Microsoft Knowledge Base, 476
      Microsoft Site Server Express, 434
      support for multiple, 70-71
Web Application Manager, *see* **WAM**
Web Service counters, Performance Monitor, 419-423
WebMaps
   creating, 424-425, 458-460
   navigating, 460-461
   printing, 460
   quick searches, 461-462
   searching, 461
WebVirt Properties dialog box, 170-171
Welcome messages (FTP), 159-160
Windows NT Server 4.0, 5
   Content Analyzer, 424
   Event Logs, 277
   integration with IIS, 70
   Network Monitor, 391-394
      capturing data, 393
      displaying data, 394
      utilization rates, 395
   NTFS permissions, 205-208
   Performance Monitor, 395-397
      counters, 403-423
      disks, 402
      exporting data, 400
      logs, 399-400
      memory, 401-402
      networks, 402-403
      processors, 403
      viewing data, 397-398
      views, 398-399
   Registry, configuring, 108-112
   security
      disabling services, 208-210
      TCP/IP, 210-211
      user accounts, 211-212
Windows NT Challenge/Response Authentication, 49-51
Windows NT Option Pack, installing NNTP Service, 296-297
Windows Scripting Host, *see* **WSH**
wizards
   Expiration Policy, 305
   NNTP Service Rebuild, 310
word breakers (Index Server), 335
Wordlists (Performance Monitor counter), 406
workstation security, 209
World Wide Web Committee, *see* **W3C**
Write (access permission), 132, 163-164

Wscript object (WSH), 375
WSH (Windows Scripting Host), objects, 374-375
WWW (World Wide Web), 4
    functionality, CGI (Common Gateway Interface), 52-55
    Index Server, troubleshooting, 491-493
    service-specific entries (Windows NT Registry), configuring, 110-112
    sites, Content Analyzer, 424-425
    Web servers, 5
    see also WWW service
WWW service, 118
    configuring, 120-122
    error messages, customizing, 142-144
    HTTP headers, 141
    ISAPI filters, 142
    performance parameters
        bandwidth, 145-147
        expected hits, 147
        HTTP Keep-Alives, 147
        user connection limitations, 144-145
    Web sites
        creating, 123-126
        default documents, 138-139
        directories, 127-135
        directory security, 139-140
        host headers, 126-127
        identification configurations, 136
        IP addresses, 122-123
        user administration, delegating, 137-138
WWW Service Master Properties dialog box, 128

X-Y-Z

XHdr Commands (Performance Monitor counter), 413
XHdr Commands/sec (Performance Monitor counter), 413
XOver Commands (Performance Monitor counter), 413
XOver Commands/sec (Performance Monitor counter), 413
XOver Entries (Performance Monitor counter), 416
XOver Entries/sec (Performance Monitor counter), 416
XPat Commands (Performance Monitor counter), 413
XPat Commands/sec (Performance Monitor counter), 413
XReplic Commands (Performance Monitor counter), 413
XReplic Commands/sec (Performance Monitor counter), 413